P9-CAG-322

CONRAD BERGENDOFF'S FAITH AND WORK

A Swedish-American Lutheran, 1895-1997

Thomas Tredway

Augustana Historical Society
Swedish-American Historical Society

Copyright © 2014 by Augustana Historical Society, Rock Island, Illinois

ISBN 978-0-910184-01-4

This book is dedicated to my wife, Kate.

ACKNOWLEDGMENTS

I am grateful to many people who helped me with this project. Philip Anderson, President of the Swedish-American Historical Society, and Ann Boaden and Kai Swanson, successive Presidents of the Augustana Historical Society, have been supportive and encouraging through the entire process of bringing the text to publication. Jamie Nelson and Sarah Horowitz of Special Collections at Augustana College helped my research in countless ways from its very beginning. Quan Vi, Creative Design Director at Augustana College, was instrumental in lay-out and design and manifested great patience and dilligence in guiding the book through the process. Dag Blanck of Uppsala University and the Swenson Swedish Immigration Research Center at Augustana offered insight into the Swedish and Swedish-American background against which Conrad Bergendoff's life developed and was a senior partner in the endless conversations which preceded my writing of each of the chapters. Joel Thoreson of the Evangelical Lutheran Church in America archives was very helpful in securing photos and in guiding me to other church resources. Heidi Anoszko of the University of Minnesota Archives also helped with a photo. Proof readers for the text included Philip Anderson, Dag Blanck, Ann Boaden, Carolyn Erickson, Sarah Horowitz, Phillip Johnson, Dorothy Parkander, Kai Swanson, Kate Tredway, and Roald Tweet. They found a good many mistakes in my draft; other errors, still lurking in the text, are my own fault.

I had known Conrad Bergendoff first when I was a student at Augustana and then later when I became involved in teaching and administration at the college. His work and his thinking intrigued me at that time. More recently I have encountered him more fully through study of his long bibliography and his extensive personal papers, and through the memories of the many people who knew him during his one hundred and two year life. As is often the case in this kind of work, my own life and thinking have been influenced and changed by this decade-long investigation of the career and ideas of a man who personified the American Lutheran intellectual in the twentieth century, so I am thankful for the opportunity to write this book.

Thomas Tredway

TABLE OF CONTENTS

THE PLAN OF THE BOOK

It is a bright fall morning in the Illinois river town. Under a high blue sky, President Conrad Bergendoff is walking into a four storey limestone building whose dome looms over the Mississippi Valley, about half-way between St. Louis and St. Paul. In his early sixties, he is a hiker, so his stride is strong and purposeful. Bergendoff is on his way to speak to several hundred of his charges, young men and women from all over the country, who are used to gathering, not entirely by choice, twice a week. They will sit before a tall bright window of stained glass with an abstract geometrical design and listen to six or seven minutes of remarks from Dr. Bergendoff. Facing that window stretching up two stories on the east side of the building, they will also sing a hymn and attend the reading by the college dean of the daily announcements. After that they rush off, back down the creaking wooden steps from the college chapel, to classes in French or physics or philosophy.

Right now at the height of his professional and personal powers, Bergendoff is slender, an inch under six feet tall. He's wearing one of his several clergy-college president suits, all of them dark grey or blue or black. As he enters Old Main, he looks up to his right, through a thatch of full but light Scandinavian hair, to a freestanding Swedish bell tower just south of the limestone building, smiles to himself at the memories it evokes, and then heads up to the chapel. The late adolescents gathering to hear him give the college president some room as he goes up the steep stairs to the chapel. They clearly respect him, and,

Chapel at Augustana College in the fifties. Pres. Bergendoff is speaking, the Dean of the College is just behind him, and students are in their assigned seats.

in fact, most of them are in some awe of his presence. Certain of them will, however, look around to check how many of their professors, *not* required to be there, have made it to chapel. They are starting to wonder about compulsory worship services, as well as about other college rules. Included in the company of those wondering was, until he graduated the preceding spring, a history major from Buffalo, New York, decades later the author of the present volume.

It's October in the late 1950s. For the first time since the forties a team not from New York has won the World Series. On his way to chapel, Bergendoff himself may not be considering whether students should *have* to be there, but you can be pretty sure he isn't mulling over the victory of the Milwaukee Braves. Sports are rarely on his mind, except when his college's teams lose too often, and the alumni complain—which they have been lately. He is certainly not thinking about buying a new Edsel, just introduced to the car-hungry American public; his salary is way too small for a new Detroit car, and he is not much interested in consumer goods, anyway. Soon the first Toyotas from Japan will arrive in the US; even one of them will be out of his price range. He does not have the time to see the new movie about the late war between Japan and the West, *Bridge on the River Kwai,* when it gets to the Fort Theater downtown. *Music Man,* set right across the river in Iowa and just now being staged in New York, is also not in his plans. Most of this man's obligations beyond the

Augustana campus are church related, and if not overseas to Northern Europe, his travels are in the regions of the US where Lutherans have settled. Bergendoff will surely not buy Ayn Rand's newly published *Atlas Shrugged* to read on one of his train trips; he has repeatedly made clear what he thinks of selfish modern materialism.

Sputnik, just put into orbit by the USSR, may be on his mind; Bergendoff's college, founded by Swedes, has a strong interest in the physical sciences and in technological achievements. Or his concern for social issues may mean the college president is reflecting on President Eisenhower's decision two weeks earlier to send troops to Little Rock, Arkansas, to integrate Central High School. He may recall with some satisfaction that only a few people on his campus wore Adlai Stevenson buttons a year ago, when the current president was re-elected. There are a few Democrats lurking at the college, but the president, the faculty, and the students are mainly Republicans; so is the Church that supports the school. Of course, the Reverend Doctor Bergendoff is probably not thinking about politics at all. More likely he is planning a train ride over to Chicago or up to Minneapolis, where he and a number of co-religionists will talk about merging their ethnic-religious denominations. Or maybe certain plans, formed in concert with the college's Dean of Men, to shut down the initiation rites of the school's Greek letter clubs are on his mind. The galley proofs for an academic book review he's done for a political science journal are back on his desk in the college library. The secretary who types his articles can trust his handwritten drafts. They have few mistakes. Beyond that, his work is recognized for its scholarly directness. That quality is already in the first drafts.

It is decades before Google or Map-Quest. Right now, in October, 1957, there is not one computer on the Augustana campus. But if you could follow Conrad Bergendoff with Map-Quest fitted out with a special mind-read feature, you might get some inkling of what he is thinking about this autumn morning. You would probably marvel at the extent of his interests. If you dialed the map down fine, saw him and his thoughts close up, in detail and large scale, your appreciation of their depth and precision might grow. And if you zoomed back out to see the broad landscape on which he thought and wrote, you might also be surprised. In their widest scope and range, his close-up, everyday ideas and efforts touched fundamental questions about all human life, its origins, purpose, and destiny. These are questions that have occupied people making their daily rounds to their daily duties since the earliest human records have been kept. When he rode the Rock Island Lines to church meetings, spoke in the Augustana chapel up the hill from the railroad depot, sailed across the North Atlantic to world ecumenical conferences, or struggled with college budgets and student disciplinary questions, the man was in fact dealing with issues that lie at the core of the human experience.

Conrad Johan Immanuel Bergendoff had a head start on the twentieth century by five years. He died, age one hundred and two, in 1997, three years shy of the third Christian millennium. Many of his intellectual contemporaries took paths that followed the secularism and materialism that Bergendoff, with sorrow, believed dominated his age. But this man was *homo religiosus* to the core, one of the shrinking cadre of twentieth century academics who maintained the faith of their ancestors. The religion so central to Conrad Bergendoff was, of course, Lutheran and Swedish. By the time of his maturity he had become its most convincing American spokesperson. Many who shared his background sought to meld it with the values and ideals of the age. Others, doubting the great claims of the tradition and frustrated with its seeming provinciality, simply abandoned it. But this man held to it unalloyed and without apology. He became one of the first representatives of this ethno-religious tradition to operate effectively in wider ecclesiastical and academic circles—well beyond its boundaries. But wherever he went, he was guided by the religious ideas and values he had learned in his own Church, the "Augustana Synod."

As Bergendoff aged, his persona softened, but his commitments did not. He continued to believe that only a meaning that came from beyond the world of sight and sense could explain and give that world purpose. And he persisted in thinking that the faith he had learned in his parents' home and church was as full an expression of that meaning from beyond it as could be found in the world of sense and sight. Some who knew him must have wondered if his long life was itself a reward for his constancy. For thirty-five years after he no longer stood beneath the high, bright, colored chapel window, speaking to students as president of their school, he would continue to walk across his college's campus, still greeted by people who knew and respected him. Of course, they also knew that what had until 1962 been Bergendoff's college and Church were of necessity changing, adjusting to the new realities of the later twentieth century.

Life in a Church—and Beyond

During his ten decades Conrad Bergendoff dealt with many of the questions and tensions within his own religious tradition, the Swedish and Lutheran branch of the Christian faith, that seemed particularly to have occupied it during the twentieth century. But of course, they were questions not limited to Lutheranism. Indeed, whenever human beings have taken the religious quest seriously, these issues have been raised. And therein lies the larger, even universal, significance of the man's life and work: standing firmly within a very specific religious-ethnic heritage, he engaged questions that seem to arise whenever people think about their place in the wide and mysterious realms of existence.

These are questions such as: How shall one's deepest spiritual experiences be spoken of? What about people who think and talk of these matters in ways that seem quite different from yours? Should the literature that records these spiritual experiences be taken literally? Is uncertainty or doubt integral to genuine religion? Can you even be sure of the sincerity of those who profess your *own* religious creed? To what extent should (or can) religious commitment be separated from the particular circumstances of your life, especially its ethnic and cultural traditions? What's the relationship between religious insight and personal moral improvement? Can faith be expected to transform not just persons, but societies as well?

That's a long list of questions, but the reader with patience to endure my prose will see that Conrad Bergendoff addressed them all. Some of them, the issue of the relationship of faith and works, for example, were older than Lutheranism, rooted in the New Testament itself. Others, such as the matter of the reciprocal ties between being Swedish and being Christian, were peculiar to Bergendoff's own tradition. Many of them are questions which have been asked by religious people, east and west, since their experiences have been shared, recorded, and the literature preserved. With regard to all of them, Conrad Bergendoff's thinking and writing were both representative of his own tradition and provocative in a larger sense. His work was some of the best going on in American Lutheranism, and it provoked questions that are still being considered by people standing within, and well beyond, his own tradition. That tradition itself morphed and expanded during his lifetime, and Bergendoff had much to do with that, as well.

While Lutheranism on both sides of the Atlantic dealt with these questions during the twentieth century, it seemed to relax and to open up. So did Conrad Bergendoff—gradually, just as his Church did. He was born into one of the ethnic enclaves in which many Americans spent the late nineteenth century; at home the family spoke Swedish. In the late twentieth century, Swedes who heard him speak in his parents' tongue were themselves carried back to the turn-of-the century expressions and cadences of their grandparents. But his papers and sermons in English manifested a complete mastery of his other "native" language as well, one he did not learn until entering elementary school.[1] The even and unemotional manner of his delivery almost belied the intensity and complexity of Bergendoff's thinking.

As the circles of his knowledge and associations widened, Bergendoff found himself being read and heard by persons who as a boy in Connecticut he felt his family and he did not really belong with. They were old line Yankees, and he was Swedish and Lutheran, the son of newcomers to New England. But, like his Church itself, he held to his creed. The wider Christian world, if

Synod Founders. In 1890 eleven of the men who had been present at the founding of the Augustana Synod thirty years earlier gathered in solemn remembrance.

it did not always agree with everything he believed, came to think it worthy of careful consideration. After first and cautiously befriending other Lutherans in America—Danish or English or Finnish or German or Norwegian speakers—Bergendoff and his Swedish-rooted Augustana Lutheran Church developed a commitment to seek organized unity with them. Bergendoff and his Church also listened to and addressed non-Lutheran Christians, and as they did so, they began to realize that there might be as much to learn as there was to teach. In the skein of personal relationships he enjoyed in his home community, Conrad had friends well beyond the family of Christians, and the great regard in which Jewish or humanist friends held him was evidence of the deep humanity they sensed in him as well as of their respect for his strong commitment to his own tradition.

Bergendoff's reverence for his father and the fathers of his Synod only deepened through his long life. When in 1919 he was summoned back to their Midwestern theological school to finish an education for the ministry that he had started in a Pennsylvania seminary, he obeyed. When in the next decade he got the chance to study in Sweden itself, he wrote in elegant and formal Swedish to the Archbishop of the national Church in hopes of gaining his advice and direction. The roots of the Augustana Synod in the Old World were dear to Bergendoff. But he never ignored the points of difference as well as those of unity that lay between the Church his immigrant forebears left behind and the one they founded in America. He knew his own ethnic community would eventually drop the use of the language it had brought from Europe, but his appreciation for Sweden, its history and culture, remained. He never quite figured out what to make of the growing secularism of a people whose national faith he preferred to think of as the progenitor of his own. In that too, Bergendoff was the son of his century, one that saw a growing bifurcation between traditional religion and the a-religion of the dominant culture, in both Europe and America.

Bergendoff spent one-quarter of his one hundred and two years managing a college. He claimed that it was with reluctance that he accepted the offer to be President of Augustana College and Theological Seminary, proffered to him in 1935. He felt that much of what that job called for did not lie in areas of his own inclinations or strengths. But it did put him in exactly that place where the dominant values of contemporary culture confronted his deepest commitments. Bergendoff believed the school must help young people preserve their faith as they found their way through to adulthood. It must lead them to see how they could live that faith out in their families and in their work. If it could not, there was little hope for the wider world.

To have to deal with the (usually) harmless shenanigans of late adolescents or with the (persistent) penury of a Church still emerging from immigrant status was not what Conrad Bergendoff had set out to do when he was ordained in the Christian ministry. But it was a price worth paying. If he could not serve his faith and Church in this way, what did his sense of Christian mission amount to? The way he articulated his commitment won him great respect, almost reverence, on the Augustana College campus and in his Church. Yet to some of the people in that Church or on the College Board, his concentration on the school's intellectual and spiritual life may not have left him time enough to worry effectively about its financial condition. In that way, too, Bergendoff's career is representative of the emerging conditions of church and educational life in his century. It was a time in which fiscal underpinnings as well as ideological and theological commitments had to be cultivated in colleges and denominations.

It was also the case that, once freed at age sixty-seven of his role as President of Augustana, Conrad Bergendoff became noticeably less somber. The year 1962 marked the end of the Augustana Synod's one hundred and two years of independent existence as well as the conclusion of Conrad's twenty-seven years as the leader of its oldest school. For most of its century of life the Synod expected great solemnity of its leaders. When you peer through the early histories and other celebratory publications of that Church, you wonder if some of the men pictured (the photos *are* all of men) might have actually *practiced* frowning before the hooded photographer took their formal portraits. That was the posed look of the early Bergendoff, too. The later Bergendoff stayed in full possession of his intellectual powers, but he seemed to have lightened, perhaps because he no longer lived on a campus and in a Church where public gravitas was always expected. In spite of the frailties that attend old age, he remained both lucid and healthy until near death. In his seventies he was still an active member of the local Black Hawk Hiking Club. In his eighties he broke an arm changing storm windows at his Rock Island bungalow. With the years the solemn demeanor and appearance that marked his early career as a Lutheran clergyman gave way to a gentler warmth and humor that eased the set of his face and seemed actually to brighten his eyes. He was even known to drink a small glass of wine, and was openly sympathetic with students' protests about the American military venture in southeast Asia.

Bergendoff was never naïve about what the world had endured after 1895. But what some theologians call an "optimism of grace" appeared in his thought and speech and increasingly asserted itself against the pessimism he felt about the directions that human life and culture had taken during his lifetime. In his nineties he still delighted, perhaps more than ever, in the hundreds of young people who crowded the sidewalks or classrooms of the college where he been president for nearly three decades. Concerts and lectures found him listening as thoughtfully in his last years as they had when, still a teen-ager, he first came to Augustana before World War I.

The Lay-Out

The plan of this book is to examine Conrad Bergendoff's early life, from his boyhood until his call to become President of Augustana (Chapters 1 and 2). Then we shift the focus to the multiple areas of his mature activity, including: his role within the Augustana Lutheran Church (Chapter 5); his ecumenical efforts, Lutheran and Christian, (Chapters 6 and 7); his life among Swedish Americans and Swedes (Chapter 8); and his years as a college administrator (Chapter 9). But first, between Chapters 2 and 5, two important matters must be considered. Once we have finished Chapter 2 and Bergendoff is settled in the professional campus position he held for twenty-seven years, and before we look in Chapters 5 through 9 at the wide reach of his professional life, we will examine the religious commitment that stood at the center of everything he did (Chapter 3) and also consider the way in which that faith controlled his understanding of human society and culture (Chapter 4). Of course, some of the issues addressed in Bergendoff's life and in this book could be treated in connection with more than one of themes to which Chapters 5 through 9 are devoted. For example, the 1948 separation of Augustana Theological Seminary from Augustana College could have been dealt with either in the chapter on the Augustana Synod (5) or in the one on higher education (9). Or the matter of Bergendoff's "theology of higher education" could have been treated in the chapter on Christianity and culture (4) rather than in the chapter on his years as a college president (9). I hope the reader will tolerate the decisions I have made even when perhaps wondering about them.

In none of the various spheres of his activity did Conrad Bergendoff go "from victory unto victory," as the Protestant marching hymn has it. There was plenty of push-back from many directions. He lost his share of votes and debates on the floor of Synod conventions and in college faculty meetings. We will see that often things did not turn out as he had expected they would. But in ways that mere egotism might not have, his even spirit and his strong conviction seem to have sustained him through defeats. When his causes won, he never gloated. When they lost he usually remained silent, and only his quiet reservation bespoke his unhappiness. When he was not silent, it was a sign of how deeply the matter troubled him. The significance of his victories and his losses lies in the interaction between his deepest beliefs and the demands that college, church, community, Swedish America, and ecumenical Christianity put upon him. It lies too in the way that within his world Bergendoff's life reflected some changes and caused others.

My aim is to cover what Conrad Bergendoff thought and, where it pertains to his ideas, to cover what he did. His life was not an exciting or eventful one; the ideas that drove it are where its greater significance lies. I have treated the duties, achievements, and difficulties of his years as the President of Augustana College at length elsewhere, in *Coming of Age* (2010), a history of Augustana College during the presidencies of Conrad Bergendoff (1935 to 1962) and C. W. Sorensen (1962 to 1975). Where it seems appropriate I have in the present book written briefly about the wider historical context in which Bergendoff operated, as, for example, in considering the early history of the Augustana Synod or the secular cast of mid-twentieth century Swedish culture. But this book is not meant to be a survey of such developments; I have referred to them when they directly influenced Bergendoff or when he wrote about them. The focus of this study is on his ideas, religious and otherwise, that both informed and were informed by these developments, activities, and events.

Each of the topics that are considered in Chapters 5 through 9 represents one sphere of Conrad Bergendoff's activity and influence. But in every one of them, we will see the college president-historian-churchman-theologian forming and, if needed, adjusting, his understanding of the fields in which he worked and of the wider world that impinged upon them. Historians of immigration speak these days of "identity formation." People who move from one culture, presumably the one they were born in, to another are led to ask themselves identity questions that may not present themselves as poignantly to folk who stay put. Thus Swedish historian Dag Blanck treats the question of *The Formation of an Ethnic Identity* in a 2006 book on the Augustana Synod. Maria Erling and Mark Granquist subtitle their 2008 history of the Augustana Church *Shaping Lutheran Identity in North America*. And in his Introduction to a 2011 history of Gustavus Adolphus, the Swedish-American college in Minnesota, Byron Nordstrom declares that the book will "use *identity* as a unifying, interpretive thread[.]"[2]

The circumstances of their lives almost force immigrant people to re-negotiate their identity, their sense of themselves. A Norwegian scholar at the University of Bergen, Orm Øverland, writes that immigrants created "home making myths," in which stories about their past were used to explain the contributions to, and justify the role of their particular ethnic group in, larger American society. Some of these myths or stories were more historically accurate than others, but collectively they created a deeper sense of belonging and importance in the new context.[3] One of the fascinating aspects of Conrad Bergendoff's work, academic and popular, was the way in which he used his reading of Swedish and Swedish-American history to advance his own deep need to credit his ethnic tradition with making a great contribution to national life, both in religious and broader ways. The Swedes belonged here in America and offered it much. Bergendoff's home making myths ranged from his emphasis on the cleanliness and order of Swedish and Swedish-American kitchens and barns to his elevation of the liturgical and theological contributions of Swedish Lutheranism to the American churches.

But we will also see some fundamental shifts in Conrad Bergendoff's self-understanding or identity, as, for example, after World War II when he faced the fact that among the nations and peoples the Swedes were perhaps the most secular of all. Often it seemed that it was the external lay-of-the-land that had changed, in this case the nature of Swedish culture. But as the ground shifted, so did Bergendoff. He had to. The interplay of circumstances with his mind and heart is part of the fascination his life holds. He was a person who sought heroically to preserve the best of the past; that is where he located and how he identified himself. It was how he made himself and his people at home in America, his own "home making myth." But he knew when things were changing, and, when pushed, he adjusted his self-understanding to these conditions. At moments he sensed the ironic turn that events had taken with regard to his own ideas and efforts. But I will argue that in the end his core sense of himself did not shift significantly. That sense was religious.

A Caution

Shortly we will consider the early years in which Bergendoff's sense of himself and his convictions were formed. This was also a time when he grew ever more aware that these convictions put him at odds with much of the culture around him. But first I must insert into this Introduction a notice, maybe even a caution. It touches the matter of his being essentially a religious person, who raised, as I suggested earlier, fundamental human questions about our relationship to the divine, however understood. Perhaps a 2008 *New Yorker* article about the Edwardian journalist and novelist G. K. Chesterton (1874–1936) can clarify what I mean by that "notice" or "caution." The author of the article is the American essayist and critic Adam Gopnik.

In 1922 Chesterton "went over to Rome," as the English sometimes speak of an Anglican's conversion to the Roman Catholic Church. Gopnik suggests that in the age when Chesterton (and Bergendoff) thought and worked there were three possibilities open to persons who sensed the promise, threat, and mystery of human life. One, which Gopnik (with Chesterton) dismisses quickly (though many moderns do not), is "rationalism." That is the "fatuous materialist progressivism" ascendant at the turn of the century, the time of Chesterton's early manhood (and of Bergendoff's boyhood). Presumably it was ultimately simple materialism, according to which the physical world we perceive is the only one there is. A second option is to look at the tableau of life, to be amazed, and to sense that through it shines a light from another place. In that place, hidden behind the curtain of sense, is the power that directs the things we perceive with our senses. We may wonder about the source of the light that shines onto the stage where we are acting and ask who or what is moving us. But in this view, we know that we can in the end not find out. We must live with the mystery. (That's where Adam Gopnik finds himself.)

The third alternative is to believe that back of the world of events and appearances is a hidden master. That master works in the place where the light comes from and where the action is directed. As Gopnik understands Chesterton, "the side we see is the side there is to look at," but the truth is "that the white radiance of wonder shines from inside, which is where the light is." Chesterton believed that behind the world that presents itself to the senses (the one the "rationalist" or "materialist" is satisfied with, or at least resigned to), you will perceive, as he did in his boyhood while watching the puppet theater his father built for him, the master who lightens and moves all things. It is not enough to treat the sensed world as complete in itself, nor is it satisfactory simply to recognize its wonder and mystery without seeking their source. We must look beyond the show to "where the light is."[4] Like G. K. Chesterton, Conrad Bergendoff was one of a number (perhaps a minority) of twentieth century intellectuals who were not satisfied merely to experience life's mystery with amazement and appreciation. They sought to understand who (Who) moves it and gives it meaning and plot. They thought the effort would be rewarded. Both the English Catholic and the American Lutheran did believe that behind the natural world was a supernatural one that was finally more real. That invisible world enlightened the stage and moved the actors in the world we live in. It was not a new way to look at human life. Before the time of Christ, Plato thought this too.

To understand Conrad Bergendoff's ideas about individual and corporate life, about higher education, or the meaning of the immigrant experience in America, or the rapprochement of Christian churches with each other, or any other matter presenting itself to his attention—from the errors of Darwinism to the dangers of social dancing—one must at least for the nonce grant him that belief in a supernatural power and order of existence. Of course, Bergendoff held to these ideas with characteristic dignity and reserve. There is no record of an eighteen year old Conrad turning to an Ouija Board to direct his academic plans. Nor, when he became "President Bergendoff," did he sign grant applications to study the effects of prayer on plant growth. But he surely believed that ultimate reality lay beyond the world that we sense.

And, of equal importance, he thought that his own religious tradition taught certain essential truths about the nature of that reality and about the questions that I earlier characterized as "spiritual" or "religious." Chesterton believed this about the Roman Catholicism to which he converted. Without these verities, in Bergendoff's case Lutheran, in Chesterton's Catholic, you could understand neither this world nor the one beyond or behind it. We might if we wished begin with the papers Bergendoff delivered at meetings of the Swedish Pioneer Historical Society or consider his years on the Rock Island County Park Commission. But if we did, we would sooner or later, and probably sooner, get to his religious ideas. They were the foundation that carried all the rest of his work, the basis on which he made his multiple contributions to contemporary life, in the church and beyond. The reader can certainly reserve his or her own views as to the alternatives Gopnik suggests, but it is pretty clear where Conrad Bergendoff came down. My argument is that to understand him you have to deal directly with his belief in God and in the way God, revealed in Christ, works in human life.

Getting at these matters is both easy and difficult. It is easy in the sense that Bergendoff's convictions permeate everything he wrote. But that is why the job of understanding him is difficult as well. By reading the slim books he authored in the decade after World War II, especially *Christ as Authority* (1947) and *One Holy Catholic Apostolic Church* (1954), you can discover in under two hundred and fifty pages the *Leitmotiv* in the life and thinking of the Swedish-American historian-theologian. But a glance through the bibliography at the end of this book will reveal the implausibly long list of articles, reviews, and other books, including two thicker ones, which he authored—beginning with his freshman essay about the train ride from his home in Connecticut to college in Illinois (1912) and ending with book reviews written in his hundredth year (1994). To discover the range of ways in which his fundamental ideas were elaborated, applied, and challenged, within the Christian church and beyond, you must confront that bibliography.

My approach has been to consider all of it. Just when you think you have read enough, one of his essays crops up with a new turn of phrase that delights and illuminates, or a new angle of thought that puzzles and bothers. But underlying everything—articles, books, reviews, chapel talks, letters, sermons—is a consistency that is surprising in a bibliography that extensive. Where Bergendoff did change his mind, I have tried to make that clear, and where in fundamental matters he held the line, I have marked that as well. When appropriate I have briefly spoken of some of his contemporaries' work, thinking it helps to understand him. Readers will, I hope, bring their own ideas and experiences to this study, joining the line of men and women who have been assured, troubled, challenged, and informed by this man who managed to personify the American Lutheran intellectual in the twentieth century.

But right now, let's see how it came to be that he was walking over to the Old Main Chapel, while Sputnik circled the earth and the leaves turned yellow and red in the Mississippi Valley. We turn to that fellow's early years, the time when his convictions were formed. He came to them, of course, reading Martin Luther, *not* G. K. Chesterton.

Celebrating the end of World War I, downtown Rock Island, 1918. Bergendoff is not in the photo. After teaching college English for a year, he had left the town a year earlier to do graduate study in Philadelphia and New York. In 1919 he would dutifully return to enroll in the Synod's seminary, located about two miles to the east, almost on the Moline city line.

CHAPTER 1

MIDDLETOWN AND ROCK ISLAND

If you want to understand Conrad Johan Immanuel Bergendoff you must consider the Augustana Evangelical Lutheran Church, its history and ethos. Bergendoff lived to see the passing of "the Synod," as his Church was commonly called in-house. In 1962 it merged with three other American Lutheran bodies to form the Lutheran Church in America. There had been no Bergendoff present one hundred and two years earlier when the Synod was born in a small Scandinavian settlement that straddled the Illinois-Wisconsin state line—about midway between Lake Michigan and the Mississippi River. But Conrad Bergendoff's imagination, the memories of his childhood, and his own and others' scholarship made the first years of the Augustana Church almost as real to him as the last ones—which he lived through. As Bergendoff began his professional academic career, the appreciative treatment of the Augustana Synod by its first historians had given way to a sharper examination of those early decades. Scholars, many of them Synod members themselves, took a balanced and even critical view of the events that had led Scandinavian Lutheran immigrants to form their own Church body. Though these other academics were determined to examine the Synod's founding and first decades with the impartial tools of modern historiography, Bergendoff was inclined to look at the same years with an appreciation that bordered on reverence. In a real sense his own identity as well as the identity of much of Swedish America was shaped in those decades.

The New Synod and the First Bergendoff

As the 1960 centennial of the Augustana Synod approached and with it the impending church merger, Dr. Bergendoff was asked by a Swedish church historian, Gunnar Westin of Uppsala University, to contribute an essay marking the hundredth birthday to *Kyrkohistorisk årsskrift,* a Swedish academic annual. In that essay Bergendoff held that the religious life of Midwestern Swedish Americans began with a "religious fanatic," Eric Jansson, who led a "bewitched following" of about 1,500 Swedes from their homeland to western Illinois in the mid-1840s, having assured the faithful that "I am the greatest light since the time of the apostles."[1] The Illinois frontier was hard on such prophets claiming to complete the unfinished biblical revelation, as the Latter Day Saints had learned down the Mississippi in Nauvoo, when their own, Joseph Smith, was killed by a mob in 1844. Bishop Hill, the colony the Janssonists founded about thirty miles southeast of Rock Island, did not long survive their prophet's assassination in 1850, but the immigration of religious parties from Sweden to the Upper Midwest had begun, said Bergendoff.[2] He was more favorably disposed toward the next major figure to arrive, who came bearing a gospel completed in the New Testament and preserved in the Church of Sweden. Lars Paul Esbjörn was a priest in that Church, arriving in Illinois in 1849, three years after Jansson. In spite of the fact that Esbjörn was first among the Augustana Synod's founders, some historians were almost as tough on him as Bergendoff had been on Jansson. One of Bergendoff's contemporaries, Fritiof Ander of the Augustana College History Department, said bluntly that Esbjörn would "probably have been called 'maladjusted' by psychologists."[3] Another colleague, G. Everett Arden, Professor of Church History at Augustana Theological Seminary, wrote of Esbjörn that he was "a complex figure, whose personality was characterized by strange contradictions."[4] Bergendoff remained more favorable toward Esbjörn, not speaking much of contradictions, let alone psychological maladjustment.

Both Arden and Ander recognized the blend of human warmth with suspicion, of faith with melancholy, and of Christian charity with egocentricity that marked Esbjörn's work in Illinois. Influenced by the temperance and revival movements, he had left Sweden with a rebuke from the Archbishop of the State Church ringing in his ears. Like many of his countrymen, the Swedish prelate saw emigration like Esbjörn's as a betrayal of Sweden and its Church. On first arriving in America Esbjörn was ready to cooperate with fellow Christians— Methodists and Calvinists—in the effort to reach Swedish immigrants. The America in which he landed had, of course, been rent by sectarian strife almost from the moment of the landing in 1620 at Plymouth. In that New England colony, Anglicans, less zealous than the Puritans with whom circumstance put them cheek-to-jowl, growled that those Puritans were "contentious, cruel and hard-hearted, among your neighbors, and towards such as in all points both civil and religious, jump not with you."[5]

As the heirs of the Pilgrims joined new immigrants in settling the present Great Lakes States, they together carried that contentiousness with them. Americans did not jump in religious unison in the nineteenth century West in which Esbjörn arrived. Ever more conservative, he grew doubtful about all non-Lutherans and stopped cooperating with them. His church added its voice to the cacophony of denominational discord that characterized pre-Civil War America. Esbjörn's reaction to American religious pluralism was not untypical. Martin E. Marty writes of Lutherans

Lars Paul Esbjörn, founder of the Augustana Synod.

in the nineteenth century Upper Midwest, "Most were convinced that their own piety was superior or their doctrinal integrity was profound and unique. They alone had a hold on full truth."[6] The description fits Esbjörn nicely. In 1851 Esbjörn brought the Swedish-American congregations he had helped to found into the newly formed Synod of Northern Illinois, a group that also included English, German, and Norwegian speaking Lutherans. Lars Paul himself subsequently accepted the professorship of Scandinavian at a small university in Springfield, Illinois, which the Lutherans had founded cooperatively to train candidates for the ministry. But within two years he grew doubtful about the orthodoxy of the school's leaders, though they too were Lutheran, and in March, 1860, in the middle of the academic term, he resigned from the faculty. That move was the catalyst that brought the Norwegians and Swedes to decide to form their own synod at Jefferson Prairie, the small Illinois-Wisconsin settlement, in June, 1860. For his part Esbjörn was "tired of the doings of the Americans and their spiritual outlook."[7]

The Swedes (and their Norwegian associates, who remained with them for only a decade and then left, mainly for linguistic and ethnic, not theological, reasons) were determined that their new church be orthodox to its core. They named it

Tufve Nilsson Hasselquist, Synod president, college-seminary president, newspaper editor.

"Augustana" to indicate their un-swerving loyalty to the primary Lutheran confession or creed, written in the City of Augs-burg (Latin, *Augustana*) in 1530. The Augustana men strongly resisted the efforts of some En-glish speaking Lutherans in the eastern United States to adjust the *Confessio Augustana* to Amer-ican ideas and circumstances. If later in its history Bergendoff's Synod took an ecumenical stance toward other Lutherans and even non-Lutherans, it did not in its first decades. Esbjörn himself grew disillusioned with life in America, and sensing that con-trol of the new Synod was slip-ping away from him, returned to his homeland, accepting a parish there in 1864. That left his col-league-competitor, Tufve Nilsson Hasselquist, as the principal figure both in the Augustana Synod and at the college and seminary that bore its name. He was to be a dominant force in Swedish-American life for the next twenty-five years, as a pastor, editor, Synod president, and leader of Augustana College and Theolog-ical Seminary. After wandering from Chicago to Paxton, Illinois, that institution settled near the Rock Island-Moline city line in 1875, the fifteenth year of its life.

Upon arriving in America (1852), T. N. Hasselquist had been, like Esbjörn at first, inclined to work with other denominations. His biographer, the historian Fritiof Ander, writes that Hasselquist had been something of a "radical" and a "pietist" in his years as a priest in Sweden. When he got to his first American congregation in Galesburg, Illinois, he dressed in white suits rather than the *prästrock* worn by Swedish priests and entered church services singing revival hymns.[8] But Hasselquist quickly abandoned such "reformed" and "unionist" tendencies in favor of certified Lutheran confessional rigor. And well past his death in 1891, such rigor characterized the Augustana Synod. In contrast to his views on Esbjörn, Ander considers Hasselquist to have been by nature a better-adjusted, even happier, person.[9] But for all that, he was never inclined to compromise his firm Lutheranism once he had settled into it. Hasselquist guided the young denomination through its first theological crisis. That crisis was centered on a new theory of the Atonement, the doctrine that attempts to explain the reason for and meaning of Christ's death. In the later decades of the nineteenth century, an evangelical and Pietistic priest of the Church of Sweden, P. P. Waldenström, wrote that Christ's death was not a sacrifice to appease God the Father's wrath against human sin, but was instead a sign that God had always loved humankind and sought its redemption, never needing to reconcile himself to humanity. These ideas stood in opposition to the fundamental Lutheran creedal statement, the Augsburg Confession.[10] Hasselquist and other Synod leaders fought Waldenströmian theology with determination. Waldenström himself once described Hasselquist as "a Lutheran fanatic."[11] But in spite of the "fanatic," some Swedish Americans held to the new Atonement theory and left the Synod to form the *Missionsförbund* (Mission Covenant) in 1885.

Together with other leaders—Erland Carlsson, Jonas Swensson, and O. C. T. Andren, all trained for the priesthood in Sweden—Hasselquist guided the Synod through the Atonement controversy and other difficulties financial and political. Their Church prospered, in numbers if not in finances. Protective of Lutheran orthodoxy, the Synod adopted the Galesburg Rule, "Lutheran pulpits for Lutheran ministers only—Lutheran altars for Lutheran communicants only."[12] This exclusiveness did not appear to hamper the Synod's growth. It increased from 900 members and 60 congregations in 1860 to 201,000 members and 921 congregations by 1900. By then it had spread from its origins in the Upper Mississippi Valley into nine regional conferences. There were conferences out on the Great Plains and along both coasts, as Swedish immigrants began to spread throughout the United States. By the time Bergendoff himself was ordained in the early 1920s, his Church included nearly 300,000 members in 1,250 congregations.[13] It was also rapidly being Americanized.

The Americanization process included the rise to influence of second generation, American-born leaders, the growing use of English in business and worship, and an increasing tendency to develop the sort of institutions and organizations that characterized the growth of other Protestant denominations. The Synod had a flourishing publishing house, periodicals in Swedish and English, several colleges, a theological seminary, and a wide-ranging program of foreign and home mission work. Women's and youth societies had begun to form, in spite of the misgivings of some of the old-line leadership, who feared these groups might rival the sponsoring congregations. In 1911 L. A. Johnston, the first American-born pastor to be elected Synod President, was installed in office. He was followed in 1918 by G. A. Brandelle, also second generation, who held the position until 1935, the year that Conrad Bergendoff became Acting President of Augustana, college and seminary. These two Synod Presidents,

Carl August Bergendoff.

Brandelle in particular, administered its affairs in much the same way that other Lutheran and Protestant church executives did their denominations. Churchwide boards and agencies multiplied. In 1925 an English language Hymnal and Service Book was introduced. At about that time the majority of men ordained to the ministry shifted from natives of Sweden to men born in America. Those years in the life of the Augustana Synod were also characterized by the influence of a growing number of younger men, including Conrad Bergendoff. Many of them had studied, and perhaps for a time worked, outside of the Synod's institutions, as had the scholars George M. Stephenson and Fritiof Ander. The seminary historian G. E. Arden maintains, however, that in spite of these rapid and sometimes perplexing changes in the Synod's life, "the faith it held was basically the faith of the founding fathers."[14]

That was, as we shall see, certainly the case with Conrad Bergendoff. His father, Carl August Bergendoff, had not been one of those founding fathers, but he heartily shared their beliefs. His son Conrad saw in Pastor C. A. Bergendoff the sort of life and faith that had built the Augustana Synod. As a child of eight Carl August had lost his own father, Sven Magnus Jonasson, a cabinet maker in Tofteryd, a village in Småland, a province of southern Sweden that contributed thousands of its people to North America. Though small, Tofteryd had monuments dating from the stone, bronze, and early iron ages, and its church, built mainly in the nineteenth century, contained a crucifix from the fifteenth and a baptismal font from the thirteenth centuries. Conrad Bergendoff later emphasized the antiquity of Swedish Christianity, symbolized throughout the land by such remains and relics.

Against this backdrop a family tragedy played out. Having taken an outdoor job as a carpenter, Sven Magnus had fallen when a scaffold gave way, and died after hitting his head on a stone. He lived six hours after the blow, "but never uttered another word." Hours before the accident, his wife had had a premonition that something horrible would happen that day. Sven Magnus left his widow with five children, all under ten years old. One of them, Carl August, a "poor, lonesome lad" who had ranked first in his confirmation class, grew up only to drift through the southern part of the country, taking short-term jobs. One of these, for a certain Carl Johan, had been little better than slavery, he recalled. His boss, "who professed to be a Christian, was a great miser." Landing in Gothenburg, Carl August resolved to leave Sweden and finally received the required permission to emigrate.

Before embarking in 1882 on the North Atlantic voyage the young man determined for obscure reasons to take the last name "Bergendoff." The older Swedish custom would have been to call himself "Svensson," using his father's first name as his last. And in fact Svensson was the name that he did use up until early April, 1882, but by the time he sailed from Gothenburg in the middle of the month, Carl August had become a "Bergendoff."[15] That name does not show up elsewhere in modern Sweden or Swedish America, and one can only speculate as to the reasons for choosing it. It was quite easy in late nineteenth century Sweden to make a legal name change, and Carl August may have sought to signify hope for a new life in America with a new name.[16] Or perhaps he had some premonition that one of his sons, Conrad, would so distinguish himself in the Swedish-American world as to merit the unique name.

In any event, when he landed in Boston, the new Bergendoff (evidently the only one in the world at that time) found a job in the Chickering Piano Factory and joined the city's Augustana Synod congregation. Its pastor thought Carl August would make a fine minister and convinced him to head west to Illinois for training. He did. Climbing down from the Rock Island Line with $150 in his pocket ("I had to live very frugally."), he secured a room at Augustana College and Theological Seminary. C. A. Bergendoff began his studies in the academy or college preparatory division of the school. Augustana sat in a lightly settled area about equal distances from the downtowns of Moline and Rock Island. The new arrival decided to join First Lutheran Church in Moline. In his first year in the college division, Carl August contracted malaria and lay a month recovering in the home of one of the professors. That, he later said, explained his slightly lower grades that term. After finishing the college course, he spent a year collecting funds for the institution, as his son would also later do (for much longer than a year).

Carl August then enrolled in the seminary. In 1892, he met Emma Fahlberg of Princeton, Illinois. A year later they married, just after seminary graduation. She was one of twelve children of an immigrant farm family. The couple's first son Conrad said that the greatest influence on his father during his seminary studies had been Olof Olsson,[17] probably the most irenic and ecumeni-

Carl August, Emma, Ruth, Conrad, and Ruben (in the sailor suit) Bergendoff, about 1900.

cal of the Synod leaders in the late nineteenth century. The older Bergendoff was ordained in 1893, at age thirty-two. The new Augustana Synod clergyman headed west to Nebraska, serving small congregations in Shickley (five years) and Newman Grove (two years), before moving to New England in 1900. The cabinet maker's son, who had wandered through southern Sweden and built pianos in Boston, had achieved a status among Swedish Americans that he would probably never have reached in his homeland. Influenced by the awakening that had swept Sweden in the nineteenth century and encouraged by his pastor in Boston, Carl August felt called by God to the ministry. But becoming a minister was also a means of upward social mobility for him, as it was for many Augustana clergy in that time. His oldest son recognized that fact when in 1980 he summarized his own research on the pastors of the Augustana Synod, noting that many of them were the sons of farmers or tradesmen and had minimal schooling: "Despairing of reaching their goals in Sweden many came to America."[18]

Carl August and Emma had five children, the first and last daughters. Their first son, born on December 3, 1895, in Nebraska, was Conrad Johan Immanuel, baptized on the New Year's Day following. The children were raised in the same serious Pietism that had characterized the childhoods of their parents. Daily devotions, sobriety, even a degree of legalism, ruled the parsonage. In addition to dancing, cards, and alcohol, the Sunday newspapers were forbidden. The Sunday morning service was the high point of the week; Pastor Bergendoff used the Swedish Lutheran liturgy. But his spirit was not harsh or judgmental, in the way that did mark the theology of some Synod men in that generation. When he retired, Pastor C. A. Bergendoff came back to Rock Island, and there at his funeral in 1940, his son Conrad said of him, "He represented the rank and file of the Augustana ministry whose work is done often in obscurity and without recognition." Their pastoral leadership, beginning in small rural parishes and then serving Swedish-American urban congregations, had been typical of the hundreds of men who built the Synod.[19] Whatever his feelings at the death of his father, Conrad Bergendoff chose in the funeral to speak of him as symbolizing a group of men whom he admired because of their role in establishing the Church to which he himself felt such loyalty. As often, we encounter Bergendoff's reluctance to speak formally in public about more personal thoughts and experience, in this case his own feelings about his father.[20]

A Yankee Town on the Connecticut

Carl August Bergendoff spent seven years in two Swedish settlements in eastern Nebraska after graduating from seminary, but as his first son was entering elementary school, the pastor took the call to Tabor Lutheran Church, the small Swedish Lutheran congregation in Middletown, Connecticut. It was a return to the Atlantic Coast where he had landed eighteen years earlier. From 1900 until 1912 he served Tabor Church, housed in a wood frame building built in 1893 (the year of its new pastor's ordination), just two years after the congregation had been organized. Two decades after leaving Connecticut, the oldest Bergendoff son wrote that he could still picture himself as a boy in the basement of his father's church, reading Luther's Small Catechism in Swedish, its frontispiece a picture of Martin Luther.[21] Upstairs was a sanctuary perhaps more elegant than the building's plain exterior might have suggested. The altar was central, in front of it the communion rail. Both, Bergendoff recalled, were draped in white when Holy Communion was celebrated. An altar painting by the popular Swedish-American artist Olof Grafström "in far away Rock Island" was purchased when the congregation's finances improved. So was a bell for the church tower, from whose dark belfry Conrad and his father watched Haley's comet.[22] That must have been in April, 1910, the year of Conrad's confirmation in the sanctuary below.

Two years later young Bergendoff graduated from Middletown High School, "an excellent, college preparatory school," which he remembered as being second only to the church in forming his ideas and values.[23] In a sense one could say that Conrad Bergendoff's whole life was spent moving between those two influences: the immigrant community of his home and church and the intellectual world of wider American society. One can only speculate on the reasons that Pastor Bergendoff took the call to Connecticut; most likely it represented professional improvement for him. But the move had a lasting influence on Conrad. Eastern Nebraska has its charms, but the high school education offered in Middletown clearly represented an academic model that the young Bergendoff would not have found in the schools of the rural settlements where his father had begun his ministry. In the same year that his oldest son graduated from Middletown High School and headed for college in Rock Island, Carl August left Tabor Church, filled a one year position soliciting funds for an Immigrant Home, and then moved to Philadelphia, where he served as pastor of Gustavus Adolphus Lutheran Church for fourteen years. This time the church building was made of brick. Like many pastors, Carl August may have waited for one of his children to finish high school before moving; the family left Middletown the day after Conrad's high school graduation.

C. A. and Emma Bergendoff's two daughters, Ruth and Eva, both married Swedish Americans. Eva's husband was Karl Mattson, a pastor who eventually became the President of Augustana Theological Seminary after it was separated from the college in 1948. Ruth, who attended Augustana herself, was a member of the housekeeping staff at North Park College in Chicago for many years.[24] The second Bergendoff son, Ruben, spent a year at Augustana, entered the army in World War I, and upon graduation studied civil engineering at the University of Pennsylvania. He became a partner in a major Kansas City firm, once the largest of its kind in the country. For three years, while Centennial Bridge between Rock Island and Davenport was being built by his company, Ruben lived in Rock Island, supervising construction. Among his colleagues Ruben was known as "Bergie," a nickname also given to Conrad in his teens. (Augustana College students applied it to their president only rarely—and never to his face.) The youngest son of the family, Carl, studied at Pennsylvania and Northwestern, entered banking, and ended his career as president of a bank in Glen Ellyn, Illinois. On retirement Carl August and Emma Bergendoff moved to Rock Island. In 1936 they saw their oldest boy installed as President of Augustana College and Theological Seminary there. Carl August died in Rock Island in 1940, Emma in 1961.[25]

At the turn of the century the town where the Bergendoff children were raised had 20,000 inhabitants. Middletown lay on the west bank of the Connecticut River, about sixteen miles south of Hartford. The river emptied into Long Island Sound about thirty miles to the southeast, and in the eighteenth century, Middletown had been an important seaport, the rival of New York and Boston. In the later nineteenth century, manufacturing replaced maritime commerce, and waves of immigrants—Irish, Italian, Polish, and German—were drawn to the Connecticut Valley to work in the new mills. Scandinavians, especially Swedes, also found their way there. After the Civil War, the Augustana Synod planted a number of congregations to serve them. By the turn of the century, there were twenty-four Swedish Lutheran churches in the Hartford District of the New York Conference.

Eventually (1912) these congregations and others in New England became a separate conference of the Synod. That New England Conference was understood in the Church to be one of its more "Swedish-tending" areas.[26] But it was less successful in attracting a high percentage of the Swedish-American population in the region than sister conferences in such states as Iowa, Nebraska, and Kansas. That may have been, says Dag Blanck, a Swedish scholar of Augustana history, because the membership of congregations on the East Coast, like the church in Middletown, was made up largely of Swedish immigrants who arrived later than their Midwestern counterparts had. These newer Swedes were as a whole less inclined to associate with the Church.[27] They brought with them across the Atlantic the secular attitudes into which Sweden was then settling. With the hyper-patriotism generated in the US by World War I and the passage of the Immigration Act of 1924, immigration slowed, and hyphenated Americanism became ever more dubious. That was true in the Swedish-American Augustana Synod as well as elsewhere. It grew more slowly between the World Wars than it had in its first half century.

For other Americans, without hyphens, Middletown was a cultural center. It was the home of Wesleyan University, which the town fathers lured to their midst in 1831 with the offer of financial and construction support. Founded by Methodists, Wesleyan, in contrast to many other church sponsored small schools, was not primarily intended to educate men for the ministry. Its first president, Wilbur Fisk, pioneered the teaching of the natural sciences and of modern as well as classical languages and literature as regular parts of the curriculum. So the school was a paradigm of what many other American liberal arts colleges would more gradually become. It must have conditioned Conrad Bergendoff's own understanding of higher education when, decades later, he got the chance to shape a college founded within his own Church tradition. In 1870 a building devoted entirely to the teaching of the sciences was constructed at Wesleyan, one of the first college structures in the country to be built solely for that purpose. During Conrad Bergendoff's school years in Middletown, the university admitted women. Later it repented of the move and began in 1912 (as young Bergendoff entrained for Rock Island) to refuse them. Until 1968 it maintained that all-male character; then women were again enrolled. When Bergendoff was growing up, the university was related to the Methodist Church. These ties were finally severed in 1938, though the name honoring the founder of Methodism, John Wesley, remained.

Many years after he and his family had left Middletown, Conrad Bergendoff spoke of delivering newspapers to the patrician homes that lay along the town's tree lined streets. One of his customers was an Episcopalian bishop, the father of Dean Acheson, who later became US Secretary of State. Another home on his route belonged to "a leading manufacturer, who was wont to give me a dollar bill each year as I delivered his paper on Christmas eve."[28] Bergendoff also recalled that his father's church, "not in a choice location, nor ... an architectural contribution to the city," was not one of the major established ecclesiastical institutions of the town. Those were Methodist, Congregationalist, Episcopalian, and Baptist. As Swedish and Lutheran, he wrote, he felt himself to be not quite a stranger in the town, but certainly "a newcomer in an old Yankee community." The larger churches in more prime locations "represented a kind of Protestantism that seemed to belong here."[29] It would be some decades before Lutherans were treated as equals by these mainline denominations, Bergendoff noted later.[30] That was true in Middletown and across the country as well.

Very likely language as well as liturgy and theology separated Swedish Lutherans from Methodists or Congregationalists. One supposes that the immigrant members of Carl August's congregation were hewers of stone and drawers of water to the old line "American" families of Middletown. But in his first essay at Augustana, freshman Conrad reflected with the kind of nostalgia that may descend upon a seventeen year old separated by long railroad miles and at least a few weeks from his hometown and family. For him Middletown seemed to signify a time of life now passed. It was a town that his family left as their son went off to school. That freshman essay, "From the Connecticut to the Mississippi," appeared in the student monthly, the *Observer.* Conrad recalled one of the thousand-foot hills that lay outside Middletown. On bright early mornings it shone in the quiet waters of the Connecticut. "Does the sun still rise over Cobalt Mountain? ... This is the question I would like to ask now as I am a thousand miles away from there."[31] In Conrad Bergendoff's mind Middletown was his hometown—at least for awhile. But he would return there seldom, since his own family left when he did. And in any case, Rock Island would soon replace it in his heart. Bergendoff often said that the city on the Mississippi had really been his spiritual hometown all his life.

The Swedish-American Capital on the Mississippi

After the Augustana Synod had moved its college and seminary there in 1875, Rock Island had become the religious capital of Swedish America.[32] The Augustana Book Concern, the Church's printing house, issued a steady stream of periodicals, books, tracts, and other religious and cultural materials that proclaimed "the ambitions and ideals of a people of which I was a part," Bergendoff wrote when he retired as Augustana College President.[33] He noted too that little was "borrowed in those early days from the 'Yankee' environment." Rather, "all the cultural and religious roots were in Sweden, and models were found in tradition."[34] But no matter how uncontaminated by Yankee influences the flow of thought and material from Rock Island was, the capital of Swedish America did not command equal loyalty in all the provinces. Indeed, many denizens of Swedish America quickly left its ethnic latitudes and were assimilated into the general population of their new country. Swedish Americans, within the Synod and without, knew that the majority of new arrivals never affiliated with the Augustana Lutheran Church. A subsequent chapter will address the absorption of many of the immigrants and their descendants into the general American population. It remains the case, however, that if Swedish America did have a spiritual capital city, it was Rock Island, Illinois.

Even as he grew up in the shadow of a fine small university and graduated high school with classmates who would attend the excellent universities of New England, Bergendoff could "never recall the time that I had any other ambition than to study at Augustana in far away Illinois."[35] In a 1951 tribute to a deceased Augustana colleague, Bergendoff spoke of S. J. Sebelius, a young man growing up in Pennsylvania: "But even there his thoughts turned to Augustana."[36] A few years after offering that tribute, Bergendoff said essentially the same thing about himself: "my youthful ambition was to go to college where my father had graduated, to Augustana."[37] Those statements were made at a time, the 1950s, when it was increasingly clear to Bergendoff that the conditions that had engendered that loyalty in a whole generation were vanishing. But to him those years and that tradition were still vivid. As a boy in Middletown, he, together with all his family, had eagerly awaited the weekly arrival of the Synod's newspaper, *Augustana*. The children carefully read its youth publication, *Ungdomsvännen* (The Friend of Youth), "a first class literary production" whose pictures "were welcome to us children who stumbled over the rhetoric of a cultivated language." (He meant Swedish.) His father's *Almanacka* also came from Rock Island, and along with the names and addresses of the Synod's clergy, it had astronomical calculations based on "Rock Island's horizon." Was there a better view of Heaven itself from the Mississippi River town? It was no wonder that "in my formative years Rock Island came to mean a view-point from which I saw the Christian church."[38]

Years later, when the Synod found itself struggling between an emphasis upon its regional conferences as against the central authority of the national headquarters, Bergendoff recalled that he never had felt a particular loyalty to the regional bodies; it was the stuff that came from the national Church institutions and publications that got to his home "on the very periphery of the Synod" and drew his interest to western Illinois.[39] Rock Island "was a connecting point of all I had learned in Swedish with all I knew of the church in this country." "It represented a faith and a way of life I deeply cherished and wanted to help interpret to those who, I knew, did not fully understand its meaning."[40] Bergendoff

Gustav Andreen, fourth President of Augustana College and Theological Seminary.

must have climbed off the Rock Island Railroad, as his father had decades earlier, with great expectations. Now he was at the very center of Swedish-American Lutheranism. If ever a man spent his life interpreting it to others, it would be he.

Conrad Bergendoff recognized that his Church itself held some people who "did not fully understand its meaning." Nor did most of the wider world. For Bergendoff the key to human life lay in the faith that the Synod's founders had planted in America. And the key to spreading that faith, Hasselquist and other Synod leaders believed, was a ministry trained in its own higher educational institutions. Augustana was the first of these to be founded. When Bergendoff enrolled it had about two hundred students. The major campus buildings were the original Old Main, built in 1875 at the time of the school's arrival in Rock Island; Memorial Hall, dedicated in 1889 (and after the demolition of the 1875 building, renamed Old Main, the name it still bears); East Hall, built in 1881 as a residence for faculty; and a small gymnasium to the south of Memorial Hall. In 1911 the college had dedicated Denkmann Library, a gift from the children of a leading Rock Island business family. A two-story building, Ericson Hall, acquired by the college as a gift from an Iowa donor, was used for the sciences. Intended to be temporary, that arrangement lasted until a new science hall was built in the 1930s. All of these buildings save the gymnasium were strung out along Seventh Avenue, which had been paved by the city in 1902. That thoroughfare connected Rock Island and Moline, each a town of about 24,000 persons according to the 1910 census.

The college lay at the east end of Rock Island, only a matter of blocks from the Moline city line. Students were discouraged from sampling the social life of either of the downtowns; both included taverns, pool halls, and theaters that had been forbidden to students by college policy, written in the nineteenth century.

Rock Island had been a river boat town when the college moved there in 1875, and Moline was a manufacturing center, particularly for farm machinery. College lore from the early twentieth century is full of stories in which Augustana students, breathing righteousness, marched to clean up the cities where they had come to study; a few such stories suggest that on rare occasions one or another student would have already sampled the wicked delights afforded by the worldly sides of Moline or Rock Island, there to be discovered by his shocked crusading classmates.

Gustav Andreen, an 1881 graduate of the college who held a doctorate from Yale, had become the fourth President of Augustana in 1901. After being elected president, Andreen enrolled in the seminary because he and others believed that the head of the school must be a minister. He was ordained in 1905. So dire was the financial condition of the institution that the Rev. Dr. Andreen passed most of his time travelling through the Synod seeking support. One calendar year "Prexy" had spent seventy-seven nights on sleeping cars. In the president's absence, Bergendoff's first year English professor, E. F. Bartholomew, who held the position of Vice President of the College, directed its affairs. Senior faculty annual salaries ranged from $1,200 to $1,500 in 1912. That range was competitive with similar Illinois and Lutheran colleges. Andreen's salary at the time was $2,500 (equal to $57,500 purchasing power in 2012). The endowment of $312,000 was also comparable with schools of equal size in the region. When Conrad Bergendoff left for Rock Island, Wesleyan University in Middletown had $2,000,000 in investments. In 1912 Augustana became a member of the accrediting agency for Midwest universities and colleges, the North Central Association. It was the body which two decades later would take a dim view of both Augustana's finances and some of its instructional facilities.

The curriculum under which Conrad Bergendoff studied had been restructured in 1910. Fifteen units of high school work were required for admission. They included English, classical or modern language, algebra and geometry, science, and history. For the degree Bachelor of Arts a student needed one hundred and twenty credits. Study had to be focused on one of several tracks: classical, modern languages, Latin-science, general science, or mathematics. Languages taught included French, German, Greek, Latin, and Swedish. The sciences included astronomy, biology, chemistry, geology, and physics. English writing and literature, history, mathematics, philosophy, and political science were offered, as were drawing, elocution, and pedagogy. Every student was required to take courses in the Department of Christianity each year of enrollment. Numbers of students still entered the college from a preparatory academy housed on the same campus, which was the means by which relatively

The entering class, Augustana College, 1912. Conrad Bergendoff is in the top row, second from the viewer's left.

unschooled immigrants could make their way into college-level work, as Carl August Bergendoff had. All of the students on the campus, academy, college, and seminary, attended the daily chapel services in Memorial Hall, usually about twenty minutes long. Sunday evening services were held in both Swedish and English.[41] Sunday mornings you were expected to attend a local Lutheran church.

Conrad Bergendoff had had a strong high school course; in fact, when he got to Augustana, he found a difference in level of preparation between himself and most of his classmates.[42] The implication was that the difference favored the boy from Connecticut. Conrad took his new academic responsibilities just as seriously as in high school and as he would through the rest of his life. He studied Latin, Greek, and Swedish, and accumulated credits in English, philosophy, and political science. His report cards are in the college archives. In the required Christianity courses his highest grade was "96," his lowest "80." But all of his undergraduate years in the capital city of Swedish-American Lutheranism were not spent in grinding study. After the freshman essay on his train trip to Rock Island, articles by or about Bergendoff showed up regularly in the pages of the *Observer*. In fact, to judge by its "Society" column young Conrad entered almost at once into the social scene at the college. The 1912 and 1913 issues of the student monthly reported on Christmas and Valentine parties his older sister Ruth (also at Augustana) and he hosted. Three Greek-letter groups for women and two for men had recently begun. They existed alongside the older literary and debating societies, toward which Bergendoff himself was more inclined. In a 1914 *Observer* article he lamented the fact that these ancient societies "have taken a slump, while athletics have been boosted." Conrad was also involved in religious activities during his undergraduate years. He contrasted Christianity with Marxism in another article in the college student monthly,[43] developed an interest in the unification of American Lutheranism, and listened carefully to visiting lecturers, from his own and other denominations.[44]

Bergendoff would never regard college athletics with the seriousness with which he looked at more cerebral activities, as his years as president of his college would demonstrate. The 1914 essay on athletics and the literary societies was, therefore, something of a portent. He felt that other Illinois colleges were doing much more for literary and debate groups than his. The same issue of the student publication had an article about the possible resumption of football, just approved by the Board of Directors. The matter was now pending before the Synod, which in the early years of the century had banned the sport in its colleges. Students had been more likely to boast of the quality of their football team than of their college president, historians of the Synod tell us.[45] In spite of these skewed inclinations, football was eventually resumed—with Church approval. Augustana musical groups included most notably the Handel Oratorio Society, which had presented sacred music since 1881.

Bergendoff entered Augustana with advanced credits from high school and finished his BA in three years, ranking as salutatorian in the class of 1915. The valedictorian was Margaret Olmsted, a local young woman, first in the class of thirty-five. At the beginning of the second half-century of its life, Augustana College was attracting local students as well as those from Synod congregations across the country. That was a pattern that would characterize the college well into the 1915 salutatorian's years as its president. Though he was second in the class, it was Bergendoff's speech that was the lead article in the college paper that May. Its thesis was, "Mankind changes, only as its ideals change." "The purpose of our education seems thus to have been the creation of right ideals," he told the graduates and guests. These ideals included an understanding of right and wrong and a readiness to share with others the truths that one had discovered.[46] In the brief talk there is some hint of the inclination Bergendoff had throughout his life to treat the highest ideals and values of his culture as the ones which the Christian faith supported, and to suggest that without Christian commitment these were likely to fall by the way. Bergendoff's strong emphasis upon the individual Christian's personal encounter with Christ that marked his mature theological position is not evident in this talk. Nor does this emphasis emerge in other writings and speeches that date from his late teens and early twenties; it first appears, as Chapter 3 will, I hope, make clear, after Bergendoff had finished his theological education and begun his pastoral ministry.

The Augustana College campus in 1915, the year of Conrad Bergendoff's graduation.

Advanced Study in the East

The salutatorian had, in any event, finished his undergraduate career in three rather than four years and was now ready for further study. The September issue of the 1915 *Observer* reported that "Conrad Bergendoff of Philadelphia, Pennsylvania" had received a scholarship to study at the University of Pennsylvania. The new Bachelor of Arts had returned to live with his parents, now in a new city. Fortified by the spiritual and academic ideals he had learned in his Christian-based home and college-oriented high school, and equipped with an undergraduate education at his father's alma mater, Conrad Bergendoff undertook advanced training in one of the country's secular universities, spending the academic year 1915-1916 at Pennsylvania. There, aged twenty, he earned a master's degree in English and history. So broad were academic disciplines in the early twentieth century, that such a combination of separate departments for a graduate degree was unremarkable. The two history courses he took impressed Bergendoff to the point that that discipline replaced literature as his major academic interest. The professor who most influenced him was E. P. Cheyney (1861-1947), a Quaker who taught English history. Cheyney used a number of basic "natural laws" as keys to interpreting human history. They stressed the changing and interdependent character of societies, which may well have broadened Bergendoff's perspective on the rather static and restrictive ideas about history and truth then current in the Augustana Synod.[47]

The following year the Master of Arts returned to Augustana to teach English, one in the long line of apprentice professors who would spend an interval between their MA and PhD work teaching English composition to first year students at the college. In 1917 Bergendoff turned east again, to take a course at Columbia University, to enroll at the Biblical Teachers Training School in New York City (today New York Theological Seminary), and in the academic year 1918-1919 to study at the Lutheran Theological Seminary in Philadelphia, commonly known from the neighborhood where it was located as "Mt. Airy." Bergendoff later expressed gratitude for the courses at Columbia and the Biblical School, but Mt. Airy made the strongest impression on the twenty-two year old. While it may have been located on the more liberal end of the American Lutheran spectrum, especially when compared with Augustana Seminary, Mt. Airy was generally identified as the more conservative of the two Lutheran seminaries in eastern Pennsylvania. The other one, at Gettysburg, was allied with the General Synod, while Mt. Airy was associated with the General Council, the pan-Lutheran body formed after the Civil War as a counterweight to the more liberal General Synod. The Augustana Synod was a member of the General Council, so Bergendoff was hardly venturing into the uncharted waters of American liberal religion when he enrolled at Mt. Airy in 1918, though that did not mean that he would have been welcomed into the Augustana ministerium had he finished his theological education there. But Conrad was not rebelling against his own denomination and its seminary when he studied at Mt. Airy. His family had moved to Philadelphia, so he was able at little cost to live at home with his parents while he took courses at the seminary.

In the late 1910s the Philadelphia school enrolled seventy-five students and had a faculty of seven professors. Its dean and leading figure was Henry Eyster Jacobs (1844-1932). Educated at Gettysburg College and at the Lutheran seminary in the same town, Jacobs, both a theologian and an historian, was by 1919 a major force in the eastern wing of American Lutheranism. That wing had just (1918) formed the United Lutheran Church. Jacob's *History of the Lutheran Church in America* (1893) was the definitive treatment of its complicated subject. Reflecting years later on his own work as an historian, Bergendoff said that it was Jacobs who had challenged him "to reconcile the role of the church and the secular world."[48] Further, Jacobs' ecumenical disposition and his understanding of the central themes and ideas in Lutheran Christianity had, as we shall see, a strong influence on Bergendoff throughout his career. Perhaps the most basic affinity between the professor and his Swedish-American student lay in their deep historical consciousness and the manner in which that generated a certain conservatism. In his history of American Lutheranism, Jacobs wrote, "Even where there are the best of reasons for abandoning, in some directions, the past development, it must be done intelligently, or far more may be lost than is gained."[49] Through the decades after he left Mt. Airy, that was certainly the way Conrad Bergendoff would approach questions of change, whether in the church, education, or society at large.

Luther D. Reed (1873–1972) taught liturgics during Bergendoff's time in Philadelphia; later Reed and his former student would collaborate in the effort to create a universal American Lutheran Order of Service based on materials from the Ancient Church and the Reformation. In the same years that he took courses in New York and at Mt. Airy, Bergendoff worked as an assistant to Mauritz Stolpe, pastor of historic Gustavus Adolphus Lutheran Church in New York. In fact, he lived with the Stolpe family for a time.[50] Those years in New York prefigured a decade, the 1920s, in which Bergendoff would combine pastoral work with academic study. The congregation of about one thousand was almost completely Swedish speaking, but sensed its growing isolation from the life of the city and called Bergendoff as an English speaking lay assistant. His responsibilities at Gustavus Adolphus Church included working with the Sunday School program, which he described in some detail for readers of the 1919 *Lutheran Companion*. He spent the "precious 90 minutes allotted" teaching children both Swedish and English, with particular attention to the *Högmässa* or High Mass of the Church of Sweden. "This heritage the child should receive, from the church of his fathers," Bergendoff wrote.[51] That was another pointer in the direction his career would take—interpreting their tradition to the young people of his denomination.

Bergendoff also began ecumenical exploration in those New York years. In a personal statement written two decades later, he spoke of attending Fifth Avenue Presbyterian Church in the city, "Sunday after Sunday," to listen to the minister, John Henry Jowett, and his "contemporary interpretation of the Eternal Word of God." For Bergendoff that was always the nature of great Christian preaching: relating the timeless Christian message to current situations and conditions.[52] Somehow he integrated his Sunday School responsibilities at Gustavus Adolphus Church with listening to a Presbyterian. From its founding the Lutheran congregation had been something of an outlier in the Augustana Synod, claiming its authority directly from the Church of Sweden, not from Rock Island. In any event, Pastor Stolpe seems not to have objected to Conrad's excursion into Calvinism.[53]

In 1919 Bergendoff got a summons from Rock Island that ended his two years in New York and Philadelphia. It was, he later recalled, couched "in almost harsh terms."[54] United Lutheran-Augustana feelings were running high over the Synod's unwillingness to join in the formation of the ULCA in 1918, and Bergendoff was told that if he intended to be ordained in his own Church, the Augustana Evangelical Lutheran Synod, he would need to return to Rock Island to complete his seminary education.[55] Even though the theological school at Mt. Airy had been supported by the General Council to which Augustana belonged, it was regarded in Rock Island as somewhat liberal, and the theological faculty of the Synod were not quite ready to certify one of its graduates for ministry in their midst. Bergendoff obeyed the call to return home, graduating from Augustana Theological Seminary two years later. His Mt. Airy credits evidently transferred. One of his friends from the Philadelphia school wrote to Bergendoff: "I am sorry for you. . . . I do not want to see you wasting your efforts in a Swedish church if it can be avoided. Unless, of course, you through it assume the leadership of the Augustana Synod and promise me to swing them into the U.L.C."[56] The classmate's wish about bringing Augustana into the United Lutheran Church was to be granted, though it would take another four decades. The classmate himself, Henry H. Bagger, would become the President of the Philadelphia Seminary.

Along with these condolences from Bagger, Bergendoff brought with him from Pennsylvania to Illinois a commitment to the unification of American Lutheranism. His experience studying at the seminary in Philadelphia had convinced him that the United Lutherans, of whom many Augustana leaders were somewhat leery, taught the same faith he had learned in his own Synod. He believed that he could serve the cause of Lutheran unity from within that Synod rather than by switching to another Lutheran body.[57] It may be that the time spent by that one student in Philadelphia was a contributing factor in the decision by the Augustana Synod eventually to cast its lot with the United Lutheran Church. That denomination, the result of the Lutheran merger negotiations after World War I, was the largest partner in the eventual (1962) creation of the Lutheran Church in America (LCA). The other choice for the Synod, perhaps in some ways more obvious, would have been to join its ethnic Norwegian-American cousins when in 1960 they and others formed the American Lutheran Church (ALC). For a quarter century the ALC lived on a sort of parallel track with the LCA until the two joined to form the Evangelical Lutheran Church in America in the late 1980s. More to follow.

Two More Years in Rock Island

The seminary to which Bergendoff "returned" in 1919 was conservative. Somewhat larger than Mt. Airy, it enrolled about one hundred, and had a faculty of eight, including President Andreen. Twenty-nine courses were offered to the students, who needed a bachelor's degree to begin study. Instruction was held in facilities shared with the college. Not until 1923 was the Synod able to dedicate separate seminary buildings on Zion Hill, which had to have thirty feet scraped off its oak-covered crest to hold the new construction.[58] The most influential member of the seminary faculty was Conrad Emil Lindberg, who taught theology from 1890 until his death in 1930. One historian of the Synod, G. Everett Arden, says of him, "it is doubtful if Dr. Lindberg seriously altered or drastically modified his basic and fundamental position during his years as a theological professor."[59] Lindberg's outlook had been set by the nineteenth century struggles of the Augustana Synod with the Pietists and Mission Friends, with liberal eastern Lutherans who were willing to compromise or "Americanize" Lutheran theology, and with the Methodists, Baptists, and Episcopalians who constantly sought to proselyte among Swedish immigrants.[60] Lindberg was a determined Lutheran creedalist, one of the sort of whom University of Minnesota historian George M. Stephenson, himself a member of the Synod and an Augustana College alumnus, wrote, "They would never recede one step from the position that the framers of the Augsburg Confession had formulated for all time the tenets of the Christian religion. What was the truth in Luther's generation was the truth in theirs and would be the truth in the church of their children."[61] A counterpoint to Stephenson's view was that of Hugo Söderström, a Swedish scholar writing in 1973: Augustana, he suggested, held that the confessions were the correct reading of the Bible because the alternative was everyman interpreting Holy Writ for himself.[62] In that direction lay what the Synod's leadership, fairly or not, saw as revivalist chaos.

Historian Stephenson's view about the rest of the Augustana Seminary faculty at the time of Bergendoff's student days there was just as scathing as his view of Synod doctrinal rigidity: "With but one exception, no theological professor in the last thirty years has possessed a bona fide Ph.D. degree, and critics of the seminary have pointed out that none has had a distinguished book of research to his credit." The faculty, he said, were called to be seminary professors "solely upon the basis of several years' service in congregations, sometimes in rural districts."[63] Those were hard words but true, as a glance through the seminary catalog for 1920 reveals. After he had become the seminary's dean, Bergendoff spoke appreciatively in public of its history, especially when appealing to the Synod for support, but his private recollections were not so positive. He recalled the tedium of his own student years there as well as the controversy concerning its academic standards that swirled around the school in the twenties. That eventually led, as we shall see, to his becoming its dean. Shortly after graduating he wrote to Professor S. G. Youngert that he was concerned that the school "is behind in scholastic attainments."[64] The rigid orthodoxy or "Lutheran scholasticism," particularly that of Lindberg, left Bergendoff unchallenged. He recalled that the notes he took in Lindberg's class did not differ appreciably from those his father had kept three decades earlier.[65] Interviewed in his eighties, he commented that the school had been "in bad shape" intellectually during his student days.[66]

His reaction to these two years at Augustana Theological Seminary was about as negative as Bergendoff ever got about the religious community in which he had grown up. We learn that when Bergendoff's mentor Nathan Söderblom, later Archbishop of the Church of Sweden, left home for the university, tension developed between him and his Pietist father, a rural priest. At times the student resented the gloomy dominance of the father and pitied the long-suffering depression of his mother.[67] There is no evidence in young Bergendoff of any such difficulties with his family or Church; his reaction to what he found to be the arid atmosphere in the Rock Island seminary is as close as he got to tension with, let alone rebellion against, his up-bringing and tradition.

For his part, the historian G. E. Arden notes that two of Lindberg's colleagues did in fact read works of contemporary biblical criticism, but that they always did so in the context of conservative Lutheran thought. For example, S. G. Youngert, who taught Biblical Introduction and New Testament, recognized the existence of an oral tradition behind the four Gospels of the New Testament, but also held that it was Moses himself who wrote every one of books of the Pentateuch. When Prof. Youngert died in 1939 Bergendoff spoke of his hour-long lectures, delivered without a break. Youngert's eyes looked straight ahead over the heads of his students, staring "far away into time and space," Bergendoff recalled.[68] C. J. Sodergren, who taught New Testament and Greek, recognized discrepancies in the biblical texts but firmly held to "the plenary inspiration of the Bible" as the true word of God and therefore definitive for faith and practice.[69] That was a view which fitted him to teach at the ultra-conservative Lutheran Bible Institute in Minneapolis when he left Rock Island in 1920.[70] But perhaps the most rigid member of the faculty was Adolf Hult, whose long and relentless opposition to any ecumenism would later be countered by Bergendoff's own precocious commitment to inter-church dialog—among Lutherans and, later, among all Christians. Aged eighty, Bergendoff recalled that already in 1920 he had raised questions about Hult's "ultra-orthodoxy" in that professor's class.[71]

The theological school Bergendoff entered was not compromised by any sort of "modernism" or liberalism. In maintaining this stance it was faithful to the thought and ethos of the Augustana Synod's founders, men whom Bergendoff would at less critical moments treat with something close to what historians have referred to as "filiopietism." That is the tendency of descendants to reflect upon their forebears with a deep respect that, consciously or not, tends to avoid negative criticism. Eighteen years after receiving his Bachelor of Divinity degree, Bergendoff, seeking to be affirmative, wrote that the seminary faculty members carried the school through a time of transition in the Synod. Presumably he was referring to the shift from a body of Swedish speaking immigrants to an English language American denomination.[72] And seven decades after graduating, in 1993 when he was ninety-eight, Conrad Bergendoff was favorable, at least publicly, about the seminary. He reminded the Swedish-American community that the school had become by the turn of the century a university level institution: "Altogether it is safe to assume that the Seminary in Rock Island matched most of the offerings of American theological schools of that day," he wrote.[73] He was not that upbeat when he left Mt. Airy to study in Rock Island seventy years earlier, or, for that matter, when he graduated. But he had paid his Synod dues.

Whatever he took from his years at Augustana Theological Seminary and however he remembered his time there, Conrad Bergendoff graduated in 1921 with a strong regard for his own tradition—along with a Bachelor of Divinity degree. What he did not get was a significant acquaintance with contemporary theological trends in the wider world of European and American Protestantism. His deepening knowledge of more modern developments in religious thought was evidently gained through his own reading and reflection, rather than from his class work as a seminarian. In that sense he was perhaps an autodidact with regard to contemporary theology. The entries in his early journals recording his private study are evidence of that. Bergendoff's subsequent work as professor and ecumenist was based on his own wide and thorough reading more than on his class work at Augustana, 1919 to 1921.

If his seminary years in Rock Island did not make Conrad Bergendoff's Lutheranism wider, it did make it deeper. In the early 1920s there emerged in Bergendoff's own preaching and writing a strong "Christocentric" emphasis. It would remain the core of his life and thinking thereafter. Each person, he believed, must her- or himself encounter Jesus Christ. That meeting (though Bergendoff would not have used the term) was, of course, a "spiritual" one. Only the first Christians and St. Paul had met Christ directly. But for Bergendoff the two millennia during which unnumbered humans had also encountered Christ testified to the power that changed personal lives and, to some extent, society. In this Bergendoff was certainly faithful to his Augustana Synod roots, ones strengthened by his years in its seminary. The strong evangelical cast to his thought could be traced back through the seminary faculty to the Synod's founders and past them to the evangelical awakening and the Pietism of nineteenth century Sweden. Bergendoff's thought was also resonant of the piety and theology at the Philadelphia seminary where he had studied before being summoned back to Rock Island. Beyond this, he had internalized the social mores prevailing in his Synod and seminary. That is attested to by his membership pledge to the Intercollegiate Prohibition Association in 1921.[74]

Of course, Conrad Bergendoff was not only studying Lutheran theology and tradition during these years. Back in Rock Island, he also reappeared in the columns of the *Observer.* And his interests were wider than the Bible or church history or theology. For example, an early 1920 issue had two contributions by the seminarian. In one Bergendoff took up the theme with which he had as class salutatorian hailed fellow graduates five years earlier: "The student of noble ideals is this generation's greatest asset. The conditions of to-day are the result of false and ignoble philosophies of life." And the remedy: "The Christian Student is the preserving salt of the world and its guiding light."[75] Here was the appearance of another theme that would for seventy-five years mark Bergendoff's view of the relationship between Christianity and culture. Human culture was in a steady decline; the twenty-five year old was already a pessimist in this matter. But that was balanced by the hope that Christian influence was preserving whatever goodness modern life did have. And the future might still be more positive, should secular society turn to the Gospel. Conrad Bergendoff never settled the questions of whether Christianity might turn society around or whether it even promised that in the first place.

If modern society could be awakened, it would be because God was using trained Christians to carry the message. That is where Augustana came in. The other 1920 *Observer* article, "What Think the Alumni of Augustana?" gave some inkling that the young Bergendoff had ambitions for his college. Maybe he even thought he might have some role in realizing them. Augustana needed, he wrote, a new seminary building, a science hall, and additional student housing. That would take money, and the author of the piece must little have guessed how much of his own life would later be spent looking for just such support for just that school. The 1920 appeal ended with a stirring summons: "Awake, arise, make real your faith in Augustana!"[76] Later Bergendoff's fund-raising

Bulldozers and horses scraping the top off "Zion Hill," to prepare the site for the Augustana Seminary's new buildings, erected in 1923, two years after Conrad Bergendoff's graduation and ordination.

39

style would become more subdued, but his belief that the mission of "Christian higher education" was to build a cadre of persons who could witness in the secular world to Christian truth and high moral values was never compromised. This belief correlated well with his ideas on how society might be made more Christian, which we will consider in Chapter 4.

In a March article Bergendoff enumerated the prominent scientists who had graduated from Augustana and were now listed in *Who's Who*. That was another device he was to use for many years. He believed the achievements of its alumni validated their years at Augustana. There is little notice in the college paper of the World War just concluded, but Bergendoff did argue in February, 1920, that athletics and physical education did have a place in undergraduate education: the need for conditioning had been clearly shown by the war. But beyond that "athletics is worth while as an allegorical application to life in general. . . .[I]f we are to win out in the game of life, we must play the game hard, and to the finish."[77] The writer had evidently forgiven intercollegiate sports for eclipsing literary societies in the middle of the previous Augustana decade, and his rhetoric in support of athletics now attained Jack Armstrongian heights. In all, Bergendoff wrote about twenty articles dealing with topics ranging from Christian Science to foreign missions to Bible study during his two years at Augustana Seminary.[78] He was also instrumental in organizing a "Young People's Christian Conference" which attracted over five hundred young people from Synod congregations to the campus in 1921. Bergendoff himself gave the keynote speech, which stressed the influence on the church and the world which a cadre of dedicated youth might have when they united in the interests of religious and social renewal. The *Lutheran Companion* was pleased at the seriousness and promise of Augustana youth; the editor wrote that the event had been "no mere jolification [sic] affair."[79]

§

Through Bergendoff's two years in the seminary the *Observer* had regularly been reporting his extensive activities in campus religious life and in alumni matters. There were already signs that the young man from the Connecticut River Valley was headed for a leading role in the life of Augustana, both Synod and college. He had cast his lot in his own tradition rather than sliding over into the more ecumenical and, as he judged things, more intellectually lively Lutheranism of the eastern United States, though the blandishments of his friends in the United Lutheran Church would follow him for many years. But right then the twenty-five year old in question was intent upon combining the life of a pastor with that of a graduate student, the latter to be fitted in among his new congregational responsibilities.

CHAPTER 2

PASTOR AND PROFESSOR

By the time Conrad Bergendoff got his Bachelor of Divinity degree in 1921 he had spent six years on the Augustana campus, three as an undergraduate, one teaching, and two in the seminary. Now, on a pastoral call from Salem Lutheran Church on Chicago's south side, he was ordained to the Lutheran ministry along with nineteen other candidates. That ordination and the status it conveyed was both homage to his parents' home and church and a harbinger of a life to be spent in service to his Synod (which by convention action would turn into a "Church" in the late 1940s).

To judge by photographs taken in the fifteen years between his ordination and his appointment as the President of Augustana College and Theological Seminary, Bergendoff quickly acquired the gravity expected of a clergyman and an academic in the Augustana Evangelical Lutheran Synod. Many of his predecessors in the Synod ministerium or on the seminary faculty peer at us with just that seriousness from the interleaf picture sections of G. Everett Arden's *Augustana Heritage: A History of the Augustana Lutheran Church*. But they do it with half of their faces hidden behind beards, so you have to look at their eyes to realize what an earnest business they were engaged in. Conrad Bergendoff grew no beard; thus you get the full force of his solemnity—from the chin as well as the eyes. Bergendoff said of one of his seminary professors that while lecturing he looked over the heads of his students as though peering into the far reaches of space and time. Pastor, then Doctor, then Dean, Bergendoff seemed to be looking from a soul that knew what it believed and to be regarding a world that did not. His mission was to change the latter condition by appeal to the former. Of course, he would never have held his own faith up for emulation, but he did regard it as the commitment of one man among many others to the central truth of the ages. It was a truth that had comforted immigrants, built congregations, and steered denominations.

A New Family and a New Salem

A newly ordained member of the Augustana ministerium.

Chicago's Salem Lutheran Church ("Augustana Synod," as its letterhead made clear) had once been served by Lars G. Abrahamson, one of the denomination's leading conservative voices, who had also been the editor of the newspaper *Augustana* for about three decades. In that role he sought to steer his Synod toward a closer relationship with the Church of Sweden and to some degree away from its earlier low-church Pietism.[1] But Salem, most recently led by Pastor F. T. Anderson, had not prospered in the early twentieth century. "Hopes for the future were faint," particularly because the neighborhood around the church was rapidly changing. Bergendoff had taken the call to Salem in part because it would enable him to do graduate work at the University of Chicago. But he soon discovered himself deeply involved in parish life and leadership, as it became clear that if the congregation were to survive, drastic steps must be taken.

So Conrad Bergendoff continued to spend his days among Swedish Americans. Writing about Carl Aaron Swensson (1857-1904), an American-born graduate of Augustana, college and seminary, and the founder of Bethany College in Kansas, historian Daniel M. Pearson says that a major function of one's ethnic group "is to provide an individual with his most important primary group relationships throughout his life," and adds, "intimate and informal relationships are often restricted within the ethnic group."[2]   Bergendoff, a generation younger than Carl Aaron Swensson, validates that observation, particularly in the decades before the Second World War. Along with his new ministerial role, Conrad also assumed that of pater familias. He would often assert that the years at Salem among Swedish-American parishioners were among his happiest; that may have also had to do with his marriage in 1922 to Swedish-American Gertrude Carlson, born in 1897 at Rockford, Illinois, the daughter of immigrants from Southern Sweden. He had evidently met her while a student pastor in Rockford in the summer of 1920.[3] The new pastor was still single when he arrived at Salem; he lived in a YMCA room for a year before marriage. But after a honeymoon, during which the groom read a study of Luther by Nathan Söderblom, *Humor och melankoli*,[4] the new couple quickly settled into the Salem parsonage, and a year later a son, Conrad Luther, arrived in the family. Five years later a daughter, Beatrice, was born. Their third child, Elizabeth, came after the Bergendoffs left Chicago for the deanship of the seminary in Rock Island. Like their father, all three graduated from Augustana; in 1944, 1949, and 1958. The younger Conrad entered the ministry himself, though in the United Lutheran Church—perhaps to get out from his father's long shadow. Beatrice married and moved to Milwaukee. Elizabeth married a pastor, Richard Thulin, whom she, an Augustana College student, had met when he was up the hill at the seminary. He later took a faculty position at Gettysburg Seminary, a United Lutheran institution. The course of the Bergendoff children's lives into wider American society suggests the weakening of some of the ethnic bonds that were so crucial to their parents.

In any event, Bergendoff rarely talked about his personal life, which was not unusual among Synod pastors, whose role set them apart from ordinary folk. Among the clergy, family stability was assumed and only discussed when breached. But these ministers, Conrad among them, certainly did have home lives. Gertrude addressed her husband as "Darling." In letters written to him when he was away from home on some ecumenical mission or other, she appears as a person whose interests and activities centered upon her home and local church. She writes that Bea and she cleaned the drawers in the bedroom chest, or that Elizabeth and she went to a missionary potluck supper last night at St. John's Church, where the family were members. The letters are full of the names of Rock Islanders, usually Lutherans or Augustana people well known to her absent husband. Her comments and judgments about others were usually gentle. Augustana students remembered her as a woman "whom we enjoyed because of her obvious 'joie de vivre.'" In 1966, reflecting on his own life, Bergendoff said, "I suppose I have been endowed with a temperament that doesn't get too excited about things, but when you can see how things turn out. . . my wife and I are very different in that respect and we complement each

Conrad and Gertrude Bergendoff (and others) with Prof. E. M. Bartholomew, Conrad's undergraduate mentor.

other."[5] Years after marrying and beginning a home, one of the children wrote to the paterfamilias, "I know mother bore a great share of the responsibility in raising us, with you being away and busy so often. . . . In truth I cannot think back and say you were gone too much, for the home you and mother made for me when you *were* home was the important thing." It was the case that Bergendoff did spend much of his time away and that Gertrude often carried the load of home and children.[6]

When Gertrude died in 1979, her husband wrote a memorial to her that was printed privately and distributed among friends and family. Conrad recalled that he had seen his future wife for the first time when she was singing in a church choir. He was struck by her fine soprano voice, one she shared for forty years in Oratorio Society performances at Augustana. When it finally grew too painful for her to stand in the chorus, Gertrude sat in the audience next to him, humming through the performance. His wife loved colors and flowers, he remembered, and she dressed accordingly. When the college could not afford to pay groundskeepers, she kept her own garden around the president's campus home. To see the sunsets she loved, Gertrude would urge her husband to drive to some Rock Island spot where she could watch them; the trees around her own home blocked her view of the western sky. She was fond of mixing with others and interested in everyone she met. Bergendoff remembered that his wife once arranged the hair on the balding head of a visiting Swedish archbishop to what she felt was better advantage. It was said she had shared a fried egg with Carl Sandburg at three in the morning. Her husband found in her "a childlike innocence that she never outgrew," and from his wife Conrad believed he had "learned something about purity of soul." Gertrude had been incapable of deceit, and subtlety was foreign to her. Tricky jokes she did not grasp. "Her loyalty was unbounded, though I tried to correct exaggerations in her estimate of myself." When Bergendoff retired, they traveled in America and Europe, together more often than they had been in his working years. Their passports, full of pages stamped at foreign docks and airports, still lie in the college archives where he deposited his papers. Gertrude died a week before their fifty-seventh anniversary.[7] Years later he wrote to a younger friend who had just lost his own wife: when Gertrude died, it was "as if 2 vines had gotten entwined, the one pulled apart to leave the other to survive."[8]

The Bergendoff ministry at "Old Salem" began at a time when only a few older congregants remained. The pastor wrote that the congregation's future was not bright at the time he arrived there. Once the neighborhood had been the center of a thriving ethnic colony, where doctors, lawyers, undertakers, and storekeepers carried on their business in Swedish.[9] But now, to the east "the negro population" was taking over old homes. And, Bergendoff added, the immediate neighborhood was being settled by Roman Catholic immigrants. Salem Church's ministry to either group did not appear promising. The congregation's decision to move to a part of the city where it could continue to serve *Swedish* Americans suggests how deeply its sense of mission was tied to ethnic as well as religious factors. At a later time, congregations in the situation in which Salem found itself in the twenties would probably have resolved to stay put and adjust their ministry to the needs of their new neighbors. But in the twenties, Salem conceived of its mission as one that must be focused upon Swedes. "Old Salem," as the building on the city's near south side (3100 south of the Loop) was called, was valued at about $45,000. The congregation of about two hundred and fifty communicants sold the building to Catholics for $30,000, began to meet in a school, and bought vacant property further south (7400) for $6,000. After resolving the concerns of near-by ULCA and Augustana congregations about the arrival of more Lutheran competition,[10] planning and construction were underway. Together Bergendoff and the lay leadership began a program of regular financial support from the entire membership. They were able to erect a parsonage, a parish hall, and a chapel. The Salem Lutherans even gave up their earlier practice of selling "chances" to finance their budget. The new buildings were valued in 1930 at $155,000 with a debt of $48,200 on them. There were five hundred and fifty-three members, and the Sunday School had grown from eighty-seven to one hundred and thirteen scholars.[11]

In October, 1923, during an American trip, the Swedish Archbishop, Nathan Söderblom, visited Salem and planted a tree on the street in front of

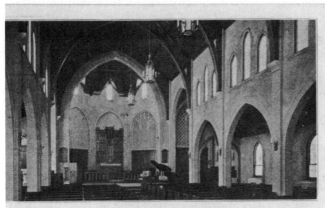

An Invitation

To you and your friends is hereby extended by the Salem Lutheran Church to worship in its sanctuary, and in case of non-affiliation with any other congregation, to m a k e this your church home, enjoying here t h o s e blessings that the Saviour offers to His people.

Conrad Bergendoff
Pastor
7352 Calumet Avenue
Vincennes 0760
Church Phone
Triangle 1788

The Evangelical Lutheran Salem Church
(Augustana Synod)
Calumet Avenue at 74th Street, Chicago
(7400 South, 350 East, One Block West of South Park Avenue)

A postcard meant to invite worshippers and possible members to the new Salem Lutheran Church, Chicago.

the new construction. By March, 1926, $26,000 had been pledged, and in that month the new sanctuary was dedicated. "New Salem" was generally recognized as "undoubtedly the most beautiful Augustana Church in Chicago." It was built in the faux Gothic style then so popular with ecclesiastical and university architects in America. The sanctuary had cost $80,000, a large sum even in those "boom days." Bergendoff later said: "God was with Salem."[12] The congregation believed that the Lord had sent their young pastor to Old Salem when but a small group of staunch members remained and "hopes for the future were faint." Pastor Bergendoff spoke of the new church as "a city or fellowship of Peace, in the midst of the sin and turmoil of this city in which the third and fourth generations of the first Salem members now dwell and work." He also recalled his own demanding participation in the rounds of meetings, prayer groups, Sunday School sessions, and men's gatherings.

The booklet printed in celebration of New Salem contained the programs and liturgies for the dedication of the new church building, but it was also filled with ads from doctors, funeral directors, insurance agencies, banks, and builders, most of them with Swedish names, though an occasional Mooney or McKay also appeared, the signs of ethnic changes yet to come. In 1922 the congregation had determined to have equal numbers of Swedish and English services, all of them more liturgical in nature than had earlier been the practice. All through his life, Pastor Bergendoff himself seems to have preferred set liturgical formulae, both ancient and recent, to the more extemporaneous expressions of faith that had often prevailed in the earlier days of the Synod, especially among Pietists. By 1928 English language worship was also the rule at Salem.[13] In 1924, at a time when the Synod came under attack for abandoning Swedish, Bergendoff defended the action of his congregation, as well as the prevailing shift to English in the entire denomination, in two forceful articles, one in the old language, one in the new. We will consider those pieces in a later chapter.

Pastoral Demeanor

The Salem pastor was also involved in synodical affairs, serving in the mid-twenties as the President of the Augustana national Luther League Council. The Synod had been somewhat dubious about youth organizations, finally deciding in 1910, after five years of debate, to permit the organization of a Synod-wide Luther League. The reservations had chiefly focused around concerns that these groups would become rivals to the very congregations that sponsored them.[14] The fact that an ordained minister rather than one of the young people themselves headed the Council suggests that the denominational fathers believed it needed mature supervision and direction. A 1925 edition of the *Lutheran Companion* pictured the President of the Luther League Council, noting that he had become "a Bible student and specialized in this work at White's Bible School, New York City."[15] Bergendoff finally resigned the Council presidency in 1928 at the same time he was finishing his doctoral work.[16] The mid-1920s had been a period of wide and intense activity for Bergendoff, both in his congregation and in the Synod. His pastorate had been, as the world might judge such things, quite successful. Salem had moved to a new neighborhood, erected a new physical plant, increased its membership, built a youth program, and raised the money to accomplish all of this. Of course, the moving and building were not entirely exceptional in the growing Augustana Synod or in American church life generally during the twenties. The editor of the *Lutheran Companion* noted with concern the drift of Synod members and churches to the suburbs and the move away from older, now changing, neighborhoods.[17]

For his part, Pastor Bergendoff insisted that the impressive growth of his congregation had been accomplished without the use of the "business" methods that had begun to characterize much American church work in the twenties. While Bergendoff was at Salem Church, *The Man Nobody Knows,* a 1925 book by the advertising executive and sometime member of Congress, Bruce Barton (1886-1967), appeared. It maintained that, contrary to common assumptions, Jesus was no other-worldly spiritual leader. Rather, he was personable and popular, always ready with a good story, a fellow who picked twelve men from the bottom ranks of business and made of them an organization that took over the Roman world. In fact, Barton wrote, Jesus had been "the founder of modern business."[18] These were not Conrad Bergendoff's views about Christ.

In 1930 Bergendoff wrote an article in the *Augustana Quarterly*, the Church's journal for clergy, in which he contrasted the "quiet, saintly pastor" with the hail-fellow-well-met now ministering in many denominations, the type whose pedigree Bruce Barton had traced back to Jesus. This modern minister, Bergendoff wrote, was "the quick, jaunty man of the world, who makes his dress that of trivial everyday life. . . . He jokes and tells stories, smokes and plays cards, cultivates always an air of polite, jovial ease and immense familiarity with the wicked world he is supposed to be endeavoring to save." But in "the bleak wilderness of twentieth century life," Bergendoff continued, the only hope lay in "the rays of light that come from a glowing fellowship of God within human hearts [and that] still illuminate the only approach possible between God and man."[19] Two years later Bergendoff lamented that in most congregations, "The office rather than the pulpit is the key position of the modern church." This was the result not "of faith but . . . of despair."[20]

That was not the ministerial style of Salem's pastor. He indicated his special position by dress as well as by demeanor, regularly wearing clerical garb. After his year in Sweden with the nation's Archbishop, Bergendoff increasingly emphasized vestments and liturgy in Salem Church, Chicago. Nathan Söderblom's time as Archbishop was seen in some Swedish and American quarters as one of *krykostât,* church pomp, marked by the reintroduction into Swedish church life of garb and ceremony that the Archbishop believed had marked the consecration of his first predecessor in the twelfth century.[21] Bergendoff later noted that in the twentieth century most Swedish bishops began to wear episcopal robes.[22] This emphasis was the very opposite, as Bergendoff saw it, of the Babbittry that was insinuating itself into American Protestantism. His skepticism about "business methods" continued through his years as a college president; it would finally grow to a point of serious tension between him and the school's Board of Directors.

So Bergendoff's personality and style were sober. In 1964, reflecting on his own experience in the ministry, Bergendoff recalled the fear with which he as a young pastor had approached people. That timidity, he said, never left him, but the reality of fellowship with God overcame it. Nothing was more pathetic than the pastor who did not believe he had "anything of certainty to give to his people."[23] Bergendoff felt it was that inner certainty—and surely not smoking or joking—that had led to the growth of Salem Church. For him the most wonderful title an ordained man could hear would always be "pastor."[24] When his first year English teacher E. F. Bartholomew died in 1946, Bergendoff preached the funeral sermon. "I don't believe you could characterize Dr.

Bartholomew as a blithe or gay spirit. I can't bring myself to think of him either as an optimist in the current meaning of that word." For the eulogist, Bartholomew's greatness lay in his sense that God was still at work in life and history. He knew that "man could never be great in a world from which he has banished God."[25] Young Bergendoff had learned more than how to write a freshman theme from his teacher. He had evidently acquired a persona, or rather may have recognized in Bartholomew qualities that his professor and he already shared, great solemnity and gravity.

A festschrift was presented to Conrad Bergendoff at the time of his retirement from Augustana. In it, one of his colleagues (and former students), Edgar M. Carlson, the President of Gustavus Adolphus College in Minnesota, wrote that while in seminary he had taken a course in the Old Testament prophet Jeremiah from Bergendoff. "There is at least a surface pessimism that runs through Jeremiah, which never gets out of hand but gives a measure of depth to the prophet's faith. And there has been that in Dr. Bergendoff also."[26] When one looks at photographs of Conrad Bergendoff during the twenties and thirties, there is a solemn set to the mouth and great seriousness in the eyes. They suggest that Carlson read him correctly, and that the qualities which Bergendoff himself felt marked the genuine pastor certainly characterized him as well. He dressed as a clergyman, did not play cards, drink, or smoke, and worried that civilization itself was on a terrible track. What he could do in the teeth of this was to witness and work for the truth that alone could save it. If his pastorate had been successful, it was all God's doing and certainly not the result of facile cheerfulness or easy optimism, let alone the application of modern American business methods.

In a revealing hand-written meditation on Psalm 23, Pastor Bergendoff considered how a Christian might carry himself in the midst of the claims and pressures of daily life. He admitted that he often judged himself by the reactions of others. If "I, rightly or wrongly, suspect that they do not estimate me highly, therefore I think myself of no great account[.]" Conversely, "should I have the feeling that by a person I am considered of some significance, . . . I act and carry myself accordingly." But, Bergendoff asked himself, would it not be better to "be myself in whatsoever company?" The key to that lay in a "piety which results from knowledge of Christ, wherein man knows well his own futility and worthlessness but wherein he knows too a redemption into a manhood that gives meaning and dignity to his life. In the hidden springs of his communion with Christ rises a spontaneous force which witnesses to men without being a demonstration of self." Through this, one finds "true joy in spiritual things amid crowding duties and oppressive cares of one's calling." "But how to keep this conviction of things unseen, or in the midst of multitudinous trifles to

A mature pastor.

follow the compass needle which directs us back to the homeland, that is the ever recurring problem, ...to catch the quiet accents of the voice of the Lord in the turbulent turmoil of a harried hurried every-day[.]"

This personal musing on Psalm 23 recognized that the temptation to go off course was great: "Before the enemy one cannot sit down in despair. Nor can one flee from this present scene. Nor is one able to assault the ramparts of the foe. . . . In the inner chamber of the heart there must be this steady communion with the Lord which gives strength and comfort to rise from the table and do the deeds of our calling in the spirit He breathes upon us and our tasks."[27] These were the deeply held beliefs about life and God that sustained Bergendoff through his heavy congregational and synodical work while he also carried on his doctoral program and began a family. The equilibratory figure who emerges from that meditation is the Bergendoff that faculty and students on the Augustana campus, fellow leaders of the Synod, and ecumenists in the nation and the world would recognize for decades. He was, in the language of the "spirituality" that emerged in the late twentieth century among Christians and fellow travelers, a "centered person," although it is by no means certain that he would have claimed that label or affirmed the mindset from which it came.

There was, therefore, an air of great solemnity about this young pastor. He was certainly cast in the mold of his synodical forefathers, who had regarded the world around them with grave misgivings and who were to a considerable degree isolated from it, both by their strong religious convictions and by their use of Swedish rather than the lingua franca of the land in which they were newly settled. The deep sense that the wider world was heading toward a debacle—this years before the advent on the world stage of Hitler or Stalin—was no mere affectation with Bergendoff. The refusal to accommodate to the easy frivolities of American life in the twenties, as clergy in other more "mainline" churches seemed to him to be doing, was the corollary of this sense of pending doom. We will see that as he became more literate in the disparate ideas and lifestyles of the twentieth century, both in America and Europe, Bergendoff persisted in his sense of alienation from them. Chapter 4 will consider his careful and detailed criticisms of secular world views emerging during his lifetime. It will shortly become clear that he was not entirely at home in the contemporary university world either, though he certainly achieved the recognitions it afforded.

A Doctorate in History

In spite of the multiple pressures, Bergendoff regarded his Salem years with great fondness. He always maintained that he had left the parish ministry with regret. He might have chosen the mission field in China, he said in 1959, but had decided instead to work in a different mission field, higher education.[28] The nineteenth century Swedish and Swedish-American Pietists who so influenced the Augustana Synod had often been called *missionsvänner,* Mission Friends. The "mission" referred not simply to foreign missions, but to the idea that every Christian must be a missionary, whether at home or overseas, and that every walk of life or occupation offered a person the chance to carry the Gospel to others. Bergendoff had that Pietistic sense of mission, so he believed that whatever his profession, his life task was to be a missionary in this broader sense.

Whether he would have preferred to stay in the Chicago ministry or become a foreign missionary, it is clear to the observer that Bergendoff certainly appeared in the twenties to be getting ready for a mission in higher education. His original reason for accepting the Salem pastoral call had been because its location would allow him to pursue a graduate degree. The call offered him an $1,800 salary and the promise that "If you are coming to Chicago to study, you can not get a better church to serve while so doing."[29] Later he said that Salem's growth and its building program had "necessitated a delay in my studies." He indicated that he had accrued "approximately 6 quarters" of credit at the University of Chicago while serving at Salem.[30] Those quarters, his transcripts reveal, were bunched in two academic years, 1921-1922 and 1927-1928. So the delay in his studies was six years long. Bergendoff earned grades ranging from "A" to "B-" in work that included American, English, Byzantine, and Christian history as well as philosophy and historical criticism.[31] The faculty member most impressing Bergendoff was the medievalist James Westfall Thompson (1869-1941), whose emphasis upon objectivity and the use of original sources,[32] would be much in evidence in Bergendoff's PhD dissertation, for which Thompson was the advisor.

Pastor Bergendoff's explanation of his reasons for entering graduate work is surprising: "I would go on to higher degrees, not for their sakes, but to prove that a higher degree did not stand in the way of an evangelical faith." And: "I wanted to ... bear witness to college students that no matter how far you go in your special field of learning you need the Word of God if you are to become a whole and healthy person." He had seen, Bergendoff held, that a great gap existed in American universities between religion and education. Much of what he read and heard in class left religion out of the account altogether. "I discovered that eminent teachers who had great reputations in their particular field avoided talking about religion, or, even worse, said things that convinced me that they knew nothing about religion, however much they knew about their subject." Though a few professors did in fact seem to be religious, most paid no attention to God.[33] These 1959 reflections came in an article in the *Lutheran Companion* that was intended to raise money for colleges throughout the Synod. The comments may perhaps have to be considered in the light of their purpose, but they do reflect again that feeling of being something of a stranger, in this case at a university.

What Bergendoff said in 1959 does seem consistent with his steady views about the relationship between human culture and the Christian Gospel. It is significant that when he began his Chicago studies they were not in the university's Divinity School, but in its History Department. That divinity faculty was dominated in the 1920s by proponents of the Social Gospel, a liberal American theology that was anathema to Bergendoff's orthodox Lutheranism. Shailer Matthews (1863-1941), a leading figure in developing the Social Gospel, was the faculty's dean. The Lutheran pastor and would-be PhD was more willing to confront plain secularism than he was to deal with deviant Protestantism. In that too he may indeed have been the son of the Augustana Synod's founders. Reflecting in retirement upon his choice of graduate program at Chicago, Bergendoff maintained that his desire to study secular history beyond that of the Christian church had figured into his decision not to enroll in the Divinity School. But the main factor seems to have been his aversion to the theology then prevailing at Chicago: "I didn't do any work in the Divinity School, I didn't like their theology."[34] Bergendoff evidently made his way onto the neo-Gothic campus of the University of Chicago in the same way he had delivered papers along the maple shaded streets of Middletown— with the sense that being Swedish Lutheran to a degree separated him from what were then "mainline" ideas and life.

While he accumulated the course credits to support his PhD candidacy and carried on his ministry at Salem and his national Luther League leadership, Bergendoff also prepared to write a dissertation. With its new building finished, his congregation agreed to give its minister a leave of absence. Supported by funds from a private source, the Westerlin family that would later make

generous gifts to Augustana College, the Bergendoffs made plans to spend a
year in Europe. The time would be mainly with the Archbishop of the Church
of Sweden, Nathan Söderblom, whom Conrad had learned to know during the
Chicago visit in 1923, when the Swedish churchman planted a tree at the site
of the New Salem. In April, 1926, Pastor Bergendoff wrote to Söderblom, with
whom he had corresponded since 1923, telling him that he had found financial
support for a year in Sweden and that his congregation had in fact granted him
a leave. He would come, he wrote, "*som en främling till Europa och till Sverige,*"
as a stranger to Europe and Sweden. Here, in spite of his own up-bringing in
Swedish-American circles, Bergendoff once more reflected the sense of being
an outsider, in this case to Sweden. But, at home in the Old World or not,
he intended to work when he got there: Bergendoff told the Archbishop that
he hoped to spend time during the coming year at Uppsala and in German
universities, gathering material for a PhD dissertation.[35]

Academic work in Europe was almost de rigueur for earlier academic
leaders in the Synod. All of the Presidents of Augustana before Bergendoff
had studied in European universities. In later years Bergendoff would
indicate that he had worked in three European institutions, Uppsala, Lund,
and Berlin. But his study was largely private research, rather than seminar
or course work. In Berlin he spent several months reading Martin Luther
in preparation for his dissertation.[36] At first he had thought to do a study
relating the Swedish Reformation to the history of the Augustana Synod, but
Söderblom had suggested that he concentrate more closely upon the work of
Olavus Petri, the principal author of the Lutheran Reformation of Sweden in
the sixteenth century. The Archbishop first proposed this to Bergendoff in a
short conversation in the Salem parsonage after the tree planting a few years
earlier.[37]

Along with visits with Söderblom to parishes in his diocese, trips to
ecumenical meetings with the Archbishop, and his own research, Bergendoff
managed to find Lars Paul Esbjörn's grave, to which he paid a solemn visit in
October, 1926. The putative founder of the Augustana Synod had returned to
Sweden in the 1860s, resumed his rural ministry, and upon his death in 1870,
was buried in the church yard in Öster-Våla, a small village near Uppsala. The
town lay on no rail line, so Conrad, Gertrude, and their toddler were driven
by an accommodating local pastor to the site, where they prayed, sang a psalm,
and, reflecting, made their silent way back from the grave to the car in which
they had arrived, an Essex sedan which, Bergendoff noted, was barely large
enough to hold the small company. The simple gravestone said, "Here rests the
professor and pastor, Lars Paul Esbjörn, the founder of the Swedish Evangelical
Lutheran Church in America." "It was a gripping time," Bergendoff reported

in *Augustana,* the Synod's Swedish language periodical, "for we thought about what this man meant in the Augustana Synod and what he had endured for its sake."[38]

In fact, the whole year was gripping. Along with the research, Bergendoff actually wrote his PhD dissertation itself, which was ready by the fall of 1927. Those who read the finished manuscript suggested that it was publishable, and Bergendoff contacted the MacMillan Company in New York. Their representative replied that the draft had been reviewed by "several of our most competent advisors, and while they speak well of it as a piece of historical writing, they do not encourage us to undertake the full responsibility of publication." If Bergendoff could put up $1,000, the firm would, however, "manufacture and catalog it." The author could have five hundred copies himself and would earn 10% on all copies sold. Bergendoff took the deal.[39] The $1,000 represented about one-third of Pastor Bergendoff's annual salary at Salem Church; it was a considerable investment in the book's publication, equal to $13,200 in 2012 buying power.

Olavus Petri and the Ecclesiastical Transformation in Sweden appeared in 1928. The cover indicated its author was "Conrad Bergendoff, M.A." That author suggested that he would present material that was new to Americans. As the Foreword said, the book did truly "shed some additional light on a man and period known too little outside of his native country, and in this country hardly at all."[40] Bergendoff took a full load of courses during the 1927-1928 academic year and at its end received his PhD, so he did not have the higher degree in hand when the book was published. The sequence of his doctoral work seems unusual. A more typical program would have had the student completing course work *before* finishing and publishing a dissertation. It was also the case that Bergendoff had not been much in actual residence at the university. He had done solid work in his first year of courses (as he did six years later) and had managed to have his dissertation published, but his graduate work had been interrupted and then completed while he was either at Salem or in Europe.

Bergendoff began and finished a PhD in the same years that he grew increasingly involved in Synod affairs and guided Salem Church through a period of growth and church construction. It is not surprising that he began to be considered by many in the Synod as something of a *Wunderkind,* destined for a major role in its mid-twentieth century affairs. He must have had little time for the kind of leisurely intellectual banter and playful reflection that have for centuries marked the lives of many apprentice scholars in their relationships with academic comrades-in-arms. What Bergendoff did demonstrate in those years at Chicago was that an evangelical Christian could earn a doctoral degree in a demanding program; that, as he said years later, was just what he had set out to prove. The question now was what he would do with the new credential.

Back to Rock Island (for Good)

The personal materials which Conrad Bergendoff included when he left his papers to the Augustana Library contain a number of job invitations or letters exploring opportunities that he received in the twenties. During the time at Salem it became increasingly clear that he was headed for "bigger things" (though he would never have used such a term). A number of important Lutheran congregations considered him as a pastoral candidate, and several educational institutions sought him as well. Perhaps he might have stayed to teach at Chicago.[41] Three Synod schools offered him positions, including Gustavus Adolphus, Upsala, and Augustana itself. The seminary at Mt. Airy was also interested in Bergendoff. The salaries offered were in the range of $2,500 to $3,000; Bergendoff had started at Salem for $1,800. He had already turned down an offer from Samuel Miller at the Minneapolis Lutheran Bible Institute, who had "mentioned this in prayer to God many, many times[.]" Bergendoff had even received a call to the mission field in China.[42]

Conrad Bergendoff was not the first Augustana young man to earn a doctorate in a nationally recognized university rather than joining the hosts of fellow churchmen who relied upon honorary degrees. Gustav Andreen, the fourth President of Augustana College and Theological Seminary, had received a PhD from Yale, and other contemporaries did graduate study at leading schools. Many of these persons took positions outside of the Augustana Synod, though they continued to be interested in its affairs. Augustana alumni from Bergendoff's student decades were faculty members at the universities of Chicago, Iowa, Minnesota, Northwestern, Pennsylvania, and Texas, among others. Some of these persons, like the Minnesota historian George M. Stephenson, Class of 1910, sought to apply the techniques of modern scholarship to a critical examination of their own ethnic and religious tradition. For his part, Bergendoff intended to stay within the Synod, and he undertook the examination of his Church in a mood of appreciation, perhaps reverence.

The call which finally drew Conrad Bergendoff away from Salem Lutheran Church came in 1930, when his former Professor of Theology, Conrad E. Lindberg, died unexpectedly. Lindberg had been dean of the Rock Island seminary since the turn of the century. Restlessness about his leadership and teaching had grown, both in the Synod and in the seminary student body. The Board of Directors appeared uncertain as to the direction they should now take. One of their younger reform-minded members was historian Stephenson, who believed that the moment for an overhaul of the entire faculty had come. He was one of those critics who held that the staff of the school must be

George M. Stephenson, Professor at Minnesota and historian of the immigration of Swedes to America.

upgraded by appointing persons with advanced graduate degrees rather than simply long pastoral experience. It was an opportunity that Stephenson and other Young Turks in the Synod had hoped for, though the sudden death of Lindberg presented it to them sooner than they had expected. Almost every member of the existing faculty was at a career stage where he could be retired or returned to some other form of ministry—voluntarily, or at the Board's direction.[43]

The students of the seminary were also determined that the academic quality of the faculty and program must be improved. The reform faction on the Board of Directors (which governed both the college and the seminary) prevailed; four members were asked to leave the faculty, and the Board set about rebuilding it.[44] Most of the departing professors returned whence they came—to pastorates.[45] The key person in the reformers' plan to reconstruct the faculty became Conrad Bergendoff, the holder of a new PhD. At its August, 1930, meeting the Board determined to call him to replace Conrad Lindberg as Dean and Professor of Theology.[46] He had, as suggested earlier, other choices, including an invitation to join the staff of the United Lutheran Seminary at Mt. Airy in Philadelphia. Bergendoff had been able to stay out of most of the sharper debates in the twenties about the character and direction of the Augustana Synod and was identified with no particular party, progressive or conservative. Thus he represented a choice for the deanship who could receive support on the floor of the Synod's annual convention, where calls to the theological faculty had to be ratified. Even his early tentative ecumenism, focused mainly on joining his Synod with other American Lutherans, did not redound to Bergendoff's discredit, for, unlike his mentor and friend Nathan Söderblom, the Swedish American did not stand accused of liberalism, of accommodating Lutheranism to other Christian theologies, or of looking for revelation in non-Christian religions.[47]

The Synod had witnessed a growing difference of opinion among its clergy about its theological and confessional life, particularly through the late 1920s. Debates involved questions about biblical inspiration and historical criticism of the Scriptures, about the role of the Lutheran confessions in the modern church, about ecumenical relationships, and even about the future role of Swedish in the Synod's life. The arguments which enlivened the pages of the *Lutheran Companion* had been particularly focused on a collection of essays, *What Is Lutheranism?*, edited by Vergilius Ferm, an Augustana graduate teaching at the College of Wooster in Ohio. Ferm's call for a "reinterpretation of the Lutheran theological tradition in the light of contemporary reality" had led Samuel Miller, the head of the Lutheran Bible Institute in Minneapolis, to demand in the pages of his *Bible Banner* that Ferm be removed from the Synod—on the grounds of heresy.[48] Bergendoff's view of Ferm was that "when he got in to American theology . . . , he lost his bearings in Lutheran theology."[49] But, on the other hand, neither did Bergendoff join the call for Ferm to be hauled up for a heresy trial.

So Dr. Bergendoff kept out of that controversy (which did not in the end result in Ferm's expulsion from the Synod ministry). One of his contemporaries noted in reviewing some of Bergendoff's work that it "has avoided the extremes of today both to the right and to the left."[50] That was his general approach in church politics as well as in church history. Another clue to Bergendoff's disposition in these matters lay in his treatment of Olavus Petri in his 1928 book. There he wrote of the Swedish Reformer and his relationship to the work of Luther and the German Reformation: "No genius can be more worthy than that which fits measures conducive to a noble goal."[51] For Petri that had meant carrying forth and adapting the work of Martin Luther to Swedish conditions. For Bergendoff that meant fitting the Augustana tradition, rooted in Sweden, to the circumstances of twentieth century America, ecclesiastic and secular. His own strong commitment to that tradition and to Lutheranism generally was spelled out in a 1929 article he had written for the *Augustana Quarterly*, "The Significance of the Lutheran Reformation of the Sixteenth Century for the Church of the Twentieth." He had become one of the editors of the *Quarterly* in 1928, a role he filled for two decades thereafter. This particular essay was focused upon Luther, but it was programmatic for Bergendoff's own life as well. Its most telling statement was perhaps the author's declaration that whatever modern secular scholarship might make of Luther's encounter with Christ, that experience was as much a plain fact as anything that modern science studied.[52] That, Bergendoff believed, was a fact his own life shared with Luther's: a religious experience as real as the laws and phenomena of nature. It was the foundation of his and his Synod's life.

Firm in that understanding of the experience Luther and many Christians shared, Bergendoff took the Augustana Seminary deanship. The offer did not come at a tranquil time in the Synod's history. The issues which had emerged in the twenties persisted. The Church was growing out of the relative ethnic isolation that had understandably characterized its first half-century. It was wrestling with the challenges that contemporary scholarship was bringing with regard to biblical studies and church history, even including the Synod's past. The Church's relationships to other American Lutherans, to the Church of Sweden, and to other Christian churches were being debated. A corps of newly trained academics was emerging. Both Board and students at the seminary knew that their school must have higher academic standards. All these and other factors may have caused Bergendoff to be somewhat hesitant in accepting the call to be dean of a school which many, himself included, believed needed extensive academic reconstruction.

But the most important reason for Bergendoff's hesitation, he later maintained, was his reluctance to give up the pastoral ministry. His personal files are filled with letters from members of Salem congregation telling him that for their part they were beseeching the Lord that he guide their pastor to remain with them. Reflecting on his career in 1959, he recalled how happy he had been in the pastorate. It had been hard to leave. "I will not use the word sacrifice in describing my leaving the parish for Augustana, for I recall the words of [the missionary] Grenfel of Labrador who decried the use of the word by any missionary because a man cannot be said to sacrifice when he gains the knowledge that he is doing the Lord's work."[53] That sense that he must remain a missionary when taking a new position was one that would be repeated in Bergendoff's career, when other invitations would come to him. But if his way was to linger over such decisions, it was not to act indecisively once he had agreed to take a job.

Though he had at moments considered a career outside of the Augustana Synod, Dr. Bergendoff now resolved to accept the proffered dean- and professorship in Rock Island. The president of the Pennsylvania seminary that had offered him a position wrote to Bergendoff that while "Your duty may ultimately lie there [at Augustana]," five years elsewhere might enable Bergendoff to grow from a "promising young scholar and pastor" into an "experienced teacher with a recognized position in [the] whole Church and with important connections already formed."[54] To his parents Bergendoff wrote, "I feel that it is perhaps my duty to accept the call to Rock Island. I am not enthusiastic about it and would prefer to stay where I am. And for the purpose of teaching I would rather have gone to Philadelphia. But I can't get myself to decline the call, which means that I will have to accept it."[55] Bergendoff's deep loyalty to his own Synod had evidently trumped his fond memories of the lively year he had spent at Mt. Airy. One gets the sense that he now *trudged* back to Rock Island—just as he had when summoned back to study there in 1919.

The salary at Augustana was set at $3,100 with an additional stipend of $300 for serving as dean. There had been some back-and-forth between the candidate and the Board of Directors about their first offer, which he told them was $800 to $1,000 less than his compensation at Salem. The Board must "make it possible for me to be relieved of financial worries and for me to center my thought and energy in the duties of my office, which will be great enough to tax all of a man's time and ability." The Board agreed, and adjustments were made. Though his doctoral and master's training had been in history, Bergendoff now became Professor of Theology, succeeding Conrad Lindberg in that role, as well as in the deanship. What fit him for the particular professorship was, therefore, not extensive and advanced formal training in theology, but his own reading and experience, the breadth and depth of which now became evident. (His bibliography indicates that by the time of his retirement Bergendoff would write over eighty book reviews in journals ranging from *Augustana Quarterly* to the *Annals of the American Academy of Political and Social Science*.) He was thirty-five years old when he asked the Board for an additional year at Salem Church before moving his growing family and his personal library to Rock Island.[56] He evidently felt he needed more time to read in preparation for the new job.

Dean and Professor of Theology

In the fall of 1931 Dean Bergendoff was installed as Dean and Professor of Theology. Four years earlier he had reported in the *Lutheran Companion* on a visit to the twelfth century cathedral at Lund, deeply impressed by its Romanesque solemnity. The Augustana Synod, he wrote, had no such monumental sanctuary looming above an ancient crypt, but it did have its seminary, and that school played the role in the American church that the great cathedral did in the Swedish.[57] Medieval cathedrals had deans, the heads of the chapters or groups of clergy attached to the churches; now Bergendoff was the dean of the closest thing the Synod had to such a cathedral. The school in Rock Island was, Bergendoff thought, the center of his Church's life.

The reformers on the Board of Directors had called other new men to the faculty. They included A. D. Mattson, Eric H. Wahlstrom, and Carl A. Anderson. Mattson had been teaching in the Department of Christianity at the college, had studied at Yale, and held a Doctor of Sacred Theology degree from Augustana Seminary itself. Both Wahlstrom and Anderson had been in pastorates, and each had also done advanced graduate work.[58] For decades Mattson was to argue that his Church must recognize the implications of

Christianity for social as well as private life. He had been impressed with the thought of Walter Rauschenbusch (1861-1918), one of the earliest proponents of the Social Gospel, and this sometimes put him at odds with the new Dean of the Seminary, who was no friend of that school of theology.[59] Wahlstrom taught New Testament and sought to steer his students away from a full verbal or literal view of scriptural inspiration and toward an understanding that "God speaks in and through the entire Bible, and yet the entire Bible bears upon each page the imprint of the human[.]" Anderson's field was Old Testament, and while the most conservative of the new faculty, he did make use of contemporary biblical scholarship and shared the ecumenical perspective of his colleagues.[60] Augustana Seminary was not a large school; by the time of its separation from the college in the late forties the faculty included seven full-time members. Four of them held PhDs.[61]

The historian of the Synod, G. Everett Arden, would write years later, when he had himself long served on the seminary faculty, that "the Augustana Church over the years has developed a number of skillful practical churchmen, but few outstanding theologians."[62] Erling and Granquist offer no direct assessment of Bergendoff's overall significance as a theologian, but they do treat him as "the leading theological voice of the synod."[63] An historian of the Evangelical Covenant Church, a sister Swedish-American denomination, speaks of Bergendoff as one of the Augustana Synod's "leading theologians."[64] Somewhere on the scale of those three statements lies the reality of the new dean's role in education and the church over the next thirty-five years. As Dean of the Theological Seminary Bergendoff had a position from which to exercise direct and formal influence on his Church. He did this, as we shall see, by bringing the light of historical study to bear upon theological questions rather than by examining them as though they were independent of the circumstances and contexts in which they arose. His theological work was always placed in its historical context.

In this sense Bergendoff was not the sort of scholastic theologian that Lindberg had been. Bergendoff's predecessor had dealt with doctrinal questions *sub specie aeternitatis,* as matters of eternal truth considered in their essence, independent of historical factors. One biographer of Nathan Söderblom characterizes Bergendoff during the year he worked with the Archbishop in Sweden as a "competent systematic theologian."[65] Bergendoff would have accepted the implied compliment graciously. But if "systematic theology" is the effort to elaborate a complete structure of theology that examines and explains in order the principal doctrines of Christianity (God, Christ, Spirit, the Church, Salvation, Resurrection, etc.), that description does not exactly apply. Karl Mattson, Bergendoff's successor as President of Augustana Theological

The Augustana Seminary faculty in the early forties. Bergendoff, by now seminary president, continued to teach liturgics. On opposite sides of the picture (as they were in matters theological) are, on Bergendoff's left, A. D. Mattson, a strong advocate for social justice, both within the Synod and beyond, and, holding the straw hat, Adolf Hult, long a conservative voice in the Synod and an opponent of what he regarded as the over-eager ecumenism of Nathan Söderblom and, by implication, Conrad Bergendoff.

Seminary, wrote in 1960, the centennial of the Synod, that while it cannot be isolated from the church, "theology moves in a realm which stands above the relativities of history."[66] Bergendoff, on the other hand, invariably began theological reflection with consideration of the historical circumstances in which ideas developed, as an historian, rather than as a systematic theologian might have. He was concerned with the way in which Christian ideas had developed through time within their historical framework. In fact, one of his Lutheran theological contemporaries noted in reviewing *Christ as Authority,* that his one criticism of the book was the "low estimate it places upon philosophy and conceptual analysis, a point easily explicable by the fact that the author is a historian, not a systematician."[67]

The approach to theology used by Bergendoff did not try to elaborate a system marked by complete congruence between individual doctrines. That had been the way of the theology he (and his father) had studied in the Rock Island seminary. As Bergendoff dealt with doctrine, historical development was the key. Still in the Salem pastorate, he had written *The Making and Meaning of the Augsburg Confession* (1930), the title of which itself suggested that the meaning of the document was tied up in the process by which it had been written, its making. Writing of "The Lutheran View of the Lord's Supper" in the *Lutheran Quarterly* two decades later, he said that "from earliest times

Christian doctrine has been framed in answer to opposite interpretations." For Bergendoff that was a principle that "should be recalled for otherwise it is easy to view the Lutheran doctrine as an absolute statement without regard to the origin of the form in which we have received the doctrine." Further, he came increasingly in his professional career to hold that "The truth in Christ is far more than correct intellectual concepts." That did not mean that he ignored doctrinal questions or treated them cavalierly, but it did signify his sense that the truth must always "be spoken in love." "[W]e are speaking of Him who is the Truth, and He found no discrepancy between truth and love."[68] So it was that as he assumed the role of Professor of Theology, Bergendoff persisted in operating as an historian. But he was an historian who accepted the Pauline priorities in the First Letter to the Corinthians: "Now abide these three: faith, hope, and love. But the greatest of these is love."

Later, after the college and the seminary in Rock Island were separated and Bergendoff, the erstwhile president of both, had chosen to stay with the college rather than to head the seminary, Conrad Bergendoff's credibility in Synod affairs, especially with regard to ecumenical relationships, was due to his proven record of involvement and leadership rather than to his formal title and position in the seminary. The Synod, after all, had four other *college* presidents. Bergendoff had begun to earn his ecclesiological clout before he got to the theological faculty, but it was his role in the seminary that firmly established his bona fides. That did not mean, of course, that Synod leaders or Synod conventions always acceded to his views, as we shall see. Augustana Lutherans spoke the truth in love to one another, or at least tried to, but they did not always hold the same understanding of that truth.

The new seminary dean had not himself led the "revolution" that had reconstructed the seminary faculty. He had accepted leadership at a time when many in the Church and at the school believed that an academic up-grade was long overdue. His installation as dean was more a sign than a cause of the changes. And Bergendoff's teaching, while it clearly introduced new thoughts and thinkers to the theological life of the Synod, did not itself constitute an overthrow of its deepest values and traditions. It would have been unthinkable for Conrad Bergendoff to take a role in that kind of effort. What he did do was to introduce contemporary theology, especially that which was rooted in historical Protestantism. That newer thought took its place next to the works of classical Lutheranism on which Lindberg had concentrated. "Such names as Aulén, Nygren, Bring, Söderblom, Barth, Brunner, Niebuhr and Tillich became part of the daily vocabulary on Zion Hill."[69] Along with new faculty and new ideas, other innovations also entered the ten-year-old buildings on that hill overlooking Old Main and the College Gymnasium. Class assignments grew more demanding, and the curriculum was revised to conform to prevailing practices in wider American theological education.

Perhaps the most significant of these changes was the introduction of an "intern" year. Previously the course of study for a Bachelor of Divinity degree had been three years long. Now an internship in a congregation under the direction of a senior pastor, preferably to be taken after the second and before the final year, was required of all students. The hope was that it would give students actual pastoral experience before they were ordained. In earlier decades students often had such experience before entering seminary, but that was not so much the case by the 1930s.[70] Many congregations, themselves strapped by the Depression, were probably happy to have interns to assist with the pastoral work load. The dean himself explained the new internship program to the wider world of theological education in a 1935 article in the journal *Christian Education.*[71] The faculty also recognized that the changes to the seminary's program required increased concentration on the Bachelor of Divinity course and decided to drop the Doctor of Sacred Theology program that it had offered until then.[72]

The new Dean of the Seminary did not hold his position long, however. After serving as President of Augustana College and Theological Seminary since 1901, Gustav Andreen, seventy years old in 1934, was due to retire. The same Synod factions that had been unhappy with the condition of the seminary and its faculty had grown increasingly impatient with Andreen's leadership of the entire institution. One of them labeled Augustana a "rudderless ship."[73] The question of when "Prexy" would retire was soon eclipsed by speculation over who would be chosen to replace him. The *Observer* ran a story in May, 1935, suggesting that it would be Dean Conrad Bergendoff, though the newspaper was not sure he would take the offer.[74] Neither was Bergendoff. The possibility of making him president had been raised a year earlier by the Augustana Board of Directors. Now, at a Board meeting in 1935, he was offered the position. But he had reservations, finally agreeing that he would serve as *Acting* President for an academic year. The salary was set at $3,600 with a $400 housing allowance.[75]

Evidently the Directors were themselves uncertain about electing Bergendoff to that role, for a motion to rescind the call was offered in the afternoon Board session, directly following the morning meeting in which the call was first extended; it lost eight to five. The cryptic minutes do not explain the reasons behind that motion to rescind. Thus, upon Andreen's retirement in the college's seventy-fifth anniversary year, Bergendoff assumed the acting presidency. The Board soon decided to make the appointment permanent. At their meeting in February, 1936, the Directors read a letter from Bergendoff "stating his reaction to the call to the presidency of the institution and presenting some of the problems in regard to the office that remain unresolved as yet in his own mind." That letter was "discussed very frankly and at considerable length by nearly every member of the Board." Here too, one is left to speculate on the nature of Bergendoff's reservations. Possibilities range from his characteristic caution in assuming important positions (recall his hesitancy over the seminary deanship) to concern over the financial condition of the school, now caught in the toils of the Depression. Nor do the minutes reveal what the Board's individual members said. But the offer to assume the permanent presidency of the school was extended and accepted. Now Conrad Bergendoff was answerable for both the undergraduate college and the graduate seminary.[76] (The academy at Augustana had closed in 1931, so Andreen was the last president to have administered that branch of the school.) The historian G. Everett Arden writes that "The growing independence of the Seminary in relation to the College was temporarily restrained" by Bergendoff's election. His concern for integrating the two Augustana branches was the reason the president continued, for a few years at least, to teach classes in the seminary.[77]

The clergyman and historian who had intended to be a pastor, had considered the foreign mission field, had earned scholarly credentials, and had headed a theological faculty now assumed the role of college president. That did not keep him from wide involvement in Synod and ecumenical circles, Swedish-American affairs, scholarship both theological and historical, and community life. Bergendoff's papers, deposited by him in the Augustana College archives, record his work in all these areas. They also contain frequent letters to railroads requesting clergy passes. Passenger trains steaming toward Los Angeles or Chicago rolled regularly into the Rock Island Depot, just below the Augustana campus. They carried Bergendoff to church, educational, and cultural meetings in all the directions that the Rock Island and connecting lines ran. He must have written many of the articles and reviews that fill the pages of his long bibliography while he rode those trains. How else could he have done it all?

§

The following chapters of this book will examine the next six decades of Bergendoff's life, years in which he devoted himself to Lutheran unity, ecumenical work, activity in Sweden and Swedish America, college management, research and scholarship, and the affairs of the Augustana Synod. But first we must give attention to what he believed was the factor or force that integrated and gave meaning to everything he did—his religious faith. He had learned this faith in his childhood home, in his Church, and at its institution of higher learning.

It had carried him through the busy years at Salem and the university. For Bergendoff a personal religious experience must be the central point of every Christian life, including his. Some who read the next chapter will believe that they know exactly what he meant. Others will find it surprising—perhaps even disconcerting. But if one wants to understand Conrad Bergendoff, one must, I think, take him at his word and begin where he thought his own life began and ended.

The Swedish-American artist Olof Grafström (1855-1926) did this idealized picture of the Augustana campus in the 1890s. In fact, industrial developments had begun to line the Mississippi, but the idyllic painting does capture a vision of the school that seems to have expressed Conrad Bergendoff's ideas about education in general and Augustana in particular.

CHAPTER 3

CHRIST AS AUTHORITY

Conrad Bergendoff maintained that the core of Christianity was not faith in the Bible—even the Gospels. Nor in the Church—even the Lutheran. Neither was it a way of life, fulfilling obligations and multiplying good deeds.[1] He liked the way the Swedish theologian Gustaf Aulén put it: redemption is a drama, one in which God sent his Son, Jesus Christ, to do battle with humanity's ancient enemies, sin, death, and the devil. In his life and particularly through his death Christ overcame these foes, freeing human beings from their power. For Bergendoff, as for Aulén, Christianity was centered on certain human lives, particularly one life. At its core Christianity was a series of events whose leading characters were those of the Bible. "God's method of revelation was not a doctrine, but a life, the life of a Moses, an Elijah, a John the Baptist, a Paul, and supremely the life of His own Son."[2] In the wider family of Christians, Lutherans are often known for their doctrinal focus and precision. But for Bergendoff not even pure doctrine (what orthodox German Lutherans spoke of as *die reine Lehre*) was finally the core and measure of Christian faith.

In Bergendoff's mind, doctrine—even Lutheran—could be over-valued. In 1932, newly installed as Dean and Professor of Theology at Augustana Seminary, he wrote, "I venture the remark that the purity of doctrine has been more consistently maintained than the purity of our practice."[3] Perhaps he meant that Lutheran thinking had been more correct than Lutheran living. But neither pure doctrine nor pure practice was at the heart of the faith. In a radio sermon delivered twenty years later, he told NBC listeners that, like St. Paul on the road to Damascus, or like St. Francis, or Martin Luther, or John Wesley, each person must her- or himself *meet* Jesus Christ. Through that meeting one's own story or drama was changed by the story or drama of Christ himself. The encounter took place when God's Spirit brought a person into the presence of Christ, either directly through the Scriptures or through the testimony of people who had already encountered him.[4] It was an ecumenical sermon—a Catholic and a Methodist got equal billing with Luther.

Christ and Jesus

Of course, as Conrad Bergendoff knew from his own inter-church involvement, the wide variety of Christian denominations testified that there were different ways of meeting Jesus Christ. The Apostle Paul met him on a desert road, the Reformer Luther in the monks' latrine. Paul had a direct *vision* of the risen Lord, while Luther reached a new *perception* of what Christ had done for him. And in the course of Christian history, even the Jesus Christ who is encountered had been seen and understood differently. One of the present author's own seminary professors once remarked in a lecture that the wide range of Christian thought and experience can be divided and categorized in many ways. One of the most basic, he said, was that some Christians tend to speak more frequently of "Jesus," others of "Christ." If one refers more regularly to Jesus, it is probably as Teacher and Example. If to Christ, it is probably as Lord and Savior. Jesus theologians are concerned with a way of life he has given humanity to follow, Christ theologians with a plan of redemption in which he plays the central role. The former think of a Palestinian peasant who went about the countryside preaching, healing, and teaching, the later of a cosmic figure who existed before the creation of the world and who changed the very nature of reality. One type or system of theology stresses Jesus, the other Christ.

Each of these theological types must face particular problems arising from the very literature that has transmitted him (Him) to us. A Christianity focused upon Jesus has to contend with the question of the historical reliability of the source documents about him, the Gospels. And one centered on Christ must deal with issues arising from other sources, especially the letters of Paul, whose complex trains of thought and attitudes on social questions present problems for many moderns. These were issues floating in the very theological air that Conrad Bergendoff breathed in the mid-twentieth century. He knew the questions well. They were clearly current in the Augustana Synod itself. For example, in the twenties Bergendoff's older contemporary, the Reverend Doctor O. J. Johnson, President of Gustavus Adolphus College, an institution of the Minnesota Conference, told a "Forum of Faiths" at the state's public university in the Twin Cities that "The crucial moment of modern youth has come[.] It must decide whether to accept Christ as a guide and teacher or, as the Bible declares Him to be, a Savior."[5] Like President Johnson in Minnesota, President Bergendoff in Illinois knew where he stood on the question of whether Jesus Christ was simply a guide and teacher or whether he was the divine savior of humanity.

Dr. Bergendoff understood that many earnest Christians were merely looking for a central and simple ethical meaning that could be distilled from Jesus' life and teachings. Bergendoff's graduate programs included courses in US history, so he was familiar with the strong tradition in American religious thought that emphasized Jesus and sought to separate him from the theological accretions of two thousand years. The *Jefferson Bible* was the third American president's effort to extract from the New Testament a simple version of "The Life and Morals of Jesus of Nazareth." Many of the Founding Fathers had little taste for the *doctrinal* history of Christianity, but they believed in Jesus' life and teaching as the revelation of a God-given pattern for humanity. That was also the core of the twentieth century Social Gospel theology that dominated many mainline American divinity schools in Bergendoff's student days and what he wanted to avoid when he prepared to do PhD work. American liberal theology, against whose Social Gospel iteration Conrad Bergendoff so strongly reacted, was oriented throughout its history toward Jesus. One American church historian writes, "Ethical imperatives became central to the Christian witness, and the Sermon on the Mount was often regarded as the heart and core of the Bible."[6] Such theologies, which emphasize Jesus as teacher and example, are apt to focus upon the first three gospels in the New Testament and also perhaps on the moral prophets of the Old. And that begs the question of the accuracy and reliability of the biblical accounts, especially those about Jesus himself.

The well-read Bergendoff was familiar with the scholarly effort that, beginning in mid-nineteenth century Europe, sought to uncover the "historical Jesus." That effort had adherents even among European Lutherans. Of its practitioners Bergendoff said, "Freed from traditional views of the meaning and authority of Scripture, they stressed its human side." They treated it "as any other human book."[7] In the nineteenth century the techniques of modern "secular" historiography (in which Bergendoff himself would later be trained at the Universities of Pennsylvania and Chicago) were turned on the New Testament. David Friedrich Strauss' *Das Leben Jesu* (1836) and Ernest Renan's *Vie de Jesus* (1863) were exemplars of that effort.

Strauss and Renan died in the nineteenth century, but the Nobel laureate Albert Schweitzer (1875-1965), himself the son of a Lutheran pastor, was a living international icon during Bergendoff's lifetime. A recognized scholar of

Scripture, Schweitzer criticized Strauss and Renan strongly in his own *The Quest of the Historical Jesus* (English translation, 1910): their works said more about their mid-nineteenth century authors than they did about their purported subject, Jesus. Bergendoff agreed. Of such men he said, "They read God's revelation in the mirror of their own depths and reflected their own ideas in the explanation of it."[8] But that is as far as he would go with Schweitzer. Bergendoff would never have doubted the sincerity of Schweitzer's discovery of universal ethical meaning in the life the Gospels presented. Nor did he discredit Schweitzer's subsequent abandonment of his scholarly career to study medicine and then to spend his life in a mission in what was French Equatorial Africa (now Gabon). He referred to him as "this talented and consecrated personality[.]" But the American Lutheran found a different central meaning in the New Testament than did Schweitzer and many of the German researchers who followed him. Speaking in 1950 of Schweitzer's well-known philosophy of "reverence for life," Bergendoff said: "there is something nebulous about a reverence for life that fails to distinguish between the lives of men and nature and the life of the Son of Man." Schweitzer's quest for the historical Jesus left Bergendoff with "a vague uncertainty as to what was found."[9]

British biblical scholarship yielded results more to Bergendoff's liking. In 1932 he reviewed favorably James Moffatt's *Grace in the New Testament*. The Scot Moffatt (1870-1944) understood that Christianity was about God seeking man, not man searching for God: "God does not save man. There is nothing savable in man. Instead, the grace of God is the creation of a new life in man."[10] That was an idea Bergendoff would often return to. He was also drawn to the work of the Welshman C. H. Dodd (1884-1973). Dodd found a unified message in the New Testament, an essential agreement among Paul, Luke, Peter, and John on the central Christian gospel of human redemption. If in spite of variations among them, the apostolic generation agreed on essentials, so could divided twentieth century Christians, Bergendoff thought.[11]

The quest to find the Jesus of history was not the only feature of contemporary biblical interpretation that confronted Lutherans such as Bergendoff. There were more edgy issues, often concerned with the contrast between the Gospels and the writings of the Apostle Paul. Thomas Jefferson has had successors. Some contemporary intellectuals who have been taken with the teachings and life of Jesus are dubious about Paul. Unlike Bergendoff, they find the doctrinal aspects of Christianity at best problematic, and for them Christian doctrine can be traced to Paul, not to Jesus. The American literary scholar and critic Harold Bloom is an example. He writes that one can comb all the authentic epistles of Paul and never know that Jesus, like Amos and the other prophets, spoke for the poor, the sick, the outcast. There is almost no mention in Paul's letters of the events of Jesus' life. For Bloom, "Pragmatically Paul's argument became what could be called 'not Jesus but Christ.'"[12] A contemporary British scholar, Charles Freeman, writes that Paul "failed to absorb, or at least express in his letters, any real awareness of Jesus as a human being[,]" and adds, "Paul is the only major Christian theologian never to have read the Gospels, and one cannot be sure that he interpreted Jesus' teachings, on the Law, for instance, with accuracy."[13]

The converted persecutor of the Church is seen by those who share this perspective as the real founder of "Christianity." That is understood as a system of doctrines and precepts which stands in contrast with the simple life and statements of the Jesus recorded, with whatever degree of accuracy, in the Gospels. The Apostle Paul was the genius who, for better or worse, devised what became historical Christianity—with the difficulties attending it. In his epistles Paul condones slavery, advises women to be silent and subordinate, and condemns homosexuality. So he is not simply the creator of a theological interpretation—as "Christ"—of Jesus' life and meaning. Paul's critics think he also sanctions two millennia of the oppressive thought and behavior of some Christians. For those who make the distinction between Jesus and Christ, the Gospels are full of simple stories and sayings, while the letters of Paul contain lines of thought sometimes difficult to follow and at points offensive to modern humanistic sensibilities.

Bergendoff did not accept this positioning of Jesus and Paul against each other. But it is interesting to note that Bergendoff himself spoke of "Jesus" infrequently. For well over half a century his own work consistently referred to "Christ" and not very often to "Jesus."[14] Early in his advanced study Bergendoff had encountered Professor Henry Eyster Jacobs at Philadelphia Lutheran Seminary, who as a young theologian had translated into English the classic *Compendium locorum theologicum* by Luther's successor at Wittenberg, Leonard Hutter (1563-1616). Hutter's *Compendium* referred steadily to Christ's theological significance as Savior and rarely at all to Jesus' earthly life.[15] Hutter was deemed so faithful to Martin Luther himself that he was often called "Luther redonatus." Jacobs' translation of the *Compendium* exercised a strong influence in the American Lutheran circles where Jacobs operated and where Bergendoff had studied. Late in Bergendoff's career, on a 1962 ecumenical trip to the USSR set up by the National Council of Churches, the American Lutheran told his Russian Orthodox hosts that "In general theology in America has moved toward a Christological understanding of the New Testament rather than toward the human Jesus of a previous period."[16] Presumably the "previous period," concerned with "the human Jesus," led to the Social Gospel and the liberal theology of the early twentieth century.

Opposed to the latter was a "Christological understanding." Whatever else that meant, it focused upon Christ's work of redemption, as lined out by Paul and reaffirmed in Lutheranism. It was not so much occupied with the moral teachings and example of the historical Jesus. Clearly Bergendoff understood these different emphases as alternatives. It was also clear which of them he preferred. Speaking again of Gustaf Aulén, he noted with approval that the Swede understood the "fact that the Christian faith is Christocentric."[17]   In terms that theologians still use, Bergendoff could be said to have had a "high Christology." Such a Doctrine of Christ would attribute to him full divinity, equal to that of the Father, and give to the Son the central role in the whole cosmic or eternal drama of redemption. (Jefferson or even Schweitzer might be said to have had less elevated Christologies.) Bergendoff's own Lutheran view of Christian life, intellectual and moral, was that first a person had to undergo a life-transforming encounter with God as revealed in Christ, in the way Paul and Luther had, and that only *after* such a meeting was he or she given the divine power to be re-made in an ethical or moral sense. No personal act of will could make one's life like Christ's.

This understanding of the core experience of the Christian life did not spring Athena-like full-grown from Bergendoff's mature theological mind. It had a long history in his Synod and in the Swedish Pietism by which the immigrant founders were nourished and shaped. The historians of Augustana such as George M. Stephenson, O. Fritiof Ander, and even G. Everett Arden do not discuss in any detail or at length the theological thought of the founders such as L. P. Esbjörn, T. N. Hasselquist, Erland Carlsson, Eric Norelius, and others. Perhaps they simply take it for granted. But all of these historians recognize the Pietistic character of the faith which the pioneers brought with them from Sweden and which they held on to in the New World. At the core of that faith was an emphasis on Christianity as personal experience rather than simply assent to orthodox doctrine. Augustana Seminary professor Arden does write, "the approach to religion was, on the whole, pietistic in the sense that it was subjective rather than objective, stressing the emotional aspects of a personal experience of conversion[.]" Further, says Arden, it was moralistic, at moments even legalistic, and "conceived of Christianity as *praxis* rather than as intellectual assent to dogma and doctrine." But it was not separatist and sought to remain within the Church of Sweden. It held on to the basic teachings of historic Lutheranism.[18]

It was also the case that Bergendoff was influenced in his understanding of the role or place of Christ in religious experience by other, non-Scandinavian, Lutherans. For example, his teacher at Mt. Airy, Henry Eyster Jacobs, wrote in the opening section of his *History of the Evangelical Lutheran Church in the*

United States that "Lutheranism is a mode of viewing and receiving and living the truths of Christianity; or rather of viewing and receiving and living in mystical union with Him who is the beginning and end of all these truths." If Lutheranism is a doctrinal faith, Jacobs wrote, "Christ is really the center of the system; for justification by faith alone means nothing more than justification by Christ alone, through faith which clings to Christ as its Saviour." That faith meant for Jacobs an affirmation of St. Augustine's teaching on original sin and forgiveness: "Lutheranism accepts Augustinianism on original sin; for as self is depreciated Christ is exalted, and as sin is excused or explained away faith in Christ is rendered needless." Lutheranism admitted of no priestly intermediary between the believer and Christ, Jacobs added: "So intimate is the union between the Saviour and the soul whom he has saved, that there is not room between them for any order of men to conciliate that favor, of which the redeemed soul already enjoys the most indubitable proofs."[19] Bergendoff's personal copy of Jacob's history, still in the Augustana College Library, has most of these passages marked in the margin or underlined, evidence of its owner's thin-penciled assent.

The now brittle yellowed pages of *Augustana, Lutheran Companion*, and *Augustana Quarterly* editions published in the decades in which Bergendoff began and completed his formal education are also filled with articles that reflect this understanding of the Christian message. Pastor A. F. Almer's series in the opening 1922 numbers of the *Quarterly, "Det andliga nutidsläget och den kyrkliga förkunnelsen,"* (The Contemporary Spiritual Mindset and the Preaching of the Church) or the "Devotional" columns of the *Companion* which reached the Middletown parsonage in Bergendoff's high school years are among almost countless exemplars of this emphasis on personal religious experience centered on Christ. There are articles as well which defend orthodox Lutheran doctrine, such as "The Future Belongs to the Lutheran Church" or "Justification by Faith" in the 1912 *Lutheran Companion*. Often these pieces contrast Lutheran truth with the allegedly more lax versions of Christianity then floating through the American atmosphere. This is just that balance of Pietism with confessional Lutheranism that marked the Swedish awakening and much of the work of such dominant nineteenth century religious figures as C. O. Rosenius and (prior to his deviation on the Atonement) P. P. Waldenström. It also characterized the spirit of the Philadelphia Lutheran Seminary during Bergendoff's time there, after he had graduated from Augustana College and returned to live with his parents in the East.

Bergendoff's first book published following his dissertation put the emphasis on orthodoxy. *The Making and Meaning of the Augsburg Confession,* a hundred-twenty-seven page volume, selling for the even then low price of seventy-five cents, appeared in 1930. According to a review by W. E. Garrison in the *Christian Century*, Bergendoff seemed to defend what might be called a "hard saying" in the Augsburg Confession. Garrison, a leading member of the Disciples of Christ denomination, said of that difficult passage in the Confession that its "central meaning is that salvation consists not in the development of man's natural virtue, but in the implantation of a new nature from a supernatural source."[20] That was not evidently a view Garrison shared. Nor was it an idea prevalent in Social Gospel circles. But Bergendoff hewed to the orthodoxy of the Lutheran creeds, on this point and throughout *Making and Meaning*. Thus, in 1930 and for six decades thereafter, he held to the idea that the Christian life began when the old human nature was replaced by a new one, created by divine action. You did not become a new person simply by developing qualities already in you. But the "hard saying" and the view of becoming Christian it implied was tempered by Bergendoff's Pietistic emphasis upon personal experience, a strand that ran through the Augustana tradition. This balance between personal Christian experience and orthodox Lutheran doctrine was worked out in one Bergendoff book in particular.

Faith in Christ

Christ as Authority was published in 1947 by the Augustana Book Concern, the publishing house of the Augustana Synod. "ABC," as the company was popularly known, had emerged from a series of sometimes bitter nineteenth century rivalries among firms competing for readers in the literate Swedish-American immigrant community. By Bergendoff's time, it had become the Synod's official and sole publisher, its motto "The printed word also proclaims the Gospel." In addition to publishing religious books (increasingly in English by the time of World War I), ABC produced a steady stream of tracts, study materials, journals, and newspapers. It was also the purveyor of textbooks and sweatshirts to the college student body. In Bergendoff's professional years, the firm controlled the *Lutheran Companion,* which by then had become the principal weekly organ of the Synod.[21] The Augustana president was a frequent contributor. ABC headquarters, located just on the edge of the Augustana College campus, also stood ready to print and sell his more extended written efforts.

The 1947 book was one such, a small work of six chapters, one hundred and forty-five pages of text and two of notes. Each of the chapters was, as one reviewer noted, "a unit in itself."[22] In addition to the first, in which the central theme was set forth, there are chapters on the authority of the Bible; Christian involvement in the natural world, especially scientific; concern for social issues; the nature of the Christian church; and ecumenical questions.

Another reviewer suggested that if Bergendoff's "Christ-centered view of divine revelation" did not run through the book, the six chapters would seem disconnected.[23]   It was, in any event, a series of essays tied together by Bergendoff's belief that Christ was the authority who held the volume, the issues it treated, and indeed all of life, together. The book was bound in a Swedish blue cover, the title and author's name stamped in gold letters. As he had with his dissertation, Bergendoff sent complementary copies to leading schools and scholars.

But if the book was a small collection of essays, it was not insignificant, especially to those who might want to understand the core of Bergendoff's personal intellectual and spiritual commitments. *Christ as Authority* contained the substance of his ideas about the relation of individuals to Christ, which was in turn the central meaning of the Gospel and, indeed, of the universe. The argument it developed was as clear an expression of the author's understanding of the Christian message (and probably of himself) as one is apt to find in the case of this man who was not given to extensive and public self-presentation or examination. The book does not offer ideas which in any significant way run counter to what Bergendoff had been saying throughout the twenties, thirties, and forties. Nor did he change his mind in the five decades that followed its appearance. Decades after its publication, Bergendoff told a younger colleague in the ministry that it was his favorite among the books he had written.[24] It is possible to read this work and to look in both time directions from its publication without discovering major shifts in Bergendoff's mind on its subject. That is how we will proceed: by treating *Christ as Authority* as a base point from which to consider the decades during which the Augustana historical theologian held firm to what he regarded as a biblical and truly Lutheran view of Christ's meaning for human life, history, and culture. Some of the questions addressed in chapters past the first one (Scripture, science, the church, etc.) will be considered at other appropriate points in this study.

Bergendoff's book appeared at a time when American theology was well under way toward the Christocentric focus that Bergendoff told the Russians about during an ecumenical visit to their land about fifteen years later. It was written to indicate how Bergendoff understood the long history of a core Christian idea. That idea was that a person's life, and by extension and to a degree, the life of society as well, could be changed by a personal meeting with Christ. In addition to being an historical exposition, *Christ as Authority* was certainly a statement about where its author had stood, did stand, and would for the rest of his life. And as such it was one of the works that both reflected and generated the shift toward a Christocentric emphasis in American Protestant theology, away from more liberal thought and toward a body of theology

Conrad Bergendoff in the mid-forties, at the time of writing his Christ as Authority.

descending from the Reformation. Considered in its immediate historical context the chapter on Scripture also clarified Bergendoff's opposition to the kind of literalist theory of biblical inspiration then prevalent in many corners of Lutheranism. It was published at a time when Bergendoff's Synod found itself increasingly involved in the efforts of American Lutheran groups to reach understanding with each other and possibly to unite to form larger church bodies. With respect to these developments, the book presented a position that firmly established the Augustana man's commitment to a Christ-centered Lutheranism that was free of the biblical literalism which the author regarded as un-Lutheran. As such the book represented an important setting of stakes in the intra-Lutheran theological and ecclesiastical negotiations that would take place in the next decade (and that will be considered in Chapter 6). But that seems to have been a by-product of its more fundamental intention—to illuminate the core of Christian experience as Bergendoff understood it.

The first chapter of the book is as close to a *locus classicus* for this matter as Bergendoff wrote. He hit his stride at once—on page 1. The great question of his age, he began, was the question of "Whom to obey, whom to follow?" "We must obey some superior power, some force outside of and beyond us." Written near the end of two decades in which brown shirts had marched through Germany and red flags had flown over Russia, *Christ as Authority* was understandably concerned with the question implied in its title. For Bergendoff fascism and communism had been perverted answers to the human quest for an authority by which to live.

Of course, some contemporary intellectuals would not have bought into Bergendoff's view that the great question of the age was "Whom to obey?" Indeed, an alternative floating in many great universities, in small colleges, and in the columns of *Harper's* or the *Atlantic,* was that the mark of a liberally educated person was to abandon the quest for some external authority in favor of the careful and difficult life-long effort to develop one's own understanding of the nature and purpose of existence. Many persons in the western world who thought themselves enlightened believed that freedom from all authoritative thought schemes and world views, including religious ones, was the true hope for civilization. In any event, questions about the nature and legitimacy of authority were certainly abroad in the land at the time Bergendoff wrote *Christ as Authority*. Widely read, *The Lonely Crowd* (1950) by David Riesman, Nathan Glazer, and Reuel Denney differentiated three types of Americans: tradition-directed persons who lived by inherited and long-standing value codes; inner-directed persons who had internalized the values of their elders; and other-directed persons who flexibly responded to peer groups, the media, and the marketplace. Few of the first type were left in mid-century; the other two were characterized as having a gyroscope or a radar respectively.

The Lonely Crowd has been considered one of the most important sociological works of its time; within three decades of its publication, it had become the best-selling American study ever published in the field.[25] Conrad Bergendoff, should he have come into the purview of the trio who authored it, would have been typed somewhere between the first and second categories, certainly not in the third. His gyroscope came from the works of Luther and the fathers of the Synod, and he certainly did not need any intellectual or moral radar apparatus with which to scan the horizon for new ideas, fads, advertisements, or newspaper stories to steer his life by. However, noting that, we also must observe that within ten years or so of the publication of *Christ as Authority* (and of the Riesman book), the autos of Augustana College students were sporting "Question Authority" stickers on their dented bumpers. Even in a Lutheran liberal arts college, the prevailing winds had shifted toward the assumption that each of the car owners must decide individually which pieces of the inherited past and the ideals of the elders might be retained—and which jettisoned.

But Bergendoff would stick with Luther, who understood humanity to be so created that each person must find an authority to live by. After Luther had rejected all human claims demanding obedience, "The authority which [he] recognized as final was none less than Christ Himself." All other authorities were ultimately false. Though Bergendoff did not, he might at this point have referred to the Reformer's image that a person is like a beast of burden that will be controlled by one rider or another; in the end a person was under the power of either God or the devil.[26] What Bergendoff did say was that "Man's seemingly innate impulse to join a group or a party is an illustration of his inadequacy to form his own conclusions."[27] The question in human life was whether to live under the authority of Christ or under some other—and all other authorities of whatever stripe finally came down to being opposed to the divine will for humankind. (We will address the way in which that view of human nature did or did not dovetail with Bergendoff's ideas about liberal education in Chapter 9.)

Some of Luther's followers may have identified the churchly functions of Word and Sacrament as the final authority in the Christian life, but, as Bergendoff understood the Reformer, these were only the means by which one is brought into relationship with Christ himself, not ends in themselves.[28] It was in this sense that Bergendoff insisted that Christianity was not primarily a way of life or system of ethics, not faith in the Bible or the church or doctrine or the sacraments. Without Christ there would be none of these secondary marks of the faith.[29]

For the Augustana College theologian and historian the question was how one might come to an encounter with Christ. It was certainly not through "some mystical apprehension." To Bergendoff the peril of mysticism was "that men conjure up out of the depths of their own subconscious being the Christ they think they have found." That was not the Christ of the New Testament. The nineteenth century Dane Søren Kierkegaard (1813-1855), whom Bergendoff quoted frequently in the thirties and forties, understood that the Christ of Scripture was not the messiah people might have expected to be sent by God. The very fact of his unexpectedness was "the guarantee that He is not a human product."[30] We can, *Christ as Authority* argued, go back beyond Kierkegaard and Luther to Paul himself, who had never seen Christ before the crucifixion, but who had to his surprise encountered him later. Paul did not hold that every Christian must have a vision experience such as his own, but his writings did refer "to a presence of Christ which is available to every believer." Even after centuries the resurrected Christ still "is in the midst of His people whom faith apprehends and follows." For Paul there was a remarkable parallel between the power that raised Christ from the dead and "what God does in the believer." "There is a relationship between the resurrection of Christ and the life of the Christian which begins at the very start of Christian experiences."[31] Both are risings from the dead.

The first chapter of *Christ as Authority* ended with this statement about that encounter: "When therefore we speak of the authority of Christ it can mean nothing less than the authorship of faith in the Christian by a meeting between Him and the believer which results in a personal decision."[32] Bergendoff described that meeting at a number of other times, both before and after the 1947 book. In an ordination sermon preached at the seventy-fifth anniversary of the Synod in 1935, the Seminary Dean, about to become acting president of the entire institution, emphasized the aspect of forgiveness that entered this encounter with Christ: "[I]n the solitude of my soul to which I ultimately must retreat I know that my sins are mine." The forgiveness which Christ bestowed was thus a defining feature of Christian experience.[33] Forgiveness was the foundation of the harmony that now characterized the divine-human relationship; without it one could not be at peace with God.

Thirty years later Bergendoff quoted Luther, who held that outside of divine grace in Christ a person "sins incessantly" in all that he does because "his center is self rather than God."[34] But then, through Christ, one was given "a new center of knowledge, a new motive power for action, a reorientation." Beforehand all of human life was "out of proportion" for lack of faith. But now there was "A new world view, a new birth, even a new heaven and a new earth," all of this through the "new contact with a Person whose presence makes for a new world."[35] In a sermon preached in 1952 at the Sunday Evening Club, the sponsor of ecumenical services held weekly in Orchestra Hall on Michigan Avenue in Chicago, the college president declared again that the Christian believed in "another world," one that was seeking to break into the present one.[36] That new world meant that a person's whole scale of values changed, one's interests shifted as he or she turned from self-seeking to doing the will of God. In 1962 Bergendoff wrote, "There is nothing more profound in human experience than this discovery of a Person who becomes the absolute ruler of the individual. For Christ is a Reality, a Person, as near and dear to us as our dearest friend. We live in His presence each moment and every word and act is judged by His approval or disapproval."[37] That was "Christ as Authority."

The Nature of the Encounter

In some of his work Bergendoff described more closely this life-changing experience. It was, he believed, both rooted in the nature of the cosmos itself and essential for every human being. The event occurred in the human will and the emotions, he said in the mid-1960s in a paper given as part of ecumenical dialogs with leading American Reformed-Presbyterian scholars, Protestants with a Calvinist background. Bergendoff was part of a team representing the recently founded Lutheran Church in America. In an essay on "Justification and Sanctification," issues on which Calvinists and Lutherans might have diverging views, he presented the Lutheran understanding of conversion. The topic he had been assigned as a member of the dialog was "Liturgy and Ethics." But Bergendoff could not discuss matters of ritual and morals without first dealing with the core Christian experience out of which Christian worship and values sprang. So he did. Conversion is "the process wherein the will of man decides, on deliberation, to alter its course. The will is affected, rather by a deep emotional experience wherein man comes to realize the unspeakable mercy of God in Jesus Christ."[38]

This process was, of course, preceded by the mind's having received the Christian message, but the essence of the event for Bergendoff seemed to have been volitional and emotional, not intellectual. He knew, of course, that people heard the Christian message constantly, but did not respond to it. The Augustana College chapel and the pews of the Synod's churches were, alas, sometimes occupied by such folk. With their minds these people registered the Christian message, but did not respond in their will and emotions. By itself intellectual understanding did not bring about the meeting with Christ. In a 1950 contribution to a festschrift in honor of Anders Nygren, Bergendoff noted that "*Reine Lehre* [pure doctrine] is intellectual, pure faith is an experience of the will."[39] He seems to have thought that once the will and emotions had undergone conversion, the philosophical matter of the rational metaphysical truth of Christianity was secondary. As we have seen and will yet, he felt that this faith was self-validating, needing no rational justification. That view put him in the company of such fideists as Martin Luther or Karl Barth.

So for our Swedish American the mind or intellect was not the problem. In the 1965 essay on Sanctification and Justification quoted earlier, Bergendoff spoke in terms of what might be called a "faculty psychology," a perspective from which one looked at persons in terms of the different aspects or faculties of their personalities. There was a long tradition in Christian thought of such an effort to understand how people became Christian, what "conversion" meant in terms of the individual's personhood, including the intellect, emotions, and will. But a "subjective" or "person-centered" analysis was not the way in which Bergendoff generally spoke and wrote of the meeting between the individual and Christ. Late in his career he wrote a critique of the then much-in-vogue field of pastoral counseling. No mastery of the techniques of modern counseling psychology "can cover up a lack of spiritual reality. Compassion or empathy is never enough. To understand the other person with whom we are seeking to communicate is certainly essential, but what if I have nothing to say once the line is connected?" And: "What I am trying to say is that there is a gospel, a message, a substance of knowledge and of faith that precedes any teaching or preaching." Healing could only take place when "the counselor himself has a living faith."[40]

Thus, no analysis of a person's feelings and will in themselves could discover God, a divine presence within that person, if the Christ encounter had not taken place. The encounter was objective reality. It had either occurred in a man or woman or it had not. It came from the "objective revelation of God [which] calls forth faith in those who hear and receive."[41] As a young pastor in Chicago who had just finished an advanced degree in history, Bergendoff wrote that the faith experience was an objective fact as real as the law of gravity.

Neither philosophers nor psychologists could explain it away: "It is not for thinkers to determine what religion is, but for religious men and women to determine what shall be thought about religion." That meant that mere academic or scholarly examination of the Christian experience would never correctly understand it; you had to undergo it yourself. "[T]he spiritual fact is not less, but rather more, a reality than the physical fact. Religion as truly as life itself is its own sufficient proof." Therefore the meeting with Christ was its own validation. Luther's experience, Bergendoff continued, "is evidence of a world where souls move in an orbit determined by their relation to the central source of energy, God Himself." And, the author added, Luther's discovery was more important for the meaning of human existence than Copernicus'.[42] Herein lay Bergendoff's fideism.

It is noteworthy that Bergendoff treated the experience of meeting Christ as the basis for Christian life and at times as the "objective fact" which validated the Christian Gospel itself. For him, as one reviewer of *Christ as Authority* wrote, Christ was "the deepest reality and the highest authority in the world."[43] Of course, the assertion that the experience of meeting Christ was as real as the law of gravity did beg the question of objectivity-subjectivity. The phenomena on which the law of gravity was based were, at least in the thought-world of Newtonian physics, "objective" physical events independent of the mind of the observer. The religious experiences that Bergendoff asserted were as real as the law of gravity were inner events in the subject who experienced them; in that sense they were "subjective" in a way that physical facts such as a rock falling from a cliff into the ocean were not. It could be argued that in spite of the claim that the meeting with Christ was an "objective fact," there was a sort of "subjectivity" that asserted itself in Bergendoff's thinking. The experience itself was, when regarded from the outside, i.e., when considered by someone other than the person undergoing it, an inner event in the subject or person apparently experiencing it, rather than an observable external event in the physical world.

This was also the tenor of the criticism of *Christ as Authority* in a 1949 review that appeared in the first volume of the *Ecumenical Review,* the journal of the newly formed World Council of Churches. The reviewer's concern was that Bergendoff's emphasis upon the encounter with Christ left Christianity open to the danger that it would be understood, in the end, to be based upon subjective human experience. The reviewer wrote that "It seems as if for the author Christian 'experience' is the ultimate authority[.]" That reviewer wanted a more objective standard by which the ecumenical movement could bring together disparate Christian groups and people: the church "must, therefore, find an expression which is independent of our subjectivity." There were too many sorts of Christian experience to make that the standard by which Christians could be brought together.[44] There was, therefore, some irony in the fact that the very experience of meeting Christ, which Bergendoff claimed was the objective center of Christianity, was found by other theologians to lead to a subjectivism that might frustrate ecumenical reconciliation.

But the "objectivity" of the Christian revelation and of the experience it brought about were themes to which Bergendoff stuck his whole life. The faith was, he acknowledged, a "faith," but that did not mean it was a "whim created by human fancy." "It has grown out of the facts of creation itself and out of the experience and sufferings of centuries of human history. It is no day-dream of human wishful thinking but the outline of the significance of all that humanity has experienced."[45] That statement appeared in a 1958 essay contrasting "the Modern Imagination" with the Christian concept of the Image of God. So for decades the Augustana theologian maintained that Christian experience was an objective reality, not in the end reducible to some category or explanation other than itself. When he spoke of the "objectivity" of the Christ encounter, Bergendoff did seem to assume that the experience was essentially the same for everyone who had it; therein lay its objectivity. Just as physical human life itself was self-evident, so was the re-born life of a person who had met Christ. This was, he also insisted, the key by which all else in human life and the cosmos itself could be understood.

Conrad Bergendoff found other twentieth century theologians who tended in this direction. By the 1930s the wave of neo-orthodox theology that had begun with the Reformed German professor Karl Barth (1886-1968) and other Europeans after World War I had swept across the Atlantic. When he wrote *Christ as Authority* just after World War II, Bergendoff, who had reservations about much in neo-orthodoxy (it was after all not originally Lutheran), had come to appreciate at least its emphasis upon the fact that the Christian revelation was "self-authenticating." That meant that its truth was not established or proved by reference to any other human reality or field of knowledge "derived from history, comparative religion, natural science, or philosophy." For Bergendoff Christianity carried its own proof with it. "Its truth lies within itself, even as its authority must be experienced by each individual within himself. Religion does not live by crumbs falling from the table of more independent lords of wisdom. Christian faith has a table of the Lord which gives sustenance to a life unique and autonomous."[46]

In retirement Bergendoff claimed that he had "always been interested in finding out what the reasons for unbelief are. And I have found that they [unbelievers] haven't any better reasons than I have for my belief."[47] But that did not mean that faith and unbelief could be balanced. Unlike a number of modern thinkers who see doubt as just as meaningful for the religious life as faith, Bergendoff regarded doubt and faith as opposites. He noted in the 1947 book that, for Luther at least, doubt was "the greatest of all sins," just as its opposite, faith, was the source of all virtue.[48] This accounts for the hard words Bergendoff had for the French Catholic mathematician Blaise Pascal (1632-1662) and his oft-cited wager. This kind of faith wager, he preached in the 1952 Chicago Sunday Evening Club sermon, tells us to "live *as if* God existed, *as if* our faith were true, on a sort of gamble that it *might* be true." If it's not, the wager maintains, not much has been lost, and if it is true, heaven is gained. But this, Bergendoff declared to the Orchestra Hall faithful, is not the Christianity that has created the church and changed men and women. The Christian faith is not "the making of a bet." Pascal's *as if* has at its center "a corroding doubt."[49] Pascal may have been what one historian calls a "doubting believer,"[50] but for Bergendoff, as for Luther, that was not a viable combination. Doubt was not simply the shadow of faith. It was its enemy. That was the reason that when a student at Augustana College gave up reciting the Apostles' Creed because of his young religion instructor's views on such "myths" as the Virgin Birth or the Gospel miracles, President Bergendoff admonished the faculty member that "The world hardly needs to be told more of what not to believe—men are hungry for what to believe."[51] (The instructor left the faculty the next year.)

A "Set Term"

Many modern minds bump up against affirmations and episodes like these and are, to say the least, nonplused. For the center of *any* human life to be defined by a religious experience and by creeds that are meant to be normative for *all* human lives is, as Bergendoff himself realized, not the way most of his (or our) contemporaries view matters. James O'Donnell, a scholar at Georgetown University, has written an insightful biography of Augustine (354-430), the fifth century Bishop of Hippo in North Africa and the intellect whom many scholars see as the dominant theologian of the Western Church prior to the High Middle Ages. O'Donnell speaks of the fact that many of Augustine's contemporaries (and ours as well) "would fret at the ways of a god who could condemn little babies to hell" (as the African bishop taught God did). O'Donnell says of the Bishop of Hippo: "God was for him a *set term*, absolute and inviolable, beyond question or doubt (italics added)."[52] That is not unlike the case of our twentieth century American Lutheran college president-theologian and his own set term, "Christ." For him Christ was a set term, beyond question or doubt.

Bergendoff's doctoral dissertation quoted a text from a 1537 Swedish devotional tract attributed to Olavus Petri: "God Himself came from heaven to become a mortal man."[53] That was the keystone of Bergendoff's theological understanding: Christ was God come to live on earth. But it was more than a concept or idea; it was the core of his self-understanding and his inner devotional life. In the rare moments when we get a glimpse of that private devotional life, it is clear that it was centered on Christ. This was the relationship that carried him through the 1920s, as pastor, Synod leader, and doctoral student. Two decades later, waiting for the US Army plane that would carry him across the North Atlantic to lecture in German universities in 1949, Bergendoff noted in his journal that for practice he had been reading St. Paul in Greek and German (rather than English or Swedish, his native languages): "In both German and Greek, Christ lives!"[54]

In a lecture on "The Sphere of Revelation" which Bergendoff gave at Harvard in 1948 he argued that God does not reveal his full nature to mankind. Beyond his nature as revealed in Christ, God cannot be known. Except for this revelation humanity is not competent to speak of the divine being and nature.[55] He advanced the same views in an article for a festschrift in honor of the Swedish theologian and bishop Anders Nygren published in 1950. There he went so far as to speak of "the agnosticism of the believer." Here again is the same refusal to speculate on or speak about the nature of God except as revealed in Christ. In the essay for Nygren he criticized, as he did at other points as well, the Dutch Christian humanist Erasmus, who in his debate with Luther on free will and election argued that it was possible to explain all of God's will and work. For Bergendoff to think that you could fathom all the divine doings was to lose the distinction between the knowable and the unknowable.[56] It was in this sense that Christ was the final or ultimate word about God, a set term, behind which lay the unknowable and hidden God, the *deus absconditus*. Toward that God one could only be agnostic.

Contrast this, for example, with the young Uppsala student and eventual Archbishop, Nathan Söderblom, writing in his diary: "Never forget that behind all revelation there is the one, eternal divine reality. Look for that, as [your] goal, not the expositions thereof. Do not focus on the books of the Bible, for remember they are only the means. As you read . . . do not ask: What kind of God was Isaiah's God? but rather: What did Isaiah know of the one, eternal divine Reality—God?"[57] Söderblom was, as we shall see, one of the most important figures in Bergendoff's life. His biographer Bengt Sundkler writes that Söderblom underwent a kind of Pietistic conversion in his mid-twenties. But even after that there remained a constant impulse in the Swede to find the truth that lay behind all religious thought. That was how he approached his doctoral dissertation on Persian religion (1901); he intended "to study the other God-revealers who have given to others their particular solutions of the problems of religion." Söderblom believed that Christ was the greatest among these "God-revealers," but he did not think that the other religions of the world had none.[58] Rather, as the Swedish scholar Sven-Erik Brodd says, the belief in God was seen by the future archbishop as having grown "in an evolutionary way . . . out of what are called 'primitive' religious forms."[59]

In Bergendoff, young or old, we do not find the urge that was present in Söderblom to look for the divine revelation or truth that lies behind all religions. For Bergendoff Christ is the last word, and there is no greater truth beyond him to which he points. Christ does not represent some deeper ultimate reality of which he is the symbol or spokesman. He is *himself* the Truth. That is why the Augustana historian-theologian gently demurred when in the mid-sixties an American study of Söderblom called the Swede a "Theologian of Revelation." Considered in this sense, the Archbishop had found revelations of God in many religions, but Bergendoff made an (at least to him) important distinction. What Söderblom meant by "revelation," Bergendoff explained, might in English have been better rendered "interpretation." So put more carefully, Söderblom had found interesting "interpretations" of divine reality in the world's religions. "His keen intellect was trained on finding how God has revealed himself in the experiences of men and women," Bergendoff said years later. As his American student and friend viewed him, Söderblom "was, I make bold to assert, a theological artist rather than a scientific theologian." For Bergendoff "revelation" ought perhaps to be reserved for God's revealing himself in Christ. That distinction between revelation and interpretation was one reason that some critics, confusing the two concepts, had doubts about Söderblom's orthodoxy, Bergendoff conceded.[60] In 1966 Bergendoff remarked about Söderblom, "I don't think he was a great theologian—I think he was a great Christian Churchman."[61]

One supposes that, for the Augustana man, artists looked for interpretations, "scientific" theologians for revelation. Thus a "theological artist" might find traces of God everywhere. But writing carefully, Bergendoff held that there lay back of Christ only the hidden God about whom neither Luther nor he was inclined to speculate. Such an effort was pointless at best, and when you pressed it, it could become discouraging or, worse yet, misleading. To be a Christian meant to believe that so far as humanity was concerned, the merciful God revealed in Christ was truly and fully God. Christ did not point to some deeper truth; he *was* the truth. The closest Bergendoff came to presenting Christ as the bearer of a meaning beyond himself was when he treated commitment to Christ as the means by which a person's character was changed—"for knowledge, for compassion, for tolerance, for friendship, for beauty, for faith, love, work."[62] But even these Christian qualities were secondary to the sheer fact of meeting Christ himself.

The sense of the term, Christ, was established, Bergendoff thought, early in Christian history. After retiring Bergendoff wrote a short essay summarizing pre-Reformation church history. It was the first chapter of a book tracing the history of Lutheranism. He began by considering the fourth century Council of Nicaea, the gathering of Christian bishops and theologians which asserted that "Christ reveals to man the nature of God, is Himself God, and is the Head of the Church."[63]   It is significant that Bergendoff opened this account of Christian history with the church council that declared the full divinity of Christ and his equality with God the Father, rather than with a discussion of Jesus Christ's earthly life and the lives of the apostolic Christians. For Bergendoff the doctrine of the Trinity, especially in the form in which it developed in the western half of ancient Mediterranean Christianity, was fundamental to his idea about the role of Christ in Christian life and thought in his own day. He held that Christ was, as Nicaea and subsequent church councils affirmed, fully and truly God, as fully and truly as the Father or Creator of all things was. The Father created, the Son redeemed, and the third person of the Trinity, the Holy Spirit, brought the truth of this to humanity.

In the eastern and Greek speaking areas of early Christendom, the emphasis was upon three separate centers of divine being, Father, Son, and Spirit. That is sometimes called a "societal" view of the Trinity. The three members of the Trinity together constituted the Godhead, itself a sort of society or fellowship of the three, Father, Son, and Spirit. But under the influence of Augustine, the western, or Roman, Catholic Church emphasized the unity of God and held that the three persons of the Trinity were, like the masks or *personae* worn by actors in ancient drama, the ways God presented himself to Christians. Bergendoff, via Luther, stood in that western or Augustinian tradition. For him when you met Christ you met God. What of the other two members of the Trinity? The Holy Spirit had nothing to say about himself; he pointed to Christ, and in Christ one learned the truth about both his own work of redemption and about creation, the work of the Father.

Based on the ancient doctrinal formulation of the Trinity, Bergendoff presented his own understanding of the reality of Christ and of the Christ experience. He spoke of these matters as simple facts—plainly, flatly, sometimes eloquently. The Christ-centered view of existence needed no defense beyond its proclamation. Bergendoff knew very well that everyone who heard the Christian message did not accept it; that was part of "the mystery of faith." When he went on to explain more fully what happened when the soul met Christ, he was not seeking to justify his view; he was simply presenting it more completely. The essentially volitional-emotional experience was for him a fact as real as those that science examined. It should also be noted that Bergendoff rarely uttered threats regarding the ultimate destiny of those who did not know Christ. He did not raise the specter of eternal punishment. In this regard at least, Bergendoff took leave of Augustine, who was not reluctant to speak of the dire consequences of human sin: most of the human race would spend eternity damned.[64] In contrast, the only time the college president seems to have talked about hell was in an occasional chapel talk at Augustana, and there the term was reserved for a description of the kind of lives students who drank, danced, and ignored their studies were living in Rock Island, Illinois—there and then.

One might mistakenly conclude from many of Bergendoff's presentations of the Christ encounter that it was only a sort of principle or theme for the Swedish-American theologian and historian. It may have been a principle, but it was quite personal as well. When he said these things Bergendoff knew whereof he spoke. They were realities in his own life, though he seldom talked directly about himself. That may have been because he was by nature modest, or because Swedish Americans tended to be reserved in the first place, or simply because his faith itself enjoined humility. But, reluctant to talk about himself or not, Bergendoff had learned these things on his mother's lap, believed them as his father preached. Christ was his set term, the center of life and, indeed, of the universe. A life with Christ in it had meaning and purpose. Without him there was ultimately none, no matter how much one's secular contemporaries fooled themselves on that count.

The author of *Christ as Authority* was especially bothered when he found the alternative to his understanding stated bluntly, as in Julian Huxley's *Evolution: the Modern Synthesis* (1942): "If we wish to work toward a purpose for the future of man, we must formulate that purpose ourselves. Purposes in life are made, not found." For Bergendoff this was "wholly wrong."[65] The purpose in his own life had not been "formulated" by Conrad Bergendoff. His father, his Church, and he himself had not made up the encounter with Christ; it was objective reality. Looked at in another way, that encounter was also for Conrad Bergendoff a "set term"—in all his thought and during his entire life. It took place in the will and emotions when the Christian message was made real by the Holy Spirit of God acting upon the revelation of Christ in the Holy Scriptures. After that it became a fixed point in the mind or intellect; a point from which Bergendoff strayed neither personally nor intellectually. It was how he understood himself, his ultimate identity shaper.

The Spirit Acting upon Scripture

The meeting with Christ occurred when the Spirit of God gave life to the teachings of the Bible, either because one had read it directly or heard it spoken of by others. Always when he spoke of "the Spirit" Bergendoff was referring to the Third Person of the Christian Trinity, as when he spoke of "Christ" he was, of course, referring to the Second. He was not interested in some sort of "World Spirit" about which philosophers and prophets from other religious traditions had spoken. The second chapter of *Christ as Authority* dealt with the action of the Spirit upon the Bible, which brought Christ into a human life.

The chapter did *not* deal with modern biblical criticism, a scholarly effort that did not bother Bergendoff to the degree that it did some other Christians. The latter insisted that the truth of Christianity rested upon the full divine inspiration of the *ipsissima verba*, the very words of Scripture. That position was sometimes referred to as "verbal" or "plenary inspiration." It was biblical literalism, and its adherents were sometimes labeled fundamentalists. To hold to such ideas, Bergendoff believed, missed the point. And insofar as some of his Lutheran brethren held this sort of view of the Bible, they misread Martin Luther. Eschewing any sort of literalism, Bergendoff insisted that in Luther and genuine Lutheranism it was the interrelationship between the living person of Christ and the description of him in Holy Writ where divine inspiration lay, rather than simply in the words of the Bible themselves.[66] Inspiration came not from the text in itself, but from the text's coming to life through the work of the Spirit in bringing a person into relationship with Christ. The question of the nature of the inspiration of the Bible was one that had troubled inter-Lutheran conversations in the years between the wars and would continue to be a factor in merger talks in the forties and fifties.[67] For Bergendoff it was a false issue, disloyal to Luther.

The Reformer's understanding of the distinction between the Word of God and the words of the Bible enabled Bergendoff to avoid biblical literalism. He was, therefore, less troubled by the uncertainties created by biblical criticism than were more literalist Christians, in whose number stood some of his American Lutheran confreres. For Bergendoff any effort to define precisely the role of the Bible in developing faith was doomed to fail. The attempt to use the doctrinal statements of the churches as the keys to the meaning of Scripture (a tendency marked among Lutherans, who often claimed their confessions were an adequate précis of the teachings of the Bible) was in the end no help. There existed a wide range of doctrinal positions among Christians, all justified by reference to the Book. In Bergendoff's mind it was also profitless to speculate whether it was the Bible that created the church, or the church the Bible. That was an issue important to Roman Catholics, who rested ultimate authority in the church rather than in the Scriptures as Protestants seemed to do. The agent that Bergendoff thought created believers, individually and in community, was the divine Word. He held that the Word existed before the biblical texts were written and collected into their present form.[68]

Bergendoff understood that there were differing ways to understand the term "Word of God." He stood with the Reformer's description of the Bible as the "manger in which Christ lies."[69] With Luther he saw Scripture, "the Word of God," as the vessel that contains the "Word that is God," Christ himself. So unless one found "Christ, the Word" in "the Bible, the Word," reading and appealing to Scripture was profitless. Lacking the vitalizing Spirit, "the objective facts and statements of Scripture are but as archeological ruins testifying to a life which used to inhabit these regions."[70] For Bergendoff, Christ, the Word of God, was as much the key to understanding the Old Testament as he was the focus of the New. He spoke of the "Living Christ of the Old and the New Testaments."[71]

To treat the Bible as offering "a sort of prepared prescription" which, if you could find the right verse, would offer a solution to all of life's difficulties, was for Bergendoff "a mechanistic and legalistic" use of Scripture. He rejected it.[72] Along with avoiding biblical literalism on the one hand and remaining untroubled by historical criticism on the other, Bergendoff also wished with Luther to "see to it that you do not make of Christ a second Moses, or of the Gospel a book of laws and doctrines."[73] Legalism must be avoided. Of course, Bergendoff agreed with Luther that the Bible had a legal meaning for "those who do not find Christ in this book." It was still a divine message, but now not of salvation, but of judgment.[74] Thus for Bergendoff, the central, and in a real sense the only completely positive, meaning of the Bible was to bring a person to a meeting with Christ. Otherwise it led to judgment on life apart from God's will; that was its legal meaning or role.

As to the matter of scriptural authority, Bergendoff held that the Bible, like the meeting with Christ itself, was ultimately self-authenticating. "Scripture needs no other proof than it itself produces."[75] In one sense, then, the authority of the Bible and the authority of Christ were finally one and the same, each reciprocally affirming the other. In the final analysis, the Bible as the Word of God and Christ as the Word of God were identical. In 1974, reviewing his already long life, Bergendoff wrote that what he had said in 1947 he still said. Faith in Christ was inseparable from the Bible.[76] But that did not make him a biblical literalist, as many of his seminary teachers had been. For Bergendoff the experience of faith was always much more than "mere adherence to Scriptural statement." He made that clear in an *Augustana Quarterly* article written five years before *Christ as Authority*. "Any experience of a living God" must be based on the Bible as its means, but "The emphasis was not on the subjective experience (the bane of modern empirical theology), but on the truth grasped in experience—a truth beyond experience, but glimpsed and sensed in experience sufficiently to become for the believer an absolute authority."[77] The experience took place in the emotions and will, but it led to the apprehension of an eternal truth which was seen to be factual and separate from the experience itself. No matter what his critics said, Bergendoff would not have conceded that the experience was merely subjective.

A decade after his book on Christ's authority, Bergendoff insisted again that the faith encounter was not ours "to be handled, stored, preserved, possessed, and controlled." It did not depend on us; it was a gift of God.[78] Luther made it clear that "I cannot by my own strength believe in Jesus Christ or come to Him." Only through the Holy Spirit could one grasp the revelation and understand the true meaning of Christ.[79] The radical Anabaptists of the sixteenth century, the left wingers of the Reformation who made Luther wonder whether he might better have remained in the Church of Rome, thought they could seek the guidance of the Spirit directly without reference to the Bible.[80] So did some of Bergendoff's contemporaries. But for both Luther and for Bergendoff it was the Holy Spirit making alive the Word in Holy Scripture that was the key to valid Christian thought and experience. He further insisted that it was not the subjective experience Luther had undergone that was vital: "It is not Luther's experience per se, as a religious phenomena, [sic] which is significant. The importance lies in *what* he experienced, the object of his experience."[81] That "object" was the Spirit acting on Scripture.

Those who sought to find Christ outside of Scripture were for Bergendoff doomed to disappointment, or in the case of the mystic, to self-deception. As we saw in the last chapter, he would have had little sympathy for the "new spirituality" that emerged in the later twentieth century, often attempting a syncretistic melding of Christianity and eastern religion, sometimes garnishing itself with the insights of pop psychology. Neither did he think that God lies deep within every person and rises up within each man or woman, as for example, we are told that the non-canonical and lately discovered Gospel of Thomas teaches—in distinction to the Gospel of John, which sees God coming to us from outside of ourselves. For John we must come to the divine light that is Christ. For Thomas that divine light lies in every person: "If you bring forth what is within you, what you bring forth will save you."[82] That was not the Augustana Synod métier, nor was it Bergendoff's.

His method or style was to make direct assertions about the authority of Christ, about the meeting with him that was the core of the Christian faith, and about the self-validating nature of Christian experience when the Spirit acted upon Scripture. By both personal temper and intellectual inclination Bergendoff was not disposed to try to argue people into accepting his ideas. Like his Augustana College chapel talks to nineteen- and twenty-year-olds, at its core his method was not to exhort. Of course, other theologians, and perhaps at moments Bergendoff himself, recognized certain questions and challenges to his assertions. The reader will probably have some as well. We turn now to a consideration of certain of these difficulties. They include the question of predestination, the matter of the similarities and differences between Bergendoff and "evangelistic" American Christianity, and the nature of Christian holiness or sanctification. In each of these areas Bergendoff's thought manifests inner tensions, some of which he recognized and some of which he did not seem to be aware of.

Another Paradox

Bergendoff never addressed head-on the question of why the experience of meeting Christ came only to some people. He said repeatedly that it was impossible to account for the Spirit visiting one person and not another. For him that matter was "hidden." Was it predestination, he asked.[83] He asked, but he did not answer that question. The troubling problem of God choosing some and not others was not one that Bergendoff ventured into readily. But it has been an important problem through the history of the church. Augustine, Aquinas, Luther, Calvin—all of them addressed it. Even Paul had spoken to it. The Swedish-American theologian did not really want to. He knew the labyrinth of paradox into which consideration of predestination led. He conceded the impossibility of creating a thoroughly consistent system of theology. It was better simply to assert "the truths of Christianity in all their paradoxical form."[84]

Of course, Bergendoff could not completely avoid dealing with the paradox with which the classical expressions of predestination also contended. When Bergendoff spoke of the divine-human meeting from the perspective of the person undergoing the experience, he saw it as a volitional and emotional one. That implied that a person could decide whether to enter into the new relationship with Christ for her- or himself or, in the case of the many who had been baptized as babies, whether to continue in the life which the parents had committed one to follow. But at other points Bergendoff treated Christian faith as entirely the gift of God and acknowledged that he could not say why some were given it and some were not. Bergendoff wrote that in the Bible "Saints, therefore, are not those who present their virtues to God, but are they who through an inscrutable purpose of God are chosen by Him to receive the purity and righteousness which He requires. This is a gift apprehended only by faith."[85] That was penned for lectures given in 1953.

Here again, Bergendoff got close to arguing for predestination. But it's as close as he wanted to get. A few pages later he moved away from the suggestion that this "inscrutable" electing of saints is entirely the work of God acting unilaterally. He referred, as he often did, to Luther, whose theology he believed to be rooted in Scripture. Luther spoke of making "a *personal decision* of faith (italics added)."[86]   That implied some degree of human participation in accepting or rejecting Christ. When he had to discuss it, Bergendoff was willing to put the matter of why some people had faith and others did not in the category of the "truths of Christianity in all their paradoxical form." Theological paradox involves stating ideas which seem to stand opposed to each other and not attempting to resolve the opposition. That is what Bergendoff did with the question of whether the meeting with Christ was one in which God and a person cooperated or whether it was entirely the work of God.

Conrad Bergendoff saw the history of Lutheranism as one in which the strong predestinarian position of Calvinism had for the most part been avoided. The Formula of Concord, a Lutheran creedal statement from the 1570s, said that "The Will of God is that all men should be saved." Why then God's will was not completely realized in this regard was a question that neither the Formula of Concord nor Conrad Bergendoff addressed. Bergendoff and his Church did not hold the view that in the end all people will be saved, as, for example, did American Universalists. To suggest that God wanted everyone saved, but then to allow that some persons were not, would be to suggest that God's will was not ultimately all-powerful. That was not a position that Lutherans usually took, either. Again, better to label the whole matter a paradox.

For Bergendoff, as for his Church, the basic and *positive* use of the idea of predestination was to guarantee that salvation was understood to be entirely the work of God.[87] The landscape of nineteenth century American Protestantism was, of course, littered with the detritus from the debate about free will versus divine election. For their part Swedish-American Lutherans kept out of the argument, one that destroyed the ecclesiastical unity of their Norwegian-American relatives for a time. In *The Church of the Lutheran Reformation* Bergendoff noted the split among these ethnic cousins of Augustana, but he did not discuss the relative theological merits of the differing factions.[88] Martin Luther once remarked that divine election was something best left for scholarly theologians to consider. It was not a matter for ordinary Christians. Conrad Bergendoff was no "ordinary Christian," but he seems to have preferred not to probe too deeply into the question, though Luther would probably have thought him fit to join the discussion. Perhaps it was his very scholarly and careful mind that kept the Augustana man from wandering into a question that had rent the peace of Christianity long before the Norwegian Americans found themselves caught in its snares.

Evangelical and Evangelistic

Readers familiar with both historic and current American Christianity may find some similarity between the Christ-encounter, foreordained or not, that Conrad Bergendoff spoke and wrote about and the experience of being "born again" that has been, and still is, preached in what are currently called the "evangelical" churches.   In the German Lutheran background which Bergendoff knew well, *evangelisch* (evangelical) was a term used to distinguish Protestants, both Lutherans and Calvinists, from Roman Catholics. Considered generically, all Protestants were "evangelical." That was the way Bergendoff and his Lutheran contemporaries used the term. However, when "evangelical" became "evangelistic" there was an aura of revivalism about it. That was not an Augustana emphasis.

It is nonetheless the case that much of what Bergendoff said about the individual's meeting with Christ shared certain elements with the evangelistic Christianity of the mid- and late twentieth century. In both cases the encounter was transforming and had implications for every aspect of one's personal and social existence. No area of life was exempt; the experience totally remade an individual. He or she was "born again," though that was not a phrase Bergendoff used often. The term comes, of course, from the third chapter of John's Gospel, but for Bergendoff it was redolent of Swedish Pietism or American revivalism, which he regarded as "meager" substitutes for mature Christian thought and worship.[89]

However, Bergendoff's emphasis upon individual Christian experience as an essential part of the Gospel did represent an affinity with the Pietistic elements in Swedish church history, especially when these elements are contrasted with the corporate emphasis of earlier periods. In 1939 a Swedish church historian at Lund University and a contemporary of Bergendoff, Hilding Pleijel (1893–1988), wrote that with Pietism "individualism broke into Swedish religious life." There emerged a new type of person with a wholly different mentality than the one that had prevailed earlier in the unified orthodox national Church. "Pietism placed the individual person with his religious needs and experiences in the center of spiritual life." Pleijel said that earlier, prior to the nineteenth century emergence of this Pietistic individualism, "Preaching was more concerned with the community than with the individual and sought to raise general folk morality rather than to give direction to the individual in religious questions and difficulties."[90] Bergendoff's emphasis upon encountering Christ certainly shared this Pietistic individualism that had replaced the earlier religious collectivism described by Pleijel.

But the idea that the new life was a gift of God rather than something the individual him- or herself autonomously decided to accept was an important distinction between Bergendoff and those "evangelicals" who used "evangelistic" revival methods. Although Bergendoff skirted the question of predestination, he balanced his sense that a person could decide to follow Christ with a repeated emphasis that in the mysterious workings of God, faith itself was a divine gift. Evangelical revivalism was predicated on the idea that the individual had free will and could decide for oneself to be a Christian. And Bergendoff's adherence to a Lutheran understanding of Christ himself as the Word of God (and the Word of God not being the literal sum of the words of the Bible) is another distinction by which he kept his distance from "evangelical" or "evangelistic" Christianity as it developed in modern times, both in America and beyond. Further, he never spoke or wrote in a "hell-fire and brimstone" mode; we have already noted that he was rarely hortatory or threatening when he wrote and preached, at least as regarded the individual, though when it came to contemporary culture, he did issue rather dire warnings, as we will see. Yet another difference in emphasis between Bergendoff and evangelistic American Protestantism was Bergendoff's reluctance to speak about his personal religious experience or to hold it up as a paradigm. Rather, he wrote and preached about the normative Christian experience which we have just described in this chapter. One is left to assume that he himself had that experience too, but he did not put forth his own testimony as a model in the way that American revivalists did.

But perhaps the most important practical distinction Bergendoff made between revivalism and Lutheranism regarding one's relationship with Christ, is that in the former the decision to become a follower of Christ was usually seen as a choice made by a grown person at a specific moment. In Lutheranism the process was more gradual, said Bergendoff in a series of 1956 lectures on *The Doctrine of the Church in American Lutheranism*. That process began with baptism, almost always administered to infants. Bergendoff's read of nineteenth century American church history was that even in those groups that baptized babies, "it was often necessary to validate one's right to be called a Christian" by deciding for Christ when the age of accountability had been reached. For these groups, "One should be able to point to a date of conversion."[91]

On the other hand, in Lutheranism, Bergendoff said, the encounter with Christ was seen as one of growth and development that began even before a person was rational and accountable, almost with birth. And it continued by means of nurture and learning in the family and in the church. It was a life of discipline and prayer. This view of the relationship between Christ and the believer was one from which American Lutheranism wavered at times in the nineteenth century American church milieu, almost seduced by the prevalent revivalism, as well as by some strands in its own Pietistic heritage.

But Bergendoff thought that from this episode Lutherans "emerged clearly as a church of Word and sacraments."[92] So preaching and Holy Communion were the primary ways in which congregations nurtured the person's relationship to Christ, once she or he had been baptized. Prayer and Bible study further supported the corporate efforts of the Christian community. That was certainly the character of Conrad's own younger days in Middletown and at college in Rock Island. Here were traces of the communal or corporate Christianity described by the Swede Pleijel.

In a small tract, *Living in the Grace of Baptism,* published in the forties by the Augustana Book Concern, Bergendoff underlined the fact that the Christian life was always one in which the new person who was created through the encounter with Christ struggled with the unregenerate old person with its selfish desires and unwillingness to turn life over to Christ. Of course, Bergendoff supported that view with quotes from Paul's letter to the Romans, which spoke of the struggle between "two laws or wills—the will of Christ in the new man, the will of sin in the old man." This, said Bergendoff, was the "normal Christian state in this world." A "fall from grace" meant that the old nature had dominated a person who had been baptized and committed to the new life. However, "if you live in repentance, you walk in baptism, which not only signifies such a new life, but also produces, begins and exercises it." But, contra Christians who held that the new life began with conversion and then made steady progress toward holiness or sanctification, Bergendoff wrote, "We may have doubts as to our sanctification. There should be none as to our justification." That meant that while one could never be certain that the old person had been completely conquered and replaced by the new, there was no doubt about Christ's having saved one—justification by grace through faith.[93] One stood justified in the sight of God, though she or he might or might not have become a completely new person so far as living on earth was concerned. Here again we see a contrast with American revivalism, especially the variety that stressed sanctification or holiness, as many of the conservative Wesleyan churches did.

Christian discipline was therefore a crucial factor in cultivating the Christian life. This raises the question of what sorts of behavior might result in a person's being denied full fellowship in the church. In the mid-nineteenth century American Lutherans could be quite specific about the grounds for excluding a member from Holy Communion. The Norwegian Lutherans in 1853 listed them: "cursing and swearing, drunkenness, frivolous and unchaste speech, malicious backbiting, disobedience to parents, cheating in business transactions, etc."[94] Not to be out-done by Norwegian Americans, twentieth century Swedish Americans offered their own list, issued in 1923 by the President of the Augustana Synod,

G. A. Brandelle: "indifference, materialism, greed, worldliness, pleasures of all kinds, gossip, slander, the dance, card playing, profaning Sunday, especially at harvest time, the inroads of secret societies, motion pictures, socialism, and the misuse of automobiles."[95]   One wonders how many were barred from Communion in Synod churches for violations of that second list.

But Conrad Bergendoff understood the Christian life as a struggle. He knew how difficult it was to keep the youth of the Synod from such transgressions as Brandelle had enumerated. Happily there is no record of any Augustana College students of his day being expelled for gossip, profaning Sunday, for socialism, playing cards, or even the misuse of automobiles, the last sin a particularly troublesome possibility at a college. And secret societies with Greek-letter names had certainly made inroads on the Rock Island campus. Often Augustana students, members or not of such groups, ran into a morality of "Don'ts," or what Synod historians called "Code Morality."[96] It had found its way into the life of American Lutheranism, and was the basis of the lists iterated above. It was, if we can trust the English playwright John Osborn's *Luther*, the sort of moralistic Christianity which the monk Martin Luther made silly— by over-scrupulously observing it. The most recent history of the Augustana Synod suggests that "The constant drumbeat from synod leaders to maintain the code's standards may have been due, in large part, to the fact that it was not being universally observed, even within Augustana institutions."[97]   One of those institutions was the college in Rock Island, and some of President Bergendoff's chapel talks to undergraduates could, like the Lutheran Church leaders' prohibitions in the last paragraph, get rather specific about dancing or drinking or cheating or laziness.

It was the case that when it was time to flesh out a description of the Christian life as it was understood in the Augustana Synod or at Augustana College, what emerged beyond the list that Brandelle had issued was a model of middle class American respectability. Divorce, homosexuality, excessive drinking, the unsavory parts of town—these must be avoided. Bergendoff said apropos of alcohol at the college, "Our young men are being taught . . . to keep away from the stuff entirely."[98] The administration tried to keep cigarette ads out of the college newspaper.[99] Lapses in sexual morality were even more serious. In the late thirties a faculty member suddenly skedaddled from Rock Island under a cloud of suspicion. The man was a published scholar who subsequently landed a good job at a national university, but when Bergendoff was asked for a recommendation, he wrote: "While [he] was known for his scholarly abilities while on our campus, he seems not to have heard of a certain commandment about his neighbor's wife, for when he left he took the wife of one of our other faculty members." And the president added, "Personally

I believe the moral influence of a teacher is equally as great as the intellectual influence, and with this conviction, I cannot give a recommendation."[100]

But it should also be understood that the moral code that seemed to function in the Augustana Synod was more than simply a list of prohibitions and warnings. The positive side of that code was a strong emphasis on service— to others, to the church, and to society at large. Bergendoff's college sent thousands of people into careers in the ministry, education, and social service. In fact, Augustana administrators sometimes worried that so many of its graduates had believed so deeply in the lives of service that they been inspired to lead, that the college did not have a body of wealthy business alumni to support it. The Augustana Church carried on eleemosynary work in hospitals, children's and elderly homes, facilities for the handicapped, and the like. Its programs of youth work and foreign missions were exemplary. At the seminary, Professor A. D. Mattson persistently reminded the church of its obligations to labor and the poor.[101]

As a theologian Bergendoff, like Luther, knew that particular lists and episodes like those cited earlier, perhaps even a list abstracted from his own policies at the college, might make the Christian life look trivial. He understood the larger meaning of Christian service and lived and taught it himself. In the end, that did not mean, however, that a church could tolerate all kinds of behavior in its members or that an individual Christian could be excused from the constant reexamination of her or his own faithfulness. Once a person had met Christ, it took resolution to continue to live with him. Even when dealing with late adolescents or wayward professors, Bergendoff sought constantly to move from specific "don'ts" to a deeper understanding of Christian sanctity.

Christian Sanctity

Conrad Bergendoff confronted matters more serious than a bill of particulars for judging sinners. As regards the deeper and ultimately authentic marks or characteristics of Christian living, the reader might wonder what precisely the Augustana theologian and educator thought. How did the encounter with Christ generate a change in a person who had experienced it as a "fact," as Bergendoff spoke of it? Was there moral improvement that skeptics for their part or sincere seekers for theirs could observe? That kind of question is as old as human religion itself: does it make a difference? The law of gravity could be measured and tested. Could you measure and test the Christ experience, which (recall) for Bergendoff was as real as any fact that science observed? He had steadily insisted that Christianity was not a code of conduct. But *did* it change lives—and how? In his book on Christ's authority the author acknowledged that most church goers fell into Kierkegaard's category, "disciple at second hand."[102] He himself "in the dark moments of the present" was frequently discouraged about the behavior of church people, he admitted in a 1952 baccalaureate sermon.[103]

Presumably Bergendoff was speaking of world conditions in that sermon, but, as suggested earlier, as he looked out at the college graduating class, he might also have been reflecting on matters closer to home. In Rock Island tensions over permitting social dancing at college events, long prohibited by the Synod, were rising. So were troubles with the Greek fraternities and sororities and their fondness for finishing their initiation rituals with "Hell Week." There was, President Bergendoff held, "a marked chasm between what we preach and what our youth do."[104] Though he did on occasion chastise students for specific moral failings, Bergendoff had long maintained that "our emphasis should be less on certain accepted standards of conduct and more on man's knowing the fullness of the grace and knowledge in Christ."[105]

"Forgiveness of sins implies, too, a relationship to Christ that inspires willingness to do His will." Christ's death, which brings forgiveness "means the death of the self" and a life of good works that "come, almost spontaneously, from a heart made new by faith."[106] Those words were written in an article about Scandinavian Lutheranism in which Bergendoff held up the Christian life of those northern lands as paradigmatic. But when he wrote them Scandinavia itself was well under way to becoming home to what many observers now regard as some of Europe's most secular modern societies. So, whether at Augustana College, the oldest American college founded by Scandinavians, or in the *hemland* itself, the tricky problem of the relationship of faith and works persistently reasserted itself. That was the case even for Lutherans, who saw faith as always prior to deeds and who often, with their founder, found troublesome the words of James in the New Testament that "faith apart from works is dead." Early in his ministry Pastor Bergendoff noted that "Lutheran preaching is so much afraid of good deeds as the cause of justification that it neglects good deeds as the fruit of that act."[107]

Theologians discuss these issues under the heading "Justification and Sanctification." Shortly after his retirement Bergendoff, representing the newly formed Lutheran Church in America, became formally involved in a discussion of these questions with American Presbyterians.[108] Justification, he held, is the act or process by which a person receives God's forgiveness and is declared righteous by him because of the work of Christ. Sanctification is the attributing of holiness to, or the acquiring of holiness by, the person who has been justified. There is a difference between those who hold that sanctification is *attributed* to a person and those who say it is actually *acquired*. If attributed, the Christian is understood to be held righteous by God, though measurable moral improvement may or may not be observable. If acquired, the person through grace actually becomes a better man or woman. A different form of the same question is whether this holiness is a moral quality and, if it is, whether it can be measured. On these questions even Lutherans differed, a fact Bergendoff well understood.

In the forties a Danish Lutheran theologian, Regin Prenter (1907-1990), published a seminal study of this question. His book, *Spiritus Creator*, was translated into English in 1953, and Bergendoff read it. Prenter was influenced by currents in both British and continental theology and was closely aligned with the Swedish "Lundensian" theologians in whom Bergendoff himself took great interest. Among these scholars at Lund University, in southern Sweden, just across the Kattegat from Denmark, were Gustaf Aulén, Anders Nygren, and Ragnar Bring. Their work was characterized by an effort to find the central themes or motifs in Christianity and to re-affirm these themes as historic realities independent of philosophy and human culture in general. Bergendoff maintained that the core of this Swedish theological renaissance was "primarily a study of Luther." Attention had shifted from an occupation with later Orthodoxy and Pietism to the Reformation.[109] That put the Lundensians in opposition to much of nineteenth and twentieth century theological liberalism.

These issues matched Bergendoff's interests, and he became one of the Swedes' chief American advocates. On the question of whether holiness was simply attributed he may not have been quite as aligned with the Dane Prenter as he was to the Lundensians, in the main because of the strong position Prenter took on the question of Christian sanctification. Prenter held, arguing from Luther, that sanctification was wholly "forensic." In the terms used in the preceding paragraph that meant that it was attributed to a person but not necessarily acquired by that person. Through the work of Christ an individual was judged by God to be holy, though in observable fact no particular quality of moral sanctity was evident in her or his behavior. In other words, in the Lutheran tradition as Prenter understood it, Christian holiness was not seen to be necessarily moral or ethical. "Forensic" meant that because of Christ, God viewed the person to be holy; he *attributed* holiness to him or her. But, as Prenter said, it was not "empirical piety."[110] Presumably that term meant acquired piety that could be observed and measured.

A Swedish scholar, Axel Gyllenkrok, also investigated Luther's view of holiness or sanctification, as Prenter had. The Swede offered a view that modified the Dane's. In a 1952 study, Gyllenkrok argued that Luther did allow for some signs of moral improvement in the lives of Christians, though he agreed that for Luther sanctification began with a Christian being declared righteous by God *before* the development of any moral goodness. This was the "alien" or forensic holiness about which Prenter wrote. Said Gyllenkrok: "The individual is fully righteous in Christ's 'alien' righteousness and in part actually and observably righteous in terms of personal growth in Christian living." [111] The Swede's more moderate view struck a middle point on the question of whether sanctification was entirely the work of God or the result of human effort, and it was an approach more congenial to Bergendoff.

In a certain sense Bergendoff wanted to hang on to both sides in this matter. He knew both Prenter and Gyllenkrok's work and had met them both at conferences. Bergendoff cited Prenter in his lectures on *The One Holy Catholic Apostolic Church,* written six years after his work on Christ's authority and, again, published as a slim volume by the Augustana Book Concern. He agreed, he wrote, that in the Old and New Testaments, "Holiness is not an ethical, but a religious term. It has to do with a man's standing before God, and since no man is good enough to appear before God, God must Himself do something to enable man to come into His presence." In the Bible saints were those to whom God gave the righteousness they could never on their own attain. [112] But having been thus justified, that is *held righteous,* through faith, Christians go on to *act* rightly. Here Bergendoff seemed to prefer the approach which the Swede Gyllenkrok had taken, one that recognized the classical Lutheran concept of alien or forensic righteousness and at the same time allowed for signs of a person's faith in the way she or he acted. For Bergendoff, you needed only look at Scandinavia to see such persons, as we shall discover in Chapter 8.

So sanctification for Bergendoff was not simply a question of one's standing before God; it had implications for how one lived. The Augustana president insisted that throughout the history of Christianity there had been "an ethical aspect of holiness unknown in other religions." He conceded that it was emphasized more in John Calvin than in Martin Luther. [113] The thought that sanctification or being made holy did have ethical or moral implications and that human choice was involved seemed to have been something Bergendoff was more comfortable in discussing, both in these lectures on *One Holy Catholic Apostolic Church* and elsewhere. He would, of course, hardly have admitted to moving away from Luther toward Calvin. But in arguing that holiness does have an ethical dimension he did seem closer to the latter, though he shied away from Calvin's strong doctrine of predestination.

Along with the Calvinists, American Methodists exercised a dominant influence on American religious life and thought in the nineteenth century that continued into the years when Bergendoff was studying and beginning his ministry. The Swedish-American pastor and historian would not have gone so far as John Wesley (1703-1791), the founder of Methodism, who held that Christian sanctification meant that a believer must take seriously Jesus' injunction, "Be perfect as your Father in heaven is perfect." Methodism held that progress toward holiness must be both moral and measurable. It was the necessary sign of a serious Christian life. The Swedish Pietism of many Augustana Synod founders was influenced by this Methodism, which saw holiness or sanctification as meaning that in daily living a Christian must display the marks of moral improvement that characterize the true believer. For his part Wesley had some reservations about whether Luther understood this. In a sermon "On God's Vineyard" Wesley asked concerning Luther, "And who was more ignorant of the doctrine of sanctification, or more confused in his conceptions of it?"[114] In Wesley's view, Luther was a fine guide on the matter of justification, but his understanding of sanctification was inadequate and unsatisfactory, since it denied the reality of the measurable moral progress toward perfection that Christ enjoined on his followers.

Bergendoff, for his part, had some doubts about Wesley: the Englishman was never clear about the nature of human sin, original and actual, so it was no wonder that he lacked clarity on Christian perfectibility as well. So Conrad Bergendoff was no Methodist. He did not leave open the possibility of earthly Christian perfection about which Wesley spoke. But he did agree that a Christian's sanctification had a moral dimension that others could see, even though this was not its essential quality. In fact, after criticizing Wesley, he lamented the fact that Lutherans needed to clarify their own ideas about Christian sanctification.[115] In 1941 he wrote that the encounter with Christ "inspires a willingness to do His will." And, he continued to think that "good works . . . come, almost spontaneously, from a heart made new by faith in Christ."[116] One assumes that Bergendoff thought you could observe these good works.

We have seen that he himself never quite ironed out all the wrinkles in his understanding of sanctification, and that he did not regard it as one of the essential doctrines upon which Lutherans must agree. With regard to both Calvinism and Wesleyanism, forces that shaped the American character deeply, Bergendoff was attracted by their moral earnestness and was willing to grant that Christian holiness had an ethical character. But he was not ready to abandon his reservations about the over-optimism that the Calvinists, and especially the Methodists, seemed to manifest. He held to a middle course. On one side lay the pessimism of some Lutheran theology with regard to the moral progress of individual Christian life (the pessimism to which Wesley objected and from which Calvin moved away). On the other was what Bergendoff saw as the facile confidence of much American religion (which Bergendoff thought the American Methodist and Presbyterian Social Gospel heirs of Wesley and Calvin exuded). Bergendoff wanted to stand in the middle. In *Christ as Authority* Bergendoff spoke of "Christian growth in the obscure men and women who in the Scriptures have found a power transforming their own existence, and more than they know changing the history of the world."[117]

In the chapter on "The Holiness of the Church" in his 1953 book on *The One Holy Catholic Apostolic Church,* the author shifts back and forth, at moments treating "holy" as "good" and at others as "sacred." The latter term might or might not imply moral improvement. In a related matter, Bergendoff did not speak favorably of the "puritan" impulse in church history which desires to have a holy congregation made up of pure people whose lives manifest the works of the Holy Spirit.[118] The question of whether a community or congregation of truly pure Christians is ever a possibility is a central one in the history of the church. It is one to which Bergendoff returned often, particularly with reference to the Pietistic strains in Swedish-American Lutheranism that marked its early history and eventually caused the break-away by some Pietists from the Augustana Synod. We will deal with that later. Here suffice it to say that Bergendoff believed that through the Christian message, "there is yet hope of a new social order, or at least of better men and women." "There is no salvation of society as such, but there is a salvation of society by the redemption of individuals who contribute to the making of society."[119]

§

In the next chapter we turn to the matter of Bergendoff's understanding of Christian social ethics and his hopes and fears for society. But for now it is clear that he thought that you could see the change in people who had encountered Christ. They were "better men and women." Always in the church there were those whose "hearts and wills and minds" had been transformed in the image of Christ himself.[120] "Through faith in a forgiving God, the transforming of the whole personality of man proceeds." That change is centered in the human will, Bergendoff wrote.[121] Therefore, in spite of his realism, he was hopeful, if not altogether confident, about human possibility. The Augustana theologian was, in any case, not satisfied with viewing Christian sanctification as non-empirical or only "forensic," as the Dane Regin Prenter argued that Luther had. Bergendoff preferred the way the Swede Axel Gyllenkrok read Luther on this count. Any way of looking at human life that did not recognize that God's will for each person was that she or he experience the transforming encounter with Christ was finally erroneous. Further, that encounter would manifest itself in the way a person lived.

CHAPTER 4

CHRISTIAN SOCIETY AND THE ALTERNATIVES

Conrad Bergendoff did not attend many of the arguments to which he was invited. But an article by H. W. Weigert in the January 21, 1942, *Christian Century* succeeded in drawing the college president out. Weigert, just then a college professor in Ohio, was a refugee from Prussia, where he had served in the Ministry of Justice. His article, "Freedom and the Germans," argued that Luther had played a major role in shaping the German national character, not always positively. The article contended that the Reformer had betrayed the German peasants during the social upheavals of the mid-1520s. The peasants had foolishly believed he would support them against their oppressive feudal lords. But, Weigert wrote, Luther had instead sided with the princes of the land who brutally put down the Peasants' Revolt. As Weigert read him, Luther believed the Christian must accept the world as it was and submit to the authorities in power, and in this passive attitude to government an "almost direct connection" ran from Martin Luther through Otto von Bismarck to Adolf Hitler.[1]

Bergendoff wasted no time in firing off a letter to the editor of the *Christian Century*. The college president was ordinarily unwilling to name and directly have at a person whose ideas he opposed. But this time he set mildness aside. "Should one laugh or weep at the perennial habit of dragging Martin Luther into court every time Germany goes to war [!] and explaining the psychology of a whole nation by pointing an accusing finger at the reformer!" Who was the "nodding *Christian Century* editor" who let Weigert get away with the claim that Luther had no ethical principles? Could the *Century* not spare its readers "a type of propaganda which . . . gives offense to members of a denomination who know a Luther seemingly lost to some contemporary Germans and Americans?"[2] He followed the letter with an article in the *Augustana Quarterly* in October spelling out his strong disagreement more fully.[3]

In both the letter to the *Century* and the article in the *Quarterly*, the Augustana Synod Lutheran recognized that Luther was "lost" to many modern theologians standing in other church traditions. So much the worse for them. Of course, Bergendoff knew Luther well, having spent months during his year in Europe in the late twenties reading Luther at several universities. Thirty years later, Bergendoff, by now a recognized Luther scholar, edited one of the fifty-five volume series of an English edition of the Reformer's works. His contribution was a volume on "Church and Ministry." So it is not surprising that in 1942 he leapt to defend Luther. However, it was not simply that the founder of Bergendoff's branch of Christendom had been attacked. Weigert's sin in this regard was egregious enough. But his criticism of Luther also touched a nerve, in that it went directly to Bergendoff's fundamental understanding of the relation of the individual Christian to society.

Like Luther, Bergendoff wrestled with the question of what influence the Christian faith might appropriately be expected to have on the political, economic, and cultural affairs of humanity. If, as critics claimed, Lutheranism had bred into the German people a passive willingness to accept civil authority of whatever character, then more was at stake than simply its founder's good name. Bergendoff was not willing to blame Luther for Hitler. Beyond that he was not ready to accept that Lutheranism had no ethic other than one for individuals. But to stake out his ground, Bergendoff had to find his way between equally unacceptable alternatives. He held neither to a theory that separated government from the church (as in modern American political thought) nor to a theology that saw government as derivative from the church (as in medieval Catholicism).

Individuals and Society

We have just seen that Bergendoff believed that a direct one-to-one relationship between the individual and Christ was the essence of genuine Christian experience. The views which he held on a variety of specific social issues, as well as his basic understanding regarding the possibility of creating (or recovering) a "Christian" social order, depended on that belief in the regeneration of the individual. After the encounter with Christ, according to Bergendoff, the person went into the world to work toward remaking it. "Through faith in a forgiving God, the transforming of the whole personality of man proceeds."⁴ He said this to the Synod clergy in 1933; eighteen years later Bergendoff told the alumni of Augustana College that "a mind that is in Christ sees the whole world differently."⁵ The person has "a new life issuing out of the new relationship between the believer and his God." These transformed persons had an influence on corporate human life.

In regard to this idea that the individual Christian must engage in society in order to bring it closer to the divine will, it is important to note, as we often have and will again in this study, that Bergendoff was very much the heir of the Swedish awakening and of Pietism and their emphasis upon individual Christian decision and experience. It had not ever been thus in Sweden. We have already noted that the Lund church historian and contemporary of Bergendoff, Hilding Pleijel, held that the sense of the individual Christian experience being prior to the corporate and collective social expression of religion was a crucial development in Swedish religious life. Before the rise of Pietism, Pleijel said, the land was characterized by a sense of Christendom that had been "stamped by the Old Testament." As Pleijel understood it, in the homogeneous orthodox Swedish Church, "consideration for corporate well-being weighed more heavily than concern for the individual's improvement, and the church's strict discipline was aimed more at warning against law breaking and enforcing an outer morality than it was at bringing about an inner transformation and moral renewal."⁶ Interestingly, the Church of Sweden seems to have sensed this shift toward individualism and in response to it issued a new catechism in 1878 which stressed that "one is not 'a Christian by his own hand,' but only in solidarity with the congregation."⁷ But for the Pietists and for Bergendoff (in this regard perhaps their unwitting heir), social improvement as well as personal rebirth would come only through individual Christians who had undergone the personal moral transformation brought about by meeting Christ.

Bergendoff, of course, believed that he stood with Luther in this matter of individual regeneration. The Reformer did not think that a better society could be created simply by persons of good will who came together in a common cause, even if under the Church and the priesthood. Bergendoff contrasted with Luther's views those of his contemporary, Desiderius Erasmus (1466–1536). As Bergendoff read him, the Dutch humanist considered Christian life, individual and corporate, to be a matter of deciding to live up to the highest values of one's culture. Christianity was for him a *Bildungsreligion*. Bergendoff translated that as "refinement religion." The Swedish American insisted that this sort of "universal humanism" was entirely the opposite of the complete reorientation of the whole being through a relationship with Christ, "beside which nothing else can be of equal importance." Christianity was not just one of several positive elements in the life of a good person.⁸ Nor was it one among many forces for betterment that went into building a just social order. In Bergendoff's mind, "There is not much of virtue and integrity in the world that has not in some way stood in connection with [Christ's] kingdom."⁹ To try to find such virtue and integrity apart from the context of personal regeneration and to treat the Christian life simply as a commendable effort at moral living guided by law, in the way that Erasmus and other humanist Christians did, was in the end to rely not upon divine grace but "on laws to produce righteousness."¹⁰

Short of full personal regeneration it took binding law to produce righteousness—both individually and collectively. Therefore in Bergendoff's mind some sort of middle ground, such as the hope that well-meaning humanists like Erasmus (or modern Social Gospelers) harbored about building a Christian society, was untenable. Whether you were a sincere humanist like the Dutch Erasmus or simply a self-seeking scoundrel like the Italian Machiavelli, you would have to be controlled by law. As Bergendoff used the term "law" it meant, of course, the Ten Commandments as well as the restraints (against, for example, murder or theft) and the demands (for, say, military service or payment of taxes) which an ordered society placed upon its members and which were in the end derivative from the Commandments of God. This secular law set the minimal level below which one could not fall without incurring punishment appropriate to whatever the offense, of omission or of commission.

Human nature was either turned over to the power of Christ, or it was caught in sin and had to be controlled by law. In that sense the humanists were fooling themselves; they too were trapped in sin. As Bergendoff understood it, the Christian was obligated to the society's law too, but he or she fulfilled the will or law of God out of gratitude. The rest of the human race obeyed law by compulsion. That law had its origin in the will of God, even if those who were compelled to obey did not recognize that fact. Here Bergendoff was very much in the Lutheran tradition, which understood both law and grace to be derived from God. As he saw it, the non-Christian obeyed this God-given law because he had to, the Christian because he wanted to. And the Christian went beyond or above that minimal law. In no case did law itself provide the motive force to regenerate a person.

Enforced legal obedience to God's commandments would never create a society that was Christian. In his early career Pastor Bergendoff was somewhat more sanguine about the possibility of seeing such a "Christian society" come into being than he was in 1947, when he wrote *Christ as Authority*. He believed that the social order would improve only to the degree that it became Christianized. And that would be when the church fulfilled its true mission in society, which was "not to make laws, but to make disciples of Christ." The idea that Christians had a social mission separated Luther, as Bergendoff understood him, from the Pietists, who retreated from society. Luther had elaborated a "Christian philosophy of life in this world."[11] Another Protestant solution, put forward by the Reformed or Calvinists, was to attempt to regulate society by laws based on Christian principles. At a time when the country was in the midst of Prohibition, Bergendoff wrote that the zeal of "our Reformed brethren" to pass laws to make America righteous had little hope of success.[12] In Bergendoff's mind, Catholics represented still another choice: the Church must simply control society. The key to a Lutheran theory of society was not to retreat, nor to legislate, nor to control. Lutherans "are preaching regeneration." Regenerated men and women will "create new forms and influence the world around them."[13] That is why Bergendoff's youthful association with the temperance movement, mentioned earlier, did not lead him to become a fervent Prohibitionist; Prohibition represented an effort to reform society by controlling it through law.

In *Christ as Authority* (1947), Bergendoff explained that the reborn person, having turned his or her life over to Christ, saw all things in a new perspective. Now God was understood to be "the God of the whole." "There are no autonomous provinces in human experience except as they have rebelled against His rule. All history, not only Biblical history, is the object of His government." No science that ignores God, no state that is wholly separate from the church, is possible for the Christian. But, the gospel of forgiveness holds that "there is yet hope of a new social order, or at least of better men and women."[14]

That last statement raised, at least by implication, a critical question touching the relationship between the rebirth of the individual Christian and the regeneration of society. Is there hope for "a new social order," or must we simply settle for "better men and women"? Is it only individuals who are regenerated, or should we seek a regenerated society as well? In his 1947 book on Christ's authority, Bergendoff maintained that "There is no salvation of society as such, but there is a salvation of society by the redemption of individuals who contribute to the making of society."[15] And: "Out of these forgiven hearts come new minds and bodies and spirits which build a society reflecting the will of Him who has become Lord in their lives."[16] This appears to mean, as Bergendoff had earlier suggested, that an entire society might at least ideally contain so many Christian women and men that it would be rebuilt, released from the control of selfish persons seeking only their own interests.[17] Here a fine line was walked: society as a whole could not be "Christianized;" rather individual Christians could influence it to the point that its character changed for the better.

Therefore all of human life and culture was at stake. Bergendoff had been thinking about this, to use one of his phrases, "for some while," particularly after becoming the president of a church-owned liberal arts college. In 1939 he wrote: "[W]e claim that only in Christian culture is the complete answer to what men [sic] shall think of himself and his fellows and what he shall do in his life in this world." For Bergendoff that involved "the relating of the whole body of human knowledge to the Word, the revealed truth and grace of God, who is Jesus Christ." That statement was in an essay on "The Elements in Christian Culture" in the *Lutheran Companion*. Here he defined "Christian culture" as the "relating of all the conditions of social intercourse to Him," and elegantly posed this question: "Is there, I ask in all earnestness, any other theory of universal society than that which has come to the western world through Jesus Christ and His Church?"[18]

A year later in the *Augustana Quarterly*, the scholarly journal for Synod clergy, Bergendoff wrote in a similar vein: "That culture is Christian wherein all the knowledge and experience of life are related to the revelation of God in Jesus Christ." The Christian and the non-believer, he continued, would never agree on a definition of culture: "Christian culture is itself the Christian interpretation of the world and its life, and to the Christian any culture which leaves out Christ is a very defective culture[.]" In fact, it is "no culture at all." Bergendoff conceded that rarely if ever was such a Christian culture "found in isolation or pure form, but was to be thought of as operating in the midst of other forces and materials." It was, he held, a leaven which worked on a society from within.[19] But to have abandoned the ideal would have been for Bergendoff to surrender the whole case: without the Christian paradigm society would be entirely lost. In his view, therefore, Christianity offered the hope for a better order of things. It sent into the world forgiven individuals who would bring that order to some degree of reality—out of gratitude, not because they were forced to be good.

The Possibility of Christian Society

One reviewer of *Christ as Authority* wondered in 1948 whether Bergendoff had "no further word as to the nature of the order which forgiveness produces."[20] It was a fair question. In the first decades of his professional life Bergendoff spoke of "Christian culture" or a "Christianized" social order.[21] He believed that in such a society, people would recognize that all truth and goodness came from God and that the divine will would be the constituting power in it, not necessarily through the church, but through individual Christians. From his pastor's study at Salem Church he had even suggested in 1924 that the Lutheran Churches might have a role in "the making of America into a

Christian nation."[22] The *Lutheran Companion* and the *Augustana Quarterly* essays just quoted suggest that right up until the entry of the US into World War II, his hope for a Christian society or culture persisted. When the War followed on the heels of the Great Depression, that earlier optimism seemed to have dissipated.

Other American theologians, facing the realities about humanity's inclinations and the prospects that began to reveal themselves in the thirties, especially with the outbreak of war in 1939, had also been thinking about the relationship between the Christian Gospel and human society and culture. One of the most important and widely read statements about these issues was *Christ and Culture*, published in 1951 by H. Richard Niebuhr (1894-1962), after decades of lecturing and reflecting on the problem. Niebuhr, the younger brother of Reinhold Niebuhr, grew up in a German Reformed church and studied at that denomination's college in Elmhurst, Illinois, then at Yale University, eventually joining its faculty. The adequacy and usefulness of Niebuhr's Christ-culture grid are still being discussed by ethicists, historians, and theologians, but it is instructive to see how this prominent contemporary of Bergendoff might have categorized or typed him.

The younger Niebuhr delineated five ways in which Christians had related their faith to human culture. The first three were: Christ against culture (many early Christians, Tolstoy, Mennonites), the Christ of culture (Abelard, Locke, Jefferson), and Christ above culture (Thomas Aquinas). The first type, Christ against culture, withdrew in the name of Christ from the sinful world; the second, the Christ of culture, identified Christ with the highest values in culture; and the third, Christ above culture, saw Christ as ruling human culture. Niebuhr's fourth and fifth types are the ones that are especially germane for our purposes. They are: Christ and culture in paradox (Luther) and Christ transforming culture (Calvin). According to H. Richard Niebuhr, Luther did not think that the creation of a Christian social order or culture was possible, believing that persons, even after they became Christians, were both justified through Christ and sinful by nature (*simul justus et peccator*). Though the person was counted as justified in God's sight because of Christ's work, human sinfulness was in fact still operative. That sinfulness would always be reflected in human culture and society, even in the Christians who sought to regenerate it. From this perspective, human culture and the claims of Christ would inevitably be in conflict, since each made demands upon the Christian which were sometimes in opposition. That was Christ and culture in paradox. Calvin, in contrast, thought that it would be possible to transform human culture under the influence of the Gospel, and worked at doing so in the sixteenth century Swiss city which he so greatly influenced, Geneva. This view was Christ transforming culture.[23] Niebuhr's contemporary, Conrad Bergendoff, who usually spoke of the Calvinists as the "Reformed," believed that in America they were trying to transform human society through making laws. That was an effort to transform culture by "Christian" legislation.

But in the sense of these types or categories, the pre-World War II Bergendoff did to some degree incline toward Niebuhr's fifth type, Christ the Transformer of Culture, at least as concerned the possibility of there being Christian society. Of course, he never would have admitted to it and would have pointed out that while the Calvinists or Reformed wanted to legislate, he believed society could be made more Christian not though laws, but by the efforts of regenerated people. Precisely at this point he would have differed with Niebuhr's interpretation of Luther. Bergendoff did not agree that for Luther persons who knew Christ were still so compromised by inherent sin that they could not act out of genuinely Christian motives. Rather, as Bergendoff read the German Reformer, Christ and culture did not have to remain in paradoxical relationship. As we have seen, the Swedish American would have been able to cite contemporary Swedish scholarship in support of this position. And more importantly, at least to the Bergendoff of the pre-World War II years, Sweden itself offered an instance of a culture in which social values and corporate as well as individual life had been shaped by Christians. This understanding of Sweden will be discussed more fully in Chapter 8.

A colleague at the seminary in Rock Island was, in Bergendoff's mind anyway, closer to a Calvinist or Reformed view than he was. The president of the institution recalled years later that this colleague, A. D. Mattson, had studied with Niebuhr and had in him "a good bit" of the Yale professor's outlook concerning the Christian's role in society.[24] That probably meant that Bergendoff thought Mattson was inclined to see some possibility of transforming society through collective Christian action, perhaps even legislation. At times Mattson's stance on social issues (such as his support of labor unions) was not well received in all Augustana corners, and Synod leaders (including Bergendoff) had to respond to complaints.[25] But before the war Bergendoff may have in fact shared some of that optimism about changing culture, even if not by passing laws. In any event, if Bergendoff were to be classed with the Calvinists rather than with Luther on the question of whether Christians could reshape society, he was himself certain that the Calvinists and he (and probably Mattson as well) differed on whether you could reform it with legislation.

Leading up to the war, Bergendoff continued to be somewhat sanguine about the reborn individual Christian and his possible role in society. But by war's end he had clearly taken a position about human culture that H. R. Niebuhr would have typed as closer to Luther, becoming ever more reserved about the possibility of Christianity transforming culture or society so that it might be spoken of as "Christian." Already in a 1941 article in the *Augustana Quarterly,* he wrote that "the paradox of Lutheran ethics" was that they did not hold that a Christian social order was possible, but that they called upon the regenerated individual to live up to the ideal and to seek its realization in the life of the community as much as possible. Here he already admitted that Lutherans were somewhat reluctant to say precisely what the kingdom of God in present human life would look like. Their views were "not always clear or consistent," he said.

As Bergendoff saw it, beyond recognizing that the kingdom exists to the extent that Christ comes to the individual believer who "goes on to redeem gradually, slowly, imperceptibly his area of community life," Lutheran ethics did not offer any plan or program for society. Again, this was an important way in which Lutheranism contrasted with prevailing "American ideals" about defining and building the kingdom of God. Those ideals were, Bergendoff thought, rooted in European Calvinism, carried by the Puritans to the New Word, and proclaimed in the earlier twentieth century by the proponents of the Social Gospel.[26] One reviewer of Bergendoff's 1954 *One Holy Catholic Apostolic Church,* himself standing in the more mainstream American Protestant tradition, found that the book "suggests, without affirming, the traditional Lutheran detachment of the 'Word and sacraments' from all problems of man in his social relationships."[27] That reviewer caught a sense of the tension in which Bergendoff stood; the Augustana man wanted to affirm the transcendent Gospel which stood above all human thought and effort and at the same time to argue for its relevance to the human social condition.

After having flirted early in his ministry with the idea that Lutherans might have a share in "Christianizing"America by seeking"to make disciples of Christ," Bergendoff grew less hopful as World War II unfolded. Reporting on mid-war Augustana College campus life in the *Lutheran Companion,* he reminded readers that Christianity did not teach the idea of steady human progress, but rather "a dire struggle between opposing forces, seeking the heart of man." Christians must try to shape modern life without supposing that they could control it.[28] Reacting to the theme "Man's Disorder and God's Design" from the 1948 Amsterdam Assembly of the World Council of Churches, Bergendoff wrote in the *Lutheran Quarterly,* a new pan-Lutheran scholarly publication of which he was editor, that "one does not need to believe in man's disorder. The difficulty is to believe in anything else."[29] By mid-century Bergendoff had shifted from thinking about ways in which individuals might work to build a culture that was controlled by Christian values to reminding others and himself that they lived in world where light and darkness were in perpetual conflict.

The views in *Christ as Authority* about Christianity and the social order reflect the post-war Bergendoff. "There is no salvation of society as such." That was his understanding in 1947. "A distinction must be made between the kingdom of God as a goal and as a process. In this world the nature of the kingdom is the latter." Here Bergendoff uses the "kingdom of God" in the sense of the rule of God in a society ordered by Christianity, "a completed order of righteousness supplanting the present order of things."[30]   His view was that such an order must always remain as a goal. Christians must struggle toward it, but it would never be realized "in this world." In the world of 1947 as Bergendoff found it, and in any human situation of which he could conceive, men and women who knew the forgiveness of their sins would exercise their influence in every area of life. "And it should be added that the manifestation of the kingdom is primarily in Christ's forgiveness of today's sins in today's human life. He can forgive the businessman, the prostitute, the educator, the statesman, the farmer, the student, the artist, the journalist, if each of these confesses and is repentant over the sins he or she commits in his or her calling." People who understand themselves this way will bring "an order of things different from that where unforgiven sins prevail and thrive."[31]

But for Bergendoff post-war, that sort of "order of things" is only in the process of coming into being. It is never fully achieved "in today's human life," whenever "today" might be. In the wake of the frightful events of the earlier twentieth century and of the post-war revelation of the depths to which humans could descend, Bergendoff, like many of his theological contemporaries, grew less optimistic about human possibility, individual and collective. It was not merely the Social Gospel that went by the boards; Bergendoff's more modest Lutheran brand of optimism also was trimmed to the prevailing winds. Now there was no thought of a Christian social order being created. One is reminded of the aphorism of the conservative English Catholic historian and journalist Paul Johnson: "Christianity is an exercise in the impossible; but it is nevertheless valuable in stretching man's potentialities."[32]

If a truly Christian society governed by divine grace infused into humanity was unattainable, the matter of the role of law again came up. Sixteen years after the end of World War II, Bergendoff addressed it once more, this time in an article in the 1961 *Lutheran Quarterly* on "Christian Love and Public Policy in Luther." What was the relationship between these forgiven Christians and the laws under which their society lived? Contra the radical left-wing Anabaptists of the Reformation era, Bergendoff was definite that Christians were not exempt from obeying those laws. They remained the same for both believers and non-Christians. Church members "have no higher wisdom than that of reason; they cannot invoke any special revelation[.]"[33]

At this point Bergendoff suggests that there is a sort of double or two-sided relationship between Christian individuals and the ordering of civil society. First and simply, redeemed Christians must obey the law, though their motive for doing so is different from the rest of humanity. Even after the Nazi era and the Second World War, Bergendoff did not address head-on the question of which circumstances might lead a Christian to refuse to obey the laws of his society. That was the darker side of the matter. It involved questions about the moments when human laws oppose divine law and when revolution against the existing order might be justified. Bergendoff was by personal temper and intellectual conviction not inclined toward revolution. Luther's answer, of course, was that the Christian should make his witness by acting against unjust civil authority, and then accept and suffer the penalty. This world was in any event passing away, and a better one awaited the believer: "Let goods and kindred go, this mortal life also. The body they may kill. God's truth abideth still. His kingdom is forever," says Luther's hymn, *A Mighty Fortress.*

Bergendoff also saw a problem when human law was treated as absolute, as though by fulfilling it, one would achieve some kind of righteous status denied to lesser mortals. He touched on it in the 1961 piece on "Christian Love and Public Policy in Luther" in the *Lutheran Quarterly.* For Luther, as Bergendoff understood him, "There is no unchanging set of laws which Christians obey in every age and thereby become righteous." Rather, "The spiritual life is creative and finds the way in which to express itself." Thus, "If we hear the Word, it will direct us to the will of God, and we must trust it to open our eyes to the means by which that will can be done by us."[34]

So the law of human society, insofar as it is consistent with the law of God, sets a line below which no person must fall. But as a positive factor in guiding the Christian in developing a stance and plan of action toward the difficult issues of his own time, law could not be taken as an instrument for a "Christian" policy or program. It does seem, therefore, that for Bergendoff "law" was understood in a minimalist way. It was the set of regulations and policies that kept order in society. When the society was challenged by questions beyond the minimal level which guaranteed order, a Christian was left to use reason and a "creative spiritual life" to determine his or her thinking and action. Bergendoff wrote this essay on "Christian Love and Public Policy" in the early sixties, and there is a slight hint of the "situational" or "contextual" ethics that were then being advanced by a number of Christian theologians.

By this time, Bergendoff was not as certain as he had been earlier that the law of God could be fully known and embodied in a human society. Never, early or late in his career, did Conrad Bergendoff offer a particular prescription for the ills of the contemporary world or a specific program to create a new

Christian order. It was up to individual Christians to engage in their societies, listen to the voice of the Spirit, and work out their own answers to social problems. In this sense it might be better to speak of God's will, rather than of divine law, at least beyond the Commandments. The Christian must seek to know what God willed in a particular situation, rather than simply turning to a code that expressed the divine will or law for society in any and all circumstances.

Reviewing in 1951 a new work on Christian pacifism, Bergendoff was critical of the assumption that pacifism was the truly Christian position regarding war. Christians, he wrote, should respect each other's efforts to work out the implications of their faith, recognizing that they might reach different conclusions.[35] A decade later he addressed the question of a Christian position regarding nuclear war, again writing that Christians would have differing views on the matter. Varying circumstances would lead to different positions, he said, though that did not mean that the will of God was unclear or ambiguous.[36] He made no effort to reconcile the unambiguous and clear will of God with his statement that Christian positions would vary. That was, of course, the nub of the problem. Presumably the divine will was clear, but individual perceptions of it were not. What Bergendoff steadily did maintain was that forgiven men and women would act out of love, and that through their work things would get better. The Lutheran Church could tell the ordinary folk of the land, "in Christ you will find new motives and a new devotion which will bring blessings to your people in their internal and their foreign relations."[37] The sense that society could be made better, not by church control nor by programs of Christian legislation, but simply by the work of Christian people within it was what one Synod historian called "the traditional Lutheran position that society cannot be saved until individuals become Christian."[38] This was a perspective that Bergendoff and his Synod shared with his mentor, the Swedish Archbishop Nathan Söderblom.[39] This understanding of the nature of the Christian person and her or his capacity to act from a Christian stance does seem to have been characteristic particularly of Scandinavian Lutherans.

While at times waiting for that Christian leavening of society to come to pass and at other moments doubting that it would, Bergendoff had plenty to say about the ills of the modern world. A contemporary historian, Jennifer Hecht, writes of the twentieth century intellectual climate, "There is a deep skepticism about our ability to know the world, to say anything true, to find a universal value."[40] Conrad Bergendoff would have agreed, though it troubled him greatly. A Swedish historian of ideas, Svante Nordin, remarks of Bergendoff's mentor, Archbishop Nathan Söderblom, that "it was obvious that he was the right man to reconcile the Swedish Church with modern culture."[41] His Swedish-

American student and friend, President Conrad Bergendoff, seems never to have conceived that such a reconciliation was possible. For that matter, perhaps it was not even desirable.

Contemporary Society

So level was our subject's temper and so becalmed his personality that many who listened to his sermons or read his essays were at first surprised at the severity of his judgments on the culture in which together he and they lived. Even now to read the strong condemnation of the condition and direction of his society, one cannot help being caught short by the intensity and extent of his criticism.   One who examines Bergendoff's roots in the Augustana Lutheran Church will perhaps be a little less surprised. Many of the historians of that Church have noted that within a decade of landing in America, the Swedish-born first generation of its leaders recognized that both the other American Christian churches and the wider secular society threatened their sense of themselves as Lutheran Christians. The "morality of don'ts" that they developed was more than a simple prohibition of specific acts and behavior. Behind the condemnation of dance and drink, of pool halls and movie houses, even of football, was the feeling that the culture in which their Synod had been planted undermined its basic assumptions about life and morality. An historian of American immigration, Jon Gjerde of UC Berkeley, calls this attitude "particularism," which he defines as the "pronouncement by church authorities that they represented the one true faith." One of the important implications of this particularism, Gjerde says, is that these church groups "remained skeptical of an emerging liberal world [and] illustrated growing discomfort with American life[.]" The Swedish Lutherans in America, he concedes, were somewhat more open to "Americanization" than were their German cousins.[42]   But if the Germans were even more resistant, the Swedes were not by a long shot ready to be absorbed, either.

Bergendoff's one-time seminary professor, Adolf Hult, had kept that tradition of resistance to Americanization alive in the early twentieth century with a long string of warnings to the Synod's congregants about the dangers of modernity.[43] And while Bergendoff differed with Hult on many issues, he echoed him in this respect anyway. Further, as we already noted, the Synod fathers, Professor Hult, and Bergendoff himself breathed the spirit that called for the Christian to stand apart from the ways of the world. The Lund church historian Hilding Pleijel wrote of Swedish religious life that "with the demand [in Pietism] for personal religious experience there readily followed an attitude that tended to reject everyone who did not share this experience. In these circles a certain reaction arose against various expressions of cultural life, especially luxury and self-indulgence."[44] Some Swedish conservatives, who were certainly not Pietists themselves, found the source of many of Sweden's ills in the growing influence of American culture. Early in the new century one wrote: "Modern Americanism should be combated, whether it reveals itself in the form of King Dollar or in the stifling Jesus cult of the chapels."[45]

That sense that American culture presented a double threat—its crass materialism and its sectarian religiosity were equal dangers—was present across the Atlantic among Augustana's leaders at the beginning of the century as well, and Bergendoff would carry it from his youth forward into the decades before and after World War II. Sometimes, as we shall see presently, he would hold Sweden up as a positive example of a land whose people and culture were shaped by the Christian faith. But the fact was that many of the Augustana Church's early leaders left a Sweden that they believed had been besotted with drink, a land whose clergy were often more worldly than their pious peasant congregations. Those plain rural folk had been touched by the temperance and awakening movements. Along with their Bibles and prayer books, the immigrant pastors carried with them to the new land a negative attitude to the State Church, both to the general concept of a government controlled and supported church and to its particular expression in Sweden. They were equally disapproving of the character of Swedish society at large. When they got to America that sense of separation from the world around them was heightened by their use of a "foreign" tongue in the English speaking landscape of the Midwest. So they were to a degree alienated—both from the land from which they sailed and from the one in which they landed. They knew that Christians were pilgrims and strangers on earth.

Recall that young Conrad himself had a sense of distance from the dominant Yankee culture of the New England town in which he grew up. When one adds to the scales the fact that the mature Bergendoff was a person of studied solemnity and a degree of pessimism, one can perhaps understand better the jeremiads that came from pulpits when he preached and from journals when he wrote. He understood himself as a missionary: "The Augustana Synod's task in America is a missionary work," he wrote in his early days as a minister. "Her pastors see themselves first and foremost as the church's missionaries[.]"[46] Such missionary-pastors were somber men, and they issued dire warnings. He was one of them. By the first decades of the new century there was the sense among Swedes on both sides of the North Atlantic that certain aspects of American culture, its sectarian religiosity as well as its rampant materialism, must be combated.

We have seen that the younger Bergendoff held out some possibility that the missionary Christian faith he shared with others in his Synod might be spread widely enough through society that one might speak of its "Christianization" or of "Christian culture." In the forties that hope began to fade. He continued to think that individual believers who had through divine grace had their selfishness transformed into Christian goodness would bring change to society. But he doubted that that would mean the transformation of the existing order. With the years his ideas about the Christianizing of society evolved. There was not that same degree of development in Bergendoff's assessment of contemporary culture, whether it was during the inter-war decades or in the years after his own retirement. He steadily condemned it. As a newly ordained minister he lamented that he and his congregation must live on the "arid plains of modernity." "We are fed from springs as the daily newspaper, the vapid magazine, the evanescent movies, the worldly office, and the careless home."[47] As he left Salem Church for the seminary deanship a decade later, he spoke of "the futility, the bitter disappointment, the sense of being lost, in the kind of world man has made for himself."[48]

In 1935, at the Luther League Convention celebrating the Augustana Synod's Seventy-Fifth Jubilee, President Bergendoff warned the teen-agers that "The battle ground is clearing these days, and we begin to see that the Church must do nothing less than set itself against the whole current modern materialism and sensualism, and create within the ranks of the Church a new life of individual and community so that the world may see something of that kingdom which is within the soul but not of the world."[49] There is here some whiff of Pietistic withdrawal from the world to establish a Christian order within one's own small community, though that was an idea that Bergendoff at other times criticized. His underlying sense that the church and the modern world were at war was deepened when Bergendoff attended the ecumenical Oxford Conference on Life and Work in 1937. Reporting in the *Lutheran Companion*, he wrote that "Much of modern life aims at the destruction of the Church," and that the sense in Oxford had been "of a beleaguered city" in the face of German fascism and Russian communism.[50] It is understandable that in the threatening climate of the late thirties, even the mainline churches were inclined to build battlements.

In the post-war years Bergendoff was particularly troubled by the character of current literature. At his college's 1952 commencement he scored, among others, Ernest Hemingway, John Dos Passos, F. Scott Fitzgerald, and Norman Mailer, all the authors of best-sellers, all proclaiming that life had no purpose, ideals were illusions, and common values had been abandoned.[51] Five years later in a series of lectures in Oregon he went after literary awards, even those bestowed by Swedes: "[T]he kind of literature that takes the Pulitzer prise [sic], or even the Nobel prise is the kind of literature that describes how depraved man can be, how mean he can be, how low he can live."[52] After his 1962 retirement Bergendoff did not let up. He advised the 1964 graduates of the Mt. Airy seminary where he had once studied that they should escape to "the fresh, clean air" in which Thomas a Kempis, Luther, or Kierkegaard wrote, the better to get away from "the sooty atmosphere and gaseous fumes of our tawdry literature and earth-crawling dramas."[53]

What most disturbed Bergendoff in contemporary novels and plays was the view of humanity that they assumed in the name of "realism." He warned Augustana students assembled in chapel that in the twentieth century human beings were understood to be simply creatures of nature, driven by a few instincts—for food, sex, power.[54] Dr. Bergendoff was never over-weight, and he did not dwell on the instinct to over-eat, but in 1960 he picked out the other two: "Our worship of sex approaches the licentiousness of the Ephesians or the people of Pompey. Our dependence on force is not much different than that of the worshipers of Mars or Thor. Our selfishness is more refined, but quite akin to that of the cultured Greeks and Romans of Paul's own time." Confronting a "generation that in its way is interested only in the luxurious materialism of the 20th century," the church would have "to begin all over again to convert the world."[55] When Salem Lutheran Church celebrated its centennial in 1968, Bergendoff, now retired, was still pessimistic about contemporary life. In the congregation's commemorative booklet he wrote: "These are days of great peril, terrible tragedy, and gross unbelief." The cure, as ever, was to seek the working of the Spirit of God "according to His own plans."[56]

The contrast between the debased reality of humankind and the facile sense of its progress that floated in the twentieth century air particularly bothered Bergendoff. The theory of evolution combined with the "anti-Christian character of modern culture" to produce that "naïve optimism." He wrote that in a 1933 issue of the *Augustana Quarterly,* comparing "The Secular Idea of Progress and the Christian Doctrine of Sanctification." Already in consternation at age thirty-eight, Bergendoff admitted, "Sometimes I am driven to feel that against this insidious poison of our times it is well-nigh useless to preach growth in grace, and a building-up of the body of Christ." To some degree that gloom contrasts with his later recollection of his Salem pastorate being the happiest time of his life, the parish ministry the way of life to which he always longed to return. Newly named the seminary dean, he now specified that the problem was that "the popular consciousness has been captured by the idea of human progress." But that was "an illusion which rests on no Christian foundations." Bergendoff cited J. B. Bury's *The Idea of Progress* (1920), which traced the concept back to the early modern period. Bury held it to be rooted in the work of a number of early moderns such as Francis Bacon (1561-1626) and René Descartes (1596-1650), who had detached their view of humanity's needs and prospects from Christian moorings. They ended with nothing more, as Bergendoff saw it, than a mere "faith in the destiny of mankind" that was ultimately humanity's faith in itself.[57]

A corollary of the concept of progress, Bergendoff believed, was the individualism that dominated much modern thinking, especially American, about human nature. Newly arrived home after a 1951 trip to Britain and Sweden, the college president told Augustana College chapel listeners that the United States was trapped in a sort of adolescence.[58] That quality in American life could be traced to what he once called a "religionless" educational system.[59] It was a system that had replaced God with mankind, believing that "no truth exists apart from man's experience, and out of experience man must make as inclusive aims as he can, but ... no revelation from any other source can be determinative for him."[60] Once the divine factor and the possibility of meaning from that source were removed from the calculation, only the human could stand in their place. And the rule of the people, no matter what dignity might be claimed for them, could be as tyrannical as any other sort of government.[61]

"The Dignity of Man" was therefore a "half truth." Christianity neither taught nor guaranteed individual worth. "Man has no other worth than that which God puts upon him. In himself he has no values except what he can make other men agree to. Individuals and nations proclaim their own worth[.]" But, "The glory and the worth of the individual are bound inextricably with the Christian religion. The guarantee of the worth of man is faith in God."[62] That was Bergendoff's view in *Christ as Authority* as well as in the scattered smaller pieces just quoted. "The New Testament knows nothing of the freedom of the individual in the sense of modern liberalism, a self autonomous and free and neutral with regard to powers above him, whom he may choose or not choose to serve."[63] Early in the book Bergendoff cited John Dewey (1859-1952) as an instance of that kind of modernity, one that accepts no authority or standard beyond "a formula of the way to respond when specified conditions present themselves."[64] Bergendoff lamented the fact that many Lutherans had themselves "drunk deep at the well of Dewey's pragmatism."[65] The injunction to choose whatever alternative seemed most functional in a given situation was a corollary of the hyper-individualism that left it to each person to devise her or his own set of values.

An Inverted Trinity

But John Dewey was the least of it. Bergendoff's most pointed criticism was reserved for a modern trinity that had replaced the ancient Christian doctrines of creation, redemption, and sanctification. That unholy threesome was, of course, Charles Darwin (1809-1882), Karl Marx (1818-1883), and Sigmund Freud (1856-1939), or rather the three schemes of thought which they and their minions had propounded. The worship of these idols, Bergendoff thought, had become a parody of devotion to the true God. That only proved that you could not avoid the Christian questions about creation, redemption, and sanctification, even when you did not accept the Christian answers. Whatever useful insights the evolutionist, the socialist, and the psychiatrist had gained into the human condition had been absolutized into substitutes for Christian concepts about how the world had come into being, how society must function, and how the inner life of humanity might best be understood.[66]

In his later years at Augustana, President Bergendoff was particularly troubled that popular Darwinism seemed to have become a sort of ersatz creed: "The Christian considers the picture of man which emerges from an irreligious use of the theory of evolution as superstition and idolatry." The operative word here was "irreligious." The idea that God's creative power could have been stretched out over millions of years was in itself not inconsistent with Christianity, said Bergendoff, never the biblical literalist.[67] What was objectionable was simply to think that "there is some kind of blind force that has made everything that is in the world."[68] "We can accept the data Darwin gathered, but the wild notions that followed in his train regarding the relationship of man and other forms of creation need a critical analysis for which we are still waiting. . . . To go on and deny to man any unique character because of real or fancied relationships to the bodily structures of other creatures betrays a lack of reason rather than any fair use of it[.]"[69] The error was not that popular Darwinism denied the innate and natural dignity of men and women. So did Christianity, as Bergendoff understood it. It was rather that Darwinism did not hold that humanity was created by God and could achieve dignity only in following his law and gospel. It offered "a picture of a human animal who is the product of forces of nature and nothing more." "I am disputing the right . . . to interpret [Darwin's] data so as to make of man a whim of unreasoning powers of nature, with no unique beginning or end, and intervening life as a tragic and meaningless fantasy."[70]

The last century had seen the interplay of Darwinian evolutionary thought with the revolutionary theories of Marxism, wrote Bergendoff in 1958. Of course, by temper and conviction he was likely to be more favorably disposed to evolution than to revolution, though not evolution blindly producing biological species, humanity included. Revolution of any sort was problematic for him; Marx's brand was downright heretical. With Karl Marx and his disciples, as with the Darwinians, the idea of change had been "converted into idolatry." In the case of the Marxists, the heavenly kingdom had been turned into "an earthly economic order" which was controlled by a dialectic process that, like the biological evolution postulated by Darwin, was mindless and undirected. "We are dealing with a way of thought and life based entirely on naked power."[71] Such thinking was, said Bergendoff, "every bit as metaphysical as any theories of theology."[72] Bergendoff rejected both Darwin and Marx because neither believed that God was in control of the process of life, biological or social. He held that whether you were positing a self-caused universe in which cold power governed or believing in one created by a benevolent deity that stood outside of it, you were making a philosophical statement. Marx was as metaphysical as St. Paul. *Which* metaphysic was the issue.

The American mood of the fifties was fearful of the Soviets and suspicious of communists in the US, so Bergendoff's rejection of Marx did resonate. In a 1954 commencement speech at Augustana he allowed as how there was some legitimacy in Marx's criticism of social injustices, but the "radical revolutionary" had gone too far and thrown out "the whole Western tradition." Not only had the greedy traders been expelled, the entire temple had been pulled down. As Bergendoff saw it, that temple had been erected on Old and New Testament foundations.[73] So again the question of the possibility of a Christian society was implicit, though the speaker did not deal with it directly during that Monday morning graduation.

In his last President's Report, sent out to alumni and friends of Augustana College in 1962, Bergendoff proclaimed that church colleges were "a fortress against Communism." For whatever reason, when he was seeking to advance the interests of his school against the godless contemporary forces that threatened its ideals and values, Bergendoff was inclined to hold American culture up as an alternative to Marxism and to argue that it was built on biblical foundations. But as we have seen, at other moments he did not speak of America that favorably; rather he hoped that it *would* turn to the teachings of Scripture, though it certainly had not. The ground he most often took in these matters was to treat Christian faith as "the very condition of the preservation of civilization."[74] This suggested that, as in the Old Testament, the whole city might be spared because of the presence of a faithful remnant, in this case persons with Christian ideas and values. That remnant was all that stood between whatever stability and order the present set-up did have and the chaos and collapse that threatened it. In Bergendoff's final decade as a college president, Marxism was the threat *du jour.*

It should be noted that Conrad Bergendoff was not opposed to socialism per se. He distinguished it from communism. He sometimes got letters at Augustana from persons who were troubled by Sweden's socialism. To one such letter he replied in 1952, "It does not seem to me . . . that socialism is anti-Christian[.]" There were "competent scholars who argue that socialism has prevented some countries from becoming communistic." There was no necessary tie between capitalism and Christianity. "[T]he Church in all ages has inclined to take sides with those who have rather than those who have not," but Christ himself took the part of the have-nots, he continued.[75] For a Midwestern college president even to intimate in the 1950s that socialism's egalitarian impulses were consonant with Christianity took some courage. For the moment at least, it represented something of a move away from the conservative Republican inclinations common to both Bergendoff and the Synod. The American interest in the Swedish social experimentation of the 1930s had included President Roosevelt as well as many American intellectuals and academics,[76] but it was after the war that Bergendoff found himself defending Swedish socialism and distinguishing it from Russian communism. However, his opposition to Marxism was not simply a play for wider support of his school as "a fortress against Communism." What he found abhorrent in Marx was his atheism. If a country such as Sweden could seek a more equitable distribution of life's goods through socialism and still maintain its State Church, Bergendoff did not think that the arrangement was self-contradictory. His speeches and articles in the fifties did often express his horror of Marxism and did appeal to Americans to oppose it, but that was in the main because it offered a chance to preach the Christian alternative, not because Bergendoff was cravenly playing to the McCarthy crowd in the gallery, hoping to gain support for Augustana. By the fifties, he had forgiven FDR's flirtation in the thirties with socialism, perhaps particularly because the Democrat had found a model in Sweden.

The Freudians constituted the third party of the inverted trinity. In 1942 Bergendoff served notice that he was repelled by those who spent their time "stirring around with Freud and Jung in the dismal abysses of human swamps."[77] In a 1958 essay he quoted Lionel Trilling (1905-1975), the literary critic and Columbia University professor, who argued that Sigmund Freud had at least made some order out of the chaos bequeathed to contemporary life by centuries of confused literature and philosophy. The Viennese psychiatrist had located the real problems within the human mind rather than in external reality, Trilling wrote (at least as Bergendoff read him). For Freud "sex" was one aspect of that human chaos, part of the race's drive to self-perpetuation. When he quoted Trilling, Bergendoff did not mean to imply entire approval of the Columbia professor's understanding of Freud, but he did take away from his reading of Trilling the sense that modern writers had become preoccupied with the sexual and physical.

Literature, art, and drama had turned to probing the mysterious depths of the sexual, an effort Bergendoff frequently denounced. Of course in his mind, Christianity knew the darkness of the human soul long before the Freudians found out about it. Like the Darwinism to which it was tied, Freudianism made humanity the product of "hidden, biological forces." And having perceived that these forces existed, the Freudians had no power save that of psychological analysis with which to fight them. For Bergendoff, of course, only Christ could cleanse the heart of "human passion" and set it in the right relationship to other people and to God.[78] As we saw in the last chapter, he was never inclined to believe that a psychologist or psychiatrist could counsel another person toward the right way if the counselor was not on that path himself. The content of counseling was critical; it must be Christian to do any good. Here as elsewhere, there was a certain either/or quality to Bergendoff's thought. He knew his Kierkegaard.

The History of the Problem

Of course a modern culture saturated with the paganism of Darwin, Marx, and Freud did not come into existence accidentally. A long history lay behind the modern mindset, and as an historian Dr. Bergendoff had a particular view of that history. Nathan Söderblom, also an historian of religion, understood the contemporary dichotomy between Christianity and secularism to have ancient sources. The Greek spirit, the archbishop-scholar said, embraced the noble ideal of self-definition and self-control. The spirit of the Gospel, in contrast, was symbolized by a thorn-crowned brow, "a humiliation of the self in order that the will of God, that which we should be, may come in its place." The Augustana president recognized the contrast of the Greek with the Christian that was made by the Archbishop.[79] In a 1952 baccalaureate sermon at Augustana, Bergendoff said that on the secular or Greek side two ancient images seemed to have survived to dominate modern life. Prometheus stood for human self-assertion in a world where there was really no divine power in control (Zeus being meaningless). Sisyphus represented the belief that life was a senseless striving.[80]

Bergendoff spoke approvingly of the Swedish ethicist and bishop Einar Billing (1871-1939) who also contrasted alternative understandings of the relationship between religion and morality in the ancient world. The Greeks sought to develop a self-standing philosophical structure to undergird morality, while the Old Testament prophets preached that such order comes from God and is already given. It does not need to be created by man. For Bergendoff humanity's hope lay in submitting to that order, which rested on ancient and immovable religious foundations.[81] Both Söderblom and Billing stressed the differences in antiquity between Greek and Jewish thought. That was a dichotomy that many American theologians in the decades after World War II, including Bergendoff, also recognized. They used it to heighten the uniqueness of the biblical message. A syncretistic effort to blend Christianity into a larger worldview with antecedents in many historical locations, Judeo-Christian and pagan, had characterized much American thought in the earlier twentieth century. Lutherans like Bergendoff had kept their distance from that. He often maintained that the only place throughout western history where morality and religion were firmly bound together was in the biblical tradition.

Judaism's sense of uniqueness was carried into Christianity, Bergendoff believed. Once that unique message had been received in the world, the job of the church was to protect, preserve, and transmit it. The early Christians were determined to maintain the purity of doctrine which they had inherited from the apostles, he said in his lectures on *The One Holy Catholic Apostolic Church,* given at the Disciples Divinity House, Chicago, in 1953. That pure teaching was the "tradition," whose guardians were the bishops of the growing church. There were some who claimed that they had received new revelations that ought to be added to the ones given to the apostles. But only the preservation of the true apostolic tradition prevented such a "disintegration of Christianity." "The ministry of the Church had the function of repudiating false doctrine, not the making of doctrine."[82]

Bergendoff regretted that the church nonetheless began to incorporate the ideas of Plato and Neo-Platonism into its thought and, to that extent, departed from apostolic purity.[83] But that was not the only compromise made in the first millennium of Christian history. From the time of the emperor Constantine in the fourth century, the church fell under the shadow of the sword, Bergendoff said in *Christ as Authority*. And after the disintegration of the Roman Empire, the papacy inherited that sword. "Western civilization bowed to the Papacy and its courts. The church was the authority over the spirit of man, and most men were satisfied to have it so."[84] For Bergendoff the first millennium began with a determination by the successors of the apostles to preserve the purity of the church. But compromises with Greek philosophy and with Roman government meant that the distinctive qualities of the Old and New Testament tradition were vitiated, as Christianity accommodated to the culture in which it found itself.

It was the Reformation and particularly the work of Luther that called the church back to the purity that fifteen centuries had seen diluted. As Bergendoff read Luther, the Holy Spirit bringing the Scriptures to life was the standard by which the church must be judged. John Calvin (1509-1564), the reformer of Geneva, went beyond Luther in emphasizing the inflexibility of the apostolic teaching and was more inclined than the German to entrust the preservation of doctrinal purity to the organizational or governmental structures of the church. Further, said Bergendoff, for Calvin only that which was explicitly authorized by the Bible was permissible. For Luther, in contrast, anything that was not prohibited was allowed. That distinction was the seed of the Protestant disunity that had persisted to Bergendoff's own time.[85] Apparently Bergendoff understood Lutheranism to be willing to accept the guidance of God's Spirit in settling matters that in the Calvinist churches were handled by church government appealing to a carefully defined apostolic tradition. We have already seen that Bergendoff saw Calvinism as preaching the law, while Lutheranism held to grace alone. At this point Bergendoff put less emphasis on the importance of confessional documents in the history of Lutheranism, speaking rather of the guidance of the Spirit. At other moments, as we shall see, he maintained that such doctrinal statements were the important condition of dialog among various Christian groups. Without them how did you know what the other fellow stood for?[86]

The Augustana theologian recognized that in spite of its intentions, the Reformation did not in the end restore the unity of apostolic Christianity. Nor did the early Protestants reach agreement on just which of the several versions of pure teaching ought now to govern the church. Though the Reformers did emphasize the distinctiveness of the gospel from the theological and political accretions of the centuries, they did not finally serve the visible unity of Christendom. Of course, Bergendoff would never have conceded to Roman Catholics such as Christopher Dawson (1889-1970) or Jacques Maritain (1882-1973) that medieval society and thought had achieved a unity or synthesis of the gospel with human culture that could still be paradigmatic for the twentieth century. Those two one-time Protestants had converted, finding in Thomas Aquinas (1225-1274) and the Church of Rome the antidote to modern secularism.

Bergendoff had difficulty with Roman Catholicism, especially because of its stand-offishness from the modern ecumenical movement. But together with Dawson, Maritain, and others, he did regret both the on-going divisions that plagued Christianity and the secularism that threatened all Christian variations. Once in a while (like Luther) he even let himself wonder whether "breaking away from Rome in order to set up spiritual autonomy has been altogether a profitable change."[87] It was the case therefore that historian Bergendoff regarded with ambiguity the medieval effort to build "Christendom." He would never cede ground to certain Roman Catholic scholars, who argued that the Middle Ages had been a truly Christian era and who lamented its passing. But neither was he positive toward the secular modernity that had replaced it. Just where in history there had been a time on which a Lutheran such as he could hang his hope remained a troublesome question for Bergendoff. We will see that he gave Sweden a try on that matter.

Though he had deep reservations about the values of the American government and of wider society, President Bergendoff worked well in the context of both. Here, Suzanne Johnson, Miss Illinois, 1959, gives Bergendoff the keys to a new Buick, a gift of the college Board, alumni, and friends,. The Illinois Secretary of State, Charles Carpentier has just presented him with a license plate numbered 1860, recognizing the college's centennial.

In *The Church of the Lutheran Reformation*, written in 1967, Bergendoff addressed the course of western history since the Reformation. That work was written in the first years of his retirement, at the invitation of Concordia Publishing House, an agency of the Missouri Synod. It was considerably longer than the smaller books which he had published in the late forties and mid-fifties. This volume was text-book size and might well have been used in seminary courses in Lutheran history. The dust jacket proclaimed that "This book tells the whole story of Lutheranism for the first time in English." (It went on to say that Bergendoff had treated Lutherans "as a family." Whether the Missouri Synod in America continued to see itself as a member of a single Lutheran family would be problematic in the later decades of the century.) In an autobiographical comment, "The Meandering of an Historian," made fifteen years after the 1967 book, Bergendoff confessed that if he had known what he was taking on when he agreed to do the project for Concordia, he might have declined.[88] The book is a fact-crammed survey that covers the iterations of Lutheranism from central Germany to the isles of the sea. A friend, Theodore G. Tappert of the Mt. Airy Seminary, applauded the book in a review in *Church History*, but did allow that "the reader may, if he is not very attentive, lose sight of the Lutheran identity which remains as the continuing thread of the story."[89]

Some of the ideas which control the 1967 historical treatment of Lutheranism were anticipated in comments Bergendoff made in a 1940 issue of the *Augustana Quarterly*, where he specified the Renaissance as that point at which "knowledge of man" replaced "knowledge of God" as humanity's central concern, to the degree that God "was ruled out altogether." The Renaissance saw knowledge as a means to power and unlimited freedom and sought both the substance of power and the reputation for having gained it: "It is no mere coincidence that the men of the Renaissance were the most greedy of fame, honor, and reputation of any persons known to history." Most recently, human culture descended from the Renaissance had, as Bergendoff understood it, "become the antithesis of Christian culture," its purpose "to disassociate all human thinking and living from the revelation of God in Jesus Christ."[90] Bergendoff's read of the secularism of the Renaissance is echoed in the work of many scholars, such as the 2011 National Book Award winner, Stephen Greenblatt.[91]

In *The Church of the Lutheran Reformation* Bergendoff offered a clear sense of which specific points in modern western history he identified as the ones where western political and social theory confirmed Renaissance secularism after the break-up of the medieval synthesis of church and society. The Dutch jurist Hugo Grotius (1583-1645), Bergendoff wrote, believed that there was a natural law from God that established norms of justice. It could be studied scientifically. But "the development of the idea was to be in the direction of a justice determined by human reason apart from God." Grotius' contemporary, the Frenchman René Descartes (who died of pneumonia in February, 1650, in dark and icy Stockholm, where he been enticed to adorn the court of the enlightened twenty-three year old queen, Christina, daughter of Gustavus Adolphus), was not content with the assurances of either science or religion and "made doubt a principle—everything was to be doubted until the mind had satisfied itself of its truth." Thus did the "mind determine the nature of God." Descartes'"new science of self-consciousness made man the center of all truth." These and other theorists of the European Enlightenment replaced the Holy Spirit with reason. So theology, yielding the supernatural, fell "victim to the dominance of the natural." It was for Bergendoff an age of "superficiality, materialism, and skepticism."[92] Except for Jews and Christians, the ancients had seen history as an endless cycle, lacking any purpose outside of itself, Bergendoff thought. That Christian sense of purpose remained in the historical understanding of western culture through the Reformation until early modern times. Voltaire, for example, took God out of his understanding, but left the sense of purpose in. However, "Human history cannot be understood from within itself," Bergendoff contended in a book review written in 1949.[93]

In a 1939 sermon Bergendoff had noted that while the American and French Revolutions had served the cause of human freedom, neither had brought peace on earth or good will among men. What they had achieved was freedom *from* something.[94] In *The Church of the Lutheran Reformation,* written three decades later, he offered his assessment of that "Quest for Freedom." The cultural transformation of the late eighteenth century had been as revolutionary as the political. In England deism gave way to skepticism and eventually to "an explanation of man and society in purely secular and materialistic terms." In France there arose after Rousseau a "realism that denied the reality of Christian theology and ethics." In contrast, "Germany showed its deep-seated religious heritage by an idealistic view of life that preserved religious terms." But Bergendoff warned the reader not to be deceived. In Georg Wilhelm Friedrich Hegel (1770-1831), "Sin, evil, forgiveness, revelation—all of religious experience—were swallowed up in the world mind which was God." German poetry found that "The glory of life was in the variety and richness of human personality." There was no room for revealed religious truth; what individuals thought and felt was what mattered. Here was the subjectivism that bothered Bergendoff wherever he found it: in mysticism, in psychological counseling, and in some contemporary spirituality.

According to Bergendoff, Immanuel Kant (1724-1804), "the keenest intellect of his age," analyzed the human mind and found it so constructed that it could judge only on the basis of what the senses reported to it. Reason could only work with what we perceive. But not satisfied with leaving it there, Kant taught that there is "a realm of practical life" in which we recognize our sense of duty, the existence of God, and the soul's immortality. So, perhaps without fully intending it, German thought and literature "helped relegate religion to the mystical intuition of the individual." [95] What Bergendoff thought about mystical intuition uncontrolled by the Spirit bringing the Bible to life, we already know. In sum, Bergendoff believed that in modern times, "Western civilization was following an illusion of progress while itself progressing on a path that brought it to the brink of disaster—the World War of 1914-1918."[96] If that was the course that politics and letters had taken, was there something better to be expected from modern science?

Science and Nationalism

The two constituting forces of the modern world, Bergendoff maintained, were science and nationalism, so they must be reckoned with in any discussion of the contemporary predicament.[97] Bergendoff presided over a college that was earning recognition for the achievements of its faculty and graduates in the natural sciences. As he assumed its leadership in the throes of the Depression,

Augustana's academic accreditation had just been saved by the construction of a new science building. He knew these fields of study were as essential to a small school's standing as they were to the reputations of the great universities of the country. For Bergendoff it was "one of the glories of the Augustana Synod that our ranks have never been torn by discussion on the relation of science and religion."[98] But of course Darwin, Marx, and Freud had all claimed to be scientists, and we have seen what Bergendoff's judgment on them was. He believed that scientists' attempts to answer questions about ultimate reality and values, until the Renaissance the province of religion, were a prime cause of the "secularism that is but a renewed form of paganism."[99] Bergendoff understood that, as one historian of science puts it, "the modern age of science began as a free-for-all." That writer, Edward Dolnick, maintains that the governing idea of seventeenth century British science was to find out for yourself, rather than to believe what someone else told you: "The Royal Society's motto was 'Nullius in Verba,' Latin for, roughly, 'Don't take anyone's word for it,' and early investigators embraced that freedom with something akin to giddiness."[100] Conrad Bergendoff, like most college presidents, was leery of free-for-alls, intellectual as well as social.

Even so, Bergendoff would have been able to accept untrammeled investigation *so long as* it was confined to looking into the natural world. For him it was crucial that science operate in the particular area of its competence. If it did so without attempting to offer answers to religious questions, its work could be carried on by Christians as well as by others. Because the Christian "believes this world is the work of an intelligent being he is convinced that there may be meaning in his applying his intelligence to studying it."[101] There was nothing in modern science which was in itself inconsistent with the Christian faith, he insisted.[102] "Instead of fitting Christianity into a scientific procrustean bed, the Christian will hold to his faith while he keeps in suspense the answers to questions which deal with the nature of matter and the age or destiny of the planets."[103] These views are not particularly startling now, but in the Augustana Synod that had emerged from its own late nineteenth century isolation and that lived in a twentieth century religious atmosphere where many conservative Christians were leery of science (witness the Scopes Trial), Bergendoff's ideas were rather progressive. Of course, three centuries earlier, at free wheeling meetings of the Royal Society in London, they might have seemed rather cautious. Context is crucial.

In a 1949 article in the *Christian Century*, Bergendoff sought to refute the Director of the World Health Organization, who had just publically declared that the "dreadfully damaging concept of original sin" must be overcome if humanity was to advance. Such a claim, Bergendoff said, was not science at all. Rather it was itself a faith, one that sought to set up its own norms rather than to be judged by a divine standard. The health official was passing off secular relativism as science.[104] In *Christ as Authority* Bergendoff noted with approval that contemporary science was abandoning absolutism, ceasing to see the world as a machine. It now understood the interrelatedness of matter and mind, just as centuries earlier Christianity had perceived the unity of body and soul. Scientists had jettisoned the centuries-old vocabulary of Newtonian physics and abandoned the concept that the universe is a "closed system of laws which God Himself can not break[.]" The "rigor of law" had been replaced by measurements now made in terms of statistical probability.[105] Religion could rise from the procrustean bed into which modern naturalism had thrown it.

Some of Bergendoff's contemporaries saw in the new physics a positive ally of Christianity, one offering clues to the way in which divine creativity worked. The Protestant Charles Hartshorne (1897-2000 [!]) and the Catholic Pierre Teilhard de Chardin (1881-1955) are examples of theologians who saw God working through the process of evolution, not simply in biological life, but in the whole cosmos. But Bergendoff was no "process theologian." He did not hope for some new synthesis of modern science and a demythologized Christianity. He found the efforts of Henry N. Wieman (1885-1975) to give a scientific explanation of God ("whom" he defined as the interaction between people and groups that promotes the greatest good) to be entirely unscientific. Why was it that the contemporary theologians attempting to construct "scientifically verifiable theologies" all seemed to arrive at differing results? Was it not the case, Bergendoff asked, that *real* science produced the same outcomes when its procedures were followed?[106] But "scientific" theologians all came out with different answers. The use Bergendoff made of the new science was more limited and perhaps negative. Quantum physics, he thought, was clearing the decks of the older scientific worldview that he feared had choked off the possibility of a God who was actively present in the natural and historical worlds.[107] He seemed to welcome this escape of science from unbreakable "law." It was analogous to the release of Synod theology from "dogma," the sort of scholastic Lutheranism that his predecessor as Professor of Theology at the Rock Island seminary had taught.

What about the fields that attempted to apply scientific rigor and research to humanity, socially and individually? While the natural science faculty at Augustana College had improved in credentials and numbers during the twenty-seven years Bergendoff was the president, the size of the staff in the social sciences had also increased. Here the issue was one of quality. Bergendoff was concerned that it was difficult to find Christians trained in the study of social issues who properly understood their mission and its relationship to Christian teaching. And he seems also to have questioned whether these fields were actually "sciences." For many years the academic cluster at the college in which the departments of economics, history, political science, psychology, and sociology were grouped was called the "Division of Social *Studies*." That may have reflected Bergendoff's own reservations about their being scientific. He was concerned that people teaching these subjects must help students find the way to build society into a "healthy community."[108] Their proper mission was to build "healthy" social structures and institutions by beginning with individuals, not with organizations. In a Christian understanding of society, "A never-ending chain of individual rebirths is implied, else the apostolic succession is broken, and only the empty forms remain."[109]

In Bergendoff's later years in higher education, the "behavioral sciences" at many universities were attempting to establish their position as legitimate empirical disciplines, and as they did so it was important for them to be "value neutral," operating as "pure" science rather than acting as social advocates. For Bergendoff the difficulty was that many trained psychologists or sociologists saw as clearly as anyone the complex problems of modern life, but refused to understand that the cause lay in human selfishness and pride. What President Bergendoff wanted was for these academics to use their training to work for humanity's well-being rather than simply to analyze its failings.[110] He believed that all fields, whether considering nature or humanity, could be taught so as to "reveal the handiwork of God."[111] Here, as in his judgment on the modern natural sciences, Bergendoff insisted that the value assumptions on which the study of human life and society was conducted should be Christian. Otherwise, scholarship simply contributed to the modern secularism that was really paganism *redivivus*.

The factor that along with science had shaped the modern mind, Bergendoff maintained, was nationalism, the rise of the state and the claims it placed upon individuals. In modern times these claims had become absolute. The state demands "supreme sovereignty," he said as World War II was about to break out in Europe.[112] After the war, the situation as he understood it had not changed: "[T]he modern state has usurped the throne of God" and recognizes "no ultimate norms except its own requirements."[113] As in many other matters, Bergendoff was inclined to dissect the problem by beginning with Luther and his understanding of Scripture.

The Reformer's contribution to political history, Bergendoff wrote in 1942, was "his denial of the right of any ecclesiastical organization, in the name of religion, to presume to control the whole life of man." Luther saw the rights of the state as coming directly from God, not through the church. The fact that government derives its legitimacy directly from God and that many of the people on whom its power is exercised are not Christian means that it cannot be based on Christian principles. Rather, it rests on "reason, wisdom, and the sanction of the use of force," Bergendoff held. After the Reformation, nation states began to deny any authority higher than themselves. For its part the Lutheran Church grew pessimistic about "its ability to convert the state." Other denominations were "more sure of their hold upon the total life of society." Lutherans saw their duty "to change the minds, heart, and wills of sinners. If that be done, the church has made an immense contribution to social life." In this sense Bergendoff and Lutheranism as he understood it saw believers as "salt in a world of corruption."[114]

The claims of the modern state to absolute authority must be checked by two factors, Bergendoff seemed to think. One was the fact that all political authority came from God; the second was that God also established the church. But how would the church check the claim of government to ultimate control over human life? There was a degree of passiveness in Lutheran political thought, Bergendoff admitted. We saw at the beginning of this chapter that he had resisted vehemently the idea afoot in English-speaking Protestantism in the late thirties and early forties that a line of descent ran from Luther to Hitler. But Bergendoff did recognize "a certain inwardness" in his own theological tradition.[115] That he said in 1942.

By the late forties, when the full extent of the Nazi horror had emerged into daylight, Bergendoff conceded that "the Achilles heel" of Luther's political ideas was the question of what to do when the government did not recognize its responsibility to God and set itself above divine law. Bergendoff confessed that there was a tendency in Lutheranism to take Paul's "pastoral counsel" that "the powers that be are ordained of God" and make out of it a theory of government. He defended Luther by pointing out that the German did not foresee modern circumstances. (That was in a way to step back from what George Stephenson had called the sense in the Synod that the fathers of Lutheranism had stated Christian truth once for all.) There were, of course, those who claimed that the monk-turned-reformer had prepared the ground for modern dictatorial statecraft. But Bergendoff assigned the blame elsewhere.

In a 1949 article on "The Lutheran Christian in Church and State," he spoke of Machiavelli. It appears that Bergendoff could still hardly contemplate writing about Luther and Hitler in the same essay; he blamed the Renaissance Italians instead. The wiles of the Renaissance popes, not any ideas coming across the Alps from Lutheran Wittenberg, were Machiavelli's model, and it was he who provided the rationale for modern tyrants. But in the end, it was not Italian but German history that Bergendoff had to address in the 1949 essay. His prescription for

Germany, as for the rest of the world, remained, "Society is the sphere where the Christian life is to be lived, and the state the arena in which they are to run who have received the torch of truth from the altar of the Church."[116]

Interestingly, as a corollary of this, Bergendoff believed that the concept of the separation of church and state had been over-emphasized in America. "For there never was a Lutheran country where state and church were altogether divorced, and in our Lutheran thinking we have unconsciously, or subconsciously, continued to think in patterns of the one influencing the other." That did not mean, as in Roman Catholicism, that the church as an institution should control government. But Bergendoff held that individual Christians should work within the state. And all Christians would, in a democracy at least, act as responsible voters. If, as in the United States, the people are sovereign, "how can we speak of a state which is entirely separated from the Church?" The same persons were members of both.[117] Bergendoff's concern was, of course, that as the forces of secularism slowly over-powered those of Christianity, as he often said they were doing in contemporary America, the society would become as pagan as ancient Rome had been.

§

So as he contemplated the rise of the modern state and of the science and technology that he thought developed at the same time as nationalism, Bergendoff came full circle, ending as he began: with the individual believer. His views about that person's meeting with Christ were the foundation on which he predicated Christian involvement in politics, as in all of society. Bergendoff limited himself to arguing that things would improve when enough Christians listening to the Spirit had leavened the whole lump. If that did not happen, the land would decline into pagan secularism. The hope was that people who were changed by meeting Christ would act as a positive force in human culture, science, and technology. So far as optimism was concerned, that was the best Dr. Bergendoff seemed to be able to muster. His work in his own branch of the Church Universal was his contribution to the effort to turn society around. We consider it next.

Until his untimely death in 1900, Olof Olsson, the third president of Augustana, lived in this Rock Island home south of Old Main. It stood along the river bluff on top of which Bergendoff's own presidential home would be perched. Olsson's irenic spirit and his love of the arts, especially music, were balanced by a deep commitment to the Lutheran confessions. That balance was reflected in Bergendoff's outlook and disposition, though the fifth president of Augustana College and Seminary more often spoke of and appealed to Olsson's predecessors, L. P. Esbjörn and T. N. Hasselquist, than he did to Olsson. Still, Bergendoff, when enmeshed in one Synod controversy or another, as Olsson too had been, might have recalled the latter's lament (quoted in Bergendoff's college history): "Why should a sensitive person as I have to bear the burdens of this office?"

CHAPTER 5

UNDERSTANDING THE SYNOD

The Augustana Evangelical Lutheran Church came of age during Conrad Bergendoff's lifetime. Indeed, it matured to the point where it realized that the role it had played during the period of the great emigration from Sweden to the New World was, like the emigration itself, over. By mid-twentieth century, Augustana's destiny appeared to be as part of a unified national Lutheran Church. One wonders whether Bergendoff and his contemporaries in, say, 1935 really imagined that within three decades their Synod would merge into a much larger body that would *not* include the other sizeable group of Scandinavian Americans, Lutherans with a Norwegian background. Instead it would involve the more liberal wing of American Lutheranism, the United Lutheran Church, a group with roots in colonial times. That was a segment of American Lutheranism about which the founding fathers of the Synod would probably have had, at the least, reservations. The future twists of American Lutheran history would hold some surprises for the generation of historians who were reexamining the history of the Augustana Synod.

Bergendoff was one of those historians. None of them might have guessed a few decades earlier what future merger negotiations in American Lutheranism would hold for Augustana. But if the future was unclear and debatable, so was the past. All interested parties did not share a common understanding of Synod history. At points the tensions existing among interpreters was palpable. For example, the Augustana College historian O. F. Ander maintained that as he was preparing his 1931 manuscript on T. N. Hasselquist, Bergendoff, along wih others, had urged him, pre-publication, to temper his pointed criticism of certain Hasselquist contemporaries, especially L. P. Esbjörn.[1] Or recall that when George M. Stephenson's *The Religious Aspects of Swedish Immigration* appeared in 1932, it was reported that one Rock Island seminary professor grew "violently nauseated after scanning a few chapters," and the Augustana Book Concern refused to carry the book in stock.[2] As a second generation, usually American-born, "intelligentsia" emerged in the Synod's ranks, both the past and the future of that body were being debated.

In the broader sense, this generation of scholars stood together in asserting the importance to general American history of the ethnic tradition whose development and values they traced. One of the pioneers of immigration historical writing, Marcus Lee Hansen (1892-1938) of the University of Illinois (where O. F. Ander knew him), wrote of such people, "Born of blood that is not British, trained in family institutions that are Continental, speaking very often a foreign language as well as English, these Americans have declared their independence of the traditional history that traces all the roots of national culture back to British soil." Though he spoke of immigrants in general, Hansen might well have been thinking of Swedish Americans such as Ander, Arden, Bergendoff, or Stephenson when he continued, "They say the sons of the earlier colonists have written their history, now we will write ours."[3] In their commitment to the importance of the history of their own ethnic tradition, these men were of one mind, but when it came to interpreting its meaning, there turned out to be disparate perspectives. Often enough, these differences about the Synod's past became differences in projecting its future as well.

The Swedes who founded the Synod themselves had a keen sense of the historical importance of their work. They saved documents, collected them, and published the materials.[4] However, the earlier generation did not include persons trained in historiography, as Bergendoff, Ander, Stephenson, Arden, and others were. This group of young Augustana historians, all with advanced graduate training, emerged in the years when American universities were themselves establishing and regularizing PhD work in history. None of them, including G. Everett Arden, Professor of Church History at the seminary, approached the cast of characters and parade of events more positively than did Bergendoff. But he did not always prevail when he took a position about the Synod's future course. Now we examine both these matters: Bergendoff's read of Augustana Synod history and his personal role in shaping its future.

The Pietistic Roots

Given his deep loyalty to his own tradition, it is no wonder that a great part of Conrad Bergendoff's religious experience and theological reflection was formed by the Augustana Synod's roots in mid-nineteenth century Swedish religion—at the time of the great emigration. We have already determined in Chapter 3 that much of the emphasis in his *Christ as Authority* is stamped by Pietistic qualities. The central role that a one-to-one meeting with Christ played in Bergendoff's understanding of Christian life is resonant of this Pietism that shaped the lives and ideas of the Synod's founders. But Bergendoff was not uncritical of Pietism, in both its historical and current forms. As against the cold formalism of much of the life of the nineteenth century Church of Sweden, the emphasis of the Pietists on a personal relationship with Christ and their concern for each individual's own devotional life was one which Bergendoff appreciated deeply. He found these qualities in the lives of Esbjörn, Hasselquist, Carlsson, and the other fathers of the Augustana Church. He once noted that many of his Swedish relatives were Pietists, some of them, in fact, Mission Friends.[5] But he was not patient regarding the theological divergence of the Pietists from orthodox confessional Lutheranism. In characteristic fashion, he tended to find a middle way, hanging onto his belief in the need for each person to know Christ for her- or himself, while noting the problems that emerged when Swedish Pietists such as Carl Olof Rosenius or Paul Peter Waldenström, the successive editors of the newspaper *Pietisten*, used their journal to advance views which Bergendoff found un-Lutheran.

Williston Walker (1860-1922), Titus Street Professor of Ecclesiastical History in Yale University, offered the early twentieth century seminary students who used his textbook a functioning definition of Pietism. His *History of the Christian Church* also gave a glimpse of how a "mainline" Protestant scholar viewed Lutheranism generally. Walker's book was published when Bergendoff was beginning his formal theological studies. Its definition of Pietism is useful, though Bergendoff did not wholly approve of the book.[6] Walker said that the Lutheran Orthodoxy that followed the Reformation had replaced "that vital relationship between the believer and God which Luther had taught [with] very largely a faith which consisted in the acceptance of a dogmatic whole." The layman was left passive, to accept the doctrines proclaimed from the pulpit, take Communion, and baptize his children. Against this "dead orthodoxy," Walker wrote, Pietism asserted the primacy of the feelings in Christian experience, the active role of the laity in Christian life, and an ascetic attitude toward the world.[7] In the case of the Swedish Pietism with which Bergendoff and fellow historians of the Synod were particularly concerned, other characteristics might be added to Walker's description: steady devotional reading of the Bible, an emphasis on conversion or being "born again," and a concern for social mission, especially through the temperance movement.

One way Bergendoff found to accommodate the fact that such Pietism was both vital to his forebears, yet (as he understood it) theologically off-center, was to argue that in fact the solid elements in Pietism could be traced back to Luther himself.[8] In his *Church of the Lutheran Reformation,* Bergendoff reviewed the process by which orthodox German Lutheranism morphed into the early Pietism that eventually found its way to Sweden. The lapse into "dead orthodoxy" produced, as Walker's textbook suggested, a reaction. In the late seventeenth and early eighteenth centuries German Lutherans such as Philipp Jakob Spener (1635-1705) and August Hermann Franke (1663-1727) experienced conversions which included emotional rather than simply intellectual elements and began to emphasize the experience of sanctification as the fulfillment of the classical Lutheran justification by faith. They started charitable works such as orphanages and schools. Through the efforts of Nicholas Ludwig, Count von Zinzendorf (1700-1760), missions to America were initiated. Zinzendorf himself visited both Sweden and America and in both places, Bergendoff pointed out, ran afoul of orthodoxy—in the persons of officials of the State Church in Sweden and of the Lutheran patriarch Henry Melchior Muhlenberg (1711-1787) in America. In each case the objections to Zinzendorf's Pietism were its over-emphasis on emotion and its tendency toward separatism from mainline Lutheranism. Those were, of course, Bergendoff's own criticisms. Swedish students went to Germany to study with the Pietists, returned home to produce a Swedish Pietist hymnal, *Songs of Moses and the Lamb,* and to advocate what one of their ecclesiastical critics called "the damnable new birth which they have now begun to proclaim."[9] Of course, the author of *Church of the Lutheran Reformation* would not have cussed, but he did object to viewing the new birth simply in the way the Pietists did. It smacked of American revivalism.

Bergendoff's 1967 survey of historical Lutheranism included an extended appraisal of Pietism, and though the author put these judgments in the minds and mouths of "the orthodox," most of the criticism seemed to be his own as well. The "extreme emphasis on conversion and individual experience meant a decline in the significance of the church and the clergy." Christianity itself became "a private matter," and the church was seen as "a collection of like-minded people with common religious experiences." The Pietistic turning away from the world looked to many critics like "a renunciation of learning and culture, a disregard of beauty in nature and art, and a denial of responsibility for a social and economic order." Further, "Introspection, the keeping of diaries, and interest in emotional satisfaction all looked like the emergence of a new type of personality."[10] We have already seen (in Chapters 3 and 4) that this emphasis upon personal religion represented a shift in Swedish religious life. Presumably Bergendoff found that inwardness overly self-centered and did not indulge himself in it..

The college president thought a healthy interest in the natural and cultural worlds and a concern for the social and economic well-being of society would rescue one from that self-centeredness. In short, it could be avoided by a Christian liberal arts education. Just retired, Bergendoff did allow that much of the Pietists' criticism of the dead formalism of church and clergy was fair, that better pastoral care and education were needed, and that "Christian activity as a sign of Christian life" was appropriately emphasized. How could one quarrel with an emphasis upon personal reading of the Bible and a life "of prayer, discipline and spiritual growth"? But finally, "The spiritual experience was often expressed in terms of intimacy with the loving Savior whose blessings were personally appropriated. Luther's teaching of a 'hidden God' *(Deus absconditus)* who cannot be known but whose awful power inspires humility and ineffable reverence was lost in pietistic self-analysis." Withdrawal from the world and the emphasis on one's own salvation suggested that "Pietism had no understanding of the salvation of the world for which Christ died." The Pietists pulled back into their own gatherings "as they waited for the end of the world."[11]

In Sweden the reaction against Pietism led to the passage of the Conventicle Act of 1726, which forbade religious gatherings outside of the control of the State Church. Bergendoff recognized that by the time of the 1858 repeal of "the hated act," irreparable damage had been done. The Pietists left the Church of Sweden. Further, they no longer required of their preachers subscription to the Augsburg Confession, and "the unity of the folk church was broken."[12] But before that shattering of formal unity in the homeland, many priests of the State Church had emigrated, often taking numbers of their parishioners with them. Many of these folk, clergy and lay, were the founders of the Augustana Synod. Historians such as Fritiof Ander and George M. Stephenson made no bones about it: the mood of the Synod had steadily been Pietistic.[13] To a degree such Pietism involved reservations about formal university training and about emphasis on a caste of clergy. Years later Karl Olsson, an historian long associated with North Park College in Chicago, wrote in a leading Swedish scholarly journal that in the nineteenth century the secular Swedish-American press "never wearied of ridiculing the Swedish[-American] pastors, partly because they were so pietistic and partly because they were uneducated and lacked the proper social graces."[14]

Bergendoff preferred to think of the Synod founders in a slightly different light. He lamented the fact that their university roots seemed to have been overlooked and that many in the Synod had fallen into the habit of thinking of them as "unlettered, undereducated men." Their children had let the "poor Swedes attitude dim the excellence of their attainments."[15] In fact, of the twelve original Swedish-American pastors who had been present at the 1860 founding of the Synod at Jefferson Prairie, Wisconsin, five (including Esbjörn and Hasselquist) had been graduates of Swedish universities, four had some formal training, either in Sweden or the US , and three had been ordained without formal schooling.[16] Bergendoff wondered whether the prevailing low estimate of the intellectual and academic preparation of the founders came from the secular Swedish language newspapers' persistent negativity toward the Augustana clergy. He saw to it that the Augustana College catalog corrected any misimpressions:"graduates of the ancient universities of Uppsala and Lund" were the founders of the Synod's oldest educational institution, it proclaimed. One of Bergendoff's favorite devices was to refer to the antiquity of Swedish religious and academic traditions, rarely noting that Swedish Christianity had existed for just one-half of the two millennia since Jesus Christ and the apostolic church. Still, in comparison to much of the Christianity the Swedes encountered on the American frontier, their religion was "ancient."

In contrast to Bergendoff's emphasis on the academic credentials of the Synod's founders, G. Everett Arden, the Augustana Seminary church historian, noted that L. P. Esbjörn was certainly no intellectual and had in fact suffered from a "lack of a thorough theological training in Sweden." Visiting Uppsala in 1937, Arden had discovered from records that Esbjörn had taken a shorter, more practical, and less demanding course of theological studies at the university.[17] Bergendoff chose rather to emphasize that Esbjörn had been at the "ancient" (founded in 1477) university in the first place. He took no notice of Arden's discovery about the "short course."

Books published in the thirties by historians Ander and Stephenson considering the early decades of the Synod set its historiographical pot boiling. In a 1932 *Augustana Quarterly* review of their work, Bergendoff, who once in a while got blunt even with his friends, made clear his view. Not only had these two historians, his contemporaries, underestimated the academic achievements of the synodical fathers, they had also overestimated the extent of disharmony and secessionism in the late nineteenth century Augustana Church. Maybe that was because neither Ander nor Stephenson (both laymen) understood the theological issues that were so crucial to the life of that Church. In that review article on the Ander and Stephenson books, Bergendoff also discussed a third work, a scholarly treatment of the Atonement controversy that had rent the world of Swedish Lutheranism on both sides of the ocean in the 1870s.

That third book was the Swedish historian Ernst Newman's *Den waldenströmska försoningsläran i historisk belysning* (*The Waldenströmian Doctrine of the Atonement in a Historical Light*). Bergendoff agreed with Newman that a central problem lay in the Pietistic view of the death of Christ which had been elaborated by Waldenström. In over-stressing divine love and in ignoring the objective need for dealing with sin through the death of Christ, Waldenström had distorted Luther's doctrine of God, which always emphasized both the mercy and the justice in the divine nature. Bergendoff's book reviews were often more pointed than his heavier and more cautious theological articles. In this review he wrote with irony: "It is a curious light that the history of these times casts on many pages of Church History—those who carry on most about the importance of the Bible emphasize not the God who is revealed there, but the man to whom the revelation comes."[18] That seemed to mean that the God of Scripture had, as Luther said, two sides, justice and mercy, and that those who, like Waldenström, stressed only the latter side fell into a sort of human-centered subjectivism that ignored the divine majesty sometimes spoken of as God's "otherness." Bergendoff was never friendly to "subjectivism," whether he found it in mystics, psychologists, or Pietists.

As it turned out, that was also the objection to Waldenströmian Pietism that the third President of Augustana College and Theological Seminary, Olof Olsson, had raised a half century earlier. In his early years attracted to Pietism, Olsson underwent a sort of conversion to Lutheran confessionalism, much as his predecessors, L. P. Esbjörn and T. N. Hasselquist, had. Olsson wrote that a long-standing question was whether it was God's power or his grace which brought men to him. He argued that these two, divine power and divine grace, must be balanced with each other. Otherwise one would fall into a sort of Unitarianism which did not understand the two sides of the divine nature, one side issuing divine law, the other offering redemption from human failure to live up to it. Further, Waldenström's whole approach reflected the sort of rationalism that had characterized the Unitarian heretics of the Reformation period.[19] For Bergendoff, who thought Olsson's paper was the best response made in Swedish America to the Atonement controversy,[20] it was by their fidelity to the teaching of Luther and the Augsburg Confession that the fathers of the Synod had kept the ranks of Swedish-American Lutherans united, even if certain second-generation historians did not properly understand the theological issues involved. He could also not resist noting in his review article that according to a current study, "The present high standard of education for the ministry in the Augustana Synod (according to Fry, *The U.S. Looks at Its Churches*—the highest in the country) is not something new."[21] So much for any hint that the Synod's founders—or for that matter, their twentieth century progeny—were either poorly educated or theologically indifferent. Bergendoff himself was willing to criticize the seminary, and, as we have seen, did so at times unsparingly. But

Olof Olsson, third President of Augustana College.

he did not respond well to such criticism by others.

Overall, Bergendoff clearly stressed the religious factors that had played into the decision of the Synod fathers to emigrate. That interpretation was common to his generation of historians, including Ander and Stephenson. John S. Lindberg, writing in 1930, offered a more economic and sociological view of the emigration in general, but he shared that perspective on the importance of the religious factors among those leaving Sweden for America: "To dissenters, the religious freedom of America looms as a great, almost inestimable advantage, worth nearly any sacrifice." Lindberg maintained that had much to do with the nature of the Swedish Church: "When the emigration began, the external forms of the Swedish State Church were rigid and rather antiquated. The Church represented the State from the religious side."[22] In his Pulitzer Prize winning *The Atlantic Migration,* Marcus Lee Hansen had also taken that view: "In Norway and Sweden dissatisfaction with the established Lutheran Church also caused many to look to America, where religious freedom might be enjoyed along with superior economic opportunities."[23] A new generation of Swedish historians, working in the so-called Uppsala Project in the second half of the twentieth century, took a different stance. Their conclusion was that "religious factors cannot be considered a definite cause of the spread of mass emigration behavior." They recognized that this was a view diverging from earlier historians. The Uppsala scholars mentioned for example, George M. Stephenson, who "concludes that Swedish emigration can largely be seen as a reaction to religious intolerance in Sweden."[24] Perhaps the newer emphasis might be traced to the changing Swedish context in which the Uppsala study was being carried on, as well as to the careful data that seem to have driven the work. We will see in Chapter 8 how Bergendoff himself reacted to the cultural and religious shifts in Swedish society.

The Earliest Years

Of course Bergendoff, ever the historian, knew that the single reason his forebears had departed Sweden was not simply that they wanted a better life in the New World, whether economic and social, religious and spiritual. They were also dissatisfied with the life they left behind. And that was not just because of difficult economic conditions, social inequalities, and their own limited prospects, whether clergy or lay. It also had to do with the Church of Sweden, its authoritative government, and its hostility to what the emigrants regarded as the positive elements in the awakening and temperance movements. Bergendoff recognized that "serious-minded observers in the early decades of the 18th century complained of the low level of life even among those who made much of faith."[25] That judgment was particularly directed against the brittle scholasticism of Lutheran theology in the eighteenth century, but Bergendoff knew that it might as well be applied to subsequent periods in Swedish history. As committed as he was to the idea that the Synod was the direct descendent of the Swedish Church, Bergendoff had also to contend with the negative estimate of certain aspects of that Church's life and history persisting in the first decades of his Synod's existence.

Bergendoff understood too that those complaints carried into the next century: when the emigrants left for America, they wanted "to build a spiritual home that would be independent of shifting political, social, and economic forces." They sought freedom from a Swedish Church that was dominated by the government.[26] And Bergendoff recognized that in spite of the "tendency to overdraw the factor of incapacity among the earliest pastors" to which some of his fellow historians had succumbed, it took a different sort of fellow to make it as an early Augustana pastor in America than it would have taken to succeed at home in the Church of Sweden. Yes, Swedish priests were well-trained, "But most of the clergy of the state church would have been as successful on the prairies of the Great West as were the brilliantly uniformed officers of Braddock's army in guerilla warfare with the French and Indians."[27]

If early Synod history was not exactly guerilla warfare, it did, said Bergendoff, include a threat to the deepest commitments of the first of the founders to arrive, Lars Paul Esbjörn. "He found in America a kind of church activity which challenged fundamental Lutheran doctrines."[28] And that challenge arose not only from without but from within the ranks of American Lutherans. A pivotal episode in the formation of the Synod was Esbjörn's sudden decision to leave his teaching post at the joint Lutheran educational venture at Illinois State University in 1860. He quit not because he feared Presbyterians or Methodists, but because he believed that fellow (non-Swedish) Lutheran faculty of that small institution in Springfield had strayed from pure doctrine in their

G. Everett Arden, Professor of Church History at Augustana Seminary.

teaching. While other Augustana historians would take a somewhat dim view of Esbjörn's precipitous departure, Bergendoff spoke of "the courageous attitude of L. P. Esbjörn in 1860 that resulted in the founding of our oldest institution and of the Synod."[29]

This reference to Esbjörn's "courageous attitude" was written in 1923, and when the books by Ander and Stephenson that were critical of Esbjörn appeared in the next decade, they did not dissuade Bergendoff from his view of Esbjörn as hero. That was clear in his 1932 *Augustana Quarterly* review of their books as well as in his own later work. Stephenson saw Esbjörn's resignation as a "spur of the moment" matter and wrote that "Only a most extraordinary set of conditions can justify the resignation of a member of the faculty in any institution in the middle of a semester, without a word of warning." Stephenson remained unimpressed with Esbjörn's several attempts at justifying his exit from Springfield.[30] To him, whose entire career was spent a faithful tenured member of the Minnesota History Department, abandoning one's teaching post in mid-term was unthinkable. But in 1969, writing his history of Augustana College, Bergendoff differed: "From the first Esbjörn had been unhappy in Springfield so that his sudden departure after less than two years was not a precipitate action."[31]

In the narrow space between "sudden departure" and "not a precipitate action" Bergendoff located the founding of the Synod. So did his colleague, the seminary's church historian, G. Everett Arden, who, writing in the early 1960s, allowed that Esbjörn had been a man of difficult temperament but was nevertheless "under the guidance of God, the chosen vessel called to found on American soil a new church." Arden was more ready than Bergendoff to accept that God might have worked through a man given to "frequent periods of melancholy and depression," who possessed a "morose and suspicious nature," had "a strong streak of egocentricity," and was "not an intellectual." Bergendoff preferred not to dwell at all upon these less attractive qualities of the first President of Augustana

College and Theological Seminary. (That generosity also extended to his successors at Augustana.) He must have been more inclined to the brighter side of Arden's picture of Esbjörn, who was in Arden's final judgment a person of "heroic proportions."[32] Both historians, Arden and Bergendoff, understood the development of the Augustana Synod and Esbjörn's role in it to have been a part of what, following earlier German work, American theologians and church historians in the mid-twentieth century referred to as *Heilsgeschichte,* the history of salvation, which began with God's dealings with humanity in the Old Testament, was supremely expressed in Christ's life, death, and resurrection, and could be seen through the subsequent history of the Christian church. The life of the Swedish-American Synod was one later expression of that *Heilsgeschichte.*

For his part, Arden seemed willing to live with an Esbjörn whose heroic proportions included serious, though not fatal, flaws. The farthest Bergendoff seems to have gone in that direction was to hint just slightly at the darker side of Esbjörn and his role in the infancy of the Synod. That was in a 1960 article in the *Swedish Pioneer Historical Quarterly.* There he acknowledged that after the Synod's new school had, against Esbjörn's wishes, been moved from Chicago to Paxton, Illinois, about one hundred miles to the south, "The next step we now think was unfortunate." That next step was that Esbjörn "in disappointment" went back to Sweden.[33] It is not clear in that article whether Bergendoff meant that the unfortunate quality of Esbjörn's departure inhered in Esbjörn himself, leaving in disappointment, or rather that it came from conditions in America, that caused the exit from the New World of the man who in order of arrival stood first in the Synod's ranks.

Bergendoff did at moments refer to the spiritual poverty of nineteenth century America, which he contrasted with the *tusenårigt andligt arv* (thousand year spiritual heritage) that Esbjörn brought with him.[34] But the other reason Bergendoff seemed not to have been willing to criticize Esbjörn to the degree that Ander, Arden, and Stephenson had was tied, I think, to his whole understanding of the relationship between the spiritual and moral qualities in an individual and that person's work, especially in the church. He was, as we saw in the third and fourth chapters, inclined to believe that one's Christian commitment was necessarily reflected in actions and was less ready to recognize the continued mixture of sin and goodness, of pure motives and psychological difficulties, that even Arden, in his treatment of Esbjörn, was willing to live with.

O. F. Ander's biography, replete with footnotes, depicted a Hasselquist who grew tired of Esbjörn's complaints of "homesickness." A Swedish pastor who knew Esbjörn before he emigrated once remarked that "He had the

Oscar Fritiof Ander, Professor of History at Augustana College.

temperament of a bishop."[35]   But Esbjörn did not bring the new Synod under his control, and returned to Sweden.   His rival for leadership in the new church, T. N. Hasselquist, wondered what would become of the new Synod if all its pastors were pining to go home to Sweden.[36]   For Ander, "the keen rivalry between Esbjörn and Hasselquist played a very important part in the formation of the Augustana Synod."[37] Ander's treatment of the tensions (he called them "dirty politics") between Hasselquist and Esbjörn may, at the least, have made for interesting reading, but it did not serve Bergendoff's more respectful view of the Synod's first decade, one which tended to equate regard for the patriarchs with a refusal to air their disagreements. Bergendoff admired Hasselquist's leadership of Augustana College and Theological Seminary, the *läroverk* (educational institution) begun by the founders in the same year as the Synod. Conrad was, after all, Hasselquist's third successor.

Paying no mind to the feistiness that Ander found in Hasselquist, Bergendoff dwelt rather upon the success with which the patriarch carried the burden of Synod president, president and professor at Augustana, newspaper editor, and pastor, often simultaneously.[38] In particular Bergendoff approved of Hasselquist's effort to combine the best of the Swedish and American educational traditions, a European emphasis on faculty primacy and general education melded to the elective system that had developed in American colleges.[39]   Bergendoff also noted with less approval that in his pastorate Hasselquist had given up the use of the Swedish *Kyrkobok* in favor of a looser form of worship than that then used in the Church of Sweden.[40]   It was difficult to picture the "low state of Lutheran liturgy in America" when the fathers of the Augustana Synod brought Swedish worship forms to the new land.[41] As Bergendoff understood him, the newly arrived Hasselquist was evidently not one of the major bearers of the Swedish liturgical tradition to America. For Bergendoff the transmission and preservation of the liturgy of the Swedish church was crucial to the identity of the Augustana Synod. It was also as rich a heritage as could be found among the American churches; the Synod had no need to look to the Episcopalians—it had the Church of Sweden as a liturgical source and model.[42]

Winning the Immigrants and Their Children

If bringing the Church of Sweden's liturgy to America was in the Augustana Synod a point of continuity with the homeland, there were also significant differences between Swedish Lutherans in Europe and America. Among those was the fact that while the Swedish Church, at least nominally, included nearly the entire population of the country, the Synod never enrolled a majority of Swedish Americans. Both Augustana's early leaders and the later students of its history understood that fact. Writing in 2006, the immigration scholar Dag Blanck of Uppsala University argues convincingly that the Synod was in fact the most important institution that shaped a Swedish American identity in the United States. But he also notes that its membership rolls never included forty percent of the people of Swedish extraction living in America. In 1870 about one-third of them belonged to the Synod. That rose to thirty-eight percent by 1880, but within a decade it had fallen back to about twenty percent, and it hovered at that level past the First World War. However, Blanck writes, many persons not formally associated with the Church sought its ministrations when they baptized children, married, or buried family. Therefore the reach of the Synod was wider than its formal membership might suggest. No other group came close to including the numbers that belonged to the Synod: in 1880, 75,000 members; in 1900, 210,000; in 1920, 291,000.[43] Other than the churches, the only Swedish-American organizations of any size were the secular mutual-aid societies or lodges that began to be established in the late nineteenth century. In the 1920s the Vasa Order had 50,000 members, the Svithiod and the Viking Orders, 15,000 each. Bergendoff's own assessment was that Augustana probably never had "more than ½ of the immigrants in its sphere of activity."[44]

Those numbers and estimates suggest that it would be a mistake to minimize the relative institutional influence of the Augustana Synod upon Swedish America. Still, leaders of the Synod itself were troubled by their failure to win even a bare majority of the immigrants and their children. Conrad Bergendoff himself once remarked that the two greatest missteps his Church had taken were to lose the Pietists who in its first decades left the Synod over the Atonement controversy and its failure to attract a greater number of those from what he regarded as its natural constituency, immigrants from Sweden and their descendants. His wistfulness over the loss of the Mission Friends was evident when he spoke with Covenanters as well.[45] From his perspective the Augustana Church had survived and grown between two difficulties.

On one side stood what Swedish church historians had called the "Hyperevangelicals." Today "hyper" connotes excitability and excess, but Swedish scholars had used *hyperevangelisk* to label nineteenth century Pietists. As these historians saw it, the Swedish Pietists stressed God's love and mercy without balancing it with an emphasis upon divine law and justice.[46] As we have seen, that was the criticism of their position which American Lutherans took as well. The Augustana Synod survived the 1885 secession of the Pietists, whom historians such as G. Everett Arden and George M. Stephenson also called "hyperevangelicals."[47]

In the other direction, the Augustana Church faced the fact that, as Arden noted, "the Synod had from the very beginning conceived its chief task and responsibility to be that of winning for the Church the great masses of incoming Swedish immigrants."[48] As the twentieth century dawned, Synod leaders began to realize that they were not attracting numbers of the Swedes who continued to land in American ports. They recognized that many of these folk came from a country that was itself becoming less religious. They had "another mindset than those who founded Swedish America," and had perhaps been "contaminated" by socialism.[49] Bergendoff quoted Synod President Eric Norelius, who early in the new century had already taken the same general view: "we wish to affect the multitudes that come here, provided they are loyal to the Swedish Church."[50]

Preaching in the thirties to new ordinands, Bergendoff declared that now the Synod's task had become "to win and keep for the Church a remnant of Swedish immigrants." This was one part of the larger job, "the transformation of the pagan life of our country so 'that it may be conformed to the body of His glory.'"[51] A decade after the 1962 merger of the Augustana Church into the Lutheran Church in America, Bergendoff sought to interpret what he himself realized had been very partial success in that effort. He echoed the analysis of earlier Augustana apologists: the post-1880 immigrants were hostile to the church, arriving from a land which appeared to be steadily becoming more secular. In 1960 one American church historian even suggested that perhaps the problem lay not simply in the secularism of the newer immigrants. Maybe it was due to a degree of complacency in the Augustana Synod, which never underwent the sort of dissension that divided Norwegian-American Lutherans. If there had been splits "strong enough a hundred years ago to provoke the founding of two rather than one Swedish Lutheran Church in America, the outreach among Swedish-speaking peoples would have been doubled. (It would have had to treble to equal Norwegian-American Lutheranism!)."[52] Bergendoff's thought on this was that the debates among the Norwegians "kept them alert."[53] Perhaps a little competition among the Swedes would have been healthy; look what it did for the Norwegians!

Would a denominational division among the Swedes have resulted in keeping more of them Lutheran? Bergendoff never addressed that question, which belonged to the same species as St. Paul's question in his Letter to the Romans, chapter 6: "What then, shall we sin that grace may abound?" What Bergendoff did believe was that it was resentment among the people toward the Swedish clergy that secularized the immigrant stream; in spite of that resentment the common people who remained in Sweden continued to respect the liturgy and the sacraments of the national Church.[54] He thought it may have been the fact that Swedish pastors were in some respects officers of the government, registering births and deaths of the entire population, which contributed to the anti-clerical sentiment.[55] Franklin Scott (1901-1994), the preeminent American historian of Sweden in his generation, was more blunt, speaking of "pastors who were the petty lords of the parishes and to whom men had to tip their hats."[56] In general Bergendoff stuck to a tempered interpretation of the growing secularism and religious indifference of the Lutheran homeland, though he grew increasingly disturbed by the direction Swedish society was taking in the years after his retirement from Augustana College in 1962.[57] He was troubled by the a-religion of the Swedes, recognized it with hesitation and regret, and wrote about it in a very gingerly fashion.

There was in fact some tension in Bergendoff's own consideration of the subject. We will see that he was willing to adduce a strong and continuing connection between the stable and humane quality of Swedish society and its four centuries of being Lutheran, at points arguing that Sweden and its Scandinavian neighbors were the nations where one could most clearly see the results of a Lutheran social ethic. At other moments, especially when grappling with the inability of his own Augustana Synod after 1890 to enroll the majority of the American daughters and sons of Sweden in its congregations, he spoke more directly of the secularism that seemed to be gripping the homeland. In an ideal world the Synod would have enrolled the great majority of the Swedes coming to America, and in Sweden those who stayed home would have remained faithfully Lutheran. Then the Synod would have functioned as the "folk church" of Swedish America. But there was a greater connection between the homeland and the new land than Bergendoff, who usually tried to defend that connection, was in this case happy to admit. Now the secularism of Swedish society was being carried across the Atlantic by the immigrants along with their trunks of clothing and family photos, and by no stretch could the Augustana Synod be construed as a folk church for the whole immigrant community. Most of them didn't join.

The Maturing Synod

The ecumenical relationships of the Synod's founders were also of considerable interest to Bergendoff. He believed that his Synod had taken a position in America half-way between the doctrinal rigidity of the early Missouri Synod and the lax Lutheranism of some eastern English-language Lutheran pastors.[58] Bergendoff recognized that both Esbjörn and Hasselquist had upon first arriving in the Middle West accepted financial support from non-Lutheran Protestants and become involved in the cooperation with them which that entailed. But Esbjörn soon began to "sense the strength of his heritage" and took "a clear stand on what he believed." And Hasselquist was "firm in maintaining the faith and order of the church."[59] One Swedish student of its first four decades, Hugo Söderström, writes that collectively the Augustana Synod came increasingly to emphasize sound Lutheran doctrine: "From having been willing to cooperate with all Christians who *sincerely* believed in Christ, they wanted only to cooperate with those who *correctly* believed in Christ."[60] And Philip J. Anderson, an American church historian, says of the developing Synod: "Augustana shed its own origins in the pietistic renewal and became increasingly structured, confessional, hierarchical, rigid, and protective. No one represented this shift more than Hasselquist, who as a young ordained priest in Sweden had been a radical revival preacher, but now in America became an establishment arch-conservative."[61]

Those judgments by a Swede and by an American were written in the later twentieth century. It would never have been easy to have made an ecumenist of the ever-more-orthodox Esbjörn, but for his part Bergendoff preferred not to let go of the idea that in contrast Hasselquist believed that "we could be good Lutherans in this new land without condemning all other Christian bodies."[62] Written in 1951, that statement reflected Bergendoff's own growing ecumenical involvement as well as Hasselquist's somewhat more measured willingness to share the soil of the New Land with other Christians (preferably Republicans). Bergendoff knew very well that in its first years the Church as a whole had been "suspicious in its dealings with non-Lutheran church bodies and cautious in its relations with Lutheran synods in America[.]"[63] As usual, he looked on the positive side, finding precedents for his own ecumenism in the history of his denomination.

Of course, some of what Bergendoff regarded as Hasselquist's commendable openness may have been due to internal problems within the Augustana Synod itself. These were difficulties which demanded almost all of its leader's attention and energy and left him little time to wrestle with Presbyterians or Methodists. Those difficulties had the two foci mentioned in an earlier chapter: the confrontation with the Pietistic Waldenströmians, who in 1885 formed the

Mission Covenant, as well as the growing inability of the Synod to attract the majority of the immigrants from Sweden who kept pouring through East Coast ports on their way to the prairies of the Middle West—as Carl August Bergendoff himself had.

But as the Swedish Americans who did join Augustana Synod congregations grew in numbers (though not as a percentage of total Swedish immigrants), they also began to prosper. Bergendoff wondered in a 1943 *Lutheran Companion* article if more than the current $1.50 per member per month could be raised in the Church to meet the cost of expansion. There were "no signs of anybody tired or exhausted" or even "exertion beyond the ordinary." The Synod members' "well-furnished homes" and "well-kept farms with modern implements and bulging barns" suggested that more could be accomplished for church and school if only more were given.[64]   At moments Bergendoff let himself get lyrical about the tidy conditions and sturdy people that prevailed in the part of Swedish America that lay under the Synod's influence. After spending time in 1933 at a church youth camp in the Pacific Northwest, he had written about "the righteous strength of the young men and the pure charm of the young women of our Church in the wonderlands of the West." He was even more taken with those young people than with the wild flowers spreading over the mountain meadows.[65] Twenty years later Bergendoff must have been gratified at the news from a Luther League convention on the other coast. Following a "Bean Feed" on the Boston Common, the fastidious Leaguers had picked up after themselves. The clean-up crew hired to do the job were sent home.[66]

The college president was not unwilling to appeal to the nobler qualities and attractive appearances of Swedish-American folk, homes, and farms when asking for money. Sometimes he traced these features of his ethnic community to its roots in the Lutheran faith. After his 1926-1927 dissertation year in Sweden, he attributed many of the same qualities he found in Swedish America to the people of Sweden and to their connection to the Church. In 1962, as his Church got ready to merge with other Lutherans, he recalled that the immigrant generation had not only been tidy; they had "known who they were." They enjoyed life in the Synod with others who shared that clear sense of identity; now their children faced a new Church and a society that had "no anchor."[67] Of course, the Church of Sweden was one place where Bergendoff believed the Synod was anchored.

This emphasis on the Synod's ties to the mother Swedish Church was one of the ways that Bergendoff's interpretation of the Synod's history was, at least when compared to the views of other contemporary Augustana historians, unique. Also somewhat particular to Bergendoff were his stress on the high educational records and standards of the founders and his view that at least some of them, notably Hasselquist, had a strong ecumenical orientation. And in contrast to fellow historians, Bergendoff preferred to focus upon the areas in which Esbjörn, Hasselquist, and others worked harmoniously, not dwelling on the points of tension and disagreement among them that others wrote about more openly. In these ways what he said about the first Augustana generation was as close to a "party line" as one is apt to encounter. That applies to his work when compared with that of Fritiof Ander or George Stephenson, or even with that of the earliest historian of the Synod, Eric Norelius, himself one of the patriarchs, who was quite candid about some of the dissension and rivalry among the founders.

Bergendoff's stress upon concord among the Synod's fathers may say as much about his own temper and outlook as it does about the first decades of the Synod. It is also the case that Dr. Bergendoff's relationship to his Church in his own professional lifetime was generally one of harmony and accommodation, much as he thought its ur-history had been. But there were also moments when he and the majority of the members of the Augustana Lutheran Church did not see eye to eye, points at which his sense of what direction their denomination ought to take in the future was challenged, and in some cases thwarted, by actions its leaders and its conventions took. We turn to some of those now, not simply because, as Ander, Arden, and Stephenson knew, discord is intriguing, but because these episodes, and in particular one of them, have much to say about Bergendoff's own understanding of Christianity in particular and human moral and intellectual life in general.

Disagreements

If he had been forced to declare himself, Conrad Bergendoff would have sided with L. P. Esbjörn in the tensions that other historians posited between Esbjörn and T. N. Hasselquist. But he found qualities in Hasselquist that were admirable, his ecumenical disposition chief among them. Another such quality was emphasis upon the national character of the Synod. The first Augustana historian, Eric Norelius, wrote that Hasselquist was *"en centralisationens man."* That meant that "He advocated *one* synod, *one* higher educational institution, *one* newspaper, *one* central administration and as much as possible the concentration of the Swedish Lutheran congregations in respect to geography."[68] Bergendoff was also "a centralization man," so that was another quality the fifth president of Augustana admired in the second. For Bergendoff the regional conferences of the Synod, and the growing number of agencies and institutions of the Church ought so far as possible be administered from the capital city of Swedish-American Lutheranism, the town where, not coincidentally, the institution Bergendoff led was located.

The opposite tendency to the centralization that Hasselquist and Bergendoff favored was an emphasis upon the regional conferences and *their* charitable and educational institutions. As immigrants from Sweden settled in Minnesota, on the Great Plains, and in the Northeast, they founded colleges which drew strong support from congregations around them. The Rock Island school found itself among competitors. The fact that the Synod had one seminary but in addition to Augustana (1860) a number of colleges—Gustavus Adolphus (founded 1862), Bethany (1881), and Upsala[69] (1893), as well as a two-year school, Luther (1883)—meant that the effort of the Rock Island school to keep Synod-wide support for its college division met with opposition from the alumni and supporters of the other undergraduate colleges.[70] The influential Synod President, Eric Norelius (held office 1874-1881 and 1899-1911), "lent the weight of his influence to these decentralizing tendencies."[71] Particularly as regarded higher education, Bergendoff was a centralization man; he felt that his school was *primus inter pares* in the Synod, and that it was in the interest of the entire Augustana Church to keep it so.

The problem emerging in the twentieth century was that other centralization men, often officers of the entire Synod, did not take that position; for them the seminary ought be the *one* national higher educational effort of the Synod. Attempts were repeatedly made on the floor of conventions and in the politicking that preceded and followed those meetings to assign Augustana College a place as one of the several regional colleges, supported by congregations in the Illinois, Iowa, and Superior Conferences, just as the other schools were by the conferences immediately around them. Those efforts found, from time to time, support from the leadership of the Synod. So while Bergendoff favored centralization as a general principle, he did not always welcome the views of the central leadership, especially when they ran counter to his own ideas about the place of Augustana College and Theological Seminary in the Church's scheme of higher education. And there were other specific episodes when tensions grew up as well. In retrospect some of those problems seem dated and perhaps even trivial. But at the time they, too, were felt to be of solemn import.

In his role as President of Augustana Bergendoff sometimes found himself explaining and/or defending actions and positions taken by faculty, staff, and students at the school which were met with doubts and opposition in the Church. Usually it fell to the President of the Synod to channel this opinion back to the campus. During his professional career Bergendoff dealt in the main with three Synod Presidents. They were Gustav Albert Brandelle (President, 1918-1935), Petrus Olof Bersell (1935-1951), and Oscar A. Benson (1951-1959). Brandelle, who for the first five years of

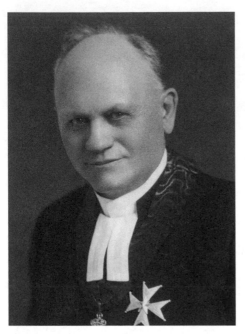

Gustav Albert Brandelle, Synod president, 1918-35.

his term also served as the pastor of a congregation in Rock Island, presided over a time of rapid Americanization in the Synod, marked particularly by the widespread switch to the use of English in worship and business. He was one of the founders of the National Lutheran Council and of the American Lutheran Conference, both inter-Lutheran agencies that sought closer co-operation among the various Lutheran bodies in the US. He also represented the Synod in Europe at ecumenical meetings during the inter-war period.

P. O. Bersell guided the Church through the social upheavals of the Depression and Second World War and directed an administrative reorganization that set up administrative boards composed of clergy and lay members which supervised the work of an executive director or secretary who carried on the business of the agency or department (e.g. foreign missions, youth work, parish education, etc.). Upon his election, Bersell moved his family from Ottumwa, Iowa, where he had served a congregation, to Minneapolis, establishing the first permanent synodical headquarters there. That was probably centralization in the wrong place so far as many Rock Islanders saw it. Decades later Bergendoff recalled that the move to the Twin Cities had been sudden: Bersell "went to Minneapolis and set up headquarters without any resolution of Synod to that effect. It was entirely a personal matter—he wanted to live in Minneapolis." Bergendoff thought it had worked out in the end, but that the move and the new and efficient way of operating that Bersell introduced did reflect "the influence of American business." He felt Bersell was "very ambitious."[72] We know what Bergendoff thought about the intrusion of ambition and business methods into church life. Oscar Benson, who had been President of the Illinois Conference, was Synod president in the fifties during the complicated negotiations that resulted in the Synod's joining three other groups to form the Lutheran Church in America in 1962. All three of these men were, of course, graduates of the Rock Island seminary, and two had B.A. degrees from

Augustana, Benson from Upsala College.[73]

Part of the heritage of the Augustana Church was an "Ethic of Don'ts." We saw earlier that President Brandelle had issued a list of particular sins which Augustana Lutherans were to avoid. It included movies, cards, socialism and the misuse of cars. Even skipping church during harvest time was on that list. For a while the Church had prohibited football at its colleges. That *Verbot* had been lifted, but throughout the first half of the twentieth century, another one, directed at a different type of physical activity to which the young were inclined, remained in place. "The Dance" was prohibited at the colleges in Illinois, Minnesota, Kansas, New Jersey, and Nebraska. The Church of Sweden which Bergendoff had come to know in the twenties was, like its American counterpart, leery of dancing and the sexual behavior to which it supposedly led Christians.[74]   So from his church work on both sides of the Atlantic, Bergendoff had been made aware of the dangers to which The Dance could lead.

But from the day in 1935 when he accepted the position of Acting President of Augustana, Dr. Bergendoff found himself in a tug-of-war between students, Lutheran and otherwise, who wanted to swing and sway, and the Church, which flatly prohibited it. Bergendoff had no sooner moved into the President's Office than he was confronted with the fact that many of Augustana's undergraduates were dancing, sometimes on the sly in the dormitories and often more openly at off-campus parties. And even in the pre-war years, when colleges had neither the inclination nor the staff to set up and direct the extensive student social programs that were characteristic of campuses in the later twentieth century, Augustana tried to find alternatives such as literary societies, parties, and even treasure hunts. But students, Lutherans or not, wanted to dance. When word spread through the Synod that the army air cadets stationed on campus during World War II were dancing, pastors grew gravely concerned.

That concern increased after the war when veterans, who had jitterbugged and waltzed at USOs all through their military service, arrived on campus with their tastes and habits firmly in place. One veteran told Bergendoff that all the students wanted was to be able to dance on campus without "some barfly blowing his beery breath over their shoulders." The college administration pretended it did not see students dancing in the student union building, through a technicality not considered a part of the campus, or at hotels and restaurants where Greek letter groups held their annual "formals" (never labeled "formal *dances*"). The pressure to legalize dancing grew at the other Synod colleges as well. Finally, after long and weighty consideration by boards, committees, and Church conventions, the Synod decided in 1950 that while there could be no "official sponsoring of dances on or off the campus by the colleges," it would (as per a last minute amendment to the original resolution) permit its schools to "supervise" off-campus dancing when it was not "officially sponsored." The original proposal before the convention suggested that 1950 was no time for youth to be asking about dancing when this age of crisis "with its dominant note of threatening tragedy" demanded that they "give themselves to the conflict that lies ahead in all seriousness." But that section was amended out of the final resolution.[75] We are left to wonder which of the crises threatening America in the fifties the authors of the resolution had in mind with the reference to "the conflict that lies ahead."

Through all this Bergendoff seems to have understood that he must play Janus. In 1935 he told two women who had been caught dancing in the Women's Building that he could not "go beyond what those who support and maintain the institution have declared shall be the policy of the institution."[76] In the same year he told the Synod that its social standards "often seem quite negative."[77] Bergendoff wrote to one pastor that there was no more dancing on campus by Lutheran students than there was by congregation members in their hometowns. He wrote that he kept reminding students of the Church's position, but often those who most vehemently "talked back" to him were themselves the sons and daughters of pastors, even conference officers.[78] On the other side of it, however, when students petitioned in 1949 to rescind the prohibition and permit a Homecoming Dance on campus, Bergendoff reminded them that the Synod had its reasons: "There is plenty of evidence as to what dancing may lead to." And, he added, a college was more than just its students. A solution must be found that would be acceptable to all those in "that constituency which we call Augustana."[79] The solution was the compromise mentioned in the last paragraph.

Bergendoff came back from the 1950 national convention of the Synod where that compromise had been reached and reported with some jaundice that the debate on dancing "went all around the subject without touching it."[80] What troubled him most in the whole business was that there was "a marked chasm between what we preach and what our youth do." Was the Church losing its youth? "It is in the field of conduct that I feel the Church has no deep hold upon them."[81] Here, on the hundred acre campus in the capital city of Swedish-American Lutheranism, Bergendoff confronted in miniature the weighty issues of how Christians behaved in society, issues he had wrestled with in scholarly quarterlies and church paper articles for three decades. No simple univocal solution afforded itself here, any more than it seems to have in his professional theological work. One thinks of Augustine administering a small North African diocese while setting the theological agenda for western Christendom for the next thousand years. Bergendoff may have had to settle for being the leading twentieth century theological spokesman of a half million American Lutherans, but he did wrestle with the same sort of mundane-celestial matters the Bishop of Hippo had.

As if the dancing debate had not been troublesome enough, Bergendoff ran into difficulties with the Synod on a matter considered by many of its pastors and presiders still more ominous, a violation of Christian decorum more egregious than waltzing or jitterbugging. This time the difficulty was entirely centered at Augustana College. The other Church schools avoided the distinction which fell to the Synod's oldest college of being the first in Christendom to have sustained a "Panty Raid." In February, 1949, about a dozen male students, masked with paper bags over their heads, invaded the women's dormitory in search of female underwear. They left successful, but a neighbor called police. The college newspaper reported that "Several co-eds had hysterics," and the local, then national, media announced that "a Panty Raid" had occurred.

Synod pastors were outraged. P. O. Bersell, President of the Augustana Church, wrote with sly generosity that he would not join in judging the college and its president until Bergendoff had been given "ample opportunity for defense." "Whether he goes too far in presenting extenuating circumstances or excuses is not for me to say at this juncture." What was at stake, said "PO," was "the Christian character of the school."[82] Bergendoff told the Board of Directors that it had been "a foolish prank" by a few students, played up by "a hungry press." Further, "none more than myself has suffered in this experience, for my whole aim has been to build up confidence in the school." If Augustana did not enjoy such a high academic reputation, the papers would not have taken notice of it at all, he said.[83] Right after the episode Bergendoff departed for Germany where, under the sponsorship of the US Army, he delivered a series of theological lectures to German scholars and students who had been separated from the rest of world Christianity during the Nazi years.

Again, one catches the juxtaposition of the ignoble and the sublime that seems regularly to have asserted itself during two Christian millennia in general and in the first century of Swedish-American Lutheran life in particular. Bergendoff left behind a Rock Island controversy that in retrospect seems to have been relatively harmless but that at the time was a matter of great weight; he went forward to participate in the reintegration of European civilization after the Nazi era. With regard to the former problem, Bergendoff appears to have indulged himself in some perhaps justifiable self-pity: "none more than myself has suffered in this experience." Some of that tone might be explained by a defeat which he had suffered in the same years—over a matter even more important to him than dancing or dorm raids.

A Persisting Problem

The major confrontation between the college-seminary president and his Church in the forties came over a question which had from time to time agitated the Synod through most of its existence: the relationship of the denomination and that of its various geographical sub-units or conferences to its oldest educational effort, the college and seminary in Rock Island. In its earliest years Augustana, *läroverket,* had been a sort of hybrid high school-college-theological institution preparing relatively unschooled immigrants (Carl August Bergendoff was an example) for ministry in Augustana, *synoden.* T. N. Hasselquist had stoutly maintained that the Church must continue to treat the Rock Island institution as the single one to be supported by the *entire* Church. But as schools were founded in other parts of Swedish America, it became clear to many that it was the seminary, now a branch distinct from the college, the academy, and the music school, in which the real interest of the entire Synod rested. Seen this way, these latter three divisions of the Rock Island institution should be the concern of the geographical conferences immediately around the school (Illinois, Iowa, and Superior), at least as folks in other conferences saw it.

At Synod conventions in 1886, 1890, and 1894, the question of separating the seminary from the college was discussed, often at the behest of partisans of one or another of the colleges in Minnesota, Kansas, Nebraska, and (in 1894) New Jersey. But the problem of equitably dividing the property of the major branches of the Synod's oldest school was an obstacle. George Stephenson saw the issue as one aspect of the struggle between the centralization faction and the regionalists of the Augustana Church. The Minnesota historian attributed the settlement of 1894 that maintained the status quo (seminary and college joined) to a plea from President Olof Olsson. Combined with the sobering effect of the hard times across the country during the depression of the early nineties, Olsson's eloquent opposition to separation had prevailed.[84]

Again in 1921 it appeared that the advocates of decentralization (many of whom also favored moving the seminary out of Rock Island) were silenced, when the Church voted to erect theological buildings on Zion Hill, the high knob that stood on the campus south of Old Main and east of the gymnasium. A Church-wide campaign for the seminary had raised nearly $400,000 for the project. Accordingly thirty feet were scraped off the hill and the fill deposited to the west and south. The Swedish Americans, engineers like their Nordic forebears, reconfigured the very landscape of the Mississippi bluffs. Bergendoff's history of the college, 1860-1935, says that from then on, "The seminary site dominated the campus."[85] Over the following decades he was thought to be particularly satisfied with this topographical expression of his belief that at Augustana the other arts and sciences clustered around theology, their center.

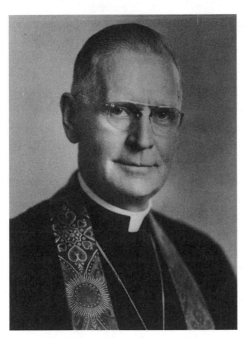

Petrus Olof Bersell, Synod president, 1935-51.

It was a lay-out worthy of Thomas Aquinas. In any event, the parties that had hoped to remove the seminary from Rock Island altogether (perhaps to Chicago) were now, it seemed, silenced.[86]

But both the seminary faculty and the regionalists of the Synod would not let the matter be. At the convention of 1926 in Philadelphia, a proposal reached the floor which called for the separation of the seminary from the college "as to property, funds, management and control." Further, the two institutions should be "placed under separate Boards, *providing* the three conferences, Illinois, Iowa and Superior are willing to take over Augustana College."[87]

The conferences were not. A compromise directed the Augustana Board of Directors to set up a Seminary Committee consisting of the presidents of the Church and the school and six other Board members. The idea was that the seminary would now get the special consideration in Board of Directors affairs that its protagonists felt it had not theretofore enjoyed. That did not satisfy the proponents of separation, however. In the early thirties, Kansas supporters of Bethany, their college now struggling to stay afloat financially, petitioned the Synod for separation at Augustana and for a division of assets between the branches.

After considering the matter for two years, the General Board of Education of the Synod reported back to the annual convention. That meeting set up a Seminary Commission of five members, presumably representing the full range of views on the issue. Conrad Bergendoff, now Dean of the Seminary, was a member. The special commission agreed that more careful separation of the assets and funds of the seminary from those of the college be instituted, and that, anticipating "possible and probable developments in the field of theological education within the Lutheran Church in America," the seminary be moved to Chicago. The report, presented in 1933, just ten years after the new buildings had been opened, was issued over the signatures of all five members, and there was no dissenting opinion attached to it. Thus, writes

G. Everett Arden, it was not unreasonable to assume that Bergendoff agreed with its recommendations, including separating the seminary and moving it to Chicago.[88] The new seminary dean had only recently moved from Chicago. He was one of the Lutheran ecumenists who hoped for a pan-Lutheran center of theological study in the Midwest. Such an arrangement might have brought his Synod's theological school into co-operation or eventual merger with the United Lutheran Church's seminary in Maywood, southwest of the city. Conrad Bergendoff was always ready to ally with the ULCA. So it might be reasonable to assume he concurred in the report.

In the post-war years, when the issue again heated up, Bergendoff insisted that he had not agreed with the majority, though he had been chairman of the commission in 1933. "My own recollection is that I voted against the proposal to move [the seminary to Chicago]. It was not until 13 years later that I found myself accused of having taken a stand which is inconsistent with my present one." With a backward twist Bergendoff held that his later recollection that he had opposed moving was supported by the fact that at the time of the report no one in the Synod who opposed the move to Chicago ever reproached him for favoring it.[89] As Bergendoff remembered it, the commission had been split, two against two, with the fifth member of the commission finally swinging it toward recommending the move.[90] It is tempting to conjecture that what had actually happened lay between Arden's claim that the absence of a minority report indicated unanimity and Bergendoff's later offer of a kind of convoluted circumstantial evidence that the commission had been split. Perhaps neither the unity which Arden alleged nor the opposition Bergendoff claimed to have offered had been quite so clear.

The 1933 motion to move to Chicago lost by 125 to 110 votes, but the division of monies was approved. Seminary assets were reckoned at about $500,000, its annual income at $28,000. Seminary faculty member G. Everett Arden wrote three decades later that the fact that in the depths of the Depression a margin of only fifteen votes kept the school from being separated and moved to Chicago suggested that "a long step in the direction of independence and institutional integrity had been taken."[91] Though he was alleged to have supported the proposal when it was made, Bergendoff's later comment on the 1933 vote to stay in Rock Island was that it had been "a sensible response to a costly proposal."[92] Arden, like most of the seminary faculty, seems to have favored the separation; for him it involved "institutional integrity." Seven of the ten persons teaching at the school in the forties (including part-time faculty) held Augustana BAs, but that seems not to have lessened their desire for independence from their undergraduate alma mater.

By now, of course, Conrad Bergendoff was president of the whole institution, college and seminary. As G. Everett Arden writes, "at no time in the history of the Augustana Church . . . has the suggestion for separation ever been espoused by the central administration of the school."[93] A charge that particularly troubled Bergendoff was that the seminary faculty had been given subordinate status by his institution's Board and administration. That "causes me to throw up my hands in despair." The seminary professors had complained more about their pay than any other group at Augustana. But Bergendoff felt that their salaries were entirely fair. "There are times when I have to restrain myself to keep aloft my estimation of the high office of theological professor."[94] Strong words. Presumably Bergendoff's role as president may have influenced his point of view, at least on a practical level, about the question that had agitated the Synod almost from its founding. It appears that in the late thirties and on into the next decade, some distance was developing between the President of Augustana and fellow pastor-scholars on its theological faculty.

The war, of course, put the question on a back burner. Enrollment in both the college and seminary declined, as men were called into the military. But the issue would not go away. As soon as it appeared that the conflict was ending, the Synod again took it up. It was clear that in many quarters a consensus was taking shape. Bergendoff remembered thirty years later that he had been called to a Chicago meeting of the Synod Executive Council in 1945 and that "Bersell announced when I came, 'We've decided to separate college and seminary,' which was not a very diplomatic move on his part."[95] The college should be assigned to the Illinois, Iowa, and Superior Conferences, and the seminary alone should remain "the object of unified Synodical support." With Synod approval a "Separation Committee" was set up. It proposed a plan for dividing assets and drew up a constitution for the seminary. Historian Arden is clear that the President of the Synod, P. O. Bersell, strongly supported this, giving "the forces agitating for separation" a certain "aggressive leadership which was able to sweep all opposition before it." For Bersell, writes Arden, "the present arrangements had been for many years—and continued to be—the cause of discord, disunity, and sectional friction throughout the Synod." The Synod President was not "primarily motivated by philosophy or theory." Indeed, it was characteristic of "the Bersell regime" first to inaugurate a program and only later to offer a theological justification for it, Arden says.[96] Theoretical or simply practical, President Bersell was blunt about his position: "In fact, it is my considered opinion that we will never get very far in the solution of this whole problem until Augustana College is given the same status as the other colleges under conference ownership and management."[97]

The separation of the two units of Augustana was carried through by Synod vote, and on July 17, 1947, Articles of Incorporation for Augustana Theological Seminary were filed in the county court house in Rock Island.[98] The functioning separation went into effect on August 31, 1948.[99] Bergendoff and the Board of Directors were left to consider what Bersell had referred to in a letter to the college president as "the readjustment in the control of Augustana College."[100] That readjustment did not, however, end up turning ownership of the school over to the three conferences, Illinois, Iowa, and Superior. As had been the case in the twenties, the conferences rejected the offer.[101] But it was determined that these three geographical units would, in fact, be the source of the Church's annual operating grants to Augustana, though technically the college remained owned by the entire Synod. In view of this, each year until 1958 Bergendoff made a report to the annual Synod meeting; after that only the Chairman of the Board of Directors and the Treasurer of the College continued to do so.[102] Evidently the other Augustana Church colleges had to be content with reporting to the annual meetings of their respective regional conferences. They still got no opportunity to plead their causes before the national conventions.

Opposing the Divorce

The alliance which finally succeeded in effecting the seminary-college separation included the leadership of the Synod, the seminary faculty, and the supporters of the other colleges. A major figure in the opposition which was swept away in the mid-forties was, of course, Conrad Bergendoff. As he sought to prevent the separation of the two major parts of the institution he headed, Bergendoff applied several lines of argument, often intermingled with each other. One was historical: this was the way the founders had established their seminary and college; who were we to change it? Another was practical: the present set-up was functioning well; why change it? And the most forceful argument was theoretical or theological. We shall deal with that presently.

Over Bergendoff's name an article, "A Divorce in 1948?" appeared in the April 3, 1946, issue of the *Lutheran Companion*. The Synod had recognized that the break-up of marriage (actual not metaphorical) was a growing American problem. In 1939 it had passed a statement recognizing that "Whenever divorce occurs it is the result of sin," taking place because of "the hardness of men's hearts."[103] And while the Church made the effort to consider the problem as one requiring pastoral guidance and counseling, faculty members had left Synod colleges over such personal failings as divorce, usually because they had been invited to do so by the institutional presidents. So to refer to the separation as a "divorce" was to anticipate in the title of the article its tenor and conclusions. "Is it to celebrate a divorce that the meeting will be held in Rock Island two years hence?" Bergendoff asked, referring to the 1948 celebration of the centennial marking Swedish settlement of the Middle West, a festival whose celebration he greatly anticipated. All that the committee favoring separation could argue, Bergendoff continued, was that the present arrangement was not satisfactory. But it had worked for eighty-six years. The Synod had repeatedly rejected separation. How would assigning the college to the three Midwestern conferences make it easier for the other regions of the Church to support their colleges? Maybe *all* the schools should be assigned to the entire Church. Or if the tie to Augustana College did not seem to be not working, maybe the seminary should be assigned to one of the other colleges. [104] By that point Bergendoff was almost ridiculing the opposition, perhaps with a sarcasm not usually charcteristic of him.

But Bergendoff was not given to idle levity; a truth was hidden in the jest. If as Synod historian Arden suggests, P.O. Bersell's reasons for supporting the separation were ultimately practical and political, Bergendoff's were not. They were predicated on his understanding of Christianity and its relationship to culture. Here lay his theoretical or theological arguments. They were rooted in his boyhood in Tabor Lutheran Church and Middletown High School, in his student days in Rock Island, college *and* seminary, and in a perspective on the Christianity-culture issue that he had been elaborating for two decades. And they were certainly made from the position he had assumed in 1935, as head of a school that he believed was the institutional embodiment of his ideas about religion and culture. I have suggested earlier that Bergendoff never worked all the kinks out of these views and that, at least at points, they were perhaps not entirely shared by other Lutheran theologians and historians. Some critics might even have wondered whether at moments Bergendoff had lapsed into a view of the relationship between the Christian gospel and human society that was tinged with Calvinism. But Bergendoff believed that Augustana College and Theological Seminary was the visible expression of these ideas, and his objections to separation were ultimately theoretical, not simply practical.

In a 1946 article in the *Lutheran Church Quarterly* Bergendoff, then filling a term as the President of the American Association of Theological Schools, had spoken of the current state of Lutheran education for the ministry: "There is something musty about some . . . Lutheran theological training—as if fresh air had for long not been let into these realms." When he visited the seminaries he got a feeling "akin to that which descends upon me when I visit people in the eighties and nineties, who dwell amidst their trinkets and the tokens of an era long, long ago." [105] The mustiness you could sniff in Lutheran seminaries was, Bergendoff believed, to a considerable degree the result of their separation from the wider fields of learning. He was no friend of the secular versions of the arts and sciences dominating the contemporary university world, but it was just for that reason that he felt the Church's seminary and its liberal arts colleges must stay together. In 1947 he wrote again in the *Lutheran Companion*: "It is for the Church's sake that I have sought to integrate the programs of the College with the Seminary. On the front of higher education the Church meets the most insidious of its foes." He warned, "If our forces are divided and out of contact with each other on this front, neither the College nor the Seminary will be able to witness powerfully against the hosts of wickedness in high places."

Implicit in that 1947 plea, written at a time when the separation was essentially a *fait accompli,* is a view of the interrelatedness of all learning that had informed Bergendoff's work at Augustana for a decade and a half. "Some may not like the description Augustana College *and* Theological Seminary, but to my mind it expresses the faith of our Church that [all] truth stands in relationship to the revelation of Jesus Christ."[106]   G. Everett Arden noted that Bergendoff's election as Augustana president to succeed Gustav Andreen signaled a time of growing integration of the seminary and the college. Now, in a statement which was a sort of rear guard action in a campaign already decided against him, Bergendoff spelled out again his belief that theology must both inform and be informed by the wider arts and sciences. His view of the relationship between Christianity and human society remained unshaken, though the Synod seems not to have been persuaded. The seminary faculty in Rock Island, just up the hill from his office, and the leadership in Minneapolis Church headquarters, now four hundred miles from the one-time capital of Swedish-American Lutheranism, went about their business respectful of Bergendoff's opinions. They were given full expression in the Church's weekly. But they were not going to prevail.

In his President's Report for the 1947-48 academic year, Bergendoff spoke even more directly. What had taken eighty-six years to create had been torn down by just two years of Synod action. Bergendoff simply would not acknowledge the length or the strength of the move to separate. He spoke of a "sudden" decision and "just two years of Synod action." And then, continuing, "That it should fall to my lot to conclude this chapter of Augustana history was not imagined when I accepted the Synod call to become president in 1935 of an institution which had been one as long as the Synod itself." History was on his side: "Every one of my predecessors—Esbjörn, Hasselquist, Olsson, Andreen—the men we honor this Centennial year—had wrought and fought for the unity of the program of higher education." Bergendoff understood himself to stand in that succession: "Convinced, as they were, that the progress of college and seminary went together and that the success of one aided the other I have worked for 17 years to give outward expression to that idea that the Christian faith gives a wholeness of interpretation of the truth which no university can give except it confess that faith."[107]

At the 1948 convention of the Synod, held in Rock Island to commemorate the centennial of the Swedish immigration to the Middle West, a motion to rescind the separation was offered, but it lost, 424-493.[108] While Bergendoff was preparing his statements and probably consulting with others who had opposed the separation and who still sought to un-do it, the new seminary Board of Directors went about electing Karl Mattson, President of the New England Conference (and Conrad Bergendoff's brother-in-law), as seminary president. After approval by the Synod convention, Mattson took office in September, 1948.[109] He had written to Bergendoff assuring him that he had no intention of putting up "a spiritual or literal hedge around the Seminary Campus."[110]

To read the Church publications, minutes, letters, and the later scholarly treatments of this episode in the Synod's history is to gain the impression that the division of the college and seminary was almost inevitable. But as 1948 drew near and at a time when it was already clear that the forces favoring the separation would prevail, Bergendoff had gone about the business of representing the seminary, of which he was still president, as though the present arrangements would continue indefinitely. For example, in the June 4, 1947, number of the *Lutheran Companion,* he reported that the enrollment of twenty first-year seminarians at Augustana compared acceptably with enrollments at the ULCA seminaries in Philadelphia (21) and Gettysburg (22). Augustana Seminary had one of the best physical plants in the country, he wrote, though it did need a new library. He also noted that "the President of the Seminary" was serving a year as president of the national association of theological schools.[111]

Bergendoff's strategy seemed, at least here, to treat the possibility of separation with less seriousness than it in fact deserved. While the debate was heating up in the forties, he did not publicly acknowledge the weight of the arguments advanced by the other colleges, nor did he seem to appreciate the depth of their advocates' sense that his college did not deserve the preferential position implied in its status as the only *synodical* college. Nor did he seem to be persuaded by their sense that an arrangement whereby congregations in Kansas had to support both Bethany and Augustana, or those in Minnesota both Gustavus Adolphus and Augustana, was unfair. To him these were "petty regional factors[.]"[112] One recalls that Plato had treated the problem of evil by calling it *me on,* non-being: ultimately, though it seemed to, evil did not exist. That is almost how in the lead-up to 1948 Bergendoff treated his opponents' plans—as though they did not exist—even as those plans matured and were carried out.

But once it was done, Bergendoff could not overcome his deep disappointment at the separation. He told P. O. Bersell that it was "like a knife cutting through my dreams and plans for Augustana." Any chance of developing the school into a small Lutheran university, perhaps like Valparaiso over in Indiana, had gone a-glimmering. This was a repudiation of Bergendoff's leadership of higher education in the Synod, "a shaking of my whole educational philosophy." He wrestled with his feelings constantly: "I pray daily for peace and that God would take all bitterness out of my heart[.]"[113] Now Bersell, who one biographer says was often thought to have an "unemotional, sphinxlike personality,"[114] took on the role of counselor, writing to Bergendoff that he must not "bring in the personal element." "I cannot follow you when you say that it is 'the shaking of your whole educational philosophy[.]'" And, also a practical churchman, the Synod President added: "I have heard it said over and over again that Bergendoff can personally have anything he wants of the Augustana Synod."[115] Bergendoff too remembered that: Bersell had told someone in his Minneapolis office that "The only man I cannot do anything with down there in Rock Island is the president of the college and seminary."[116] One wonders whether that comment by Bersell reflected a degree of *avundsjuka* (*avund* – envy; *sjuka* – sickness); or was Bersell ever so slightly *hånande* (taunting)? Whatever Bersell meant, for Bergendoff that was just the point: the one thing he most wanted just then was to keep the college and the seminary under a single administration—his. And that is what he could not have.

Further, the decision to separate attacked Bergendoff's sense that he understood the Synod and that, with whatever suitable modesty, he was the spokesman for its long tradition and deepest values. The matter *was* personal. And Bergendoff never understood why the President of Synod had raised the question when he did: "Usually Bersell was pretty astute and I don't quite see why he insisted on it at that time. There was no particular reason for it at that time."[117] It left Bergendoff "confused about my future in the Synod." He was not sure he knew its mind.[118] It was not only his educational philosophy and his vision for Augustana that were threatened. As Bergendoff saw it, his long years of loyalty and service and his sense of the history and ethos of the Augustana Synod had been put into question. And he continued to feel that he had been blind-sided: "In other words the thing was settled before I was even brought in on it. They probably knew how I felt, but that's no reason why I shouldn't have been consulted."[119]

Permanent Opposition

In a nasty irony, all of this came at a time when Dr. Bergendoff was President of the nation's Association of Theological Schools. He was, of course, given the choice by the Synod of either presidency, college or seminary. Both Bersell and the faculty of the seminary hoped that he would decide to be its president.[120] Bergendoff's loyalty to the Synod, damaged, but certainly not destroyed by the action of the convention to separate the seminary and college, might have prompted him to remain with the seminary. In 1943 he had written: "In my own mind there is no doubt about the most important single institution of our Synod—without hesitation I say that it is our Theological Seminary."[121] But five years later he decided for the college. His statement to the new seminary Board reflected his disappointment: "For seventeen years the Synod has had no occasion to complain of maladministration in the Seminary. For Synod then suddenly to make this drastic change in the structure of the institution without either any clear reason for the change or any clear objective to be realized by the change, leaves me without any other program for the Seminary than I have pursued all these years." Everyone in the Church had always understood what he had worked for, Bergendoff continued, but clearly that was no longer so. "I have no other alternative but to abide by my decision and to ask to be relieved of further responsibility for the administration of the Seminary."[122]

When the deed was done and the separation finalized in 1948, Dr. Bergendoff got dozens of letters of sympathy and support from the Augustana College faculty. To read the file that still contains the many notes that he saved is to think for a moment you are reading messages of condolence following a funeral. There are pledges of undying loyalty to the college president from History Department chairman O. F. Ander (who was not always quite so faithful), aspersions on the motives of Bergendoff's opponents from Religion Department head V. R. Pearson (who was himself one of the Synod clergy), and elegant sentences marveling at ecclesiastical intrigue from English Department chairwoman H. C. K. Naeseth (who also took the opportunity to get in her request for additional departmental staff). From the Lutheran seminary at Gettysburg came a job offer: "Why not give yourself some release from the burdens of administration and get yourself a chance to do some of that writing you have so long wanted to do!"[123] Apparently the ULCAers in the East saw a chance finally to swoop in and take Bergendoff from the Midwestern Swedes. Those tempting invitations he resisted.

The Rock Island *Argus* was also interested in what was going on over at the campus on the east end of town. To an inquiry from a local reporter about a recent action taken by the seminary Board, Bergendoff coolly replied, "I am not a member of the Seminary Board. I yet do not know what that Board did. . . . Under the circumstances I think a protest might be lodged with the Seminary Board for not giving the local papers the story."[124] A year later at the Minneapolis Synod convention he told the delegates that the move had been a "serious mistake."[125]   That's how he continued to regard it.   All the Synod President could say in response to a letter from Bergendoff reflecting his on-going distress at the separation was that "I am exceedingly sorry about the general attitude your recent note suggests[.]"[126]

To a colleague at the *Christian Century* Bergendoff wrote after the fact that "The few clear arguments advanced for the separation were all in the field of administration, some believing that the Seminary would receive more attention when separated from the College, and its appeal made more direct to the Church."[127]   But having made his choice to be President of Augustana College, Bergendoff began to think and write particularly about the role of laymen and women in the church.   It was a theme that had always been important to him, but now it had particular relevance.   In 1947, as it appeared that the separation was going to occur, Bergendoff translated a Swedish work written in the early twentieth century, *Our Calling (Vår kallelse)* by Einar Billing, in which the implications of Luther's doctrine of the priesthood of all believers were worked out.[128]   (The alternative was, of course, the more exclusive idea that only ordained men exercised the priestly office.)   In *Lutheran Quarterly* articles in 1949 and 1951, Bergendoff stressed the need to reassert this view of the priesthood of all believers and to flesh out further its implications for the Christian's role in modern society.[129]   One shadow side to the Augustana Synod's heritage for Bergendoff was that, like the Church of Sweden, his Synod had "given little room for the laity in the government of the church."[130]   In this sense the Synod held a "high" doctrine of the ministry; for example, a congregation without a pastor was not allowed to vote in the annual convention of the Church.[131]   Now Bergendoff was sympathetic with the strand in Lutheranism which had understood the office of the ministry itself as deriving from the doctrine of the priesthood of all believers rather than a counter view, which believed the ministry to be directly instituted by Christ and therefore not dependent on the congregation of lay persons for its authority.[132]   Of course, an undergraduate college would play a central role in preparing lay Christians as well as the clergy they appointed to be their pastors.

In *Augustana: A Profession of Faith,* Bergendoff did belatedly recognize that "Some did feel that Augustana was in a favored situation as a 'synodical' institution," and then added, "but these hardly recognized that in some respects the college suffered because of the wider interest in the seminary."[133]   That, written in 1969, was a twist on the arguments of the "seminary separatists" who believed that it was the seminary which suffered from neglect. The issue would remain troubling for the rest of Bergendoff's life.   G. Everett Arden writes that "This episode stirred the temper and emotions of the Synod as nothing else had done, perhaps, since the Waldenström controversy in the preceding century."

He continues, "In the heat of the debate words were spoken, accusations were made, threats were hurled, and pressures were exerted which caused rifts and wounds which will remain as long as some of the active participants are among the living."[134]   In 2010 Nils Hasselmo, a scholar and Augustana graduate who over the years had come to know the president emeritus well, wrote that the episode "seemed to have been a bitter experience, the pain of which had not dissipated even after all these years[.]"[135]

So Conrad Bergendoff never reconciled himself to the divorce. In his own words in 1977: "Augustana [Seminary] had a very good reputation, and all of a sudden to put the ax to it—I didn't understand. I still don't."[136]   Of course the seminary faculty and the proponents of separation did not think the seminary had been chopped down, "the ax put to it." And in a longer view, the matter was about a seminary-college relationship that was not to be long-lived anyway. It concerned a period of about fifteen years, for in 1962 the Rock Island seminary, together with seminaries from the other synods which were forming the Lutheran Church in America, was merged into the Lutheran School of Theology at Chicago, a new institution to be located near the University of Chicago. In his President's Report for 1948, Bergendoff, perhaps in unintentional but prophetic mode, had said that the inevitable result of the 1948 decision would be "the removal of the Seminary to another location." It was in a sense a strange comment for him to make, if by it he implied that such a removal would be negative, for he had himself at moments suggested that a theological school combining the institutions of several American Lutheran synods should be built near a university.

In conversations recorded three decades later for Church archives by Glen C. Stone, Bergendoff recalled that he had wanted to use the joint college-seminary as "leverage" in negotiations over a merged Lutheran Church, though he did not indicate how that might have worked. Maybe he was thinking again about a Lutheran university. He also noted that "I think I said at the time that when we separate college and seminary it's the beginning of the end of the Augustana Church, which is exactly what happened. And should happen as far as that's concerned."[137]   So Bergendoff seems, perhaps indirectly, to have recognized that the separation of college and seminary had to be seen in the light of the wider trajectory of Lutheranism in America, one toward church merger and the integration of educational institutions. When that did occur, it was prompted more by the inter-Lutheran ecumenism that Bergendoff so ardently supported for theological reasons than it was by the Augustana separation of 1948 he so ardently opposed, also for theological reasons.

For the new LCA to maintain three or four seminaries in separate middle western locations, each representing one of the merging synods, was not going to be. In any case, the seminary buildings in Rock Island were bought by the college and used for academic, administrative, and student housing purposes. The chapel continues as a place of worship, now for undergraduates. Augustana kept the seminary's buildings—if not its program. But administration, finances, and buildings were never the core issue for Bergendoff. In this, the most significant defeat of his long career in the Augustana Evangelical Lutheran Church, Conrad Bergendoff, once he became President of Augustana College and Theological Seminary, had argued for the institutional embodiment of a particular view of the relationship of Christianity to culture and for the unity of all knowledge. Those were ideas that had informed his life since his own college and seminary days. They trumped his read of the Synod's mood and leadership, his sense of collegiality with the other Synod colleges, and even to some degree his Lutheran ecumenism, which until he became President of Augustana had led him to agree on the need for a strong united pan-Lutheran theological school in the Middle West. Six decades later one comes away from sifting through the now-cold ashes of this controversy with the impression that for Bergendoff it was all about a theological-educational issue: "the Lordship of Christ over higher learning." In his mind, practical concerns were of little importance compared to that.

Perhaps as residue of the debate over the independence of the seminary, Bergendoff also experienced resistance from the Synod over the question of membership on the Augustana Board of Directors. That matter developed concurrently with the seminary-college issue. The President of the College was not a voting member of its Board; the constitution stipulated that he was "advisory." When the college-seminary separation took place, Bergendoff asked—with the support of the Board—that the President of the College be made a voting member of that Board. "The idea that the president is an employee of the Board, and that all the faculty members are employees of the Board, is a policy derived from American business corporations. But a college is not a bank or an insurance company."[138] He resisted the implication that directors and faculty were in some sense opposed: "I vigorously protest against the idea of setting faculty and Board against each other, as if [the faculty] has to be kept in control by the Board."[139] But in 1950, when the proposal got to the floor of the Synod annual convention, it lost. Bergendoff reported back to the campus that "No fight had been made on this point."[140] The President of the Illinois Conference assured Bergendoff that the refusal to grant him voting Board membership "is not based on any lack of confidence in the president now or in the future." We are left to speculate on why the Church resisted making the change, but not until the creation of the LCA and Bergendoff's retirement from the school, was the President of the College made a voting

Board member.[141] Perhaps the simplest explanation of the change itself is that it came when a new Church, a new Board of Directors, and a new President of the College were in place. At Augustana there were many carry-overs from its years as a school of the Synod, but the persistent unwillingness to make the President of the College a member of the Board was not one of them. Whatever the objections to that had been, they evaporated in 1962.

§

It is impossible to imagine Bergendoff accepting the theoretical and theological implications of the 1948 separation. But neither can one picture him abandoning the Augustana Synod in response to it. As he addressed twentieth century human life and twentieth century Christianity, he stood firmly on an understanding of himself and of society that he had formed in the Swedish-American Lutheran community. But ironically, the Synod was both the source of the strongest convictions of his life and the cause of the deepest disappointment of his career. Both were inextricably bound up with Augustana College *and* (till 1948) Theological Seminary. The next chapter will address the questions of how Bergendoff interpreted his Synod's relationship to other American Lutherans and what he thought about the role a unified American Lutheranism might play in a nation and world that he believed to be careening toward ever greater disasters. These were catastrophes beside which panty raids and even institutional separations paled.

Salem Lutheran Church (Augustana Synod), Chicago. Though theirs was perhaps the finest Lutheran sanctuary in the city, the congregation, when planning and building it, had to calm the concerns of other Lutherans on the South Side that the neighborhood was being over-built with churches of their denomination(s).

CHAPTER 6

LUTHERAN UNITY

Conrad Bergendoff generally preferred to look for the strands of continuity that ran through history, especially that of the Christian Church. But with regard to his Synod's attitude and relationship to other Christians, including Lutherans, he recognized that an important and dramatic shift had occurred between the first and the second halves of Augustana Synod history. In the centennial year 1960 he spoke of "The transition from an older Augustana, suspicious in its dealings with non-Lutheran church bodies and cautious in relations with Lutheran Synods in America, to a synod friendly in its attitude toward other Protestants and active in furthering co-operation within Lutheranism[.]" This represented not simply an effort to relate to other American Lutherans in formal organizations, but "the breaking-away from an isolationist policy of non-co-operation with other non-Lutheran bodies, and a conscientious entrance into participation with Christians of other denominations in common interests."[1]

The writer was uniquely entitled to make such statements because he had been one of the principal advocates for this outreach. In fact, at some moments Bergendoff had played a critical role in influencing a shift in Synod opinion in favor of specific steps, not simply toward informal friendliness with other church bodies, but aimed at eventual merger with other Lutherans and at formal association with ecumenical organizations, American and international. And when the Augustana Church committed itself to merger negotiations with other American Lutherans, he was one of the major participants in the talks. If the separation of the college and the theological seminary represented the major defeat of his long and loyal membership in the Synod, his ecumenical work perhaps represented his major success.

Early Augustana Ecumenism

As the Bergendoff statements just quoted suggest, the early decades of Augustana history were marked by very cautious inter-church contacts, even with other American Lutherans. Two associations or confederations of Lutheran groups had developed in the course of the nineteenth century, and Swedish-American Lutherans had at moments been associated with both. The Evangelical Lutheran General Synod was formed in the eastern states in 1820. Bergendoff noted that by the Civil War the General Synod was made up of bodies that included two-thirds of the 235,000 Lutherans in the United States.[2] One of its leading figures was Samuel Simon Schmucker (1799-1873), the founder of Gettysburg Seminary. He advocated modifying the classical Lutheran creedal statements in an effort to fit European Lutheranism to American ideas and conditions. Bergendoff was not favorably disposed to Schmucker who, he wrote, "became enamored of an American spirit that spent its energy in a vague ambition to unite the Protestant churches to counteract the Church of Rome." That was "spineless Lutheranism." Schmucker had "failed to see that the course of Lutheranism was not an imitation of revivalist practices and confessional indifference."[3]

When they first arrived in the US, several Swedish Lutheran pastors, including L. P. Esbjörn and T. N. Hasselquist, did for a time associate with the General Synod. That was through joining and taking support from the Synod of Northern Illinois, one of the member bodies of the larger national group. But after Esbjörn's 1860 withdrawal from the joint Lutheran educational venture at Illinois State University in Springfield and the subsequent founding of the Augustana Synod, the Swedes grew increasingly opposed to the "American Lutheranism" represented by the General Synod and Schmucker. Bergendoff saw Esbjörn and his compatriots as part of the tide of Germans, Norwegians, and others who swept American Lutheranism toward stronger confessionalism, a commitment to classical Lutheran theology, rather than toward accommodation to existing American religious life and thinking.[4]

Ten years after the 1860 formation of their own Synod, the Swedish immigrants associated with a second group, set up by more conservative Lutherans, many of them in what was then the "West." This was the General Council, established just after the Civil War, and it subscribed to the *Unaltered Augsburg Confession*. It was meant as a counterweight to what the conservatives saw as the doctrinally relaxed General Synod. If the latter had emphasized the "practical life of the church," the General Council, wrote Bergendoff, focused upon theology and doctrine.⁵ Its "Principles of Faith and Church Polity" (1867) was a documentary declaration meant to contrast with the *Definite Synodical Platform* (1855) of Schmucker and his allies, which had rejected such traditional Lutheran concepts as baptismal regeneration and the real presence of Christ in the Lord's Supper. Bergendoff saw the development of the General Council as a return to the strict orthodoxy of the Swedish Lutherans who settled along the Delaware River in the seventeenth century. Those Swedes, along with their German and Dutch fellow Lutherans, had been "clearly confessional."⁶ Their settlements had, of course, gradually been absorbed by surrounding colonists; their Lutheranism also disappeared and the churches became Episcopalian. But confessionalism revived, and most of post-Civil War Lutheranism, said Bergendoff, "refused to conform to contemporary culture."⁷ As we have seen, when Bergendoff said that, it usually signified his approval.

The *Unaltered* Augsburg Confession to which the Synod's founders had subscribed and which Bergendoff steadily insisted was the adequate and the sole grounds upon which American Lutherans must agree for union or merger between their myriad councils, synods, and churches had, of course, a long history. Written not by Luther but by his trusted colleague Philipp Melanchthon (1497-1560), the document had been presented in 1530 to the Emperor Charles V in the south German city whose name it bore. Meant to explain the position of the Lutherans, it was part of an effort to unite the religiously divided German princes in the face of the Turkish threat to Europe from the east. (Luther himself was still officially an outlaw in the Holy Roman Empire and as such could not come to Augsburg.) While a "studiously measured statement which he [Melanchthon] hoped would be acceptable to moderate Catholic opinion," the summary of Lutheran teaching did not produce the hoped for concord. Instead, says a leading contemporary British church historian, it found "a new career as the 'Augsburg Confession', theological cornerstone for a new branch of Christendom[.]"⁸ Melanchthon's irenic effort at compromise did not, however, conceal the document's strong commitment to the doctrine of justification by faith and its rejection of certain practices of the medieval church such as clerical celibacy, the Mass as the repeated sacrifice of Christ's death, the necessity of confession, invocation of the saints, denial of the cup in Communion, and monastic vows.

But these were not the teachings of the Augsburg Confession which came most into dispute among nineteenth century American Lutherans. Schmucker's revision, published in his *Definite Platform,* indicated that Melanchthon's original document contained five errors: the approval of the Mass, the permitting of private confession, the denial of the obligation to observe the Sabbath, the assertion of baptismal regeneration, and the affirmation of the real presence of Christ in Communion. Within years the majority of American Lutherans, beginning in the East and spreading to the Middle West, had rejected Schmucker's alterations to what they understood to be true Lutheranism, and a document which three centuries earlier had been intended as a moderate statement of Protestant teaching, steering a course between Rome and the more left-leaning Reformers, had become the battlement behind which a revival of Lutheran orthodoxy occurred among Lutherans in the new land.[9] When a Lutheran congregation erected a new sanctuary, it often inscribed "UAC" on its cornerstone, and countless aging buildings in the American heartland are still mute witness to the determination of their laymen and pastors to remain true to the "Unaltered Augsburg Confession." It was this rejection of "spineless Lutheranism" that Conrad Bergendoff treated as the founding principle of his own Synod.

But by the turn of the century, the threat of Schmucker's compromise had for the most part passed, and American Lutherans settled into certain newer alignments. Augustana would remain affiliated with the General Council until the latter, having settled its differences with the General Synod, joined with it to form the United Lutheran Church in America in 1918. By that time it was clear that the position on the far right of American Lutheranism had been firmly occupied by Lutherans of the Missouri Synod, a body of German-American origin that regarded almost all other Lutherans with reservations as to their orthodoxy and that for the most part kept itself clear of any entanglements with them. Missouri formed its own cohort, the Synodical Conference, in 1872. The two major groups in that alliance, which finally dissolved in the early 1960s, were the Missouri Synod and the smaller Wisconsin Synod, though for a time one Norwegian-American group did belong to it. General Synod-General Council-Missouri Synod: that was the topography of the American Lutheran landscape in the first half century of the Augustana Synod's existence, until the point when the Swedish Americans began to realize that the time had come to seek tighter ties and perhaps even organic union with other Lutherans.

One possibility for the Augustana Synod would have been to join the new United Lutheran Church in America (ULCA) in 1918. That Church was formed from the General Council, the General Synod, and the General Synod, South (created as a result of a split at the time of the Civil War). Bergendoff, right then" studying in the East, attended the New York meetings where the ULCA had been born and reported sympathetically on them in the *Lutheran Companion*. He agreed with the Governor of New York's assessment that this had been "the greatest religious event of the year" and noted happily that the new Church was not condescending toward the Scandinavian-American

Lutheran bodies.[10] *The Lutheran*, a periodical of the General Council, was not so generous when the Swedish-American Lutherans declined to join; the journal said that Augustana had "subordinated unity of faith to unity of race" when it stayed out of the ULCA merger.[11] That referred to Augustana's assertion that it must continue as a separate body in order to minister to immigrant Swedes. An historian of American religion, Robert T. Handy, writes of American Lutherans collectively that they "had to focus much of their efforts on meeting the needs of the newcomers, and in trying to find proper organizational forms for their sprawling, diversified, theologically strict movement."[12] In that light the Augustana reticence to merge into the ULCA is not uncharacteristic, especially of Lutherans in the Middle West. For his part, Bergendoff was gratified that the ULCA had a deep commitment to "the larger ideal of a church as one against the non-Christian views in movements in the nation or other Christian organizations." One supposes that "other Christian organizations" referred to the variety of Protestantism that at this early stage in his career Bergendoff already regarded as a sell-out to liberalism and secularism. He also remarked approvingly on the hope within the ULCA that it would be able to merge itself into a "truly United Lutheran Church in America."[13]

In the long and labyrinthine maneuvers toward Lutheran unity during the following decades, Bergendoff continued to treat the ULCA merger of 1918 as paradigmatic. That was because the ULCA held to the Unaltered Augsburg Confession and accepted as legitimate the attestations of loyalty to it by the merging Lutheran parties. But a concern for the continuing spiritual needs of Swedish immigrants and their descendants and fear that the new ULCA might be too liberal prevailed in the Augustana Synod, and it stayed out of the 1918 merger. For Bergendoff, "language and structure peculiarities" were the factors that kept Augustana from joining.[14] "Language" meant the larger question of the ethnic ministry of the Synod, and "structure" probably referred to the fact that Augustana had a more centralized form of government than the new ULCA, in which regional bodies were predominant. In 1924 the young pastor wrote that the reason for the Synod's continuing "independent position" even toward other American Lutherans was its desire to preserve "the spirit of the Swedish church as it expresses itself in Sweden's best days and personalities."[15] An American church historian, non-Lutheran, non-Scandinavian, and presumably neutral, writes that "In this wrestling with transplanted nationalism the Lutherans provided the principal object lesson."[16] But for Augustana it was not simply loyalty to its Swedish roots, but a sense of mission to Swedish speaking immigrants and a respect for their heritage from the Church of Sweden that led the Synod to maintain an independent identity in 1918.

Augustana did, however, join the National Lutheran Council, a loose confederation of Lutheran bodies that had dual origins: in plans to celebrate the four hundredth anniversary of Luther's Ninety-five Theses and in joint Lutheran efforts to minister to servicemen at home and in Europe. The Luther anniversary celebration in the U.S was somewhat dampened because of anti-German sentiments awakened by World War I, but the Council's post-war efforts focused on European relief, national publicity, the gathering of statistical information, and work in the growing industrial urban areas of the country. Most of the ethnic and regional Lutheran bodies, the Missouri Synod excepted, joined.[17]

Fault Lines and Theses

The major fault line running through the National Lutheran Council lay between the new United Lutherans and the also-newly-formed Norwegian Lutheran Church in America (1917). The Norwegian Americans, many of whom were stout confessionalists, were suspicious that the ULCA paid only lip service to the Lutheran Confessions. The Norwegian Americans developed doctrinal statements intended as tests to be taken by the latter as proof of confessional orthodoxy. The most important of these doctrinal test statements originated with H. G. Stub (1849-1931), President of the Norwegian Lutheran Church and, according to historian Mark Granquist, "strongly inclined toward the Missouri Synod and a strict Lutheran confessionalism."[18] The first of these tests was known as the Chicago Theses (1919). Not content with it, Stub and his allies issued a revised and more explicit standard, the "Minneapolis Theses," (1925). Beyond insisting upon strict confessional loyalty, the 1925 version added statements against lodge membership and supporting an inerrant view of biblical inspiration. Tellingly, the Chicago statement had received support in the pages of the Missouri Synod's official newspaper.[19] A counter statement, named after its authors (who were leaders of the ULCA), the Knubel-Jacobs Theses, embraced a more ecumenical position. Based on a paper entitled "The Essentials of a Catholic Spirit" by F. H. Knubel (1870-1945), President of the ULCA, these 1920 theses held that no signed agreements beyond the historic Lutheran Confessions should be needed to demonstrate true Lutheran identity and that no one Lutheran group had any grounds for doubting the sincerity of any other in this matter.[20]

The position taken in the Knubel-Jacobs Theses was the one Bergendoff held consistently through the decades. His sympathetic report on the 1918 creation of the United Lutheran Church was early evidence of these views. Bergendoff platted this ground in a 1937 article for the *Augustana Quarterly*: one Lutheran body could judge another simply by its official declarations. If it were said that a certain body's actions betrayed its confession, then there could be no unity even on a local level, for failure to live up to a profession of faith was the bane of congregational as well as denominational life. Further, Bergendoff concluded that a careful reading of the Minneapolis Theses of the Norwegian Church and of the ULCA's constitution revealed no doctrinal differences; the two bodies "may be considered as united in faith." Bergendoff was "more interested in unity than in a rationalization of divisions."[21]

Some of the tensions that continued between Lutheran bodies in the United States, Bergendoff believed, could be traced to the fact that they were overly preoccupied with theological and doctrinal questions. That was particularly true of their seminaries, whose strength—concern for theological clarity—was also their weakness. Too quickly the separate Lutheran denominations, each with its own theological school, assumed they possessed the full Christian revelation. And they gave narrow scope to that revealed truth. So much of their writing came from controversy that Lutherans did not know "how to state Christian doctrine without assuming an attitude almost pugnacious. Speaking truth in love is still an unattained art among us."[22]

But agreement could be reached on a much simpler basis. In the 1952 *Lutheran Companion,* Bergendoff offered his definition of a Lutheran: a person who subscribed to the Augsburg Confession. According to that document, "It is enough to agree concerning the doctrine of the Gospel and the administration of the Sacraments." It was not necessary to reach concord on "every minute interpretation of every problem in the Bible." In fact, to ask for this was to be untrue to the Lutheran Confessions and to make sanctification rather than justification the central doctrine of Lutheranism.[23] We determined in Chapter 3 that Bergendoff's view of sanctification shifted from time to time, but that, as Chapter 2 suggested, his understanding of justification remained steady—from his early years as a pastor through his long retirement. He would not hold fellow Lutherans to more consistency than he himself managed in these questions, so variation on sanctification was permissible, while agreement on justification was essential. Bergendoff began his series of 1956 Lectures on "The Doctrine of the Church in American Lutheranism" with the declaration that the most significant result of three centuries of Lutheranism in America was "a common attitude toward the confessions of the Lutheran Church."[24]

We have seen and shall see that many American Lutheran bodies, including Bergendoff's own, had at moments doubted the Lutheran bona fides of other ones. Following the promulgation of the Chicago-Minneapolis Theses and the countervailing Knubel-Jacobs Theses, one of the Scandinavian bodies might accuse another of straying from the straight and narrow. But for the century of Bergendoff's life no one Lutheran denomination so regularly insisted that the others demonstrate their fidelity to the confessions as did the Lutheran Church, Missouri Synod. Breathing some of the intensity of their Saxon German ancestors and certain of their own fidelity to an earlier Saxon, Luther himself, the founders of the Missouri Synod and their heirs occupied the conservative end of the American Lutheran spectrum. When Conrad Bergendoff expressed his hope for the union of all American Lutherans, he included the Missouri Lutherans.[25] In fact, he had succeeded in 1942 in gathering a conclave of Lutheran theologians at Augustana which, along with members of the American Lutheran Conference and the United Lutheran Church, included professors from the Missouri Synod.[26] But he knew that Missouri joining any merger with Augustana, let alone the United Lutherans, was unlikely. That was clear at that 1942 meeting in Rock Island, where he had been concerned about whether the Missouri representatives would even agree to worship together with their Lutheran brothers.[27]

The Augustana president had already spoken to the questions that lay between the Lutheran Church, Missouri Synod, (LCMS) and other Lutherans. In 1939 Bergendoff defended his Synod's teaching and practice against Missouri doubts about them in an article "Here We Stand!" in the *Companion*. It was with regard to the Missouri Synod's attempts to set the standard for intra-Lutheran fellowship that he was most pointed: "I question the method of attaining fellowship which consists in one party offering a document to the other to be signed on the dotted line." Further, "You treat us as non-Lutherans. We resent it."[28] Bergendoff always insisted, contra Missouri, that no doctrine of scriptural inspiration beyond that in the Augsburg Confession was needed. In a 1945 letter he wrote that Missouri persisted in subscribing to a very narrow idea of biblical inspiration. "I shall continue to teach that the Augustana Synod should refuse to try to put the truth of inspiration into some strait-jacket formula." Further: "Faith in Christ was present long before there was any definition of inspiration. Indeed, one's attitude toward inspiration is determined by faith in Christ; faith is not dependent on a theory."[29]

In 1961, as the Lutheran Church in America was being formed, Bergendoff addressed Missouri Synod concerns about Augustana's ecumenical ties. He noted that in the Connecticut town where he grew up there had been Missouri and Augustana congregations, "but there was no more fellowship between these two Lutheran churches than if the Baltic Sea had separated them." (It had their ancestors.)   Bergendoff hoped that a new attitude toward other Christians, Lutheran and non, would develop in the Missouri Synod and suggested that "drawing a confessional curtain between ourselves and all other Christians is a sign of weakness rather than strength." But even while writing this, Bergendoff called himself one of the Missouri Synod's "admirers" and recognized it as a part of the American Lutheran community.[30]   To many Christians outside of that circle, the Missouri Synod was not that admirable. An English ecumenist and church historian writes of the LCMS that it "has proved a serious obstacle to union even among Lutherans." She continues that it "has taken up a rigidly confessional and uncooperative position on the basis of all the Lutheran symbolic books, and refuses to enter into any kind of co-operation or union with the World Council or any other body, such as would in its view compromise the revelation of truth which it has received through the Holy Scriptures in their Lutheran interpretation."[31]

In all of his own comments on Missouri, Bergendoff stuck to the simple view that if one said he agreed with the *Confessio Augustana* that was good enough; no further demonstration of true Lutheranism was needed. At one

Bergendoff being awarded an honorary doctorate at Concordia Seminary, St. Louis, 1967.

point he even turned the tables, arguing it was those who demanded more than this who were really the ones in violation of the Lutheran Confessions.[32] He did get a number of letters from leaders in the United Lutheran Church congratulating him on his "frank and kindly" reply to questions from the Missouri Synod. They agreed that he had "hit the nail on the head" when he insisted that no one group of Lutherans could determine what all others must believe.[33] In spite of these difficulties, however, Bergendoff maintained all his life that he personally had enjoyed cordial relationships with many Missouri leaders and seemed proud of having received an honorary degree from the Missouri Lutheran seminary in St. Louis.[34]

Suspicions between Lutherans did not go away, however, regardless of personal friendships and honorary degrees. For the more conservative church bodies one of the troubling tendencies in the more liberal ones was their alleged "unionism." Both elements in the National Lutheran Council rejected unionism, but in the conservatives' minds the fact that the United Lutheran Church and to a degree the Augustana Synod were involved in ecumenical relationships with non–Lutherans belied their protestations of innocence. For his part, Bergendoff defined unionism as the effort to establish church fellowship in a way that ignored present doctrinal differences or treated them as unimportant. It made a "pretense of union which does not exist."[35] He recognized that in the Lutheran circles he moved in, "Unionism has come to be tinged, even as a word, by an ill-odor, and the Lutheran scholar needs watch his step when he discusses the topic, for the burden of proof is all on his shoulder, if he assays to proclaim that the unity of the church is also an article of the Lutheran Confession."[36] That was in a 1939 lecture delivered at Gettysburg Seminary, founded by S. S. Schmucker, a man whose over-all theological position Bergendoff rejected, but whose spirit of openness he did appreciate. So Bergendoff spoke, at least in this matter, to friends. He long held the view that "Granted that some unionism is not healthy, certainly it is not a wholesome symptom when parts of the Church glory in sectarianism, and publish to the world that they will have nothing to do with any other Christians."[37]

The Swedish-American scholar came from a tradition where the existence of a State Church which included almost all the national population meant that unionism had not really been an issue, of course. The opposition to unionism came "from conditions unknown to Lutherans of Scandinavian background, and to the latter the sharpness, even bitterness, of tone found in German Lutheran references to 'unionism' is somewhat puzzling."[38] That in Bergendoff's 1956 lectures before a United Lutheran audience, again among friends. The German conditions to which he referred included the 1817 government-enforced union of Lutheran and Calvinist churches in Prussia. The Nazis had also compelled the merger of Protestant denominations in the Third Reich. The "ill-odor" of such enforced unity was still in German-American Lutheran nostrils. Any approach to non-Lutheran Christians was likely, at least in some twentieth century American Lutheran quarters, to be regarded as unionism and thus grounds for suspicion, if not the breaking off of relationship with the offending church body. Bergendoff, of course, was not so put-off by it, though he did not, as we shall see, favor the pretense of union which did not exist.

Two Camps

But Bergendoff's views and voice did not dominate, either in the National Lutheran Council or in the Augustana Synod, and efforts at reaching theological unity in the Council failed. Within the NLC two camps settled into uneasy co-habitation. Augustana found itself in the middle, tugged at one moment and in some of its precincts toward the conservative Norwegians, at other times and places toward the United Lutherans. By 1930 tensions had not dissipated, and at a Minneapolis meeting the more conservative members of the National Lutheran Council agreed to form a new confederation, the American Lutheran Conference. It was this development that elicited from Bergendoff the articles in his own Synod's publications concerning what precisely constituted true Lutheranism that have just been discussed.

In any event, the National Lutheran Council continued to operate, while the Augustana Synod, along with Norwegians, Danes, and two German-American bodies, joined the new sub-group, the American Lutheran Conference. They maintained NLC membership as well. The two NLC camps now consisted of the Norwegian Americans and their allies on one side and the United Lutherans on the other. The Augustana Synod wavered between them. Thus, in the same year as the American Lutheran Conference, including Augustana, was formed, the Synod resolved to continue negotiating with the ULCA. Erling and Granquist write, "Augustana seemed to want to have it both ways[.]"[39] And their predecessor as Synod historian, G. Everett Arden, says, "The endeavor to face, as it were, in two directions at once, was perhaps ingenuous and naïve, but even in these early stages of inter-Lutheran relationships, Augustana assayed the role of intermediary[.]"[40] For his part, Bergendoff steadily maintained a view he first stated in 1933: the American Lutheran Conference would not endure so long as it intentionally excluded the United Lutheran Church.[41] At that point his predictive powers faltered, at least insofar as they covered the next two decades. Tensions, theological and otherwise, certainly did continue in the Conference; in fact at times, we are told, the Norwegian (-American) Lutherans resented "the pushiness of the Swedes," who wanted the ULCA included in any merger discussions. One historian, E. Clifford Nelson, says that in considering these tensions "sociological" matters were not to be underestimated; he seems to mean ethnic and personal factors.[42]

Of course, the Synod itself was not of one "ingenuous and naïve" mind on these questions. In fact, parties developed. One included important Synod leaders. It appeared that President P. O. Bersell and Editor of the *Lutheran Companion* E. E. Ryden tended toward the American Lutheran Conference and thought that the best hope for Augustana's merging with other bodies lay with the developing efforts of that Conference toward an organic union, minus the ULCA. In the late forties, in fact, the Synod was invited to join formally in negotiations aiming at a merger with the other American Lutheran Conference bodies. A Committee on Lutheran Unity was established by the Augustana Synod, and it met with the Joint Committee on Union that had been set up by the other four Conference denominations. After agreeing on the theological statement that the Joint Committee on Union had developed (one redolent of the conservative Chicago-Minneapolis Theses of 1919 and 1925), the Augustana negotiators surprisingly and almost simultaneously stated their desire that merger talks be open to all the members of the National Lutheran Council. That meant that the ULCA should be brought in, for that body made no secret of its long desire to be included. But the American Lutheran Conference bodies were not ready for that.

This was Augustana wanting it both ways, facing in two directions. For a second party had emerged within the Synod. These people's views were made clear in an April, 1952, *Lutheran Companion* article by S. E. Engstrom, Augustana's Executive Director of the Board of American Missions, who was by some irony to be elected President of the American Lutheran Conference seven months later. Engstrom argued that his Synod must stay committed to unity with *all* the members of the National Lutheran Council. If the American Lutheran Conference's Joint Committee on Union would not agree, Engstrom wrote, Augustana should open talks with the United Lutheran Church and any other bodies wishing to join them. (Two other groups, as it turned out, were interested: small Finnish and Danish churches.) For Engstrom the Augustana Church's ecumenical ties to the National and World Councils of Churches were crucial; it was likely that the American Lutheran Conference bodies, which had stayed out of ecumenical organizations up until then, would not permit those affiliations in any church they formed.[43] The Engstrom article also noted that while the National Lutheran Council was the inter-Lutheran agency where real work was being accomplished, the American Lutheran Conference was merely a "talking fraternity" and a "friendly debating society." As its president, he seemed entitled to say so.

These views stood in contrast to those of the Editor of the *Companion*, E. E. Ryden, who editorialized in favor of the American Lutheran Conference, asserting that its churches and Augustana had no doctrinal differences and had "arrived at complete agreement in all matters pertaining to faith, practice and life[.]"[44] There was, at least implicitly, some tension between Ryden, the Chairman of the Augustana College Board of Directors, and the President of the College on the question of which camp the Synod should now line up with. And the fact that they lived a few blocks apart in Rock Island as well could only have underlined their differences. Each of them, Ryden and Bergendoff, represented a strong body of opinion within the Synod about Lutheran unity.

The issue was joined. It was clear that the 1952 Synod convention, set for mid-June in Des Moines, would be centered upon the question. Which direction should the Synod take: the conservative American Lutheran Conference Joint Committee on Union or the more ecumenical and pan-Lutheran possibilities still beckoning through Augustana's ties to the National Lutheran Council and the United Lutheran Church? Conrad Bergendoff, certainly smarting from the 1948 defeat over the relationship of the college and seminary, had not been a member of the Augustana Committee on Lutheran Unity. But his ecumenical credentials were unquestionable, and he had by now demonstrated his willingness to live with Synod actions which he had opposed. The histories by Arden and by Erling and Granquist both make clear the crucial role Bergendoff played in Des Moines. In a certain sense that assembly represented the Augustana College president's reemergence into Synod life—at full throttle. He had swallowed his disappointment over 1948 and now addressed again a question with which he had been occupied since becoming an Augustana College Bachelor of Arts four decades previous: what would it take for American Lutheran unity?

The *Companion* article that reported on the Des Moines meeting included a photo of Conrad Bergendoff speaking forcefully into a microphone on the convention floor—and in the blazing Iowa heat that had even the newly elected President of the Church presiding in his shirt sleeves.[45] The Executive Council of the Synod had endorsed a recent theological statement, the United Testimony on Faith and Life, of the Joint Committee on Union of the American Lutheran Conference. That United Testimony essentially maintained the position taken three decades earlier in the Chicago and Minneapolis Theses. Bergendoff, at the time a member of neither that Synod Executive Council nor its Committee on Lutheran Unity, addressed head-on the issue implied in that endorsement of the United Testimony. To sign it would be to concede that "we have to prove that we *are* Lutherans." And: "We are never going to get anywhere in any unity negotiations if we must rewrite the confessional books of the Lutheran Church. What we must try to do is to get Lutherans to recognize Lutherans. Unity is not made; it is acknowledged." At his best when one of the fundamental assumptions on which his mindset and life path had been built was threatened, Bergendoff belled the cat: "To be brutally frank, the United Lutheran Church is left out purposely. How can we have union with one of the greatest Lutheran bodies in our country ignored?"[46]

The man who had sympathetically witnessed the creation of the ULCA and had studied a year at its Philadelphia seminary was not willing to watch his own denomination turn its back on that body, even in the interests of a union with other Scandinavians (some Germans also invited) in the Middle West. What Bergendoff hoped for was a new Lutheran Church that would include all the members of the National Lutheran Council. That meant, he recalled years later, consigning the Minneapolis Theses (and the United Testimony based on them) "to limbo where they belong."[47] Speaking for himself and his party, he affirmed at the microphone in sweltering Des Moines, that "we believe so strongly in the union of the entire Lutheran Church that we would prefer to wait longer for the real thing than to accept something else."[48]

However, the "real thing"—unity of *all* members of the National Lutheran Council—was not just around the bend. Still performing a balancing act, the

1952 Des Moines convention approved statements declaring that it agreed substantially with the United Testimony of the American Lutheran Conference, but that it was also "unwilling to continue in unity discussions which are not open to all Lutheran general bodies and which do not include the consideration of the subject of ecumenical relations."[49] By now Augustana was firmly involved in the modern ecumenical movement, the taint of "unionism" notwithstanding. So its unwillingness to give up its ties with non-Lutherans was taken by the American Lutheran Conference to mean that Augustana was not going to join its efforts, restricted as they were to those Lutherans whose orthodoxy had been certified by signing the United Testimony. By the end of the year, the division between Augustana and its erstwhile Scandinavian and German brethren of the American Lutheran Conference was clear. Now Conrad Bergendoff, fresh from demonstrating his influence at Des Moines, assumed a place on the new Augustana Committee on Lutheran Unity which would negotiate church merger. That committee was appointed by the Executive Council.[50] If in the process Bergendoff had reasserted his own role as a force in the Synod and carried the day against the inclinations of an Executive Council (led until his retirement a year ago by President Bersell) that four years earlier had thwarted his ideas about higher education, that was probably beside the point.

One might say that in the early days of the Augustana Synod, the dominant concern about the Augsburg Confession had been to keep it from being watered down (especially by Schmucker and his supporters). But by Bergendoff's time, especially with him and those who thought as he did, the concern was to keep zealous defenders of the Confession from adding to it—with statements of their own designed to test the orthodoxy of others (such as the ULCA) who claimed to adhere to it. The unexpected twist was that from having sought to keep the *Confessio Augustana* safe from those who sought to subtract from it, Augustana now began to be troubled by those who seemed to want to add to it.

ALC and LCA

In 1951 a new President of the Synod, Oscar A. Benson, had assumed the office held till then by P. O. Bersell. Bergendoff seems to have thought for a moment that he himself might be called upon to assume the Synod presidency, for he prepared a statement turning it down: "I have searched my heart and mind in seeking an answer to the call you ask me to accept." But, "I must decline[.]" Later across the top of the inked draft declining the offer he scrawled in pencil, "Not given—unnecessary!"[51] Many years afterwards in a taped interview, Bergendoff said of the effort to elect him, "The moment I saw it I said, 'I am not a candidate.' I didn't want it. I would not have accepted it."[52] No matter, for the new president, Oscar Benson, was in sympathy with the views

Bergendoff had expressed in Des Moines.

Benson made that clear in November, 1952, at a meeting in Minneapolis; his Church had not changed its stance about including all National Lutheran Council bodies in union talks. Nor would it give up its ecumenical memberships. In that Minneapolis meeting the American Lutheran Conference delegates expressed their "deep regret over the situation which has developed by the decisions of the Augustana Lutheran Church." But they were "without authority from their respective Church bodies to include all other Lutheran bodies in said negotiations." In response President Benson told the meeting that his hands were tied by the action of his Synod: "If and when our Church shall decide differently, we shall be at the service of the Church." He thanked the representatives of the other churches for the "forthrightness of your statement" and assured them that "we understand its implications." Then: "This is our valedictory for the moment. I suggest we be permitted to be excused so that you may go on with the work that is so important, and which, I pray God, may mean much for the days that lie ahead."[53] In the *Companion,* Ryden reported, "It was a solemn moment, and everyone present sensed its significance as the Augustana representatives arose and walked quietly from the conference chamber while the other committee members sat in silence."[54] Ryden himself had, of course, hoped that his Synod would stick with the other Midwesterners in the American Lutheran Conference.

These soft but certain tones with which Augustana left the American Lutheran Conference negotiations had in 1952 replaced the more forceful rhetoric of ecclesiastic and theological disagreement from earlier moments in Lutheran history (e.g. Luther-Erasmus or Hasselquist-Waldenström). But nonetheless the matter was settled. One historian of American Lutheranism, E. Clifford Nelson, says of the period that followed, "the events of the decade from 1952 to 1962 had all the elements of a Greek drama moving irreversibly to its denouement."[55] As a matter of principle the Synod could not for now cast its lot with the other major Scandinavian-American Lutheran body, choosing rather to ally itself with a group, the United Lutheran Church, whose orthodoxy the Norwegians and their allies wondered about, but whose Lutheran credits Bergendoff had never doubted. If "the real thing" he had spoken about earlier in Des Moines was unity that included at least all the members of the National Lutheran Council, it was at best postponed. And, in fact, the real thing (still minus one-third of American Lutheranism, the Missouri Synod) would wait for another quarter century, until in the late eighties the Evangelical Lutheran Church in America was formed from the two bodies that resulted from the negotiations of the nineteen fifties.[56]

Those two bodies were the Lutheran Church in America (ULCA, Augustana, and two smaller Danish and Finnish groups) and the American

Lutheran Church (Norwegians, other Danes, and a Midwestern body with a German background). The LCA, Conrad Bergendoff insisted, had preserved what the Augustana founders had contended for: loyalty to the Unaltered Augsburg Confession.[57] But a merger including all the National Lutheran Council members had not taken place. Instead the sub-group within the NLC that had set up the American Lutheran Conference, now minus Augustana, formed the new ALC (American Lutheran Church). Other members of the National Lutheran Council, now including Augustana, founded another denomination, the LCA. Apparently the American Lutheran Conference had become beside the point.[58] In one more of the turns that characterize this story, it was an Augustana pastor, S. E. Engstrom (who had pre-Des Moines advocated the opening of merger talks to all Lutheran bodies), who presided over the last meeting of the Conference in 1954, declaring it dissolved.[59]

Bergendoff played an important role in the creation of the LCA. Reflecting later on the work of the Joint Commission on Lutheran Unity, he noted with some satisfaction that "we lost no time in doctrinal discussions."[60] That meant, that as he had written for decades, theological unity was assumed; no group doubted the others' Lutheran credentials. And the college president, long experienced in the difficult matter of church control of theological education, must have supported the principle that the seminaries of the LCA would be administered by a single national board, though the question of how much central control would be exercised from headquarters in New York was left unsettled. The negotiators also determined that the LCA would avoid any statement that smacked of an inerrant or literalist theory of scriptural inspiration, so the freedom to carry on biblical scholarship was assured. Bergendoff felt that on the matter of a doctrine of scriptural inspiration, "back of different, stammering descriptions of the meaning of Scripture, we [Lutherans] all have the same faith that this is the Word of God."[61] That was good enough.

Dr. Bergendoff also offered the Joint Commission a suggestion that led it out of the seemingly small but tricky question of whether clergy could belong to lodges. The question, said Bergendoff later, almost caused Augustana to break off the negotiations. In the ULCA lodge membership had not been prohibited, and many of its pastors belonged to such groups. The Augustana Synod, like many other conservative Lutheran bodies, did forbid lodge membership. Bergendoff felt that many of these fraternal organizations "professed a deism not in accord with the Christian faith."[62] In 1937, as he contemplated relations between the United Lutheran Church and the American Lutheran Conference, Bergendoff had warned that lodge membership was the "one distinct and different [sic] between the practice and theory of the two bodies." Since it was not a confessional issue, the ULCA ought to be willing to concede the point, he wrote.[63] In the actual merger talks of the 1950s,

The Joint Commission on Lutheran Unity, 1956. Bergendoff is in the second row from the top, his successor at Augustana, C. W. Sorensen, in the bottom row, second from viewer's right.

Bergendoff proposed a statement that no candidate who held membership should be ordained and that clergy of the new Church who were in lodges should be disciplined or censured.[64]   After a ten minute caucus led by their president, Franklin Clark Fry, the ULCA Commission members gave way, and Augustana, which might even have abandoned the negotiations over the issue, stayed in.[65]   It was never clear that all of the ULCA pastors who did belong to lodges subsequently quit them.   One Missouri Lutheran historian called the agreement between the ULCA and Augustana on this matter "a curious wedding of principle and expediency."[66]   But for Bergendoff it had been important. Along with his unease over the deistic theology on which many lodges were founded, he felt that "a minister should not have peculiar ties to certain members of his congregation."[67]

With that hurdle passed, the Joint Commission continued with drafting a constitution for the new Church. Bergendoff was asked to write a preamble, and, assisted and nudged by ULCA President Fry, "he came up with a beautiful and profound statement."[68]   However, his most important contribution had been right after the opening of the negotiations.

The Idea of the Church

It was clearly Bergendoff's paper on the "Lutheran Doctrine of the Church," presented at the opening meeting of the Joint Commission in December, 1956, which represented his major work in the negotiations.[69]   That paper was the core of Bergendoff's 1956 lectures and book on *The Doctrine of the Church in American Lutheranism*.   In that paper and in the book he argued again for his view that Lutherans must accept at face value each other's professions of loyalty to the Lutheran Confessions without further need of proof, particularly in the form of signing further doctrinal statements.[70] Of course, at that point he was preaching to the converted, since by implication its very participation in the talks suggested that a denomination agreed with that premise. That was the issue more than any other which had set the American Lutheran Conference Churches on a separate path from that which led to the creation of the Lutheran Church in America. Bergendoff's paper also argued that American Lutheranism had found a balance between the congregation as "the basic unit" of the church and the regional or ethnic synods, which took care of matters such as training for the ministry, uniformity in liturgy, and printing materials.[71]

In a lecture at Augustana Seminary given while he was preparing the 1956 lectures and book, Bergendoff had also made explicit his long-held views on the nature of the Christian Church and on his own denomination's "Idea of the Church." In the lectures which had resulted in the 1956 book on *The Doctrine of the Church in American Lutheranism,* Bergendoff had responded to an "assignment" to treat the matter of Lutheran *doctrine,* in this case on the Christian church. Left to his own inclinations, as he was in the lecture at Augustana Seminary, he spoke about his own Synod's ideas on that matter. The use of that term, "Idea," rather than "Doctrine," which had a somewhat more rigid sense, itself indicates a degree of openness in Bergendoff's approach.[72] (Similarly, he entitled a 1952 article on the Lutheran understanding of Holy Communion, "The Lutheran View of the Lord's Supper," again avoiding the term "doctrine."[73])   That willingness to treat as an idea or view what others regarded as a doctrine or dogma suggests a flex that would be crucial in the inter-Lutheran negotiations and inter-confessional discussions that had sprung up after the war. It recalled the Swede Gustaf Aulén's 1912 work, *Till belysning af den lutherska kyrkoidén* (On the Lutheran Idea of the Church). Balancing his deep conviction that unity around a creedal statement was vital, Bergendoff displayed a certain willingness to relax "doctrine" into an "idea" or a "view."

Bergendoff had steadily held that no particular form of church government had been set up in the New Testament. He also argued that his own denomination had steered a middle course between the all-inclusiveness of the Church of Sweden and the exclusiveness regarding membership of many American churches. This had been a critical issue between the Synod and the *missionsvänner* who left Augustana's midst after the Civil War. In Bergendoff's view, they had argued that the true church must be pure, consisting only of Christians whose confession and whose life were consistent. They had stressed the "separatedness of the Church from the world."[74] Of course, he knew that many early Augustana pastors, Olof Olsson in Lindsborg, Kansas, for example, had hewed to the position that church membership must be restricted to "those who have been gently but thoroughly tested by the pastor and the deacons according to the Word of God, as to their true conversion." Lutheran orthodoxy was not good enough, and Olsson had seen to it that even his wife was examined, to be certain that along with doctrinal correctness she had truly been born anew.[75] But as greater numbers of immigrants arrived from Sweden in the seventies and eighties, the Augustana Synod had begun to admit them to membership. If they had been communicants in the Church of Sweden and wished to be associated with the Augustana Synod, they were welcomed, even when they did not always manifest the Fruits of the Spirit, which Paul had said were the marks of genuine Christian living. Even Olof Olsson had given way on the question, abandoning his idea of a pure church of tested true believers. Bergendoff believed that you could not maintain a church by demanding that it be made up only of pure Christians: "Holiness is not inherited. . . . There is no succession of holiness."[76]

Bergendoff also thought that it was not the goodness of its members but a faithful ministry that assured the continuity of the church. He recognized that there were varying ideas about the ministry among American Lutherans and said that Augustana held a higher view of it than other nineteenth century American Lutherans.[77] Here a "higher" view seemed to mean that the pastor of a congregation was seen to be its leader in matters having to do with its everyday life as well as in spiritual and theological questions and that congregations without pastors could not participate as voting units of the Synod conventions. At the same time, Bergendoff recognized in the volume of *Luther's Works* on *The Church and the Ministry,* which he edited in 1958, that for Luther the Christian Church was made up of congregations built around the proclamation of the Word by a pastor authorized to do so by "the call of a congregation."[78] The implication of this was that the ministry was "a function which the members delegate to a certain few to serve in the ministry of Word and sacrament." An alternative was to see the ministry as an order established directly by Christ himself, independent of the congregation. In the former case, the ministry derived authority from Christ *through* the congregation, not directly. But in his lectures on *The Doctrine of the Church in American Lutheranism,* Bergendoff held that either of the alternatives was within Lutheran boundaries, so the matter should not keep Lutherans apart. [79]

It was the case that Bergendoff's "Doctrine" or "Idea of the Church" emerged in segments or stages, as he contributed to inter-Lutheran dialog in the decades after World War II, trying to bring historical light into the process of uniting American Lutherans. In this case he operated theologically, as he usually did, by considering the historical circumstances in which doctrinal positions emerged within churches. In keeping with his own approach, we might consider the circumstances that led to the works in which Bergendoff's "ecclesiology" appeared: *The One Holy Catholic Apostolic Church* (1954), "Augustana's Idea of the Church" (1955), and *The Doctrine of the Church in American Lutheranism* (1956). All of these works were issued in the fifties, the heyday of inter-Lutheran ecumenism in America. So Bergendoff's idea of the church was meant to serve the cause of Lutheran unity. He thought that a church must be organized or centered around a statement of its beliefs, its creed or confession. It should accept as members those who said they believed in that creed. Its holiness came from having been founded by Christ, not ultimately because of the goodness or holiness of its members. Ministers would serve the congregations of the church through preaching and administering the sacraments, but no single theory of how they derived their authority was essential. The earthly church or denomination, made up of its many congregations, could be governed by bishops, by colleges or synods of clergy, or by the corporate will of its congregations when they met together.

It was important to Bergendoff that any earthly Christian body recognize that it was not co-terminal with that true Church of Christ of which the New Testament and the Reformers spoke. That meant there were Christians outside of as well as within each organized earthly denomination or church. "Invisible church" is not a term Bergendoff used much, but he wrote that Lutheran theologians seemed unable to avoid at least the idea it contained. "For they agree that no church is identifiable with the Kingdom of Christ. There is a body of Christ which can be comprehended neither in one denomination nor in one definition."[80] That meant that each organized church or denomination must make an effort to understand and to seek fellowship with Christians outside of its structures or membership, even though that effort would often be difficult and might not result in full communion and understanding. That was Bergendoff's "Idea of the Church."

We recall that Bergendoff had been a "centralization man" so far as the question of the role of the national office of the Augustana Synod had been concerned, even though that office had not always held views that he shared. By the early fifties, in the years when the LCA negotiations were not yet going on at a rate of three and four meetings a year as they did in the second half of the decade, he seems to have moved to some degree toward modifying his position about central authority. In the *Lutheran Companion* he argued several times against some "great Lutheran bureaucracy which gathers power in some 'headquarters.'" Perhaps an alternative might be synods in each region or state; these synods (now no longer ethnic and national as his Synod had been) might be given a relative degree of autonomy, with a national convention meeting triennially.[81] Bergendoff, who had reacted early in his ministry against the intrusion of business methods into congregational life, still argued for keeping the "business model" where "all is planned, controlled, and judged by a powerful central authority" out of the new Church. "The Lutheran Church has good reason to go slow in rebuilding a hierarchy to which Luther dealt a staggering blow."[82]

Perhaps Bergendoff feared that his denomination, much smaller than the ULCA, would be swallowed up by a strong national office after the merger.[83] He also realized that what was developing in American Lutheranism were two (three if the Missouri Synod were taken into account) bodies, the eventual ALC and LCA, which might conceivably have stood off from one another for many decades, especially if vested interests should develop in the leadership of one or both of them That, of course, did not happen. What did turn out was that for the quarter-century of its life, the LCA had perhaps more national direction and authority than had been the case in the United Lutheran Church, the largest partner to the merger.[84] A strong national office did not block the ALC-LCA merger of the late eighties, though Bergendoff had feared that "Powerful Lutheran Churches opposed to each other may be a greater disaster than weaker Lutheran synods overlapping each other."[85]

In 1958, as two sets of negotiations proceeded, the President of the National Lutheran Council called on the two groups to make one more effort at exploring the formation of one church rather than two, but these hopes were not realized.[86] The NLC also sponsored "conversations" with the Missouri Synod in which Conrad Bergendoff participated, 1959-1961. Bergendoff was by this time convinced that there was little hope for rapprochement. "Most disconcerting" was that Missouri wished the other Lutherans to accept their *damnamus* of other church bodies. That condemnation of other Christians "makes all cooperation impossible," he maintained in a paper presented during the meetings.[87] There are indications that Bergendoff's position toward Missouri had hardened. During these "conversations" he got a note from the Executive Director of the National Lutheran Council. It brought up Bergendoff's unwillingness to debate Missouri on what the Augustana man regarded as Missouri grounds and suggested that Bergendoff's attitude might be an impediment to continuing the talks between the Missouri Synod and the NLC Churches. In spite of Bergendoff's objections, Paul C. Empie, the NLC officer, had been willing to discuss the Missouri view of Scripture. To the Augustana man that seemed like engaging in "a battle with Missouri on a 'proof text' basis."[88]

Something did eventually come of these efforts to bring the Missouri Synod into a relationship with the churches of the National Lutheran Council: the formation in 1967 of the Lutheran Council in the United States of America.

It established a Washington office and did carry on some cooperative work between Missouri and the other major Lutheran bodies.[89]   But theological difficulties proved its vulnerable point, especially after a conservative shift in the Missouri Synod in the 1970s.   The Lutheran Council in the USA broke up, and dissidents who left Missouri during its shift further to the right eventually united with the LCA.

A New Denominational Home

For the most part, Conrad Bergendoff was at home in the new Lutheran Church in America. What he would miss, as his Augustana College history (1969) and his *The Augustana Ministerium: A Study of the Careers of the 2,504 Pastors of the Augustana Evangelical Lutheran Synod-Church, 1860-1962* (1980) suggested, was the comradery of life among Swedish-American Lutherans. That slowly but inevitably dissolved in the LCA. So did the ties and personal associations which the Augustana Church had maintained with another smaller Swedish-American body, the Evangelical Covenant Church, descended from the Pietists who had broken with the Synod in the nineteenth century. In the paper he had delivered in 1956 at the opening session of the negotiations that led to the LCA's formation, Bergendoff noted appreciatively that Pietism had, in spite of its emotionalism, awakened the church through its Christocentric emphasis and its stress on the universal priesthood of all believers.[90] He seems to have realized that in the new denomination there would be some loosening of the ties with the Covenanters which the Augustana Church had maintained, though, as we shall see, he also thought that important issues remained outstanding between their tradition and his. The Covenant historian Karl Olsson, writing as the Synod merged into the LCA, observed that "Distrust and opposition but also wistfulness have marked these [Augustana-Covenant] relations."[91] When it came down to it, wistfulness was more characteristic of Bergendoff's attitude than distrust and opposition had been.

Augustana historian Arden, writing at the time of the creation of the LCA, spoke of its formation as the "consummation of the story of Augustana Lutheran Church" and entitled his chapter tracing the course of the Synod's involvement in the merger "Destiny Fulfilled."[92] Writing forty-five years later, Maria Erling and Mark Granquist are not so sure: "But both in Augustana during the 1950s, as well as among some later observers, the question has been asked as to whether the two separate Lutheran mergers of the 1960s were not more of a mistake than an advance, more of a sidetrack than a way forward."[93] For his part, Bergendoff regretted that much of the distinctiveness of the Augustana Synod had inevitably been lost in the new Lutheran Church in America. Ties to Sweden had been "not severed, but certainly weakened."[94]

He did feel, however, that strong liturgical interest, social consciousness, the doctrine of the ministry, an ecumenical concern, and an "evangelistic strain" that pointed to the distinctiveness of Christian faith and life were emphases that the Augustana Church brought into the LCA.[95]

For Conrad Bergendoff, who retired from the Augustana College president's office in the year the LCA came into being, the new Church seems to have been both a step forward and a disappointment. The LCA embodied the open and ecumenical Lutheranism which he had long represented and advocated. However, it was at best a partial realization of his hopes for American Lutheranism, leaving out 2.3 million Lutherans with whom he and his Synod had long been in fellowship, not to mention 2.7 million who were members of the Missouri Synod. Of course, he could tell himself that it was the Norwegians and their allies in the ALC who had turned away his Swedish-American Synod and the other bodies advocating *pan*-Lutheran rapprochement. The ALC folk, of course, took a different view; for them it was Augustana's position that had led its representatives to walk silently out of the meeting in November, 1952, to seek union with the United Lutheran Church.

Bergendoff accepted an assignment from the new Church: to study its theological seminaries. Each of the merging churches had carried on its own theological education, and the ULCA had several schools, two of them located quite close to each other in Philadelphia and Gettysburg. Bergendoff set about visiting all of the soon-to-be LCA seminaries. President Emeritus of the Augustana Church P. O. Bersell had urged Bergendoff to take the assignment, writing to him that "your appointment would do more than anything else . . . to calm the rising storm that is growing in Augustana." The implications went beyond the seminary issue. "There is now in our group a serious suspicion that we are being 'annexed' by the U.L.C.A. despite all the beautiful talk of this being a real merger and a new Church." Bersell felt that it was unfortunate that in the merger negotiations the Augustana people had failed to bring these seminaries of the new Church under "direct church control."[96] Bergendoff did take the job. Thus did the two old colleagues, each the President of an Augustana, find themselves in a concert of opinion over an issue—theological education—which had put them at odds fifteen years earlier.

The result was the somewhat controversial "Bergendoff Report." One historian of the LCA suggested that it "minced no words."[97] Bergendoff's assessment was that over half of the students enrolled in the schools might not have been admitted to university graduate study and further, that because of the low faculty to student ratios, the education offered in the seminaries was very expensive. High costs had not necessarily achieved high quality. That was not complementary of the academic level of the Lutheran ministry in general. And the helter-skelter proliferation of institutions, notably in the ULCA, "hardly exemplifies planned parenthood." The study recommended merging several of the schools and locating them close to university campuses.[98] That was consistent with thinking in the Protestant churches generally. One prominent ecumenical leader took a cue from Bergendoff and predicted interdenominational clustering of theological schools near universities throughout the country.[99] One such merger of Lutheran schools did take place, combining ULCA seminaries in suburban Chicago and Nebraska with the seminary in Rock Island and bringing in Danish and Finnish schools as well. The new Lutheran School of Theology at Chicago, adjacent to the University of Chicago campus, was dedicated in 1967. Catholic, Congregational, Presbyterian, and other schools were also located there. The two Lutheran seminaries that were close neighbors in eastern Pennsylvania, however, are still operating separately., As the dust settled around the controversy, Bersell again wrote to Bergendoff: "We are both aware of the sectional, provincial and institutional resistance that will develop. It is a pity that the Church was not given full authority in this matter."[100] In Bersell's mind ULCA localism had prevailed over Augustana centralization, the Bergendoff Report notwithstanding.

World Lutheranism

When the Evangelical Lutheran Church in America was formed from the LCA and ALC a quarter century later (1988), Bergendoff was ninety-two years old and while in good health, mind and body, had largely withdrawn from denominational affairs. But he must have been gratified that the American Lutheran Church had agreed that the new ELCA should hold membership in the National and World Councils of Churches and that it still remained true to the Lutheran Confessions—without asking for further signed documentary evidence of sincerity. Whereas many of his colleagues in the Augustana Synod had seen the issue in American Lutheranism as one that lay between the groups that formed the American Lutheran Church in 1960 and those who two years later joined in the Lutheran Church in America, Bergendoff had steadily held that the real division ran between the Missouri Synod and the rest of Lutheranism in America. Missouri held that any new church should be so built as to leave no doctrinal question unanswered, whereas others thought that where Scripture gave "no clear or direct indication," freedom and variation were possible.[101] The Evangelical Lutheran Church in America included the two-thirds of American Lutherans who had finally come to agree on the latter position. In this matter Bergendoff had been something of a seer. His hopes included the union of most American Lutherans into one body and the coming together of world Lutheranism as well. However, neither of these goals was entirely fulfilled in the way he had hoped they would be.

Just after World War II, the Augustana Synod found itself involved with other Lutherans on a world scale. That involvement was focused on the formation of the Lutheran World Federation. Developments in the period between World Wars set the groundwork for formal establishment of that body in 1947. The Lutheran World Federation had its roots in a predecessor group, the Lutheran World Convention, which was established in 1923 at Eisenach in the (Weimar) Republic of Germany, the town where Luther had been hidden for protection in the Wartburg Castle after his "Here I stand" before the Holy Roman Emperor at the Diet of Worms. Subsequent meetings in Copenhagen (1929) and Paris (1935) were marked by tensions between Germans and Lutherans from other countries, mainly because of the Treaty of Versailles and continuing German efforts to extricate their nation from its obligations. A fourth session set for Philadelphia in 1940 was cancelled due to the outbreak of war.

European and American churches were the constituting bodies of the Lutheran World Convention, and even the mission churches were often represented by Europeans and Americans. With the Allied victory in World War II, efforts to revive world pan-Lutheranism resulted in a gathering at Lund in (neutral) Sweden in 1947. It was dominated by three blocs: German, American, and Scandinavian Lutherans. German Christians had in 1945 confessed to war guilt, so the tensions that existed between them and the other two blocs over responsibility for the First World War had to a degree dissipated. The election of the Swedish theologian-bishop Anders Nygren (1890-1978) to head the Federation was itself a sign of the mediating role that the Nordic Lutherans assumed in the new organization. The Lutheran World Federation was meant to be a tighter confederation than its predecessor from the inter-war period had been. One ecumenical historian ventured that the LWF was "by far the best organized" of the international denominational bodies, "with its head offices overtopping those of the World Council in Geneva."[102]

The LWF focused on four concerns: post-war relief, missionary needs, theology, and ecumenical involvement. During Conrad Bergendoff's working lifetime, assemblies were held in Lund (1947), Hanover (1952), Minneapolis (1957), Helsinki (1963), Evian (1970), Dar es Salaam (1977), Budapest (1984), and Curitiba, Brazil (1990). Bergendoff attended the first three, in the fifties sitting in meetings of the first LWF Commissions on Theology and on Liturgy.[103] The 1970 meeting of the LWF had been scheduled to be held in Brazil, but conditions in that country, then under a military government, resulted in a last-minute decision to shift the assembly to Evian in France. Bergendoff, reflecting on the twenty-fifth birthday of the LWF, said that the shift from Brazil to France was the most critical moment in LWF history. The Brazilian government used oppression and torture, and "Prudence and regard for Western delegations took precedence over courage[.]"[104]

Bergendoff further lamented the fact that the LWF had corporately decided not to press toward a common declaration of faith to the world; in fact, at Helsinki in 1963 it had failed even to achieve a unity of faith among Lutheran Churches themselves.[105] That assembly in Finland had been presented with a statement on justification, but had rejected it, a decision which portended a shift in the LWF from the functional and theological leadership of well-known scholar-churchmen (such as Nygren) representing European and American churches (such as Bergendoff's) to rising Third World influence and direction over the Federation.[106] Today the largest body in the LWF is the Church of Sweden (still claiming most Swedes as members), and the ELCA is the fourth. The second and third largest Churches are in Tanzania and Ethiopia. Membership numbers and commitment in the latter bodies may be more solid than in the Swedish or American groups. Many of the southern or third-world Lutheran Churches seem to be concerned that the European folk or state churches and the American denominations are "strikingly susceptible to the virus of secularism." In the newer (formerly missionary) churches, "the value of preserving the Reformation heritage has been seen in the light of failings, if not apostasy, of the older churches." For these former mission churches, justification by faith must be considered relative to its implications for social, political, and economic issues.[107]

The LWF had stated in its original constituting documents that membership was open to any church which found in "the Unaltered Augsburg Confession and Luther's Catechism, a pure exposition of the Word of God."[108] Bergendoff's reflection on the entire history of the organization was that "It is a sobering thought that Lutheran unity has been promoted by international catastrophe[.]"[109] He meant war. For him theological unity should have been the under-pinning of whatever else the Lutheran World Federation undertook. That unity could, of course, be found in the *Confessio Augustana,* and he must have been somewhat puzzled that a further statement on justification was needed in the first place. Perhaps the LWF should have been more familiar with the history of American Lutheranism. For Bergendoff at least, the experience of his own co-religionists in America had made it clear that statements beyond the Lutheran Confessions turned out to be more productive of discord than of unity, just as they were at Helsinki in 1963.

At the 1984 assembly in Budapest the LWF finally did agree that all its member churches were in pulpit and altar fellowship with each other, this on the basis of their assent to the Augsburg Confession and the Catechism, as specified in the Federation's constitution. It was also at this assembly that two South African churches were suspended from membership because their continued support of the system of apartheid was deemed to be a violation of their declaration of Lutheran faith. Still, the Budapest assembly's statement on "The Unity We Seek" has often been taken as a definitive expression of the ecumenical ideal of "reconciled diversity." It reads: "The true unity of the church . . . is a communion in holy baptism and in the eucharistic meal, a communion in which all the ministries exercised are recognized by all as expressions of the ministry instituted by Christ in his church. It is a communion where diversities contribute to fullness and are no longer barriers to unity."[110]

§

The 1984 Budapest actions of the Lutheran World Federation embodied both Bergendoff's sense of what constituted Lutheranism and his idea that this faith had consequences. Bergendoff's prescription for Lutheran unity had always been simple: people and groups which said they held to the Lutheran Confessions, particularly the Augsburg Confession and Luther's Small Catechism, should be taken at their word and should be able to commune together. Indeed, by mid-century he thought they should merge. In spite of his sense that doctrine was not the core of the Christian life, he believed that creedal statements were the way in which Christian bodies identified themselves and related to one another. Without them you did not know where the other person or church stood.

Once American Lutherans had emerged from their ethnic enclaves and agreed that they stood together—on the base of their confession—the question became, "What next?" There were obviously other Christians in the United States. It was in encounters with these people that the self-understanding of the Augustana Church was tested and modified. Conrad Bergendoff's own ecumenical involvement would, in the course of the twentieth century, reach far beyond the boundaries that enclosed him and his Church in the early years of his career. The Synod, though lagging behind, did in the end come with him, at least to the point of encounter and conversation. The question that now emerged was whether they—our subject and his Church—would cross the line that they had drawn by their stout affirmation of the Unaltered Augsburg Confession. Across that line all sorts and conditions of Christians were praying, working, worshipping. To what degree could Lutherans pray, work, worship with them?

Rock Island Spires. Perhaps this view of Augustana, taken from Lincoln Park, reminded Bergendoff of the spires of Oxford, which he first saw in 1937. He used this photo on the jacket of his 1969 history of the College. Here were faith and learning, properly situated.

CHAPTER 7

OTHER CHRISTIANS

"After more than 25 years of association with the ecumenical movement, I testify for myself that I have gained rather than lost, that I am no less loyal to my own Church, but that I have gained something which is a common treasure of all Churches."[1] That was Conrad Bergendoff reflecting in 1954 on his past encounters with non-Lutheran Christians. It also represented the frame of mind with which he would carry on the work of representing his denomination to other churches for decades to come. While that statement does not reflect any break with his past attitudes and ideas, it does indicate an important shift, perhaps a maturation, in them. In 1936 his tone had been different: "Because I believe that the Lutheran Church, above others, has kept true to the Word of the Lord and thus made possible the clearest, the fullest, the best balanced Christian life, I wish to be part of the Lutheran Church and to derive from her the means of the grace of Christ." Bergendoff commented on the opening up that took place at about the midway point in the history of the Augustana Synod with regard to ecumenical involvement, as we saw in earlier chapters. A similar shift, at least in emphasis and mood, had also taken place in his own thinking.

In that 1936 *Lutheran Companion* essay, Bergendoff staked out the position with which he would sail to Britain for the 1937 Oxford and Edinburgh meetings of world Christendom (less the Roman Catholic and some evangelical churches). He was not sure, he wrote, that everyone involved would be "a fellow Christian," but he did know that he was not "the only true Christian."[2] One assumes that he believed some non–Lutherans would be in the latter category. To what extent he felt the full force of the contradiction between Christian faith and the existence of hundreds of church bodies, many of them claiming to embody the fullest expression of that faith, is not clear. One recalls Arnold Toynbee (1889-1975): "In the freest flight of imagination it would be difficult to conceive of a sharper contradiction of the essence of Christianity [than in] the impact of Parochialism upon the Western Christian Church[.]"[3] In the mid-thirties Bergendoff did not reflect Toynbee's sharp sense of the utter contradiction between splintered Christendom and the faith it professed.

But after the 1937 trip to Britain, Bergendoff's experience did reflect (or, indeed, anticipate) what American church historian Martin Marty predicted in 1972 might develop in the ranks of denominational historians: they "can re-explore their own assumptions and may be able to discern the ethnic aspects in what they had earlier regarded as their universal points of view."[4] That is the dynamic that characterized Bergendoff's thought and work as an ecumenist. He slowly but steadily came to the view that much of what he earlier had regarded as the universal truth in his tradition was in fact deeply conditioned by its own ethnic particularity, if not parochialism. One sees this clearly in his scholarly and inter-church efforts just before and after World War II.

Even in the Augustana Synod, which its historians believe took the lead among mid-twentieth century American Lutheran bodies in commitment to ecumenism, Bergendoff's position was sometimes lonely. Many of Augustana's people, clergy and lay, believed with the Bergendoff of 1936 that above others their Church had kept true to the Word of God and that it offered the best opportunity for leading a Christian life; they were not particularly troubled to reach out to other Christians. But Bergendoff's frame of mind was adjusted after returning from his 1937 ecumenical foray to Britain. He noted that his own profession, church history, had paid a great deal of attention to the dissent and discord that had marked religious history, but he wondered who would recognize those who sought through ecumenical involvement to keep the church from falling into "sectarian chaos[.]"[5]

In 1946 Bergendoff wrote that Lutherans had for decades been preoccupied with their own affairs. A few conspicuous pathfinders had gone out "onto the highways of world Christianity rather than [having] found themselves on those highways by virtue of their seminary's direction."[6] Still (for two years) the president of one such seminary, he evidently knew whereof he spoke. He had sometimes gone ahead, attending and contributing at ecumenical events and meetings, when some of the folks back home had not been as certain as he was that this was God's work. Sometimes he traveled at his own expense.

Not everyone in his Synod was as ecumenical as Bergendoff. And it was also the case that most other species of Lutheran in the US were not as ecumenical as the Swedish Americans and their seminary in Rock Island. So when one ventured forth to meet and discuss points of agreement and difference with Anglicans or Presbyterians or Methodists, he was in a real sense a pioneer. That was true even in Bergendoff's own Church, let alone in the variety of other Lutheran bodies in the United States, some of which found (and still find) such meetings and discussions to be out of keeping with doctrinal purity.

American Ecumenism

In spite of reservations in many quarters, the twentieth century saw the rise of inter-church encounter to a degree that earlier centuries since the Protestant Reformation had not. These encounters involved Protestants and Orthodox Christians, and on very rare occasions, some Roman Catholics. Most often this ecumenism developed in the English-speaking context, and the names of its early champions are often Anglo-sounding. But a German-American Lutheran, the oft-criticized (in Lutheran circles) and oft-admired (by other Protestants) Samuel Simon Schmucker, provided much of the impetus to the formation of nineteenth century American and British ecumenical groups. Chief among these groups were the Evangelical Alliance in Britain (1846) and its American counterpart (1867). One historian of ecumenism writes that Schmucker's "thorough exposition of the necessity of Church union, his candid facing of the evils of the denominational spirit . . . provided the arguments for the 20th-century ecumenical movement. He did work that did not need to be done again."[7]

As we saw in the last chapter, that was not how many American Lutheran church historians, including Conrad Bergendoff, viewed Schmucker. For them his views represented "spineless Lutheranism." It was around such differences of perspective that some of the fundamental issues in the twentieth century ecumenical movement developed. Bergendoff himself came increasingly to represent an approach to inter-church efforts that sought to balance confessional loyalty with openness. He wanted to preserve the distinctive doctrinal and liturgical qualities of his own tradition while at the same time acknowledging the fundamental Christian commitments of other church families. One of the questions that would occupy churchmen for decades was whether Christian groups might join in service and worship while preserving what they saw as their own doctrinal integrity. It was a question that Bergendoff struggled with throughout his career. His involvement in long rounds of committees, assemblies, lectures, and seminars, all of them efforts at inter-church understanding and perhaps cooperation, did bring about a marked development in his own thinking. He had not reached such openness quickly. In 1924 Bergendoff had written in the *Lutheran Companion* that "there is a limit to assimilation." The Lutheran Church "must know where she can give way and where she must remain firm."[8] If it did not simply repeat it, that statement recalled the mood of the 1875 Galesburg Rule to which the Synod had subscribed: "Lutheran pulpits for Lutheran ministers only; Lutheran altars for Lutheran communicants only."

Bergendoff maintained this reserve toward non-Lutherans for decades, responding to an inquiry in the mid-fifties by asserting that if the Lutheran Church exchanged pulpits and altars with other denominations, people would wonder if there were no differences between the groups: "an exchange implies unity of faith." It would be acceptable to hold Thanksgiving services together or cooperate in baccalaureates, but not to hold full worship jointly.[9] The letter just quoted suggests that as late as the 1950s Bergendoff, like Wolfgang Goethe, found "two souls in his breast." He entered ecumenical dialog with serious reservations, but he could not but recognize the deep commitment and faith of people who came from other confessional traditions.

Most higher-level (or supra-local) ecumenical encounters were held under the auspices of one or another of the national and international associations of Christian churches whose development was one of the major aspects of twentieth century Christian history. In 1908 the Federal Council of Churches (FCC) was organized in the United States. Its membership included most American Protestants, the major exceptions being Southern Baptists, Lutherans, and the Protestant Episcopal Church. (The Episcopalians soon got involved.) The early focus was on temperance and social service, but by World War II the Federal Council's work included almost all areas of churchly concern, ranging from race to radio. Such matters as foreign missions and religious education were the foci of other single-purpose American organizations. The Federal Council was the main channel through which American churches related to the international ecumenical movement. On that level the founding of political bodies such as the League of Nations and the United Nations was paralleled among Christians by the establishment of inter-church groups. The "Faith and Order" and "Life and Work" movements that grew between the World Wars led to the World Council of Churches in 1948. (Indeed, the Swedish Archbishop Nathan Söderblom had thought that the international political organizations were the "body" of international life, while the Christian ecumenical structures were their "soul."[10])

The Augustana Church, like its Lutheran sisters, did not join these organizations, and that became a source of some tension between the Swedish-American Lutherans and "mainline" Protestantism. We have noted that, among many others, its president, Eric Norelius, had warned during the Synod's fiftieth anniversary against any "unionism," the move to fellowship with other Christians, even other Lutherans, with whom they were "not in complete doctrinal agreement."[11] That tension became palpable at the point the Augustana Church sought to take part in the Oxford and Edinburgh Assemblies of the late 1930s. The leaders of the Federal Council viewed non-member churches as outsiders. For their part, many Lutherans found much in the Federal Council to be concerned about in the inter-war decades, especially since it appeared to them to be dominated by the liberal Social Gospel mindset of American Protestantism. The mere fact that the Augustana Synod was sending representatives to the 1937 assemblies and that it was therefore by implication consorting, even once removed, with the Federal Council, caused Synod President P. O. Bersell to caution Bergendoff. Augustana, he said, needed to focus on bringing American Lutherans together before attempting "approachment" to other churches "far afield."[12]

Bergendoff himself harbored continued doubts about ecumenical involvement. In 1930 he had written an article on the Augsburg Confession that was rather negative about the Federal Council and the *Christian Century*, which he apparently regarded as its mouthpiece. They appeared to be dominated by Calvinist influences inimical to Lutheranism. "Somehow or other, something of the Zwinglian or Calvinistic conception of Church and State still adheres to the Reformed Church, so that church unity means little more than the unity of all within a state under the influence of a political church."[13] Bergendoff recognized that, in the Augustana Synod language of the thirties, "Reformed" generally meant most American Protestantism.[14] In a way, Bergendoff's pronouncement reflected the sense that he and his fellow Lutherans stood apart from the main stream of American church life. That came from his personal boyhood experience as well as from his theological stance. There are hints in the 1930 article of a sense of necessary isolation from the rest of Protestantism. Fidelity to the faith demanded this of Lutherans. That makes the growth of his Church's and Bergendoff's own ecumenism all the more noteworthy. By the end of the decade in which this article was written, Bergendoff's experience in the 1937 assemblies in Britain resulted in growing openness to other Christians—in the US as well as overseas. He had also taken part with the American evangelist and missionary, E. Stanley Jones (1884-1973) in evangelism tours on behalf of the Federal Council in the thirties.[15]

The Second World War brought further adjustments to the Synod and its mindset. The leadership of the Augustana Synod had been very careful about associating with the Federal Council of Churches. As he did sometimes, President Bersell occupied both sides of the question. For example, in 1942 he wrote to Bergendoff that he had had his attention drawn to a story in the *Argus* (of Rock Island) in which Bergendoff was identified as the general chairman of a local program arranged under FCC auspices. Bersell told the college president that he needed a statement from him "that will clear you of any suspicion of having done something that is contrary to the spirit and decisions of our own Church."[16] On the other side of the matter, Bersell did think that he himself deserved some credit for having been the only American Lutheran leader to have appointed an official delegation to the 1937 Oxford and Edinburgh ecumenical meetings (more of which shortly). He believed he had "stuck my neck out" by moving ahead of the "pharisaical isolationism" of many of his fellow Lutheran Church presidents. What he and Bergendoff might do, he suggested, was to sit down together and talk the business over. Bergendoff needed to understand the delicacy of Bersell's position; the Church President had to be cautious and could not appear to be running too far ahead of the Synod.[17]

But three years later Bersell decided to recommend that the Synod consider membership in the Federal Council. Bergendoff was one of three persons commissioned to study the question. By the time they reported back to Synod, a new national inter-church body was being formed. In 1950 the Federal Council absorbed a number of other agencies and morphed into the National Council of the Churches of Christ in the United States of America. This was one moment when Bersell and Bergendoff were of a mind; "you and I have seen very much eye to eye in regard to these matters," Bersell wrote.[18] With that agreement between its leaders, the 1950 Synod convention voted to accept membership in the National Council of Churches. Augustana was the first Lutheran body in the US to do so. It was a significant step, though the Church was already a member of several of the agencies which merged into the National Council. Bergendoff had been a "fraternal observer" at the fortieth anniversary celebration of the Federal Council held in Cincinnati in 1948. The FCC, he wrote, has thrown "the light of the Gospel into dark corners of American life where individual Christians have been unwilling or unprepared to go alone." It was on solid ground, defining Christ as "God and Savior."[19] Both in its confessional basis and in its efforts to spread Christianity into the secular reaches of contemporary America, the FCC had Bergendoff's approval, so he welcomed the formation of the National Council in 1950.

Lutherans were welcomed heartily at the Cleveland constituting convention in 1950. P. O. Bersell led the opening worship service, and Franklin Clark Fry of the United Lutheran Church presided at the business sessions. Conrad Bergendoff was one of the ten Augustana delegates. In 1960 Stephen Neill, an Anglican ecumenist and historian, wrote cryptically of international ecumenism that "It was thought wise from the start to have the Lutheran churches of the world closely associated with the high command of the ecumenical movement."[20] Whether that was because of the Lutherans' leadership abilities, their theological acumen, their sheer numbers, or simply because they had stayed out so long, Neill does not say. In any event, the generalization seemed to apply in the United States; the Lutherans had arrived, taking a place among the twenty-nine Protestant and Orthodox churches (representing almost 32 million Christians) that became members of the National Council of Churches.[21] In 1951 the body included five Presbyterian-Reformed, four Methodist, four Baptist, and three Lutheran denominations.[22] Of course many American Lutheran churches hung back, including the other four members (beside Augustana) of the American Lutheran Conference, as well as the Missouri Synod.

The World Church

The Augustana Church's entry into the National Council of Churches seemed ground-breaking, but in fact the earth had been prepared for decades. Bergendoff was part of that spade work. In the early years of the twentieth century, the Synod had been stand-offish to approaches from international ecumenism. President Norelius had spurned a 1911 invitation to join a world-wide Protestant Conference on Faith and Order, responding that the Augustana Synod considered "an outward union of different churches ... to be futile and no union at all."[23] One historian, Byron Swanson, writes that the Synod's "complex system of scholastic confessionalism" was marked by a "polemic, defensive, intolerant, and absolutistic claim of pure doctrine[.]"[24] But the election of G. A. Brandelle as Synod President in 1918 portended a shift in Augustana attitude. The destructiveness of the Great War and the growing Americanization of the Synod itself contributed to that shift, as did the change in Synod leadership. Bergendoff noted with approval that in 1925 Brandelle was present among the six hundred delegates from thirty-seven countries who gathered in Stockholm at the Universal Christian Conference on Life and Work.[25] That Conference "was the child of one heart and one brain; Nathan Söderblom, Archbishop of Uppsala, *was* Stockholm 1925."[26] It may well have been that it was the invitation from the Archbishop of the Church of *Sweden* that brought the Augustana men to Stockholm—along with the effects of the war, the language shift in the Synod, and the change in its leadership. Söderblom was determined not to allow theological differences to block efforts at uniting Christian churches in response to the devastating results of the war. Hence the emphasis upon "life and work."[27] The other main stream in inter-war ecumenical life, "faith and order," dealt with questions of doctrine and polity. Lutherans were a little more skittish about getting involved in these matters.

The Stockholm meeting was followed by a gathering two years later at Lausanne, this one the first official conference of the Faith and Order movement, which had been formally organized on a sort of parallel track to Life and Work. No Augustana representative was present among the four hundred delegates from over one hundred churches. But continental Lutherans were there. It is possible that conservative reaction in the Augustana Synod after Stockholm 1925 and the fact that in Lausanne *Faith and Order,* implying doctrinal issues, were to be dealt with, kept Augustana from crossing the Atlantic for these sessions in Switzerland. After Stockholm one Rock Island seminary professor had written in the *Lutheran Companion* that he feared "close fellowship with people whose religious views and aims are suspicious to say the least." It appeared that "the Stockholm Conference is but a step in the direction of an ecumenical council on Faith and Order."[28] He was right.

For their part, the German and Scandinavian Lutherans at Lausanne 1927 were somewhat cautious about its proceedings and results. It appeared that "difficulties of language and the use of Anglo-Saxon methods of procedure unfamiliar to the Lutherans had prevented them from making their due contribution to the discussion, and rendered them hesitant to assume responsibility for the decisions reached."[29] The Germans (and the Swedes as well) were set off balance when during informal theological sessions one of them would venture an opinion and then be asked by the presiding English speaker, "Do you want to make that a motion?"[30] Söderblom, who had reservations about discussing Faith and Order, fearful that it would lead to theological disagreement, had left Lausanne early, which had further vitiated its effects. He had acted not simply as a leader; he had been a bridge between the English-speaking delegates and continental Protestants.

It was also the case that, faced with questions of Faith and Order, the Swede himself had pulled back slightly from his characteristic ecumenical openness. He joined with other Lutherans in a statement of their own which, says one biographer, "may be regarded as possibly the first embryo of confessional grouping in the organized ecumenical movement[.]"[31] Söderblom's death in 1931 was nonetheless a blow to that movement, but plans proceeded apace for a 1937 gathering on Faith and Order in Edinburgh, to be held shortly after Life and Work meetings set for the same summer in Oxford. By now it was clear that whatever the reservations of Söderblom's Lutheran heirs about discussing doctrine, it would not be possible to separate practical from theological issues. One's view of society's problems and needs could not be kept apart from one's theological position; Life and Work was gradually but certainly converging with Faith and Order.[32]

Oxford and Edinburgh

But by the mid-thirties things were also changing in the Augustana Evangelical Lutheran Synod. Conrad Bergendoff had closely followed reports from Stockholm 1925 and Lausanne 1927 and, anticipating the great gatherings planned for England and Scotland in 1937, expressed his hope that the Augustana Synod would be there.[33]   Six men were eventually chosen to represent Augustana at one or the other of the conferences, Bergendoff at both. Bergendoff's recollection in 1963 was that he had set out for Britain having purchased his own ticket and that only en route did he learn that the Synod had appointed him and the others delegates.[34]   One imagines a wireless message from Synod headquarters in Minneapolis reaching the ship in mid-Atlantic; it was 1937.

At first the Augustana position at Oxford and Edinburgh appeared to be slightly dubious, at least in the eyes of the Federal Council of Churches leadership, since the Synod was one of those "communions which are outside the Federal Council."[35]   That was in a letter from the General Secretary of the FCC. In February another leading American ecumenist wrote to Bergendoff concerning "a difficult point about which I must be quite frank.   Our first responsibility is to the cooperating Churches, and we must not use these special rules to admit to the Conference any persons except those who have the full approval of the authorities of their own Churches."[36]   The sticking point appeared to be that the Synod itself had not accepted the invitation to the conferences, but had authorized its Executive Committee to send delegates.[37] The ruffled feathers were, however, smoothed, and the Augustana delegates, holding the full approval of their Church's authorities, took their places at both meetings.   Bergendoff was assigned to the Oxford section on "The Church and Education" and to the section on "The Church of Christ and the Word of God" at Edinburgh.

Of the four hundred twenty-five delegates at Oxford, three hundred were from the US and the British Commonwealth.   None came from Germany, the Nazis having forbidden attendance; they locked up certain of the churchmen who meant to be there.   There were, accordingly, no problems with Germans being put off by Anglo parliamentary procedures.   As had been the case in the 1920s, a plenary Holy Communion was not celebrated, though the Church of England did invite all baptized and communing members of the Conference to a service it sponsored.   Evidently, the Augustana delegates did not accept that invitation.   Bergendoff reported in the *Lutheran Companion* that there had been unity of "pulpit and pew," but not at the altar.[38]   Given the ancient Galesburg Rule (Lutheran pulpits for Lutheran pastors), that represented at least a dawning possibility that other Christians might some day at least *speak* in Lutheran churches. Before adjourning, the Conference, with only two dissenting, voted to join with Faith and Order to form a World Council of Churches.

One week following adjournment at Oxford, Bergendoff and two other Augustana representatives were among the three hundred and forty-four voting delegates at Edinburgh. WilliamTemple, Archbishop of York, chaired the general sessions, whose most important result was an "Affirmation of Union in Allegiance to Our Lord Jesus Christ." While it did not stipulate what the specific marks of visible Christian unity would be, the statement became an important basis for the subsequent work of the World Council of Churches. The delegates at Edinburgh also approved joining the WCC. "We have lifted our hearts in prayer, we have sung the same hymns; together we read the same Holy Scriptures."[39] In 1938 representatives of the two movements, Faith and Order and Life and Work, met in Utrecht to begin developing a constitution for the projected World Council.[40] The outbreak of war postponed formal establishment of the WCC until 1948 at Amsterdam.

The Augustana Synod was kept informed about the proceedings and results of Oxford and Edinburgh in the *Lutheran Companion* and the *Augustana Quarterly*. Bergendoff reported that two opinions had emerged with regard to the major issue at Oxford. That issue concerned how the kingdoms of the world might be transformed to become the Kingdom of Christ. One group believed that humanity, individually and collectively, must work together to bring this about; the other held that human power could not accomplish it. In Lutheran ears the former position sounded like American liberal religion. Bergendoff was troubled by the inability or unwillingness at the Conference to define the distinction between the church and the world in such a way that it became clear that only the power of Christ could transform the present order into the Kingdom of God. In spite of these differences, however, he did think that a sense of a "higher, holier, more perfect Church" had emerged in the meetings and that it was clear to all (Augustana delegates included) that no one extant denomination had that church's fullness.[41]

What seems to have encouraged Bergendoff about the Oxford meeting was that American liberal theology had been eclipsed, "a fact which made some of us suspect that in the face of critical conditions that theology has not much to contribute." "To an American, used to the loud and insistent voices of liberal theology in the Protestant Churches of his country, this language sounds a new note of faith and hope." He was pleased at the agreement among Anglican, Lutheran, Orthodox, and Reformed theologians at Edinburgh that salvation was entirely the work of divine grace, appropriated by faith, which was itself a gift of God. This "left little to be desired by the most thorough of the Lutheran theologians."[42] Some of the growing involvement of Bergendoff and his Synod in world ecumenism seems to have come from their sense that it was no longer dominated by the liberal or Social Gospel frame of mind that they believed had been so prominent in earlier inter-church circles, especially in the States.

This shift toward ecumenism did not, therefore, come entirely from changes in Lutheran hearts and minds. Much of it was due to the Lutheran perception that mainline Protestant Christianity had also undergone a change. That was particularly Bergendoff's perception. He liked the Social Gospel as little in the late thirties as he had in the early twenties, but by the late thirties his experience in the 1937 assemblies in Britain would result in a new disposition in his encounters with other Christians. Bergendoff had already spent the year with Archbishop Söderblom when he expressed his grave doubts about the FCC and the *Christian Century* in the 1930 article on the Augsburg Confession that was cited above. It appears, therefore, that his later insistence that it had been the Swedish churchman who brought him to ecumenism[43] should be balanced with the changes brought about by his experiences at Oxford and Edinburgh when the factors that produced the shift in his thinking are being weighed. The time with the Archbishop of the Church of Sweden was spent, with a few exceptions, in the company of Lutherans; it was in Britain in 1937 that Bergendoff passed protracted and intensive weeks listening, talking, and worshipping with "all sorts and conditions of men," as the Anglican Book of Common Prayer had it. A year with the Swedish ecumenist or not, he continued up until 1937 to hold back from an involvement of both head and heart in inter-church encounters. Thus, when a reviewer of Bergendoff's 1954 *One Holy Catholic Apostolic Church* identified the author as a thirty-year ecumenical veteran,[44] he was being generous by a decade, for Bergendoff had not really become a committed ecumenist until Oxford and Edinburgh.

However, it is also true that the dilemma that Söderblom had faced in the twenties became in the thirties Bergendoff's own: "Yet, as the ecumenical meeting with others made the sense of confessional loyalty vivid, there was also the question whether ultimate loyalty was with tradition and confession or with Christ."[45] Simply to pose the alternative this way, confession or Christ, was to have moved from the earlier stance of the Synod and even of the younger Bergendoff, in which loyalty to Christ was precisely understood to be expressed *through* loyalty to the Lutheran confessions. And Bergendoff knew it. In early 1938 he reported to readers of the *Augustana Quarterly* that few delegates "came back from the two world Conferences of the Churches held last summer in Great Britain quite the same as they were before their attendance and experiences there." The realization had dawned that "there is already an essential unity in the Church, despite its many divisions." Now he was not sure "whether agreement on every point of doctrine was necessary before Christians acknowledged each other as fellow followers of Christ." His own "previous notions of what constituted the Church of Christ on earth were unfortunately narrow and unforgivably self-centered."[46] From his comments at the time and later, it was clear that Bergendoff had been particularly moved by the joint worship services and devotional meetings he had attended. They were themselves evidences of a unity with non-Lutherans he had not expected to find when he sailed for Britain. The $80 underwriting for his expenses which the Synod allotted Bergendoff[47] was money well spent, assuming that the Synod was heading in the same direction as Bergendoff himself, yet needed a strong voice to urge it on.

Before 1937 Conrad Bergendoff's understanding of Christian unity might perhaps be characterized in this way: Unity exists when Christians can agree upon how they state their faith. After 1937 his view became: Unity, a gift of God, already exists among Christians and the purpose of ecumenical work is to find ways to give visible expression to that unity. This change had implications for the way Bergendoff regarded the doctrinal statements of his own Church.

International Ecumenical Involvement

So it was that with his ecumenical blood up, our subject got involved in a number of international activities and agencies in the forties. In 1940 the Synod's Committee on Reference and Comity, Conrad Bergendoff, Secretary, recommended that Augustana join the World Council of Churches, stipulating that representation be on a confessional rather than regional basis. The Synod's annual contribution to the WCC should be $150.[48] Bergendoff himself was Chairman of the Chicago Committee of the WCC.[49] The point of seeking confessional rather than regional representation was that Lutherans did not want to be lumped in with other Americans, most of whose churches were far more liberal in matters of doctrine than they. A year later Bergendoff's Synod committee reported that the annual contribution should be upped to $300. (The WCC had asked for $375, so some bargaining appeared to have been going on.) By now Bergendoff had been travelling to ecumenical sessions with growing frequency, sometimes as a private churchman, sometimes on behalf of his Church. In the late thirties he had been appointed to the board of *Christendom,* the official publication of the American section of the nascent WCC.[50] Soon articles under his name began to appear in its issues.[51] In 1941, prior to Pearl Harbor, the Federal Council anticipated that the war would raise fundamental issues about the international order. Bergendoff was asked to serve on an FCC Commission to Study the Basis of a Just and Durable Peace, the Presbyterian layman John Foster Dulles its chairman.[52]

After Pearl Harbor Bergendoff was active on the Commission on the Relation of the Church to the War in the Light of the Christian Faith (another of the FCC groups whose function was quite adequately described by its title).[53] In 1946 he took a seat on the American Study Commission planning for the 1948 Amsterdam Assembly, the actual founding session of the World Council of Churches. And Bergendoff and two others were appointed to represent the Synod at the 1950 WCC Central Committee meetings in Toronto.[54] That session issued the "Toronto Statement" of the WCC Central Committee which made it clear that the organization was not meant to be a "Super Church," a reservation about the WCC that the Augustana Church certainly shared.[55] Bergendoff was one of two Augustana delegates to the Third World Conference on Faith and Order in Lund in 1952, and he was, of course, involved in the 1954 Evanston Assembly of the WCC. At that meeting, the theme of which was "Christ—the Hope of the World," it was apparent that the Americans continued to be more optimistic about that hope being realized in the present world than the Europeans, who tended to see Christian hope in an eschatological framework.[56] Ever the Lutheran, Bergendoff took the European perspective.

Following the Amsterdam assembly of the World Council (which he had not attended), Bergendoff insisted in a 1948 *Christian Century* article that most of what Christian groups knew about each other was an amalgam of non- and mis-information.[57] As he saw it, that principle operated locally as well as internationally. Bergendoff joined efforts to form a Rock Island County Council of Churches, acting as president of a group of about thirty congregations whose number included not only the mainline Protestant groups, but the Church of the Nazarene, the Gospel Temple, and the Salvation Army, and also the local Mission Covenant and Evangelical Free Churches, both Swedish-American congregations. Activities ranged from organizing a World Day of Prayer to advocating the restoration of the salary line for a local probation officer.[58] Bergendoff had become perhaps the leading ecumenist among Middle Western American Lutherans. Of course, a number of ULCA men, notably Franklin Clark Fry, president of his denomination since 1944, were also nationally prominent ecumenical leaders.

Conrad Bergendoff's most significant ecumenical activity in the post-war years resulted from being asked by the US Army, Religious Affairs Division of the Military Government, to spend three months in 1949 lecturing in Germany. The Augustana Board of Directors granted him a leave, and on April 5 he found himself waiting for a military plane to cross the Atlantic. In sessions in Heidelberg, Tübingen, Erlangen, and other Evangelical centers, he met hundreds of students, churchmen, and academics, including Helmut Thielicke (1908-1986), Edmund

Schlink (1903-1984), and Hanns Lilje (1899-1977), all important ecumenists. Some of his encounters with German Lutherans, who had been isolated from Western Christendom through the *Hitlerzeit*, were cordial; in others he discovered a rigid confessionalism that he himself had begun to transcend. He wrote in his journal, "Need to consider what really unites. Too much of theology, without fruit. Yet need clarity of conviction."[59]

When he returned home, he arranged for relief packages from Rock Island to be sent to some of the people he met on the trip. One German Lutheran pastor replied in a thank-you letter: "It is naturally a bit painful for me to accept help from a Baptist church, although the gift has really been a great help to us."[60] Together with his impressions of "the ghastly horror of war," the trip seems to have been one more factor contributing to Bergendoff's growing openness, perhaps in reaction to the entrenched exclusiveness he sometimes met from German Lutherans, nervous about taking gifts from American Baptists. He began to refer to that conservatism as "Missouri-ness."[61] He wrote home to Gertrude that while in Germany he spoke in English, though he did understand most of what the Germans were saying.[62] He evidently understood enough to distinguish types and degrees of Lutheranism.

Whatever the causes, in the forties Bergendoff elaborated an ecumenical theology on which he operated for the rest of his life. Always an historian, he based it upon his read of the centuries since the Reformation. The first ecumenical efforts had been chiefly carried on by individuals. In his 1953 lectures on *The One Holy Catholic Apostolic Church* at the Disciples Divinity House in Chicago, Bergendoff singled out a string of lonely souls—from the Strasbourg reformer Martin Bucer (1491-1551) to the Scot John Dury (1596-1680)—who sought to bridge the gap between Lutherans and Calvinists. Those individual efforts were superseded in the nineteenth century by the formation of associations such as the Evangelical Alliance of 1846 which brought individual Christians into league with each other, though not their churches. Interestingly, in speaking of the Evangelical Alliance, Bergendoff did not mention the central role Samuel Simon Schmucker, the compromiser of the Augsburg Confession, played in founding it.

It was not until the twentieth century that denominations themselves began to form alliances, most notably the World Council of Churches. But Bergendoff offered a caution: "One illusion needs to be removed from our thinking before we try to see the true nature of the Church's unity, namely, that in all the centuries of Christianity there has ever been a period of an undivided Church, in the sense of one all-embracing organization." It was crucial to understand that "We are not going back, in the ecumenical endeavor, to something once existing and now lost. Rather we are feeling for a kind of fellowship in which the love of Christ is the constraining power, and where each part voluntarily brings its contribution to a whole which comprehends all the life of Christendom."[63] Writing in the *Christian Century* as he was preparing the 1947 lectures on *Christ as Authority,* Bergendoff condemned the "supreme sovereignty of churches" as a concept just as "immoral" as that of the ultimate sovereignty of nation states. "The World Council offers the best hope of modern history for the integration of the communion of Christendom into a pattern where faith indeed is a great standard, where hope has its sovereign place, but where love is the greatest of all."[64]

Many of the church unions which had been achieved theretofore, Bergendoff held in these 1953 lectures on *The One Holy Catholic Apostolic Church*, had come as the result of political pressure from governments which in the end controlled them. The Lutheran-Reformed union in nineteenth century Prussia was an example. And many of the off-shoots of dominant churches, off-shoots such as English Presbyterians or Dutch Mennonites, had developed because they believed themselves to be fuller expressions of the apostolic faith than the churches they left. "I accept the denominations as they are. I take them to be what they profess to be." Hope lay in the fact that each group would increasingly recognize that it alone did not reflect the fullness of the holy, catholic, apostolic church. For Bergendoff the focus must shift from bodies seeking to preserve their own version of the Gospel to the recognition of "the limitless love of God and a Christian attitude toward every man who bears the name of Christ[.]" That did not mean, he argued, that churches should seek for unity with one another. Rather the goal should be harmony, a recognition that the other is seeking to respond to God's revelation of his nature in Christ.[65] Early in those lectures he called for a conciliar approach: "A council of churches must have a part in the final resolution of differences which are caused by a single church's claim that only their's [sic] is the correct understanding of the divine Word."[66]

In *Christ as Authority* (1947) Bergendoff had already posited these alternatives, which he discussed more thoroughly in his 1955 *The One Holy Catholic Apostolic Church*. In these two books the mature post-war ecumenical stance of the Augustana man was spelled out. One option would be to aim for "one united church." Although the plan had its advocates, "I can not join them." To try to overcome differences by suppressing them would be to exchange one confusion for another. A second choice would be to operate on a "conciliar theory" of unity. Bergendoff explained this: "Let each of the groups be heard and then identify their differences. Recognize that no single communion is self-sufficient; each has a part of the truth."[67] Thus, he saw existing denominations as contributing their genius to the total Christian impact in the world. This was what one reviewer of *The One Holy Catholic Apostolic Church* characterized as "the typical Lutheran view."[68] ("Typical Lutheran" it may have been by 1955, but it had certainly not been two decades earlier, when any ecumenical involvement at all was dubious in most American Lutheran circles.) Ultimately Bergendoff placed love above even faith as the quality that might bring churches together in a federation: "And recall that even greater than faith is love." No faith which separated Christ's followers had the fullness of Christ's own love.[69] The idea that mutual love rather than common doctrine constituted the ultimate bond between Christians was one of the grounds upon which Bergendoff defended his own Church's decision to join the National Council of Churches as well as the World Council.

"The Lutheran Churches which isolate themselves will have to answer for themselves," he wrote in 1951 in a *Lutheran Companion* piece. Bergendoff argued that the ascendency of modern secularism had placed Christians in a defensive stance and made it all the more important that they stand together. Now, at least for Synod consumption, his argument was not simply from the essential nature of the Christian Gospel itself, but from the threat of enemies. For his part, he assured readers, ecumenical involvement had made him more aware of the reasons he was a Lutheran. His definition of "pure" Lutheranism had developed over the past two decades; now it included openness to other Christians and recognition that one's own faith must be willing to consider that of others.

The appeal Bergendoff made in this article to Synod history also stressed its early ecumenical caste rather than the circle-the-wagons Augustana disposition that some of his fellow historians had characterized in work published in the twenties and thirties.[70] Thus, when a reviewer of Bergendoff's 1967 history of Lutheranism wrote that it was discouraging to note the assertion that "many Lutherans have little interest in worldwide organizational unity unless there is first confessional unity,"[71] he was, if he attributed that position to Bergendoff himself, mistaken. Bergendoff had persistently favored membership in the National and World Councils of Churches, where confessional agreement was not requisite. But that did not obviate certain doctrinal differences.

Unresolved Issues: Holy Communion

Bergendoff was his Church's leading theological and ecumenical spokesperson and one of its knowledgeable historians. As such he could not ignore that, however deep the love of Christ that bound the many Christian denominations together, certain matters between them remained outstanding. Through the decades of Bergendoff's involvement these difficulties persisted. None was as obvious as the matter of inter-communion, common participation in the

Eucharist or Lord's Supper. In 1952 the German Edmund Schlink, a Lutheran who had done a doctorate with the Reformed theologian Karl Barth, wrote in the *Ecumenical Review,* "where there is no communion at the Holy Supper, there is not true organic diversity but disorder and shame."[72] And George M. Stephenson, the Minnesota historian who had skewered many of the Synod's early isolationists, wrote to Bergendoff in the fifties, reminding him that the refusal to share in Holy Communion was a "grim caricature of the Savior's will."[73] That was clearly the sense of persons, lay and clergy alike, who were involved in inter-church dialog in the years after the war. But it was not the way that many Augustana Lutherans had seen the matter before 1939.

Conrad Bergendoff was in that latter company. In 1926, acting as Söderblom's secretary, he accompanied the Archbishop to an ecumenical meeting in Berne. The session was a follow-up to the Stockholm 1925 assembly. After the Berne meeting Bergendoff noted in the *Lutheran Companion* that "Christians can meet together and consider each other as friends rather than enemies, and if we cannot work or worship together, we can live together."[74] Given the realities of American church life into which the Augustana Synod had been born, to be "friends rather than enemies" was probably a step forward. Bergendoff himself was cautious. In 1930 he observed that "It is going to be increasingly difficult to maintain confessional Lutheranism in America in the atmosphere of fraternization now so prevalent."[75] It was what he regarded as casual fraternization that troubled him. So far as the Lord's Supper was concerned, he wrote in 1934, Lutherans would have to steer their way between Roman Catholicism, which had turned the gift of Christ into the sacrifice of the mass, "far away from the simple Lord's Supper," and most Protestants who had almost done away with Communion altogether, which explained why "you have such looseness in Reformed worship." The Lutheran pastor should celebrate Holy Communion at least once a month, he believed, and keep a record of who attended. That was the best index of which members of a congregation were truly faithful.[76]

It was important, Bergendoff felt, that only those who understood that Communion was neither a simple memorial nor a sacrifice be permitted to partake in a Lutheran church. Communicants must "understand what they do." Instruction of children in this matter was essential. Once a person, youth or adult, accepted Lutheran teaching, why would she or he not become a member of the congregation? [77] Bergendoff wrote in 1936 to a pastor in the Upper Peninsula of Michigan concerning non-Lutherans communing that the pastor should explain the Lutheran position to them, and if they agreed with it, he should admit them "to this particular celebration."[78] That was a reference to a united service of worship. When such joint services were the question,

Bergendoff believed that a Lutheran could be part so long as no one was proclaiming non-Lutheran teaching from the pulpit. But to have the Lord's Supper when there was no agreement on the atonement of Christ underlying it was a mistake.[79] Bergendoff thought that one's view of the Lord's Supper was a piece with the rest of one's theology: each church body "has cut the Sacrament to suit the requirements of other doctrines which the denomination has guarded."[80] Of course, the core of Lutheran teaching on Communion was that Christ's words, "This is my body; this is my blood," were interpreted in "the classical tradition of the Church which since the first century had taught . . . Christ was himself bodily present with those who communed." Both early and late in his career, Bergendoff maintained that this was simply the New Testament view.[81]

The idea that theological or doctrinal agreement was essential for people to commune together was one of the foundations of Lutheran church life in the first three-quarters of Augustana's century of existence. If you took Communion with people who did not believe what you did about it, doctrinal laxity was implied. Bergendoff agreed.[82] He did, however, recognize that non-theological factors also played into the formation of a denomination's understanding of the Sacrament: "the Ecumenical Movement has hardly done more than reveal how nationalistic the religious groups have been." That meant that considerations of "history and heritage" as well as concerns for pure doctrine had to be taken into account.[83] Bergendoff was too much the historian to discount those. And his disposition to examine questions historically came to play a role in his attitude toward sharing Communion with non-Lutheran Christians.

The Beginnings of a Thaw

After 1937 Bergendoff's outlook began to change. By 1948 he had come to think that the possibility of inter-communion should be at least a goal, if not one quickly to be reached. "We will attain no unity by trying to get away from this goal, nor in getting around it." Bergendoff by now wondered whether joint worship might help overcome dogmatic differences.[84] That would reverse the order of things; now the possibility was that worshipping together might lead to doctrinal agreement rather than representing theological concord already reached. Bergendoff's writing in the 1950s reflected some uncertainty about the question. This was a move away from the negative certainty he had expressed in the thirties.

In an important 1952 article in the inter-Lutheran journal *Lutheran Quarterly,* entitled "The Lutheran View of the Lord's Supper," Bergendoff began by noting that "There has been bitter quarreling at the table of the Lord, and sometimes it seems that Christians have been more hostile towards fellow Christians with different views of the Supper than towards those who are outside the household of faith." He wrote that Lutheran teaching regarding Communion must be understood in its historical context, having developed in reaction both to the Roman idea that the bread and wine actually changed into the body and blood of Christ (transubstantiation) and to the extreme Protestant position that the Sacrament was simply a memorial celebration of Christ's death. That was not a new idea with Bergendoff. Neither was his assertion that the simplest interpretation of Christ's words, "This is my body; this is my blood" was to believe them, accepting the great mystery implied in identifying bread and wine as containing the body and blood of Christ. There was no point in attempting to explain this with philosophical categories as the Roman Church did, nor in denying it as many Protestants did. The central truth of the Gospel, the Incarnation of God in Christ, was at stake, as Bergendoff understood it. But, "we ought in all honesty realize that the doctrine of the sacrament is not a revelation dating from the Wartburg, 1528 [where the Lutheran position had been developed], but a matter of a living Church which in the twentieth century may no longer be contained in the compartments of the sixteenth." And then, as he had begun: "The most unseemly quarrel in the world is the quarrel of His disciples at His table."[85] Important in this piece were Bergendoff's recognition that the failure to commune with non-Lutheran Christians was regrettable, even deplorable, and that the Lutheran understanding, though he continued to hold it, was the result of historical conditions which no longer prevailed. That way lay hope, if not an immediate ecumenical breakthrough. And, as already noted, simply to use the word "View" rather than "Doctrine" in the title of the article suggested a degree of openness.

Clearly two realities persisted in Bergendoff's and in many other Lutheran minds as well. One was that it was essential to keep sacramental fellowship with other Christians as a goal. The other was that disagreement as to its meaning and nature kept inter-communion from being achieved. The relationship between inter-communion and doctrine continued to trouble Lutherans. This was the "Ecumenical Paradox" Bergendoff had written about for decades. In a 1954 article by that name he tentatively and pensively asked a question—of himself as much as of his fellow Augustana members: "Dare we unite at the table of the Lord with those who believe in the forgiveness of sins through Jesus Christ, or are we going to set up requirements which go beyond Christ's own requirements? Is this His table or ours?" That question had been a crucial one in the debate about open and closed communion for centuries: Was it the *Lord's* Supper, or did it belong to one denomination or another? In the next paragraph of that 1954 article Bergendoff spoke hazily of "some sort of relationship between all those who are in Christ."[86] But that did not seem to mean inter-communion right now, though he continued to hope for it. He personally recognized that the question persisted as to whether formally establishing inter-communion among denominations implied approval of their differing theological views. He was not entirely at ease with suggesting that it did not matter at all.

Here, in his full theological maturity, we find Bergendoff wrestling with the question that Samuel S. Schmucker had put to Lutherans in the prior century, that had troubled the Archbishop of Sweden in the twenties, and that Edmund Schlink had raised after World War II. But even then our Swedish American was not quite ready to recommend to his Church that it approve communion with other non-Lutheran Christians. The members of the World Council of Churches, he wrote in his history of Lutheranism (1967), all acknowledged common baptism and faith in Christ as the Son of God. They shared in services of prayer, in mission to the world, and in the study of Scripture. But the historical record, as Bergendoff read it, clearly indicated that Lutherans were not ready for open communion with non-Lutherans, though they might see it as a worthy goal.[87] On the larger denominational scale the reality was that Lutherans continued to hold back; Bergendoff was asked to use his contacts to find a location for the separate Lutheran Communion Service at the 1954 World Council Assembly in Evanston.[88]

Nevertheless, by the time of his retirement and his gradual backing out of active ecumenical work, Bergendoff was asking of himself and his Church questions which he was not quite ready to answer, either in the affirmative *or* in the negative. "Are we going to set up requirements for fellowship which go beyond Christ's own requirements? Is this His table or ours?" Was "ultimate loyalty with tradition and confession, or with Christ?" One might at this point simply note that even to have asked these questions of the fathers of the Augustana Synod would have been to risk a stern reply from some and outright wrath from others. The best answer Bergendoff could give was to keep aiming at the goal of full communion, recognizing all the while that it was "eschatological." That meant that unity would be realized only after the *eschaton*, the end of this world. But it also meant that it was "the last word," the final goal of Christians still on earth.

Maybe, Bergendoff thought, the answer was going to be found locally and personally rather than through meetings between denominational families: "I believe this problem will have to be attacked and solved on the parish level and in terms of individuals rather than by group action."[89] Interviewed after retiring, he remarked that the range of student religious backgrounds at Augustana and his other church contacts in and around Rock Island had contributed significantly to his ecumenical impulse.[90] One supposes that

Conrad Bergendoff himself did take Communion with non-Lutherans, though he understood his denomination was not ready formally to approve it. Of course, by the end of the century the Evangelical Lutheran Church in America would be in communion with Episcopalians, Moravians, Presbyterians, Reformed, and the United Church of Christ. (Indeed, in 1999 Lutheran and Roman Catholic theologians issued a joint statement on the meaning of Justification by Faith, though Lutherans were not subsequently welcomed to Mass.) That such developments could have occurred within decades of the mid-century struggles over the issue suggests that Conrad Bergendoff's patient and deliberate efforts had not been wasted and that Lutheranism itself was moving at what in matters ecclesiastical was considerable speed.[91]

On a less speculative level, Bergendoff was involved with the effort in his own tradition to refine its worship services. This was partly because he believed that in the liturgical renaissance which Lutherans were experiencing in the mid-twentieth century lay a recognition of the centrality of the Eucharist in worship that might be paradigmatic for other Christian churches as well. Fellowship with Anglicans and Orthodox in the National and World Councils, each with its own tradition of liturgical worship, led Bergendoff to examine his own. He concluded that the inheritance of the Augustana Synod from the Church of Sweden was one of the richest. American Lutheran worship itself was in a low state when Esbjörn, Hasselquist, and others brought the *Church Handbook* with them from Sweden and began to conduct worship according to its ancient order. Bergendoff wrote of this "conservative position of the founders" as regarded worship, noting that in America they also soon began to wear the priestly garb of the Swedish clergy.[92] He himself regularly wore clerical garb in his pastoral work, and appeared so dressed often in the pre-war years at Augustana College and Theological Seminary. Only after the war, did he begin to show up regularly in shirt and tie for college photographs.

In the forties Bergendoff represented the Augustana Synod in the effort of the American Lutheran Conference to develop a common liturgy for its members,[93] and when in the fifties and sixties the attempt was made to involve all the branches of American Lutheranism in developing a common form of worship, he was also a member of the commissions working on a hymnal and book of worship.[94] The new *Service Book and Hymnal* ("the red hymnal") was published in 1958. It was one of the most successful of the National Lutheran Council's efforts at inter-Lutheran cooperation.[95] He must have been gratified when, after sending a copy to Gustaf Aulén, he got a reply telling him it was *"ett mycket imponerande arbete,"* a very impressive work.[96] Bergendoff saw the liturgical form in which Holy Communion was celebrated as one of the gifts of Lutheranism to the wider family of churches, especially in the US. Otherwise, he believed, worship would be structured "at the whim of influential ministers."[97]

Bergendoff argued that de facto all churches had their rituals. "The main question was, should we choose an order of service composed by some individual preacher according to his fancy and likes? Or shall we follow an order that has grown up in the Christian Church through two thousand years of experience in Christian worship?"[98] Bergendoff was committed to developing an order for Lutherans that reflected those two millennia. Apropos of the individual's devotional life, he suggested that the ancient "forms and customs which surround the sacrament are more effective than the definitions he has learned." You got more out of proper worship than you did by rote doctrinal formulae, even from Luther's Small Catechism. And he noted the difference between "the abstract, polemical, often violent language of the schoolroom which Lutheran dogmatics represent" and the "quiet, simple, worshipful spirit, the atmosphere of the sanctuary."[99] That again suggested the possibility, gleaming in the distance like the spires of a cathedral seen far off, that worship might unite Christians, when doctrinal definitions could not.

The Apostolic Succession

Along with questions about admission to the Eucharist and the nature of worship generally, an issue of church government that some Christian groups raised to the highest level of theological significance also stood between church families. That was the matter of "the Apostolic Succession." It involved the claim that the present bishops of a specific church had been consecrated in their office by bishops who in turn had been consecrated by bishops in a chain that reached back to the apostles of Christ themselves. This view held that for a church to be properly constituted, it must be governed by such bishops and that the only true priests or ministers were those ordained by bishops who stood in that apostolic succession. The Anglican communion of churches, including the Episcopal Church in the United States, claimed such succession (though the Pope repudiated that in 1896).[100] The Anglicans recognized other churches which had that succession, notably the Orthodox churches *and* the Church of Sweden. The Anglican recognition of that latter body brought Conrad Bergendoff in the United States of America into the consideration of the matter. The apostolic succession had not been preserved by the priests who came to America from Sweden to assume the role of pastors in the Augustana Synod. The founders, themselves mere priests, had ordained new clergy, and therefore, at least in Anglican eyes, the episcopal chain back to the apostles had been broken. The Swedish historian Ulf Beijbom suggested that "the abolition of the episcopacy satisfied the revival-influenced nucleus of the synod."[101] It was also probably simply a matter of convenience on the American frontier.

Bergendoff preferred to think that the episcopacy had been dropped for more theological reasons: it was not essential to the church. While the Church of England explored the matter of inter-communion and the mutual recognition of priestly orders with the Church of Sweden,[102] he insisted that it was no matter. "The doctrine of the apostolic succession has never been congenial to Lutherans, and assuredly the Swedish Church has never made any claim to have conveyed charismatic power [by it]."[103] Bergendoff did know that when the Swedes were unable to supply their early churches on the Delaware River with clergy, they happily consigned them to the care of priests of the Church of England. But he was glad to note as well that when the Churches of Sweden and England did explore inter-communion, the Swedes said that so far as their Church was concerned, any Christian belonging to a body that accepted the Augsburg Confession was readily admitted to the Eucharist in Sweden.[104] He was probably also happy that while his mentor Nathan Söderblom valued the apostolic succession, he believed that to treat it as essential would be a "conflict with the basic principle of Lutheranism."[105]

In retirement Bergendoff recalled that in the mid-twenties Söderblom had told him, "Go back to Augustana and have them introduce the bishop system and we'll ordain the bishop[.]" Bergendoff's comment was, "I didn't give him much hope on that."[106] Fifty years after Söderblom said it, the remark sounds quite casual, but the Archbishop had a record in that regard, having consecrated a Lutheran bishop for Estonian Lutherans in 1921. He spoke to fellow Swedish churchmen of making of the Baltic a "Lutheran inland sea."[107] Söderblom did believe that episcopal government was the best, if not essential, type of Church polity and that because of retaining it the Church of Sweden had "a stronger and more faithful continuity with the institutions of the Church of the Middle Ages than any other non-Roman section of Western Christendom."[108] The other Scandinavian Churches which had bishops did not claim the apostolic succession, so the Church of Sweden was the only body in Lutheranism that did. For Bergendoff the churches of Denmark and Norway, like his own, were as fully catholic as any claiming apostolic succession. The "wholeness of the church, which the term 'catholic' was originally meant to express, . . . is not primarily concerned with a form of government."[109]

As a participant in Episcopal-Lutheran conversations (which did not at the time issue in any formal agreement between the two Churches), Bergendoff discovered in the mid-thirties that his Episcopalian counterparts were honorable men and good company, but he remained unconvinced by their argument for the necessity of ordination through the apostolic succession.[110] President Brandelle was less delicate in regard to accepting it: "the Augustana Synod would never, never, never go with anyone on that point."[111]

Bergendoff remembered vividly another episode reflecting his own Synod's view of the episcopal office and insignia, one that had roiled Synod waters in the early thirties. Just before his death in 1931, Nathan Söderblom had sent a gold Swedish bishop's cross to the Augustana Synod as a token of the ties between the two Churches. But President Brandelle, avoiding any hint of episcopal high churchliness, had replied that while grateful for it, "we do not hereby adopt any episcopal insignia to be worn by the incumbent of the presidential office." [112] In the 1970s Bergendoff recalled that when P. O. Bersell had been installed in office after Brandelle's 1935 retirement, the latter had worn the cross and then passed it to Bersell, who went into the sacristy "and came out and preached without the cross." (Here as at a few other points in these taped interviews the transcript records "Laughter.")[113]

According to Bergendoff, three great streams ran through Christian history so far as the forms of church polity and government were concerned: episcopalian—government by bishops; presbyterian—government by synods or conclaves of ministers (presbyters); and congregational—self-government by the local Christian community. Lutherans in America had adopted the presbyterian or synodical form.[114] Medieval history was evidence enough of "the inadequacy of the episcopal system to keep the Church apostolic, holy, and catholic."[115] One reviewer of *The One Holy Catholic Apostolic Church* did note that though Bergendoff did not believe that episcopal government was one of the essential marks of the church, it did seem that the office of bishop was preferable to the "rather clumsy system of synodical and district presidents for which there is neither Scriptural nor historical warrant."[116] Maybe replacing that "clumsy" American Lutheran system with bishops was what Archbishop Söderblom had in mind when he offered to come over and set up episcopal government for them. But for Bergendoff the matter of government by bishops in a direct line from the apostles should be no impediment to church unity, though it was for his Episcopalian brothers and sisters. But other doctrinal issues were not quite so peripheral.

Theological Clarity

In his view of the encounter of the individual with Christ as the heart of the Christian life and in his understanding of the necessity of love which was the core of personal encounter with Christians outside of one's own communion, Bergendoff maintained that doctrine stood subordinate. When he and others met to plan the Lutheran Church in America, he noted that they quickly passed over doctrinal questions. It was not that doctrine did not matter; in this case the point was that they already agreed upon their theological position, loyalty to the Augsburg Confession. But when one sought to represent one's own

Church to other confessional bodies, it was unavoidable that theological or doctrinal issues should come into consideration. So it was that in spite of his view that doctrine could never replace Christian love in one's inner life and or in one's dealings with others, Bergendoff argued that greater theological clarity was what was needed in the ecumenical movement. "We need not less theology, but more, to discover wherein unity can be achieved." Without a doctrinal base, you had no church at all.[117] For Bergendoff it was "an obligation of faith no less than of love to recognize those other churches for what they do teach and not to judge them only by what they do not teach."[118]

Here lies a crucial point in Bergendoff's mature ecumenical position. He did not call for theological clarity from others nor did he seek to be clear himself so that he could *refute* those who differed from him. He entered ecumenical dialog because he wanted to understand other Christians. His choice of history as his field of advanced study, his long interest in other cultures, his amicable relationships with people in his own community who held other religious ideas than his—all these were evidence of a curiosity about and respect for people who differed from him. He wanted to understand their premises and assumptions and to explain his to them. That applied to his ecumenical work as well. When he wrote in a review of Karl Olsson's *By One Spirit,* a history of the Evangelical Mission Covenant Church, that Covenanters' unwillingness to adopt a creed made it hard for others to grasp what they stood for, he was not, intentionally anyway, denigrating their Church. He sought a creedal statement so he could know what the Mission Friends believed. He thought that Olsson himself recognized that without such a statement one understood neither what orthodoxy was nor where heresy lay. A Christian community needed to say what it believed so that others might understand what it was about.[119] "We cannot avoid putting into words what we believe, if we are to make known our Christian faith."[120] Bergendoff's informal comment about his reaction to Olsson's book was, "I poke a little fun at the title of the thing 'By One Spirit' because there are all kind of spirits in the book." Some of the Mission Friends he knew while they were students at Augustana had his sympathy, because they "would like to be along with us who really believe something." And: "Well, when you think of these kind of groups—the Lutheran Church can at least say 'this is what we believe.'"[121] This was Bergendoff in the mood or frame of mind of the creedalist, one he did not always work in.

Beyond simply believing something, however, Bergendoff came increasingly to think that it was his own creed, the Augsburg Confession, that forced him to listen as well as to speak to Christians of other denominations. Lutherans said that they believed in "the one Church." That meant that they either had to claim that theirs was that one Church, or look for it in concert with others who were not Lutheran.[122] Of course, in all of this Bergendoff took people at their word, refusing to get around behind them to see if they *really* believed what they said they did. That was the path he took to Lutheran unity, and he stayed on it when he encountered non-Lutherans. That must surely have been one of the reasons why he achieved such recognition as an ecumenist; while some fellow Lutherans began their encounters with other Christians suspiciously, he took them for what they said they were and sought assiduously to avoid impugning their authenticity or sincerity.

Another characteristic of Bergendoff's ecumenical work was that it was dialogic, but in a way that did not always immediately seem to be. In none of his work was he given to the sort of interchange in which Person A made a point, Person B responded, A replied, eliciting an answer from B, and so forth. That back-and-forth might be called "conversational dialog." It was not the sort of academic conversation that characterized his graduate training, nor did it seem to be the way Bergendoff conducted his pastoral ministry. The kind of dialog that suited him better was one in which an individual representing a particular position made a careful, often extended, scholarly statement representing those views, and others were given time and the opportunity to make responses, usually in formal academic papers which they presented themselves. The dialog would often continue in the minds of each of the participants long after the adjournment of the meeting in which the initial statements had been made, and opportunity to meet again would be arranged so that the dialectic could advance. That was the nature of the ecumenical encounters in which Bergendoff often found himself involved, and it was from these that, over the years, his openness to other Christian viewpoints matured. There was not a drop of iconoclasm in his blood—and little impatience—so he was particularly suited to such precise and extended exercises.

Again, Bergendoff understood that all creeds and confessions were themselves the creatures of historical forces and circumstances. That had freed him for ecumenical encounter: "I've had not too much difficulty with the Confessions myself because my approach has not been from the systematic which I think makes it more difficult, but from the Historical point of view."[123] This was a different view from that held by the fathers of his denomination who, as the historian Stephenson put it, believed that the Augsburg Confession stated for all time the eternal truths of New Testament Christianity.[124] Just as with his views on inter-communion, Bergendoff's ideas about the role of doctrine in ecumenical affairs evolved. After his year in Sweden with Nathan Söderblom, he wrote, "When the Lutheran Church comes to see itself as a branch of Christendom instead of as a bunch of self-assertive little twigs, it may have a larger place in the Tree of Life than it now fills."

Further, "If the Church of the Reformation has the truth, it need not lock it up within the safety vaults of an exclusive Lutheranism[.]"[125]

Already, when Bergendoff wrote that (1929), the matter of Lutheranism's relationship to other Christian groups and theologies was in play. At that point Bergendoff's primary concern was that his own confessional family get its house in order. A year later, perhaps wistfully recalling Söderblom's openness, he judged that the present ecumenical prospects were not promising: "As Lutherans we have no better standard than the Augsburg Confession. But to hold it means a continued division from Rome and separation from the rest of the Protestants."[126] To recognize the historical circumstances that surrounded every creedal statement did not mean that creeds should be dismissed. It would not be possible, he said in 1939, simply to forget history; Luther spoke of "one mind and understanding" as well as of "one faith, one love."[127] He said that to a meeting of the Federal Council of Churches, as though to serve notice that Lutherans were still afar off as concerned entry into its ranks.

But the war saw a softening of that view. Faith, said Bergendoff in 1944, is always a gift of God, and it appeared that God had given different people different ways of being Christian. No one part of Christendom, even the Augustana Synod, could claim to be the whole body of Christ.[128] It was essential to get over the idea that each Christian had been personally confronted by the many denominational creeds and made a deliberate and considered individual choice, he noted in *Christ as Authority* (1947).[129] Most people belonged to a church because of historical factors. Obviously that applied to Lutherans, including the writer, as well as to others. Bergendoff did not wish to underestimate the importance of theological choices, he wrote a year later, but as the ecumenical movement went forward, it would be vital to examine carefully the traditions and doctrines of other groups as well as of one's own. That was, he thought, the only way to steer a course between two equally unattractive alternatives. One was to see religious differences as deep and almost impossible to resolve, since they arose from the most basic issues of human existence. The other was to hold that since these differences produced antagonisms, one should hold faith tentatively and experimentally.[130] (We have seen what he thought of Pascal.) The most fruitful *modus operandi* would be to take your own doctrinal position seriously and to attribute the same sincerity to others.

By the time of his lectures on *The One Holy Catholic Apostolic Church* (1953), Bergendoff had concluded that such careful examination of the others' traditions and beliefs ought to begin with an effort to understand the apostolic message. That was actually the key ecumenical question: what did the apostles teach? Current New Testament research might help to illuminate this, he said, pointing particularly to the work of the British scholar, C. H. Dodd. Professor Dodd

Bergendoff and Swedish Archbishop Erling Eidem at the 1948 centennial celebration in Rock Island. The two men were ecumenical bridge figures, especially with post-war Germans.

concluded that there was a wide range in the interpretation of the apostolic *kerygma* or message, but that in all this variety its essential elements were knowable. "With all the diversity of the New Testament writings, they form a unity in the proclamation of the one Gospel." That had three implications, Bergendoff thought. One was the variation itself, for example, between Paul and John, Peter and Luke. Allowance must be made for this when you met other Christians.   A second implication of the unity of the New Testament message was that "we may not make any but apostolic elements the points of separation from our brethren." And third, "we may find that the road to unity will lead less through the barren wastes of controversy in which each finds fault with the other, and more directly through the fruitful fields of study in the elements of the apostolic kerygma."[131]

These comments, delivered to an ecumenically disposed audience at the Disciples Divinity House in Chicago, were as full an expression of Bergendoff's search for creedal or theological unity among branches of Christendom as can be found. They must, of course, be balanced with his long history of loyalty to the confessions of his own Church, particularly the one after which it was named. They must also be considered in view of Bergendoff's early and continuing caution about sharing in the Lord's Supper with people who held other creeds. The lectures do beg a question: was the *Confessio Augustana* itself a statement of the apostolic faith beyond which one could not go? Or could you perhaps get, as

C. H. Dodd suggested, back to the apostolic kerygma itself? Rather than offering safe and settled answers to such questions, Bergendoff's 1953 lectures represent an exploration of terra incognita, at least so far as the Synod was concerned. As such, they are the work of a man who, again, had not resolved all the problems and even contradictions in his position, but who was willing to venture out of safe haven anyway. It was what his father had done when he boarded ship in Gothenburg, bound for a New World.

Neo-Orthodoxy

When he did range outside the confines of his Synod, Bergendoff encountered a theological scene far more lively than that of his seminary days in Rock Island. He lived in one of the church-changing theological periods in Protestant history. Indeed, this theological renaissance was often referred to as the "new Reformation theology" or "neo-orthodoxy." Bergendoff read the representatives of the movement thoroughly and had plenty to say about them, though he confessed he did not like the term "neo-orthodox" itself.[132] Towering over the movement, however named, stood the Swiss-German, Karl Barth. Schooled in the liberal theology of the late nineteenth century, Barth reacted against the identification of Christianity with culture, especially after many of his German mentors supported the Kaiser's aims in the First World War. When he read Barth in the thirties, Bergendoff recognized his importance at once. Barth's power lay in his insistence that "only something greater than man-made doctrines can save the world." Bergendoff liked Barth's warning that people came to church to hear the divine word, not to listen to pieces of the preacher's wisdom.[133] But Barth's over-emphasis upon God's transcendence was "a road that leads nowhere," Bergendoff felt. The roots of that lay in Calvinism.[134] That over-emphasis was corrected in Lutheranism, as Bergendoff understood it, by a view of Christ as the mediator between God and humanity. Nonetheless, the Swedish American welcomed Barth's break with liberal theology, his denial that Christianity was one more human effort to find God, and his recognition of the depth of the chasm that separates humanity from God.[135] For the moment, seeming to forgive Barth's Calvinism, Bergendoff lauded him for asserting God's authority over "the idols of mankind" in a 1935 sermon at the diamond jubilee Synod convention.[136] It was, of course, the Great War which had done much to generate this shift in European theology. Nicholas Hope, a British historian of northern Protestantism, writes, "It took three brutal years of total war for an understanding of the darker side of human nature—an issue raised at the Reformation by Luther . . . —to sink in: a full 400 years after the Reformation."[137]

Interestingly, Bergendoff found one leading American representative of the new theology, Reinhold Niebuhr (1892-1971), to be "the voice of despair." Niebuhr's assertion that society was ruled by selfishness, that Christianity might influence the individual but not society as a whole, and that at moments a sort of violence might be needed to bring change about, was "a confession of defeat."[138] Here, once more, Bergendoff steered a middle course between abandoning culture to pagan values and thinking that it could be signed over entirely to the control of Christians. Many observers saw Niebuhr as an heir of Luther as much as of Calvin, but, as Bergendoff viewed him, Niebuhr erred in the direction of a pessimism that bordered on cynicism. Christians could not simply abandon society to power and force. In a sense, therefore, Bergendoff's criticism was that Niebuhr's realism had given up altogether on the attempt to influence society with Christian values. Oddly, it was as if Niebuhr had too readily abandoned the Calvinist effort to legislate morality, which Bergendoff had also roundly criticized. We saw in Chapter 4 that what the Swedish-American Lutheran really wanted was a culture influenced by the work of individual Christians, rather than one where "the Reformed" sought to legislate Christian living.

When war broke out in 1939 and as he realized that many of his German Lutheran confreres stood behind Hitler, Bergendoff wondered what Lutheranism had to put in the place of that Calvinist effort to legislate morality. He confessed in a private letter that it was a fair criticism of his own theological tradition that it had not figured out how Christian love should be translated into social action.[139] That was an issue that bothered Bergendoff through the rest of his days. He recognized that Luther had "recalled us to the paradoxes of faith."[140] But how to apply those paradoxes to making ethical decisions, either individually or socially—that remained the issue.

In both Barth and Niebuhr, then, Bergendoff detected the deep influence of Calvin, who in contrast to Luther had an all-absorbing concern for the sovereignty of God.[141] It was surprising, therefore, that Bergendoff maintained in the Lutheran-Reformed conversations in which he participated in the sixties that Calvinism had no key central doctrine which united it in the way that justification by grace did Lutheran theology.[142] One might have supposed that Calvin's emphasis upon absolute divine sovereignty was such a central theme. As Bergendoff saw it, Barth's expression of divine sovereignty led him to a "dead end," that is, to fail to see the gap-bridging work of Christ. Niebuhr's problem, also stemming from the Calvinist emphasis upon God's transcendence, was that he gave up all hope of Christian influence in society and culture. So far as social theology and ethics were concerned, Bergendoff criticized some Calvinists for seeking to govern society by laws which the church had a determinative voice in establishing. He believed that other Calvinists committed the opposite mistake: abandoning society to the pagan standards which he believed were coming to dominate it.

As was the case with his criticism of the Calvinists, original or neo, Bergendoff found any effort to create a linear connection between the Gospel and social programs to be at best ill-advised. What was needed was not a "Theology for the Social Gospel," Bergendoff wrote in 1938, but Christians who would let the light of Christ's gospel shine through their works.[143] Three years later he addressed the American Lutheran Conference, arguing that the current concept of "social righteousness" had been separated from divine revelation. For Paul and for Luther, social goodness did not come by human programs or legislation. Man's highest goodness and the righteousness of God were in opposition to one another, Bergendoff insisted. Christian righteousness began with a confession of sin.[144] Bergendoff was put off both by what he regarded as the facile optimism of the Social Gospel and the pessimism of neo-orthodoxy. To the extent that mainline American Christianity seemed in thrall to either, he did not think he could fall into company with it. We have noted the relief with which he discovered at Oxford and Edinburgh that many non-Lutherans were no less dubious than he about the possibility of humanity fixing its own enormous problems, but that they were willing to confront the challenges of the times with the Christ of the New Testament. By 1937 a higher Christology seemed to prevail at the ecumenical conferences in Britain; that matched Bergendoff's inclinations.

Catholic Thought, Roman and Non

The other strand in Christendom which Bergendoff had persistent problems with was, of course, Roman Catholicism. In this he stood firmly in the long, steady tradition of the Augustana Synod.[145] Early and late his own writing was full of strong anti-Roman assertions, none of which was particularly unique to Bergendoff, but many of which were quite pointed. Bergendoff himself never soared to the heights of eloquent animosity reached in a 1912 editorial in the *Lutheran Companion,* which labeled Roman Catholic services "séances of musty mysticism, muffled mummery, and melodramatic mockery."[146] (So much for anybody who thought the Swedish Americans had not mastered English!) But he was as dubious as that editor about the history, the government, and the current state of the Church of Rome.

Bergendoff knew the work of such Roman Catholic apologists as Christopher Dawson, Jacques Maritain, and Emmet John Hughes (1920-1982). He regarded all of them, Hughes in particular, as a "brilliant example of the use of history for purposes of propaganda." The propaganda lay in maintaining that the Roman Church had been the spine of western civilization and that medieval society was a golden age.[147] That was, thought Bergendoff, a false reading: "Some day an historian with a true perception of the real value of history will write a history of the Church in which most of the mass conversions of early and medieval ages will be described as more or less farcical."[148] (Did he include the conversion of the Swedes?) The unholy medieval alliance between secular authority and the church could not be maintained, but in the Inquisition, Bergendoff said, a last desperate effort was made to enforce obedience from society to the church. Despite claims of sovereignty over them, the Catholic Church grew increasingly dependent on national governments to hold its dominant position.[149] Ignatius Loyola (1491-1556) Bergendoff treated as an example of "Spanish fanaticism." The Church saw "no inconsistency in making saints of popes and Jesuits who in the name of Christ had pitilessly tortured and exterminated thousands whose only crime was their search for a purer faith[.]"[150]

Implicit in the claims of the Roman Church was, of course, the idea that Protestantism was a late contrivance of heretics. But, Bergendoff held, the Lutheran Church goes "back through the Middle Ages to the Day of Pentecost." Archbishop Söderblom had assured him that the "riches of past history are as much our rightful property as Rome's."[151] Bergendoff had made his own contribution in support of the Archbishop's assertion. His *Olavus Petri* had traced Swedish liturgy and piety back through the Reformation to the earlier life of the church. With its own claim to history, Lutheranism, as Bergendoff saw it, had no need to apologize to Rome: "We can go no farther today than did Melanchthon towards Rome. Since then Rome has retreated farther from us."[152] The doctrine of papal supremacy was the sticking point.[153] "There is no more anti-catholic Church than one which sets itself up as the exclusive institution of salvation and takes Christ's place as the governor of mankind. We do deny the pretensions of the Church of Rome . . . to have any right to rule in His place."[154] No unity could be reached among Christians by submission to one man's authority or to a ministry dependent on that authority, which was alleged to be the sole agency "competent to know the will of God."[155]

During the Second Vatican Council of the early 1960s, Bergendoff felt that the "triumphal tone of former ages" had been quieted. But the Church of Rome, he cautioned, was not giving up its core doctrine concerning the role of the Pope. Some "small degree of unity in faith" had been achieved in the Roman Church's recognition that there were Christians who were not in communion with it. Lutherans would hardly be stirred by that. But they should greet with approval Vatican II's Declaration on Religious Freedom. Implicit in it was the renunciation of force as a means of maintaining the Catholic

In 1930 Archbishop Söderblom presented Synod leaders with a cross like the ones worn by Swedish bishops. Seeming too high churchly, it was received with near reluctance. But two decades later, the Americans began to use the pectoral cross as a symbol of the Synod's presidency. Here, in 1951, P. O. Bersell passes the sign of office to his successor, Oscar Benson.

Church's position in countries where it was dominant.[156] In *The Church of the Lutheran Reformation* (1967) can be found what is perhaps Bergendoff's most conciliatory judgment on Vatican II and the Roman Catholic Church. He acknowledged a "remarkable change," one perhaps prompted by the losses which western Catholicism sustained in World War II and the Soviet take-over of Eastern Europe. The recognition of Protestants as "separated brethren," was a step forward, and the use of the vernacular in the mass, the collegiality of bishops, and the greater role of the laity—all these recalled the demands of the Reformers four centuries earlier. But the condemnations of *sola fide* (faith alone), the veneration of Mary, and the continuing position of the Church on mixed marriage all remained as difficulties.[157] The "totalitarian Roman Church" that sought "spiritual rule of the world" which Bergendoff warned his Lutheran brethren about before World War II[158] had moderated its position; the question was whether its essential claims had been modified. Bergendoff was not so sure. He did not expect that Lutherans would "return to Rome" any more than they were likely to have fallen into step with the Social Gospel in the twenties and thirties.

Amidst the general jubilation at its 1960 centennial convention in Rock Island, the Augustana Church had found time to express its concern about the possibility of a Roman Catholic being elected President of the United

States in the impending November election. The Synod took action that put it in the company of the Southern Baptist Convention and the Assemblies of God, passing a resolution that cautioned its members that it would be a "misuse of tolerance" to disregard the "ideological beliefs and affiliations" of candidates for national office. That was certainly a coded reference to the candidacy of John F. Kennedy. The report on which the action was based maintained that "there are grounds for reasonable doubt that a Roman Catholic president would be free of institutional control and from desires to promote in special ways the ends of the Roman Church." [159] This hostility to the Church of Rome that had characterized the Swedish-American Church from its founding did not dissipate until after the formation of the Lutheran Church in America, which followed by two years the solemn warning from the Synod about electing a Catholic president—issued to no avail, as it turned out. At the school of which Conrad Bergendoff had been president, a sort of de facto détente with Rome took place beginning in the later sixties, as an increasing number of Catholics enrolled. In fact, within two decades of Bergendoff's retirement, there were as many Roman Catholics as members of the LCA in the Augustana College student body, and a priest, indeed, a Jesuit, had joined the campus ministry staff.

But these developments came later; it was clearly the case that the ecumenical ventures which Bergendoff and his Church had undertaken in the decades after World War II did not include all those calling themselves Christians. It was not likely that Augustana and its leading ecumenist would have entered as heartily into inter-church dialog if the Social Gospel theology of the twenties had continued to dominate American Protestantism. And we know that Bergendoff saw no possibility that Lutherans, bewitched by Vatican II, would "go over to Rome," in the nice phrase used in the preceding century when Anglicans like John Henry Newman converted. So liberal Protestantism and conservative Catholicism were out. But Lutherans like Bergendoff were drawn into conversation with Presbyterians and Congregationalists and Episcopalians. After World War I many theologians in these denominations were attracted by the rise of a school of thought that found its roots in the Reformation and in careful exploration of the central New Testament message that the Reformers claimed to have rediscovered. A theological conversation arose in which Lutherans could listen and be listened to, for the parties were using a vocabulary and perhaps even operating on assumptions with which Luther's heirs were familiar.

Augustana historians have remarked upon the shift in the Synod toward ecumenical involvement that took place during the thirties. It was at Oxford and Edinburgh that the Augustana Synod "identified itself with the mainstream of the modern ecumenical movement," writes G. Everett Arden.[160] Maria Erling and Mark Granquist's *Augustana Story* entitles a chapter "Augustana's Ecumenical Vision." And Byron Swanson's doctoral dissertation, *Conrad Bergendoff: The Making of an Ecumenist* carefully traces the influences on Bergendoff which led to his becoming the leading ecumenical voice in his Church. There is no question about the Augustana Church being on the leading edge of American Lutheran inter-denominational engagement. The impetus to that came, Bergendoff believed, from the understanding of Luther and the Lutheran confessions, which held that the Holy Catholic Church was greater than any one earthly organized expression of it. In the case of Augustana and Bergendoff himself, it also came through the influence of the Swedish Lutheran ecumenist Nathan Söderblom. And the other ecumenically inclined American Lutheran body, the United Lutheran Church, was for Bergendoff paradigmatic, a view he developed both because of his year in its Philadelphia seminary and his on-going contacts with its leaders and theologians.

But along with these impulses coming from Lutheranism itself, the seismic shift in non-Lutheran Protestantism must be taken into account when the engagement of Augustana and other American Lutherans in inter-church conversations and organizations is considered. When the American theological scene was dominated by what Lutherans regarded as a shallow and over-optimistic liberalism that they believed represented not just the opposite of their own more profound theological tradition but a superficial reading of the Bible itself, American Lutherans remained aloof from national and world-wide ecumenical encounters. When the tilt to a new Reformation theology, neo-orthodoxy, took place, Lutherans were ready to talk. Such conversations would not force them to compromise their deepest convictions just to convene the meetings.

Conrad Bergendoff was in on the early stages of that process of getting acquainted and then engaged. By the time of his retirement from the process, he had begun to wonder if others did not in fact believe what he did, though they had not signed the *Confessio Augustana*. Maybe if these others meant what the Confession meant, and more important-ly believed what the New Testament said, there was a chance you could worship together with them—and at least consider the possibility of holding a Communion service together. That was hardly in the offing when Bergendoff had been ordained into the ministry of the Augustana Synod in the early twenties. At that time, the Swedish Americans were just emerging from the splendid isolation that Bergendoff himself later said had marked their first half-century in the New World.

§

Through its developing ecumenical involvement, the Augustana Church and its leading theological spokesman believed they were standing in the company of the Church of Sweden. The figures of its late Archbishop Nathan Söderblom and its bishop-theologians, particularly Anders Nygren and Gustaf Aulén, were powerful influences in this turning to inter-church dialog. That was, however, but one of the ways in which the Swedish-American Synod in North America and the land from which its founders sailed were bound together, for better and for not-so-better, in the twentieth century. And just as nobody in Augustana took place ahead of Conrad Bergendoff as an ecumenist, nobody stood ahead of him in the line of those who sought to understand and strengthen ties with his father's homeland. That is the subject of the next chapter.

CHAPTER 8

SWEDISH AMERICA AND SWEDEN

When the Lutheran World Federation was formed after the Second World War, the largest church to join it was the Church of Sweden, and a Swede, Bishop Anders Nygren, was elected President of the Federation. The State Church counted as the largest Lutheran body in the world, because virtually everybody living in Sweden was reckoned to be a member. Conrad Bergendoff had no trouble with that. He thought that to be Swedish was to be Lutheran and, further, that to leave the Church of Sweden was like leaving the country itself: "One leaves too much of oneself, one's heritage and hope."[1] When a Missouri Synod pastor impugned the orthodoxy of the Church of Sweden and the Augustana Synod's ties to it, Bergendoff reminded him that "Sweden and Lutheranism are more of a unit than Germany and Lutheranism." Germany was populated with Catholics and Calvinists as well as Lutherans, while Sweden was almost entirely Lutheran. What was more, for the Augustana Synod to reject the Church of Sweden would be to violate the commandment to honor father and mother.[2] Bergendoff liked to think of his Synod the way the Gettysburg Seminary church historian Abel Ross Wentz did: "The Augustana Lutherans came to America from the land of Lutheran archbishops and cathedrals, of high Lutheran liturgies and firm Lutheran loyalties."[3]

This was a great tapestry as Bergendoff saw it; tug on one thread, and the whole weaving changed. When a Swede left his Church, he was just about giving up his nationality, and when an outsider doubted the Swedish Lutheran

Church, the Lutheran loyalty of the Augustana Synod came into question as well. The problem was, of course, that the tapestry *was* being rewoven. Both Swedish and Swedish-American life were transforming quickly in mid-century. In Sweden the national culture was growing ever more secular, and in the United States the ethnic character of the Augustana Synod was disappearing. So shortly would the Synod itself. That left Conrad Bergendoff in a position where he had to renegotiate his own sense of history, to reconstruct his "narrative" (to borrow a term now shared by scholars with TV news anchors). Bergendoff was not quite willing to consider himself a relic, one of the last of those for whom the identities Swedish and Lutheran were almost synonymous. Yet once in a while he did wonder whether he had become the champion of lost causes or perhaps a dreamer of "impossible dreams."[4] Maybe, he mused in 1966, he belonged "more to the old than the new."[5] While at moments regretting that some changes had come to pass, at others he faced them, though often with reluctance. The purpose of this chapter is to trace his shifting understanding of Sweden and Swedish America and their relationship to the Lutheranism that was so essential to Bergendoff's identity.

Explaining the Facts

We noted in Chapter 5 that the Augustana Synod never enrolled most of the Swedish immigrants arriving in the United States and that among others Conrad Bergendoff was considerably troubled by that fact. By the time the teen-aged Conrad had enrolled at Augustana, over one million Swedes had sailed for America. Sweden sustained the loss of perhaps twenty percent of its population in the course of that mass exodus. Chicago became the world's second largest Swedish city, after Stockholm. In time the emigration to America came increasingly from Swedish cities, and these urban Swedes were apt to be less religious than the immigrants who had come to America previously from the countryside. The earlier arrivals in America, according to the last President of Augustana Theological Seminary, Karl Mattson, had been younger, aged twenty to thirty-five, from rural Sweden, poor (just able to afford the trip), and married with families.[6] The newer immigrants settled in cities rather than on farms. Reflecting their urban backgrounds, they sought work where it could be found—in America's booming cities.

Rock Island, one hundred and fifty miles to the west of the world's second largest "Swedish city," was often seen as Swedish America's cultural-spiritual capital. That may have pointed to the tendency of many of the newer and more secular Swedes to assimilate more quickly to American life. In 1910 Chicago's population was 2.2 million; Rock Island's 24,000. It appeared, in spite of the persistence of its ethnic neighborhoods, to be far easier to be absorbed in the town on Lake Michigan than it was in the one on the Mississippi; in teeming Chicago, only eighteen percent of the immigrants from Sweden belonged to the Augustana Synod in 1880.[7] And the Swedes in Chicago were a small percentage of the city's millions; in Rock Island there were a college, a seminary, and a publishing house to preserve the Swedish Lutheran identity, as well as a much smaller town, where Swedes could not hide from each other in the first place.

The common view about the two-thirds of the immigrant Swedes who did not identify with Augustana was that they adjusted to American life with relative ease.[8] Indeed, that fraction of the Swedes in America may have included many who no longer sought or needed a headquarters for their particular ethnic sub-culture. To the degree they were melding into wider American society, the majority of Swedes may have been losing interest in their ethnicity. Of course, the Swedish Americans who were on Synod membership rolls surely did feel the influence of the religious institutions headquartered in Rock Island, and to the extent that the Augustana Synod retained its Swedishness, the people in its sphere did.   But things were changing as the twentieth century unfolded. In 1959 Bergendoff admitted that in the rush of American life the Swedish America he had known had been "passing away before our very eyes."[9]   That included the Swedish America influenced by the Synod.

At least a priori, one supposes that two factors caused that "passing away." One was the influx of less religious immigrants from Sweden in the twentieth century and the other was the process of Americanization within the Synod itself. Of course this did not diminish the commitment Bergendoff felt to the ecclesiastical and cultural institutions based in the Mississippi River town that continued in the first half of the twentieth century to focus the loyalty of those Swedes who did observe the Lutheran faith of their forebears.

For Bergendoff the Church was still the most important agency to shape the life of Swedish America. He would have agreed on that count with the assessment of the Swedish scholar Dag Blanck.[10] But Bergendoff went a little farther: "outside of the immigrant churches nothing worthy of mention has been accomplished in America by the descendants of Sweden."[11] Of course, "The Augustana Synod may not have succeeded in gathering within its fold the vast majority of the Swedes in America—and that is not altogether its own fault—but it is nevertheless practically the only organization of Swedish Americans that has built for the future and made a successful attempt to perpetuate the rich spiritual and cultural inheritance that is ours by birthright." Many Swedes who had concern only for their "temporal welfare and pleasure" were fast disappearing into general American society; they would leave no lasting monument to their lives and work, Bergendoff grimly continued. The

Gertride Bergendoff (viewer's right) and friends, dressed up.

assumption seemed to be that only religious Swedes would leave a legacy in the New World. Bergendoff thought the others would *spårlöst försvinna* (disappear without a trace).[12]

That was written in 1923, but Bergendoff continued through the following decades to believe that the only Swedish culture that seemed to have persisted in the New World was that conditioned by the church bodies, especially his own. It was almost as though one had to be Lutheran (or at least a church member) to preserve one's Swedish heritage—in America as in Sweden. That raises again the question about the relationship between being Swedish, or in this case Swedish American, and being Lutheran. We are left to wonder whether Bergendoff was perhaps myopic about religion and the Synod when he claimed that little of value had been left by the Swedish Americans outside of the institutions that the Synod and the other Swedish-American religious bodies had founded. A 2002 article by Dag Blanck, for example, makes clear that in the later twentieth century Swedish Americans found numbers of ways, few of which were explicitly religious, to continue to affirm their ethnicity. They ranged from mid-summer festivals to dinner menus to academic conferences.[13]

But often Bergendoff did not like the pictures of Swedish-American life that he encountered in alternative readings of Swedish immigrant history. He was troubled, for instance, by the depiction of life among the immigrants that emerged from the 1960s work of the Swedish author Vilhelm Moberg (1898-1973). Bergendoff warned of peril if all you read were the novels in Moberg's *Emigrants* tetralogy: "These were not the emigrants from Sweden who created the church and institutions with which I have been associated through all the years of this century. Fortunately there were other types who came to this country who laid cultural and religious foundations that now look back on a long history."[14] What Bergendoff found objectionable in Moberg was his concentration on an earthy selfishness in the immigrants that was untempered by religious faith. Carl Sandburg's work was more worthy of the pioneers, Bergendoff said. Sandburg pictured "the sturdy and honest citizens, the men and women who built churches, hospitals, schools, and whose sons and daughters early became identified with the best forces in American society." The mid-twentieth century had enough of the kind of "realism" Moberg represented; Bergendoff was "deeply disappointed" in him. This low estimate of Moberg was not improved by the fact that the novelist himself had been quite critical of what he found to be the hostility of the Augustana Synod to higher culture.[15]

Bergendoff still hoped someone would write "the story of the immigrants who made the Swedish name respected and admired in America[.]"[16] In 1976 Bergendoff wrote that he applauded the attention that the novelist had given to the common people, but that "another Moberg" was needed, one who would recount the intellectual and spiritual achievements of the immigrants "who did not live by bread alone."[17] One assumes he meant the members of the Synod. By 1976 that body was, of course, gone from the scene, merged into a larger Church, where ethnicity had little influence beyond nostalgia. That transition in American Lutheranism, particularly in Augustana, began decades earlier, and its most important feature was probably the shift, almost entirely, to the use of English in both worship and Church business.

The Language Transition

Bergendoff had presided at Salem Church over the shift from Swedish to English. Four decades later, he recalled "how closely the Swedish language was connected with our experience of the Lutheran faith."[18] But in the twenties, change was in the offing, and it fell to Bergendoff himself to argue that if the qualities Swedish and Lutheran had to be separated, his Church and he would remain Lutheran. We recall that the Salem congregation had moved from what had once been a Swedish neighborhood on Chicago's near South Side to one much farther south where no single ethnic flavor, Swedish or otherwise, was as pronounced. In retrospect the changes in the character of the entire city seem to have been inevitable. That included the dilution of *svenskhet*, Swedishness, among the immigrants and their children. But of course in the first decades of the century that dilution was not taken for granted. Indeed, in some quarters it was not accepted at all.

The most focused opposition to the Americanization of the immigrants and of the Augustana Synod in particular came from Vilhelm Lundström, a Gothenburg professor and newspaper editor. Like T. N. Hasselquist in Illinois, Lundström combined careers in journalism and academe, though he did not manage, as Hasselquist had, simultaneously to lead a church body. In the first decade of the new century Lundström became the head of *Riksföreningen för svenskhetens bevarande i utlandet,* The Society for the Preservation of Swedish Culture in Foreign Lands. He was also the dominant voice in the organization's biweekly publication, *Allsvensk samling.* From its first meeting in Stockholm's Grand Hotel in 1907, the organization had conceded that the overseas Swedes would never again be under the political sway of Sweden, but it believed deeply that they must remain in the Swedish cultural and ethnic orbit. Lundström maintained that there were, in fact, two fatherlands. The first was "the kingdom to which we belong politically." The other "consists of all Swedes throughout the world, *the Swedish stock,* or from the purely linguistic viewpoint, our language area." The use of Swedish became the key to the preservation of Swedishness. Without it "one cannot belong entirely to the Swedish nationality; race and blood, pure as they may be, do not suffice in themselves." One-third of the nine million Swedes in the world lived outside the Kingdom, Lundström reminded his readers; they must be kept for the second, cultural and ethnic, fatherland.[19]

In 1910 an American sister to the Swedish organization was founded in connection with the fiftieth anniversary of the Augustana Synod. Headquartered in Sweden-America's "capital city," *Föreningen för svenskhetens bevarande i Amerika* regarded Augustana College and Theological Seminary as its epicenter: "May the day never come when the Swedish tongue falls silent within its walls or the Swedish spirit dies within the hearts of its teachers or students. Hail to the fifty-year-old bastion of Swedish culture in the mighty land between the great oceans."[20] And asked to serve as treasurer was Conrad Johan Immanuel Bergendoff. He agreed, but not without his fingers crossed. Years later he would write that "all along I realized that it was a losing cause. I stayed with it because of my love for my heritage."[21]

In the first stages of his movement, Professor Lundström would not have conceded to the Treasurer of their American affiliate, nor even to the Swedish government, that *svenskhetens bevarande,* preserving Swedishness, was a losing cause. When US policy during World War I restricted the activities of the foreign language press, the Swedish language newspaper grew increasingly alarmed, and following the war, the efforts at Americanization (which among other things meant the use of English) seemed to continue. The editor railed

against the "unbridled tyranny of a dominant language." In the early twenties
Allsvensk samling decided that the greatest perfidy really lay in the Augustana
Synod itself and began to suggest that the move in the Church toward English
was in fact the result of deliberate policy on the part of its leadership. Articles
such as "How the Swedes Are Seeking to Kill the Swedish Language in
America" appeared.[22] Finally, in 1924, after three years of steady attacks from
Lundström and his allies, the lukewarm sometime Treasurer of *Föreningen för
svenskhetens bevarande i Amerika* and Pastor of Salem Lutheran Church, Chicago,
decided to respond directly. Right then, in the homeland, Professor Lundström
himself was growing weary, even disillusioned, with the struggle. Neither the
Swedish folk nor their leaders seemed greatly concerned about his cause. A
contemporary Finland-Swedish historian, Bengt Kummel, notes that after
World War I, the government had little interest in pursuing policies, domestic
or foreign, that would have supported the *allsvensk* movement.[23]

Yet it was just at that moment that Bergendoff sent an article, "*Augustana-
Synoden och svenskhetens bevarande*" to Lundström's newspaper, which published
it in April. Writing in the Swedish he had learned from his family and from
the publications of the Synod steadily mailed to the parsonage in Connecticut,
the author said he had noted "the tone of wonder, of fear, even of complaint"
in *Allsvensk samling* about the Synod's position toward the preservation of
Swedishness. He had waited for the Synod's defenders to speak, but since
nobody else seemed ready to, Bergendoff, "as one of the members who was
born and reared and now serves within that church and who at the same time
reckons himself among the friends of Swedishness in America," now presumed
to express himself on the matter. The Synod's position must be judged from a
churchly not a cultural standpoint, he insisted. Language was a means of ministry
for the Church, which from the beginning would use whatever instruments
were at hand to "win the world for Christ." The Gospel was not intended only
for Swedish speakers. The best thing a Swedish-American Lutheran could give
to the new country was the Faith. (Here again, the identification of Sweden
and Lutheranism.)   But there were places the Church did not seem well
received. "It must be said that the church works gladly where it is welcome
and that the later immigration from Sweden has not shown itself to be disposed
to the ministry of the church." It was not the Synod's responsibility to teach
language; it had neither the time nor the money for that. The Synod must
advance the Gospel, even when it did so in English.

Then, hitting his stride, the twenty-nine year old pastor adduced two Swedes,
both of whom made it clear that Lutheranism and the Swedish language were not
necessarily correlatives: Gustavus Adolphus (who gave his life for "the evangelical
Lutheran faith") and the current Archbishop of Sweden (who had written to "the

undersigned" that the Synod was "Swedish-America's core"). The implication was that both the seventeenth century king and the contemporary prelate had advanced the interests of the Lutheran faith of Sweden in places where Swedish was not spoken. Sweden's psalm book, worship service, Christian art, holy days, her churchliness and piety—all these could be preserved in America, even if the language could not. These were reasons enough for the continued life of the Synod, independent of other American Lutheran communities. "Whatever tongue she speaks, the Augustana Synod's heart is still Swedish!" And finally, Bergendoff added a word about language. Those speaking Swedish because they could not use English were "Swedish-minded" of necessity, not love. And a warning: anyone who thought to elevate Swedish culture by belittling American would never win friends for his cause.[24]

It is noteworthy that the position which Conrad Bergendoff took— insisting that the Synod's prime responsibility was the propagation of the faith rather than the preservation and advancement of Swedish language and culture in America—was one which the editors and writers of the *Lutheran Companion* and predecessor publications of the Synod had been advocating steadily through the first decades of the new century. For example, one of the chief proponents of that view was Pastor Adolf Hult, in most other matters an ultra-conservative. In 1905 Hult wrote in the *Augustana Journal*, a forerunner of the *Companion,* "We would reach souls. We may not be able to give our children Swedish. The latter is a question of this world, the former of the world to come."[25] Born in Moline in 1869, Hult may have been one of the very conservative theological voices in the Synod, but as one of the Augustana clergy to be born in America,[26] he was also an advocate of the use of English. So Bergendoff was not staking out new ground in his *Allsvensk samling* essay in 1924; that ground had been occupied two decades earlier by the man who would later become one of Bergendoff's least favorite seminary professors. (Hult taught at the seminary, 1916-1943.) The Synod was clearly being forced to make a decision between two of its essential identifiers: Swedish and Lutheran. Both Hult and Bergendoff knew where they stood, and at least in this regard, if in few others, they stood together. Faced with the choice of preserving either its Swedish or its Lutheran character, a choice the Synod would perhaps have preferred not to have to make, Augustana, at least in the persons of these two second-generation Swedish-American pastors, had no doubts about chosing to protect its religious identity, even at the expense of its ethnic. The "world to come" was, of course, more central to their concerns than this one.

Americanization and Melting

The younger (by twenty-six years) of these two defenders of the use of English also wrote a second piece on the Swedish-English language transition, this time in English. "The Americanization of the Augustana Synod" appeared in the *Lutheran Companion* in two installments in August, 1924. Here Bergendoff declared apropos *svenskhetens bevarande i Amerika,* "the phrase is not a happy one." If its users were aiming at creating a "Sweden in America," Bergendoff had little sympathy with them. But one's Swedish heritage could be defended. The people of the Augustana Synod should develop fellowship with the "American churches" not as poor orphans, but with "a self respect born of a noble heritage and history and strong in a faith as old as any in the Protestant world and adorned with a spiritual culture equal to that of any other church in the world." Here the implication was that the Augustana Synod (and Conrad Bergendoff himself) belonged in America as much as any other church (or person). He continued: "the Americanization of the Augustana Synod should mean not that America remakes the Synod, but that the Synod remakes America." And here was the young Bergendoff's optimism about the possibility of Christianizing the country, now coupled with a defense of his own denomination's heritage. That heritage was both cultural and spiritual. Bergendoff made little distinction between these qualities in Swedish life, as we shall shortly see. What he was concerned about just then in his Synod was its importation of Sunday School literature, church architecture, and revival hymns from "the Reformed." (Here the latter term seemed to mean general unwashed American Protestantism.) Better for Augustana to stick to its own inheritance.[27] That was why Pastor Bergendoff, supporting the publication of Augustana Synod material in English, argued in the mid-twenties that "Doctrinal literature in the language of our land must be provided for the growing generation."[28]

The 1924 English language essay was organized around three "American national characteristics," each of which, Bergendoff argued, could be turned to Augustana's advantage. These national characteristics were: independence, unity, and idealism, all essentials of the American spirit. In Bergendoff's application, independence meant the preservation of his Swedish-American tradition; unity, the readiness to unite with other Lutherans in the "attempt to Christianize America;" and idealism, the willingness to join sensible (an important qualifier for Bergendoff) reform efforts being undertaken by non-Lutheran Christians.[29] The essay was in many respects a programmatic statement for Bergendoff's churchmanship for the next fifty years. Each of those qualities— keeping tradition, pan-Lutheranism, and cooperation with other Christians in reasonable reform—was vital to him. However, each of these underwent a kind of revised understanding or interpretation in the course of the following decades, as we have seen. Above all, it was important to the author that to be truly American did not mean giving up your heritage. While he recognized that cooperation with non-Lutherans on "social and civic problems" might be in order and that his Synod must emerge from its "splendid isolation," he was not willing to abandon firm loyalty to the Augsburg Confession; "there is a limit to assimilation."[30]

The "melting pot" metaphor, the image of America as a great vessel into which poured folk from around the world, there to be recast into one new people, was a strong one in the America in which Conrad Bergendoff grew up and worked. He did not like it. The two essays just considered make clear that in the twenties Bergendoff had argued for the preservation of the unique elements in his own inheritance. He thought them as just as noble as the ideals and values of the wealthy New Englanders to whom he had delivered newspapers when a boy and whose universities he had passed up in favor of an immigrant college on the Mississippi. This was one example of what the Norwegian scholar Orm Øverland calls the effort to develop "home making myths," which ethnically oriented Americans used to form and strengthen their sense of belonging in the broader national society. Another student of the immigrant experience, Jon Gjerde of UC Berkeley, argues that the First World War was an important factor in the homogenization of these groups:"the heterogeneous minds of the Middle West, though they continued to exist, were being forcefully merged in a world at war into an American whole."[31]

Even after World War II, which had gone a long way toward further blending the sons and daughters of the Augustana Synod into the great American composite, Bergendoff held out against the melting pot image and the realities it represented. The "Melting-Pot simile," he wrote in 1968, "is pernicious because it blurs or obscures the true place of the immigrant in our national life." Melding architectural and musical images, he continued: "Rather America is an incomplete architecture and the Swedish immigrant was a participant in the production of a new world symphony which is still unfinished."[32] And in 1971, noting the broadening of the work of immigration historians from consideration of specific ethnic groups to the search for the common elements in all immigrant experiences, he wrote:"We are not a people, but a congeries of peoples and cultures, unlike any other in the ancient or modern world."[33] He would have agreed with the assessment of a professional colleague and friend, Carl Wittke, who noted the stress that was placed by factors such as war in Europe upon the assimilation of ethnic groups, including Swedes, into general American society.[34] But just that recognition that there were commonalities in the experiences of all immigrants was itself an indicator of the melting that had been going on—even in Rock Island. So were the broadening mix of family names among Augustana College students, of course. The choice which Augustana, Synod and College, faced was one common to Scandinavian-American institutions. One scholar, Elder Lindahl, writing about the language issue, recalls two adages from North Dakota: "Churches were established because Swedish was popular; Churches were closed because Swedish was unpopular."[35] That went for colleges as well as churches.

So while the churches Americanized, their colleges did as well. The study of history at Augustana had long since broadened into the mainstream. In 1948 History Department Chairman O. F. Ander had succeeded in luring to the Rock Island campus the annual meeting of the Mississippi Valley Historical Association. That was the national organization dedicated specifically to the study of American history. Ander wrote to President Bergendoff reminding him that leading academics such as Theodore Blegen at Minnesota, Carl Wittke at Western Reserve, Ray Allen Billington at Northwestern, and Merle Curti at Wisconsin were exploring American immigration history on a wider scale, and would welcome a visit to Augustana, there to learn what historians of Swedish America were up to. Along with the academic papers they read to each other, the scholars evidently enjoyed the smorgasbord served up by the college.[36] The MVHA meeting, including its dinners, had been set up to coincide with the 1948 celebration of the one hundredth anniversary of Swedish immigration to the Middle West.

Of course, so far as scholarship was concerned, Augustana did continue to be particularly interested in its own tradition. In the fifties Dr. Ander told Bergendoff that the Swedish Central Bureau of Statistics had offered to the school a large body of documents dealing with nineteenth and twentieth century Swedish life, and after some reluctance on Bergendoff's part to accept it because of concern over where it might be housed, Ander prevailed, and the "ton of material" was located in the well-supported attic of sturdy Denkmann Library.[37] One supposes that a good part of the stuff depicted Swedes in a way that was consonant with Bergendoff's views of their character. So it was that the Swedish language (still being taught to late teen-agers at Augustana, of course) became an instrument of research, valuable and important, but a far cry from the preserving agent for *svenskhet* that *Allsvensk samling* had believed it must be. By the last third of the century, academics were examining ethnicity as a factor in the history of American religious development.[38] But while the importance of ethnic influence in the country's history was being recognized and examined by scholars, the melting of ethnic Lutheranism went on.

Roots in Sweden

Whether you accepted the Melting Pot metaphor or not, the language shift was evidence of the changes in Swedish America. But through his career, Bergendoff believed that his Church and the culture it embodied were the direct descendants of Sweden and its Church. Some of the scholars who looked at the Synod's relationship with the Church of Sweden labeled the claim that the American body was the "daughter" of the Swedish "unhistorical."[39] But for Bergendoff the relationship and the metaphor were self-evident and self-justifying.[40] Two years after his defense of the language shifts in the Synod, Bergendoff actually went to Sweden, there to work with the Archbishop of the mother Church, Nathan Söderblom.[41] To judge by the frequency with which he later spoke of that trip and the degree to which he thought of Sweden in terms of the impressions he had formed of it in that year, it must be rated as one of the formative events in his life, together with his student years at Augustana, his sojourn at the Mt. Airy seminary, and his years in Chicago.

The family of three Bergendoffs had nearly decided to live in the Söderblom household, at the last moment finding a small place in the Church of Sweden Mission Home, where the boy, age two, would not disturb the Archbishop.[42] But that did not keep the American from traveling with Söderblom through his diocese, the country, and much of Europe. Years later Bergendoff said of the Archbishop, "Few could keep up with him."[43] But the young Augustana pastor did try and in doing so got a picture of Swedish church life that left a strong impression on him. The national Church in the twenties was in the midst of crucial changes, though Bergendoff did not often speak about many of them, either at the time or later. A number of the issues the Church faced arose as the result of social and political developments, the most obvious of which was the coming to power of a Social Democratic government. Women had been granted suffrage in 1919. A year later the revisionist or gradualist Marxist, Hjalmar Branting (1860-1925), became Prime Minister in the first of three short-lived Social Democratic governments that he led prior to his death. Branting maintained, in contrast to revolutionary socialists such as Lenin, that a just social and economic order could be reached by steps and without violent revolution. When Branting's party came to power in the twenties, the nation of six million was growing increasingly secular. A leading newspaper, *Dagens Nyheter,* estimated in 1927 that on an average Sunday in November that year just over five percent of the population attended services.[44] In 1926, when the Bergendoffs arrived in Sweden, the first in a series of alternating Liberal and Conservative governments was elected, but the social reforms and the reduction of the military which Branting had led remained in place. So did a degree of anti-church sentiment.

One contemporary Swedish church historian, Ingmar Brohed, writes that criticism of the Church came from several directions: from the free churches, from the low-church faction in the State Church, from the Social Democratic party, and from a secularized middle class. The question of where precisely ownership of the Church's property lay—with the Church itself or with the state—was under discussion, as was the matter of disestablishment. When the twelve Swedish bishops or when annual *Allmänna kyrkliga mötet* (the General Church Convention) proposed moderate measures to modernize and democratize the authoritarian ecclesiastical regulations and procedures that were hanging over from the last century, it was not uncommon for the government, which ultimately controlled the Church, simply to respond with silence, a passive-aggressive style applied to politics. The Social Democrats themselves were split between those who favored disestablishment as quickly as possible and others who believed that democratization of the Church could be carried off with government direction. So strong were the currents and counter-currents that swirled through Swedish national religious life in the inter-war period, that even questions about how one might leave the Church of Sweden, either in life or in death, could not be settled. The *rätt till fritt utträde ur Svenska kyrkan* (right freely to leave the Church of Sweden) and the more morbid question of whether every Swede had to be buried according to the rite of the national Church were heatedly debated, usually with most of the bishops in opposition to the proposals to relax either membership or funeral requirements. The leaders of the Church appeared reluctant to let go of their ecclesiastic hold upon the country, up to and including burial, though all the while their services of worship were less frequented by the people, and the Church's influence over them diminished.[45]

It appeared that already in the nineteenth century the Swedish clergy, sensing some of the validity in the criticism of their status as officers of the state as well as pastors of their flocks, grew weary of being regarded, as one Swedish church historian puts it, *"som statens megafon"* (as a megaphone for the state) and of leading services which were set up *"som en statlig angelägenhet"* (as a state affair). That was the down side of acting as salaried official registrars of birth, marriage, and death for all Swedes and of announcing changes in government ordinances and regulations as part of worship services, all in a land where even attendance at Holy Communion was regarded as a civic duty as much as it was as a spiritual act.[46]

The Church responded to these criticisms in many ways. As Conrad Bergendoff increasingly acquainted himself with Sweden and her Church, two of these responses especially impressed him. One was the *Ungkyrkorörelse* or Young Church Movement formed in the first decade of the century by men who had studied at Uppsala, including Nathan Söderblom, Einar Billing, J. A. Eklund, and Manfred Björkquist, all later bishops. Its motto, *"Sveriges folk, ett Guds folk"* (Sweden's people, a people of God), captured the movement's effort to bring its countrymen to see the Church as God's gift to them and to rediscover their deep religious and cultural roots. The movement published a newspaper, founded a folkschool, visited congregations, and sought to establish contacts with the growing workers' movement in Sweden. Björkquist took a rather nationalistic line in several political controversies, including one about naval armament and national defense, in the years before the First War. That actually had the unintended effect of splitting rather than uniting the Church, as other less conservative clergy and laypersons held different political and economic views.[47] Therein lay a certain irony, for, as a recent Uppsala dissertation says, the conservatives maintained that society was an organic whole in which the institutions of the state, the family, marriage, and the Church were understood to be the orders of God's creation.[48]

The principal theological thought-line behind the Young Church Movement came from Einar Billing, a Bible and Luther scholar at Uppsala and eventually Bishop of Västerås (about 60 miles northwest of Stockholm). Billing (1871-1939) elaborated a "Folk-Church Theology" that emphasized "grace as *offered* rather than *received*." That meant that God's grace was offered through the national Church to all the Swedish folk, not simply to those who, as in the free churches, decided to accept it. For Billing the Church of Sweden had an obligation to minister to all the people of the land, and such a ministry was itself the expression of the divine grace that was no respecter of persons. It was important to realize that rather than being simply a State Church, an ecclesiastical body supported through taxation and ultimately controlled by the government, the national Church was a folk church, a divine gift to all Swedes.[49]

Bergendoff found that to be a powerful idea, and he much preferred to speak of the Church of Sweden as Billing thought of it: a folk church.[50] The folk church idea protected the Church of Sweden on two fronts. It was a contrast with the evangelical view, often asserted in the free churches, but also present in the national Church, that the local congregation must be made up of true believers.[51] It was also, of course, an effort to preserve the role of the Church in Swedish society as the country's national religious institution. This was not unlike the position of the Augustana Synod in the United States, which sought to guard itself against the excesses of the Pietists on one side and on the other hoped to enroll the majority of the wave of new immigrants. In any event, Billing's theological justification of the national Church was the second of the responses to the rising secular tide that especially impressed Conrad Bergendoff.

The tendency that emerged in Sweden in the first decades of the twentieth century to forge a sense of Swedish homogeneity and unity made an appeal to both nationalism and Lutheranism, says one Swedish historian, Kjell Blückert. In the interwar period the attendant "rhetoric became more aggressive, and more integrated in the societal and ecclesial life." At the same time, it tended toward a certain "banal nationalism," according to Blückert: "The concepts 'home', 'church', 'land', 'people' and 'king', with their synonyms, are all employed pell-mell, in the imagery of both the church and the nation."⁵² This applied to the time when Bergendoff himself came to know Sweden directly, rather than only through the recollections of his parents and older friends. He seems to have been impressed by the ideas of Söderblom, Billing, Eklund, Björkquist, and others. The intellectual framework which he got from these theologian-bishops melded with the impressions he took from his own travels with the Archbishop. Together they generated the somewhat idyllic view of the impress of Lutheranism upon Swedish culture that we will shortly discuss.

Here we simply note that in contrast to this general tendency to identify church and nation, others, including the author of the Atonement theory which had in part led to the departure of the Pietists from the Augustana Synod, held that a territorial church to which everyone belonged by birth was foreign to the New Testament. As P. P. Waldenström read it, the Bible clearly said that individual faith and commitment were requisite for being Christian, and he seems to have understood that not everyone would come away with the same reading of that book. The American scholar Mark Safstrom points out that Waldenström was not distressed by the plurality of religious and social ideas that had begun to replace the earlier unanimity of Swedish society. Indeed, a central strand in Waldenström's career was recognition of this pluralism; he sought to develop a deliberate strategy for dealing with the conflicts that it had begun to generate.⁵³

Waldenström also thought that the Augustana Synod had sought to replicate the Swedish folk church model and that as that concept was increasingly articulated by some of the leaders of the Church of Sweden (just as pluralism began to characterize the country), it was reflected in the Synod's sense of its mission in North America.⁵⁴ Bergendoff became one of those reflectors. But we have seen earlier how much it troubled him and other second generation Synod leaders that they had never enrolled even half of the immigrants. That failure nagged at their sense of being the heirs of the Swedish folk church. If it did not give the lie to that sense, it certainly did raise doubts about the Synod's role as the Swedish folk church in America. Some Swedish students of the Synod's early history have argued convincingly that the basic reason for Augustana's existence separate from other American Lutherans was ultimately neither theological nor political; it was to serve immigrants from Sweden.[55] In this light it is understandable that the failure to win a majority of them deeply troubled its leaders, Conrad Bergendoff among them.

For his part, Bergendoff would not give up on the national Swedish Church; he persisted in thinking that "the so-called state churches have answered a role of bringing the gospel to bear on all aspects of national life[.]" He recognized that free church leaders had problems with this. Yet he argued that even those same free churches sought to influence the country, not simply by trying to convert the land person by person, but through social and political programs.[56] (Shades of the Reformed in America!) There were also persons *within* the Church of Sweden, notably the priest and Social Democratic Riksdag member, Harald Hallén (1884-1967), who believed it would be possible to erect a righteous socialist society that was based on the common ethical values which the Swedish Folk Church represented.[57] He was less willing to abandon the church-state set-up than were the free churches, which for their part had long since given up on it. With very rare exceptions, the Swedish Lutherans on the western side of the Atlantic did not flirt with any possible hook-up between socialism and Christianity.[58]

The *Swedish* Reformation

But for all of the issues surrounding Sweden and its Church when he got there, Bergendoff had crossed the Atlantic to write a dissertation as well as to get to know the land from which his father had emigrated forty-four years earlier. Convinced by Archbishop Söderblom, he determined to focus on the work of the Swedish Reformer, Olavus Petri. In the history of the Swedish Church and its turn to Lutheranism, Bergendoff found many of the qualities that he believed persisted into the twentieth century life of the land. The Sweden he came to know in the 1920s may have been in the process of very significant change, but he preferred to think of it as a land that was still the heir of its sixteenth century Reformation— to which he now turned his scholarly attention.

Most of Bergendoff's subsequent work, especially the short books written during his twenty-seven years as a college president, had a theological focus and often dealt with historical developments in broader strokes that sustained Bergendoff's themes or arguments. But *Olavus Petri and the Ecclesiastical Transformation in Sweden* was an exact and detailed examination of source documents, replete with careful comparison of variant texts and with extensive footnotes. The study established the view of Swedish church history which the author would maintain for the rest of his life. Its bibliography consisted almost entirely of Swedish sources, primary and secondary. The

Foreword reminded readers that little was known in the United States about Olavus. And the concluding paragraph was a statement of the mood and outlook of the entire work. "Olavus Petri knew the power of destruction. He preferred the power of construction. The heart rather than the altar must witness the first reformation."[59]

In the two hundred and fifty pages between those statements, Bergendoff presented the work, though little of the personal life, of the architect of a Swedish Lutheranism that would last for four centuries. He recognized the Erastian or state-controlled character of the Reformation in Sweden. Gustav Vasa (ruled 1523-1560) established national freedom from two outside agencies: the Kings of Denmark (who had under the terms of the Union of Kalmar of 1397 controlled all Scandinavia through the fifteenth century) and the Roman Popes (who since the conversion of the Swedes at the beginning of the second millennium had ruled the Church of Sweden). Attracted to Lutheran teaching, not least because of its denial of the temporal power of the Church, Gustav made a break with Rome in 1523, just six years after the posting by Luther in Wittenberg of his Ninety-five Theses. Struggling to consolidate his power, the king was not formally crowned until 1528 at Uppsala, but on that day, wrote Bergendoff, "an evangelical preacher preached the coronation sermon for an evangelical king in the archiepiscopal church of Sweden."[60]

The evangelical preacher was, of course, Olavus Petri (or Olof Petersson, if one did not mind giving up the academic Latinism). Bergendoff traces the events that brought this smithy's son first to the new university in Uppsala (established 1477) and, as was then common with Swedish students, on to advanced work at the (also newly-founded) university in Wittenberg, 1516-1518. In Germany Olavus came into Luther's orbit, or as Bergendoff said ornately: "His Swedish disciple revealed in future works that he had taken impress from the position Luther had attained to, in this period."[61] Bergendoff spent most of the remainder of his *Olavus Petri* in careful consideration of these "future works." The ecclesiastical stance developed by the Swedish Reformer and his brother Laurentius, consecrated Archbishop in Uppsala in 1531, was based upon the Lutheranism that emerged in these early Reformation years.

Carried north, that Lutheranism had a decidedly Swedish character according to Bergendoff, who always insisted that it was a misconception to regard the Lutheran Church as essentially German.[62] What Olavus had achieved was to fit Luther to Swedish needs and conditions: "The genius of the Swedish Reformer ... manifests itself not in the creation of new forms and doctrines, but in selection of material produced by the German Reformation and emphasis on what he considered essential and best. No genius can be more worthy than that which fits measures conducive to a noble goal."[63] That statement was a kind of credo that underlay almost all of Bergendoff's historical work as well as his attitude toward contemporary church affairs: some might regard genius simply as breaking new ground, but for Bergendoff greater genius lay in forming a worthy goal and then carefully adjusting current conditions to that goal. The spiritual transformation of Sweden was much more gradual than the political changes carried through by the king in the decade 1521-1531. Bergendoff thought that the result of this gradual spiritual transformation shaped Sweden ever after. And it was no mere German import. "The first literary production of the Swedish Reformation is not a copy of Luther, but an independent work[.]"[64] That is how Bergendoff treated the translation of the New Testament, as well as the devotional, liturgical, theological, and polemic literature from Olavus that he considered in the dissertation. It was important to Bergendoff to make clear that Swedish Lutheranism was sui generis, no mere footnote to the Reformation down on the Continent.

In the dissertation and in a number of essays and articles that followed it, Bergendoff put the Swedish Reformation in longer historical perspective. Scandinavia was "Last to join the papacy and among the first to leave it, [and] never experienced the worst of medieval abuses," he wrote in the *American-Scandinavian Review* in 1940. "Here is a unity of history as well as geography and culture, almost unique in the modern world." In Sweden even the Reformation represented continuity rather than a rupture.[65] And the cathedrals of northern Europe, Bergendoff believed, had never been fully Roman Catholic; they were, in fact, built in protest "against the empty forms of Romanism" well before Luther.[66] In spite of the fact that in 1542 Olavus Petri had barely escaped execution at the hands of his erstwhile champion, Gustav Vasa, over the question of royal control of the Church, Bergendoff maintained that in Sweden the Church had never surrendered autonomy to "an all-absorbing state." Through the Reformation the Swedish bishops had kept their dioceses, and the clergy had held their position as one of the estates in the Riksdag, so both continuity and a degree of autonomy had, in Bergendoff's view, been preserved.[67] Of course, the matter of continuity involved the question of the apostolic succession of bishops, which Bergendoff never felt was an essential element of Lutheran faith. And the autonomy of the church would inevitably be in question when it was in the end under royal control. Thus both the continuity and the autonomy were to a degree problematic.

But it was certainly true that, however the ecclesiastical history of Sweden might be parsed, for Conrad Bergendoff it was positive. That was how, moving from the sixteenth to the seventeenth century, he considered Sweden's *stormaktstid* (Age of Great Power). Remember that Bergendoff cited Gustavus Adolphus (ruled 1611-1632) when defending the switch to English in the

Bergendoff and college history professor O. F. Ander had rather differing views on Synod and Swedish history but were also good friends. Here they are with their wives, Ruth Ander and Gertrude Bergendoff.

Augustana Synod. The defense of non-Swedish Lutheranism was, of course, the least of the monarch's virtues and significance: "all his aims and ideals were suffused with a religious fervor, raising them from the level of expediency to the realm of the kingdom of the Spirit." Unlike the contemporary kings of England or France, Gustavus Adolphus was not "a king above his people."[68]   Bergendoff believed that in Sweden the law was always understood to be superior to the crown.[69]   And the King was "Protector of the Faith," not as in England, "Supreme Head of the Church."[70]   Gustavus Adolphus lived and fought in the same conditions as his men on "the bleak shores of Finland and Russia," and died in the thick of battle, protecting the faith.   His wars were "the price the Swedish people had to pay for their independence."[71]   Bergendoff's upbeat heroic read of Swedish church history was here, in a speech given as a tribute on the three hundredth anniversary of Gustavus Adolphus' death, extended to its early modern political and military development.   That was the time when, save for the great king's death in battle defending Protestantism, Sweden might have emerged to permanent great power status.   But though the nation itself never again attained that Gustavian glory, for Bergendoff Sweden's Church and the culture he believed it created remained paradigmatic.

Bergendoff's Sweden

That was why Conrad Bergendoff had some difficulty confronting the growing secularism of the Swedish.   In the early thirties, reviewing George M. Stephenson's *Religious Aspects of Swedish Immigration,* he insisted that the author underestimated the present strength of the Church of Sweden.   For Stephenson to speak of it as "a mere shadow of its former greatness" and of its "impotency" and "declining influence" was to make "superficial judgments,"

Bergendoff wrote. If the Swedish Church was as weak as the Minnesota historian claimed, how did he explain its survival and growth and, Bergendoff added, the flourishing of its American offspring?[72]

Thus, one wonders what Bergendoff made of a 1939 letter from another historian, his Augustana colleague, O. F. Ander, at the time carrying on research in Sweden. Ander wrote that he was shocked of a Sunday morning to discover that the church he attended was only half full. And he reported talking with a Swedish couple in their fifties who intimated to Ander that they never prayed. Neither did a young student he met, who told him "Swedes were too intelligent for such a superstition." Ander understood how Bergendoff (whose direct experience of Sweden had been in the mid-twenties, but who had enjoyed several ecumenical encounters with Swedish churchmen in America and Britain since then) would feel: "I know that this is going to hurt you; it has hurt me so deeply that some nights I have been unable to sleep."[73]

Years later came a personal letter from Bergendoff's old friend-nemesis Stephenson. Historians have long memories, so Bergendoff should not have been surprised when the scholar (still at Minnesota but long since cured of studying immigration by the bitter reception *Religious Aspects* received in the Synod) wrote to him with what seemed like gentle taunting about the "present state of impotency of the Church of Sweden and the flourishing (by contrast) of the free churches[.]"[74] Whatever Bergendoff made of mid-century Sweden, the direction it was headed was clear. That raises for the Bergendoff interpreter a number of interesting questions.

The fourth chapter of the present work discussed Conrad Bergendoff's ideas about the relationship between the Christian message and human culture. He never completely settled the question of the extent and depth to which the Gospel could reshape social life, rejecting the medieval Catholic idea of church control over it, the Reformed effort to legislate Christian goodness, and the Pietistic tendency to withdraw from society. His hope was that regenerated men and women who knew Christ would move into responsible roles in politics, education, economic life, the arts, science, etc. and would, listening to the voice of the Spirit, gradually transform society. This begged the question whether that had ever actually happened—anywhere, anytime. Bergendoff's answer is interesting.

At moments Conrad Bergendoff actually suggested that Sweden was as close as you could get to finding such a society, which is why, whatever letters he got from a sleepless Ander or a skeptical Stephenson, both of whom were actually in the country more than he and saw first hand the empty pews, Bergendoff did not seem to want to stare too directly at mid-twentieth century Sweden. There was, in both his formal writing and his passing comments about modern Sweden, a double sense. He considered Swedish society to be paradigmatic in some regards, and yet he also realized, especially after making post-war visits of his own, how secular it was becoming. Prior to World War II, Bergendoff spoke of Swedish culture as a worthy pattern more often than he did after the war. Before 1939 he was also more optimistic about the degree to which Christians could move society toward conforming to the values of their faith. The over-lap was not coincidental.

We saw that in 1926, when he was arranging his visit to that land, Bergendoff had written to the Archbishop that he would come to Sweden *"som en främling"* (as a stranger). But during his 1926-1927 sojourn, he quickly learned his way around, in part because Söderblom had taken him under his wing. After visiting parishes and Church institutions, Bergendoff began to sense that he knew the country well. The recollection of his father's memories of his own boyhood and youth and the retelling by Swedes in the congregations in Middletown and Chicago of their stories—these and other experiences seem to have helped Bergendoff overcome his status as *främling* rather quickly. And of course he spoke elegant turn-of-the-century Swedish fluently.

So as a man who soon felt at home in Sweden, Bergendoff reported to readers of the *Lutheran Companion* on his impressions. After time spent at the Sigtuna Institute, founded as a part of the Young Church Movement, and smitten with blue skies and water divided along the horizon by green-black pines and firs, Bergendoff told readers that "Even more glorious was the Christian piety that everywhere expressed itself in the lectures, in the simple chapel, in the outings, in the fellowship." The experience had been "proof abundant that in many youthful hearts in Sweden lives the Spirit of God[.]"[75] Visiting parishes and schools with Söderblom (who had a diocese of his own, Uppsala, to care for, in addition to being head of the national Church), Bergendoff was taken with "the order and obedience that prevail in Swedish schools." The Archbishop had asked children if they could name their *farfarsfar*, great grandfather, and the answers were always sharp and certain. Could American children do that?[76]

With time to reflect back on his experience in Sweden, Bergendoff did not grow less positive. In a 1941 article on "Lutheran Ethics and Scandinavian Lutheranism" in the *Augustana Quarterly,* he elaborated his ideas about the strong ties that bound the "deeply religious fervor of Norwegian and Swedish folk" to everyday work and home life. These were the people who made modern Scandinavia. "The neatness of the Northern home, the cleanliness of the cities, the skill of peasant weaving and of folk art—the visitor to Scandinavia who has himself been brought up in the spirit of a Lutheran home never doubts that there is a relationship between the parish church and the parish life." The point of the 1941 article was to argue against those who felt that contemporary

German history discredited Lutheran social theory. "Lutheranism in Scandinavia has more fully than in Germany realized the Lutheran doctrine" and "the deflection is in Germany." Following Einar Billing's theology of the folk church, Bergendoff wrote that the key lay in the assurance of the forgiveness of sins that the folk church proclaimed. "The Christian is taught that he is a member of the universal priesthood, but the place of his ministry is in his shop, on his farm, in his home, in the regular routine of daily tasks." And, "receiving forgiveness, he goes on to redeem gradually, slowly, imperceptibly his area of community life, and thus righteousness enters that area."

In 1947 Bergendoff translated a small book by Einar Billing, *Our Calling*. The original Swedish version, *Vår kallelse,* had been written in 1909. It argued that it was in the Reformation that the Germanic peoples began to see their daily work, whether elevated or humble, as a calling from God. This was, Billing said, why, in an economic and social sense, the Germanic folk were ahead of the Romance peoples. The Germanic treated their work as a form of worship; their understanding of the religious life was crucial. The more a Roman Catholic became religious, the more he withdrew from ordinary life; the more a Protestant became religious, the more he entered everyday life—as a calling.[77] That willingness to hold up northern Europeans as a model of Christian involvement in society carried over to Bergendoff, who applied it in particular to Scandinavia. Of course, by 1947 he was not as ready as Billing had been in 1909 to include the Germans themselves.

The criticism of this view of Lutheranism's social effects, Bergendoff recognized, was that it "makes for a decaying conservatism in social life." The Lutheran answer is that "the Kingdom cometh not by calculation." The most the Christian can do is to live day by day. "If the world's individuals did the same we might begin to understand the nature of a Christian order of society." These are, of course, the ideas we encountered in the chapter on Bergendoff's view of society. The point here is that he believed that it was in Scandinavia that these ideas came closest to being lived out. That accounted for the clean farms and neat kitchens, the children who knew their great grandfathers' names. But, Bergendoff admitted, even in these northern lands, the essential paradox of Christian social ethics prevailed. The Christian was obliged to seek the realization of the Gospel in the life of the community, while recognizing at the same time that it would never be fully reached.[78]

It is difficult when reading the 1941 article on "Lutheran Ethics and Scandinavian Lutheranism" to avoid wondering whether its author wanted it both ways. Charmed by Swedish life and attributing its virtues to Christianity, he also was a Lutheran and believed that society as a whole would never be fully Christian. But Bergendoff steered his course carefully, adducing the folk life of Sweden and Norway as evidence of the deep influence of Lutheranism upon society without quite claiming that these were "Christian societies." The paradox, as Bergendoff saw it, did not lie in Scandinavia, but in the very nature of Christianity. It enjoined upon its adherents the effort to strive for a goal which it also told them they could never reach. It was the daily knowledge that their sins were always forgiven that Bergendoff believed enabled such people to live in that paradox or tension, at the same time sinners and justified. In the end, that went for Swedes and Norwegians as well as for everyone else. Still, Bergendoff clearly believed that the Lutheran Nordic lands came as close to realizing a Lutheran Church-permeated society as any place on earth.

As indicated, some of Bergendoff's impressions of the piety of Swedish religious life, especially in rural parishes, came from his own experiences traveling through the Uppsala diocese with Nathan Söderblom. They were certainly reinforced by his acquaintance with the person and writing of a church historian at Lund University, Hilding Pleijel, who was one of the visiting Swedish dignitaries at the 1948 Pioneer Centennial (more of which shortly). Along with his more formal academic work, the Lund historian authored a number of popular small books depicting the stable and ordered life of rural Swedish congregations in the eighteenth and nineteenth centuries. Pleijel pictured the women of the parish who made their way to services carrying in one hand a bouquet of flowers, in the other their hymn books, given to them on the day of their weddings. They and their husbands gathered on the sloping lawns of the country churches, chatting until the bell called them to worship. These were folk who by the diligence of their pastors were steeped in the catechism and the psalm book, "both of which set their seal on country life."[79] Pleijel inscribed one of his books to Bergendoff, "*Till Conrad Bergendoff med tack för oförgätliga dagar i Rock Island 1948,*" (with thanks for unforgettable days in Rock Island, 1948). This aspect of Pleijel's work must have charmed Bergendoff and confirmed him in his belief that once a more settled and truly Lutheran world had existed—in the Swedish countryside which the ancestors of Augustana Synod folk had left for America.[80]

Bergendoff's more positive read of the Swedish ecclesiastical situation had some precedent in the way his teacher, the American Lutheran historian and theologian Henry Eyster Jacobs of the Philadelphia Lutheran Seminary, had also written of the Lutheran Church and "the humble, quiet, sincere lives of hundreds of thousands of her people, who, in all meekness, are slow to give their confidence to those whom they do not know, but who at the same time, cordially love and submissively obey and considerately care for all that has once established itself as worthy of esteem."[81] These qualities in European Lutherans, especially Germans, were of course viewed more dubiously after the *Hitlerzeit,* but Jacob's phrases did anticipate the mood of his Swedish-American student. Decades after studying with Jacobs, Bergendoff sketched out a depiction of Scandinavian Lutheran folk piety which tended to ignore the problems involved in the melding of state and church, of the secular with the sacred, that had characterized much of life in the Church of Sweden since the Reformation.

Bergendoff was, however, not alone among his contemporaries in thinking that the over-all effect of the ecclesiastical set-up in Sweden was positive. There were others who were as impressed as he had been in encountering Scandinavian society and who believed that the finer qualities of the homeland had been carried to the New World. Even the iconoclastic Minnesota historian George Stephenson commented that visitors among Swedes in America "noted the cleanliness and neatness of the Swedish peasant homes and the high standard of living as compared with those of certain other [!] national groups."[82] And an "American" (meaning in this case non-Swedish-descended) churchman had complimented both the Swedes and his own countrymen by noting that the former were "more nearly like Americans than any other foreign peoples[.]"[83] The fathers of the Augustana Synod were able to sing that hymn as well. During a visit to Sweden L. G. Abrahamson, who had served Salem Church before Bergendoff, had flattered the Swedish clergy "by rehearsing the American preference for immigrants of Nordic stock."[84]

Conrad Bergendoff, who sometimes ignored the problems implicit in the church-state arrangement of Scandinavian society, also noted that in America Swedes did not plunge into politics the way the Germans, Irish, and Norwegians had. That was probably because they "looked on the turmoil, hysteria, and corruption of the party system in America with little admiration. Their sense of order, justice, obedience to law, was violated by the arbitrariness and dishonesty of the American party system." Bergendoff believed that the Swedes "helped to keep alive the voice of conscience."[85] He also assured both the Swedes and his own countrymen that the immigration had not left Scandinavia bereft of solid citizens. Those who stayed in Denmark, Norway, and Sweden had, he said at a 1936 community anniversary celebration in Minnesota, raised their lands to "a point of well-being which is envied by all the rest of the world." Care of the old and sick, neutrality in the Great War, stable currencies, co-operative movements, even the Nobel Prize—all were reasons for that envy.[86]

Modern Sweden

Apropos of envy, in 2005 an Uppsala professor of missions notes that "Sweden was the only [Scandinavian] country that managed to stay out of World War II. This led to envy from the other countries during and after the war."[87]

That shrinking of Scandinavian neutrality to Sweden alone was but one of the important shifts that had taken place in the Nordic lands by the middle of the century, when it was only Sweden that had stayed out of both the war and NATO. Bergendoff defended the morality of the Swedish position. In fact, right up to Pearl Harbor he had strongly opposed American involvement in the Second World War. He little cared for what he saw as Franklin Delano Roosevelt's desire to enter the war and at one point wrote to a member of the US Senate, "May plain citizens not hope that Congress will cease giving the President blank checks[?]" Further, "I am opposed to surrendering the really vital decisions of our national life to any one individual, be he a president in this country, or a Fuehrer in some other."[88] In late 1941, he voiced the hope regarding Sweden that if its clergy were called on to rise to the heroism of their Norwegian counterparts, the Swedes would stand up to the Nazis with the same courage as the Norwegians had.[89]

However, Sweden stayed out of the war, and Bergendoff found himself defending that stance. He recognized other realities as well. Secularism was seeping into every corner of Swedish society. Between the wars a Swedish court chaplain complained that in the smallest peasant homes, people knew what was going on in Paris; through the movies they could take part in *"Newyorks nattlivs ruskigheter,"* the nastiness of New York nightlife.[90] Whatever was cause and whatever effect, it was clear that as the twentieth century devolved, so did the influence of the Church in Sweden. The modern culture which Bergendoff had so strongly been criticizing since his days as a Chicago pastor had now found its way to Sweden—assuming it had not been there already.

In fact, the Sweden to which Conrad Bergendoff returned after the war was well on its way to becoming what in a 2008 book American sociologist Phil Zuckerman calls one of the world's "Least Religious Nations." (The other country distinguished in this regard is Denmark.)[91] Those changes could and can be seen in almost any direction one looked or looks. One of the most fundamental shifts in public sentiment came just after the war. During the conflict the tension between the Social Democrats and the Church had been for a time reduced. A unity government headed by the Social Democrat Per Albin Hansson (1885-1946) concluded a sort of concordat with the Church. Photos showed Archbishop Erling Eidem (whom Bergendoff later knew well) signing an agreement with Gösta Bagge, the government Minister of Ecclesiastic Affairs. It declared, "The Swedish way is the Christian way."[92] But hardly had the Russians and the Western Allies begun to quarrel over Berlin, when that era of good feeling ended in Sweden. So did the religious character of national life reflected in the concordat and the slogan.

Perhaps the most telling evidence of that shift away from religion was the public controversy over the book *Tro och vetande* (Faith and Knowledge), published by an Uppsala philosopher, Ingemar Hedenius (1908-1982). This 1949 work became the center of a lively debate in both the press and academe about the validity of certain value judgments or affirmations. Hedenius had attacked both Nazism and Communism, claiming that their value or faith assertions were irrational. But after the war, he began a debate focused on religious faith and values. In a letter to a friend written several years pre-*Tro och vetande,* Professor Hedenius confided he was considering setting aside "higher philosophy" and looking for *"något roligt"* (something fun) to work on: "For example to pounce on the theologians and the bishops."[93] His criticism "was directed almost entirely against Swedish Lutheran theology as [Hedenius] encountered it through leading Swedish theologians and bishops."[94] The philosopher stuck to churchmen in his own country because he felt he did not know British or Catholic religious thought adequately. Hedenius seemed to have had no quarrel with the study and presentation of Christianity as an historical phenomenon, but he insisted that it should be done by scholars standing apart from their own religious commitments. That had certainly not been the case, he claimed, particularly with the Lundensian School that included Gustaf Aulén, Anders Nygren, and Ragnar Bring (all oft-cited friends of Conrad Bergendoff). For Hedenius, these churchmen smuggled their religious commitments under the guise of objective scholarship (*vetenskap)* into their work, and in so doing violated his standards for truth. The Christian faith contained assumptions and ideas which could not be proved rationally or scientifically. Nor could it convincingly be communicated to non-believers. And it contained internal contradictions.[95]

The Swedish public seemed to swing toward Hedenius in the debate, and both Christian and non-Christian observers in Sweden judged that he got the better of Nygren and company.[96] An historian of philosophy wrote: "Where the theologians were surly and confused, Hedenius was brilliant and jolly."[97] And a church historian: "The debate not only weakened the Swedish Church's position in the culture debate, but even brought into question Christianity as a view of life worthy of belief."[98] By the seventies theological study at both Lund and Uppsala had been separated from the Church of Sweden, morphing into faculties of "the science of faith and world views" and "the science of church and societies."[99] One American observer speaks of "the doldrums into which Swedish theology fell after the age of the giants, Aulén, Nygren, and Bring."[100] Archbishop Söderblom and the religious renaissance that attended his prominence in the twenties notwithstanding, the trajectory of Swedish life and thought in mid-century was toward the secular.[101] Disestablishment lurked in the wings.

Swedish Bishops

What Dr. Bergendoff would have thought of these developments should by
now be clear. The Sweden and the universities he had known were passing—
not disappearing altogether, of course, but taking on new character. So was the
Church of Sweden. It would not be until the end of the millennium that the
Church would be disestablished, but that it was headed in that direction was
clear decades earlier. Probably the two twentieth century Swedish Archbishops
best known within and beyond the borders of the kingdom are Nathan
Söderblom (Archbishop 1914-1931) and K. G. Hammar (Archbishop 1997-
2006). The changes within the Church are symbolized by these two men, their
thinking, and their archiepiscopal work.

Bergendoff tended to consider the bishops of the Swedish Church not
simply as its titular leaders but as the men who determined the tone and character
of its theological and devotional life as well its polity. The historian George
Stephenson noted that the nineteenth century Archbishops of the Church
of Sweden, especially "that prince of high churchliness" Henrik Reuterdahl
(Archbishop 1856-1870), regarded Augustana "with no little distrust."[102] The
feelings were mutual. For his part, Bergendoff may have been troubled in
1939 when the Synod president passed along a report from a Norwegian-
American colleague that one Swedish bishop had made a speech to European
and Americans Lutherans "in which he criticized and ridiculed the Augustana
Synod and the Swedes in America."[103] But Bergendoff generally paid little
mind to those more sour aspects of nineteenth century American-Swedish
Lutheran church relations.

Bergendoff had, in fact, become, especially through his relationship with
Söderblom, one of the Swedish bishops' chief American apologists. Believing
that the inclination to appoint academic theologians to the episcopacy was
one more mark of the health of the Church of Sweden, Bergendoff had
been one of the early transmitters of the work of Aulén, Nygren, Bring,
and others to the English-speaking world. A contemporary of Bergendoff,
the English Methodist theologian Philip Watson, had himself spent time in
Sweden before the war, translated Nygren's *Agape and Eros* into English, and
wrote of the experience, "It was in Sweden a dozen years ago that I found a
Luther in many ways other and greater than I had heard of in either England
or Germany[.]"[104] As a result of his time in Sweden, Bergendoff had also had
such an awakening to a Luther he had not known before. In bringing Swedish
theology to America, Bergendoff acted in his homeland much as Söderblom
had in Sweden, where as a professor (before being appointed Archbishop)
he had introduced new trends in German theology to the Swedes.[105] For
Bergendoff the Swedish bishop-theologians were paradigmatic and symbolic:

nowhere else in Christendom was there such a "long line of distinguished bishops" as in the Church of Sweden.[106] In spite of his steady insistence that episcopal government was not essential to the Christian churches, it is likely that during his year in the twenties with Söderblom he formed the impression that the Swedish bishops were in fact the very soul of their Church, even if once in a while a Norwegian American overheard one of those prelates making fun of the Swedish Americans.

Nathan Söderblom towered over the Swedish, the European, and the world ecclesiastical landscape for the seventeen years he served as Archbishop and, for that matter, for years after his death in 1931. Holding a doctorate from the University of Paris that he had earned while pastor of the Swedish Lutheran congregation there, he was professor at Leipzig (while keeping his professorship at Uppsala as well), when word came to him that against expectations he had been selected by the government as Archbishop of the Church of Sweden.[107] Moving back to Uppsala from Germany, Söderblom went with enthusiasm at the job that had come as a surprise. But reservations about his orthodoxy and his background as a student of world religions dogged him—in America as well as in Europe. L. G. Abrahamson, who represented the Augustana Synod at Söderblom's 1914 consecration, was favorably impressed, but back in the US doubts about the new man and his Church persisted. At the Rock Island seminary Professor Adolf Hult was particularly concerned, labeling Söderblom "the most dangerous man in the Lutheran Church" and a "skillful evader" in theological matters. Of course, the Lutheran Bible Institute in Minneapolis shared Hult's fears; its dean, Samuel Miller, worried that the Archbishop consorted with liberals.[108] Judged by Miller's lights, he did.

In 1923 Söderblom determined to accept an invitation to visit the United States, first issued by the Federal Council of Churches. After the Swede indicated that he did not wish to offend American Lutherans by traveling entirely under the auspices of an ecumenical body toward which many of them harbored suspicions, L. G. Abrahamson arranged that the Augustana Synod would also issue an invitation.[109] Söderblom, a master of French and German, spoke passable English as well. The Archbishop lectured in the East and then made his way to the Midwest, everywhere delighting audiences with his sense of humor and, as always, "creating around him an atmosphere of joyous festivity." One Swedish historian wrote after Söderblom's death that "As a prince of the church he developed a grandeur . . . and yet was the most modest and unaffected of men."[110] Photos show a man of medium height, a sturdy Scandinavian face, often smiling, and a high forehead topped with full but wispy hair. They reflect a fellow with an almost dapper demeanor. One of his countrymen spoke of Söderblom's "sunny personality,"[111] but another suggested that in fact Söderblom's bonhomie was "glittering above mysterious depths" in which there lay a certain melancholy.[112] (He had suffered a serious heart attack in the early 1920s.) That shadowed side cannot have been much in evidence in 1923 in America, though the Archbishop did lecture on "Humor and Melancholy in Martin Luther" at the University of Chicago during his visit to the city. Even George M. Stephenson was charmed by the Swede's ebullience. But not one to pass up the chance to wrap a jibe inside in a compliment, Stephenson noted that Söderblom was more "democratic and informal" than many of the dignitaries of the Synod,[113] some of whom, of course, came along on the Archbishop's trip through the US. Years later

Nathan Söderblom.

Bergendoff remembered that, along with his intellect and charm, Söderblom had tremendous energy, which had to be balanced by his wife Anna who "cooled him down a little bit at times, I think, because he was so excitable in some ways."[114] The Archbishop was, for his part, troubled by the lack of understanding and cooperation among the several American Lutheran bodies he encountered during the trip.[115]

The October night before Söderblom planted a tree in front of the Salem Lutheran Church construction site, he addressed a banquet at the LaSalle Hotel in the Loop. Oyster cocktail, crème of fresh mushrooms, filet of sole, filet mignon, heart of lettuce, and petit fours were served, as were a rendering of "The Blind Ploughman," two violin solos, and many prayers. Along with Söderblom's address the audience heard one from the Reverend Doctor A. P. Fors, Pastor of Bethel Lutheran Church, Chicago, "*Dotterkyrkans skuld till moderkyrkan*" (The Daughter Church's Debt to the Mother Church). The next day at Salem the bilingual assembly sang "A Mighty Fortress" and "*Med Gud och hans vänskap*" (With God and His Friendship).[116]

Söderblom had not been the first Swedish bishop to visit the Synod. The Bishop of Visby, on the Island of Gotland, Knut Henning Gezelius von Scheele, had done so three times, most recently during the fiftieth anniversary of the Synod in 1910. But 1923 was the first glimpse Augustana people had of a Swedish *Arch*bishop, and, accompanied by his wife Anna and seventeen year-old son Jon, Söderblom went a long way toward dispelling the undercurrent of hostility toward the Swedish Church that had been carried by the Synod's founders to the New World and had run through the Synod for decades.[117] The Swedish historian Sven-Erik Brodd remarks that the Archbishop was one of the first modern Christian leaders who "chose to work publicly."[118] He was evidently somewhat canny about publicity.

After 1923, Swedish bishops visited often, and Bergendoff was invariably involved in making arrangements for them. The war did, of course, delay the wave, but after 1945 it swelled again. In the later forties Gustaf Aulén (1879-1977), Bishop of Strängnäs, about 60 miles west of Stockholm, and a prominent theologian, and Archbishop Erling Eidem, appointed upon Söderblom's death, came to the US and Augustana. Aulén told Bergendoff in 1946, "I could not think of being in America without going to Rock Island."[119] He preached the baccalaureate sermon there in 1947. Bergendoff had met Eidem (Archbishop 1931-1950) in Britain in 1937, and right after returning home, he wrote him to "solidify relationships with the Swedish Church[.]"[120] Eidem was at the 1948 centennial of the immigration of Swedes to the Midwest. Sometimes while episcopal itineraries were being arranged Bergendoff would get a letter wondering, *"Hur mycket skall besöken kosta?"* He usually answered in English that the visit's costs would be shared between the nervous hosts in Lindsborg or Minneapolis and the agencies sponsoring the trips.[121]

Contrast the status and perspective of those Swedish prelates with the standing and outlook of K. G. Hammar, the Archbishop who presided over the severing of the tie between Church and state in Sweden, finally consummated in 2000 A.D., just after Dr. Bergendoff's death. Hammar writes: "Now the historical situation is completely different. The Church has no power left in Swedish society." For Hammar the present powerless situation of the Church is more consonant with its deepest values and mission than in the centuries when it lived with compulsory tax support and government control: "That the Church in this regard must be designated as 'powerless' can only be interpreted as a step forward, a historic development that is entirely in line with the Church's innermost understanding of its faith and of the conditions for the mediating of that faith."[122] Hammar, who was criticized for everything from his reservations about the literal Virgin Birth to his political opposition to Israel, welcomed the disestablishing of the State Church, believing that powerlessness *is* the essential Christian condition, at least when judged by the standards of the world. There is not the slightest hint in Hammar of the possibility of

Christianizing society, little thought of exercising influence over the politics or culture of the land. "KG," as he is known by TV interviewers and the public in general, was trained as theologian and historian, as both Söderblom and Bergendoff had been, but thought-worlds as well as church-decades separate his outlook from theirs. Whether the philosopher Hedenius at mid-century or the churchman Hammar at century's end, many leading Swedish voices spoke directly of changes about which Bergendoff was more inclined to be circumspect. Whether Hedenius was gloating or Hammar simply making a virtue of necessity is beside the point.

Coping with Changes

These developments may well have been the inevitable to-be-expected results of factors operating everywhere in the western world. But given the high view of the culture and Church of Sweden that he held, they must have been disconcerting for Bergendoff. More clearly than any other person of his generation, he expressed the ideas that we have sketched about the mother-daughter ties that bound Swedish and Swedish-American Lutherans. Connected to that was an understanding of Swedish culture that must have been rooted in his family's experience. That understanding seems to have been strengthened during the year he spent with Söderblom, 1926-1927. Bergendoff, whose jeremiads about modern culture we considered in Chapter 4, was never quite as hard on contemporary Swedish life in particular as he was on western culture in general. But with the passing of the post-war decades, he came increasingly to recognize the reality that when it came to secularization, Sweden was very much in step with, if not out ahead of, the rest of the West.

In an address at the 1948 centennial celebration, Bergendoff said that through its history Sweden had linked piety and learning to a remarkable degree.[123] But a year later, after his summer trip through Germany visiting theological and ecclesiastical institutions, he declared that in Europe generally, as in America, learning and religion were being separated. As bad as the ruins from war were, the detritus that really needed to be cleared came from intellectual and moral destruction. Post-war despair was coalescing into nihilism.[124] Following several visits in the fifties and sixties, he wrote in 1967 of modern Scandinavia that "Despite brilliant leadership, solid scholarship, improvement of places and ways of worship, and modern means of communication, attendance at church services and at Holy Communion remained small. The ties between church and school slowly dissolved." And: "The churches in Scandinavia retained inherited privileges, but their influence steadily declined among a religiously indifferent population. Secularization and materialism seemed to grow with each new invention."[125]   Now the Swedish Church had to confront "modern pagan secularism."[126]   Seven decades earlier Henry Eyster Jacobs, Bergendoff's professor at the Philadelphia Lutheran Seminary, had quoted one of the Synod's founders, Eric Norelius, who had seen the hand of Providence in the fact that "the Swedish Evangelical Lutheran Church in America was founded before the time when the tide of laxity in doctrine and practice swept over the old Fatherland[.]"[127]   It appears that in the 1950s Conrad Bergendoff faced these (to him) unpleasant realities about the direction of Swedish religion and culture during the twentieth century.

This reappraisal was evident in book reviews Bergendoff wrote in the early years of the decade.   In 1950, reviewing a work on the relations between religion and education in Sweden, he said that the greatest need of the land was "for the enunciation of a Christian humanism" by the theretofore complacent Church.[128] In 1952 he reviewed a small book by the Lund historian Hilding Pleijel which considered the historic Lutheran theory of the three orders into which society was by God's will divided—government, the church, and the family.   Bergendoff remarked that the book was "sobering because it suggests that even the twentieth century church still thinks in terms of a by-gone social order and is unprepared for the revolutionary changes swirling around it today."[129]   A year later in reviewing a treatment of the Swedish free churches, Bergendoff called for rethinking by Lutherans of their ideas about the church and the ministry: "A church as well as an individual may so love its privileges that it loses its life."[130]   In these cases, the reviewer seems to have recognized the inability (or unwillingness) of the Swedish Church to abandon its old assumptions about its dominant place in society and to adjust to the new realities.

That shift in Bergendoff's view of modern Sweden was quite clear in a review of a 1967 biography of Dag Hammarskjöld.   In this piece, the retired college president observed with a touch of grim satisfaction that many Swedes who began to read Hammarskjöld's autobiographical *Markings* believed, incorrectly, that they knew their countryman.   "Themselves superficial they thought they were intimates with the famous figure.   When the 'profile' of his personality emerged, they were confused.   Half pagan, they could not endure this confrontation with a deeply spiritual character, least of all his confession of Christianity."   Some critics resorted to personal attacks upon Hammarskjöld.   "The reception of *Markings* casts a startling light on the abyss of modern culture and on those of its spokesmen, taunting a man who after probing all its vaunted glory finds the secret of human life in the Scriptures."[131] Here was Bergendoff, who ever since emerging into adulthood had blasted modern life and values, now conceding that his castigation applied as clearly to contemporary Sweden as it did elsewhere. The hostility *Markings* evoked in Sweden demonstrated that.

That Bergendoff did not misread the Swedish reaction to Hammarskjöld's book is evidenced by the comments on *Markings* made by Tage Erlander, who when the book came out was Swedish Prime Minister (1946-1969). In his diary Erlander wrote:"Hammarskjöld's posthumously published book has frightened me! . . . Has Hammarskjöld in a few years so formed his Jesus-identification that he has become a really dangerous person? Supermen are dangerous. Not least he who lets his dreams of superman be crystalized into a God before whom people humbly bow their knees."[132] As he had with Söderblom, Bergendoff to an extent appropriated Hammarskjöld for his own purposes; now he cited the United Nations diplomat as evidence that thoughtful moderns could still be Christian. But in doing so he was forced to the uncomfortable corollary that contemporary Sweden, clean homes and well-kept farmyards notwithstanding, had become as secular as the rest of the western world—perhaps more.

When you compare the views Bergendoff had expressed in the twenties and thirties about Swedish life with his own later statements, you are left to ask how he accounted for what, to judge by his own comments, was a rather precipitous Swedish descent into "half pagan" secularism that was often hostile to religion—as Erlander's comments were. This was a country Bergendoff had just decades earlier held up as a model of the way in which a Church, through its members, could leaven and change a society. Of course to a certain extent the decline could be attributed to qualities which Bergendoff found inherent in *all* people, Scandinavian or not. The Scriptures and the Lutheran Confessions taught the sinfulness of every human, even Swedes. But the question remained: How did Swedish Lutheran culture fall, at least by Bergendoff's lights, so far so fast? How did he cope with its having been paradigmatic (at least for him) earlier in the century, into a society where a man like Hammarskjöld could be misunderstood, even mocked in public and labeled dangerous in private, for being Christian?

The present author is not competent to offer a careful analysis of twentieth century Swedish history and society. But even a cursory reading of modern Sweden suggests that Bergendoff's interpretation of "The cleanliness and tastefulness of the housewives' rooms, the delicacy of the coffee table . . . matched by the orderliness of the fields" was perhaps overly sanguine. That was particularly so if his purpose was to demonstrate a necessary link between these features of Swedish life, the faith of the State (or, as he preferred, Folk) Church, and underlying national values and characteristics. And to do that does seem to have been his purpose:"These folk put into practice the Lutheran teaching of daily life as a 'kallelse' a vocation," he wrote in 1943. "The children

Elizabeth, the Bergendoffs' younger dauhter, as Sankta Lucia, December, 1957.

of the Church of Sweden" lived this sort of ordered Christian life in both Sweden and America, as Bergendoff understood it.[133] When he wrote that, of course, Bergendoff was reflecting on the Sweden he had seen in the company of Nathan Söderblom.

The point here is not to deny that Swedes on both sides of the ocean had tidy homes and farms. It is rather to ask whether the pre-war Sweden Bergendoff had come to know was not already in the process of secularization, a process whose mature results Bergendoff encountered in his post-war visits as well as in his reading. A British church historian, Nicholas Hope, writes that already by the beginning of the nineteenth century, "Swedish Lutheranism lost its congruence with Swedish citizenship[.]"[134] Bergendoff, of course, would have dated that loss of "congruence" much later. But the Young Church Movement ("The people of Sweden, a people of God") was as much a protest against the growing secularization of Sweden in the early twentieth century as it was evidence of deep folk piety.[135] The war years had seen a temporary suspension of the Social Democratic opposition to the state-Church arrangement ("The Swedish way is the Christian way"), but the immediate post-war period witnessed the debate over Professor Hedenius' *Tro och vetande,* in which the sympathies of the literate public seem to have swung to the Uppsala philosopher, not to the Lund theologians whom he ridiculed. By the time the Swedes who *thought* they knew Hammarskjöld woke up to his Christianity, it was clear that his private spirituality did not match the inner lives of many of his countrymen. In fact, it put them off, as it did the Prime Minister.

It must also be remembered that Bergendoff's ancestors had *not* left a nineteenth century Sweden which they themselves held up as a model. The authoritarian quality of Church life, the wide-spread drunkenness and poverty, and the lack of social mobility had made many of the Augustana Synod's founders into opponents of the State Church pattern, glad to be a free church in America.[136] It was not until well into the twentieth century that members of Bergendoff's own Church had truly reconnected with what they now, in the words of the Synod historians Maria Erling and Mark Granquist, came to regard as "the Charming, Modern Church of Sweden."[137] That body was a far cry from what one American historian calls "the formalism and the barren overintellectualized theology of the state church" that had marked the religious life of Sweden in the preceding era.[138] Bergendoff's position during this bridge building with the Church of Sweden (of which he was a major architect) was to see that Church as both pattern and source for what he always regarded as the unique Lutheran character of Scandinavia. He believed that the ways the Nordic churches had shaped national life were themselves the evidence and example which demonstrated that his ideas about the individual Christian life and its possibilities for leavening all of society were not naïve. They showed that there was in fact a way for Christians to influence culture short of church control or legislation. However, in all of this he was not able to quote T. N. Hasselquist or Eric Norelius on the paradigmatic nature of the Swedish society they had left or on the desirability of its Church-state set-up. It is difficult to avoid the thought that Bergendoff held up as an example a country and Church which were neither what during his own life he hoped they were, nor what, as they left their homeland, his immigrant forebears had seen them in reality to be.

Honoring and Being Honored

His idealistic academic and ecclesiastical efforts to reestablish the historical connections between the two countries he knew and loved (at least in their ideal expressions) led to Bergendoff being recognized widely in both cultures. Recognition came because of certain specific pieces of his work and because in general he was among the most important and active Swedish Americans seeking to understand and preserve ties between the two countries. His dissertation on Olavus Petri had, of course, received notice in Sweden, and Bergendoff developed contacts with academics at both Uppsala and Lund. In 1938, the year of the tercentenary of Swedish settlement on the Delaware, Bergendoff and George M. Stephenson were awarded honorary doctorates by the Uppsala Faculty of Theology.

It is most likely that the principal advocate of the honors for the two Americans had been Gunnar Westin, Professor of Church History at Uppsala, the first member of a free church to hold that position. Westin, a Baptist, had come to know Bergendoff and Stephenson through his own work in American religious history. He once remarked that he had formed a rather *"mörk bild"* of the Augustana Synod through his contacts with Stephenson and had been pleasantly surprised upon meeting Bergendoff and Fritiof Ander. That "dark picture" of Augustana had been brightened through Westin's contacts with these latter two representatives of a more progressive Synod generation than the one that alienated Stephenson.[139] The newspaper, *Upsala Nya Tidning,* reported of the 1938 doctoral award ceremony at the university that "during Bishop Runestam's Latin oration many listeners, more Anglo-Saxon than Latin, were startled at the words, 'Rock Island, Illinois;' it was the foremost scholar of the Swedish Reformation Dr. Conrad Bergendoff, Rektor of Augustana College and Theological Seminary, Rock Island, Illinois, U.S.A., who was promoted *in absentia* to the honorary doctorate." Bergendoff had "enhanced and spread the name of Sweden in America. With gratitude we send our greetings and congratulations to him across the seas," read the citation.[140] The ThD degree *honoris causa* was not lightly bestowed by the Swedish university, and for the relatively young Bergendoff (age 43) to be granted the honor was the more remarkable. In the Augustana Synod, by way of contrast, honorary Doctor of Divinity degrees were freely bestowed by the denominational colleges, were not uncommonly the cause of jockeying for favor and of envy among the clergy, and were thus a bane of Bergendoff's life, as he himself often remarked.

President Harry Truman seemed to enjoy the 1948 centennial celebration at Chicago Stadium; Swedish Prince Bertil sits between Truman and a pensive Bergendoff.

The year 1938 was the three hundredth anniversary of Swedish settlement on the Delaware River. Certain celebrations were planned in the East, but they were not an Augustana Synod production. A few Swedish Americans were on the original planning committee, which included, along with them, a DuPont, a Samonsky, and several Irish Americans. Bergendoff was a member of the Reception Committee for Tercentenary Lecturers, along with the Presidents of the Universities of Pennsylvania, Purdue, Iowa, and Illinois, and of Knox, Pomona, Gustavus Adolphus, and Bethany Colleges.[141] Synod President Bersell wrote a peeved review of the tercentenary ceremonies in the *Lutheran Companion*. A Swedish male chorus, he said, had failed to show up at a Synod-sponsored Lutheran service, though they must have been somewhere nearby, for they sang later that night at a secular celebration in Philadelphia. Neither had any Swedish royalty come to the Lutheran service. Bersell, in dyspeptic mood, warned the Swedish bishops who *were* present that this would lead to a "sorry aftermath" (no particulars specified).[142] Bergendoff's conclusion from the celebration and the disappearance of those Delaware Swedish settlements long before their three hundredth birthday was that the settlers had not "learned to be both Lutheran and American; [they] remained American and became Episcopalian."[143]

In addition to concluding that settlers must struggle to be both Lutheran *and* American, Bergendoff seems to have learned from the Delaware tercentenary that if Lutherans and other Swedish–American Christians were to be given due place in such festivals, they better take charge of them. That is what happened with the 1948 centennial celebration of the arrival of the first Swedish immigrants in the Middle West, though that too was not without problems. Dr. Bergendoff became the head of the "Swedish Centennial Association," and determined that "The Jubilee will be of an ecclesiastical character." Nils William Olsson, brother of the North Park historian Karl Olsson and an American academic and diplomat, became the Executive Secretary of a parallel organization, the "Pioneer Centennial Association," and the two groups worked well together, melding into a "Swedish Pioneer Centennial Association, Inc." Carl Sandburg was the Honorary Chairman, and people from North Park College and the Covenant Church and other Swedish–American denominations as well as Augustana Lutherans were heavily involved. The ceremonies attracted visits from Prince Bertil and Archbishop Eidem in the summer of 1948, and the governors of several Midwestern states were involved as well.[144]

One of the Stockholm newspapers, reporting on the plans, identified Bergendoff as "the foremost scholar of the history of the Swedish Reformation and a promoter of the cultural ties between Sweden and America." It also indicated this celebration would be much more meaningful than the 1938 tercentenary events.[145] That was certainly Bergendoff's perspective; the newspaper probably got it from him. In his view, the seventeenth century Delaware settlements had been absorbed into colonial America; their principal remains were the church buildings themselves. But colleges, hospitals, congregations— you could still see "the fruitage" of the mid-nineteenth century immigration.[146] And an important academic result of this centennial was the founding of the *Swedish Pioneer Historical Quarterly,* which

King Carl XVI Gustav and Conrad Bergendoff, April, 1976.

quickly established itself as the leading scholarly journal publishing work on the immigration and Swedish-American life.[147]

Dr. Bergendoff's efforts to shape the 1948 centennial were to a degree checked by certain persons and factors in his Synod. In fact, the result was a sort of dual track for the festivities; there were actually parallel celebrations, one by and for the Synod, another involving the wider Swedish-American community. The Church's ranks included persons who were "very much afraid of a Swedish emphasis in our Centennial celebration, not the least the possibility of a 'Church and State' impression." That was in a 1948 letter to Bergendoff from Oscar Benson, at that time the President of the Illinois (or Central) Conference and later President of the Augustana Church. Benson indicated that some of the brethren were also concerned "that we are adopting some kind of unwholesome ecumenicity[.]" And he was worried about creating the impression that "we are 'one' with the Swedish lodges." Further, the Synod must avoid "Any fanfare with respect to the Swedish government dignitaries in connection with the service."[148]

Evidently everyone in the Synod did not support Bergendoff's efforts to arrange a pan-Swedish-American event in Chicago or to promote observation of the 1948 anniversary in other Swedish-American population centers in the US. So—by itself—the Synod sponsored its own celebration, for its own people. This was cast as marking "A Century of Blessings" and focused on the Centennial Synod Convention of 1948, held at Augustana College and Seminary. Included in the convention program were trips for all the delegates to New Sweden, Iowa, site of the first Lutheran congregation to be organized by Swedes in the Middle West, and to Andover, Illinois, location of the "mother church" of the Synod, Jenny Lind Chapel (so named because of a nineteenth century gift from the "Swedish nightingale").[149] The delegates and others were also treated to an historical pageant performed out-of-doors at the Rock Island High School football stadium that came "to a close with a great outburst of music and singing by a massed choir."[150] Historian Arden tells us that as a result of the Centennial Thank Offering, a fund drive that President Bersell had long planned as an accompaniment to the actual festivities, "no less than $2,181,776.53" was raised by convention time.[151] That 1948 conclave was, of course, also the one that finalized the separation of Augustana Seminary from Augustana College, so it must have been a bitter-sweet event for Bergendoff. He does not seem to have been greatly involved in planning the Synod celebration.

The then cool relationship with the Synod leadership may be one reason that Bergendoff turned instead to developing a series of events that paralleled the Synod's, but did not overlap with them. These commemorations were meant to include *all* Swedish Americans, Lutheran and free church, religious and secular. Sponsored jointly with the several Swedish-American denominations and with a number of secular organizations, this second celebration did result in a particularly spectacular night at the Chicago Stadium in June, 1948. President Harry Truman, Swedish Prince Bertil, Carl Sandburg, and 18,000 others were present. Along with the obligatory historical pageant, music and speeches were the order of the evening.[152] The Augustana Synod's publications took little notice of that gathering, which involved "unwholesome ecumenicity," "fanfare with respect to Swedish dignitaries," and "the Swedish lodges." You could peruse all the 1948 issues of the *Lutheran Companion* and hardly figure out that the Chicago Stadium event had ever taken place at all. Similarly, you can read Conrad Bergendoff's short article on the Pioneer Centennial in a 1969 issue of the *Swedish Pioneer Historical Quarterly* and gain little impression of the Synod's in-house 1948 celebrations.

There were several currents eddying around the floor of the Chicago Stadium (usually a venue for hockey and basketball) at the great rally on June 4, 1948. Although he had determined that the centennial should be "of an ecclesiastical character," Dr. Bergendoff, as president of the association planning the event, had gone ahead and included in the celebration just those elements which Conference President and fellow pastor Benson had warned him against. In fact, Bergendoff, who had found the 1938 Delaware Tercentenary too secular and un-Lutheran, now led in the planning of a massive rally that included Mission Covenanters and Methodists, members of the Order of Vasa, and a Swedish prince, not to mention the Democrat who was, at least for the nonce, in the White House. But Bergendoff seemed in no mood to submit to a Church which was just then in the process of carrying through—over his strong objections—the separation of the Rock Island seminary and college. And Truman, a long-shot at re-election, surely found himself among an ethnic group which, to judge by the editorials that kept showing up in the *Lutheran Companion,* had little sympathy with his presidency or policies.[153] But in a victory that stupefied the predictors, the President did carry Illinois that November, so his appearance before the American Swedes at the Chicago Stadium may have paid important political dividends. We can guess that notwithstanding the fact that Truman showed up at the Chicago rally, Bergendoff did not cast his ballot for the Democrat from Missouri.

Bergendoff's fidelity to causes ethnic continued to be recognized. In 1975, aged eighty, he was again commended for his long loyalty to Swedish America and Sweden, when the Consul General of Sweden in Chicago came to Rock Island to elevate him to the rank of Commander, First Class, in the Royal Order of the North Star. The Swedes no longer granted noble rank to their own citizens, but did recognize people outside the kingdom who had made important contributions to its interests and causes. Bergendoff wrote a letter after the ceremony, asking the Consul to convey his thanks to King Carl XVI Gustav for the recognition.[154] The title still came bestowed by the monarchy.

§

A year later, reflecting on the world he had grown up and worked in, the North Star Commander penned these lines:

> Those days, those people, are gone. Like the continent that legend says sank in the Atlantic, the community that was Swedish-America has disappeared beneath the waves of time. But as men once thought they heard, in the evening stillness, tones coming from the submerged race, so we too, if we try, can hear music of past festive occasions, and heartfelt prayers of those who sought a land truly good, in soul as well as soil.[155]

That wistful elegy could as well have been written about the Sweden Bergendoff thought he knew as about the Swedish America he really did know so well.

CHAPTER 9

A COLLEGE PRESIDENT

To have begun a career as a college president in the Depression, served through World War II and a good part of the Cold War, and to retire during John Kennedy's presidency was no mean feat. To have done it with grace and patience and to leave the position with the affection and respect of the staff and students with whom one had worked for nearly three decades was even more remarkable. Readers may well have forgotten that the occupation our Swedish-American intellectual and churchman listed on his tax returns was "college president." But that was the role that paid Conrad Bergendoff's salary, modest though it was.[1] By now we know that it was Bergendoff's firm footing in the faith of his fathers and his determined ideas about what he regarded as the most important questions of human life that sustained him in a job that grew in difficulty and complexity with the decades.

President of Augustana College and (for a time) Theological Seminary was a role Bergendoff assumed reluctantly and one he left willingly, though not without pressure from the Board of Directors. Financial questions had certainly troubled his first years as president, during the height of the Depression. In the last years of his service, financial problems reemerged, now in the boom times of the late fifties. In the thirties the problem had been that nowhere in American society did there seem to be money to support higher education. In the fifties the American economy was expanding, and many universities and colleges were taking advantage of it, strengthening both facilities and finances. Now the problem was that Augustana did not seem to be seizing these opportunities. Certain members of its Board of Directors and alumni constituency feared their college was falling behind other schools, some of them Lutheran institutions in the Middle West with histories and prospects very much like Augustana's.

As the demands of the job grew more varied and pressing and the quest for resources more intense, Bergendoff persisted in believing that no aspect of his service mattered as much as his continuing effort to proclaim the reasons why the position was so important. It was not important because it was *he* who held the position or because the mere act of speaking was crucial. Rather, Dr. Bergendoff believed that whoever served in church-sponsored higher education was at the very front of the struggle between the Christianity in which he had anchored his own spirit and the modern world about which he harbored such doubts. It was in colleges like Augustana that the New Testament gospel confronted the dominant secular view of the world. Compared to that confrontation, finding resources was secondary, so far as its president was concerned.

Christian Higher Education

As in everything else that mattered in human life, Bergendoff maintained that to be carried on rightly, higher education must be under the authority of Christ. The role of a college of the Church was "to re-call mankind to its obedience to a Lord who has sovereignty over all of mankind." That sovereignty

Bergendoff Hall of Fine Arts at Augustana College, finished in 1955, was named in honor of the fifth President of the College upon his retirement.

included higher education; apart from God's rule, humanity, including its educational activity, had no ultimate meaning: "The glory of Humanity is in its relationship to a Head who gives all the members what significance they possess." This manifesto appeared in the *Lutheran Companion* in 1948, but as with much else that Bergendoff wrote, it stated ideas which he had held since the time of his own formal education and that he would maintain through the rest of his life. "When the professions . . . lose the sanctity of the divine call, the cold hand of selfishness gradually clutches them and squeezes out their life... Even the pursuit of knowledge itself is prostituted to the lure of selfish gain."[2] In a 1950 speech before a group of Ohio college presidents Bergendoff said that as an educator he could speak "only in the name of those who believe that Christ is the head of all faculties," and asked rhetorically when the colleges and universities of the country would "accept his lordship."[3] In 1988 Bergendoff, retired from the Augustana presidency for a quarter century, still held these views: "the individual, like Archimedes, has to find some place to stand in order to move his own world." Every intellectual position involved an act of faith, and for Bergendoff there was one true faith in a world filled with false alternatives. The centuries bore witness to its truth. Systems of thought, cathedrals, higher learning, the arts—all were evidence of "the new understanding of human life" which came through Christ.[4]

These were clear sentiments, expressed at age ninety-three. They were consistent with what Bergendoff understood to have been the views of the founders of his Church and school and with what he believed from his earliest years in higher education. "A Christian interpretation of all knowledge" is what the men who began Augustana, Synod and College, sought, one that was anchored in the "revelation of God in the Christ of the Bible." That meant that religious faith must pervade the natural and social sciences, humanities, philosophy, arts, and all the other disciplines taught in modern universities.[5] In a 1937 radio sermon Bergendoff insisted that "modern man" wanted more than the shallow secularism that surrounded him. Moderns were searching for answers to the vital questions of life—about its origin, purpose, and destiny. Here the Christian venture in higher education was, he said, "on the front line, defending a coming generation from unbelief and from all the strange foes of the modern world."[6] Ten years later in his *Christ as Authority,* Bergendoff wrote that for any field of human knowledge to exclude Christ was but an admission that it was without God and therefore without hope.[7]

But our subject did depart from many contemporary advocates for "Christian higher education" in his insistence that *all* fields of study were appropriate for church-related institutions. The church must make use of every kind of intellectual and scientific work, Dr. Bergendoff wrote in 1939. That included the scholarly efforts of both Christians and non-Christians.[8] Each aspect of human life ought to be investigated; none should be excluded from consideration.[9] Accordingly, historians note that at a time when Genesis and geology were presumed by many Christians, including Lutherans, to be opposed to each other, Augustana and other colleges of the Swedish-American Synod taught the subject.[10] We have seen that Bergendoff's own understanding of the relationship of the Bible to religious faith was never literalist or fundamentalist, so he saw no conflict between the accounts of creation in Genesis, which he did not read literally, and the work of nineteenth and twentieth century geology. Nor did he believe that evolutionary biology was of necessity opposed to a Christian view of human life and origins. The key issue was whether one understood God to be in control of the process or not.

The twenties and thirties saw a powerful resurgence of a Protestant (and to a degree Roman Catholic) fundamentalism that fought with renewed vigor against the "Godless" secular materialism (sometimes alleged to be abetted by liberal religion) that it feared was seeking to dominate public American education, thought, and life.[11] The struggle had reached epic but cartoonish proportions in the 1925 Scopes "monkey" trial over the teaching of evolution in the Tennessee public schools. We know that President Bergendoff held no brief for the secular materialism he found prevalent everywhere in modern society and that he had reservations about Darwinism. But neither did he want to make common cause with American fundamentalism. He was at times suspect among other American Lutherans because of his disavowal of biblical literalism. So he was determined that his college (and his Church) should find a middle way between these equally unattractive alternatives. Appropriately for a president whose school taught both evolutionary biology and geology, Bergendoff recognized the "dynamic" character of the religious faith that must govern true education; it might "express itself differently in changing environments."[12] As the natural and social science programs burgeoned at Augustana College after World War II, Bergendoff argued that they too must be brought "under His captivity."[13] He resisted the suspicion that he found in some types of Protestantism where "education and piety do not mix very well."[14] Sydney Ahlstrom, an American church historian who was himself a son of the Augustana Synod, wrote that in contrast to fundamentalism, the revival of orthodoxy that occurred in American religious thought in the twentieth century held a "deep respect for the scientific, scholarly, and artistic achievements of men."[15] As a scholar who was himself part of that revival, Bergendoff shared that deep respect and greatly advanced the interests of the sciences, scholarship, and the arts at Augustana.

Louis Almen, a member of the Augustana College Department of Christianity in the fifties and sixties, writes that the integration of all fields of knowledge with theology is a particularly Swedish emphasis, and finds

Bergendoff's insistence upon it to derive from his heritage.[16] Separating the college and seminary divisions of Augustana in 1948 troubled Bergendoff deeply, not simply because it meant that he would have to choose between these two in continuing his own career as president, but because he believed the move suggested some bifurcation between religion and the rest of human knowledge.[17] The physical layout of the Augustana campus, with the seminary on a hill surrounded by the other buildings on lower ground, where the humanities, arts, and sciences were taught, had been an architectural expression of Bergendoff's own view of how the fields of knowledge ought to be organized. For him the revelation in Christ must control all of university study, not simply religion and theology.   "Rather the Church maintains that only the Christian Faith makes a universe of the chaos of facts, and that the Christian virtues of faith, hope, and love, transcend knowledge, and give to knowledge itself the significance it has."[18] No field of study was forbidden to the Christian—precisely because that person alone of all others understood that humanity by itself could not discover the ultimate meaning of existence.

In 1940 Bergendoff wrote, "There are fruits of truth which man can not receive unless it be given him. The sin of man is his assumption of a role wherein he presumes to judge the Creator and make himself equal to God." When a person does that, he allies himself with "that prince of evil whom Jesus characterizes as the father of lies."[19] Three years later in a weekly column in the *Lutheran Companion* entitled "From College Windows" he told readers that "God and the 'father of lies' are contending for victory, and that man most easily yields to the latter," adding, "It makes all the difference in the world on which foundation culture is built—pagan or Christian."[20] Bergendoff seldom personified evil, and his reference to "the father of lies" suggests a cosmic ethical dualism, a view of human life as a struggle between opposing forces, that carried over to a somewhat bi-polar view of culture and education. They were Christian, or they were pagan.

The deep sense of the power of evil may have come in some part from the terrible news about the destruction being wrought by the war. In a 1947 commencement address, Bergendoff declared that "If our education does not lead towards Him, it can only lead towards hell, and the best educated of our age have given us a glimpse of the mouth of hell. There is no neutral. [sic] No-Man's land between Heaven and hell which education can prepare us to inhabit. If God be left out of American education, American youth will be outside the Kingdom of God." The atomic bombings of Japan were evidence of the horrors that knowledge separated from faith could produce.[21] The role of Christian scholars was "to rescue the liberal arts from the captivity into which paganism wanted to confine all education. Literature, history, philosophy and art, in their [Christian] hands become instruments to the understanding of a life far more glorious than

Bergendoff and the Augustana Board of Directors at his inauguration in 1936.

the sordid purposes to which faithless men would commit the knowledge of man."[22] One remembers that Bergendoff said that he entered graduate study to prove that a Christian could win advanced degrees without surrendering his faith. You could be a cultured student in the best American university tradition and still believe in the "Living Christ of the Old and New Testaments."[23] As the president of his Church's oldest school, Bergendoff sought faculty who had survived the rigors of graduate study, as he had, with their religious faith intact.[24]

The Worldly Alternatives

These were the uncompromising ideas that governed Bergendoff's thinking during the twenty-seven years that he served as Augustana's president. Of course both he and his counterparts in other less religious institutions understood that all American colleges and universities were not built on the same assumptions. Because of (and at moments perhaps in spite of) his own strong religious assumptions, Bergendoff was well regarded in higher education both within and beyond the borders of American Lutheranism. He filled a number of roles in the North Central Association, the regional accrediting body for higher education in the central US, and was often invited to speak to and for that body. A year before his retirement, he talked about "Quality Education for All" at the Association's annual meeting, adducing both Aristotle and Erasmus [!] in support of his thesis that every religious or humanistic institution must educate its students in "honor and virtue" as well as in skills and methods.[25]

At a 1952 Phi Beta Kappa address at Knox College in Galesburg, fifty miles down US 150 from Rock Island, the President of Augustana addressed "Building a New Humanity" and said that all good education seeks the unity behind the outward appearances of both nature and culture.[26] A decade later at Northern Illinois University's commencement, Bergendoff spoke about the leadership that educated persons must assume in society and reminded the graduates that, ultimately, a learned person must seek and find answers to the great questions of human life. At that ceremony in nearby DeKalb, he did not specifically suggest that it was the Christian faith that offered those answers.[27] Here again he did not present the Christian position as forcefully as he might have at his own school or in the pages of the *Lutheran Companion*; the tone is somewhat less dualistic. I noted earlier that Bergendoff seldom spoke in the hortatory; he used that restraint when addressing educators in DeKalb or Galesburg who did not share the religious axioms on which he believed his own college was built. One assumes that when he spoke of the search for purpose and meaning in human life, he did so hoping that his listeners would, like St. Augustine, remain "restless till they rest in Thee."

That did not mean that the Augustana man endorsed or approved of the current condition of American higher education. It was precisely its lack of a center, its unwillingness to concentrate upon the essential task of seeking the true answers to the great issues of human life, that most troubled him. He could make common cause with private schools which encouraged that quest in their students, and he hoped that public universities would do so as well. Bergendoff was bothered by a 1939 PhD dissertation written at NYU on church-related American colleges. It maintained that Protestant schools did not perpetuate "the theological bias of any particular religious group, but teach courses in Bible and ethics primarily as an aid to character formation."[28] He resisted that kind of generic Protestantism, believing that Lutheranism must avoid it.

Furthermore, Bergendoff feared that American higher education was in fact headed in the opposite direction, abandoning even the bland lowest-common-denominator teaching of religion. The Augustana president's reaction to the mood prevailing in American universities was not simply cantankerous or idiosyncratic. It is not clear that he read the 1951 essay of a recent Yale University graduate, *God and Man at Yale*. But that graduate, William F. Buckley, Jr., a Roman Catholic, found the same antipathy to religion, Christianity in particular, at his university that Bergendoff decried in American higher education generally. Against expectations, young Buckley's book caused a firestorm; many historians regard it as having initiated a renaissance in American conservatism, after F.D.R., the New Deal, and the Second War. Bergendoff would not have gone along with the author's attempt to couple Christianity with conservative economic individualism; remember that Bergendoff maintained that Christianity and socialism were not in essence opposed to each other. But he would certainly have agreed with Buckley's criticism of the value-free indifference, even hostility, toward religion that prevailed in most of American higher education by mid-century.[29]

That may be why Bergendoff was at times ready to make common cause with, or at least to borrow arguments from, intellectuals with whom he normally had problems. For example, we saw in Chapter 4 that Bergendoff had little patience with the Roman Catholic elevation of medieval European civilization as the pattern by which modern society might be brought back into harmony with Christian ideals. He found the views of Catholic historians such as Christopher Dawson and Jacques Maritain not to be consonant with his own Lutheran understanding of the Christian ethic for society. Yet at the same time Bergendoff joined them in lamenting the irreligion of modern culture. It was a mistake for Lutherans reacting against Rome to align with contemporary "secularists and skeptics" in abandoning the search for the will of God in the life of the world. Bergendoff's Church must undertake again the "difficult and dangerous task of effecting a new harmony of knowledge,"[30] even if the result was not the medieval synthesis redux.

Thus, in spite of John Henry Newman's aversion to Protestantism, Bergendoff found the Anglican convert to Rome to be spot on when he argued in his *The Idea of a University* for the central role of religion in higher education. Newman (1801–1890) was right to ask whether a university should be limited to teaching what was available to the senses, thus denying a place to spiritual realities that transcended sense.[31] Beyond that, what Bergendoff wanted was a distinctly *Lutheran* idea of the relationship of faith and culture. We recall that he was not content with the view often characterized as Lutheran that held that the two realms, secular society and the church, were separate from each other, the former governed by God's law, the latter by his grace. He believed that in Scandinavian Lutheranism, an effort, successful to some degree, had been made to influence social and public life by the precepts of the Christian faith.

Similarly, it was in its colleges that the American Lutheran Church must develop a view of the relationship of Christ to culture that brought all of human life under his sovereignty.[32] At the present time the unity of knowledge under the authority of Christ had been lost: "When theology is excluded, the other sciences move into its place, not only eliminating its influence, but magnifying their own out of all due proportion."[33] As Bergendoff saw it, "In their heterogeneity, their sprawling disconnectedness, their lack of unity, the universities of today but mirror the disjointedness of modern society. ... Lacking cohesion in themselves they disclaim any guidance of individual character, and claim no higher purpose than the discovery and dissemination of facts."[34] In a 1952 sermon at the Chicago Sunday Evening Club, Bergendoff castigated the "intellectual superciliousness on the part of some who may be Ph.D.'s in one field of culture but who don't know the ABC's in the field of religion."[35] Such academics were the products of universities with the disjointed curricula and indifference to religion that Bergendoff, along with Roman Catholics, ranging from John Henry Cardinal Newman to William F. Buckley, Jr., lamented.

These views of Bergendoff are not identical with the medieval concept of "Theology, the Queen of the Sciences," but they are in some ways reminiscent of it. Bergendoff's Lutheran twist was that university teaching was understood not to be under the direction of the church and its authorities but controlled by the view of Christ and his authority which he developed in the 1947 book on that subject. Rather than ecclesiastical determination, a university curriculum properly constituted would be submitted to Christ, that is to a view of the world that was based on the revelation of God in Christ, and perhaps even more directly, to the Christ living in persons who had encountered him themselves, in the emotional-volitional experience that Bergendoff believed stood at the heart of genuine Christianity. Bergendoff therefore argued for *intellectual* and *spiritual* control of higher education by Christianity, rather than *institutional* control by the organized church. What he objected to in secular higher education, in contrast, was "the rise of a philosophy of religion which makes of Christianity one of many religions of the world, all of which are of importance, none of which is particularly unique."[36] That was written in 1935, but for the rest of his professional career and beyond, Bergendoff held to that idea: Christianity was not simply one of several paths to God. Because it was the revelation of God's will for humanity, it was uniquely fitted to govern the organization of the higher fields of knowledge and to give them their ultimate meaning. So he was not favorably disposed to the American Council on Education proposal for the "objective teaching of religion," though he did suppose that it was better than excluding religion altogether from public institutions.[37]

There is, therefore, in Conrad Bergendoff's thought about university education an important distinction from much of the thinking about it that emerged in Protestant higher education, even in the American Lutheran churches, during the later twentieth century. Richard Solberg's *Lutheran Higher Education in North America* (1985) makes the point that after World War II, American Lutheran colleges and universities were places where "The worship of God and the open proclamation of the gospel in the midst of the academic community" were accepted and freely practiced.[38] For Bergendoff that certainly represented an improvement over public institutions, where the American idea of separation of church and state kept Christian proclamation and worship off-campus.

But at an earlier stage of their histories, and certainly in the understanding of their nature which Conrad Bergendoff held, these Lutheran schools were institutions where the *controlling* concept over all that was taught and done was the "Lordship of Christ." For him a Lutheran college was not simply a school where the Christian message could, among other ideas, be proclaimed in an academic community. That might also happen through campus ministry programs on secular university campuses. Bergendoff maintained that at a Lutheran college, Christ must be Lord.[39]

Authority in Higher Education

The key to Bergendoff's ideas about higher education was his sense that every person, aware of it or not, seeks an authority and that most modern people were not really able to develop their own ideas about which authority they would believe and live by. The first pages of *Christ as Authority* (1947) said, "Man's seemingly innate impulse to join a group or party is an illustration of his inadequacy to form his own conclusions. Even the great independent thinkers have arrived at their positions by reactions to their fellow men, and by some intuitive perception that they were themselves following some one or some thing outside themselves."[40] That perception of the human condition and its

Bergendoff presents a copy of his history of Augustana College, A Profession of Faith, *to C. W. Sorensen in 1969.*

need for an authority was the keystone of the 1947 book. Implicit in it was a view of human nature and responsibility somewhat different from one that lay behind such statements as those in the later "official publications" of Bergendoff's own college, issued in the decades after he had retired. In the later Augustana declarations, the assumption was that students must form their own world views and come to personal religious commitment, hopefully Christian, during their college years. That would happen after thoughtful examination of the many possibilities which culture and scholarship presented to them. The two ways of looking at what should occur during college, Bergendoff's and the later one, were not unalterably opposed to each other, but there was a significant shift in tone and emphasis.

The difference is clear when one contrasts Augustana College statements from the fifties with those of a decade later. In Bergendoff's last years as President of Augustana, the annual academic catalog declared that the college "seeks to fulfill its vocation to testify to the character and destiny of man manifest in the gospel of Christ and to make known the obligation that rests on every man, especially the educated man, to answer for his life and thought to the Alpha and Omega of all life and truth." In 1964, two years after C. W. Sorensen had succeeded Bergendoff as president, a visiting North Central Association accrediting team found that "the statement of purposes in the Catalog has a poetic, pulpit-like ring which is unrealistic and, in part, lacking in real content." The team suggested a shorter and more specific one.[41] Thus, the 1969 catalog said simply and in less pulpit-like fashion: "Students are encouraged to make rational judgments and personal commitments that are consistent with moral integrity and the Christian faith."

Changes of the same sort are evident in the college constitution. The document under which President Bergendoff operated for twenty-seven years stipulated that higher education at Augustana should be carried on "under the direction of a faculty motivated by the Christian faith." Further, a stated constitutional purpose of the school was, "To teach youth the way of life determined by the revelation of Jesus Christ in the Word and the Church." By the end of the century, that statement in the constitution had been changed, prompted by educational authorities of the State of Illinois, who indicated that if the purpose of the college was to teach "the revelation of Jesus Christ," public monies could not be used to do it. The governing document was altered to read that the college's aim was to offer a higher education "consistent with the life and mission of the Lutheran Church in America."[42] State funds continued to reach the Augustana exchequer.

Gustavus Adolphus College was a sister institution to Augustana, as close in size, character, and history to the Rock Island school as American higher education included. A 2011 history of Gustavus Adolphus relates a similar shift toward a kind of religious pluralism, though it may have come a decade later. The 1970 Gustavus catalog read that "we consider God, from whom all things come forth and to whom all things return, to be the ground and source of our life." The 1984 catalog said: "Gustavus students see campus religious life differently, according to the emphasis they have developed for themselves[.] In this variety are diverse religious philosophies."[43] It is tempting to conclude that, at least as concerned the colleges' self-understanding, a wave of religious pluralism spread through Lutheran-related schools in the sixties and seventies, from the Eastern states, through Ohio to Illinois and thence up toward Southern Minnesota. That pluralism admitted the possibility of several religious options being present among students and encouraged them to exercise their own judgment when making commitments. Here the assumption was that students were capable of finding their own authority. That was not Conrad Bergendoff's view.

Seven years after its 1962 founding, the Lutheran Church in America itself issued a statement, *The Mission of LCA Colleges and Universities,* which had been drawn up by a group of Church administrators, pastors, and college officials and adopted by the Board of College Education and Church Vocations of the Church. Augustana president C. W. Sorensen was one of its members. That document spoke of development through education of "all aspects of the human character—e.g., the intellectual, the personal, the moral and the religious" so as "to maintain . . . the wholeness of the human personality." The Church sought "to provide an educational setting in which students, faculty and administrators may encounter the Christian gospel." The *Mission* statement said that LCA colleges had a particular responsibility "to provide opportunities for the study of mankind's religions" and to "see their lives and responsibilities in the context of the Christian faith." The colleges must create Christian community within the academic setting which "may not include all members of the college as active participants, [but which] touches all."[44]

Again, there is nothing in this 1969 statement that is wholly inconsistent with the views stated by Conrad Bergendoff through his four decades in higher education, but the tone and mood are clearly different. Now the Church supports institutions whose primary purpose is not to teach the Christian way of belief and life; rather it is educational. Within that academic context, opportunity is to be provided for members of the colleges to encounter and consider the Christian view of human life. Everyone in the school might or might not wish to participate in that. Students should be able to study "mankind's religions." George Marsden, the historian of American higher education, writes of such emphasis shifts as these, which appear to have been characteristic of many colleges with Protestant roots, "It also meant dropping anything that might be characterized as religious indoctrination." It was important to show, "that students were being taught to think for themselves, as opposed to 'conformism' or submission to 'authoritarianism.'"[45] Perhaps the simplest gauge of the shift at Augustana, as at most LCA colleges, is that, by the last third of the century, attendance at Christian worship was not required of all students. Chapel was no longer compulsory.[46]

As the merger in the late eighties of the LCA with the American Lutheran Church approached, it was clear that the LCA supported a wider range of institutions and of ideas about church-related higher education than did the ALC. The LCA maintained that the Church was "a mediator of the means of grace," but said that its colleges were educational institutions, not churches. The ALC adopted a position that emphasized "a redemptive and reconciling role for education, in addition to its investigative and creative dimensions."[47]   Bergendoff would probably have found the ALC position closer to his own.   One recalls that many persons in the Augustana Synod of the fifties felt that their Church would be more at home with the groups that did eventually form the ALC. But Bergendoff argued, convincingly as it turned out, that if his Synod had to choose, it must go with the United Lutherans, since they were in principle open to merger with all American Lutherans.   His views prevailed, and the Augustana Church joined the LCA, while other Midwestern Scandinavian-American groups formed the ALC. When Augustana merged into the LCA it encountered colleges with a much less evangelical sense of their mission than the four-year colleges of the Swedish-American Lutherans—Augustana, Bethany, Gustavus Adolphus, and Upsala—had.

At least as regarded higher education, the Synod, and perhaps Conrad Bergendoff, might have found the ALC more congenial.   Nearing retirement, he wrote, "We dare construct our curriculum, as no state school can, on the principle that religious knowledge is as important—and as true as any knowledge of science or philosophy. . . . Here converts are made from pagan humanism to Christian humanity."[48]   But in the following decades there was little talk at Augustana of converting students, not even by the Augustana Campus Church, whose program of voluntary worship and service had in the mid-sixties replaced required chapel as the principal formal agency of Christian proclamation on the Rock Island campus.[49]

However much the rhetoric about the role of the church in higher education may have shifted in the decades after Conrad Bergendoff's retirement from Augustana, there is no doubt that he was his Church's most articulate spokesman for a view that prevailed in the Synod's colleges for the century of its existence.   It was also held by most of the other Midwestern Lutheran bodies which supported colleges in that region of the country.   Bergendoff believed that the encounter with Christ was an emotional and volitional experience.   It was what he meant when he said in 1988 that every person must find a faith, and that every intellectual position ultimately rests upon one such faith or another.[50]   Christian faith came to intellectual expression *after* a person had made the initial commitment to follow Christ.   In articulating the relationship of that core Christian experience to learning, the mode became intellectual and academic as well as emotional and volitional.   This intellectual mode rose to what Bergendoff called in his 1936 Augustana inaugural address "spiritual discernment of Him Who put the atoms together and upholds the stars[.]"[51]

It was this discernment of the divine source of all things studied and taught that Bergendoff looked for in the faculty he recruited for his school. He sometimes complained that it grew increasingly difficult to find scholars that understood and could articulate the relationship of their own fields to that overarching concept of Christ's control.[52] When the majority of the college's faculty had done their undergraduate work at Augustana itself or at schools such as Gustavus Adolphus, Bethany, Luther, and St. Olaf, all Scandinavian-American institutions which operated in a shared world of discourse about Christianity and education, this was not a problem. But after the war, people began to join the staff who had a far wider range of undergraduate training, often at secular public universities. Bergendoff felt that in his own conversations with such staff, the issue of relating academic and religious commitments grew more problematic. In 1958 he therefore applied—successfully—for a foundation grant to finance study and conversation on these matters at Augustana. That project had significant influence upon the college's 1964 self-study prepared for the North Central Association accreditation visit, which, as we have seen, in turn generated some changes in the way the college spoke about the place of religion in its curriculum and life.[53] But those changes were not always in a direction the President Emeritus might have welcomed.

Bergendoff only very rarely spoke directly to individual faculty about how they might teach their specific courses:"They knew their subjects; I didn't. What could I tell them about how to do their jobs?"[54] But he did have ideas about how academic fields might relate to the college's Christian mission. It was easy to understand how music, especially vocal, could fit with the gospel; one could "find in music that which God himself would reveal to you so that you might praise Him and so that life itself becomes a song."[55] In the emerging social sciences Bergendoff was bothered by the contemporary emphasis on value-free objectivity; he sought faculty who would help students discover ways to form "a healthy community."[56] Still in the Salem pastorate, he had written of the American psychologist John B. Watson (1878-1958), often regarded as the founder of American behaviorism; Watson gave us "an interpretation of life in harmony with this machine age." Now that mechanistic view of humankind permeated current literature, art, philosophy, and science.[57] As for the physical sciences, it was important to recruit professors who saw the natural world as God's creation. At times, said Bergendoff, he "despaired of finding scientists who not only know their subject but want to teach it as a Christian vocation."[58] Of course, Christian values must prevail in the teaching of the humanities, in spite of the sordid realities on which much of current literature was focused. For example, Bergendoff was left to wonder about the Swedes: "why Sinclair Lewis should be adjudged the outstanding American author by the Nobel Literature

Committee." (Lewis' work, in Bergendoff's view, evidently reflected Watson's mechanistic behaviorism.)[59]

So there were many ways in which Bergendoff believed that the entire college curriculum must be subject to Christ. Faith enlightened reason and gave all of its discoveries and insights ultimate meaning. That was the "spiritual discernment" Augustana looked for in its faculty. Through the years of Bergendoff's presidency, Augustana professors did not work on annual contracts; the letters setting forth salary and the other terms of employment were "calls" to the teaching staff. The implication was that theirs was a religious vocation; they were as surely in the service of the Church as were the clergy. In 1949 Bergendoff told a colleague at another church-related college that Augustana insisted "that they [faculty] understand and be loyal to Christian attitudes and convictions." When possible, he said, he tried to get a letter from the prospective person's pastor. Academic credentials were not the whole story; it was essential to know about a member of the faculty's church relationship.[60]

Behind his vision for the Augustana faculty—the hope that scientists would sense the presence of God in nature or humanists focus on the noblest literature—lay Conrad Bergendoff's ideas about the relationship of the individual Christian to human culture. We have seen that he resisted the "Reformed" idea that you could legislate a Christian society. At the college that meant that no administration or governing board should tell individual scholars what or how they could teach; no effort was made to mandate a "Christian curriculum." As we noted, the college fully supported the teaching of subjects that at some more "Reformed" schools were not considered. Geology is the notable example. What Bergendoff looked for was "spiritual discernment" in faculty; he hoped that they had encountered Christ in the way that he believed was essential to being Christian in the first place. After that, he trusted such people to teach their fields in a manner consistent with their religious experience, just as one hoped that individual church members would go out into general society, not with some standard set of regulations or laws with which to make it Christian, but, whether a carpenter or a nurse, seeking to translate his or her own commitments into everyday life, thus gradually transforming society. It was, the Augustana president thought, a particularly "Lutheran" way to look at higher education, one that combined core faith with intellectual and academic liberty. In this sense, Bergendoff's "theology of higher education" had a double aspect. Seen as an expression of his understanding that a relationship with Christ must lie at the center of any rightly oriented human life, it seems conservative, perhaps even authoritarian. Bergendoff sought faculty who shared that faith. But he insisted that, once hired, these people had the right to teach how and what they chose.

In that regard he seems to have offered far wider latitude and freedom than many contemporary "Christian" educators, some of them Lutheran, were willing to grant. In this latter sense he stood firmly for academic freedom.

Vision and Reality

Bergendoff's ideal was that higher learning go on freely in a community of Christian scholars. Schools like his were "the Church's instrumentality to seek to win education, even the highest, for the view of life revealed in Holy Scriptures."[61] That was the ideal. At the same time, the Augustana man understood that the situation on the ground in Rock Island, as at many other places in society and church, did not always match that ideal. Indeed, Lutheran thinking, perhaps more than varieties of more sanguine Protestantism, accepted and even expected that there would be differences between vision and reality. For twenty-seven years Bergendoff administered the life of an American liberal arts college, and in one sense his career seems to have been spent along the boundary that ran between his high vision of Christian higher education and quotidian life of the campus. He rejoiced when the two—vision and reality—were synchronous, and he bore patiently the days when they did not quite seem to be. Such days included, for example, the one when the local Daughters of the American Revolution complained that one of his faculty had been critical of American capitalism. On another day he heard from parents whose son had given up reciting the Apostles Creed because of the "radical" views of one member of the Religion

The Augustana campus in the 1940s.

Department faculty.[62]   Bergendoff had hardly moved into the new office as Acting President in 1935 when he had to write a female student reminding her that it was not acceptable to dance in front of the double doors in the Women's Building lounge.[63]

The author of the present work has treated elsewhere (in a history of Augustana College, 1935-1975) student life at the college when Bergendoff was president. But some data may be in order here so that the reader gets a sense of the *Sitz im Leben* in which "Dr. B" operated. Early in his years as president, Bergendoff declared that "Augustana is primarily for students from Augustana congregations." And he wondered about what kind of a college Augustana would be if Lutheran students became a minority.[64] In the years before the war, about half of the enrollment at the college came from the area around Rock Island and the other "Tri-Cities." Lutherans were 57% of the student body in 1935, 55% two decades later. Colleges such as Luther in Iowa or Gustavus Adolphus in Minnesota had higher percentages of both Lutherans and residential students and might be assumed therefore to have had more homogeneous student bodies than the school in Rock Island, where nearly half of the students commuted to campus and were usually not Lutheran.

In 1941 the college paper, the *Observer,* headlined the fact that "50% at Augie Do Not Belong to Lutheran Church."[65]   Student life at the college was also probably more diverse and polyglot than one might suppose from official rhetoric. If reality and rhetoric had entirely matched, Augustana would have been a rare college indeed. Whether it was regarding drinking, dancing, fraternity and sorority life, or just worldliness in general, Bergendoff became disturbed at moments. He wondered how it could be that the students who resisted his assumptions and methods were often themselves the children of pastors and Church conference officials.[66]   But facing the other direction, he could express impatience with the strictures of the Church, which "often seem quite negative."[67] He warned the college's Board that "there is such a marked chasm between what we preach and what our youth do that we face a serious moral situation." How should the college fix the social problems of youth, when the whole Church had not been able to correct them over many years?[68]

One particularly poignant and illustrative encounter between the idealistic President of Augustana and the reality of student life occurred in March, 1954, at the height of fraternity initiation. Arriving to eat with the men of Andreen Hall in their Dining Room, Bergendoff encountered a number of would-be Greeks dressed in their dirty and messy initiatory garb; it was "Hell Week." Bergendoff told the *Observer* he had had no idea that this was how pledging went on; pledges would in future not be allowed in the dining hall in that condition. Further, he was deeply troubled by the "'subhuman' cries emanating from the intramural field" during pledging. (As it was, that field lay directly below Bergendoff's campus home on the river bluffs.) When asked by the student reporter what he would suggest to the fraternities to replace their initiatory rituals, Bergendoff said, "That's your problem."[69] Efforts to curb unseemly behavior and in particular to rein in the Greek letter societies, which seemed to be the epicenter of such behavior, did not achieve notable results, however. By the year of his retirement Bergendoff sighed: "I would have been happy if this change would have been effected in my administration, but I cannot report success."[70]

While the student body grew from about five hundred and fifty to about twelve hundred during Bergendoff's tenure as president, the faculty of liberal arts and music increased from thirty-seven to seventy-six. The ratio of faculty to students increased, often taken as a sign of quality in a small liberal arts college. The percentage holding doctorates was a point of pride for Bergendoff; he pointed out that Augustana rated in the upper quartile of Midwestern colleges and universities in this regard.[71] Students continued to hold "excellence in teaching" above even formal credentials and scholarly publication. Bergendoff had always agreed with those priorities.[72] Interestingly, the two scholars best known in their respective national professions were probably Fritiof Fryxell, who managed to combine his research into remote geologic time with strong Christian faith, and Fritiof Ander, whose personal Lutheran commitment seemed not to be vitiated by his somewhat caustic views about "dirty" church politics in the Augustana Synod's early history. The debate director, Martin Holcomb, and the choir conductor, Henry Veld, were also recognized across the country for the excellence of the students whom they coached and led.

Faculty salaries remained a grave concern for the President of Augustana, from the nineteen-thirties to the sixties. As the Depression eased, the pay cuts which the faculty had been willing to accept in the interests of institutional survival were slowly restored, though the war so skewed things that comparisons are difficult. By the later years of Bergendoff's service, restlessness about compensation did set in among the teaching staff. The president had long been concerned as well: "We want the best, but we can't pay for the best." There was nothing particularly "Christian" about the assumption that teaching as a Christian calling should mean a sacrifice in pay, he wrote.[73] But by 1959 the local chapter of the American Association of University Professors had grown impatient; colleagues at other Synod colleges were better paid than at Augustana, they told the Board of Directors. Bergendoff was not so sure and wrote to his counterparts at the other schools in Kansas, Minnesota, and New Jersey: "We have an active AAUP chapter that gathers figures faster than I can keep up with." The three replies, alas, told him that the AAUP chapter was correct; salaries in Rock Island did lag behind.[74] This was a situation which the college was not able to correct until several years into the administration of C.W. Sorensen (1962-1975).

President Bergendoff seemed particularly pleased that so many Augustana alumni had themselves pursued advanced degrees and were teaching at many of the country's leading colleges and universities. Many graduates of the school in Rock Island received prestigious fellowships when they began advanced study. Bergendoff was also gratified when the college was awarded a chapter of the national honor society, Phi Beta Kappa, in 1949. At the time only one other Lutheran-related school, Gettysburg College in Pennsylvania, already had a chapter. Augustana held a place among the stronger liberal arts colleges in the region and among Lutheran institutions during the Bergendoff presidency.

Of course, the curriculum continued to be a hybrid of "pure" liberal arts and more career-oriented or applied studies, such as education, business, and nursing. In 1960 the majors most frequently chosen by the graduating class of two hundred and thirty-six were: education (13%), history (8%), business (8%), mathematics, speech rehabilitation, geology, and music (5% each), and philosophy and nursing (4% each). One in three of the graduates took one of the "practical" majors that presumably led directly to a job.[75] But whether one's major was accounting or English literature, each student had taken one-third of the work for the BA degree in general education courses, distributed among the humanities, arts, religion, and the social and natural sciences. The school's claim to be a college of the liberal arts and sciences rested, therefore, to a considerable extent on these core graduation requirements.

Perhaps in part because of the president's own scholarly profile and his high visibility in American and international ecumenical circles, Augustana in fact enjoyed a stronger reputation as a liberal arts college by the time Bergendoff retired than it had when he took the presidency in 1935, when the lack of adequate science facilities had threatened its accreditation. The President of the College continually emphasized the central role that the humanities, arts, and sciences must play in the Christian encounter with the secular modern mind. He never wearied in chapel talks of reminding listeners (each in her or his assigned seat, attendance being checked by secretaries perched in the balcony of the Old Main Chapel) that, just as many of the present faculty had, they too could assume lives of service in academe. That would put them at the forefront of the confrontation between the values of Christianity and the secular world of American higher education. That effort was for him the very soul of Augustana.

Conrad Bergendoff had long hoped to see the creation of a Lutheran university in the United States,[76] one that would rank with those begun by Congregationalists in Cambridge and New Haven, Presbyterians in Princeton, or Methodists in Nashville and Evanston. Perhaps he even dreamed that Augustana itself might be the core of such a venture. In any case, the Lutherans' university would remain faithful to the presence of Christ at the core of learning, however far from that Congregationalists, Presbyterians, and Methodists might have drifted. But the separation of the seminary and college had stifled that university possibility, he thought. Augustana became a small liberal arts college in part through the conviction of its leaders and in part because it lost the chance, as Bergendoff saw it, to develop into a university when the seminary and the college were split by Synod action.

Finances (and Football)

One student of Bergendoff's life, Ann Boaden, has written that Bergendoff's time as a parish pastor provided a model for his work at the college.[77] That thought has implications for understanding life at the school during the twenty-seven years he led it. It suggests the concern for individual members of the staff and student body that prevailed in the President's Office and recalls the metaphor of "the Augustana family," heard often on campus during the Bergendoff years. The esprit that prevailed at the college was rooted in a sense of collegiality and mutuality which Bergendoff personified and fostered. It is also the case that the pastoral model conditioned Bergendoff's daily work as president and shaped his administrative style. He clearly understood his role to be that of academic and religious leader of the school and was usually willing that others, especially certain members of the Board and administration, should carry primary responsibility for its financial and physical well-being. Two other ordained Synod clergy, Knut Erickson and E. E. Ryden, served as College Treasurer and as President of the Board for most of the Bergendoff presidency. They watched over the books and accounts and did most of the campus planning. Bergendoff's principal concerns were intellectual and spiritual.

Besides that of pastor, another model for Conrad Bergendoff's role at Augustana came from the presidencies of great intellectuals who had towered over some of the country's leading universities in his own boyhood years. Most notably, during his forty-year presidency Charles William Eliot (1834-1926) turned Harvard from a provincial New England college into an internationally recognized research institution. His vision for university education drew attention and support by virtue of the passion for learning it evoked rather than simply because of the clever cultivation of constituencies through what Conrad Bergendoff would have labeled "business" methods. Bergendoff's years at Augustana were directed by his own ideal of what Christian higher education must be—not by a quest for resources. He believed those would come when the college's supporters caught his own high vision for Augustana. So whether we think of him as a dutiful pastor of his college or as a visionary intellectual in his Church, we have a Bergendoff who was not oriented toward the search for money. Higher things were at stake. In that sense his Augustana years embodied a time-honored idea about college presidencies, one rooted in the late nineteenth century. But by the middle of the twentieth century, during Bergendoff's last years in his office, the great public and private universities, as well as many schools like Augustana, began to apply fund raising methods more likely to be taught in business schools than in liberal arts colleges or seminaries. The assumption was that great intellectual and academic achievements required solid fiscal underpinnings. To bring Harvard to the preeminent position it enjoyed by the time of his retirement in 1909, even Eliot had had to be concerned for those underpinnings too.

The financial situation which confronted Bergendoff when he assumed the presidency of the school in mid-Depression was a near debacle. So grim was it that one wonders whether it was a principal reason that the Dean of the Seminary, who sat in on the Board of Directors meetings and may be presumed to have been familiar with the fiscal condition of the institution, was hesitant about taking the position that Gustav Andreen had held for thirty-five years. An auditing firm, called in to examine the books, determined that there were in place neither procedures for monitoring the annual operating budget nor measures for "safeguarding the Institution's funds." Their recommendation was that monthly control of the annual budget should be set up, that only budgeted expenditures be permitted, and that projections for the future be based on "actual expected income," rather than gifts only hoped-for, many of which had not been materializing.[78] The college's investments were in no better shape than the annual budget: "the stocks and bonds held by the College in its investment portfolio are in a precarious state and it cannot be corrected in a few minutes or in a few days time." "A loss of at least 40% will have to be taken," the Board learned. The real estate investment situation was equally dismal: "this loss will be a rather substantial sum."[79] It turned out that the endowment was almost two-thirds in real estate, most of it in Chicago, and that certain agents in the city had, it appeared, approached the edges of fraud in their dealings with Augustana.[80]

The wreckage of the Depression was almost cleared away when the war broke out. Of course, the school's finances were greatly skewed by the shifts in enrollment caused by the draft. Some federal money did flow into the college, especially through a program for training Army Air Cadets. By the later forties, the finances of the school had been regularized by careful cooperation between the Board and the Reverend Doctor Knut Erickson, the Treasurer. Enrollment increased, particularly because of the flood of veterans on campus. Efforts to gain support from the Tri-City community as well as from the Church were successful. By 1962 endowment funds stood just under $3 million, with indebtedness of about half that amount. Augustana was certainly not one of the nation's more affluent liberal arts colleges. It enjoyed an academic reputation that exceeded what one might have expected given its finances. But at least these finances had been stabilized. The question now was whether the school would develop, as other similar institutions in its region and in the Lutheran churches had, an aggressive effort to find gifts for buildings and endowment.[81]

In the years after World War II, Augustana did receive a number of sizeable bequests. They strengthened its facilities significantly. A new residence hall for men, a woman's residence complex, a fine arts building named for the president, and a concert hall seating 1600 were built with these funds, as a new science building had been in the mid-thirties (preserving the college's accreditation).[82] Several of the gifts which financed these projects were in the range of over one-half million dollars and came from persons with roots in the Augustana Church. In sum, gifts received in the later nineteen-forties and fifties amounted to about $5 million. (Allowing for inflation, $5 million in 1958 would have equaled over $38 million in 2012.) Bergendoff continued to regard the Synod as "a living endowment." He saw it as the major source of funding for the annual operations of the school as well as the field where prospecting for special grants and estate gifts should continue.[83] As late as 1961 Bergendoff maintained that church-related schools should not accept federal government support; it "might drain off the Christian influence."[84] Better to stick with the Church.

But as the merger of the Augustana Church into the Lutheran Church in America loomed, many people in the Church, some of them on the Board of Directors, indicated that they did not believe that the major operating support for the school would continue to come in the form of annual grants from the regional conferences (or in the LCA, "synods") of the Church. Neither, they suggested, would large special gifts. O. V. Anderson, the President of the Illinois Conference of the Augustana Church, admonished the college to "get a new place in the sun."[85] The Board continued to press the college administration to carry on more aggressive fund-raising. In response to a direct question from one of the pastors on the Board as to whether the school was in fact looking outside of the Church for money, Bergendoff answered "partly yes and partly no."[86]

That ambiguity did not sit well with a cadre of newer Board members elected in the late fifties, and they began to insist that a more thorough "development" (the then current euphemism for fund-raising) program and staff be set up. In 1957 Bergendoff had responded to an inquiry from another small liberal arts college. He reported that Augustana was allocating approximately $10,000 annually to fund-raising, with three staff (Directors of Alumni, Field Services, and Public Relations) each spending part time at it.[87] Most colleges were devoting larger staff and funding to these activities, and the Augustana Board wanted much more attention given to the effort. Finally in 1961, thinking that the task could not be left to the current administration, the Board undertook to recruit and hire a Director or Vice President of Development on their own, simply going around

Bergendoff.[88] By now the matter had raised some tension between the college's president and its Board. The two parties agreed that Bergendoff would step down from his position in 1962.[89] It was a development that Bergendoff accepted with his usual even spirit.

In 1942 President Bergendoff and his seminary colleague Eric Wahlstrom had translated a piece by Gustaf Wingren (1910-2000) for the *Augustana Quarterly.* In it the Swedish theologian and bishop had argued that in Luther's view of the Christian's earthly calling, no effort to justify oneself or to earn God's favor is necessary: "it is a task *(Aufgabe)* in which he does not need to make himself righteous; he *is* righteous through the gospel." That frees the Christian to carry out his work with humility and in a spirit of service.[90] That was how Conrad Bergendoff understood the role he believed God had assigned him at Augustana. So far as his feelings mattered, he had agreed to fill the college presidency reluctantly, and he gave it up readily.

The Board Minutes in the first years of the administration of C. W. Sorensen, who succeeded Bergendoff, are clear that getting a Development Program up and running was his and the Board's top priority. Sorensen recruited an able staff to manage that program, and the income that resulted from their efforts placed the academic staff and curriculum of the college on a much more solid footing. [91]

Along with the matter of fund-raising, another area of the college's activity seemed to need more aggressive attention from the administration, at least as the Board and alumni saw things in the late fifties. That was athletics. After the Synod decided in the early twentieth century to allow the resumption of football at its colleges, the Swedish-American schools, including Augustana, enjoyed some success, perhaps too much, in intercollegiate competition. Gustavus Adolphus College had its membership in the Minnesota Intercollegiate Athletic Conference suspended for the 1941-1942 year because of an alleged "systematic defiance of conference rules,"[92] and at Augustana Bergendoff was receiving letters from other colleges complaining of the overly aggressive "solicitation" efforts of the football coach. He wrote to that zealous winner of football matches: "I am therefore very desirous that Augustana shall be among the schools that stand for the highest standards in this matter of soliciting students."[93] The coach in question left the college, and when the war ended and athletics resumed full blast, Bergendoff was, to say the least, no longer plagued with complaints about Augustana taking unfair advantage of other colleges in athletics. The faculty's and president's stance was that "Augustana does not encourage students whose only interest is athletics and neither recruits nor subsidizes such students."[94]

The football record, 1951 through 1958, was 23-41-1, which did not trouble Bergendoff, but which did upset certain Chicago area alumni, weary of reading about lop-sided losses in the Sunday morning *Tribune*. From these alumni the Board got "Certain communications for getting better football teams . . . one was a petition incorporating specific suggestions." The coach resigned, telling the college paper he was "tired of losing." He respected the president's academic priorities, but couldn't keep up with other teams supported with far greater resources than Augustana gave to athletics. When the new coach began again to recruit forcefully, Bergendoff reminded him that "We cannot afford to have students who are not in sympathy with our requirements in Christianity or chapel attendance." He indicated his fundamental attitude toward sports when he told a prospective member of the coaching staff while interviewing him for an Augustana job, that the football "record this year hasn't been anything to boast of as far as scores go, but we are not overly concerned and think that next year may bring a brighter picture." That might have satisfied a Chicago Cubs fan, but it did not go down well with alumni. One such alumnus, a pastor, told President Bergendoff that you could find a new football staff more easily than you could replace the college's alumni.[95]

Thus the athletic record, mediocre at best, especially in the manly sport of football, became, surprisingly in our longer perspective, another issue of contention between Conrad Bergendoff and the Board of Directors, taking its place alongside the seemingly more serious questions of financial management and fund-raising. It contributed to the sense among some alumni and Board members that it might be time for a different approach, time to find a "new place in the sun" for Augustana. The relationship between the two Augustanas, Synod and College, had not always been smooth. The first President of the College, L. P. Esbjörn, had left for Sweden in disappointment after serving three years; the third, Olof Olsson, had been accused of heresy. It was not completely out of keeping with Augustana history that the fifth and last president to serve the college during the life of the Augustana Lutheran Church should part company with the Synod-dominated Board over finances (and football).

In spring, 1962, Bergendoff learned that Clarence "Woody" Sorensen, then at Illinois State University, had agreed to take the president's job. The retiring president wrote to his successor, congratulating him and warning that "It will take all that a man has."[96] Much of Bergendoff's energy, especially in his later years as president, had been spent either in fund-raising or at least in somewhat tense discussions with the Board about it (as well as about athletics). The search for generous donors or winning coaches had certainly not taken "all that a man has" when the man was one of the Church's principal intellectuals and ecumenists. But it did demand more of every American college president's time. Midway through his years as president, Conrad had written to his engineer brother Ruben that "Begging money is not my strong point."[97] The image of Lutheran pastor and the work of certain great American university presidents were, as suggested, patterns that governed Bergendoff's management of the school. We remember that he never bought into (he would have disliked that turn of phrase in itself) the kind of ministry that ran a congregation or a college with business techniques. It was one of his differences with Synod President P. O. Bersell, who was not above such methods.[98] In his last year in office, Bergendoff wrote that the miracle that most described the college's operation was Jesus' feeding of the five thousand with a few loaves and fishes.[99] After he retired, Bergendoff still spoke often on the campus, and at a Homecoming Chapel Service in the late sixties he noted in passing during a homily on the spiritual truths at the core of a Christian education that the school year had never opened at Augustana with any certainty that the books would be balanced when it was over.[100]

The Augustana Legacy

In the years following his retirement, Bergendoff lived in a new Church which he had done much to create and in which, at first, he played an important role, especially through his study of its theological education. But with time his life became centered, as it had been since the early thirties, on the Rock Island campus, now minus the seminary. He came increasingly to believe that one of the college's missions must be to preserve the Swedish-American heritage. That had been a priority for Bergendoff early in his years as president. He worried that the "American temper" did not value the past: "Our thoughts are on new things, new cars, new radios, new houses." The Swedish-American community, especially "those who have made fortunes in America," should come forward with financial support.[101] In the Synod-college centennial year he insisted that "there is hardly any Swedish American institution comparable to this educational venture, wherein hundreds of thousands of the sons and daughters of Sweden sought to build a continuing agency for the preservation of an ancient culture and its transmission to generations who are becoming a part of America." The heart of that continuing agency was "the faith which has been an inspiration of Swedish life for centuries." And, "Here an interest in education which is characteristic of Sweden has been a means of uniting an ancient heritage with a pulsating hope for a new world, not least in the Mississippi Valley." Augustana was, he claimed, "the noblest monument of Swedish immigration in America."[102]

In that 1960 article in the *Swedish Pioneer Historical Quarterly,* Bergendoff predicted that in its second century Augustana would certainly increase its influence as an American college and "even be a valuable link with modern Sweden, but it can never be again what it was in its first century—a symbol of the ideals and hope of a people on pilgrimage from one culture to another."[103] When he received the Order of Commander of the North Star from Sweden

Iverne Dowie and Ernest Espelie, editors, give the festschrift, The Swedish Immigrant Community in Transition, *to the honoree in 1963.*

in 1975, Bergendoff lamented that Swedish America had not produced "a kind of talent" that had put the immigrant experience into "lasting language." Along with gratitude for the honor, he, now age eighty, sent greetings back to Sweden from those "here at Augustana who are trying to keep alive the inherited flame."[104] However strong his own vision for and memories of Augustana, Bergendoff understood that things had changed. But he continued to think that the college could fill a vital, though perhaps reduced, ethnic role through its preservation of Synod records and immigrant materials, the Swedish Department, its reception of distinguished Swedish guests, and the summer Swedish language program. "On Augustana devolves the duty of maintaining its historic connections with the land of Sweden."[105] It bore the name of the now-departed Synod and with it the responsibility for preserving its traditions.

By the later twentieth century, therefore, both of the qualities that distinguished Bergendoff's college from other small American liberal arts institutions—the Middle West had one in nearly every county seat town—had undergone significant changes. The Augustana Conrad had known since arriving on campus in 1912 had been seen by neighbors and by educators alike as a Swedish Lutheran college. Minnesota historian George Stephenson recalled that in his own student days, "The citizens of Rock Island and Moline spoke rather disdainfully of it as the 'Swede College,' a name that described it accurately, although the student body almost to a man, perhaps, resented the characterization."[106] Betsey Brodahl, Dean of Women, who lived for years in an apartment in House on the Hill, the mansion on the Weyerhaeuser property that had been given to the college in the 1950s, remembered that when the lumber family no longer needed the land and home, they determined to "give it to the Swedes."[107] As surely as it was understood to be a venture begun by Swedish Americans, Augustana was known to be Lutheran. That characterization persisted even through the decades in which many other denominational colleges had shed their religious identities. Conrad Bergendoff, as well as many of his "American" neighbors, believed, perhaps in the teeth of certain evidence, that to be Swedish *was* to be Lutheran. Of course, the Augustana man did realize that his college's Swedishness was certainly changing in obvious and significant ways; hopefully it was not simply disappearing. We have seen how the Augustana president maintained that it was its religious orientation that continued to set his college apart from most of American higher education, even education carried on in relation to other denominations. If the school's ethnic tradition was inevitably being diluted, its religious heritage must not be.

§

Just as the college's academic stature increased from 1935 to 1962, in the case of these two particular qualities—Swedish and Lutheran—Augustana underwent important changes during Bergendoff's years as its leader. These changes continued in the following decades as well. From having been a Scandinavian-American enclave in American higher education, the school developed into a strong (though under-financed) and to some degree typical Midwestern liberal arts college. It was also a repository for the records of a vanishing ethnic sub-culture and a center for the study of the immigration from Sweden that had now slowed to a trickle. The founding of the Swedish Pioneer Historical Society and the Augustana Historical Society, in both of whose beginnings Bergendoff played a leading role, strengthened the preservation and study of Swedish-American history. But neither the Augustana College basketball roster nor the Swedish 101 class lists were dominated by Scandinavian surnames any longer. And, of course, by the later twentieth century the very identification of "Swedish" with "Lutheran" disappeared, both in Europe and in Rock Island as well. We have already discussed the fact that the college's understanding of its Lutheran orientation had changed, as had the sponsoring Church itself. So it appears that the Bergendoff years were one stage in the evolution of Augustana, as the presidential periods before and since have also been.

The administration of C. W. Sorensen that followed Bergendoff's was a time of improvement and stabilization of the school's fiscal position, of the over-all academic profile of the faculty, and of Augustana's efforts to attract, retain, and graduate strong students. Still, for many alumni of the thirties, forties, and fifties, the Conrad Bergendoff years are remembered as halcyon ones, when the college came as close to realizing the high vision of its founders and of its fifth president as ever it had or would. The college had found a course, as had its president, between the secular materialism that marked much of American life in the twentieth century and the evangelistic fundamentalism that characterized much of the response to it.

Egon Weiner, Chicago sculptor, with the bust of Bergendoff done in recognition of the subject's retirement in 1962.

THE COURSE OF A LIFE

As it had been since he returned to be Dean of the Theological Seminary in the early thirties, the Augustana campus continued to be a home base for Conrad Bergendoff after 1962. Immediately following retirement the former college president carried on a two year study of theological education in the new LCA. It took him across the country. But when that was completed, he settled again into Rock Island and there remained for three decades until his death in 1997, age one hundred and two. He did travel to represent the Lutheran side in theological conversations with Presbyterian-Reformed churches and went to the USSR with a National Council of Churches delegation in the sixties. Gertrude and he traveled for pleasure as well. But mainly, he was a presence on the college campus where he had first arrived at age sixteen in 1912. In the nineteen-sixties, seventies, and eighties, Dr. Bergendoff was a regular in the library and at concerts and lectures, and from time to time even showed up in the lunch room. In 1975 one young faculty member bumped into the retired president—literally—while she was swimming laps in the college pool; a half-hour discussion with Bergendoff about her dissertation, then in the works, ensued.[1] No ceremonial occasion was complete without the President Emeritus. His meditations, homilies, and prayers continued to express for many in the college community their own vision and hope for the school.

Gertrude and Conrad at the Stockholm City Hall.

In those years, Bergendoff authored three major books: a history of Lutheranism (1967), a history of Augustana College (1969), and a guide to the careers of all of the pastors of the Augustana Synod during its own hundred and two year existence (1980). He represented the LCA in ecumenical work, reviewed historical and theological books, and authored a number of articles, especially on Swedish-American themes. Because Conrad was less involved in college and church affairs, Gertrude Bergendoff and he spent more time together than they had since his years as a pastor in Chicago in the 1920s. Their passports, still in the college archives, reflect their international travels, invariably focused on, though not limited to, Scandinavia. When Gertrude died in 1979, it was a hard blow; in 1995 Conrad wrote to a friend, "My world changed in a way I cannot fully understand even now after 16 years."[2] But Bergendoff continued to be involved on the college campus well into his nineties. Sundays you could find him, usually in a dark blue college president's suit, at St. John's Church, just east of the college on Seventh Avenue in Rock Island.   He favored a pew on the north side of the sanctuary with the stained glass windows whose dedicatory inscriptions in Swedish recalled earlier leaders of the college and the Synod.

As his hundredth birthday approached, Bergendoff's circle of friends in the Swedish-American community prepared a festschrift, *Aspects of Augustana and Swedish America,* in his honor. It was the second such book to be presented to him. He had received the first, *The Swedish Immigrant Community in Transition,* thirty years earlier, at the time of his retirement. In 1995, Herbert Chilstrom, just retiring as the first Presiding Bishop of the new Evangelical Lutheran Church in America, visited him at his apartment in a Rock Island assisted living facility just before the actual hundredth birthday. The bishop and his wife brought the donuts; Bergendoff prepared the coffee. For devotions Conrad read from Dietrich Bonhoeffer, translating from German on the spot.[3] His correspondence files, kept carefully right up until the time of his death, contain birthday congratulations from a granddaughter, telling him about her managerial prospects in her new job at K-Mart, and from a great-granddaughter thanking him in laborious and careful print "for beeing my great grandpa."[4]

Honors continued to come to Bergendoff during his retirement. Lutheran Social Services of Illinois made him Amicus Certus (a True Friend), Luther Seminary in St. Paul gave him its Christus Lux Mundi Award, and he (along with Dag Hammarskjöld, Edgar Bergen, Carl Sandburg, and Charles Lindbergh— they all posthumously) was named by the Swedish Council of America as a recipient of one of its Great Swedish Heritage Awards. The college over which he had presided for twenty-seven years established an endowed professorship of humanities in his name. Bergendoff took it all with customary grace and self-deprecation. When his portrait was hung by the Augustana Board of Directors, he was relieved that "being hanged" did not hurt.

Changes, Some Ironic

The merger of his denomination into the Lutheran Church in America had coincided with Bergendoff's retirement from Augustana. By the time of that union with three other American Lutheran groups in 1962, Bergendoff had experienced some ecclesiastical victories and some set-backs, and he understood

Bergendoff and his great-grandson, also Conrad.

it. The separation of the seminary from Augustana College was the most important instance of the latter, just as the Synod's insistence that any new merged Lutheran Church must be open to ecumenical membership was an instance of the former. But after the LCA was formed, there seems to have been little doubt among former Augustana Synod people that Conrad Bergendoff interpreted and carried its tradition forward, as no other single person did. That may have been in part because he lived so long, and in full possession of his intellectual powers. But it was also due to the fact that Bergendoff understood and articulated as few others did the core ideas in the tradition into which he was born and in which he would live for over a century.

Bergendoff's career began in one of the many ethno-centric synods that characterized the American Lutheran landscape before mid-century. He participated in the formation of clusters of these bodies that eventually, later in his life, developed into national denominations that gradually began to establish ties to non-Lutheran churches and, by the end of his days, were in communion with them. Given the length of his life, it is no wonder that Bergendoff experienced, as few of his contemporaries were able to, the extent of the changes which his confessional tradition underwent in the twentieth century.

With the passing of the denomination and the merging of its seminary with three others, the principal "Augustana" left in America was the college in Rock Island. But at that institution things were rapidly changing as well. The sixties were never undone at the school. The challenge to authority and tradition, the rise of student and faculty power, the insistence that varying religious and ethical perspectives be given place—these and other factors did not cause the institution to sink away, but they certainly altered both the appearance and substance of its collegial life. It would never again be the tight-knit community with the homogeneous vision of its purpose over which Bergendoff had presided. Maybe that was why to many the President Emeritus represented that vanished and longed-for homogeneity all the more.

Bergendoff also realized that Swedish America was fading. The world of ethnic neighborhoods, lodges, taverns, anniversary rallies, Mid-Summer Day picnics, and Sankta Lucia coronations had been a vibrant reality. Now it was becoming the subject of scholarly investigation or nostalgic local celebrations, punctuated at moments by staged royal or episcopal visits and the occasional awarding of a medal or certificate to honor some keeper of the flame. But Swedish America was hardly the living community it had been between the Civil and the Second World Wars. As Bergendoff himself said, the world he had grown up in had sunk, like Atlantis, beneath time's waves.

As we have seen, Bergendoff sometimes speculated that he had been the champion of lost causes. That was perhaps an over-statement (unless he was simply referring to his failure to keep the seminary at Augustana from being separated from the college). It was, however, clearly the case that his own thinking on matters such as inter-church relationships, higher education, Swedish culture, to name but a few, had undergone significant changes. He was a man who at moments brought about and at others reflected some of the most important developments in the tradition in which he grew up and spent his years. As few had with such insight and such persistence, he dealt with the questions and tensions that his tradition had had to face as it grew, altered, and confronted the realities of American and world history during its last two-thirds century of independent existence. Sometimes he was ahead of the curve of events, sometimes behind it. It may be well in concluding this study of Conrad Bergendoff's faith and work to review and summarize his achievement. It may also be appropriate to consider certain areas in which things did not turn out as he had expected. More of that shortly.

The line of the development of this book has, the author hopes, been clear. We traced Bergendoff's life up to the point he became President of Augustana College and Theological Seminary. Then we considered his ideas about the core religious experience of his own and other Christian lives and sought to trace the implications of these ideas for Bergendoff's understanding of larger societal questions. After that, a chapter was devoted to his work within his own denomination, where these ideas were developed, confirmed, and at moments challenged. We saw that his work for unity of his own Synod with other Lutherans was predicated on his strong belief that their mutual adherence to the Lutheran creeds, especially the Augsburg Confession, was enough to bring them together. When he began to be involved in encounters beyond Lutheran borders with other Christian churches, Bergendoff found himself wondering whether creedal agreement was essential to full fellowship with them. We looked at the shifting relationship between his ethnic tradition, both in

America and Sweden, and his religious ideas. And finally, a chapter summarized his work as an educator.

In the Introduction, I enumerated certain fundamental questions about the Christian faith, questions which Bergendoff addressed and which in more generic form have arisen in many religious traditions and contexts. On some of them, for example, the necessity of literal interpretation of the sacred texts of his religion, Bergendoff's position was clear: he was no literalist. On others, like the possibility of Christian regeneration of society, he was somewhat equivocal. As certain as he was about the nature of the core experience of Christian life, or about the need to organize all learning around that core, Bergendoff was less sure about how fully to join with non-Lutherans or whether he could continue to hold up Scandinavian culture as paradigmatic. I hope that I have made it plain—both when he was clear and when he was not.

Now, in conclusion, I want to examine certain issues which Bergendoff's faith and work raised in several areas of his activity. These issues derive from some of the universal human religious questions which I think Bergendoff addressed; I hope consideration of them will help to locate him within his own religious tradition and in wider twentieth century Christianity as well. Easy and unequivocal solutions to these issues are still pending, and they continue to animate the lives of the institutions and the people that are his heirs. They have to do with: the relationship between personal and corporate religion; between Lutheranism and ecumenical Christianity; between Swedish culture and American culture; between the Christian message and the liberal arts and sciences; and between Bergendoff's understanding of religion as offering the answers to the deep questions of human life and the fact that often the answers he reached in their turn provoked new questions. In the case of each of these we have seen a Bergendoff who was more certain of definite answers early in his career than he was later. It is no discredit to him that this was so; he lived in the twentieth century.

In each of these situations, a sort of twist or irony emerges in the course of Bergendoff's life and work. Conditions in the wider world impinged upon his ideas and efforts, as did the dynamic or inner development of his own ideas. The irony or the incongruity lies in the differences between what Bergendoff thought and expected, especially early in his career, and what actually turned out to be the case. For the ancient dramatists, irony arose when those watching a drama knew all along that things would turn out differently than the characters moving through the action on the stage thought they would. In the incongruity between the situation as understood by the characters and the audience's knowledge of the truth lay the irony. The best known example of this in ancient drama is probably Sophocles' *Oedipus the King,* in which the protagonist, fulfilling oracular prophecy, unwittingly kills his father and marries his mother. He blinds himself at play's end, an act symbolic of not having seen the truth through the course of the whole drama. Until then only the gods (and the audience) have known the real state of affairs. Oedipus' end may be tragic as well as ironic, but it is the incongruity between what he thought was happening and what did turn out to be the case that is pertinent to this discussion.

A kind of incongruity did inhere in the relationships between Bergendoff's ideas and values, the situations which he confronted through his career, his understandable reactions to those situations, and the way things eventually turned out. After the fact, Bergendoff realized that such irony or incongruity had developed, though he had not, of course, been aware of this at first. That unawareness is of the essence of irony. In his own work on the subject, the American theologian Reinhold Niebuhr remarks, "the knowledge of irony is usually reserved for observers rather than participants."[5] Perhaps it is what our Swedish-American historian-theologian meant when he referred to himself as the champion of lost causes or a dreamer of impossible dreams. I would not, as I have said, entirely agree with that self-assessment, but it does appear that things did not always develop as he had expected they would. In that Bergendoff was like all of us. He worked and thought within the limits that his tradition and his own commitments and choices determined. The issues I have listed earlier in this concluding section of the book, and which I now intend to discuss, are still important to people who carry on the effort to interpret their religious faith in the context of their own situations in life. We are, as was Bergendoff, still liable to the ironic turns or incongruities that seem invariably to characterize human thought and effort when they deal with such weighty matters. But the questions he worked through deserve the reader's consideration, as she or he puts Conrad Bergendoff into the list of people whose life and work have mattered and whose ideas continue to challenge one's own.

Individual and Corporate Religion

The British philosopher and mathematician Alfred North Whitehead (1861–1947) maintained that "Religion is what a man does with his solitude." After his ecumenical awakening, when among others Methodists came into his circle, Conrad Bergendoff would probably have preferred the view of another Englishman, John Wesley: "There is no such thing as a solitary Christian." Speaking of the gathering of Christians, Martin Luther said simply, "No man can be saved who is not found in this congregation." That was how Bergendoff understood the Christian religion; it must be lived out in the company of other Christians. He was not taken with the solitary anchorite monks who in the early Christian centuries fled Roman society to live alone in the desert, perhaps, like Simeon Stylites, on top of a column erected above the sands.

That emphasis upon corporate Christianity marked the Swedish Lutheranism from which the Augustana Synod was descended. We have noted repeatedly that Bergendoff was not inclined to speak much of his private or solitary religious experience. He found the liturgical formulae of the Church of Sweden's prayer book a far more fulfilling and meaningful expression of his faith than he did the kind of extemporaneous personal prayers and testimonies frequent in the frontier varieties of American Protestantism among which the Synod fathers found themselves. He spoke of the respect which the people of Sweden felt toward the ceremonies and services of their national Church, especially when these were compared with what he regarded as the shallow revivalism of the free churches. Further, Bergendoff had devoted much of his scholarly effort to an examination of the collective history, in Sweden and in America, of his religious tradition and denomination. He could not think of the contemporary religious situation—his own, Lutheranism's, or that of the other Christian churches—without referring to its historic roots. Thus, I have argued that rather than being a "systematic theologian," he was an "historical theologian." History meant shared experience.

Bergendoff knew personally the Swedish church historian Hilding Pleijel, who maintained that up until the middle of the nineteenth century, Swedish Christianity had been almost entirely a social or corporate religion. Lutheranism in Sweden had provided the sanction for a stable society and at moments had exercised an Old Testament-like legalism over the country's folk. Pleijel wrote that the Church's efforts were directed at raising general folk morality rather than picking individuals out of the wider society, hoping to redeem them from its sinful midst. One could only find Christian fulfillment in solidarity with one's local congregation, not by leaving it to form some new group or sect of the truly faithful. We have seen that until Bergendoff was moved to face the hard fact that Swedish culture, especially following the Second World War, had become one of the most secular in the world, he held that culture up as an example of the way in which Lutheran Christian social values and ethics could leaven a whole society. In the North of Europe, more fully than anywhere else in the world, he wrote, Lutheranism had permeated whole countries with its stable and civilizing influence. So both Bergendoff and Pleijel maintained that, at some historical point earlier than the mid-twentieth century, Christian values had been diffused through the land of their fathers and mothers. They might have dated the shift from that kind of society differently, Bergendoff probably placing it later than Pleijel did.

Our subject also never quite made his peace with the fact that when Swedish Lutheranism was transplanted to North America, it failed to bring the majority of Swedish immigrants into its fold. And he recognized that the community in which he had grown up was not the only kind of Swedish America to develop.

There was a secular one as well. He did argue that his Synod was the only part of that immigrant community that preserved a clear identity and that created lasting institutions, asserting with an uncharacteristic degree of immodesty that the college he led was the most important of those institutions. (Bergendoff was able to boast of his college, though never of himself. The former ability is an important part of a college president's job description, the latter not really essential, though commonly encountered.) But he knew that the Augustana Synod had never achieved the place of a folk church among its natural constituency, and he also knew that it was increasingly difficult to maintain that Swedish society itself was permeated by the continuing influence of its own folk Church. He lamented the passing of corporate national Christianity in Sweden as he did the failure of his own Church to win most of the immigrants to America from Sweden. But he held, as did other historians of the Synod, both in his lifetime and more recently, that the Swedish Lutheran experience was unique in comparison with other ethnic Lutheran groups in that it had never been rent by schism. It had preserved its communal quality intact, even if it had not succeeded in becoming the folk church of Swedish Americans. That it was not a folk church was in part due to the fact that it did not enroll even half of the immigrants.

But not becoming the Swedish-American folk church was also due to Augustana's and Bergendoff's basic understanding of the Christian experience. While religion was not reckoned to be a matter of solitude, the Augustana understanding of the church was a good deal more individual or personal than the collective or community Christianity that had prevailed up until the mid-nineteenth century in Sweden. The shift toward a newer understanding of the essential Christian experience, one that stressed individual decision and commitment, is associated with the growth of Swedish Pietism on both sides of the Atlantic. So is the emphasis upon the Christian congregation as a gathering of true believers, people who have individually decided to follow Christ, not simply assuming that they are in the company of the faithful because their parents had once promised at their baptism that they would be.

The founders of the Synod had, to some degree or other, been drawn to that idea of a purer church and had only given it up gradually, as they contrasted their own Lutheran understanding of the character of the church with the more evangelistic American denominations around them. But then they had to face, as it were, the fact that they were not winning the majority of their transplanted countrymen and women. That suggested that some sort of act of will or a kind of individual decision had to be made by a person to join or to remain in the church. The church was a community made up of individuals who had personally decided for Christ. In this sense, Pietism not only generated the one split in the ranks of Swedish-American Lutheranism (which did not need to be reckoned to the Synod's account, since when it took place, the people who left Augustana no longer held to the Augsburg Confession and were therefore not technically Lutherans). Pietism also continued to work within the Synod, deeply conditioning its piety and even its theology.

By now it should be clear that for Conrad Bergendoff the decision to be Christian, whether a person made it at a specific moment or whether it was one that was quietly reaffirmed throughout life, was an individual one. In spite of his deep reverence for his Swedish Lutheran roots, he did not think one was automatically, by virtue of birth, a Christian. An individual must encounter Christ. We considered this in the third chapter of this book, and it was a theme to which Bergendoff returned throughout his life. It had enormous implications for how he viewed the rest of society, other church groups, and his work in education. We have had few glimpses of Bergendoff's own religious or inner life, but those we do get confirm his own "commitment to Christ." We see the young pastor and graduate student, unsure of himself, but willing to take on a hectic parish schedule and balance it with graduate school demands. Or we catch a look at a mature churchman, waiting in New England for the US Army plane to carry him to still smoldering Germany, there to lecture to theological faculties beginning to be rebuilt.

The Christ experience of which he wrote most often in the third person was certainly one which Bergendoff knew of in the first. I wrote earlier that for Bergendoff, "Christ" was a "set term," so it would be pointless here to add my own speculation on "what it meant" to him. To name Christ was enough for Bergendoff; he did not attempt further elaboration. The reader can make her or his own conjectures and develop an interpretation based upon them. But it is clear that the relationship to Christ was intensely personal and that it was what Bergendoff knew to be the very center of his life. It was also the standard by which all of society and culture was to be judged, challenged, and, hopefully, remade. Thus, Christianity was for Conrad Bergendoff both an essentially individual and a necessarily corporate reality.

We noted earlier that contemporary scholarship dealing with immigration has spoken often of "identity," and that several works dealing specifically with the Augustana tradition have examined and explained the way in which a Swedish-American or a Swedish-American-Lutheran identity has been fashioned and changed in the nineteenth and twentieth centuries. Bergendoff was a member of the Augustana Synod, the group which seems to have been the principal agency in forming and maintaining that identity for the largest number of immigrants from Sweden to America. But it would be a mistake to think that if you asked Bergendoff who he understood himself to be, he would have simply answered that he was a Swedish-American Lutheran or "an Augustana man." True, his

Lutheran Social Services of Illinois President Donald Hallberg presents the organization's Amicus Certus award to Conrad Bergendoff and Orion Samuelson, WGN farm broadcaster, 1996.

answer might have been closer to one of those labels in 1925 than it would have been fifty years later.

But at both moments, and before and since, Bergendoff would have answered that he was a person whose life was centered and defined by his religious commitment. And even an answer like that would have been somewhat generic; what he would have said explicitly was that he had met Christ. That is in fact how he did speak—repeatedly. His identity was *homo religiosus*. Whatever sense of himself he got from his ethnic-religious community was derivative, as that community itself was; his self-understanding was rooted, as Augustana's identity was, in personal religious experience. That experience, as we have seen, had significance for all of Bergendoff's ecclesiastical and educational work. So as for religion being a matter of what one did with one's solitude in the way Whitehead's aphorism suggests, Bergendoff would have demurred. The religious life was for him intrinsically social and cultural. But nonetheless it began with an intensely personal or individual experience. Here the irony lay not so much in the temporal development of the Augustana tradition through the decades, as it did in the inner tension of its central commitments. In this sense, Bergendoff was very much the heir of Swedish Pietism, which was one stage in the history of a people whose earlier religious life had been centered upon the community and whose later religiosity gradually dissolved into secularism. One important collateral implication of this religious individualism was that it contained within itself an important reason, along with rising Swedish secularism, why Bergendoff's Synod did not (indeed, could not) become the Swedish-American folk church. That was ironic.

Lutheran and Ecumenical Christianity

The world of Swedish-American Lutheranism had a history, a vocabulary, and a structure of thought which in many ways were shared with most European Lutheranism. In the New World the Augustana Synod understood itself to be bound by these elements to other Lutheran groups. Yet some of Augustana's piety, hymnody, and liturgy, as well as its ethnicity, were unique. Bergendoff believed that the rituals of the Church of Sweden were among its noblest gifts to the New World. He was convinced that the work of that Church's twentieth century theologians was the best being done in contemporary Lutheranism, perhaps in all Christendom. He saw Scandinavian culture, at least up through the early twentieth century, as having been permeated by the social values of Lutheranism to a degree that had not occurred anywhere else, even in Germany. And he believed that his Synod had a responsibility to all immigrants from Sweden, even if many of them did not seek those ministrations.

Thus we have encountered a Conrad Bergendoff passing up Harvard or Wesleyan for Augustana College; returning from Mt. Airy to Augustana Theological Seminary in the early twenties; marrying a daughter of immigrants whom he met when she was singing in a Rockford Swedish-American church choir; deciding to study history, not liberal American theology, at the University of Chicago; building the finest Augustana Synod sanctuary in Chicago; making a pilgrimage to Sweden to write a dissertation on Olavus Petri; declining a career elsewhere in American Lutheranism or higher education; and reluctantly agreeing to serve first as Dean of the Seminary and then as President of Augustana. All of these life moves took place within or in response to the Swedish-American-Lutheran community, which for the first half of his years was the agency beyond all others that defined Bergendoff, that shaped his identity and self-understanding. Even the religious commitment that Bergendoff believed to be fundamental to his life was made in his Synod and on terms that had deep roots in its own history and that of Swedish Lutheranism and Pietism. Bergendoff's ultimate sense of himself came from this tradition, though, of course, he believed that the tradition pointed way beyond itself—to the single most important event in human history, the incarnation of God in Christ two millennia earlier.

Right at this point lay one of the crucial pivots in Bergendoff's life. Implicit in his tradition and his own experience were elements which demanded that one go *past* the tradition, for its essence lay beyond and prior to itself. That was one vital quality of the meeting with Christ: essential though it was, it eventually but inescapably pointed past itself. One implication of that was to seek fellowship with others who had also had that experience; Christianity began with personal experience, but it sought community. At first Bergendoff, like the fathers of his denomination, maintained that the Lutheran Confessions, especially the one for which his Church and college were named, were the fullest and truest expression of the biblical message of salvation through Christ. In the mid-thirties Bergendoff said that his Church offered the opportunity for a person to live the "best balanced" Christian life; that was why he remained in it.

That meant that the full communion one hoped for with other Christians would be with those who subscribed to the Augsburg Confession. Early in his professional career, the new President of Augustana seemed to stand solidly with his Church's founders in unyielding defense of their creeds and in insisting that communion with other Christians depended on adherence to those statements of faith. To other historians, less committed to such confessional fidelity than Bergendoff, it seemed that this view really boiled down to the idea that the Augsburg Confession had for all time stated the essence of Christianity and that not to agree with it was to miss the opportunity to be fully Christian. But it was right at this point that, for his part, Conrad Bergendoff began to insist that further evidence of your Lutheran bona fides was not necessary; you didn't have to sign additional proofs of orthodoxy. The Augsburg Confession was good enough. It was necessary and it was adequate. Already he had begun to recognize ecumenical impulses in it, at least as regarded other Lutherans.

Then Bergendoff went to Britain for the Oxford and Edinburgh meetings. He listened to addresses, took part in discussions and seminars, and, most importantly, worshipped with non-Lutherans. These people, it turned out, seemed to be as loyal to Christ and the gospel as folk he had known in Augustana and in American Lutheranism. The Augustana man got involved in the work of committees, attended continuation sessions after the 1937 meetings, and argued that his denomination ought to be a member of the national and world councils of churches. These groups sought to promote encounter, if not organized unity, among different Christian traditions. Now Bergendoff's attitude about Lutheran confessional documents began to shift further. Early in his career he held that so long as other groups professed that they adhered to them, his own denomination should commune and probably unite with them. Now he began to maintain that the value of these statements of faith to which Lutherans attached such importance was that they offered the basis on which his Church could interpret and explain itself to other Christians. Rather than being a reason his denomination did not have full fellowship with others, the creeds became a basis upon which they might.

It now became important to Bergendoff that the *Confessio Augustana* recognized that the groups of those who adhered to it were not co-terminal with the Church of Christ on earth; that Church existed elsewhere in the world too, beyond the Augsburg Confession, as it were. To be faithful to that Confession, you had to recognize that fact and try to figure out its implications. That was yet another stage in his understanding of the ecumenicity implicit in the Confession. Bergendoff did not declare himself in favor of signing formal agreements for full communion with other denominational families, a position his Church *did* reach by the end of his life, but he almost certainly took Holy Communion with non-Lutherans, as he said, "on the local level." First to meet, to work together, and then to pray and sing, maybe even to take Communion with these folk, became the path to ecumenical agreement.

The shift in the use Bergendoff made of his Church's confessions, if not the fundamental understanding he had of them, both reflected and caused a growth in his sense of who were brothers and sisters in the faith, a faith that he himself had first learned in the closed communion of Swedish-American Lutherans. In a manner fully consistent with his understanding of the deliberate, even slow, way that Sweden had come to the Reformation in the first place, Bergendoff acted on what he believed were the inner and compelling dynamics of Lutheranism itself. He sought with some success to bring his Synod with him in this ecumenical opening up. He was historian enough to recognize that this represented a development in his denomination and in his own thinking as well, though he steadily maintained that, seed-like, this ecumenism lay in his tradition from the start. Perhaps the clearest way to speak of this shift in Bergendoff's experience of ecumenical relationships is to note that from having emphasized the qualities in Lutheranism that he believed to be unique to it and essential for full Christian thinking and living, he began to stress that encountering, listening, and speaking to other Christians was the true way to be a faithful Swedish-American Lutheran. Here the incongruity lay between the ethno-religious Lutheranism of the early Bergendoff and his Synod and the ecumenical openness to which he and his Church moved in mid-century. It is clear from his self-reported reaction to the inter-Church meetings he attended in Britain in 1937 that he had not expected to be as strongly influenced as he was by his encounters with non-Lutherans and that thereafter his ecumenical work took on an urgency and intensity that one might not have anticipated in the early 1930s.

Sweden and America

We have seen that the fathers of the Augustana Synod left Sweden with, at best, ambivalent feelings about their homeland. Their own career prospects in the Church of Sweden were not especially promising. They were leaving a Church which, together with the monarchy and the aristocracy, represented and defended a conservative way of life and a settled social order. The Pietism that had influenced many of the immigrant pastors was a strong force in Swedish religion in the nineteenth century, but it was never really embraced by the leadership of the national Church. Though for a time this Pietism tried to exist as a sub-order within that Church, eventually it established its own organization. The priests of the Church of Sweden who came to America had mixed thoughts about the tax-supported State Church and at the same time doubts about the free churches such as the Baptists and Methodists in the homeland. When they got to America, they were friends of neither the state church model nor the revivalist free churches. The latter were viewed as rivals preying upon immigrants who were rightfully the spiritual charges of the Lutheran Augustana Synod.

These generalizations are the picture of the relationship between the founders of Augustana and the Church of Sweden which emerges from the work of historians of the Synod such as O. F. Ander, G. Everett Arden, and George M. Stephenson. Conrad Bergendoff, who did not himself devote his early scholarly efforts to direct study of the first years of Swedish Lutheranism in America, had somewhat different ideas. He stressed the high educational attainments of the Synod fathers and their desire to preserve the theology, cultus, and folk piety of the Church of Sweden in America. He treated their differences with Sweden over church organization, i.e. state control and episcopal government, as one of the questions not essential to the faith. Sincere Christians could disagree on these matters; they were adiaphora. In this regard he was in the vanguard of those in the Augustana Synod who sought to bring about rapprochement with the Church of Sweden. With the visits by Swedish bishops in connection with Augustana anniversaries and with the growing influence of Swedish bishop-theologians in international Christianity, the suspicion between Lutherans in Sweden and in the Synod melted into a flood of good will by the Second World War. His own year with the prince of the Swedish religious renaissance, Nathan Söderblom, gave Bergendoff a deep and lasting sense of the spiritual power of Swedish religion and culture, which he longed to see prevail in his own American denomination as well.

And there was the rub. Many historians of Swedish culture regard the Söderblom years as a temporary hiatus in the steady move toward secularism in Sweden. In this view, the cooperation of church and state during World War II was another such hiatus. One is tempted to say that the picture of Swedish life that Bergendoff got from following Söderblom through his own diocese in the twenties, a picture he hung on to through the war years, was at best a partial and perhaps even a distorted one. The rude reality seems to have hit him when he discovered the scorn and even hostility in Sweden that greeted Dag Hammarskjöld's *Markings* upon its publication in the sixties. By then it was clear that the society which Bergendoff had held up as a paradigm of Lutheranism's ability to condition a whole nation had gone over to the dark side, to a secularism that was, by Bergendoff's oft-stated standards at least, ultimately pagan.

There lies a certain irony, as well as the rub. We know what Bergendoff thought about contemporary American culture; he decried its materialism, secularism, and paganism for four steady decades, from the Salem pulpit, the Augustana chapel, and the pages of the *Lutheran Companion*. He spoke of the spiritual poverty into which the immigrants to the Middle West had made their way in the mid-nineteenth century, and regarded much of the religion on the American frontier as thin revival gruel. The Swedes brought to the American religious table their far richer "thousand year spiritual heritage." For Bergendoff the substantial tradition of Reformation theology was a needed counterweight to the thin superficiality of the American Social Gospel, and he welcomed the revival of Luther's influence in mainline American Protestantism in the thirties. Indeed, it was one of the major reasons he found himself more at home than he had expected to be in ecumenical circles before and after the Second War. That is where the irony lay. As American Christianity became increasingly influenced by what Bergendoff felt was the deeper substance of the revival of Reformation theology, the land where Bergendoff believed that theology had permeated the culture was turning away from organized Christianity.

Some observers have noted that the American Revolution was never hostile to religious faith in the way the French Revolution was. The present writer is not competent to parse the implications or even to defend the legitimacy of that generalization. But it is clear that two centuries after those revolutionary upheavals, religious questions are still very much part of the public dialog in America. You cannot be elected to high public office in the United States if you are suspected of atheism; the issue would not come up in Sweden. The very fact that the anti-religious tirades of Christopher Hitchens or Richard Dawkins sell books in America is testimony to the religious cast of American life; in Western Europe atheism is last week's news. Conrad Bergendoff might or might not take some consolation in the fact that a kind of religious faith is still a factor in the public mind and conversation in the first of his "native" lands. But after the mid-twentieth century, it hardly mattered on the other side of the North Atlantic, in his second homeland. That *did* bother him, and it is perhaps the clearest example of the fact that things did not turn out as Conrad Bergendoff thought they would (or should).

The Christian Faith and the Liberal Arts

During his service as President of Augustana College, Bergendoff had sometimes worried that many of its academic staff did not fully understand, or at least that they did not very well articulate, their personal ideas about the way in which their own work related to the theological or religious underpinnings of the college itself. Bergendoff's strong condemnation of much of the culture that had evolved since the Renaissance and Reformation did not keep individual faculty and departments from considering many of that culture's achievements and aspects, whether the theater of Shakespeare or the biology of Darwin. Bergendoff himself recognized that. In his later presidential years, he had wondered aloud where Augustana might find social scientists willing to exercise Christian value judgments in their increasingly value-neutral disciplines, physical scientists who understood and declared explicitly that all nature witnessed to its divine grandeur and origin, or teachers of literature who were willing to avoid the tawdry smut of much contemporary writing in favor of Christian decency.

But while many of the college faculty explored areas about which Bergendoff himself harbored doubts, or when these academics operated with a neutrality that seemed not to take full account of the Christian gospel, they recognized that their president was the one man on campus who sought to hold all of their work together. He did it not simply by providing a physical and fiscal context in which they could teach and write—blackboard chalk and a monthly paycheck—but more importantly by trying to offer an intellectual, even theological, framework that made sense of it all. If they did not always share the depth and intensity of Bergendoff's religious commitments, they respected them. And in the years after he left the leadership of the school, Bergendoff continued for many people on the campus and in its wider constituencies to represent that integration of learning by the Christian faith, as he often put it, "under the lordship of Christ."

We have seen that Bergendoff was not threatened by the discoveries of the modern natural sciences and that in contrast to American fundamentalism, his Church and he made room in their colleges for the full range of thought and research that was going on in the contemporary university world. Free of biblical literalism, Bergendoff saw no conflict between Genesis and geology. All fields of study belonged in the curriculum. The Augustana president would never have agreed with the negative position implicit in the question of the ancient church father Tertullian (ca. 160-225): "What hath Athens to do with Jerusalem?" Our Swedish American devoted his professional life to the proposition that when the learning of Athens was brought under the spiritual direction of Jerusalem, the world, both idea and reality, would be as God meant it. Only in this way, could the disparate disciplines of the modern "*multi*versity" be made a *uni*versity.

That was the reason that Bergendoff believed that Augustana must teach all of the arts and sciences. But what he came to realize ever more clearly during the years that he administered the college, was that the newly trained scholars who joined his faculty were increasingly imbued with the idea that their academic work must be carried on free of their ideological or religious commitments. It was not disallowed to have such convictions, but they could not be permitted to interfere with the way one did one's chemistry or political science. To get people with the best training was to search for them in precincts where academic or scientific "objectivity" was absolutely insisted upon. Bergendoff recalled his own training in the twenties, when he discovered the a- or even ir-religion that prevailed in most of the modern university, even with his own greatly respected professors. So in the very insistence upon teaching all the arts and sciences and in the persistent quest for excellence of scholarly preparation in candidates for the Augustana faculty, it was necessary to court people who had been trained to keep their religious faith out of their academic work. George M. Marsden, an historian of American higher education, nicely catches the dilemma that faced colleges like Bergendoff's by mid-century: "Keeping up meant hiring faculty with loyalties to national academic standards more than to church concerns."[6]

What that meant in practical terms was that, when possible, Bergendoff hired men and women whose *undergraduate* training had been in schools like his own. In fact, outside accreditors at moments remarked, not altogether favorably, on the homogeneity of the Augustana faculty, many of whom were, like the president, graduates of the college itself, or of Middle Western Lutheran schools very much like it. The assumption of the criticism was that a wider variety of outlooks and backgrounds was desirable in the teaching staff. And in a real sense, that was the issue. In a way, Bergendoff wanted just the opposite: a faculty that saw all of its work in a Christian context and that shared a common commitment to the religious as well as the academic purposes of the college. This was another of the ironies that marked Bergendoff's work: to get the excellence which the academic substance and reputation of his college demanded, it became necessary to recruit academics who were, both explicitly and implicitly, trained to keep their personal commitments out of their professional work.

The standards of excellence which the European and American intellectual and scholarly worlds insisted upon were informed to a considerable degree by the very ideals of secularism and value neutrality which Bergendoff believed were corroding the Christian faith and undermining its place in society. In the later Bergendoff years and thereafter, Augustana became a good deal more heterogeneous. The president and senior faculty welcomed its growing academic reputation, but lamented the loss of religious community which was also setting in. These developments—increasing academic stature and growing religious heterogeneity—may not have been tied together of necessity, but, as it was, they did accompany each other. The American Lutherans had founded many colleges, the majority of them in the Middle West. It was an unhappy state in the Upper Middle West that did not have one or two of them. All of these institutions, Augustana included, had steadily maintained that there was no necessary conflict between their religious foundations and the academic excellence they sought. But it took a sturdy sort of Christian to make her way through a first-rate graduate program and to emerge with a well-thought-out religious position as well as with a PhD certifying professional competence. Bergendoff knew such folk were hard to find, especially at the salaries his school could afford to pay. It was one thing to recruit a geologist like Fritiof Fryxell, an historian like O. F. Ander, or a student of literature like Henriette Naeseth in the throes of the Depression, quite another to find such people in the competitive post-Sputnik years.

As Bergendoff saw it, there seemed to be fewer of these Christian scholars in the first place, and the competition for them was ever stiffer. Further, when you got these people to come to Rock Island, it was important to help them understand more thoroughly the relationship between their faith and their academic work. Sometimes that might mean adjusting some of the attitudes and assumptions with which they left grad school. Here the irony lay in the tension between Christian commitment and the way the liberal arts and sciences were taught and practiced in twentieth century America. In retrospect we, the audience, can see that this was the arc of American scholarly development; Bergendoff, the actor, believed it need not be so. But things did not take the course he hoped for and, to a degree, expected.

Answers and Questions

The Introduction to the present book said that Conrad Bergendoff dealt during his long career with many questions that are fundamental to the human religious experience. The reader may recall that Bergendoff was troubled when some persons and agencies in American higher education suggested that it was enough to ask these questions and to explore the many answers given to them in the classical religions of history. That was what these individuals and organizations meant by "including the religious dimension" in higher education. Bergendoff knew that the American commitment to the separation of church and state meant that in public university education it was not permissible to advocate for one particular religion's answers to these questions. He felt that the great edge which a college like his held was that it *could* maintain and teach the truth of Christianity; it did not have to feign neutrality. And although colleges and universities from other denominational traditions had cast off from their religious moorings, Bergendoff was gratified that Lutheran institutions like Augustana were anchored

Conrad Bergendoff, BA, 1915.

to the church, both structurally and intellectually.

But we have seen that in the years after his retirement as President of Augustana, Bergendoff's college and sister institutions shifted the way they thought and spoke of their missions. Whereas in the earlier decades of the century they had spoken of their purpose to "teach youth the way of life determined by the revelation of Jesus Christ in the Word and the Church," they now asserted that "students see campus religious life differently, according to the emphasis they have developed for themselves." The earlier statement was normative, the later simply descriptive. Presumably young people were now expected to work through their own answers to the great questions about the origin, purpose, and destiny of their lives, helped gently from the side by mature faculty—and even college chaplains.

That was not the way Bergendoff had grown up. He recalled the long hours that his siblings and he had spent memorizing catechetical answers to set questions. When he got back to Augustana Seminary, he was discouraged to find out that this was for all purposes the way Professor of Theology Conrad Lindberg taught would-be pastors—with formularized Lutheran answers, to be learned by rote. Bergendoff's inclination to broaden that outlook had been honed by his year at Mt. Airy, and it led him to do extensive reading in authors, historic and contemporary, Lutheran and otherwise, whose names the seminary faculty had hardly heard, let alone read. Yet, that did not mean that Bergendoff's quest was any the less for religious certainty. He eschewed Pascal's elevation of doubt to a principle for religious commitment, and found Descartes' effort to pare philosophy down to a personal core ("I think, therefore I am.") to be self-centered subjectivism.

Yet the very tradition which had given birth to Bergendoff's religious and theological experience inevitably faced questions itself. Some of these were posed by the conditions of life in the mid-twentieth century. Thus, Bergendoff confessed that different Christians would find different answers to the morality of developing nuclear weapons. Or in a matter as seemingly petty as dancing on the college campus, he recognized that what the tradition of his Church maintained did not seem to have much relevance to the people who came back to the college after the war. We know the degree to which his encounters with theologians from other traditions led him to wonder about the claims to universal validity of the theology of his own denomination. He came increasingly to understand that the Synod was itself the creature of very particular historical factors and circumstances, just as the grand centuries-long faith of the entire Christian church had been.

In his seventies Bergendoff ruefully recalled those memorized definitions that Professor Lindberg had required of his students: "how ludicrous to define God." Student Bergendoff's reaction was a far cry from the attitude of the Synod fathers who believed, at least according to one historian, that the *Confessio Augustana* had for all time defined the essence of the faith. That reaction to Lindberg's certainty points to an important distinction that should be made here with regard to the questions that Bergendoff found himself asking in the course of his career. It was one thing to have the tradition challenged from outside its borders, often from the secular culture that Bergendoff so strongly criticized. There were, for example, questions about the legitimacy of belief in God in the first place or about the doctrine of the resurrection of Christ, such as those the Swedish philosopher Ingemar Hedenius had raised with the theologians of Lund University. It was another matter to address questions that arose from the dynamic of one's own tradition, questions which came almost inevitably to be posed by the inner logic of Bergendoff's faith itself.

From within the tradition came questions about its relationship to other denominations, Lutheran and otherwise. Bergendoff said that the fact that many Lutherans in North America declared that they adhered to the Augsburg Confession meant that his own Synod had to decide whether to believe those statements or to devise further tests to determine their sincerity. Further, he argued that since the Confession recognized that there were Christians outside the Lutheran movement, Christians within that movement had to face the question of how to relate to them. These latter were "home-grown" questions, not problems imposed from outside the tradition. It should be clear that these home-grown questions were raised on the basis of the central faith commitment that Bergendoff maintained his life long.

Bergendoff did not set sail from Lutheran certainty out into the wide uncharted waters of religion in general. Nor did he tack toward the melted-down, lowest-common-denominator Christianity that he found everywhere around him in mid-century American life. He believed as firmly in 1995 as he had in 1925 that the heart of true Christianity was the encounter with Christ that was spelled out in Chapter 3 of this book. But that experience and the theological framework that supported it were not a closed system. They raised their own questions, ones which, as he reflected on his Church's history and considered its prospects, Bergendoff felt must be addressed.

These questions eventually led our subject far past the limits that had defined his life when he graduated from Augustana College, then its Seminary, and entered the ministry of its Church. Just as Bergendoff was carried in directions he might not have anticipated in the early stages of his career, American Lutheranism was also propelled beyond the certainties that had characterized many of its pastors and people in the early twentieth century. It moved toward agreements, commitments, and opportunities that few of its patriarchal leaders might have guessed lay ahead. Ironically, answers which had been thought and intended to settle matters led rather to further questions. No actor in the drama more clearly represents this shift than does the subject of our study.

Faith and Humane Irony

Conrad Bergendoff was in some regards a different man in 1995 than he had been when he emerged from childhood and traveled to Illinois to attend college. Certain tensions, even ironies, marked his century long career. I have tried to point out some of them. In the course of the decades, Bergendoff himself became aware of many of them. They arose in areas where Swedish-American Lutheran institutions and people were especially liable to the confrontation between their own beliefs and the times in which they lived. Beyond this, these folk were faced by questions arising from their core commitments themselves.

As the man who today more than any other represents the tradition of the Augustana Church and its oldest school, Bergendoff reflects the solutions and the incongruities that arose, both from these confrontations and from the dynamic of the heritage itself. We have seen that Bergendoff's self-understanding, his identity, underwent significant adjustments with regard to the matters discussed in this Conclusion. He clearly found himself tugged back and forth between communal and individual Christianity, and the claims of one did not always harmonize with the other. He moved from a defensive to an ecumenical understanding of his own Church's place in American Lutheranism and in modern world Christendom. He faced that the land he had held up as a pattern for the role of Christianity in society had itself turned away from that pattern. And he had to confront the fact that his own understanding of the preeminent and proper place of the Christian message in higher learning was in significant ways being adjusted—even at the college he had led for twenty-seven years. In these several important areas of his life and thinking, the answers Bergendoff had assumed or reached in youth and early adulthood did, over the course of the decades, lead to new questions—in his own life and in that of the institutions which had defined him and meant so much to him.

I noted earlier in this Conclusion that in the way matters developed with regard to these issues there inhered a certain irony. Things turned in directions that Bergendoff had not anticipated. He himself realized that, remarking on it later in his life. At moments he had been an actor in the drama. But later he found himself in the audience, able to look back on the action and see now how it had headed down different paths than he had expected. During Bergendoff's century-long life, 1895–1997, two leading American Christian intellectuals wrote about the irony that had characterized that period in American history. While the work of neither exactly matches the ancient Greek dramatists' sense of the ironic, both these intellectuals found an incongruity between what actors in the historical drama anticipated and what turned out to be the case. And both sought to relate that incongruity to the Christian sense of history.

Bergendoff's contemporary, Reinhold Niebuhr, whom Arthur Schlesinger, Jr., writing in the *New York Times* in 2005, called "the most influential American theologian of the 20th century,"[7] offered a theological perspective on irony. Though not Sophoclean, it is germane here. In *The Irony of American History* (1952), Niebuhr distinguished between irony, tragedy, and pathos. Pathos, which is often our reaction to natural evil, elicits our pity, but not our admiration or contrition. Tragedy, Niebuhr wrote, arises when there is a conscious choice of evil for the sake of a larger good. For Niebuhr the threat of using atomic weapons to preserve peace was tragic. Tragedy combines nobility with guilt, and it awakens both our pity and our admiration. In contrast to pathos and tragedy, Niebuhr held, "Irony consists of apparently fortuitous incongruities in life which are discovered, upon closer examination, to be not merely fortuitous."[8] The incongruity or irony seems for Niebuhr to inhere in the nature of persons and situations and in the interaction between them.

For his part, the church historian Martin Marty finds the course of twentieth century religion to be ironic, entitling the first volume (1986) in his treatment of American Christian history, 1893 to 1919, *The Irony of It All*. The book covers a period that roughly overlaps Bergendoff's younger years, at home and at Augustana College and Theological Seminary. In his introductory section, Marty recalls Reinhold Niebuhr's treatment of *The Irony of American History*. Marty notes Niebuhr's aphorism that God is "a divine judge who laughs at human pretensions without being hostile to human aspirations."[9] As did Niebuhr and Marty, Conrad Bergendoff understood that quality to lie in God. Both historian and theologian, he would have strenuously protested that no man or woman could so rise above human life as to view its arc—from the past through the present toward the future—objectively and with certainty. Marty concludes, "Irony, especially

The official portrait.

in the religious sphere, depends upon some measure of freedom and permits meaningful activity in response to the sacred, the divine, the gods, or God. Thus its perspective allows for not only human folly but also for enhancement of the humane[.]"[10]

Whether young Bergendoff's certainty that his own Church most fully expressed Christian truth or his later elevation of Swedish culture to the paradigmatic were "folly" or not, they certainly demonstrated his concern for that "enhancement of the humane." That concern is the quality that remains so winsome in his life and work. Bergendoff used his freedom in the belief that God supports human aspirations, realizing at the same time that he laughs at human pretensions. Bergendoff also thought, with Niebuhr, that only "a governing faith or world view" could make sense of the historical events in which human life plays out, bestowing dignity upon human effort, even though an ironic quality often inheres in that effort.[11] And with both Niebuhr and Marty, he believed that a Christian world view was humane. For him Christianity was in general marked by compassion and sympathy toward others and in particular committed to a humanistic culture that sought through the faith to develop the highest possibilities of human life. None of us can hope to do more than to contribute to an "enhancement of the humane," knowing all the while that our read of the trajectory of things is by its nature uncertain, and that soon some observer will note the irony in our own interpretations and efforts, perhaps even wondering in retrospect why we did not see it.

Within this framework, the importance of Bergendoff's life and thought is that he made a careful and protracted effort to relate his ethno-religious tradition to the changing religious and cultural conditions of the world in which it found itself. He believed that at the core of his tradition lay the truth about human existence which, he came increasingly to realize, had also animated other such traditions. He represented, and often to a considerable degree generated, the adjustments that his own heritage made to life in the twentieth century. But the stage which his Church and its institutions reached in his lifetime was just that— one stage. And its own commitments as well as conditions beyond itself have now carried Bergendoff's tradition past the point to which he and his generation brought it. That should not be surprising, for it lies in the nature of Christian history, as it does in human history as a whole, that this is the case: *Ecclesia semper reformanda est* (the Church must always be reformed).

Still, the faith that lay at the center of Bergendoff's life was also rooted in Christian history, and as he understood it, his commitment to that faith did not change. Of course, he took no credit that it was so. *Soli deo gloria.* I suggested in the Introduction to this study that some readers would be deeply gratified and others perhaps surprised to discover who Bergendoff thought he was. Now in conclusion, I must say this: *He was in fact who he believed himself to be.* In this lay his extra-ordinary integrity. Maybe that is the final thing to be said of him. In a century of both progress and madness, he held his course. His ideas, achievements, and contributions were rooted in that steadiness. Of course, all the questions he faced were not resolved, all his perceptions not validated, all his aspirations not realized. But what he had experienced and learned in Middletown and Rock Island held up for him—for one hundred and two years. It compelled him to the efforts in the many areas of his work for which he won deserved recognition. It grounded him through a century of change that confounded wise and famous persons. It comforted him when others opposed him and things did not turn out as he wished. Individual readers will decide for themselves whether to strive for such steadfastness in their own lives and thinking—and whether to look for it in the places Bergendoff found it. But his constancy did, in the century through which he lived, make Conrad Bergendoff a remarkable man.

ENDNOTES, SELECTED BIBLIOGRAPHY, AND INDEX

ABBREVIATIONS

The following abbreviations are used in the Endnotes; in the Bibliography names or titles of the journals are spelled out.

AQ	*Augustana Quarterly*
CB	Conrad Bergendoff
CBP	Conrad Bergendoff Papers
LC	*Lutheran Companion*
LQ	*Lutheran Quarterly*
SAHQ	*Swedish-American Historical Quarterly*
SPHQ	*Swedish Pioneer Historical Quarterly*

The following method of notation is used to refer to materials from the Bergendoff Papers. The citations that follow below on the left are examples; on the right are explanations of the citations.

CBP 9-6	Bergendoff papers, Processed, Box 9, Folder 6. (There are 81 boxes in this series.)
CBP UP	Bergendoff Papers, Unprocessed, general.
CBP UP 3	Bergendoff Papers, Unprocessed, Personal Correspondence Series in Numbered Box 3. (The series has 18 boxes of letters dating from 1930 through 1982, though it is labeled "Personal Correspondence, 1935-1962.")
CBP UP 1921-1923	Bergendoff Papers, Unprocessed, Personal Correspondence Series in the "Letters." (It has three dated boxes covering the years 1916-1923 and one box labeled "Family/Sweden.")
CBP UP Friendship	Bergendoff Papers, Unprocessed, Box labeled "Friendship Manor."

NOTES ON USAGE IN THIS BOOK

Conrad Bergendoff's books, essays, reviews, etc. are cited in the Endnotes *without the author being indicated.*

The text of this book follows current practice among historians of immigration in using a hyphen in "Swedish-American" when it is used as an adjective, and in leaving out the hyphen when "Swedish American" is used as a noun. Norwegian Americans are treated the same way, as are Norwegian-American matters.

Bergendoff and the journals in which he wrote often "Americanized" Swedish titles and other references by capitalizing words which in current Swedish practice are not. This book follows current Swedish usage, and titles in the Endnotes and Bibliography reflect this practice.

Some American journals did not print the Swedish characters å, ä, and ö; this has also been changed in this book so as to reflect Swedish spelling. But alphabetical lists in this book (as in the Bibliography or Index) treat these Swedish letters as though they were the English letters *a* and *o*.

ENDNOTES

INTRODUCTION

1   In fact, Swedish was Bergendoff's *first* language; when he began elementary school, he spoke only Swedish. Byron R. Swanson, *Conrad Bergendoff: The Making of an Ecumenist,* Th.D. dissertation, Princeton Theological Seminary, (1970), p. 132.

2   Byron Nordstrom, "Introduction," in Dave Kenney, *Gustavus Adolphus College: 150 Years of History,* (St. Peter, Minn., 2011), p. 2.

3   Orm Øverland, *Immigrant Minds, American Identities: Making the United States Home, 1870-1930,* (Urbana, Ill., 2000), pp. 8-9, 191-193.

4   Adam Gopnik, "The Back of the World: The troubling genius of G. K. Chesterton," *The New Yorker,* (July 7 and 14, 2008), pp. 52-59.

CHAPTER 1

1   Quoted in Franklin D. Scott, *Sweden: The Nation's History,* (Minneapolis, 1977), p. 355.

2   "A Century of Augustana History," *Kyrkohistorisk årsskrift,* v. 59, (1959), reprinted in SAHQ, v. 61, (Oct., 2010), p. 293; *Augustana: A Profession of Faith,* (Rock Island, 1969), p. 4. Bergendoff's ecumenical mentor, the Swedish Archbishop Nathan Söderblom, was not so dismissive of Bishop Hill. His biographer, Bengt Sundkler, writes that the Archbishop was very sorry not to be able to visit it during his 1923 trip in the U.S. To Söderblom the Illinois colony was an example of the Swedish Pietism that he had known growing up. Bengt Sundkler, *Nathan Söderblom: His Life and Work,* (Lund, 1968), p. 304.

3   O. Fritiof Ander, "Augustana-kyrkan vid sitt sekelskifte," *Kyrkohistorisk årsskrift,* v. 60, (1960), Eng. trans. by Dag Blanck and Thomas Tredway, SAHQ, v. 61, (Oct., 2010), pp. 261-263.

4   G. Everett Arden, *Augustana Heritage,* (Rock Island, 1963), p. 27.

5   Quoted in Nathaniel Philbrick, *Mayflower: A Story of Courage, Community, and War,* (New York, 2006), p. 162.

6   Martin E. Marty, *Modern American Religion, Volume 1: The Irony of It All, 1893-1919,* (Chicago, 1986), p. 169.

7   Quoted in George M. Stephenson, *The Founding of the Augustana Synod,* (Rock Island, 1927), p. 109.

8   Oscar Fritiof Ander, *T. N. Hasselquist,* (Rock Island, 1931), esp. Chs. 1 and 2.

9   This is the view Ander takes of the two men in both his 1931 monograph on Hasselquist and his 1960 article in *Kyrkohistorisk årsskrift.*

10   The Augsburg Confession, Article III, Of the Son of God, speaks of Christ's death "that he might *reconcile the Father to us and might be a sacrifice. . .* for all actual sins of men." Article IV, Of Justification, states, ". . . sins are forgiven for Christ's sake, who, by His death, *has made satisfaction* for our sins." And Article XX, Of Good Works, referring to Christ, contains the phrase, ". . . *by whom the Father is reconciled.*" (Italics added.)

11   John Norton, editor and translator, *P. P. Waldenström at Augustana, 1901: Excerpts from his Nya färder i Amerikas Förenta Stater,* (Rock Island, 2012), p. 7.

12   Arden, *Augustana Heritage,* p. 150.

13   Maria Erling and Mark Granquist, *The Augustana Story,* (Minneapolis, 2008), p. 380.

14   Arden, *Augustana Heritage,* p. 251.

15   I am indebted to Jill Seaholm of the Swenson Swedish Immigration Research Center at

CHAPTER 1

Augustana College for this information from the Center's records.

16 Nils William Olsson, "Naming Patterns among Swedish-Americans," *Swedish American Genealogist,* v. 14, (June, 1994), esp. pp. 86-87, discusses the naming practices which prevailed at the time of Carl August's emigration.

17 Byron R. Swanson, *Conrad Bergendoff: The Making of an Ecumenist,* Th.D. dissertation, Princeton Theological Seminary, (1970), p. 120.

18 "The Augustana Pastor: Saga of a Thousand Immigrants from Sweden," SPHQ, v. 31, (Jan., 1980), p. 40.

19 The sketch of C. A. Bergendoff's career in this and the preceding paragraphs is based upon information in, "On the Occasion of the Centennial of Augustana College," SPHQ, v. 11, (Apr., 1960), p. 35; "Carl August Bergendoff," MS, (1940), CBP 41-2; "Father's Notebook," MS, (n.d.), CBP UP; *The Augustana Ministerium,* (Rock Island, 1980), p. 51; Swanson, *Conrad Bergendoff,* pp. 121-125; and *Förhandlingar vid New York-Konferensens af Augustana-Synoden trettiosjätte årsmöte i Jamestown N.Y., 18-23 April, 1906.*

20 After his 1962 retirement at Augustana, Bergendoff did speak directly about the character of his family home and childhood, as well as about his own career, in two sets of interviews of which typescripts exist. The first interviews were done by Byron R. Swanson in 1966 and were recorded and transcribed in connection with Swanson's 1970 doctoral dissertation, *Conrad Bergendoff: The Making of an Ecumenist.* The second set was done in 1977 and 1979 by Glen C. Stone, as a part of the series, Archives of Cooperative Lutheranism, and was also transcribed. In addition, Swanson's dissertation refers to interviews with Bergendoff which he conducted in 1967 and 1968.

21 "The Frontispiece in Our Catechism," *The Church School Teacher,* v. 2, (Nov. 19, 1933), pp. 7-8.

22 "Augustana—A People in Transition," in J. Iverne Dowie and Ernest M. Espelie, editors, *The Swedish Immigrant Community in Transition,* (Rock Island, 1963), pp. 198-199.

23 Ibid., p. 198.

24 Philip J. Anderson, "Histories from the Inside Out: Shared Origins and Denominational Historiography in the Writings of G. Everett Arden and Karl A. Olsson," SAHQ, v. 63, (Apr.-July, 2012), p. 84.

25 This paragraph is based on the sources indicated earlier, in the notes five and six places above this one, as well as on clippings and letters scattered through Bergendoff's papers at Augustana.

26 Erling and Granquist, p. 197.

27 Dag Blanck, *The Creation of an Ethnic Identity,* (Carbondale, Ill., 2006), pp. 35-36.

28 "Augustana—A People in Transition," p. 201.

29 Ibid., p. 198.

30 "Three Score and Ten," MS, (n.d.), CBP 73-2.

31 "From the Connecticut to the Mississippi,", Dec., 1912.

32 George M. Stephenson, *The Religious Aspects of Swedish Immigration,* (Minneapolis, 1932), p. 352.

33 "Augustana—A People in Transition," p. 202.

34 "Augustana in America and in Sweden," SPHQ, v. 24, (Oct., 1973), p. 239.

35 "On the Occasion of the Centennial of Augustana College," p. 35.

36 "Where God's Glory Dwells: A Tribute to Dr. S. J. Sebelius," LC, v. 96, (June 13, 1951), pp. 9, 16.

CHAPTER 1

37 "Why I Became a Missionary," LC, v. 105, (Mar. 4, 1959), pp. 9-10.

38 "Augustana—A People in Transition," pp. 199-202.

39 "This Matter of Centralization," LC, v. 48, (Feb. 8, 1940), p. 170.

40 "Augustana—A People in Transition," pp. 199-202.

41 The information about Augustana College in the preceding paragraphs is largely derived from *Augustana: A Profession of Faith,* Chs. 9-12.

42 Swanson, *Conrad Bergendoff,* p. 139.

43 "Bread for the Hungry," *Observer,* Jan., 1915.

44 Swanson, *Conrad Bergendoff,* pp. 146-148.

45 Erling and Granquist, p. 71.

46 *Observer,* May, 1915.

47 Swanson, *Conrad Bergendoff,* pp. 151-158.

48 "The Meandering of an Historian," *Concordia Historical Institute Quarterly,* v. 55, (Winter, 1982), pp. 181-184; MS, CBP 73-7.

49 Henry Eyster Jacobs, *A History of the Evangelical Lutheran Church in the United States,* second edition, (New York, 1899), p. 2.

50 Byron R. Swanson, Transcript of interviews with Conrad Bergendoff, June 23-24, Dec. 7, 1966, p. 11.

51 "A Sunday-School Program," LC, v. 27, (Feb. 15, 1919), p. 85.

52 Untitled statement, MS, (1940), CBP 67-5.

53 Arden, *Augustana Heritage,* pp. 182-183 and Erling and Granquist, pp. 54-55, contain further information about Gustavus Adolphus Church in New York; see also Swanson, *Conrad Bergendoff,* pp. 161-166. In a memorial tribute to Pastor Stolpe, "Mauritz Stolpe—In Memoriam," LC, v. 46, (Sept. 22, 1938), p. 1192, Bergendoff recalled the cultured and dignified man under whom he had served in New York in the late 1910s.

54 Swanson, *Conrad Bergendoff,* p. 205.

55 Erling and Granquist, p. 245.

56 Henry H. Bagger to CB, Sept. 20, 1919, CBP UP 1916-1921.

57 Erling and Granquist, pp. 246 247.

58 G. Everett Arden, *The School of the Prophets,* (Rock Island, 1960), Ch. 5.

59 Arden, *Augustana Heritage,* p. 249.

60 Erling and Granquist, pp. 53-55, contains an account of Lindberg's struggles with poverty and heresy as a young pastor in Pennsylvania and New York in the 1870s.

61 Stephenson, *The Founding of the Augustana Synod,* p. 72.

62 Hugo Söderström, *Confession and Cooperation,* (Lund, 1973), p. 184.

63 Stephenson, *Religious Aspects,* p. 342.

64 S. G. Youngert to CB, CBP UP 1923-1926.

65 "Theology in the Augustana Church," MS, (n.d.), CBP 73-3.

66 Glen C. Stone, Interviews with Conrad Bergendoff, June 22-23, 1977, Oct. 4, 1979, Archives of Cooperative Lutheranism, p. 32, CBP 84; Swanson, *Conrad Bergendoff,* pp. 205-215, offers a summary of the state of the seminary in the early 1920s and of Bergendoff's reaction to it.

67 Sundkler, pp. 29-30.

68 "Dr. Youngert, An Appreciation," LC, v. 47, (Mar. 9, 1939), pp. 297-298.

69 Arden, *Augustana Heritage,* pp. 249-250.

70 Ibid., p. 285.

71 Stone, p. 8.

CHAPTER 1

72 "Dr. Youngert, An Appreciation."

73 "A Swedish University Tradition in America," SAHQ, v. 44, (Jan., 1993), p. 16.

74 Harry S. Warner to CB, May 8, 1921, CBP UP 1921-1922.

75 *Observer*, Jan., 1920.

76 Ibid.

77 *Observer*, Feb., 1920.

78 Swanson, *Conrad Bergendoff*, pp. 217-223.

79 Carl J. Bengston, "Young People's Christian Conference," LC, v. 29, (Mar. 5, 1921), pp. 146, 148; *Observer*, Mar., 1921.

CHAPTER 2

1 Maria Erling and Mark Granquist, *The Augustana Story*, (Minneapolis, 2008), pp. 205-207.

2 Daniel Merle Pearson, *The Americanization of Carl Aaron Swensson*, (Rock Island, 1977), p. xiii.

3 Byron R. Swanson, Transcript of interviews with Conrad Bergendoff, June 23-24, Dec. 7, 1966, p. 22.

4 Byron R. Swanson, *Conrad Bergendoff: The Making of an Ecumenist*, Th.D. dissertation, Princeton Theological Seminary, (1970), p. 307.

5 Swanson, Interviews with Bergendoff, p. 48.

6 The information in this paragraph is almost entirely from Conrad Bergendoff, personal correspondence and unprocessed papers.

7 *Gertrude Bergendoff, 1897-1979: In Memoriam*, (Rock Island, 1979), CBP 41-1a; Ann Boaden, *Light and Leaven*, (Rock Island, 2011), pp. 208-209; the boxes of Bergendoff's unprocessed personal correspondence contain many letters Gertrude Bergendoff wrote to her husband when he was away from home.

8 CB to George Hall, June 11, 1995, printed in *Augustana Heritage Newsletter*, (Oct., 1996), p. 4.

9 "Memories of a Vanishing Swedish-America," SPHQ, v. 10, (Apr., 1959), pp. 70-71.

10 Peter Peterson to CB, Mar. 9, 1922; John M. Bramkamp to CB, (n.d.), CBP UP 1921-1922.

11 The 1920 and the 1930 data are from Illinois Conference Minutes for the respective years.

12 $80,000 in 1926 would equal over $1,005,000 in 2012 buying power.

13 The information in the preceding paragraphs about Salem Church is based in part upon three histories of the congregation published by the congregation in 1926, 1943, and 1968. They can be found in the records of Salem Church itself, and in the archives of the Swenson Swedish Immigration Research Center, Augustana College. Bergendoff contributed sections of each booklet.

14 G. Everett Arden, *Augustana Heritage*, (Rock Island, 1963), pp. 206-210; Erling and Granquist, pp. 263-266.

15 LC, v. 33, (Sept. 26, 1925), p. 615. Bergendoff's President's Reports to the Synod are contained in a number of LC issues through the mid and late 1920s, as well as in the Minutes of the Synod. "White's Bible School" was the name by which the Biblical Seminary in New York was popularly known.

16 "President's Report of the Synodical Luther League Council," LC, v. 36, (Mar. 3, 1928), p. 207.

CHAPTER 2

17   Erling and Granquist, p. 142.

18   Bruce Barton, *The Man Nobody Knows*, (Indianapolis, 1925).

19   "The Personal Approach to Soul-Winning," AQ, v. 9, (Apr., 1930), pp. 111-112.

20   "The Church and the Gospel," AQ, v. 11, (Jan., 1932), p. 72.

21   Sven-Erik Brodd, "Nathan Söderblom—religionshistoriker, ärkebiskop och
      internationell ekumenisk kyrkoledare," in Ingmar Brohed, *Sveriges kyrkohistoria: 8.
      Religionsfrihetens och ekumenikens tid,* (Stockholm, 2005), p. 379; Bengt Sundkler, *Nathan
      Söderblom: His Life and Work,* (Lund, 1968), pp. 107-114.

22   *The Church of the Lutheran Reformation,* (St. Louis, 1967), p. 254.

23   "The Inner Being," Commencement Address, Philadelphia Lutheran Theological
      Seminary, (May 14, 1964), MS, CBP 72-2.

24   "Temple Talk," LC, v. 41, (Nov. 4, 1933), p. 1381.

25   "Our Lofty Destiny: Sermon Preached at Funeral of Dr. F. F. Bartholomew," LC, v. 54,
      (July 3, 1946), p. 14.

26   Edgar M. Carlson, "Dr. Bergendoff—Christian Scholar and Educator," in J. Iverne
      Dowie and Ernest M. Espelie, editors, *The Swedish Immigrant Community in Transition,*
      (Rock Island, 1963), p. 217.

27   Untitled MS, (n.d.), CBP UP 1923-1926.

28   "Why I Became a Missionary," LC, v. 105, (Mar. 4, 1959), pp. 9-10.

29   E. T. Anderson to CB, (n.d.), CBP 41-5.

30   Biographical sketches, MS, (n.d.), CBP 41-1.

31   Transcripts, CBP 41-3.

32   Swanson, *Conrad Bergendoff,* pp. 232-233.

33   "Why I Became a Missionary," p. 10.

34   Swanson, *Conrad Bergendoff,* p. 228; Swanson, Interviews with Bergendoff, p. 19.

35   "Biographical Data," CBP 41-1; CB to Nathan Söderblom, Apr. 12, 1926, Nathan
      Söderbloms samling, brev från svenskar, Manuscript Division, Uppsala University
      Library.

36   "The Lutheran Church and the Modern State," AQ, v. 21, (Oct., 1942), p. 317.

37   Swanson, *Conrad Bergendoff,* p. 310. In 1918 the Augustana Book Concern had
      published *Olavus Petri: The Church Reformer of Sweden* by Nils Forsander, a professor at
      Augustana Seminary. That book was written at the level of Church School literature
      rather than as a scholarly study, and Bergendoff's 1928 book did not mention it in its
      bibliography.

38   "Vid L. P. Esbjörns grav," *Augustana,* v. 71, (Nov. 18, 1926), p. 726.

39   W. H. Murray to CB, Oct. 28, 1927, CBP 41-4. Seven years later the company wrote to
      Bergendoff, telling him that, "sales in recent years have fallen off" and that they could
      no longer handle the book and would sell him thirty-two copies for thirty cents each.
      Otherwise they would dispose of their stock. Everett E. Hale to CB, May 3, 1934, CBP
      41-4. Fortress Press, the Lutheran publishing house, did re-issue Bergendoff's book in
      1965.

40   *Olavus Petri and the Ecclesiastical Transformation in Sweden, 1521-1552,* (New York, 1928),
      Foreword. Decades after the appearance of Bergendoff's dissertation, the author's
      judgment about the relative lack of knowledge about or interest in Petri seems to have
      held up. For example, neither Diarmaid MacCulloch's magisterial *Christianity: The First
      Three Thousand Years,* (New York, 2009), nor Paul Johnson's somewhat biting *A History of
      Christianity,* (New York, 1976), mentions Petri. MacCulloch's *The Reformation: A History,*

CHAPTER 2

(New York, 2003), pp. 335-336, gives Olavus and his brother Laurentius a paragraph, treating the Swedish Reformation as essentially the work of King Gustav Vasa.

41 Swanson, *Conrad Bergendoff,* p. 330.

42 Personal materials, CBP 41-5.

43 Arden, *Augustana Heritage,* pp. 286-287; Erling and Granquist, pp. 245-248.

44 Board Minutes, Aug. 6, 1930, Feb. 25, May 12, June 2, July 8, 1931.

45 Arden, *Augustana Heritage,* p. 284.

46 Board Minutes, Aug. 6, 1930.

47 See Swanson, *Conrad Bergendoff,* p. 340.

48 Erling and Granquist, pp. 242-244.

49 Swanson, Interviews with Bergendoff, p. 40.

50 A. F. Almer, Review of Conrad Bergendoff, *The Making and Meaning of the Augsburg Confession,* in AQ, v. 9, (July, 1930), p. 286.

51 *Olavus Petri,* p. 147.

52 "The Significance of the Lutheran Reformation of the Sixteenth Century for the Church of the Twentieth," AQ, v. 8, (Apr., 1930), pp. 135-146.

53 "Why I Became a Missionary," p. 10.

54 Charles M. Jacobs to CB, July 1, 1930, CBP UP 1.

55 CB [to parents], Sept 11, 1930, CBP UP Family.

56 Personal materials, CBP 41-5. Bergendoff's salary of $3,400 in 1931 would equal $51,800 in 2012 buying power.

57 "In the Cathedral of Lund," LC, v. 35, (Feb. 12, 1927), pp. 154-155.

58 Arden, *Augustana Heritage,* pp. 284-285.

59 Gregory Lee Jackson, *Prophetic Voice for the Kingdom,* (Rock Island, 1986), pp. xiii, xiv, 12-17. Jackson's biography of Mattson also points out that Bergendoff and Mattson disagreed on liturgical questions (Bergendoff high church, Mattson low), the separation of the college and the seminary (Bergendoff against, Mattson for), and the 1962 merger of Augustana to form the LCA (Bergendoff for, Mattson against).

60 Arden, *Augustana Heritage,* pp. 292-296.

61 *Augustana College Bulletin* [College and Seminary Catalog], (Apr., 1947), pp. 58-59.

62 Arden, *Augustana Heritage,* p. 100.

63 Erling and Granquist, p. 110.

64 Karl A. Olsson, "Kontinuitet och förvandling inom svenska immigrantsamfund i USA," *Kyrkohistorisk årsskrift,* v. 82, (1982).

65 Sundkler, p. 399.

66 Karl E. Mattson, "The Theology of the Augustana Lutheran Church," in Emmer Engberg et al., editors, *Centennial Essays,* (Rock Island, 1960), p. 29.

67 T. A. Kantonen, Review of Conrad Bergendoff, *Christ as Authority,* in AQ, v. 28, (July, 1948), p. 282.

68 "The Lutheran View of the Lord's Supper," LQ, v. 4, (Aug., 1952), pp. 278-279.

69 G. Everett Arden, *The School of the Prophets,* (Rock Island, 1960), p. 232.

70 Ibid., pp. 233-234.

71 "The Augustana Four-Year Plan of Theological Education," *Christian Education,* v. 19, (Dec., 1935).

72 Arden, *School of the Prophets,* p. 234.

73 Erling and Granquist, p. 249.

CHAPTER 2

74   *Observer,* May 17, 1935.

75   P. Arthur Johnson to CB, June 29, 1935, CBP UP 3.

76   The election of Bergendoff to the Augustana presidency is discussed in Thomas Tredway, *Coming of Age,* (Rock Island, 2010), pp. 93-95.

77   Arden, *School of the Prophets,* p. 235.

CHAPTER 3

1   *Christ as Authority,* (Rock Island, 1947), pp. 11-12.

2   Ibid., p. 59.

3   "The Church and the Gospel," AQ, v. 11, (Jan., 1932), p. 71.

4   NBC Sermon, MS, (1952-53), CBP 70-5.

5   Quoted in Dave Kenney, *Gustavus Adolphus College: 150 Years of History,* (St. Peter, Minn., 2011), p. 72.

6   Sydney E. Ahlstrom, *A Religious History of the American People,* (New Haven, 1972), p. 779.

7   *The Church of the Lutheran Reformation,* (St. Louis, 1967), p. 205.

8   Ibid., p. 206.

9   Review of Albert Schweitzer, *The Philosophy of Civilization,* in LQ, v. 2, (May, 1950), p. 231.

10   Review of James Moffatt, *Grace in the New Testament,* in AQ, v. 11, (Apr., 1932), pp. 171-172.

11   *The One Holy Catholic Apostolic Church,* (Rock Island, 1954), pp. 23-24.

12   Harold Bloom, *Genius: A Mosaic of One Hundred Exemplary Artistic Minds,* (New York, 2002), p. 142.

13   Charles Freeman, *The Closing of the Western Mind,* (New York, 2002), p. 124.

14   For example, in the series of "Temple Talks" appearing in the early thirties in the *Lutheran Companion,* Bergendoff refers to "Jesus" preaching, LC, v. 42, (Jan. 20, 1934), p. 69; (Sept. 22, 1934), p. 1189; otherwise regularly to "Christ." That is the case as well in his 1947 *Christ as Authority.*

15   Leonard Hutter, *Compend of Lutheran Theology: A Summary of Christian Doctrine, Derived from the Word of God and the Symbolical Books of the Evangelical Lutheran Church,* English trans. by Henry Eyster Jacobs and George Frederick Spieker, (Philadelphia, 1868).

16   "Contemporary Theological Trends," MS, (1962), CBP 52.

17   Review of Gustaf Aulén, *Faith of the Christian Church,* in *Theology Today,* v. 6, (Apr., 1949), pp. 116-118.

18   G. Everett Arden, *Augustana Heritage,* (Rock Island, 1963), pp. 9-10.

19   Henry Eyster Jacobs, *A History of the Evangelical Lutheran Church in the United States,* second edition, (New York, 1899), pp. 3-7. Jacob's reference to "mystical union" with Christ did not mean an endorsement of religious mysticism not controlled and not defined by Scripture, as Jacobs made clear in the same section of his history of American Lutheranism. Later Bergendoff would also caution against any mysticism that was not governed by the Bible.

20   Winfred Ernest Garrison, Review of Conrad Bergendoff, *The Making and Meaning of the Augsburg Confession* [and two other books], in *Christian Century,* v. 47, (June 18, 1930), p. 785. Another of the books considered in this review was *What Is Lutheranism?* (New York, 1930), edited by Vergelius Ferm, which the reviewer found more accommodating.

CHAPTER 3

Ferm was also a member of the Augustana ministerium. Essays in Ferm's book maintained that Lutheranism could adapt to modern conditions and needs and that Luther himself would hardly address modern problems simply by appeal to his own writings (an appeal presumably made often by some of his followers). Maria Erling and Mark Granquist, *The Augustana Story,* (Minneapolis, 2008), pp. 242-243.

21   Daniel Nystrom, *A Ministry of Printing: History of the Publication House of the Augustana Lutheran Church, 1889-1962,* (Rock Island, 1962).

22   Abdel Ross Wentz, Review of Conrad Bergendoff, *Christ as Authority,* in LQ, v. 1, (Feb., 1949), p. 99.

23   T. A. Kantonen, Review of Conrad Bergendoff, *Christ as Authority,* in AQ, v. 28, (July, 1948), p. 281.

24   Glen C. Stone, "Conrad Bergendoff as Churchman," *Augustana Heritage Newsletter,* (Oct., 1996), p. 9.

25   Rupert Wilkinson, "'The Lonely Crowd,' at 60, Is Still Timely," *Chronicle of Higher Education,* Sept. 12, 2010.

26   Martin Luther, *On the Bondage of the Will,* in E. Gordon Rupp and Philip S. Watson, translators and editors, *The Library of Christian Classics, Volume XVII, Luther and Erasmus: Free Will and Salvation,* (Philadelphia, 1969), p. 140.

27   *Christ as Authority,* p. 1.

28   Ibid., pp. 1-6.

29   Ibid., pp. 10-14.

30   Ibid., pp. 17-18.

31   Ibid., pp. 18-21.

32   Ibid., p. 21.

33   "A Colony of Heaven," LC, v. 43, (June 22, 1935), p. 777.

34   *Church of the Lutheran Reformation,* p. 36.

35   "The Divine Impulse in Preaching," AQ, v. 25, (Oct., 1946), pp. 313-315.

36   "The Break of Day," LC, v. 97, (Apr. 23, 1952), p. 11.

37   "Aspects of Faith—the Source of Authority," MS, (July, 1962), CBP 71-7.

38   "Justification and Sanctification: Liturgy and Ethics," in Paul C. Empie and James I. McCord, editors, *Marburg Revisited,* (Minneapolis, 1966), pp. 122-123.

39   "The Revelation and the Ministry of Grace," in Yngve Brilioth, editor, *World Lutheranism Today: A Tribute to Anders Nygren, 15 November 1950,* (Stockholm, 1950), p. 33.

40   "As the Seminary Views Clinical Pastoral Education," MS, (Nov. 7, 1962), CBP 72-1.

41   "What Kind of Unity?" LC, v. 47, (Mar. 2, 1939), p. 267.

42   "The Significance of the Lutheran Reformation of the Sixteenth Century for the Church of the Twentieth," AQ, v. 8, (Apr., 1929), pp. 144-145.

43   Wentz, Review of *Christ as Authority,* p. 99.

44   W. Schweitzer, Review of Conrad Bergendoff, *Christ as Authority,* in *Ecumenical Review,* v. 1, (Spring, 1949), pp. 345-346.

45   "The Modern Imagination and Imago Dei," LQ, v. 10, (May, 1958), p. 110; "What Kind of Unity?" p. 267.

46   *Christ as Authority,* p. 50.

47   Byron R. Swanson, Transcript of interviews with Conrad Bergendoff, June 23-24, Dec. 7, 1966, p. 45.

48   *Christ as Authority,* p. 71.

CHAPTER 3

49 "The Break of Day," pp. 4, 11.
50 Jennifer Michael Hecht, *Doubt: A History,* (San Francisco, 2003), p. 325.
51 CB to [Georg] Delbrugge, Jan. 16, 1961, CBP 19-7.
52 James O'Donnell, *Augustine: A New Biography,* (New York, 2008), p. 179.
53 *Olavus Petri and the Ecclesiastical Transformation in Sweden,* (New York, 1928), p. 195.
54 CBP UP, Travel Diary, Apr. 2-June 25, 1949.
55 "The Sphere of Revelation," *Lutheran World Review,* v. 1, (Oct., 1948), pp. 38-53.
56 "The Revelation and the Ministry of Grace," pp. 21-35.
57 Quoted in Bengt Sundkler, *Nathan Söderblom: His Life and Work,* (Lund, 1968), p. 24.
58 Ibid., p. 26. Sundkler thinks that Söderblom's Pietistic conversion had under-tones of reconciliation with his over-demanding father: "The conversion while understood by Söderblom as a return to the Heavenly Father was just as much a reconciliation with his earthly father. It may well be argued which of these came first." Ibid., pp. 29-30.
59 Sven-Erik Brodd, "Nathan Söderblom—religionshistoriker, ärkebiskop och internationell ekumenisk kyrkoledare," in Ingmar Brohed, *Sveriges kyrkohistoria: 8. Religionsfrihetens och ekumenikens tid,* (Stockholm, 2005), p. 376.
60 Review of Charles J. Curtis, *Nathan Söderblom: Theologian of Revelation,* in SPHQ, v. 18, (Jan., 1967), pp. 50-51.
61 Swanson, Interviews with Bergendoff, p. 27.
62 CBP UP, Travel Diary, Apr. 30, 1949.
63 *Church of the Lutheran Reformation,* p. 1.
64 Paula Fredricksen, *Sin: The Early History of an Idea,* (Princeton, 2012), Ch. 3.
65 *Christ as Authority,* p. 63.
66 E. Theodore Bachmann, *The United Lutheran Church in America, 1918-1962,* (Minneapolis, 1997), pp. 251-252, notes that in this regard Bergendoff's book on Christ's authority put him firmly in the camp of Joseph Sittler, a theologian of the ULCA, who had argued against "assertions of the verbal inspiration of the Scriptures" made by T. F. Gullixson, President of Luther Seminary, St. Paul.
67 E. Clifford Nelson, "The New Shape of Lutheranism," in E. Clifford Nelson et al., editors, *The Lutherans in North America,* (Philadelphia, 1975), pp. 497, 501, 505-506.
68 *Christ as Authority,* pp. 23-27.
69 Ibid., p. 42.
70 Ibid., p. 39.
71 Untitled MS, (Jan., 1951), CBP 70-1.
72 *Christ as Authority,* pp. 38-39.
73 Ibid., pp. 41-42.
74 Ibid., p. 43.
75 Ibid., p. 44.
76 "Three Score and Ten," MS, (1974), CBP 73-2.
77 "The Lutheran Church and the Modern State," AQ, v. 21, (Oct., 1942), p. 319.
78 "Knowing Whom We Believe: 2 Tim. 1: 13-14," MS, (1955-1956), CBP 71-1.
79 "The World of the Holy Spirit," [lectures in Portland, Oregon], MS, (1956), CBP 71-1.
80 *Church of the Lutheran Reformation,* p. 55. It should be noted that Bergendoff did disagree with Luther as to whether the Anabaptist movement had in its history "saints and martyrs" who stood in the long line of such men and women through Christian history. He thought, contra Luther, that the Anabaptists did. Conrad Bergendoff, editor and

CHAPTER 3

translator, *The Church and the Ministry, II, Luther's Works,* v. 40, (Philadelphia, 1958), p. 381.

81   *Christ as Authority,* p. 7.

82   Elaine Pagels, *Beyond Belief: The Secret Gospel of Thomas,* (New York, 2003), discusses the John/Thomas distinction at length.

83   Review of John Dillenberger, *God Hidden and Revealed,* in *Theology Today,* v. 10, (Jan., 1954), pp. 556-558; "The World of the Holy Spirit," MS, (n.d.), CBP 71-1.

84   Review of Aulén, *Faith of the Christian Church.*

85   *One Holy Catholic Apostolic Church,* p. 28.

86   Ibid., p. 35.

87   *Church of the Lutheran Reformation,* pp. 120-121.

88   Ibid., pp. 235-236.

89   Ibid., p. 218.

90   Hilding Pleijel, *Från fädernas fromhetsliv,* (Stockholm, 1939), pp. 57, 144.

91   *The Doctrine of the Church in American Lutheranism,* (Philadelphia, 1956), p. 41.

92   Ibid., p. 44.

93   *Living in the Grace of Baptism,* (Rock Island, n.d.).

94   Quoted in *Doctrine of the Church in American Lutheranism,* p. 49.

95   Quoted in Emmer Engberg, "Augustana and Code Morality," in Emmer Engberg et al., editors, *Centennial Essays,* (Rock Island, 1960), p. 124.

96   Ibid.

97   Erling and Granquist, p. 126.

98   CB to A. F. Quest, May 19, 1938, CBP 4-12.

99   *Observer,* Nov. 10, 1938.

100 CB to John Tate, Feb. 9, 1939, CBP 4-5.

101 See Arden, *Augustana Heritage,* esp. Ch. 16, and Erling and Granquist, Chs. 11, 16, 18.

102 *Christ as Authority,* p. 21.

103 "No Other Image," LC, v. 97, (July 9, 1952), p. 15.

104 Thomas Tredway, *Coming of Age,* (Rock Island, 2010), pp. 78-86.

105 "College Windows," LC, v. 51, (Dec. 1, 1943), p. 1360.

106 "Lutheran Ethics and Scandinavian Lutheranism," AQ, v. 20, (July, 1941), pp. 209-210.

107 "The Individual Christian's Call to Personal Evangelism," AQ, v. 5, (Mar., 1926), p. 27.

108 Bergendoff presented a paper to the dialog, "Justification and Sanctification: Liturgy and Ethics," which appears in Empie and McCord, pp. 118-127.

109 Review of Hjalmar Lindroth, *Recent Theological Research in Sweden: A Luther Renaissance,* in LQ, v. 3, (Feb., 1951), pp. 106-107.

110 Regin Prenter, *Spiritus Creator,* English trans., (Philadelphia, 1953), pp. 64-72.

111 Axel Gyllenkrok, *Rechtfertigung und Heiligung in der frühen evangelishen Theologie Luthers,* (Uppsala, 1952), p. 83.

112 *One Holy Catholic Apostolic Church,* p. 28.

113 Ibid., p. 43.

114 John Wesley, *Sermons on Several Occasions,* (New York, 1833), p. 389.

115 Review of Newton Flew, *The Idea of Christian Perfection in Christian Theology,* in AQ, v. 14, (Apr., 1935), p. 181. Bergendoff would *not* have gone so far as L. P. Esbjörn did when he lumped the Methodists' idea of sanctification together with the doctrine of sinlessness in believers that was held by the Janssonists of Bishop Hill, Illinois. Hugo

CHAPTER 3

Söderström, *Confession and Cooperation,* (Lund, 1973), p. 33.
116   "Lutheran Ethics and Scandinavian Lutheranism," pp. 209-210.
117   *Christ as Authority*, p. 31.
118   *The One Holy Catholic Apostolic Church,* p. 29.
119   Ibid., pp. 80, 85.
120   "The Significance of the Augsburg Confession for Our Own Day," AQ, v. 9, (Apr., 1930), p. 163.
121   "The Secular Idea of Progress and the Christian Doctrine of Sanctification," AQ, v. 12, (Jan., 1933), p. 63.

CHAPTER 4

1   H. W. Weigert, "Luther and the Germans," *Christian Century,* v. 59, (Jan. 21, 1942), p. 81.
2   "In Defense of Luther," *Christian Century,* v. 59, (Feb. 4, 1942), pp. 155-156.
3   "The Lutheran Church and the Modern State," AQ, v. 21, (Oct., 1942).
4   "The Secular Idea of Progress and the Christian Doctrine of Sanctification," AQ, v. 12, (Jan., 1933), p. 63.
5   "A Mind That Is in Christ," *Augustana College Bulletin,* (Dec., 1951).
6   Hilding Pleijel, *Från fädernas fromhetsliv,* (Stockholm, 1939), pp. 136-137.
7   Oloph Bexell, *Sveriges kyrkohistoria: 7. Folkväckelsens och kyrkoförnyelsens tid,* (Stockholm, 2003), p. 329.
8   "The Significance of the Lutheran Reformation of the Sixteenth Century for the Church of the Twentieth," AQ, v. 8, (Apr., 1929), p. 141.
9   "The Modern Imagination and Imago Dei," LQ, v. 10, (May, 1958), p. 112.
10   *Christ as Authority,* (Rock Island, 1947), p. 83.
11   "Towards a History of the Augustana Synod—Three Books Reviewed," AQ, v. 11, (July, 1932), p. 260; Review of Gustaf Aulén, *Church, Law and Society,* in *Church History,* v. 17, (June, 1948), pp. 148-149.
12   "Significance of the Lutheran Reformation," p. 145.
13   "The Secular Idea of Progress," p. 68.
14   *Christ as Authority*, pp. 77-80.
15   Ibid., p. 85.
16   Ibid., p. 89.
17   "Today's Pioneers," LC, v. 44, (Sept. 19, 1936), p. 1192.
18   "Elements in Christian Culture," Pt. 2, LC, v. 47, (Nov. 2, 1939), pp. 1384-1385.
19   "Significant Elements in Christian Culture," AQ, v. 19, (July, 1940), pp. 224-233.
20   Claude Welch, Review of Conrad Bergendoff, *Christ as Authority,* in *Christendom,* v. 13, (Summer, 1948), p. 398.
21   For example, "Elements in Christian Culture," Pt. 2, p. 1384, or "Significance of the Lutheran Reformation," p. 145.
22   "National Aspects of the Lutheran Church in America," AQ, v. 3, (June, 1924), p. 54.
23   H. Richard Niebuhr, *Christ and Culture,* (New York, 1951), esp. Chs. 5 and 6.
24   Glen C. Stone, Interviews with Conrad Bergendoff, June 22-23, 1977, Oct. 4, 1979, Archives of Cooperative Lutheranism, p. 30, CBP 84.
25   Maria Erling and Mark Granquist, *The Augustana Story,* (Minneapolis, 2008), pp. 136-137; Gregory Lee Jackson, *Prophetic Voice for the Kingdom,* (Rock Island, 1986), p. 22.
26   "Lutheran Ethics and Scandinavian Lutheranism," AQ, v. 20, (July, 1941), pp. 207-221.

CHAPTER 4

27   W. E. Garrison, Review of Conrad Bergendoff, *The One Holy Catholic Apostolic Church*, in *Christian Century*, v. 71, (Aug. 18, 1954), p. 977.

28   "From College Windows," LC, v. 51, (June 16, 23, 1943), pp. 742, 785.

29   "The Mind of the Church Today," LQ, v. 1, (May, 1949), p. 181.

30   *Christ as Authority*, p. 88.

31   Ibid., p. 89.

32   Paul Johnson, *A History of Christianity*, (New York, 1976), p. 516.

33   "Christian Love and Public Policy in Luther," LQ, v. 13, (Aug., 1961), p. 224.

34   Ibid., p. 227.

35   Review of Culbert G. Rutenber, *The Dagger and the Cross: An Examination of Christian Pacifism*, in LQ, v. 3, (Feb., 1951), p. 116.

36   "The Christian Conscience and Nuclear Warfare," *The National Lutheran*, v. 30, (Oct., 1962), pp. 8, 10.

37   "The Lutheran Church and the Modern State," p. 324.

38   G. Everett Arden, *Augustana Heritage*, (Rock Island, 1963), p. 378.

39   Bengt Sundkler, *Nathan Söderblom: His Life and Work*, (Lund, 1968), p. 127.

40   Jennifer Michael Hecht, *Doubt: A History*, (San Francisco, 2003), p. 428.

41   Svante Nordin, "Hundra år av religionsdebatt," in Jakob Christensson, editor, *Signums svenska kulturhistoria: 1900-talet*, (Stockholm, 2009), p. 142.

42   Jon Gjerde, *The Minds of the West: Ethnocultural Evolution in the Rural Middle West, 1830-1917*, (Chapel Hill, 1997), pp. 248, 270-272.

43   Byron R. Swanson, *Conrad Bergendoff: The Making of an Ecumenist*, Th.D. dissertation, Princeton Theological Seminary, (1970), pp. 207-210.

44   Pleijel, *Från fädernas fromhetsliv*, p. 138.

45   Adrian Molin, *Svenska spörsmål och kraf*, second edition, (Stockholm, 1906), quoted in Martin Alm, "Bilden av Amerika," in Christensson, p. 184. Molin (1880-1942) was a conservative, anti-emigration, pro-German intellectual and journalist.

46   "Augustana-Synoden och svenskhetens bevarande," *Allsvensk samling*, v. 11, (Apr. 15, 1924), p. 3.

47   "The Largeness of Life," LC, v. 29, (Oct. 22, 1921), p. 679.

48   "Theology and Our Times," AQ, v. 12, (Oct., 1933), p. 344.

49   "Victory's Call," LC, v. 43, (Feb. 2, 1935), p. 129.

50   "The Oxford Conference," LC, v. 45, (Aug. 26, 1937), p. 1095.

51   "What Are We Fighting for in America?" LC, v. 96, (June 27, 1951), p. 17.

52   "The Image of God and the Image of Man," MS, (1956), CBP 71-1.

53   "The Inner Being," Commencement Address, Philadelphia Lutheran Theological Seminary, (May 14, 1964), CBP 72-2.

54   "Three R's for Today," LC, v. 96, (Oct. 3, 1951), p. 10.

55   "Looking Ahead from 1960," LC, v. 106, (June 29, 1960), pp. 3-4.

56   "From Generation to Generation," *Century: Salem Lutheran Church*, (Chicago, 1968), p. 16.

57   "The Secular Idea of Progress," pp. 53-68.

58   *Observer*, May 10, 1951.

59   "New Year's Thoughts at Augustana," LC, v. 44, (Jan. 4, 1936), p. 13.

60   "Educational Relations," MS, (1939), CBP 46-2.

61   "What Are We Fighting For in America?" p. 9.

CHAPTER 4

62   "From College Windows," LC, v. 51, (Oct. 13, 1943), p. 1132.

63   *Christ as Authority*, p. 95.

64   Ibid., p. 9.

65   "The Secular Idea of Progress," p. 59.

66   "The Modern Imagination," p. 107.

67   Ibid., pp. 102, 110.

68   "The God Beyond Our Knowledge," MS, (1956), CBP 71-1.

69   "Theology, the Church, and the University," LQ, v. 13, (Feb., 1961), p. 7.

70   "The Modern Imagination," pp. 101-102.

71   Ibid., p. 104.

72   "Theology, the Church, and the University," pp. 7-8.

73   "Two Stations Beyond," LC, v. 99, (June 30, 1954), pp. 4, 22.

74   "What Are We Fighting For in America?" p. 10.

75   CB to Carl Swanson, Nov. 7, 1952, CBP 15-6.

76   Merle Curti, "Sweden in the American Social Mind of the 1930s," in J. Iverne Dowie and J. Thomas Tredway, editors, *The Immigration of Ideas: Studies in the North Atlantic Community*, (Rock Island, 1968), p. 159ff.

77   "Tongues of Them That Are Taught," LC, v. 50, (Apr. 30, 1942), p. 559.

78   "The Modern Imagination," pp. 105-106, 113-114.

79   "The Secular Idea of Progress," pp. 64-65.

80   "No Other Image," LC, v. 97, (July 9, 1952), p. 14.

81   "The Ethical Thought of Einar Billing," in Philip J. Hefner, editor, *The Scope of Grace*, (Philadelphia, 1964), pp. 279-306.

82   *The One Holy Catholic Apostolic Church*, (Rock Island, 1954), Ch. 1.

83   "Religion and Culture," MS, (1950-1951), CBP 70-2.

84   *Christ as Authority*, pp. 3-4, 125.

85   *One Holy Catholic Apostolic Church*, pp. 10-17.

86   Review of Karl A. Olsson, *By One Spirit*, in SPHQ, v. 14, (Jan., 1963), pp. 33-35.

87   *Christ as Authority*, p. 7.

88   "The Meandering of an Historian," *Concordia Historical Institute Quarterly*, v. 55, (Winter, 1982), pp. 181-184.

89   Theodore G. Tappert, Review of Conrad Bergendoff, *The Church of the Lutheran Reformation*, in *Church History*, v. 37, (June, 1968), p. 216.

90   "Significant Elements in Christian Culture," pp. 226-229.

91   Greenblatt, the American Shakespeare scholar, traces the recovery in the Renaissance of ancient philosophical materialism, through the rediscovery in the fifteenth century of a forgotten manuscript by the ancient Roman poet Lucretius, *On the Nature of Things*. This work contained such ideas as: the world runs without the gods; goodness and pleasure are complementary, not opposed; the universe is simply composed of small particles of matter which eternally combine and break up. The rediscovery of Lucretius, says Greenblatt, was "The Swerve" toward the secular that shaped modern science, both natural and social. Stephen Greenblatt, *The Swerve: How the World Became Modern*, (New York, 2011).

92   *The Church of the Lutheran Reformation*, (St. Louis, 1967), pp. 171-178.

93   Review of Karl Löwith, *Meaning in History*, in LQ, v. 1, (Nov., 1949), p. 472.

94   "True Freedom," LC, v. 47, (June 22, 1939), p. 779.

CHAPTER 4

95   *Church of the Lutheran Reformation*, pp. 203-204.

96   Ibid., p. 212.

97   "Theology and Our Times," p. 343.

98   "The Augustana Synod and the Augustana Seminary," AQ, v. 22, (Jan., 1943), p. 25.

99   Ibid., p. 343.

100   Edward Dolnick, *The Clockwork Universe: Isaac Newton, the Royal Society, and the Birth of the Modern World*, (New York, 2011), p. 58.

101   *Christ as Authority*, p. 63.

102   "The Modern Imagination," p. 110.

103   *Christ as Authority*, p. 50.

104   "The Kind of World This Has Become," *Christian Century*, v. 66, (July 13, 1949), pp. 40-41.

105   *Christ as Authority*, pp. 48-49. Isaac Newton himself did believe that God providentially guides the world and that he was free to act in the universe independent of the laws which he had set forth and which Newton had elucidated. Alvin Plantinga, *Where the Conflict Really Lies: Science, Religion, and Naturalism*, (Oxford, 2011), pp. 76-84. Bergendoff's point seems to be that as *commonly understood* classical or Newtonian physics taught that the universe is a closed system.

106   "Theology and Our Times," pp. 334-336. Wieman was teaching at the University of Chicago when Bergendoff did a history PhD.

107   *Christ as Authority*, pp. 49-56.

108   Report of the President, Augustana College, 1962.

109   "Significant Elements in Christian Culture," p. 231.

110   "True Freedom," pp. 779-780.

111   "Humanity and the Humanities," *Christian Century*, v. 60, (July 7, 1943), p. 794.

112   "True Freedom," p. 778.

113   "Education for Church and State," LC, v. 56, (Sept. 22, 1948), p. 11.

114   "The Lutheran Church and the Modern State," pp. 319-324.

115   Ibid., p. 323.

116   "The Lutheran Christian in Church and State," LQ, v. 1, (Nov., 1949), pp. 414-423.

117   "A Free Church in a Free Nation," AQ, v. 25, (Jan., 1946), p. 70.

CHAPTER 5

1   O. F. Ander to George M. Stephenson, May 28, 1931, Stephenson papers, Box 2, Univ. of Minnesota archives.

2   Rudolph J. Vecoli, "'Over the years I have encountered the hazards and rewards that await the historian of immigration': George Malcom Stephenson and the Swedish-American Community," SAHQ, v. 51, (Apr., 2000), p. 135.

3   Marcus Lee Hansen, *The Immigrant in American History*, edited by Arthur M. Schlesinger, (Cambridge, Mass., 1940), p. 27.

4   *Samling af Augustana-Synodens, dess konferensers och inrättningars oktrojer, stadgar och ordningsregler*, (Rock Island, 1918) is a collection of official documents published by the Synod; Eric Norelius, *De svenska lutherska församlingarnas och svenskarnas historia i Amerika*, 2 vols, (Rock Island, 1890, 1916) contains many original documents in its text. Bergendoff translated selections from Norelius' first volume in *The Pioneer Swedish Settlements and Swedish Lutheran Churches in America, 1845-1860*, (Rock Island, 1984).

CHAPTER 5

5   Byron R. Swanson, Transcript of interviews with Conrad Bergendoff, June 23-24, Dec. 7, 1966, p. 1.

6   "The Significance of the Lutheran Reformation of the Sixteenth Century for the Church of the Twentieth," AQ, v. 8, (Apr., 1929), p. 143. Bergendoff objected to Walker's assertion that though Luther was a noble and profound man, his experience was not entirely applicable to modern times. Now in the twentieth century, thought Walker, Christians were working together with God to bring his Kingdom to earth. Bergendoff, quoting Luther, did not believe that it was possible for humans to build God's Kingdom on earth.

7   Williston Walker, *A History of the Christian Church,* (New York, 1918), p. 496.

8   "The Augustana Synod and the Augustana Seminary," AQ, v. 22, (Jan., 1943), pp. 14-15. For his part the Pietist Waldenström reminded the Augustana people that Luther himself advocated conventicles and other practices for which the Church of Sweden had punished the Pietists. In Waldenström's view, Luther and Lutheranism ought to be separated from each other. See Mark Safstrom, "Defining Lutheranism from the Margins: Paul Peter Waldenström on Being a 'Good Lutheran' in America," SAHQ, v. 63, (Apr.-July, 2012), esp. pp. 103-104, 112-113.

9   *The Church of the Lutheran Reformation,* (St. Louis, 1967), pp. 155-166.

10   Ibid., p. 157.

11   Ibid., pp. 168-169.

12   Ibid., p. 217.

13   Oscar Fritiof Ander, *T. N. Hasselquist,* (Rock Island, 1931), p. 79; George M. Stephenson, *The Religious Aspects of Swedish Immigration,* (Minneapolis, 1932), pp. 285, 386.

14   Karl A. Olsson, "Kontinuitet och förvandling inom svenska immigrantsamfund i USA," *Kyrkohistorisk årsskrift,* v. 82, (1982), p. 14.

15   "The Augustana Synod and the Augustana Seminary," pp. 15-16.

16   Sam Rönnegård, *Prairie Shepherd: Lars Paul Esbjörn and the Beginnings of the Augustana Lutheran Church,* translated by G. Everett Arden, (Rock Island, 1952), pp. 268-270.

17   G. Everett Arden, *Augustana Heritage,* (Rock Island, 1963), pp. 27-28, 34. Esbjörn's Swedish biographer, Sam Rönnegård, also noted that Esbjorn did not have a "particularly thorough" theological training and that his course at Uppsala "must have been somewhat superficial." Rönnegård, pp. 8, 296.

18   "Towards a History of the Augustana Synod—Three Books Reviewed," AQ, v. 11, (July, 1932), pp. 259-266.

19   O. Olsson, *Reformationen och Socinianismen, Föredrag wid reformationsfesten wid Aug. College 1878,* (Rock Island, 1880); Arden, *Augustana Heritage,* pp. 174-188; Maria Erling and Mark Granquist, *The Augustana Story,* (Minneapolis, 2008), pp. 43-46; Ernest William Olson, *Olof Olsson,* (Rock Island, 1941), pp. 155-158; Stephenson, *Religious Aspects of Swedish Immigration,* pp. 285-286. It is interesting that the Covenant historian Karl Olsson agrees that Waldenström's Atonement doctrine, "when pushed to its logical conclusion appeared to threaten the validity of persons in the Trinity." Karl Olsson "Paul Peter Waldenström and Augustana," in J. Iverne Dowie and Ernest M. Espelie, editors, *The Swedish Immigrant Community in Transition,* (Rock Island, 1963), pp. 115-116.

20   Swanson, Interviews with Bergendoff, p. 1.

21   "Towards a History of the Augustana Synod," pp. 265-266.

22   John S. Lindberg, *The Background of Swedish Emigration to the United States: An Economic*

CHAPTER 5

and Sociological Study in the Dynamics of Migration, (Minneapolis, 1930), pp. 29, 36.

23   Marcus Lee Hansen, *The Atlantic Migration, 1607-1860,* edited by Arthur M. Schlesinger, fourth printing, (Cambridge, Mass., 1951), p. 141.

24   Hans Norman, "The Causes of Emigration. a. An Attempt at a Multivariate Analysis," in Harald Runblom and Hans Norman, editors, *From Sweden to America: A History of the Migration,* (Minneapolis, 1976), p. 155.

25   "Towards a History of the Augustana Synod," p. 260.

26   "New Year's Thoughts at Augustana," LC, v. 44, (Jan. 4, 1936), p. 13.

27   "Towards a History of the Augustana Synod," p. 265.

28   *The Doctrine of the Church in American Lutheranism,* (Philadelphia, 1956), p. 40.

29   "The Dedication of Augustana Theological Seminary and the Visit of Archbishop Söderblom," LC, v. 31, (Oct. 27, 1923), p. 683.

30   Stephenson, *Religious Aspects of Swedish Immigration,* pp. 191-192.

31   *Augustana: A Profession of Faith,* (Rock Island, 1969), p. 19.

32   Arden, *Augustana Heritage,* pp. 27-28.

33   "On the Occasion of the Centennial of Augustana College," SPHQ, v. 11, (Apr., 1960), p. 37.

34   One can hear Bergendoff himself speaking in this way in the taped recording meant to be played by visitors to the Jenny Lind Chapel in Andover, Illinois, the building first erected by Esbjörn and his band of settlers in the early 1850s. The Swedish version of Bergendoff's recorded talk also refers to the spiritual poverty of the nineteenth century American milieu into which the Swedes arrived. The English version omits that reference.

35   Rönnegård, p. 197. The comment was, in fact, made by Nathan Söderblom's father, himself a priest in the Church of Sweden.

36   Ander, *T. N. Hasselquist,* p. 57-58.

37   Ibid., p. 41.

38   *Augustana: A Profession of Faith,* p. 28.

39   "On the Occasion of the Centennial of Augustana College," pp. 38-39.

40   "The Americanization of the Augustana Synod," LC, v. 32, (Aug. 16, 1924), p. 522.

41   "Our Attitude Towards Liturgical Innovations," MS, (1945-1946), CBP 68-9.

42   Swanson, Interviews with Bergendoff, p. 14.

43   Dag Blanck, *The Creation of an Ethnic Identity,* (Carbondale, Ill., 2006), pp. 26-32.

44   "Augustana in America and in Sweden," SPHQ, v. 24, (Oct., 1973), p. 238.

45   CB to Emmer Engberg, July 7, 1955, CBP 16-2; Philip J. Anderson, "Histories from the Inside Out: Shared Origins and Denominational Historiography in the Writings of G. Everett Arden and Karl A. Olsson," SAHQ, v. 63, (Apr.-July, 2012), p. 84. Anderson's essay makes the point that the Mission Friends may, in the end, not have been Augustana's to lose; in fact, most Mission Friend congregations which became Covenant were not congregations that had left the Augustana Synod; pp. 92-93.

46   I am indebted to Dag Blanck for directing me to the work of such Swedish historians as Carl Alfred Cornelius and Ernst Newman who used *hyperevangelisk* in this way.

47   Arden, *Augustana Heritage,* p. 160ff; Stephenson, *Religious Aspects of Swedish Immigration,* pp. 264-267.

48   Arden, *Augustana Heritage,* p. 237.

49   Blanck, *Creation of an Ethnic Identity,* p. 35.

CHAPTER 5

50   "The Americanization of the Augustana Synod," p. 523.

51   "A Colony of Heaven," LC, v. 43, (June 22, 1935), p. 779.

52   Sydney Eckman Ahlstrom, "Facing the New World: Augustana and the American Challenge," in Emmer Engberg et al., editors, *Centennial Essays,* (Rock Island, 1960), p. 17.

53   Glen C. Stone, Interviews with Conrad Bergendoff, June 22-23, 1977, Oct. 4, 1979, Archives of Cooperative Lutheranism, p. 24, CBP 84.

54   "Augustana in America and Sweden," pp. 238-239.

55   "Temple Talks," LC, v. 42, (May 26, 1934), p. 645.

56   Franklin D. Scott, *Sweden: The Nation's History,* (Minneapolis, 1977), p. 361.

57   *Church of the Lutheran Reformation,* pp. 218, 255.

58   "National Aspects of the Lutheran Church in America," AQ, v. 3, (June, 1924), p. 169.

59   *Augustana: A Profession of Faith,* pp. 7, 24.

60   Hugo Söderström, *Confession and Cooperation,* (Lund, 1973), p. 21.

61   Philip J. Anderson, "Paul Peter Waldenström and America: Influence and Presence in Historical Perspective," *Covenant Quarterly,* v. 52, (Nov., 1994), p. 7.

62   "That Ye Love One Another," LC, v. 96, (Apr. 11, 1951), p. 8.

63   "Ecumenical Experiences," in Engberg, *Centennial Essays,* p. 102.

64   "How Strong Is the Augustana Synod?" LC, v. 51, (Jan. 20, 1943), pp. 72-73.

65   "Among Lutherans on the West Coast," LC, v. 41, (Sept. 9, 1933), p. 1143.

66   Erling and Granquist, p. 283.

67   Untitled MS, (1959-1960), CBP 71-5.

68   E. Norelius, *T. N. Hasselquist: Lefnadsteckning,* (Rock Island, [1900]), p. 63.

69   The university in Sweden is spelled with two *ps*: Uppsala; the college in New Jersey with but one: Upsala. At the time the New Jersey college was founded the custom in Sweden was to spell the word with one *p*.

70   The Synod also founded eight other colleges, only one of which survived—by merging into Texas Lutheran College. Erling and Granquist, p. 381.

71   Abdel Ross Wentz, *A Basic History of Lutheranism in America,* revised edition, (Philadelphia, 1963), p. 195.

72   Stone, pp. 95-96.

73   The preceding paragraph is based upon passages in Arden, *Augustana Heritage*; Bergendoff, *The Augustana Ministerium,* (Rock Island, 1980); and Erling and Granquist.

74   See, for example, Maria Södling, *Oreda i skapelsen,* (Uppsala, 2010), pp. 46-56.

75   Synod Minutes, 1950, p. 328; this is discussed at greater length in Thomas Tredway, *Coming of Age,* (Rock Island, 2010), pp. 83-86.

76   CB to Ruth Parsons, Nov. 25, 1935, CBP 1-15.

77   Report of the President, Augustana College and Theological Seminary, 1936.

78   CB to Brother Mattson, May 12, 1948, CBP 12-4.

79   *Observer,* Feb. 10, 1949.

80   Board Minutes, June 22, 1950.

81   Report of the President, Augustana College, 1949.

82   P. O. Bersell to J. B. Heid, Mar. 15, 1949, CBP 13-1.

83   Board Minutes, May 11, 1949.

84   Stephenson, *Religious Aspects of Swedish Immigration,* pp. 348-349.

85   *Augustana: A Profession of Faith,* p. 154.

CHAPTER 5

86 G. Everett Arden, *The School of the Prophets,* (Rock Island, 1960), pp. 203-204.
87 Synod Minutes, 1926, p. 63, Italics added.
88 Arden, *Augustana Heritage,* p. 352.
89 CB to P. O. Bersell, Oct. 17, 1946, CBP 11-1.
90 CB to P. O. Bersell, Oct. 5, 1946, CBP 11-1.
91 This and the preceding three paragraphs are based largely on Arden, *School of the Prophets,* pp. 226-230.
92 *Augustana: A Profession of Faith,* pp. 175-176.
93 Arden, *Augustana Heritage,* p. 347.
94 CB to P. O. Bersell, Oct. 17, 1946, CBP 11-1.
95 Stone, p. 92; Stone's transcript follows this with the notation "(laughter)"—which presumably came from Bergendoff.
96 Arden, *Augustana Heritage,* p. 348.
97 Synod Minutes, 1946, p. 18.
98 Arden, *School of the Prophets,* pp. 243-246.
99 Board Minutes, Feb. 10, 1948.
100 P. O. Bersell to CB, Nov. 2, 1945, CBP 10-1.
101 Synod Minutes, 1947, p. 121. In fact, one of the conferences, Superior, did this time accept control of the college, but the other two, Iowa and Illinois, did not.
102 Synod Minutes, 1957, 1958.
103 Synod Minutes, 1939, p. 265.
104 "A Divorce in 1948? Let Us Keep Augustana College AND Theological Seminary," LC, v. 54, (Apr. 3, 1946), pp. 8-9.
105 "An Appraisal of Lutheran Theological Education," *Lutheran Church Quarterly,* v. 19, (Oct., 1946), p. 332.
106 "Our Theological Seminary," LC, v. 55, (June 4, 1947), p. 7.
107 Report of the President, Augustana College, 1948; Synod Minutes, 1948, pp. 63-64.
108 Synod Minutes, 1948, p. 115.
109 Arden, *School of the Prophets,* p. 248.
110 Karl E. Mattson to CB, Feb. 17, 1948, CBP UP 8.
111 "Our Theological Seminary," pp. 6-7.
112 CB to P. O. Bersell, Sept. 30, 1946, CBP UP 8.
113 Ibid.
114 G. L. Bongfeldt, *Pen Portraits of P. O. Bersell and C. A. Wendell,* (Rock Island, 1950), p. 9.
115 P. O. Bersell to CB, Oct. 2, 1946, CBP UP 8.
116 Stone, p. 93.
117 Ibid.
118 CB to P.O. Bersell, Sept. 30, 1946, CBP UP 8.
119 Stone, p. 93.
120 P. O. Bersell to CB, Nov. 28, 1947; Eric Wahlstrom et al. to CB, Dec. 3, 1947, CBP UP 8.
121 "The Augustana Synod and the Augustana Seminary," p. 14.
122 CB to Leonard Kendall, Jan. 26, 1948, CBP 12-3.
123 Abdel Ross Wentz to CB, Apr. 17, 1948, CBP UP 8.
124 CB to Lynn Ash, Feb. 12, 1948, CBP 12-21.
125 Synod Minutes, 1949, p. 149.
126 P. O. Bersell to CB, Nov. 24, 1949, CBP 13-1.

CHAPTER 5

127 CB to Paul Hutchinson, June 22, 1948, CBP 12-3.
128 Einar Billing, *Our Calling*, translated with an Introduction by Conrad Bergendoff, (Rock Island, 1947).
129 "The Lutheran Christian in Church and State," LQ, v. 1, (Nov., 1949); "Wanted: a Theory of the Laity in the Lutheran Church," LQ, v. 3, (Feb., 1951).
130 *Doctrine of the Church in American Lutheranism*, p. 25.
131 Söderström, pp. 93, 171.
132 *Church of the Lutheran Reformation*, p. 296; *Doctrine of the Church in American Lutheranism*, p. 29.
133 *Augustana: A Profession of Faith*, pp. 157-158.
134 Arden, *Augustana Heritage*, p. 345. The other sponsored history of the Augustana Synod, Erling and Granquist, published in 2008, makes very little mention of the 1948 separation.
135 Nils Hasselmo, Review of Erling and Granquist, in SAHQ, v. 61, (Jan., 2010), p. 48.
136 Stone, p. 94.
137 Ibid., p. 93.
138 Report of the President, Augustana College, 1949.
139 Board Minutes, May 11, 1949.
140 Ibid., June 22, 1950.
141 Tredway, pp. 103-104.

CHAPTER 6

1 "Ecumenical Experiences," in Emmer Engberg et al., editors, *Centennial Essays*, (Rock Island, 1960), pp. 102-103.
2 *The Church of the Lutheran Reformation*, (St. Louis, 1967), p. 231.
3 Ibid., pp. 238-239.
4 *The Doctrine of the Church in American Lutheranism*, (Philadelphia, 1956), pp. 10-13.
5 Ibid., p. 80.
6 Ibid., pp. 2-5.
7 *Church of the Lutheran Reformation*, pp. 242-243.
8 Diarmaid MacCulloch, *The Reformation*, (New York, 2003), pp. 173-174.
9 A summary of the controversy as well as parallel versions of the Augsburg Confession and the "American" revisions by Schmucker et al. can be found in August R. Suelflow and E. Clifford Nelson, "Following the Frontier, 1840-1875," in E. Clifford Nelson et al., editors, *The Lutherans in North America*, (Philadelphia, 1975), pp. 217-227.
10 "Impressions from the 'Merger Meeting' in New York City, Nov. 12-18, 1918," LC, v. 26, (Dec. 7, 1918).
11 Quoted in Byron R. Swanson, *Conrad Bergendoff: The Making of an Ecumenist*, Th.D. dissertation, Princeton Theological Seminary, (1970), p. 183.
12 Robert T. Handy, *A History of the Churches of the United States and Canada*, (New York, 1977), p. 331.
13 "Impressions from the 'Merger Meeting' in New York City."
14 *Church of the Lutheran Reformation*, p. 256.
15 "Augustana-Synoden och svenskhetens bevarande," *Allsvensk samling*, v. 11, (Apr. 15, 1924), p. 3.
16 Don Herbert Yoder, "Christian Unity in Nineteenth-Century America," in Ruth Rouse

CHAPTER 6

and Stephen Charles Neill, editors, *A History of the Ecumenical Movement, 1517-1948,* third edition, (Geneva, 1986), p. 222.

17 E. Clifford Nelson "The New Shape of Lutheranism," in E. Clifford Nelson, *The Lutherans in North America,* pp. 403-414.

18 Mark Granquist, "'The Sociological Factor Is Not to Be Underestimated': Swedes, Norwegians, and American Lutheran Merger Negotiations, 1920-60," in Philip J. Anderson and Dag Blanck, editors, *Norwegians and Swedes in the United States: Friends and Neighbors,* (St. Paul, 2012), p. 158.

19 G. Everett Arden, *Augustana Heritage,* (Rock Island, 1963), p. 270.

20 Nelson, pp. 409-410.

21 "The Relationship between the American Lutheran Conference and the United Lutheran Church in America," AQ, v. 16, (Oct., 1937), pp. 318-321.

22 "An Appraisal of Lutheran Theological Education," *Lutheran Church Quarterly,* v. 19, (Oct., 1946), p. 333.

23 "The Meaning of Lutheran Unity," LC, v. 97, (Nov. 5, 1952), pp. 10-11.

24 *Doctrine of the Church in American Lutheranism,* p. 1.

25 "The Americanization of the Augustana Synod," LC, v. 32, (Aug. 23, 1924), p. 539.

26 Bergendoff's essay for the conference, "Lutheran Unity," in E. C. Fendt, editor, *What Lutherans Are Thinking,* (Columbus, Ohio, 1947), argued that "their very uneasiness in isolation" made it clear that American Lutherans *knew* they could not go on separated from each other indefinitely.

27 Edward C. Fendt, *The Struggle for Lutheran Unity in the U.S.A. from the Late 1930's to the Early 1970's,* (Minneapolis, 1980), p. 26.

28 "Here We Stand!" LC, v. 47, (Mar. 30, 1939), pp. 392-393, 399.

29 CB to C. O. Granlund, Feb. 16, 1945, CBP 9-2.

30 "A Letter to the Missouri Synod from One of Its Admirers," *Seminarian,* v. 52, (Apr., 1961), pp. 4-9; MS, CBP 71-6.

31 Ruth Rouse, "Voluntary Movements and the Changing Ecumenical Climate," in Rouse and Neill, p. 325.

32 "The Meaning of Lutheran Unity," p. 11.

33 F. H. Knubel to CB, Dec. 28, 1938; Luther D. Reed to CB, Jan. 4, 1939, CBP UP 4.

34 Glen C. Stone, Interviews with Conrad Bergendoff, June 22-23, 1977, Oct. 4, 1979, Archives of Cooperative Lutheranism, p. 87, CBP 84.

35 "The Relationship between the American Lutheran Conference and the United Lutheran Church in America," pp. 322-325.

36 "The True Unity of the Church," *Lutheran Church Quarterly,* v. 12, (July, 1939), p. 258.

37 Review of J. T. McNeill, *Unitive Protestantism,* in AQ, v. 18, (Apr., 1939), p. 167.

38 *Doctrine of the Church in American Lutheranism,* p. 68.

39 Maria Erling and Mark Granquist, *The Augustana Story,* (Minneapolis, 2008), p. 323.

40 Arden, *Augustana Heritage,* p. 280.

41 "Among Lutherans on the West Coast," LC, v. 41, (Sept. 9, 1933), p. 1145.

42 Nelson, p. 500.

43 S. E. Engstrom, "Lutheran Unity Is Desirable," LC, v. 97, (Apr. 2, 1952), pp. 8-10; (Apr. 9, 1952), pp. 10-11.

44 Editorial, LC, v. 97, (Feb. 27, 1952), p. 7.

45 E. E. Ryden, "A Hopeful Church Faces World Task," LC, v. 97, (July 16, 1952), pp. 7-9.

46 Ibid., p. 9.

CHAPTER 6

47   Stone, p. 21.

48   Ryden, "A Hopeful Church Faces World Task," p. 9.

49   Synod Minutes, 1952, pp. 374-375.

50   Ibid., 1953, p. 340.

51   CBP UP 10.

52   Stone, p. 99.

53   Synod Minutes, 1953, pp. 342-343.

54   E. E. Ryden, "Augustana Quits Merger Negotiations," LC, v. 97, (Nov. 26, 1952), p. 7.

55   Nelson, p. 505.

56   The process by which the Augustana Church ended up merging into the LCA is discussed in some detail in Arden, *Augustana Heritage,* Ch. 17, and in Erling and Granquist, Ch. 19.

57   "A Century of Augustana History," *Kyrkohistorisk årsskrift,* v. 59, (1959), reprinted in SAHQ, v. 61, (Oct., 2010), p. 310.

58   E. E. Ryden, "Dissolution or Expansion," LC, v. 97, (Dec. 3, 1952), pp. 4-5.

59   Arden, *Augustana Heritage,* p. 397.

60   Quoted in Erling and Granquist, p. 332.

61   "What Kind of Lutheran Unity? Two Sign-Posts Point the Way," LC, v. 100-101, (Jan. 19, 1955), pp. 10-11.

62   Statement regarding Franklin Clark Fry by Conrad Bergendoff, in Robert H. Fischer, editor, *Franklin Clark Fry: A Palette for a Portrait,* supplementary number of LQ, v. 24, (1972), pp. 128-129.

63   "The Relationship between the American Lutheran Conference and the United Lutheran Church in America," pp. 325-328.

64   Minutes of the Joint Commission on Lutheran Unity, Sept. 18, 1957, CBP 49-1.

65   Fischer, p. 129; Mark Granquist, "Conrad Bergendoff and the LCA Merger of 1962," in Raymond Jarvi, editor, *Aspects of Augustana and Swedish America,* (Rock Island, 1995), p. 105.

66   John H. Tietjen, *Which Way to Lutheran Unity?* (St. Louis, 1966), p. 138.

67   Stone, p. 64.

68   Johannes Knudsen, *The Formation of the Lutheran Church in America,* (Philadelphia, 1978), pp. 37-38.

69   Ibid., p. 42.

70   "Lutheran Doctrine of the Church," CBP 49-1.

71   Ibid.

72   "Augustana's Idea of the Church," *Augustana Seminary Review,* v. 7, (June, 1955).

73   "The Lutheran View of the Lord's Supper," LQ, v. 4, (Aug., 1952), pp. 278-294.

74   *The One Holy Catholic Apostolic Church,* (Rock Island, 1954), p. 41.

75   Philip J. Anderson, "'Strangers Yet Acquainted': The Personality of Religious Schism in Lindsborg, Kansas," SAHQ, v. 49, (July, 1998), p. 213.

76   *One Holy Catholic Apostolic Church,* p. 46.

77   "Augustana's Idea of the Church," pp. 11-23.

78   "Introduction," in Conrad Bergendoff, editor and translator, *The Church and the Ministry, II, Luther's Works,* v. 40, (Philadelphia, 1958), pp. xiii-xiv.

79   *Doctrine of the Church in American Lutheranism,* pp. 26-29.

80   Ibid., p. 86.

CHAPTER 6

81   "The Meaning of Lutheran Unity, a Proposed Blue Print," LC, v. 97, (Nov. 5, 1952), pp. 10-11.
82   "What Kind of Lutheran Unity?"
83   At the time of the merger the ULCA had 2,500,000 members, Augustana 500,000, and the Danish and Finnish groups 25,000 each. Albert P. Stauderman, *Our New Church,* (Philadelphia, 1962). The new LCA (1962) had 3,200,000 members, the new ALC (1960) 2,300,000, and the Missouri Synod 2,700,000 members in 1962. Nelson, p. 483.
84   Erling and Granquist, pp. 332-333.
85   "What Kind of Lutheran Unity?"
86   Erling and Granquist, p. 334.
87   "What Kind of Co-operation is Possible in View of the Discussion to Date?" MS, (1961), CBP 49-3.
88   Paul C. Empie to CB, May 11, 1960, CBP 49-4.
89   Frederick W. Wentz, *Lutherans in Concert,* (Minneapolis, 1968), pp. 171-174.
90   "Lutheran Doctrine of the Church."
91   Karl A. Olsson, "Paul Peter Waldenström and Augustana," in J. Iverne Dowie and Ernest M. Espelie, editors, *The Swedish Immigrant Community in Transition,* (Rock Island, 1963), p. 114.
92   Arden, *Augustana Heritage*, p. 411.
93   Erling and Granquist, p. 335.
94   Remarks acknowledging award of Order of the North Star, First Class, Nov. 14, 1975, CBP 73-2.
95   "Augustana in America and Sweden," SPHQ, v. 24, (Oct., 1973), pp. 238-241.
96   P. O. Bersell to CB, Mar. 22, 1962, CBP UP 14.
97   W. Kent Gilbert, *Commitment to Unity,* (Philadelphia, 1988), p. 162-163.
98   *The Lutheran Church in America and Theological Education,* (New York, 1963) is Bergendoff's report. The notes he made as he prepared it are in CBP 41-17 and CBP 48.
99   Samuel McCrae Cavert, *Church Cooperation and Unity in America: A Historical Review, 1900-1970,* (New York, 1970), p. 117.
100 P. O. Bersell to CB, Jan. 22, 1964, CBP UP 15.
101 *Doctrine of the Church in American Lutheranism*, pp. 88-89.
102 Stephen C. Neill, *Brothers of the Faith,* (New York, 1960), p. 165.
103 Jens Holger Schjørring et al., editors, *From Federation to Communion: The History of the Lutheran World Federation,* (Minneapolis, 1997), contains an historical account of the LWF, especially in Chs. 1 and 2 and in the appended "Handbook." Bergendoff is not listed in the index, but a photo of the Commission on Theology meeting in Minneapolis in 1957 shows him at the table with six other members; Carl E. Lund-Quist to CB, Oct. 23, 1952, CBP UP 11.
104 "After Twenty-five Years," MS, (1972), CBP 73-1.
105 Ibid.; the inability of the Helsinki Assembly to reach agreement on justification is discussed in Eric W. Gritsch, *A History of Lutheranism,* (Minneapolis, 2002), pp. 232-233; Gritsch also offers a good summary of the history of the LWF, pp. 233-239.
106 Schjørring, pp. 375-396.
107 Ibid., p. 48.

CHAPTER 6

108   Ibid., p. 527.
109   "After Twenty-five Years."
110   "The Unity We Seek," in Michael Kinnamon and Brian E. Cope, editors, *The Ecumenical Movement: An Anthology of Key Texts and Voices*, (Geneva, 1997), p. 122.

CHAPTER 7

1   "The Ecumenical Paradox—'Our Oneness in Christ, Our Disunity as Churches,'" LC, v. 99, (Aug. 4, 1954), p. 14.
2   "The Holy Christian Church," LC, v. 44, (Feb. 22, 1936), pp. 236-238.
3   Arnold Toynbee, A *Study of History*, v. 4, (London, 1937), pp. 221-222.
4   Martin E. Marty, "Ethnicity: The Skeleton of Religion in America," *Church History*, v. 41, (Mar., 1972), p. 19.
5   "The Church—the Abiding Monument," LC, v. 46, (July 28, 1939), p. 937.
6   "An Appraisal of Lutheran Theological Education," *Lutheran Church Quarterly*, v. 19, (Oct., 1946), p. 336.
7   Don Herbert Yoder, "Christian Unity in Nineteenth-Century America," in Ruth Rouse and Stephen Charles Neill, editors, *A History of the Ecumenical Movement, 1517-1948,* third edition, (Geneva, 1986), p. 245.
8   "The Americanization of the Augustana Synod," LC, v. 32, (Aug. 23, 1934), p. 539.
9   CB to Mrs. E. Leonard Swann, Mar. 29, 1956, CBP 17-5.
10   Bengt Sundkler, *Nathan Söderblom: His Life and Work,* (Lund, 1968), pp. 327, 376.
11   Byron Swanson, "Conrad Bergendoff as Ecumenist," in Hartland H. Gifford and Arland J. Hultgren, editors, *The Heritage of Augustana,* (Minneapolis, 2004), pp. 280-281.
12   P. O. Bersell to CB, Jan. 10, 1936, CBP UP 3.
13   "The Significance of the Augsburg Confession for Our Own Day," AQ, v. 9, (Apr., 1930), p. 67.
14   "Today's World and Today's Church," LC, v. 49, (Jan. 30, 1941), p. 138.
15   Byron R. Swanson, *Conrad Bergendoff: The Making of an Ecumenist,* Th.D. dissertation, Princeton Theological Seminary, (1970), p. 341.
16   P. O. Bersell to CB, Jan. 20, 1942, CBP UP 5.
17   P. O. Bersell to CB, Jan. 26, 1942, CBP UP 5.
18   P. O. Bersell to CB, Nov. 24, 1948, CBP 13-1.
19   "Federal Council Observes 40th Birthday," LC, v. 56, (Dec. 29, 1948), pp. 10-11.
20   Stephen C. Neill, *Brothers of the Faith,* (New York, 1960), p. 155.
21   G. Everett Arden, *Augustana Heritage,* (Rock Island, 1963), pp. 308-311; Maria Erling and Mark Granquist, *The Augustana Story,* (Minneapolis, 2008), pp. 296-297; and Philip A. Johnson, "National Council Is Born," LC, v. 95, (Dec. 13, 1950), pp. 10-11, 22, are accounts of the Augustana Church's joining the NCC. Ruth Rouse, "Other Aspects of the Ecumenical Movement, 1910-1948," in Rouse and Neill, pp. 621-624, is a good, short account of the process by which the Federal Council became the National Council of Churches.
22   Samuel McCrae Cavert, *The American Churches in the Ecumenical Movement, 1900-1968,* (New York, 1969), p. 209.
23   Synod Referat [Minutes], 1911, p. 37.
24   Swanson, *Conrad Bergendoff,* p. 2.
25   "The Holy Christian Church," p. 237.

CHAPTER 7

26 Nils Ehrenström, "Movements for International Friendship and Life and Work, 1925-1948," in Rouse and Neill, p. 545.

27 "Lutherans and Christian Unity," MS (1953-1954), CBP 70-6.

28 Quoted in Arden, *Augustana Heritage,* p. 305.

29 Tissington Tatlow, "The World Conference on Faith and Order," in Rouse and Neill, p. 423.

30 Sundkler, p. 411.

31 Ibid., p. 410.

32 Ehrenström, p. 573.

33 "The Holy Christian Church," p. 237.

34 "Augustana-A People in Transition," in J. Iverne Dowie and Ernest M. Espelie, editors, *The Swedish Immigrant Community in Transition,* (Rock Island, 1963), p. 204.

35 Samuel McCrae Cavert to CB, (n.d.), CBP 53-3.

36 Floyd W. Tomkins to CB, Feb. 11, 1937, CBP 53-3.

37 Erling and Granquist, p. 298.

38 "The Oxford Conference," LC, v. 45, (Aug. 26, 1937), pp. 1095-1096.

39 The text of the "Affirmation of Union" is in Michael Kinnamon and Brian E. Cope, *The Ecumenical Movement: An Anthology of Key Texts and Voices,* (Grand Rapids, 1997), pp. 85-86.

40 Summaries of the Oxford and Edinburgh meetings can be found in Rouse and Neill, (Oxford), pp. 587-592, and (Edinburgh), pp. 431-437.

41 "The Oxford Conference."

42 "Oxford and Edinburgh, 1937," AQ, v. 17, (Jan., 1938), pp. 25-44.

43 Biographical statement, CBP 69-9.

44 J. Robert Nelson, Review of Conrad Bergendoff, *The One Holy Catholic Apostolic Church* [and seven other books], in *Ecumenical Review,* v. 7, (Apr., 1955), p. 293.

45 Sundkler, p. 406.

46 "Oxford and Edinburgh, 1937," p. 28.

47 P. O. Bersell to K. T. Anderson, Sept. 29, 1937, CBP UP 3.

48 Synod Minutes, 1940, p. 204.

49 Swanson, *Conrad Bergendoff,* p. 340.

50 H. Paul Douglas to CB, Oct. 10, 31, Dec. 11, 16, 1938, CBP UP 4.

51 For example, "Lutheran Ethics and Scandinavian Lutheranism," AQ, v. 20, (July, 1941), and "Intercommunion: A Symposium on the Report of the American Section of the Commission on Intercommunion," *Christendom,* v. 7, (Autumn, 1942).

52 Walter W. Van Kirk to CB, Apr. 4, 1941, CBP UP 5.

53 Samuel McCrae Cavert to CB, Feb. 11, Apr. 16, Oct. 25, 1943, CBP UP 6.

54 Synod Minutes, 1941, p. 253.

55 H. Krüger, "The Life and Activities of the World Council of Churches," in Harold E. Fey, editor, *The Ecumenical Advance: A History of the Ecumenical Movement, Volume 2, 1948-1968,* (London, 1970), p. 29.

56 Ibid., p. 39.

57 "Westphalia to Amsterdam," *Christian Century,* v. 65, (Aug. 11, 1948), pp. 801-803.

58 Relevant materials are in CBP 37-10.

59 CBP UP, Travel Diary, Apr. 2 – June 25, 1949.

60 CBP UP 9.

61 CBP UP, Travel Diary, Apr. 2 – June 25, 1949.

CHAPTER 7

62   CB to Gertrude Bergendoff, Apr. 20, 1949, CBP UP 9.

63   *The One Holy Catholic Apostolic Church*, (Rock Island, 1954), pp. 75-83.

64   "Westphalia to Amsterdam," p. 803.

65   *One Holy Catholic Apostolic Church*, pp. 84-98.

66   Ibid., p. 22.

67   *Christ as Authority*, (Rock Island, 1947), pp. 133-137.

68   John R. Brokhoff, Review of Conrad Bergendoff, *The One Holy Catholic Apostolic Church* [and one other book], in *Frontiers*, v. 6, (Feb., 1955), p. 29.

69   *Christ as Authority*, (Rock Island, 1947), pp. 133-137.

70   "A New Commandment . . . 'That Ye Love One Another,'" LC, v. 96, (Apr. 11, 1951), pp. 8, 14.

71   Richard V. Pierard, Review of Conrad Bergendoff, *The Church of the Lutheran Reformation*, in *Christianity Today*, v. 12, (Oct. 27, 1967), p. 34.

72   Quoted in Kinnamon and Cope, p. 127.

73   George M. Stephenson to CB, July 27, 1955, CBP UP 12.

74   "Observations at Four Meetings," LC, v. 34, (Dec. 4, 1926), p. 1163.

75   "The Significance of the Augsburg Confession for Our Own Day," p. 168.

76   "Temple Talks," LC, v. 42, (Apr. 7, 1934), p. 421, (May 12, 1934), p. 581.

77   Ibid., (Sept 8, 1934), p. 1125.

78   CB to Elmer J. Holt, Feb. 29, 1936, CBP 1-8.

79   "The True Unity of the Church," *Lutheran Church Quarterly*, v. 12, (July, 1939), p. 273.

80   Untitled response to the Report of the American Section of the Commission on Intercommunion, MS, (n.d.), CBP 68-1.

81   *At the Lord's Table*, (Rock Island, 1961).

82   "The Holy Christian Church," p. 238.

83   Untitled response to the Report of the American Section of the Commission on Intercommunion.

84   "Christian Unity in Non-Sacramental Worship," MS, (1948), CBP UP.

85   "The Lutheran View of the Lord's Supper," LQ, v. 4, (Aug., 1952), pp. 278-294.

86   "The Ecumenical Paradox," p. 8.

87   *The Church of the Lutheran Reformation*, (St. Louis, 1967), pp. 314-315.

88   H. H. Harms to CB, Feb. 12, 1954, CBP UP 11.

89   *One Holy Catholic Apostolic Church*, pp. 94-98; Bergendoff first and tentatively took this position on the eschatological nature of Christian unity in lectures at Gettysburg Seminary given in 1939: "The True Unity of the Church."

90   Byron R. Swanson, Transcript of interviews with Conrad Bergendoff, June 23-24, Dec. 7, 1966, p. 25.

91   Eric W. Gritsch, *A History of Lutheranism*, (Minneapolis, 2002), pp. 239-244, offers a summary of the state of Lutheran relationships with other Christian churches at the beginning of the twenty-first century.

92   "Our Attitude Towards Liturgical Innovation," MS, (1946), CBP 68-9; "The Liturgical Tradition of the Swedish Church," *Lutheran Church Quarterly*, v. 21, (July, 1948).

93   Frederick A. Schiotz to CB, Jan. 24, 1947, CBP 47-1.

94   Minutes of the Committee on Liturgy and Hymnal, CBP 47-5, 6.

95   Erling and Granquist, pp. 325-326.

96   Gustaf Aulén to CB, Dec. 22, 1959, CBP UP 13.

CHAPTER 7

97   "Justification and Sanctification: Liturgy and Ethics," in Paul E. Empie and James McCord, editors, *Marburg Revisited,* (Minneapolis, 1966), p. 124.

98   *Lutheran Worship,* (Rock Island, 1961).

99   "The Lutheran View of the Lord's Supper," p. 288.

100 Georges Florovsky, "The Orthodox Churches and the Ecumenical Movement Prior to 1910," in Rouse and Neill, p. 210; Henry Renaud Turner Brandreth, "Approaches of the Churches towards Each Other in the Nineteenth Century," in Rouse and Neill, pp. 297-300.

101 Ulf Beijbom, *Swedes in Chicago,* (Växjö, Sweden, 1971), p. 238.

102 Stephen Charles Neill, "Plans of Union and Reunion," in Rouse and Neill, pp. 471-473. Neill notes that the Anglicans grew concerned when they determined that all communicants in the Church of Sweden need not have been confirmed by bishops, while the Swedish Lutherans noted in return that all Anglican communicants had not really received a thorough doctrinal education.

103 "Henry Melchior Muhlenberg," LC, v. 50, (July 16, 1942), p. 870. Bergendoff might have been bothered by the comment of a contemporary historian that, "A certain preoccupation with the idea of apostolic succession is characteristic of the Church of Sweden, earning her a privileged position at the papal court." Björn Ryman, *Nordic Folk Churches,* (Grand Rapids, 2005), p. x.

104 "Intercommunion in the Church of Sweden and the Church of England," AQ, v. 15, (Apr., 1936), pp. 136-138.

105 Carl Henrik Lyttkens, *The Growth of Swedish-Anglican Intercommunion between 1833 and 1922,* (Lund, 1970), p. 268.

106 Glen C. Stone, Interviews with Conrad Bergendoff, June 22-23, 1977, Oct. 4, 1979, Archives of Cooperative Lutheranism, p. 17, CBP 84.

107 Sundkler, pp. 274-287.

108 Ibid., p. 408.

109 *One Holy Catholic Apostolic Church,* p. 63.

110 "The Holy Christian Church," LC, v. 44, (Feb. 22, 1936), pp. 236-238.

111 Quoted in Erling and Granquist, p. 294.

112 Erling and Granquist, p. 214.

113 Stone, p. 99.

114 *One Holy Catholic Apostolic Church,* pp. 18-19.

115 Ibid., p. 64.

116 Alfred F. Kierschner, Review of Conrad Bergendoff, *The One Holy Catholic Apostolic Church,* in *Una Sancta,* v. 11, (1954), p. 20.

117 "The True Unity of the Church," p. 272.

118 *The Doctrine of the Church in American Lutheranism,* (Philadelphia, 1956), p. 89.

119 Review of Karl Olsson, *By One Spirit,* in SPHQ, v. 14, (Jan., 1963), pp. 33-35. Bergendoff recognized in this review that Olsson himself took a view like his concerning the role of creeds. Perhaps Bergendoff's comment applied more to the Mission Friends in general than to Olsson in particular.

120 "Is the Layman Lost in a Sea of Theologians?" MS, (1956), CBP 71-1.

121 Swanson, Interviews with Bergendoff, p. 42.

122 "The Ecumenical Paradox," p. 7.

123 Swanson, Interviews with Bergendoff, p. 43.

CHAPTER 7

124   George M. Stephenson, *The Founding of the Augustana Synod,* (Rock Island, 1927), p. 72.
125   "The Significance of the Lutheran Reformation of the Sixteenth Century for the Church of the Twentieth," AQ, v. 8, (Apr., 1929), pp. 138-139.
126   "The Significance of the Augsburg Confession for Our Own Day," p. 168.
127   "What Kind of Unity?" LC, v. 47, (Mar. 2, 1939), p. 268.
128   "A Sane View of Ourselves," LC, v. 52, (June 21, 1944), pp. 10-11.
129   *Christ as Authority,* p. 132.
130   "Westphalia to Amsterdam," p. 802.
131   *One Holy Catholic Apostolic Church,* pp. 23-26.
132   Review of John Dillenberger, *God Hidden and Revealed,* in *Theology Today,* v. 10, (Jan., 1954), pp. 556-558.
133   "The Church and the Gospel," AQ, v. 11, (Jan., 1932), pp. 73-74.
134   Review of W. Pauck, *Karl Barth,* in AQ, v. 11, (Jan., 1932), pp. 84-85.
135   "Theology and Our Times," AQ, v. 12, (Oct., 1933), pp. 337-342.
136   "A Colony of Heaven," LC, v. 43, (June 22, 1935), p. 777.
137   Nicholas Hope, *German and Scandinavian Protestantism, 1700-1918,* (Oxford, 1995), p. 584.
138   "Theology and Our Times," p. 340.
139   CB to B. M. Christenson, Jan. 24, 1939, CBP 46-3.
140   "Is Another Springtime Coming in Theology?" MS, (1962), CBP 71-7.
141   "The Social Philosophy of Jonathan Edwards," AQ, v. 7, (Dec., 1928), pp. 290-291.
142   "Justification and Sanctification: Liturgy and Ethics," pp. 119-120.
143   "The Divine Calling of the Layman," LC, v. 46, (Nov. 10, 1938), p. 1419.
144   "Today's World and Today's Church," p. 138.
145   Erling and Granquist, pp. 140, 143-144.
146   Editorial, "'The Divine Origin of the Priesthood,'" LC, v. 20, (Sept. 7, 1912), p. 1.
147   Review of Emmet John Hughes, *The Church and the Liberal Society,* MS, (1944), CBP 68-6.
148   "The Personal Approach in Soul-Winning," AQ, v. 9, (Apr., 1930), p. 109.
149   *Church of the Lutheran Reformation,* pp. 305-306.
150   Ibid., pp. 103-106.
151   "Temple Talk," LC, v. 41, (Sept. 30, 1933), p. 1221.
152   "The Significance of the Augsburg Confession for Our Own Day," p. 168.
153   George Shuster, the President of Hunter College and a Roman Catholic, contributed a piece to the journal *Social Action* in 1947, as did Bergendoff, on the current state of Catholic-Protestant relations in the U.S. They agreed that the doctrine and role of the papacy was the core issue. "The Contemporary Situation as a Protestant Sees It," *Social Action,* v. 14 (Jan. 14, 1948), pp. 24-33; Liston Pope to CB, Nov. 10, 1947, CBP UP 8. The Augsburg Confession itself made no direct reference to this problem.
154   "The Ecumenical Paradox," p. 8.
155   *Christ as Authority,* pp. 26-27.
156   "The Challenge of Vatican II," *Valparaiso University Bulletin,* v. 41, (Sept. 22, 1967), pp. 55-62.
157   *Church of the Lutheran Reformation,* pp. 315-316.
158   "Today's World and Today's Church," p. 139.
159   Synod Minutes, 1960, pp. 255-261; Dean Gevik, "Church Speaks on Presidency," LC, v. 106, (July 6, 1960), pp. 15-17, 23; Franklin Littell, *From State Church to Pluralism: A Protestant Interpretation of Religion in American History,* (Garden City, N.Y., 1962), p. 155.
160   Arden, *Augustana Heritage,* p. 305.

CHAPTER 8

1   "Lutheran Ethics and Scandinavian Lutheranism," AQ, v. 20, (July, 1941), p. 219.

2   "Here We Stand!" LC, v. 47, (Mar. 30, 1939), pp. 393, 399.

3   Abdel Ross Wentz, *A Basic History of Lutheranism in America,* revised edition, (Philadelphia, 1963), p. 187.

4   One gets this sense in Glen C. Stone, Interviews with Conrad Bergendoff, June 22-23, 1977, Oct. 4, 1979, Archives of Cooperative Lutheranism, CBP 84, as well as in Bergendoff's informal conversations during his later decades. See also Ann Boaden, "Weighing the Stars and Hearing the Word: Conrad Bergendoff's Idea of Christian Higher Education at Augustana College and Theological Seminary," in Raymond Jarvi, editor, *Aspects of Augustana and Swedish America,* (Rock Island, 1995), p. 80.

5   Byron R. Swanson, Transcript of interviews with Conrad Bergendoff, June 23-24, Dec. 7, 1966, p. 1.

6   Karl E. Mattson, "The Theology of the Augustana Lutheran Church" in Emmer Engberg et al., editors, *Centennial Essays,* (Rock Island, 1960), p. 33.

7   Ulf Beijbom, *Swedes in Chicago,* (Växjö, Sweden, 1971), p. 245. Beijbom reported that 7% were Methodists, 2% each Baptist, Episcopal, and Mission Covenant.

8   In a 1982 essay Dag Blanck argued that Swedes did not assimilate as quickly as Bergendoff, G. Everett Arden, O. F. Ander, and others claimed they did, citing more recent scholarship including work by Nils Hasselmo, an Augustana graduate. Based on this, Blanck held that at least at Augustana College the immigrants underwent "acculturation," the adoption of some American cultural patterns, but that they were not simply "assimilated" into wider American society losing thereby their ethnic identity. Dag Blanck, "'A Language Does Not Die Easily . . .' Swedish at Augustana College, 1860-1900," SPHQ, v. 33, (Oct., 1982), pp. 288-305.

9   "Memories of a Vanishing Swedish-America," SPHQ, v. 10, (Apr., 1959), pp. 70-72.

10 Dag Blanck, *The Creation of an Ethnic Identity,* (Carbondale, Ill., 2006), pp. 26-32.

11 "Towards a History of the Augustana Synod—Three Books Reviewed," AQ, v. 11, (July, 1932), p. 263.

12 "The Dedication of Augustana Theological Seminary and the Visit of Archbishop Söderblom," LC, v. 31, (Oct. 27, 1923), pp. 682-683.

13 Dag Blanck, "On Being Swedish in America Today," in Lars Olsson and Sune Åkerman, editors, *Hembygden & Världen,* (Växjö, Sweden, 2002).

14 "On the Occasion of the Centennial of Augustana College," SPHQ, v. 11, (Apr., 1960), pp. 35-36.

15 Henry Hanson, Jr. to CB, May 3, 1949, CBP 13-3.

16 "Review of Gustav [sic] Moberg, *Invandrarna,*" MS, (n.d.), CBP 70-5.

17 "An Ancient Culture in a New Land," SPHQ, v. 27, (Apr., 1976), p. 127.

18 "Augustana—a People in Transition" in J. Iverne Dowie and Ernest M. Espelie, editors, *The Swedish Immigrant Community in Transition,* (Rock Island, 1963), pp. 199-200.

19 H. Arnold Barton, *A Folk Divided: Homeland Swedes and Swedish Americans, 1840-1940,* (Carbondale, Illinois, 1994), pp. 179-180.

20 Ibid., p. 182.

21 "Augustana—a People in Transition," p. 202.

22 H. Arnold Barton, "Conrad Bergendoff and the Swedish-American Church Language Controversy of the 1920s," SAHQ, v. 46, (July, 1995), pp. 209-211.

23 Bengt Kummel, "Nationalism över statsgränser: Rörelser som enat och splittrat," in Max Engman, editor, *När imperier faller: Studier kring riksupplösningar och nya stater,* (Stockholm,

CHAPTER 8

1994), pp. 130-141. Kummel's article reflects in part his 1994 dissertation on Lundström at Åbo Akademi in Finland.

24 "Augustana-Synoden och svenskhetens bevarande," *Allsvensk samling*, v. 11, (Apr. 15, 1924), p. 3.

25 Adolf Hult, "Sparks from the Anvil of the English Question," *Augustana Journal*, v. 13, (Feb. 15, 1905), p. 10.

26 Hult was one of five American born members of the ordination class of 1899, which had eighteen members in all.

27 "The Americanization of the Augustana Synod," LC, v. 32, (Aug. 16 and 23, 1924), pp. 522-523, 538-539.

28 "The Board of Christian Education and Our Sunday Schools," LC, v. 33, (Nov. 28, 1925), p. 761.

29 "The Americanization of the Augustana Synod."

30 Ibid., pp. 538-539.

31 Jon Gjerde, *The Minds of the West: Ethnocultural Evolution in the Rural Middle West, 1830-1917*, (Chapel Hill, 1997), p. 325.

32 "The Swedish Immigrant and the American Way," SPHQ, v. 19, (July, 1968), p. 157.

33 "On the Fortieth Anniversary of the Augustana Historical Society," SPHQ, v. 22, (Oct., 1971), pp. 209-210.

34 Carl Wittke, "Fissures in the Melting Pot," in J. Iverne Dowie and J. Thomas Tredway, editors, *The Immigration of Ideas: Studies in the North Atlantic Community*, (Rock Island, 1968), pp. 143-144.

35 Elder Lindahl, "The Troublesome Language Question," in Jarvi, p.72.

36 O. F. Ander to CB, Mar., 1949, CBP 39-18. Ander did not list as one of the distinguished visitors George Stephenson at Minnesota who, by now weary of resentment in the Augustana Synod toward his views of its history, had moved out of the field of immigration history.

37 The negotiations between Ander and Bergendoff over this collection are dealt with more fully in Thomas Tredway, *Coming of Age*, (Rock Island, 2010), pp. 168-169.

38 In his 1972 Presidential Address to the American Society of Church History, Martin Marty called for a deeper examination of the role of ethnicity in the study of American religious history. Martin E. Marty, "Ethnicity: The Skeleton of Religion in America," *Church History*, v. 41, (Mar., 1972).

39 Stephenson, *The Religious Aspects of Swedish Immigration*, (Minneapolis, 1932), p. 176.

40 "Towards a History of the Augustana Synod;" "The Cultural Heritage of the Augustana Synod," AQ, v. 14, (Oct., 1935); "Here We Stand!"

41 Eric W. Gritsch, *A History of Lutheranism*, (Minneapolis, 2002), pp. 217-22, offers a summary of Söderblom's career, particularly in the ecumenical movement.

42 Byron R. Swanson, *Conrad Bergendoff: The Making of an Ecumenist*, Th.D. dissertation, Princeton Theological Seminary, (1970), p. 321.

43 Review of Charles J. Curtis, *Nathan Söderblom: Theologian of Revelation*, in SPHQ, v. 18, (Jan., 1967), p. 50.

44 Ingmar Brohed, *Sveriges kyrkohistoria: 8. Religionsfrihetens och ekumenikens tid*, (Stockholm, 2005), p. 18.

45 Brohed's volume 8 of *Sveriges kyrkohistoria*, especially Section 1, offers a thorough survey of the issues here briefly discussed, as well as treating shifts in theology, liturgics, church

CHAPTER 8

construction, intra-church politics, non-Lutheran churches, and related matters in the period between the wars. Shorter discussions of these matters can be found in Franklin D. Scott, *Sweden: The Nation's History*, (Minneapolis, 1977).

46 Oloph Bexell, *Sveriges kyrkohistoria: 7. Folkväckelsens och kyrkoförnyelsens tid*, (Stockholm, 2003), pp. 10-13, 172-173.

47 Alf Tergel, *Från konfrontation till institution: Ungkyrkorörelsen 1912-1917*, (Uppsala, 1974), p. 85; Bengt Sundkler, *Nathan Söderblom: His Life and Work*, (Lund, 1968), p. 76.

48 Maria Södling, *Oreda i skapelsen*, (Uppsala, 2010).

49 Brohed, pp. 26-30; Björn Ryman, *Nordic Folk Churches*, (Grand Rapids, 2005), pp. 52-54.

50 "The Churches of Scandinavia," *American-Scandinavian Review*, v. 28, (Dec., 1940), pp. 295-300.

51 Nicholas Hope, *German and Scandinavian Protestantism, 1700-1918*, (Oxford, 1995), p. 584.

52 Kjell Blückert, *The Church as Nation*, (Frankfurt am Main, 2000), pp. 256, 320.

53 Mark Safstrom, *The Religious Origins of Democratic Pluralism*, Ph.D. dissertation, University of Washington, (2010), pp. 10-17.

54 Mark Safstrom, "Defining Lutheranism from the Margins: Paul Peter Waldenström on Being a 'Good Lutheran' in America," SAHQ, v. 63, (Apr.-July, 2012), p. 116.

55 Hugo Söderström, *Confession and Cooperation*, (Lund, 1973), pp. 181-182.

56 *The One Holy Catholic Apostolic Church*, (Rock Island, 1953), p. 138.

57 Brohed, p. 36; Hallén's career is covered thoroughly in Urban Claesson, *Folkhemmets kyrka: Harald Hallén och folkkyrkans genombrott*, (Uppsala, 2004).

58 One such exception may have been Augustana Seminary professor A. D. Mattson, whose pacifism and support of labor, while not making him a socialist, did cause Synod and seminary leaders, including Bergendoff, both to defend Mattson's academic freedom and at the same time to ask Mattson himself to tone down the expression of his views. Maria Erling and Mark Granquist, *The Augustana Story*, (Minneapolis, 2008), pp. 136, 142, 152, 306.

59 *Olavus Petri and the Ecclesiastical Transformation in Sweden, 1521-1552*, (New York, 1928), Foreword, p. 251.

60 Ibid., p. 44.

61 Ibid., p. 70.

62 *The Church of the Lutheran Reformation*, (St. Louis, 1967), p. xv.

63 *Olavus Petri*, p. 147.

64 Ibid., p. 91.

65 "The Churches of Scandinavia."

66 "In the Cathedral of Lund," LC, v. 35, (Feb. 12, 1927), pp. 154-155.

67 "Lutheran Ethics and Scandinavian Lutheranism," pp. 215-216.

68 "Gustavus Adolphus in Sweden," LC, v. 40, (Oct. 1, 1932), pp. 1265-1266.

69 *Church of the Lutheran Reformation*, p. 13.

70 "Church and State in the Reformation Period," *Lutheran Church Quarterly*, v. 3, (Jan., 1930), p. 54.

71 "Gustavus Adolphus in Sweden."

72 "Towards a History of the Augustana Synod," p. 263.

73 O. F. Ander to CB, Jan. 8, 1939, CBP UP 8.

74 George M. Stephenson to CB, July 18, 1955, CBP UP 12.

75 "Observations at Four Meetings," LC, v. 34, (Dec. 4, 1926), p. 1162.

76 "On a Visitation Tour," LC, v. 34, (Nov. 27, 1926), p. 1139.

CHAPTER 8

77   Einar Billing, *Our Calling*, translated with an Introduction by Conrad Bergendoff, (Rock Island, 1947), pp. 11-13.
78   "Lutheran Ethics and Scandinavian Lutheranism."
79   Hilding Pleijel, *Från fädernas fromhetsliv*, (Stockholm, 1939); *Från hustavlans tid: Kyrkohistoriska folklivsstudier*, (Stockholm, 1951); *Hustavlans värld: Kyrkligt folkliv i äldre tiders Sverige*, (Stockholm, 1970); E. E. Ryden, "Lund at Augustana: Noted Swedish Scholars Address Ministerium," LC, v. 56, (June 30, 1948), pp. 10-13.
80   That book is now in the collection of the Swenson Swedish Immigration Center, Augustana College.
81   Henry Eyster Jacobs, *A History of the Evangelical Lutheran Church in the United States*, second edition, (New York, 1899), p. 9.
82   Stephenson, *Religious Aspects of Swedish Immigration*, p. 405.
83   Quoted in Erling and Granquist, p. 104.
84   Ibid., p. 207.
85   "The Swedish Immigrant and the American Way," SPHQ, v. 19, (July, 1968), pp. 149-151.
86   "Today's Pioneers," LC, v. 44, (Sept. 19, 1936), p. 1190.
87   Ryman, p. 49.
88   CB to Robert F. Wagner, May 26, 1941, CBP 6-6; see Tredway, pp. 138-142.
89   CB to Samuel McCrae Cavert, Sept. 10, 1942, CBP 8-1.
90   Södling, p. 42.
91   Phil Zuckerman, *Society without God: What the Least Religious Nations Can Tell Us about Contentment*, (New York, 2008). Zuckerman even notes, as had Bergendoff, the cleanliness and security of Scandinavian towns. But he does not find that tidiness to be evidence of Christian piety as Bergendoff did. Scandinavian sociologists of religion have also pointed to the rising secularism of Swedish society. See, for example, Eva M. Hamberg, "Religious Change in Sweden from 1955 to 1970," *Kyrkohistorisk årsskrift*, v. 111, (2011).
92   Brohed, p. 169.
93   Svante Nordin, "Hundra år av religionsdebatt," in Jakob Christensson, editor, *Signums svenska kulturhistoria: 1900-talet*, (Stockholm, 2009), p. 145.
94   Brohed, p. 169.
95   Ingemar Hedenius, *Tro och vetande*, new edition, ([Lidingö, Sweden], 2009), pp. 41-52; Svante Nordin, *Från Hägerström till Hedenius*, (Bodafors, Sweden, 1983), pp. 178-179.
96   *Tro och vetande* in a new edition was re-issued (for the ninth time) in 2009 by the Fri Tanke förlag (Free Thought Publishers). An Introduction by Lena Andersson says that six decades after original publication, the Swedish debate about religion has been going on as though the Hedenius book had never appeared: "That is due to no weakness in the book, but to the fact that humanity is fully capable of neglecting the clear and obvious and persisting in the illusory and murky."
97   Nordin, *Från Hägerström till Hedenius*, p. 179.
98   Brohed, p. 207. The debate and its aftermath are thoroughly discussed in a lively conservative treatment: Johan Lundborg, *När ateismen erövrade Sverige*, (Nora, Sweden, 2002).
99   Ryman, p. 131.
100   Norman A. Hjelm, "Augustana and the Church of Sweden: Ties of History and Faith,"

CHAPTER 8

in Hartland H. Gifford and Arland J. Hultgren, editors, *The Heritage of Augustana,* (Minneapolis, 2004), p. 35.

101 Nordin, "Hundra år av religionsdebatt," pp. 139-153.

102 Stephenson, *Religious Aspects of Swedish Immigration,* pp. 78, 221.

103 P. O. Bersell to CB, Aug. 14, 1939, CBP 4-12.

104 Philip S. Watson, *Let God Be God! An Interpretation of the Theology of Martin Luther,* (Philadelphia, 1947), p. vii.

105 Gustaf Aulén, "Den teologiska gärningen," in Nils Karlström, editor, *Nathan Söderblom: In memoriam,* (Stockholm, 1931), p. 65.

106 Review of Elis Malmeström, *J. A. Eklund: En biografi,* in LQ, v. 3, (Feb., 1951), p. 112.

107 Walter Sillen, "Nathan Söderblom," *Journal of Religion,* v. 28, (Jan., 1948), pp. 37-50.

108 Erling and Granquist, pp. 206-207, 236-238; Arden, *Augustana Heritage,* (Rock Island, 1963), pp. 315-316.

109 Stone, pp. 14-15.

110 Tor Andræ, "Nathan Söderblom som religionshistoriker," in Karlström, p. 25.

111 Hilding Pleijel, "The Church of Sweden: An Historical Retrospect," in Robert Murray, editor, *The Church of Sweden: Past and Present,* (Malmö, Sweden, 1960), p. 28.

112 Nils Ehrenström, "Movements for International Friendship and Life and Work, 1925-1948" in Ruth Rouse and Stephen Charles Neill, editors, *A History of the Ecumenical Movement, 1517-1948,* third edition, (Geneva, 1986), p. 546.

113 Stephenson, *Religious Aspects of Swedish Immigration,* p. 240.

114 Stone, p. 17.

115 Swanson, *Conrad Bergendoff,* p. 291.

116 Materials in CBP 41-9.

117 G. Everett Arden, *The School of the Prophets,* (Rock Island, 1960), p. 221.

118 Sven-Erik Brodd, "Nathan Söderblom—religionshistoriker, ärkebiskop och internationell ekumenisk kyrkoledare," in Ingmar Brohed, *Sveriges kyrkohistoria: 8. Religionsfrihetens och ekumenikens tid,* (Stockholm, 2005), p. 374.

119 Gustaf Aulén to CB, Sept. 20, 1946, CBP 23-4.

120 CB to Erling Eidem, Oct. 9, 1937, CBP 27-8.

121 CBP 38-3.

122 K. G. Hammar, *Tecken och verklighet; Samtal om Gud; Ecce Homo-efter två tusen år,* (Lund, 2006), p. 111.

123 "They Came with the Bread of Life," LC, v. 56, (June 23, 1948), pp. 7-8.

124 "Observations of an American Educator in Europe, 1949," *Association of American Colleges Bulletin,* v. 36, (Mar., 1950).

125 *Church of the Lutheran Reformation,* p. 255.

126 "The Unique Character of the Reformation in Sweden," in A. C. Piepkorn et al., editors, *The Symposium on Seventeenth-Century Lutheranism,* v. 1, (St. Louis, 1962).

127 Quoted in Jacobs, *History of the Evangelical Lutheran Church in the United States,* pp. 413-414.

128 Review of *Kyrka och folkbildning,* in LQ, v. 2, (May, 1950), p. 280.

129 Review of Hilding Pleijel, *Från hustavlans tid,* in LQ, v. 4, (May, 1952), p. 238.

130 Review of Arvid Norberg, *Frikyrklighetens uppkomst,* in LQ, v. 5, (Nov., 1953), p. 412.

131 Review of Henry P. Van Deusen, *Dag Hammarskjöld: The Statesman and His Faith,* in SPHQ, v. 18, (July, 1967).

CHAPTER 8

132   Tage Erlander, *Dagböcker 1963-1964,* (Hedemora, Sweden, 2012), pp. 143-144.
133   "The Augustana Synod and the Augustana Seminary," AQ, v. 22, (Jan., 1943), p. 21;
      "Lutheran Ethics and Scandinavian Lutheranism." Bergendoff had high praise also for
      Finland: "the Finn is a straight, faithful, good-natured and industrious character. He
      pays his debts. His nation has a high degree of culture and a fiery spirit of liberty."
      Bergendoff also noted during the Finnish-Russian war of 1940 that Finland was the
      "world's most Lutheran (96%) country," though he made no necessary connection
      between the Finns' Lutheranism and the other qualities he mentioned, such as paying
      their debts. CBP 38-6.
134   Hope, p. 305.
135   Brohed, pp. 26-35.
136   It should be noted that a leading Swedish student of emigration to American, Sten
      Carlsson, held that whatever the degree of religious dissatisfaction among those leaving
      Sweden, it was second to the poverty caused by several bad harvests as a motive for
      emigrating. Carlsson is quoted in Söderström, p. 166. See also Hans Norman and
      Harald Runblom, editors, *From Sweden to America: A History of the Migration,*
      (Minneapolis, 1976).
137   Erling and Granquist, pp. 206-207.
138   Scott, p. 355.
139   Gunnar Westin, *Mina unga år i skola, baptistsamfund och universitet,* (Stockholm, 1967), p.
      228ff. Westin was probably also the person who arranged that Fritiof Ander should,
      in 1960, be awarded an honorary doctorate from Uppsala for his work in Swedish-
      American history. Thomas Tredway and Dag Blanck, "Interpreting One Hundred Years
      of Augustana History: Fritiof Ander, Conrad Bergendoff, and the 1960 Centennial,"
      SAHQ, v. 61, (Oct., 2010).
140   *Upsala Nya Tidning,* June 1, 1938, p. 8.
141   Materials in CBP 27-6.
142   P. O. Bersell, "The Lutheran Tercentenary," LC, v. 46, (July 28, 1938), pp. 939-943, 946.
143   "National Aspects of the Lutheran Church in America," AQ, v. 3, (June, 1924), p. 156.
144   Materials in CBP 39-18.
145   Clipping from *Stockholms-Tidningen,* Nov. 3, 1947, in CBP UP 8.
146   "On the Occasion of the Centennial of Augustana College," pp. 42-43.
147   "The Beginnings of the Swedish Pioneer Centennial," SPHQ, v. 20, (Oct., 1969),
      pp. 161-169.
148   Oscar A. Benson to CB, Jan. 17, 1948, CBP 45-6.
149   LC, v. 56, (Feb. 4, June 9, June 16, June 23, June 30, July 7, July 14, 1948).
150   E. E. Ryden, "Heroes of Faith: A Dramatic Pageant at Centennial Observance," LC,
      v. 56, (June 2, 1948), p. 15.
151   Arden, *Augustana Heritage,* pp. 340-341.
152   Material pertinent to Bergendoff's involvement in the planning of the pan-Swedish-
      American celebrations can be found in Swedish Pioneer Centennial Association
      Records at North Park University, Chicago. On the Chicago rally see especially *Pioneer
      Centennial Newsletter No. 5,* May, 1948.
153   Through 1948 E. E. Ryden, the *Companion* Editor, steadily railed against the military
      mindset which he believed controlled Washington and argued that the growing

CHAPTER 8

confrontation with the USSR could be avoided. Ryden was non-plussed when in November Truman was re-elected in one of the great political upsets in U.S. history. The Editor's conclusion was that you couldn't trust polls. Ryden's leading position among "the most isolationist of the Swedish-American editors" is detailed in Finis Herbert Capps, *From Isolationism to Involvement: The Swedish-American Press in America, 1914-1945,* (Chicago, 1966).

154   CB to K. H. Andersson, Nov. 21, 1975, CBP UP 17.
155   "An Ancient Culture in a New Land," SPHQ, v. 27, (Apr., 1976), p. 134.

CHAPTER 9

1   When Bergendoff retired, his salary was $12,000, equal to a 2012 purchasing power of $88,100; that latter figure is about one-third of the average salary in 2012 of presidents at schools the size and character of Augustana, according to the annual survey of administrative compensation made by the College and University Professional Association for Human Resources.

2   "Education in Church and State," LC, v. 56, (Sept. 22, 1948), p. 11.

3   "Conservation and Creation in Christian Higher Education," [Paper delivered to Ohio College Association], MS, (1950), CBP 69-6.

4   "Faith and Knowledge," in Jane Telleen et al., editors, *The Parkander Papers,* (Rock Island, 1988).

5   "The Augustana Synod and the Augustana Seminary," AQ, v. 22, (Jan., 1943), p. 23.

6   "The Vacant Throne: A Radio Sermon," LC, v. 45, (May 27, 1937), p. 683.

7   *Christ as Authority,* (Rock Island, 1947), pp. 111-112.

8   "Educational Relations," Lutheran World Convention Report, (1939), CBP 46-2.

9   "From College Windows," LC, v. 51, (Dec. 15, 1943), p. 1415.

10   Maria Erling and Mark Granquist, *The Augustana Story,* (Minneapolis, 2008), p. 87; Kurt W. Peterson, "A Question of Conscience: Minnesota's Norwegian American Lutherans and the Teaching of Evolution," in Philip J. Anderson and Dag Blanck, editors, *Norwegians and Swedes in the United States: Friends and Neighbors,* (St. Paul, 2012).

11   Susan Jacoby, *Freethinkers: A History of American Secularism,* (New York, 2004), esp. Chs. 8 and 9.

12   "The Augustana Synod and the Augustana Seminary," p. 23.

13   *The One Holy Catholic Apostolic Church,* (Rock Island, 1954), p. 25.

14   Report of the President, Augustana College, 1946.

15   Sydney E. Ahlstrom, *A Religious History of the American People,* (New Haven, 1972), p. 946.

16   Louis Almen, "Conrad Bergendoff and the Augustana Heritage—A College Perspective," *Augustana Heritage Newsletter,* (Oct., 1996), p. 6.

17   See Ch. 5.

18   "Educational Relations."

19   "Significant Elements in Christian Culture," AQ, v. 19, (July, 1940), p. 228.

20   "From College Windows," LC, v. 51, (June 23, 1943), p. 785.

21   "Religion and Education in America," LC, v. 55, (July 9, 1947), p. 17.

22   "A Tribute to Prof. Carl Fryxell . . . A Faithful Servant," LC, v. 54, (Sept. 11, 1941), p. 8.

23   Untitled MS, (Jan., 1951), CBP 70-1.

24   CB to J. F. Burgh, Apr. 1, 1949, CBP 13-1.

CHAPTER 9

25   "Quality Education for All," North Central Association Quarterly, v. 36, (Fall, 1961), pp. 186–192.

26   "Building a New Humanity," MS, (1952), CBP 70–4.

27   "With All the Rights and Privileges Thereto Pertaining," MS, (1961), CBP 71–6.

28   Report of the President, Augustana College and Theological Seminary, 1939.

29   Writing in the 1990s, George M. Marsden, a critic of the secular materialism that had come by mid-century to dominate American universities, to the exclusion of the free expression of religious points of view, argues, not as Buckley did regarding Yale, that the religious commitments that controlled many American universities earlier in their histories should be reestablished, but merely that traditional religious worldviews ought at least to be allowed expression in the contemporary academy. George M. Marsden, *The Soul of the American University,* (New York, 1994).

30   "The Lutheran Church in Higher Education," in Minutes of the Evangelical Lutheran Ministerium of Pennsylvania, 1948, MS, CBP 69–3.

31   "Theology, the Church and the University," LQ, v. 13, (Feb., 1961), pp. 3–5.

32   "The Lutheran College and Culture," MS, (1950), CBP 69–8.

33   "Theology, the Church and the University," p. 6.

34   "The Church in Higher Education," MS, (1958), CBP 71–3.

35   "The Break of Day," LC, v. 97, (Apr. 23, 1952), p. 11.

36   "The Seminary and the Future," LC, v. 43, (June 1, 1935), p. 686.

37   "Religion and Education in America," p. 17.

38   Richard W. Solberg, *Lutheran Higher Education in North America,* (Minneapolis, 1985), p. 350.

39   This was a position he took as late as 1990, when speaking at the retirement celebration of a member of the Augustana Religion Department, Bergendoff maintained that the college's program was a compass and Christ was the needle which pointed to the true direction from which all other points took their direction: "The needle points to Christ, in whose name the institution exists." CB UP Friendship Manor.

40   *Christ as Authority,* pp. 1–2. Bergendoff does mention and then at once dismisses the possibility that it is not necessary to follow anyone at all, i.e., that a person need not be governed by any authority whatsoever.

41   Report of a Review Visit by North Central Association, May 3–5, 1964, Faculty Minutes, 1964.

42   Thomas Tredway, *Coming of Age,* (Rock Island, 2010), pp. 270–272.

43   Dave Kenney, *Gustavus Adolphus College: 150 Years of History,* (St. Peter, Minn., 2011), p. 156.

44   Board of College Education and Church Vocations, Lutheran Church in America, *The Mission of LCA Colleges and Universities,* (New York, 1969).

45   Marsden, p. 416.

46   Tredway, pp. 264–268.

47   Solberg, pp. 341–343.

48   "Why I Became a Missionary," LC, v. 105, (Mar. 4, 1959), p. 10.

49   Tredway, pp. 266–268.

50   "Faith and Knowledge," p. 84.

51   *Observer,* Oct. 1, 1936.

52   CB to Manning Pattillo, Oct. 13, 1958, CBP 18–7.

CHAPTER 9

53   Tredway, pp. 40-43; 157-159; 263-272.
54   Quoted in Ann Boaden, "Weighing the Stars and Hearing the Word: Conrad Bergendoff's Idea of Christian Higher Education at Augustana College and Theological Seminary," in Raymond Jarvi, editor, *Aspects of Augustana and Swedish America,* (Rock Island, 1995), p. 81.
55   *Observer,* Nov. 21, 1946.
56   Report of the President, Augustana College, 1962.
57   Review of W. P. King, editor, *Behaviorism, a Battle Line,* in AQ, v. 10, (Jan., 1931), pp. 77-78.
58   Report of the President, Augustana College, 1962.
59   Review of W. P. King.
60   CB to J. F. Burgh, Apr. 1, 1949, CBP 13-1.
61   "From College Windows," LC, v. 51, (June 23, 1943), p. 785.
62   CB to Harry Getz, Mar. 29, 1952, CBP UP 10; CB to [Georg] Dellbrugge, Jan. 16, 1961, CBP 19-7.
63   CB to Ruth Parsons, Nov. 25, 1935, CBP 1-15.
64   "Against the Stream," LC, v. 7, (May 18, 1939), p. 621.
65   *Observer,* Nov. 27, 1941.
66   CB to Brother [?] Mattson, May 12, 1948, CBP 12-4.
67   Report of the President, Augustana College and Theological Seminary, 1936.
68   Board Minutes, May 11, 1949.
69   *Observer,* Mar. 15, 1954.
70   CB to Edward Hellsted, Nov. 4, 1959, CBP 19-2.
71   Report of the President, Augustana College, 1959.
72   Faculty Minutes, Apr. 8, 1961; CB to Harold Anderson, Feb. 3, 1948, CBP 12-1.
73   Report of the President, Augustana College and Theological Seminary, 1946.
74   The letters are in CBP 18-5. The maximum salary at Augustana was $7,500; Bethany, $8,500; Gustavus Adolphus, $8,700; Upsala, $8,000. Salaries of less senior faculty were scaled accordingly.
75   Tredway, p. 150.
76   "The Augustana Synod and the Augustana Seminary," p. 19; Boaden, "Weighing the Stars," pp. 79-80.
77   Boaden, "Weighing the Stars," p. 80.
78   Board Minutes, Oct. 1, 1935.
79   Report of Board of Directors Investment Committee, 1936, CBP 33-7.
80   Board Minutes, July 8, 1936, Feb. 16, 1937.
81   Tredway, Ch. 5.
82   Glen E. Brolander, *An Historical Survey of the Augustana College Campus,* revised edition, (Rock Island, 1992).
83   Report of the President, Augustana College, 1951; CB to Floyd E. Laursen, Jan. 3, 1944, CBP 8-9.
84   "A College President's Plea," LC, v. 107, (July 12, 1961), p. 12. The college did, however, take out low-interest US loans for constructing new residence halls.
85   Board Minutes, May 21, 1958.
86   Ibid., Feb. 19, 1959. There was, of course, no simple unequivocal answer that, from the college's point of view, Bergendoff might have given. If he'd said "no," it would have

CHAPTER 9

suggested a lack of initiative; if "yes," that he was to some degree giving up on the Church as a source of funds.

87   CB to Ohio Wesleyan University, Feb. 7, 1957, CBP 17-8.
88   Board Minutes, May 10, 1961.
89   This series of events is covered in Tredway, pp. 131-134.
90   Gustaf Wingren, "The Christian's Calling According to Luther," translated by Conrad Bergendoff and Eric Wahlstrom, AQ, v. 21, (Jan., 1942), pp. 13-16.
91   Tredway, Ch. 12.
92   Kenney, *Gustavus Adolphus College,* p. 85.
93   CB to H.V. Almquist, Nov. 28, 1935, CBP 1-1; June 2, 1937, CBP 2-1.
94   Faculty Minutes, May 15, 1952.
95   These matters are covered in Tredway, pp. 57-61.
96   CB to C. W. Sorensen, Apr. 4, 1962, CBP 19-11.
97   CB to Ruben Bergendoff, Dec. 31, 1953, CBP 15-8.
98   G. Everett Arden, *Augustana Heritage,* (Rock Island, 1963), pp. 328-345.
99   CB to Mrs. Raymond Haier, Jan. 25, 1962, CBP 19-7.
100   Author's personal recollection.
101   "A Treasure Trove: Expert Finds Augustana Museum a 'Gold Mine,'" LC, v. 47, (Nov. 23, 1939), p. 1487.
102   "On the Occasion of the Centennial of Augustana College," SPHQ, v. 11, (May, 1960), pp. 43-44. Swedish Americans did, of course, build other institutions, and some of these, also enduring, might have wished to share this status Bergendoff accorded to his own.
103   Ibid., p. 44.
104   Remarks acknowledging the award of the Order of the North Star, Nov. 14, 1975, CBP 73-2.
105   "Augustana in Changing Times," MS, (1962), CBP 71-7.
106   George M. Stephenson, *The Religious Aspects of Swedish Immigration,* (Minneapolis, 1932), p. 372.
107   Author's recollection.

CONCLUSION

1   Ann Boaden, "Weighing the Stars and Hearing the Word: Conrad Bergendoff's Idea of Christian Higher Education at Augustana College and Theological Seminary," in Raymond Jarvi, editor, *Aspects of Augustana and Swedish America,* (Rock Island, 1995), pp. 77-78.
2   CB to George Hall, June 11, 1995, printed in *Augustana Heritage Newsletter,* (Oct., 1996), p. 4.
3   Herbert Chilstrom to Augustana Heritage Festival of Faith, Apr. 27, 1996, copy in CBP UP Friendship.
4   CBP UP Friendship.
5   Reinhold Niebuhr, *The Irony of American History,* (New York, 1952), p. 153.
6   George M. Marsden, *The Soul of the American University,* (New York, 1994), pp. 415-416.
7   Arthur Schlesinger, Jr., "Forgetting Reinhold Niebuhr," *New York Times,* (Sept. 18, 2005).
8   Niebuhr, pp. vii-ix. Niebuhr suggests that there is, at least in the initial stages of the apparently fortuitous incongruity, a certain degree of the comic. But it is the hidden and non-fortuitous relationship in this incongruity which moves it from the comic to

CONCLUSION

the ironic, and it is that non-fortuitous quality that I think lies in the developments in Bergendoff's thought and work that are discussed here. Niebuhr moves from these general considerations to treating the irony of American foreign policy in its relationship to Communism, but that is less pertinent here.

9   Ibid., p.155.

10   Martin E. Marty, *Modern American Religion, Volume 1: The Irony of It All, 1893-1919,* (Chicago, 1986), pp. 6, 319.

11   Niebuhr, pp. 155-156.

SELECTED BIBLIOGRAPHY

BERGENDOFF PAPERS

Conrad Bergendoff deposited his professional and his personal papers in the Special Collections of the Tredway Library at Augustana College. They fall into two groups:

PROCESSED PAPERS

Eighty-one boxes or cartons of material have been processed and arranged topically by college librarians. The first box contains a list or index of the contents of each of the eighty-one boxes. Almost all of this material dates from the years of Bergendoff's professional activity, pre-1962. As indicated above, it is referred to as: CBP, box number, folder number, (e.g. CBP 16-5).

UNPROCESSED PAPERS

These seventy boxes contain personal correspondence, papers, diaries, mementos, photos, and other memorabilia. (Bergendoff even donated his personal commemorative "1860" Illinois license plates, issued in 1960, to the archives.) Some of the material pre-dates his retirement from Augustana College, but much of it is from later. It remains in the condition in which Bergendoff gave it to the library. This material includes two series of Personal Correspondence, one in eighteen numbered boxes, and a second in three boxes dated by years. It also includes material in boxes labeled "Friendship Manor," the facility where Bergendoff lived in the mid-1990s. As indicted above, this material is referred to as: CBP UP, box number (e.g. CBP UP 3), or box date (e.g. CBP UP 1921-1923), or box name (e.g. CBP UP Friendship), or in a few cases simply as CBP UP.

PUBLISHED WORKS OF CONRAD BERGENDOFF

Bergendoff is the author of all the works listed in this section of the Bibliography, save for works he translated and edited, whose original authors are indicated. Co-authors or co-editors are listed in brackets. This Bibliography lists works used in preparation of the present book.

BOOKS

Augustana—A Profession of Faith: A History of Augustana College, 1860-1935, (Rock Island, 1969).

The Augustana Ministerium: A Study of the Careers of the 2,504 Pastors of the Augustana Evangelical Lutheran Synod/Church, 1860-1962, (Rock Island, 1980).

A Bible History for Schools, Confirmation Classes and Homes, (Rock Island, 1939), [with J. Vincent Nordgren].

The Bible Study Quarterly, v. 11. *The Gospel of the Kingdom,* (Rock Island, 1930).

Christ as Authority, (Rock Island, 1947).

The Church of the Lutheran Reformation: A Historical Survey of Lutheranism, (St. Louis, 1967).

The Doctrine of the Church in American Lutheranism, (Philadelphia, 1956).

The Expanding Horizons of the Church, in the series, Theodore K. Finck et al., editors, The Christian Growth Series of Sunday School Lessons, Teacher's Guide and Study Book, Senior

II, Fourth Quarter, (Philadelphia, 1949).

A History of the Augustana Library, 1860-1990: An International Treasure, (Rock Island, 1990).

I Believe in the Church: Confessions and Convictions, (Rock Island, 1937).

The Lutheran Church in America and Theological Education, (New York, 1963).

The Making and Meaning of the Augsburg Confession, (Rock Island, 1930).

Olavus Petri and the Ecclesiastical Transformation in Sweden, 1521-1552, (New York, 1928).

The One Holy Catholic Apostolic Church, (Rock Island, 1954).

One Hundred Years of Oratorio at Augustana: A History of the Handel Oratorio Society, 1881-1980, (Rock Island, 1981).

PAMPHLETS

The Apostle's Creed Today, (Rock Island, 1956).

Atomic Warfare and the Christian Faith, Report of a Commission of the Federal Council of the Churches of Christ in America, (New York, 1946), [with other authors].

At the Lord's Table, (Rock Island, 1961).

The Basis of Confidence, (Rock Island, 1956).

The Christian Conscience and Weapons of Mass Destruction, Report of a Commission of the Federal Council of the Churches of Christ in America, (New York, 1950), [with other authors].

The Colony on the Delaware and Augustana on the Mississippi, 1638-1938, (Rock Island, 1938).

Evangelium omriket . . . Textblad för söndagsskolan, v. 26, Jan.–Mar., 1930, (Rock Island, 1930).

A Faith That Understands, (Carthage, Ill., 1950).

The Final Chapel Talk by President Conrad Bergendoff, (Rock Island, 1962).

Framstående män och kvinnor i Gamla Testamentet . . . Textblad för söndagsskolan, v. 26, July–Dec., 1930, (Rock Island, 1930).

Gertrude Bergendoff, 1897-1979: In Memoriam, (Rock Island, 1979).

John Birger Fryxell, a Tribute, (Rock Island, 1953).

Living in the Grace of Baptism, (Rock Island, n.d.).

The Lutheran Church and Millenarianism, (Rock Island, n.d.).

Lutheran Worship, (Rock Island, 1954).

One Church: I Believe in One Holy Christian Church, (Rock Island, n.d.).

Our Attitude Toward Liturgical Innovations, (Rock Island, 1946).

Perspective in American Education, Augustana College Library, Occasional Paper no. 7, (Rock Island, 1961).

The Relation of the Church to the War in the Light of the Christian Faith, Report of a Commission of the Federal Council of the Churches of Christ in America, (New York, 1944), [with other authors].

Reports of the President, Augustana College, 1936 through 1962, (Rock Island, 1936-1962).

The Spirit of Augustana, (Rock Island, 1954).

What the Lutheran Church Stands For, (Rock Island, n.d.).

Worship in the Singing Church, (Rock Island, 1958).

ARTICLES

"The Advent of the Lord," *Pulpit Digest,* v. 39, (Nov., 1958).

"After Twenty-five Years," *Lutheran World,* v. 19, (1972).

"Against the Stream," *Lutheran Companion,* v. 47, (May 18, 1939).

"Ambassadors of Peace," *Lutheran Companion,* v. 42, (June 9, 1934).

"The Americanization of the Augustana Synod," *Lutheran Companion,* v. 32, (Aug. 16 and 23, 1924).

"American Lutherans and the Doctrine of the Church," *Lutheran Outlook,* v. 8, (May, 1943).

"The American Student of 1920," *Augustana Observer,* Jan., 1920.

"Among Lutherans on the West Coast," *Lutheran Companion,* v. 41, (Sept. 9, 1933).

"An Ancient Culture in a New Land," *Swedish Pioneer Historical Quarterly,* v. 27, (Apr., 1976).

"Andreen of Augustana," *Augustana College Bulletin,* (Sept., 1940).

"Annual Meeting of the Augustana Foreign Missionary Society," *Lutheran Companion,* v. 28, (Feb. 14, 1920).

"An Appraisal of Lutheran Theological Education," *Lutheran Church Quarterly,* v. 19, (Oct., 1946).

"An Appreciation," in *Samlade Dikter av Mauritz Stolpe,* (Rock Island, 1940).

"Are Our Universities Big Enough?" *The Christian Scholar,* v. 37, (Mar., 1954).

"Article XXI, Augsburg Confession," *Lutheran Companion,* v. 38, (Nov. 8, 1930).

"Augustana, an Approaching Centennial," *American Scandinavian Review,* v. 32, (Dec., 1944).

"Augustana and Her Foreign Mission Society," *Augustana Foreign Mission Society,* (Rock Island, Nov., 1920).

"Augustana and Her Relatives," *Concordia Historical Institute Quarterly,* v. 57, (Winter, 1984).

"Augustana—A People in Transition," in J. Iverne Dowie and Ernest M. Espelie, editors, *The Swedish Immigrant Community in Transition: Essays in Honor of Dr. Conrad Bergendoff,* (Rock Island, 1963).

"Augustana—A People's Aspiration," *The Cresset,* v. 39, (Feb., 1976).

"Augustana: A Profession of Faith," *Augustana College Bulletin,* (Fall, 1969).

"Augustana College," in Julius Bodensieck, editor, *The Encyclopedia of the Lutheran Church,* v. 2, (Minneapolis, 1965).

"An Augustana Conference on Faith and Service," *Augustana Foreign Mission Society,* (Rock Island, Nov., 1920).

"The Augustana Foreign Missionary Society," in *The Missionary Calendar of the Augustana Foreign Missionary Society,* v. 1, (Rock Island, 1921).

"The Augustana Four-Year Plan of Theological Education," *Christian Education,* v. 19, (Dec., 1935).

"Augustana in America and Sweden," *Swedish Pioneer Historical Quarterly,* v. 24, (Oct., 1973).

"Augustana in Changing Times," in *Augustana Swedish Institute Yearbook,* (Rock Island, 1962).

"Augustana in the Merged Church: How Will the College Be Affected?" *Augustana College Bulletin,* (Mar., 1962).

"The Augustana Pastor: Saga of a Thousand Immigrants from Sweden," *Swedish Pioneer Historical Quarterly,* v. 31, (Jan., 1980).

"Augustana's Idea of the Church," *Augustana Seminary Review,* v. 7, (June, 1955).

"The Augustana Synod and the Augustana Seminary," *Augustana Quarterly,* v. 22, (Jan., 1943).

"Augustana-Synoden och svenskhetens bevarande," *Allsvensk Samling,* v. 11, (Apr. 15, 1924).

"Augustana Theological Seminary," *Lutheran Companion,* v. 39, (Oct. 10, 1931).

"Aulén, Gustav Emmanuel Hildebrand," in Vergilius Ferm, editor, *An Encyclopedia of Religion,* (New York, 1945).

"The Basis of Confidence," *Augustana College Bulletin,* (June, 1956).

"A Beautiful Centennial Gift," *Lutheran Companion,* v. 106, (Oct. 26, 1960).

"The Beginnings of the Swedish Immigration into Illinois 100 Years Ago," *American Swedish Monthly,* v. 42, (June, 1948).

"The Beginnings of the Swedish Pioneer Centennial," *Swedish Pioneer Historical Quarterly,* v. 20, (Oct., 1969).

"Beyond Skepticism," *Augustana College Magazine,* (July, 1981).

"Beyond the Horizon," *Augustana College Bulletin,* (Summer, 1963).

"The Board of Christian Education and Our Sunday Schools," *Lutheran Companion,* v. 33, (Nov. 28, 1925).

"Body and Spirit in Christian Thought," *Lutheran Quarterly,* v. 6, (Aug., 1954).

"The Book of Isaiah," *Daily Devotions for Lutheran Youth,* (Rock Island, 1929).

"Bread for the Hungry," *Augustana Observer,* Jan., 1915.

"The Break of Day," *Lutheran Companion,* v. 97, (Apr. 23, 1952).

"Building on the Good Foundation," in C. G. Anderson et al., editors, *Faith in Action: The Building of the Church,* v. 2, (Minneapolis, 1938).

"Canossa," *Lutheran Church Quarterly,* v. 5, (July, 1932).

"Can We Understand Russia?" *Contemporary Club Papers,* v. 65, (Feb., 1961).

"Can Worship Be Ecumenical," *Christendom,* v. 13, (Spring, 1948).

"Catholic-Protestant Relations in America: The Contemporary Situation as a Protestant Sees It," *Social Action,* v. 14, (Jan. 15, 1948).

"A Centennial of Swedish Pioneers," *American-Scandinavian Review,* v. 34, (June, 1946).

"Centennial Planning Progress: 100ᵗʰ Year to Be Commemorated in 1959-60," *Augustana College Bulletin,* (Dec., 1958).

"A Century of Augustana History," *Kyrkohistorisk årsskrift,* v. 59, (1959).

"A Century of College and Community Cooperation," *Augustana College Bulletin,* (Jan., 1975).

"A Century of Science at Augustana," *Augustana College Bulletin,* (Apr., 1979).

"A Century-Old Monument: Augustana College's Old Main," *Swedish-American Historical Quarterly,* v. 35, (July, 1984).

"The Challenge of Vatican II," *Valparaiso University Bulletin,* v. 41, (Sept. 22, 1967).

"Changing Times-an Abiding Goal," *Augustana College Bulletin,* (Apr., 1944).

"Charles Michael Jacobs," *My Church,* v. 24, (1938).

"Christian Baptism," *The Salem Messenger,* v. 38, (Apr., 1925).

"The Christian Conscience and Nuclear Warfare," *The National Lutheran,* v. 30, (Oct., 1962).

"Christian Convention of Augustana Young People," *Lutheran Companion,* v. 28, (Nov. 13, 1920).

"Christian Faith and Higher Education," in *Papers and Proceedings,* 49ᵗʰ Annual Convention, National Lutheran Educational Conference, Atlantic City, N. J., (Jan. 12-14, 1963).

"Christianity and Christian Science," *The Lutheran Church Review,* v. 41, (Jan., 1922).

"Christian Love and Public Policy in Luther," *Lutheran Quarterly,* v. 13, (Aug., 1961).

"Christian Personality and Christian Education," in John Paul von Grueningen, editor, *Toward a Christian Philosophy of Higher Education,* (Philadelphia, 1957).

"Christian Science—and Christ," *Lutheran Companion,* v. 29, (May 28, 1921).

"Church," in Julius Bodensieck, editor, *The Encyclopedia of the Lutheran Church,* v. 1, (Minneapolis, 1965).

"The Church and Higher Education," *Lutheran Companion,* v. 55, (Apr. 2, 1947).

"The Church and Scouting," *Lutheran Companion,* v. 52, (Feb. 9, 1944).

"Church and State," in *Program Helps,* (Rock Island, 1953).

"Church and State in the Reformation Period," *Lutheran Quarterly,* v. 3, (Jan., 1930).

"The Church and the Gospel," *Augustana Quarterly,* v. 11, (Jan., 1932).

"The Church College and American Ideals," *Lutheran Companion,* v. 100-101, (June 29, 1955).

"The Churches of Scandinavia," *American-Scandinavian Review,* v. 28, (Dec., 1940).

"The Church in the World," in *Proceedings and Papers,* 27ᵗʰ Annual Convention, National Lutheran Educational Conference, Philadelphia, (Jan. 7-9, 1940).

"The Church-the Abiding Monument," *Lutheran Companion,* v. 46, (July 28, 1938).

"The Church-the Abiding Monument of the Delaware Settlements," *Journal of the American Lutheran Conference,* v. 3, (Aug., 1938).

"Civilization, Twilight or Dawn?" *Contemporary Club Papers,* v. 52, (1947-1948).

"C. L. E. Esbjörn-An Appreciation," *My Church,* v. 25, (1939).

"A College President's Plea," *Lutheran Companion,* v. 107, (July 12, 1961).

"A Colony of Heaven," *Lutheran Companion,* v. 43, (June 22, 1935).

"Comments on Brunner's Essay," *Lutheran World,* v. 7, (Dec., 1960).

"The Communion of Saints—A Lutheran Viewpoint," *Augustana Quarterly,* v. 16, (Jan., 1937).

"Conservation and Creation in Christian Higher Education," in *Transactions,* 79th Annual Meeting of the Ohio College Association, Columbus, (Apr. 21-22, 1950).

"Contending for Peace," *American Pulpit Series,* Book 13, (New York, 1946).

"Council Report to Synod," *Lutheran Companion,* v. 33, (July 4 and 11, 1925).

"Creating Resources for This Time," *Association of American Colleges Bulletin,* v. 37, (Mar., 1951).

"A Critic of the Fourteenth Century: St. Birgitta of Sweden," in James L. Cate and Eugene N. Anderson, editors, *Medieval and Historical Essays in Honor of James Westfall Thompson,* (Chicago, 1938).

"The Cultural Heritage of the Augustana Synod," *Augustana Quarterly,* v. 14, (Oct., 1935).

"The Dedication of Augustana Theological Seminary and the Visit of Archbishop Söderblom," *Lutheran Companion,* v. 31, (Oct. 27, 1923).

"Delivered from Sleep and Damnation," *Lutheran Women,* v. 6, (Mar., 1968).

"The Divine Calling of the Layman," *Lutheran Companion,* v. 46, (Nov. 10, 1938).

"The Divine Impulse in Preaching," *Augustana Quarterly,* v. 25, (Oct., 1946).

"A Divorce in 1948? Let Us Keep Augustana College AND Theological Seminary," *Lutheran Companion,* v. 54, (Apr. 3, 1946).

"Dr. Bergendoff's Welcome to Synod," *Lutheran Companion,* v. 48, (June 20, 1940).

"Dr. Youngert...An Appreciation," *Lutheran Companion,* v. 47, (Mar. 9, 1939).

"Early Moves Toward Union," *Lutheran Companion,* v. 103, (Feb. 27, 1957).

"Ecumenical Experiences," in Emmer Engberg et al., editors, *Centennial Essays: Augustana Lutheran Church, 1860-1960,* (Rock Island, 1960).

"The Ecumenical Movement in the Churches," *Contemporary Club Papers,* v. 68, (Mar. 22, 1965).

"The Ecumenical Paradox- 'Our Oneness in Christ, Our Disunity as Churches,'" *Lutheran Companion,* v. 99, (Aug. 4, 1954).

"The Educational Implications of Christian Faith," in *Creative Tensions: Papers Presented at the Proceedings of the 50th Annual Meeting of the National Lutheran Educational Conference,* (Washington, D.C., 1964).

"Educational Relations," in Lutheran World Convention Report, (1939).

"Education for Church and State," *Lutheran Companion,* v. 56, (Sept. 22, 1948).

"The Education Which Gives True Freedom," *Christian Education,* v. 23, (Apr., 1940).

"Effective Preaching," *American Lutheran,* v. 23, (May, 1940).

"Elements in Christian Culture," *Lutheran Companion,* v. 47, (Oct. 26 and Nov. 2, 1939).

"Erziehung und Weltanschauung," in *Theologische Literaturzeitung,* nr. 11, (1953).

"The Ethical Thought of Einar Billing," in Philip J. Hefner, editor, *The Scope of Grace: Essays on Nature and Grace in Honor of Joseph Sittler,* (Philadelphia, 1964).

"Faith and Knowledge," in Jane Telleen et al., editors, *The Parkander Papers: A Festschrift Honoring Dr. Dorothy Parkander,* (Rock Island, 1988).

"A Faith for These Times," in S. J. Sebelius, editor, *A Faith for These Times: Lutheran Sermons for Our Day,* (Rock Island, 1942).

"A Faithful Servant: a Tribute to Prof. Carl Fryxell," *Lutheran Companion,* v. 54, (Sept. 11, 1946).

"The Faith of Augustana," *Lutheran Companion,* v. 44, (Oct. 10, 1936).

"Federal Council Observes 40th Birthday," *Lutheran Companion,* v. 56, (Dec. 29, 1948).

"A Festive Day at Augustana: Cornerstone of Andreen Hall Is Laid," *Lutheran Companion,* v. 45, (June 3, 1937).

"Foreword," *Lutheran Quarterly,* v. 1, (Feb., 1949).

"The Founders of Augustana," *Augustana College Bulletin,* (Sept., 1969).

"The Four Hundredth Anniversary of the Presentation of the Augsburg Confession, June 25 1930," *Lutheran Companion,* v. 38, (June 14, 1930).

"A Free Church in a Free Nation," *Augustana Quarterly,* v. 25, (Jan., 1946).

"Friends of Youth," *Lutheran Companion,* v. 50, (Sept. 10, 1942).

"From College Windows," [weekly columns], *Lutheran Companion,* v. 51, (Mar. 31-Dec. 15, 1943).

"From Generation to Generation," in Roger Carlson, editor, *Century +[plus]: Salem Lutheran Church, Chicago, Illinois,* (Chicago, 1968).

"From the Connecticut to the Mississippi," *Augustana Observer,* Dec., 1912.

"The Frontispiece in Our Catechism," *Church School Teacher,* v. 2, (Nov. 19, 1933).

"Future Goals for Augustana: The Church College in a Post-War World," *Lutheran Companion,* v. 51, (Oct. 13, 1943).

"The Future of Luther in Lutheranism," *Lutheran Forum,* v. 1, (July, 1967).

"Give Until You're Happy," *Lutheran Companion,* v. 41, (Feb. 11, 1933).

"The Glory of the Risen Christ," *The Pulpit,* v. 24, (Aug., 1953).

"A Goodly Heritage," *Lutheran Forum,* v. 22, (Pentecost, 1988).

"The Gospel of Life," in Alton M. Motter, editor, *Preaching the Resurrection,* (Philadelphia, 1959).

"A Grave in Africa," *Lutheran Companion,* v. 49, (Mar. 13, 1941).

"Greetings from Our College Presidents," *Lutheran Companion,* v. 50, (Apr. 30, 1942).

"Guardians of the Past or Pioneers of the Future," in *Creative Tensions: Papers Presented at the Proceedings of the 50th Annual Meeting of the National Lutheran Educational Conference,* (Washington, D.C., 1964).

"Gustav Andreen som skolman," *Korsbaneret. Kristlig kalender för året 1941,* (Rock Island, 1941).

"Gustavus Adolphus in Sweden," *Lutheran Companion,* v. 40, (Oct. 1, 1932).

"Henry Melchior Muhlenberg," *Lutheran Companion,* v. 50, (July 16, 1942).

"Here We Stand!" *Lutheran Companion,* v. 47, (Mar. 30, 1939).

"The Holy Christian Church," *Lutheran Companion,* v. 44, (Feb. 22, 1936).

"The Hope of Missions," *Missions-Tidning,* v. 15, (Apr., 1921).

"How Great Our Love for Augustana?" *Lutheran Companion,* v. 46, (Dec. 8, 1938).

"How New is the New Liturgy?" *Lutheran Companion,* v. 104, (Apr. 23 and 30, May 7, 1958).

"How Real Is Christmas?" *American Swedish Monthly,* v. 53, (Dec., 1959).

"How Strong Is the Augustana Synod?" *Lutheran Companion,* v. 51, (Jan. 20, 1943).

"How the Augustana Church Came to Be," in Birger Swenson and E. E. Ryden, editors, *Augustana Annual, 1960,* (Rock Island, 1960).

"Humanity and the Humanities," *Christian Century,* v. 60, (July 7, 1943).

"Illinois Conference Luther League," *Lutheran Companion,* v. 30, (Feb. 25, 1922).

"Impressions from the 'Merger Meeting' in New York City, Nov. 12-18, 1918," *Lutheran Companion,* v. 26, (Dec. 7, 1918).

"In Defense of Luther," *Christian Century,* v. 59, (Feb. 4, 1942).

"In Defense of What?" [editorial], *Times-Democrat,* Davenport, Iowa, (Sept. 27, 1958).

"The Individual Christian's Call to Personal Evangelism," *Augustana Quarterly,* v. 5, (Mar., 1926).

"Inga minnen äro mig kärare än dem jag bevarar från aftonandakten," in Sven Thulin, editor, *Hågkomster och livsintryck: Till minnet av Nathan Söderblom,* (Uppsala, 1934).

"In Memory of Dr. C. G. Carlfelt," *Swedish Pioneer Historical Quarterly,* v. 5, (Oct., 1954).

"The Inner Development of the Augustana Synod," in Abdel Ross Wentz, *The Lutheran Church in American History,* (Philadelphia, 1923).

"An Inquiry into Foreign Missions," *Lutheran Companion,* v. 41, (Mar. 18, 1933).

"In Search of Self," *Swedish Pioneer Historical Quarterly,* v. 30, (Apr., 1979).

"Intercommunion: A Symposium on the Report of the American Section of the Faith and Order Commission on Intercommunion," *Christendom,* v. 7, (Autumn, 1942).

"Intercommunion in the Church of Sweden and the Church of England," *Augustana Quarterly,* v. 15, (Apr., 1936).

"An International Prayer Meeting," *Christian Century,* v. 59, (Mar. 11, 1942).

"In the American Tradition," in O. F. Ander, editor, *The John H. Hauberg Historical Essays,* (Rock Island, 1954).

"In the Cathedral of Lund," *Lutheran Companion*, v. 35, (Feb. 12, 1927).

"Justification and Sanctification: Liturgy and Ethics," in Paul C. Empie and James I. McCord, editors, *Marburg Revisited*, (Minneapolis, 1966).

"The Kind of World This Has Become," *Christian Century*, v. 66, (July 13, 1949).

"The Largeness of Life," *Lutheran Companion*, v. 29, (Oct. 22, 1921).

"Lent," *Budbäraren*, v. 35, (Mar., 1922).

"A Letter to the Missouri Synod from One of Its Admirers," *The Seminarian*, Concordia Theological Seminary, v. 52, (Apr., 1961).

"Life's High Calling," *Lutheran Companion*, v. 39, (Mar. 7, 1931).

"The Liturgical Tradition of the Swedish Church," *Lutheran Church Quarterly*, v. 21, (July, 1948).

"Living on an Inheritance," in Phil Schroeder, editor, *Seven Sermons from the 125th Anniversary Year of Augustana College, Rock Island, Ill.*, (Rock Island, 1986).

"Looking Ahead from 1960," *Lutheran Companion*, v. 106, (June 29, 1960).

"The Lutheran Christian in Church and State," *Lutheran Quarterly*, v. 1, (Nov., 1949).

"The Lutheran Church and Her Sunday School," *Lutheran Companion*, v. 28, (Nov. 27, Dec. 11 and 18, 1920).

"The Lutheran Church and the Modern State," *Augustana Quarterly*, v. 21, (Oct., 1942).

"Lutheran Church in America," in *American-Swedish Handbook*, v. 7, (Rock Island, 1965).

"The Lutheran Church in Higher Education," in *Minutes and Proceedings of the Evangelical Lutheran Ministerium of Pennsylvania and the Adjacent States*, (Philadelphia, 1948).

"The Lutheran College and Culture," *Journal of the Association of Lutheran College Faculties*, v. 2, (Dec., 1949).

"Luther and Lutheranism Today," *The Catholic World*, v. 206, (Nov., 1967).

"Lutheran Ethics and Scandinavian Lutheranism," *Augustana Quarterly*, v. 20, (July, 1941).

"Lutheran Higher Education and Government," *Lutheran Outlook*, v. 9, (Feb., 1944).

"Lutheranism," in Marvin Halverson and Arthur Cohen, editors, *A Handbook of Christian Theology*, (Cleveland, 1958).

"Lutheranism Comes to America," *Lutheran Companion*, v. 103, (Feb. 20, 1957).

"Lutheran Missions from Luther to Francke," in William K. Anderson, editor, *Christian World Mission*, (Nashville, 1946).

"A Lutheran Study of Church Unity," in *Essays on the Lutheran Confessions Basic to Lutheran Cooperation*, (New York, 1961).

"Lutheran Theology Today," *The National Lutheran*, v. 16, (Fall, 1947).

"Lutheran Unity," in E. C. Fendt, editor, *What Lutherans Are Thinking: A Symposium on Lutheran Faith and Life*, (Columbus, Ohio, 1947).

"The Lutheran View of the Lord's Supper," *Lutheran Quarterly*, v. 4, (Aug., 1952).

"Lutheran Worship," *Budbäraren,* v. 35, (July, 1922).

"Luther's View of the Church," *Lutheran Companion,* v. 103, (Feb. 13, 1957).

"Man," *The Seminarian,* Concordia Theological Seminary, v. 41, (Mar. 8, 1950).

"Mauritz Stolpe-In Memoriam," *Lutheran Companion,* v. 46, (Sept. 22, 1938).

"The Meandering of an Historian," *Concordia Historical Institute Quarterly,* v. 55, (Winter, 1982).

"The Meaning of Lutheran Unity," *Lutheran Companion,* v. 97, (Nov. 5, 1952).

"Memories and Memorials," *Lutheran Companion,* v. 49, (Oct. 9, 1941).

"Memories and Visions," *Augustana Observer,* Apr., 1920.

"Memories of Archbishop Nathan Söderblom," *My Church,* v. 17, (Rock Island, 1931).

"Memories of a Vanishing Swedish-America," *Swedish Pioneer Historical Quarterly,* v. 10, (Apr., 1959).

"The Mind of the Church Today," *Lutheran Quarterly,* v. 1, (May, 1949).

"A Mind That Is in Christ," *Augustana College Bulletin,* (Dec., 1951).

"The Modern Imagination and Imago Dei," *Lutheran Quarterly,* v. 10, (May, 1958).

"Nathan Söderblom, Archbishop and Evangelical Catholic," *Una Sancta,* v. 22, (Trinity, 1965).

"National Aspects of the Lutheran Church in America," *Augustana Quarterly,* v. 3, (June, 1924).

"The Nature and Purpose of the Religious Conference of Young People at Augustana," *Lutheran Companion,* v. 29, (Jan. 8, 1921).

"The New Liturgy: Uniting in Worship," *Augustana Lutheran [Lutheran Companion],* v. 95, (Apr. 19, 1950).

"New Year's Thoughts at Augustana," *Lutheran Companion,* v. 44, (Jan. 4, 1936).

"No Male and Female: Biblical Basis for Women's Work in Church," *Lutheran Companion,* v. 97, (Oct. 15, 1952).

"No Other Image," *Lutheran Companion,* v. 97, (July 9, 1952).

"No Royal Road," *Augustana College Bulletin,* (Summer, 1968).

"Observations at Four Meetings," *Lutheran Companion,* v. 34, (Dec. 4, 1960).

"Observations of an American Educator in Europe, 1949," *Association of American Colleges Bulletin,* v. 36, (Mar., 1950).

"Of What Are We Afraid?" *Augustana College Bulletin,* (Sept., 1959).

"Old Main," *Augustana College Bulletin,* (Dec., 1950).

"On a Visitation Tour," *Lutheran Companion,* v. 34, (Nov. 27, 1926).

"On the Fortieth Anniversary of the Augustana Historical Society," *Swedish Pioneer Historical Quarterly,* v. 22, (Oct., 1971).

"On the Occasion of the Centennial of Augustana College," *Swedish Pioneer Historical Quarterly,* v. 11, (Apr., 1960).

"On the Thirty-fourth Anniversary of the Augustana Foreign Mission Society," *Lutheran Companion,* v. 28, (May 1, 1920).

"Our Children Will Bear Witness," *The Lutheran*, v. 42, (Apr. 27, 1960).

"Our Literary Societies," *Augustana Observer*, May, 1914.

"Our Lofty Destiny," *Lutheran Companion*, v. 54, (July 3, 1946).

"Our Oneness in Christ and Our Disunity as Churches," in Vilmos Vajta, editor, *The Unity of the Church: A Symposium*, (Rock Island, 1957).

"Our Theological Seminary," *Lutheran Companion*, v. 55, (June 4, 1947).

"Our Youth for Christ," in Evald Lawson, editor, *The Master and Augustana Youth*, (Rock Island, 1926).

"Oxford and Edinburgh, 1937," *Augustana Quarterly*, v. 17, (Jan., 1938).

"The Oxford Conference," *Lutheran Companion*, v. 45, (Aug. 26, 1937).

"Past and Present," *Augustana Observer*, Sept., 1920.

"Pastor J. F. Seedoff: An Appreciation," *Lutheran Companion*, v. 47, (Sept., 1939).

"A Pastor's Core Library," *Lutheran Quarterly*, v. 1, (Nov., 1949).

"Peace and the Christian Citizen," in Philip J. Anderson, editor, *Amicus Dei: Essays on Faith and Friendship*, (Chicago, 1988).

"Peace on Earth and Good Will among Churches," *Christendom*, v. 10, (Summer, 1945).

"The Personal Approach in Soul-Winning," *Augustana Quarterly*, v. 9, (Apr., 1930).

"The Poverty of Our Age," *Lutheran Companion*, v. 29, (Aug. 13, 1921).

"The Power to Bear," *Lutheran Companion*, v. 45, (Feb. 11, 1937).

"A Prayer," [at the funeral of G. A. Brandelle], *Lutheran Companion*, v. 44, (Feb. 1, 1936).

"Praying for Peace," *Lutheran Companion*, v. 56, (Sept. 1, 1948).

"Preaching and Human Life," *Augustana Quarterly*, v. 26, (Jan., 1947).

"Preparing for Peace," *Lutheran Outlook*, v. 10, (June, 1945).

"President's Report of the Synodical Luther League Council," *Lutheran Companion*, v. 36, (Mar. 3, 1928).

"Public Sentiment," *Augustana Observer*, Mar., 1914.

"Publishing Achievements Mark Society's 50 Years of Service," *Swedish Council News*, v. 5, (Winter, 1979).

"Quality Education for All," *North Central Association Quarterly*, v. 36, (Fall, 1961).

"The Relationship between Evangelism and Education in the Mission of the Church," in R. Pierce Beaver, editor, *Christianity and African Education*, (Grand Rapids, Mich., 1966).

"The Relationship between the American Lutheran Conference and the United Lutheran Church in America," *Augustana Quarterly*, v. 16, (Oct., 1937).

"Religion and Culture," in John G. Kunstmann, editor, *The Church and Modern Culture*, (Valparaiso, Ind., 1953).

"Religion and Education in America," *Lutheran Companion*, v. 55, (July 9, 1947).

"The Removal and Reconstruction of Salem," in H. C. Nelson, editor, *A Historical Record of Salem Lutheran Church,* (Chicago, 1943).

"The Responsibility of the Church in the World's Social Improvement," *Lutheran Church Quarterly,* v. 17, (Oct., 1944).

"Retrospect and Prospect," *Lutheran Quarterly,* v. 26, (Nov., 1974).

"The Revelation and the Ministry of Grace," in Yngve Brilioth, editor, *World Lutheranism of Today: A Tribute to Anders Nygren, 15 November 1950,* (Stockholm, 1950).

"A Revision of the Communion Service," *Augustana Quarterly,* v. 18, (Jan., 1939).

"The Rock Foundation," *Journal of Theology of the American Lutheran Conference,* v. 6, (May, 1941).

"The Role of Augustana in the Transplanting of a Culture across the Atlantic," in J. Iverne Dowie and J. Thomas Tredway, editors, *The Immigration of Ideas: Studies in the North Atlantic Community,* (Rock Island, 1968).

"The Role of the University," *Campus Lutheran,* v. 5, (Jan., 1954).

"Salutatory," *Augustana Observer,* May, 1915.

"A Sane View of Ourselves," *Lutheran Companion,* v. 52, (June 21, 1944).

"The Schism between the Churches of the East and the West," *Lutheran Church Review,* v. 42, (Oct., 1923).

"The Secular Idea of Progress and the Christian Doctrine of Sanctification," *Augustana Quarterly,* v. 12, (Jan., 1933).

"The Seminary and the Future," *Lutheran Companion,* v. 43, (June 1, 1935).

"The Sender and the Sent," *World Encounter,* v. 5, (July, 1968).

"The Sermon in the Lutheran Liturgy," in *The Unity of the Church,* Department of Theology, Lutheran World Federation, (Rock Island, 1957).

"A Shipment of Swedish Books," *Augustana Quarterly,* v. 24, (Oct., 1945).

"The Significance of the Augsburg Confession for Our Day," *Augustana Quarterly,* v. 9, (Apr., 1930).

"The Significance of the Lutheran Reformation of the Sixteenth Century for the Church of the Twentieth," *Augustana Quarterly,* v. 8, (Apr., 1929).

"Significant Elements in Christian Culture," *Augustana Quarterly,* v. 19, (July, 1940).

"Singing the Lord's Song in a New Land," *Lutheran Forum,* v. 15, (Reformation, 1981).

"The Social Philosophy of Jonathan Edwards," *Augustana Quarterly,* v. 7, (Dec., 1928).

"Söderblom, Lars Olof Jonathan," in Vergilius Ferm, editor, *Encyclopedia of Religion,* (New York, 1945).

"Some Observations on the Constitution of the Lutheran World Federation," *Lutheran World,* v. 11, (Apr., 1964).

"Some Values of Athletics," *Augustana Observer,* Feb., 1920.

"Some 'Why's' About Our Church," *Lutheran Companion,* v. 50, (Apr. 2, 1942).

"The Soul of a Church School," *Augustana College Bulletin*, (Jan., 1932).

"The Source of Authority," *Lutheran Companion*, v. 108, (Aug. 15, 1962).

"The Sources of the Original Constitution of the Augustana Synod, 1860," in O. F. Ander, editor, *Augustana Historical Society Publications*, v. 5, (Rock Island, 1935).

"The Sphere of Revelation," *Lutheran World Review*, v. 1, (Oct., 1948).

"The Spirit of God and the Corporate Guidance of the Church," *Christendom*, v. 10, (Winter, 1945).

"Spiritual Growth," *Lutheran Companion*, v. 30, (Mar. 18, 1922).

"'The Story of Christian Hymnody,' An Appreciation," *Lutheran Companion*, v. 105, (July 29, 1959).

"A Sunday-School Program," *Lutheran Companion*, v. 27, (Feb. 15, 1919).

"Sven Gustav Youngert," *Lutheran Companion*, v. 47, (Mar. 9, 1939).

"The Swedish Church on the Delaware," *Church History*, v. 7, (Sept., 1938).

"A Swedish Contribution to American Education," *Association of American Colleges Bulletin*, v. 27, (Oct., 1941).

"The Swedish Element in America," *Illinois Journal of Education*, (Apr., 1970).

"The Swedish Immigrant and the American Way," *Swedish Pioneer Historical Quarterly*, v. 19, (July, 1968).

"A Swedish University Tradition in America," *Swedish-American Historical Quarterly*, v. 44, (Jan., 1993).

"Symbolism in the New Salem," in *Salem* [book for the dedication of the new church building], (Chicago, 1926).

"The Synodical Luther League Council," *Lutheran Companion*, v. 33, (Jan. 31, 1925).

"Temple Talks," *Lutheran Companion*, v. 41, (Sept. 23–Dec. 30, 1933), v. 42, (Jan. 6–Nov. 10, 1934).

"$10,000 for Salem," *Budbäraren*, v. 35, (Feb., 1922).

"Tenure at Augustana College," *Bulletin of the American Association of University Professors*, v. 24, (May, 1938).

"That Ye Love One Another," *Augustana Lutheran [Lutheran Companion]*, v. 96, (Apr. 11, 1951).

"Their Faith They Brought with Them from the Old World to the New," in John R. Nyberg, editor, *This Is My Church*, (Rock Island, 1960).

"Theological Education," [Part 6, Religious Resources and Obligations of the Church-Related College: A Symposium], *Christian Education*, v. 22, (Feb., 1939).

"Theological Education and American Lutheranism," in *Johann Michael Reu: A Book of Remembrance, Kirchliche Zeitschrift*, (Columbus, Ohio, 1945).

"Theology and Our Times," *Augustana Quarterly*, v. 12, (Oct., 1933).

"Theology, the Church and the University," *Lutheran Quarterly*, v. 13, (Feb., 1961).

"They Came with the Bread of Life," *Lutheran Companion*, v. 56, (June 23, 1948).

"Things, Tools and Thoughts," *Augustana College Bulletin*, (July, 1965).

"This Matter of Centralization," *Lutheran Companion*, v. 48, (Feb. 8, 1940).

"Three R's for Today," *Augustana Lutheran [Lutheran Companion]*, v. 96, (Oct. 3, 1951).

"The Throne and the Faculties," *The Seminary Review*, Lutheran School of Theology, Rock Island Campus, v. 18, (Second Quarter, 1966).

"Today's Pioneers," *Lutheran Companion*, v. 44, (Sept. 19, 1936).

"Today's World and Today's Church," *Journal of Theology of the American Lutheran Conference*, v. 6, (Jan., 1941).

"Tongues of Them That Are Taught," *Lutheran Companion*, v. 50, (Apr. 30, 1942).

"To the Members of Salem, Oct. 22, 1922," *Budbäraren*, v. 35, (Nov., 1922).

"Towards a History of the Augustana Synod--Three Books Reviewed," *Augustana Quarterly*, v. 11, (July, 1932).

"A Treasure Trove: Expert Finds Augustana Museum a 'Gold Mine,'" *Lutheran Companion*, v. 47, (Nov. 23, 1939).

"Tree Planting," *Budbäraren*, v. 36, (Nov., 1923).

"A Tribute," [to Dr. Adolf Hult], *Lutheran Companion*, v. 51, (Mar. 24, 1943).

"A Tribute to Dr. Christenson," *Lutheran Companion*, v. 56, (Oct. 13, 1948).

"True Freedom," *Lutheran Companion*, v. 47, (June 22, 1939).

"A True Israelite: A Tribute to the Memory of Dr. I. M. Anderson," *Lutheran Companion*, v. 97, (Feb. 6, 1952).

"The True Unity of the Church," *Lutheran Church Quarterly*, v. 12, (July, 1939).

"Two Stations Beyond," *Lutheran Companion*, v. 99, (June 30, 1954).

"Two World Conventions," *Lutheran Companion*, v. 45, (Aug. 5, 1937).

"The Under-Developed Areas of the Human Mind," in *The Small College Annual*, (1955).

"An Underground Service: A Glimpse of Postwar Misery Among German Refugees," *Lutheran Companion*, v. 57, (June 15, 1949).

"The Unique Character of the Reformation in Sweden," in A. C. Piepkorn et al., editors, *The Symposium on Seventeenth Century Lutheranism*, v. 1, (St. Louis, 1962).

"The Uniting Word," in Alton M. Motter, editor, *Preaching on Pentecost and Christian Unity*, (Philadelphia, 1965).

"The Vacant Throne," *Lutheran Companion*, v. 45, (May 27, 1937).

"Vid L. P. Esbjörns grav," *Augustana*, v. 71, (Nov. 18, 1926).

"The Vision That Is Augustana," *Augustana College Bulletin*, (Dec., 1959).

"Westphalia to Amsterdam," *Christian Century*, v. 65, (Aug. 11, 1948).

"Who Wants to Be a Missionary Now?" *Lutheran Standard*, v. 9, (Feb., 1969).

"Why I Became a Missionary," *Lutheran Companion,* v. 105, (Mar. 4, 1959).

"Within the Church," *Budbäraren,* v. 34, (Aug., 1921).

"Years at Augustana," in *Andreen of Augustana, 1864-1940,* (Rock Island, 1942).

WORKS OF OTHER AUTHORS TRANSLATED BY BERGENDOFF

Aulen, Gustaf, "Nathan Söderblom as Theologian," *Una Sancta,* v. 24, (Mar., 1967).

Billing, Einar, *Our Calling,* (Rock Island, 1947; [reissued] Philadelphia, 1964).

Church and Ministry, II, Luther's Works, v. 40, (Philadelphia, 1940).

Enander, Johan A., "A Significant Enander Document," *Swedish Pioneer Historical Quarterly,* v. 21, (Jan., 1970).

"A Letter Concerning a Life Problem of a People—To the Clergy of the Church of Sweden from Their Bishops," *Lutheran Quarterly,* v. 4, (Feb., 1952).

Norelius, Eric, *The Pioneer Swedish Settlements and Swedish Lutheran Churches in America, 1845-1860,* (Rock Island, 1984).

"A Preface to the Ecumenical Creeds," *Augustana Quarterly,* v. 24, (Jan., 1945).

"Reports to the American Home Missionary Society, 1849-1856," *Augustana Historical Society Publications,* v. 5, (Rock Island, 1935).

Wingren, Gustaf, "The Christian's Calling According to Luther," *Augustana Quarterly,* v. 2, (Jan., 1942).

BOOKS REVIEWED BY BERGENDOFF

Abell, Aaron, *The Urban Impact on American Protestantism, 1865-1900,* in *Annals of the American Academy of Political and Social Science,* v. 236, (Nov., 1944).

Acton, Lord, *Essays on Freedom and Power,* in *Lutheran Quarterly,* v. 1, (Feb., 1949).

Adell, Arthur, *Nya Testamentet på svenska 1526,* in *Augustana Quarterly,* v. 16, (Apr., 1937).

Allard, F. M., *Från Luther till Bach,* in *Augustana Quarterly,* v. 13, (July, 1934).

Ander, O. F., *T. N. Hasselquist,* in *Augustana Quarterly,* v. 11, (July, 1932).

Andrén, Åke, *Introductorium theologicum,* in *Lutheran Quarterly,* v. 4, (Feb., 1952).

Aulén, Gustaf, *Church, Law and Society,* in *Church History,* v. 17, (June, 1948).

Aulén, Gustaf, *The Faith of the Christian Church,* in *Theology Today,* v. 6, (Apr., 1949).

Bainton, Roland, *The Reformation of the Sixteenth Century,* in *Lutheran Quarterly,* v. 5, (Feb., 1953).

Benz, Ernst et al., *Die Ostkirche und die Russische Christenheit,* in *The Annals of the American Academy of Political and Social Science,* v. 270, (July, 1950).

Borgenstierna, Gert, *Arbetarteologi och altarteologi,* in *Lutheran Quarterly,* v. 5, (May, 1953).

Brilioth, Yngve, *Nattvarden i evangeliskt gudstjänstliv,* in *Lutheran Quarterly,* v. 3, (Nov., 1951).

Clark, E. T., and Cram, W. G., editors, *The Book of Daily Devotions,* in *Augustana Quarterly,* v. 12,

(Jan., 1933).

Curtis, Charles J., *Nathan Soderblom, Theologian of Revelation*, in *Swedish Pioneer Historical Quarterly*, v. 18, (Jan., 1967).

Dahl, K. G. William, *Letters Home from the Prairie Priest*, translated by Earl Helge Byleen, in *Augustana Historical Society Newsletter*, v. 9, (Spring/Summer, 1994).

Dillenberger, John, *God Hidden and Revealed*, in *Theology Today*, v. 10, (Jan., 1954).

Eddy, Sherwood, *The Kingdom of God and the American Dream*, in *Annals of the American Academy of Political and Social Science*, v. 217, (Sept., 1941).

Estborn, Sigfrid, *Under Guds grepp: En studie i Nathan Söderbloms förkunnelse*, in *Augustana Quarterly*, v. 24, (July, 1945).

Ferm, Vergilius, editor, *Contemporary American Theology*, v. I and II, in *Augustana Quarterly*, v. 12, (Oct., 1933).

Ferré, Nels F. S., *Swedish Contributions to Modern Theology*, in *Christendom*, v. 5, (Winter, 1940).

Flew, Newton, *The Idea of Perfection in Christian Theology*, in *Augustana Quarterly*, v. 14, (Apr., 1935).

Hofrenning, B. M., *Captain Jens Munk's Septentrionalis*, in *Augustana Quarterly*, v. 24, (July, 1945).

Hök, Gösta, *Herrnhutisk teologi i svensk gestalt*, in *Lutheran Quarterly*, v. 3, (May, 1951).

Holmquist, Hjalmar, *Handbok i svensk kyrkohistoria*, II, III, in *Lutheran Quarterly*, v. 8, (Feb., 1956).

Holmquist, Hjalmar, *Svenska kyrkans historia*, in *Augustana Quarterly*, v. 13, (July, 1934).

Holborn, Hajo, *Ulrich von Hutten and the German Reformation*, in *Annals of the American Academy of Political and Social Science*, v. 198, (July, 1938).

Holmström, Folke, *Det eskatologiska motivet: Nutida teologi*, in *Augustana Quarterly*, v. 14, (Oct., 1935).

Horton, Walter M., *Toward a Reborn Church*, in *Lutheran Quarterly*, v. 2, (Feb., 1950).

Höye, Bjaine, and Ager, Trygve, *The Fight of the Norwegian Church Against Nazism*, in *Annals of the Academy of Political and Social Science*, v. 231, (Jan., 1944).

Ingebrand, Sven, *Olavus Petris reformatoriska åskådning*, in *Lutheran Quarterly*, v. 16, (Nov., 1964).

The Institute of Social and Religious Research, *The Education of American Ministers*, 4 vols., in *Augustana Quarterly*, v. 13, (Apr., 1934).

Johnson, Amandus, *The Journal and Biography of Nicolas Collin*, in *Church History*, v. 6, (June, 1937).

Joyce, G. H., *Christian Marriage—An Historical and Doctrinal Study*, in *Augustana Quarterly*, v. 13, (Oct., 1934).

Justus, Karl B., *What's Wrong with Religion?* in *Annals of the American Academy of Political and Social Science*, v. 254, (Nov., 1957).

Karlström, Nils, *Ekumeniska preludier*, in *Lutheran Quarterly*, v. 3, (Aug., 1951).

Karlström, Nils, editor, *Nathan Söderblom: In memoriam*, in *Church History*, v. 7, (Dec., 1938).

Kerr, Hugh Thompson, *A Compend of Luther's Theology*, in *Christendom*, v. 9, (Winter, 1944).

King, W. P., editor, *Behaviorism, A Battle Line*, in *Augustana Quarterly*, v. 10, (Jan., 1931).

Kroon, Sigurd, *Det svenska prästmötet under medeltiden*, in *Review of Religion*, v. 13, (May, 1949).

Krumbine, M. H., editor, *The Process of Religion*, in *Augustana Quarterly*, v. 13, (Jan., 1934).

Kyrka och folkbildning, [by several authors], in *Lutheran Quarterly*, v. 2, (May, 1950).

Lilja, Einar, *Den svenska katekestraditionen mellan Svebilius och Lindblom*, in *Review of Religion*, v. 13, (May, 1949).

Lindbeck, George A., *Dialogue on the Way*, in *Minister's Information Service*, [LCA], (Jan., 1966).

Lindroth, Hjalmar, *Recent Theological Research in Sweden: A Luther Renaissance*, in *Lutheran Quarterly*, v. 3, (Feb., 1951).

Liturgical Society of St. James, *Pro Ecclesia Lutherana, vol. I*, in *Augustana Quarterly*, v. 13, (Apr., 1934).

Liturgical Society of St. James, *Pro Ecclesia Lutherana, vol. II*, in *Augustana Quarterly*, v. 14, (July, 1935).

Löwith, Karl, *Meaning in History*, in *Lutheran Quarterly*, v. 1, (Nov., 1949).

Luther Academy in Sonderhausen, *Nachrichten der Luther-Akademie in Sonderhausen*, in *Augustana Quarterly*, v. 14, (Apr., 1935).

Macfarland, Charles S., *The Christian Faith in a Day of Crisis*, in *Annals of the American Academy of Political and Social Science*, v. 204, (July, 1939).

Malmeström, Elis, *J. A. Eklund: En biografi*, in *Lutheran Quarterly*, v. 3, (Feb., 1951).

McConnell, J. C., *Christianity and Coercion*, in *Augustana Quarterly*, v. 13, (Jan., 1934).

McNeill, J. T., *Unitive Protestantism*, in *Augustana Quarterly*, v. 18, (Apr., 1939).

McSorley, Harry J., C. S. P., *Luther: Right or Wrong? An Ecumenical-Theological Study of Luther's Major Work, the Bondage of the Will*, in *Lutheran Forum*, v. 3, (June, 1969).

Melanchthon, Phillip, *The Loci Communes of Phillip Melanchthon*, translated by Charles L. Hill, in *Journal of Religion*, v. 26, (Apr., 1946).

Moffatt, James, *The Days Before Yesterday*, in *Augustana Quarterly*, v. 10, (Jan., 1931).

Moffatt, James, *Grace in the New Testament*, in *Augustana Quarterly*, v. 11, (Apr., 1932).

Moffatt, James, *Love in the New Testament*, in *Augustana Quarterly*, v. 9, (Oct., 1930).

Morrison, Charles Clayton, *The Unfinished Reformation*, in *Lutheran Quarterly*, v. 5, (Aug., 1953).

Mott, John R., *The Present-Day Summons to the World Mission of Christianity*, in *Augustana Quarterly*, v. 11, (Jan., 1932).

Murray, Robert, *Olavus Petri*, in *Lutheran Quarterly*, v. 5, (Feb., 1953).

Newman, Ernst, *Den waldenströmska försoningsläran i historisk belysning*, in *Augustana Quarterly*, v. 11, (July, 1932).

Norberg, Arvid, *Frikyrklighetens uppkomst*, in *Lutheran Quarterly*, v. 5, (Nov., 1953).

Norman, Carl E., *Prästerskapet och det karolinska enväldet*, in *Review of Religion*, v. 13, (May, 1949).

Nygren, Anders, *Kristus och hans kyrka,* in *Lutheran Quarterly,* v. 8, (Nov., 1956).

Olsson, Karl A., *By One Spirit,* in *Swedish Pioneer Historical Quarterly,* v. 14, (Jan., 1963).

Opperman, C. J. A., *The English Missionaries in Sweden and Finland,* in *Church History,* v. 7, (June, 1938).

Ottersberg, Gerhard, *Wartburg College 1852-1952, A Centennial History,* in *Lutheran Quarterly,* v. 5, (Feb., 1953).

Pauck, W., *Karl Barth,* in *Augustana Quarterly,* v. 11, (Jan., 1932).

Pleijel, Hilding, *Der Schwedische Pietismus in Seinen Beziehungen zu Deutschland,* in *Augustana Quarterly,* v. 16, (Apr., 1937).

Pleijel, Hilding, *Från hustavlans tid,* in *Lutheran Quarterly,* v. 4, (May, 1952).

Pleijel, Hilding, *Svenska kyrkans historia,* in *Augustana Quarterly,* v. 14, (July, 1935).

Roos, M. Fr., *Kristlig husandaktsbok,* in *Augustana Quarterly,* v. 12, (Jan., 1933).

Roth, Erick, *Sakrament nach Luther,* in *Lutheran Quarterly,* v. 5, (Feb., 1953).

Rutenber, Culbert G., *The Dagger and the Cross: An Examination of Christian Pacifism,* in *Lutheran Quarterly,* v. 3, (Feb., 1951).

Ryden, E. E., *The Story of Christian Hymnody,* in *Lutheran Companion,* v. 105, (July 29, 1959).

Schweitzer, Albert, *The Philosophy of Civilization,* in *Lutheran Quarterly,* v. 2, (May, 1950).

Shirer, William L., *The Challenge of Scandinavia,* in *Christian Century,* v. 72, (Aug. 3, 1955).

Skydsgaard, K. E., *One in Christ,* in *Christian Century,* v. 74, (Dec. 18, 1957).

Smith, A. F., editor, *Talking with God,* in *Augustana Quarterly,* v. 12, (Jan., 1933).

Society of St. Ambrose, *The Use of the Common Service,* in *Augustana Quarterly,* v. 14, (July, 1935).

Söderblom, Nathan, *Ett år: Ord för varje dag,* in *Augustana Quarterly,* v. 12, (Jan., 1933).

Söderblom, Nathan, *The Nature of Revelation,* in *Lutheran Quarterly,* v. 20, (Feb., 1968).

Stephenson, George M., *The Religious Aspects of Swedish Immigration,* in *Augustana Quarterly,* v. 11, (July, 1932).

Tappert, Theodore G., and Doberstein, John W., *Notebook of a Colonial Clergyman,* in *Lutheran Quarterly,* v. 12, (Nov., 1960).

Tidskrift för kyrkomusik och svenskt gudstjänstliv, in *Augustana Quarterly,* v. 14, (July, 1935).

Till, Barry, *The Churches' Search for Unity,* in *Lutheran Forum,* v. 7, (Feb., 1973).

Tomkins, Oliver S., *The Church in the Purpose of God,* in *Lutheran Quarterly,* v. 4, (May, 1952).

Van Dusen, Henry P., *Dag Hammarskjöld: The Statesman and His Faith,* in *Swedish Pioneer Historical Quarterly,* v. 18, (July, 1967).

Van Dusen, Henry P., *God in These Times,* in *Augustana Quarterly,* v. 14, (Oct., 1935).

Westin, Gunnar, *Svenska kyrkan och de protestantiska enhetssträvandena under 1630-talet,* in *Augustana Quarterly,* v. 18, (Apr., 1939).

JOURNALS EDITED

Augustana Quarterly, v. 7-27, (1928-1948).

Lutheran Quarterly, v. 1-4, (1949-1953).

OTHER PRIMARY SOURCES

Augustana College and [until 1949] Theological Seminary Catalog.

Augustana Observer.

Minutes of the Annual Convention, Augustana Evangelical Lutheran Synod [Church]; [prior to 1920 titled in Swedish as: *Referat*].

Minutes of the Board of Directors, Augustana College and [until 1949] Theological Seminary.

Minutes of the Committee on Liturgy and Hymnal.

Minutes of the Faculty, Augustana College and [until 1949] Theological Seminary.

Minutes of the Joint Commission on Lutheran Unity.

Report of the President, Augustana College and [until 1949] Theological Seminary.

Samling af Augustana-Synodens, dess konferensers och inrättningars oktrojer, stadgar och ordningsregler, (Rock Island, 1918).

BOOKS, ARTICLES, REVIEWS, ESSAYS BY OTHER AUTHORS

When a specific article or essay in a book, festschrift, or collection of articles has been cited in the text, that article in that book is listed by author. The book itself is *also* listed by the name of the editor. These are works used in preparing this book.

Ahlstrom, Sydney E., *A Religious History of the American People,* (New Haven, 1972).

Ahlstrom, Sydney Eckman, "Facing the New World: Augustana and the American Challenge," in Emmer Engberg et al., editors, *Centennial Essays,* (Rock Island, 1960).

Alm, Martin, "Bilden av Amerika," in Jakob Christensson, editor, *Signums svenska kulturhistoria. 1900-talet,* (Stockholm, 2009).

Almen, Louis, "Conrad Bergendoff and the Augustana Heritage—A College Perspective," *Augustana Heritage Newsletter,* (Oct., 1996).

Almer, A. F., Review of Conrad Bergendoff, *The Making and the Meaning of the Augsburg Confession,* in *Augustana Quarterly,* v. 9, (July, 1930).

Ander, Fritiof, "Augustana-kyrkan vid sitt sekelskifte," *Kyrkohistorisk årsskrift,* v. 60, (1960), [Eng. trans. by Dag Blanck and Thomas Tredway in *Swedish-American Historical Quarterly,* v. 61, (Oct., 2010)].

Ander, Oscar Fritiof, *T. N. Hasselquist,* (Rock Island, 1931).

Anderson, Philip J., and Blanck, Dag, editors, *Norwegians and Swedes in the United States: Friends and Neighbors,* (St. Paul, 2012).

Anderson, Philip J., "Histories from the Inside Out: Shared Origins and Denominational Historiography in the Writings of G. Everett Arden and Karl A. Olsson," *Swedish-American Historical Quarterly,* v. 63, (Apr.-July, 2012).

Anderson, Philip J., "Paul Peter Waldenström and America: Influence and Presence in

Historical Perspective," *Covenant Quarterly,* v. 52, (Nov., 1994).

Anderson, Philip J., "'Strangers Yet Acquainted': The Personality of Religious Schism in Lindsborg, Kansas," *Swedish-American Historical Quarterly,* v. 49, (July, 1998).

Andræ, Tor, "Nathan Söderblom som religionshistoriker," in Nils Karlström, editor, *Nathan Söderblom: In memoriam,* (Stockholm, 1931).

Arden, G. Everett, *Augustana Heritage: The History of the Augustana Lutheran Church,* (Rock Island, 1963).

Arden, G. Everett, *The School of the Prophets: The Background and History of the Augustana Theological Seminary, 1860-1960,* (Rock Island, 1960).

Aulén, Gustaf, "Den teologiska gärningen," in Nils Karlström, editor, *Nathan Söderblom: In memoriam,* (Stockholm, 1931).

Bachmann, E. Theodore, *The United Lutheran Church in America, 1918-1962,* (Minneapolis, 1997).

Barton, H. Arnold, "Conrad Bergendoff and the Swedish-American Church Language Controversy of the 1920s," in *Swedish-American Historical Quarterly,* v. 46, (July, 1995).

Barton, H. Arnold, *A Folk Divided: Homeland Swedes and Swedish Americans, 1840-1940,* (Carbondale, Ill., 1994).

Beijbom, Ulf, *Swedes in Chicago: a Demographic and Social Study of the 1846-1880 Immigration,* (Växjö, Sweden, 1971).

Bengston, Carl J., "Young People's Christian Conference," *Lutheran Companion,* v. 29, (Mar. 5, 1921).

Bersell, P. O., "The Lutheran Tercentenary," *Lutheran Companion,* v. 46, (July 28, 1938).

Bexell, Oloph, *Sveriges kyrkohistoria: 7. Folkväckelsens och kyrkoförnyelsens tid,* (Stockholm, 2003).

Blanck, Dag, *The Creation of an Ethnic Identity: Being Swedish American in the Augustana Synod, 1860-1917,* (Carbondale, Ill., 2006).

Blanck, Dag, "'A Language Does Not Die Easily . . .' Swedish at Augustana College, 1860-1900," *Swedish Pioneer Historical Quarterly,* v. 33, (Oct., 1982).

Blanck, Dag, "On Being Swedish in America Today," in Lars Olsson and Sune Åkerman, editors, *Hembygden & Världen,* (Växjö, Sweden, 2002).

Bloom, Harold, *Genius: A Mosaic of One Hundred Exemplary Artistic Minds,* (New York, 2002).

Blückert, Kjell, *The Church as Nation: A Study in Ecclesiology and Nationhood,* (Frankfurt am Main, 2000).

Boaden, Ann, *Light and Leaven: Women Who Shaped Augustana's First Century,* (Rock Island, 2011).

Boaden, Ann, "Weighing the Stars and Hearing the Word: Conrad Bergendoff's Idea of Christian Higher Education at Augustana College and Theological Seminary," in Raymond Jarvi, editor, *Aspects of Augustana and Swedish America,* (Rock Island, 1995).

Board of College Education and Church Vocations, Lutheran Church in America, *The Mission of LCA Colleges and Universities,* (New York, 1969).

Bongfeldt, G. L., *Pen Portraits of P. O. Bersell and C. A. Wendell,* (Rock Island, 1950).

Brandreth, Henry Renaud Turner, "Approaches of the Churches towards Each Other in the Nineteenth Century," in Ruth Rouse and Stephen Charles Neill, *A History of the Ecumenical Movement, 1517-1948,* third edition, (Geneva, 1986).

Brilioth, Yngve, editor, *World Lutheranism Today: A Tribute to Anders Nygren, 15 November 1950,* (Stockholm, 1950).

Brodd, Sven-Erik, "Nathan Söderblom—religionshistoriker, ärkebiskop och internationell ekumenisk kyrkoledare," in Ingmar Brohed, *Sveriges kyrkohistoria: 8. Religionsfrihetens och ekumenikens tid,* (Stockholm, 2005).

Brohed, Ingmar, *Sveriges kyrkohistoria: 8. Religionsfrihetens och ekumenikens tid,* (Stockholm, 2005).

Brokhoff, John R., Review of Conrad Bergendoff, *The One Holy Catholic Apostolic Church* [and one other book], in *Frontiers,* v. 6, (Feb., 1955).

Brolander, Glen E., *An Historical Survey of the Augustana College Campus,* revised edition, (Rock Island, 1992).

Buckley, William F., Jr., *God and Man at Yale: The Superstitions of "Academic Freedom,"* (Chicago, 1951).

Capps, Finis Herbert, *From Isolationism to Involvement: The Swedish-American Press in America, 1914-1945,* (Chicago, 1966).

Carlson, Edgar M., "Dr. Bergendoff—Christian Scholar and Educator," in J. Iverne Dowie and Ernest M. Espelie, editors, *The Swedish Immigrant Community in Transition,* (Rock Island, 1963).

Cavert, Samuel McCrae, *The American Churches in the Ecumenical Movement, 1900-1968,* (New York, 1969).

Cavert, Samuel McCrae, *Church Cooperation and Unity in America: A Historical Review, 1900-1970,* (New York, 1970).

Christensson, Jakob, editor, *Signums svenska kulturhistoria: 1900-talet,* (Stockholm, 2009).

Claesson, Urban, *Folkhemmets kyrka: Harald Hallén och folkkyrkans genombrott,* (Uppsala, 2004).

Curti, Merle, "Sweden in the American Social Mind of the 1930s," in J. Iverne Dowie and J. Thomas Tredway, editors, *The Immigration of Ideas: Studies in the North Atlantic Community: Essays Presented to O. Fritiof Ander,* (Rock Island, 1968).

Definite Platform, Doctrinal and Disciplinarian for Evangelical Lutheran District Synods: Constructed in Accordance with the Principles of the General Synod, (Philadelphia, 1855).

Dolnick, Edward, *The Clockwork Universe: Isaac Newton, the Royal Society, and the Birth of the Modern World,* (New York, 2011).

Dowie, J. Iverne, and Espelie, Ernest M., editors, *The Swedish Immigrant Community in Transition: Essays in Honor of Dr. Conrad Bergendoff,* (Rock Island, 1963).

Dowie, J. Iverne, and Tredway, J. Thomas, editors, *The Immigration of Ideas: Studies in the North Atlantic Community: Essays Presented to O. Fritiof Ander,* (Rock Island, 1968).

Ehrenström, Nils, "Movements for International Friendship and Life and Work, 1925-1948," in Ruth Rouse and Stephen Charles Neill, editors, *A History of the Ecumenical Movement, 1517-1948,* third edition, (Geneva, 1986).

Empie, Paul C., and McCord, James I., editors, *Marburg Revisited,* (Minneapolis, 1966).

Engberg, Emmer, "Augustana and Code Morality," in Emmer Engberg et al., editors, *Centennial Essays,* (Rock Island, 1960).

Engberg, Emmer, et al., editors, *Centennial Essays,* (Rock Island, 1960).

Engman, Max, editor, *När imperier faller: Studier kring riksupplösningar och nya stater,* (Stockholm, 1994).

Engstrom, S. E., "Lutheran Unity Is Desirable," *Lutheran Companion,* v. 97, (Apr. 2, 1952).

Erlander, Tage, *Dagböcker 1963-1964, Utgivna av Sven Erlander,* (Hedemora, Sweden, 2012).

Erling, Maria, and Granquist, Mark, *The Augustana Story: Shaping Lutheran Identity in North America,* (Minneapolis, 2008).

Fendt, E. C., editor, *What Lutherans Are Thinking: A Symposium on Lutheran Faith and Life,* (Columbus, Ohio, 1947).

Fendt, Edward C., *The Struggle for Lutheran Unity in the U.S.A. from the Late 1930's to the Early 1970's,* (Minneapolis, 1980).

Ferm, Vergilius, editor, *What Is Lutheranism?* (New York, 1930).

Fey, Harold E., editor, *The Ecumenical Advance: A History of the Ecumenical Movement, Volume 2, 1948-1968,* (London, 1970).

Fischer, Robert H., editor, *Franklin Clark Fry: A Palette for a Portrait,* supplementary number of *Lutheran Quarterly,* v. 24, (1972).

Florovsky, Georges, "The Orthodox Churches and the Ecumenical Movement Prior to 1910," in Ruth Rouse and Stephen Charles Neill, editors, *A History of the Ecumenical Movement, 1517-1948,* third edition, (Geneva, 1986).

Fredricksen, Paula, *Sin: The Early History of an Idea,* (Princeton, 2012).

Freeman, Charles, *The Closing of the Western Mind: The Rise of Faith and the Fall of Reason,* (New York, 2002).

Garrison, W. E., Review of Conrad Bergendoff, *The One Holy Catholic Apostolic Church,* in *Christian Century,* v. 71, (Aug. 18, 1954).

Garrison, Winfred Ernest, Review of Conrad Bergendoff, *The Making and the Meaning of the Augsburg Confession* [and two other books], in *Christian Century,* v. 47, (June 18, 1930).

Gevik, Dean, "Church Speaks on Presidency, "*Lutheran Companion,* v. 106, (July 6, 1960).

Gifford, Hartland H., and Hultgren, Arland J., editors, *The Heritage of Augustana: Essays on the Life and Legacy of the Augustana Lutheran Church,* (Minneapolis, 2004).

Gilbert, W. Kent, *Commitment to Unity: A History of the Lutheran Church in America,* (Philadelphia, 1988).

Gjerde, Jon, *The Minds of the West: Ethnocultural Evolution in the Rural Middle West, 1830-1917,* (Chapel Hill, 1997).

Gopnik, Adam, "The Back of the World: The troubling genius of G. K. Chesterton," *The New Yorker,* (July 7 and 14, 2008).

Granquist, Mark, "Conrad Bergendoff and the LCA Merger of 1962," in Raymond Jarvi, editor, *Aspects of Augustana and Swedish America,* (Rock Island, 1995).

Granquist, Mark, "'The Sociological Factor Is Not to Be Underestimated': Swedes, Norwegians, and American Lutheran Merger Negotiations, 1920-60," in Philip J. Anderson and Dag Blanck, editors, *Norwegians and Swedes in the United States: Friends and Neighbors,* (St. Paul, 2012).

Greenblatt, Stephen, *The Swerve: How the World Became Modern,* (New York, 2011).

Gritsch, Eric W., *A History of Lutheranism,* (Minneapolis, 2002).

Gyllenkrok, Axel, *Rechtfertigung und Heiligung in der frühen evangelishen Theologie Luthers,* (Uppsala, 1952).

Hamberg, Eva M., "Religious change in Sweden from 1955 to 1970," *Kyrkohistorisk årsskrift,* v. 111, (2011).

Hammar, K. G., *Tecken och verklighet; Samtal om Gud; Ecce Homo-efter två tusen år,* (Lund, 2006).

Handy, Robert T., *A History of the Churches of the United States and Canada,* (New York, 1977).

Hansen, Marcus Lee, *The Atlantic Migration, 1607-1860,* edited by Arthur M. Schlesinger, fourth printing, (Cambridge, Mass., 1951).

Hansen, Marcus Lee, *The Immigrant in American History,* edited by Arthur M. Schlesinger, (Cambridge, Mass., 1940).

Hasselmo, Nils, Review of Maria Erling and Mark Granquist, *The Augustana Story,* in *Swedish-American Historical Quarterly,* v. 61, (Jan., 2010).

Hecht, Jennifer Michael, *Doubt: A History,* (San Francisco, 2003).

Hedenius, Ingemar, *Tro och vetande,* new edition, ([Lidingö, Sweden], 2009).

Hjelm, Norman A., "Augustana and the Church of Sweden: Ties of History and Faith," in Hartland H. Gifford and Arland J. Hultgren, editors, *The Heritage of Augustana,* (Minneapolis, 2004).

Hope, Nicholas, *German and Scandinavian Protestantism, 1700-1918,* (Oxford, 1995).

Hult, Adolf, "Sparks from the Anvil of the English Question," *Augustana Journal,* v. 13, (Feb. 15, 1905).

Hutter, Leonard, *Compend of Lutheran Theology: A Summary of Christian Doctrine, Derived from the Word of God and the Symbolical Books of the Evangelical Lutheran Church,* English translation by Henry Eyster Jacobs and George Frederick Spieker, (Philadelphia, 1868).

Jackson, Gregory Lee, *Prophetic Voice for the Kingdom: The Impact of Alvin Daniel Mattson Upon the Social Consciousness of the Augustana Synod,* (Rock Island, 1986).

Jacobs, Henry Eyster, *A History of the Evangelical Lutheran Church in the United States,* second edition, (New York, 1899).

Jacoby, Susan, *Freethinkers: A History of American Secularism,* (New York, 2004).

Jarvi, Raymond, editor, *Aspects of Augustana and Swedish America: Essays in Honor of Dr. Conrad Bergendoff on His 100ᵗʰ Year,* (Rock Island, 1995).

Johnson, Paul, *A History of Christianity,* (New York, 1976).

Johnson, Philip A., "National Council Is Born," *Lutheran Companion,* v. 95, (Dec. 13, 1950).

Kantonen, T. A., Review of Conrad Bergendoff, *Christ as Authority,* in *Augustana Quarterly,* v. 28, (July, 1948).

Karlström, Nils, editor, *Nathan Söderblom: In memoriam,* (Stockholm, 1931).

Kenney, Dave, *Gustavus Adolphus College: 150 Years of History,* (St. Peter, Minn., 2011).

Kierschner, Alfred F., Review of Conrad Bergendoff, *The One Holy Catholic Apostolic Church,* in *Una Sancta,* v. 11, (1954).

Kinnamon, Michael, and Cope, Brian E., editors, *The Ecumenical Movement: An Anthology of Key Texts and Voices,* (Geneva, 1997).

Knudsen, Johannes, *The Formation of the Lutheran Church in America,* (Philadelphia, 1978).

Krüger, H., "The Life and Activities of the World Council of Churches," in Harold E. Fey, editor, *The Ecumenical Advance: A History of the Ecumenical Movement, Volume 2, 1948-1968,* (London, 1970).

Kummel, Bengt, "Nationalism över statsgränser: Rörelser som enat och splittrat," in Max Engman, editor, *När imperier faller: Studier kring riksupplösningar och nya stater,* (Stockholm, 1994).

Lindahl, Elder, "The Troublesome Language Question," in Raymond Jarvi, editor, *Aspects of Augustana and Swedish America,* (Rock Island, 1995).

Lindberg, John S., *The Background of Swedish Emigration to the United States: An Economic and Sociological Study in the Dynamics of Migration,* (Minneapolis, 1930).

Littell, Franklin, *From State Church to Pluralism: A Protestant Interpretation of Religion in American History,* (Garden City, N.Y., 1962).

Lundborg, Johan, *När ateismen erövrade Sverige: Ingemar Hedenius och debatten kring tro och vetande,* (Nora, Sweden, 2002).

Luther, Martin, *On the Bondage of the Will,* in E. Gordon Rupp and Philip S. Watson, translators and editors, *The Library of Christian Classics, Volume XVII, Luther and Erasmus: Free Will and Salvation,* (Philadelphia, 1969).

Lyttkens, Carl Henrik, *The Growth of Swedish-Anglican Intercommunion between 1833 and 1922,* (Lund, 1970).

MacCulloch, Diarmaid, *Christianity: The First Three Thousand Years,* (New York, 2009).

MacCulloch, Diarmaid, *The Reformation,* (New York, 2003).

Marsden, George M., *The Soul of the American University: From Protestant Establishment to Established Nonbelief,* (New York, 1994).

Marty, Martin E., "Ethnicity: The Skeleton of Religion in America," *Church History,* v. 41, (Mar., 1972).

Marty, Martin E., *Modern American Religion, Volume 1: The Irony of It All, 1893-1919,* (Chicago, 1986).

Mattson, Karl E., "The Theology of the Augustana Lutheran Church," in Emmer Engberg et al., editors, *Centennial Essays,* (Rock Island, 1960).

Murray, Robert, editor, *The Church of Sweden: Past and Present,* (Malmö, Sweden, 1960).

Neill, Stephen C., *Brothers of the Faith,* (New York, 1960).

Neill, Stephen Charles, "Plans of Union and Reunion," in Ruth Rouse and Stephen Charles Neill, editors, *A History of the Ecumenical Movement, 1517-1948,* third edition, (Geneva, 1986).

Nelson, E. Clifford et al., editors, *The Lutherans in North America,* (Philadelphia, 1975).

Nelson, E. Clifford, "The New Shape of Lutheranism," in E. Clifford Nelson et al., editors, *The Lutherans in North America,* (Philadelphia, 1975).

Nelson, J. Robert, Review of Conrad Bergendoff, *The One Holy Catholic Apostolic Church* [and seven other books], in *Ecumenical Review,* v. 7, (Apr., 1955).

Niebuhr, Reinhold, *The Irony of American History,* (New York, 1952).

Niebuhr, H. Richard, *Christ and Culture,* (New York, 1951).

Nordin, Svante, *Från Hägerström till Hedenius,* (Bodafors, Sweden, 1983).

Nordin, Svante, "Hundra år av religionsdebatt," in Jakob Christensson, editor, *Signums svenska kulturhistoria: 1900-talet,* (Stockholm, 2009).

Nordstrom, Byron, "Introduction," in Dave Kenney, *Gustavus Adolphus College: 150 Years of History,* (St. Peter, Minn., 2011).

Norelius, E., *T. N. Hasselquist: Lefnadsteckning,* (Rock Island, [1900]).

Norelius, Eric, *De svenska lutherska församlingarnas och svenskarnas historia i Amerika,* 2 vols, (Rock Island, 1890, 1916).

Norman, Hans, "The Causes of Emigration. a. An Attempt at a Multivariate Analysis," in Harald Runblom and Hans Norman, editors, *From Sweden to America: A History of the Migration,* (Minneapolis, 1976).

Norton, John, editor and translator, *P. P. Waldenström at Augustana, 1901: Excerpts from his Nya färder i Amerikas Förenta Stater,* (Rock Island, 2012).

Nystrom, Daniel, *A Ministry of Printing: History of the Publication House of the Augustana Lutheran Church, 1889-1962,* (Rock Island, 1962).

O'Donnell, James, *Augustine: A New Biography,* (New York, 2008).

Olson, Ernest William, *Olof Olsson,* (Rock Island, 1941).

Olsson, Karl, *By One Spirit,* (Chicago, 1962).

Olsson, Karl A., "Kontinuitet och förvandling inom svenska immigrantsamfund i USA," *Kyrkohistorisk årsskrift,* v. 82, (1982).

Olsson, Karl, "Paul Peter Waldenström and Augustana," in J. Iverne Dowie and Ernest M. Espelie, editors, *The Swedish Immigrant Community in Transition,* (Rock Island, 1963).

Olsson, Lars, and Åkerman, Sune, editors, *Hembygden & Världen,* (Växjö, Sweden, 2002).

Olsson, Nils William, "Naming Patterns among Swedish-Americans," *Swedish American Genealogist,* v. 14, (June, 1994).

Olsson, O., *Reformationen och Socinianismen, Föredrag wid reformationsfesten wid Aug. College 1878,* (Rock Island, 1880).

Øverland, Orm, *Immigrant Minds, American Identities: Making the United States Home, 1870-1930,* (Urbana, Ill., 2000).

Pagels, Elaine, *Beyond Belief: The Secret Gospel of Thomas,* (New York, 2003).

Pearson, Daniel Merle, *The Americanization of Carl Aaron Swensson,* (Rock Island, 1977).

Peterson, Kurt W., "A Question of Conscience: Minnesota's Norwegian American Lutherans and the Teaching of Evolution," in Philip J. Anderson and Dag Blanck, editors, *Norwegians and Swedes in the United States: Friends and Neighbors,* (St. Paul, 2012).

Philbrick, Nathaniel, *Mayflower: A Story of Courage, Community, and War,* (New York, 2006).

Pierard, Richard V., Review of Conrad Bergendoff, *The Church of the Lutheran Reformation,* in *Christianity Today,* v. 12, (Oct. 27, 1967).

Plantinga, Alvin, *Where the Conflict Really Lies: Science, Religion, and Naturalism,* (Oxford, 2011).

Pleijel, Hilding, "The Church of Sweden: An Historical Retrospect," in Robert Murray, editor, *The Church of Sweden: Past and Present,* (Malmö, Sweden, 1960).

Pleijel, Hilding, *Från fädernas fromhetsliv,* (Stockholm, 1939).

Pleijel, Hilding, *Från hustavlans tid: Kyrkohistoriska folklivsstudier,* (Stockholm, 1951).

Pleijel, Hilding, *Hustavlans värld: Kyrkligt folkliv i äldre tiders Sverige,* (Stockholm, 1970).

Prenter, Regin, *Spiritus Creator,* English trans., (Philadelphia, 1953).

Riesman, David et al., *The Lonely Crowd: A Study of the Changing American Character,* abridged edition, (New Haven, 1961).

Rönnegård, Sam, *Prairie Shepherd: Lars Paul Esbjörn and the Beginnings of the Augustana Lutheran Church,* translated by G. Everett Arden, (Rock Island, 1952).

Rouse, Ruth, and Neill, Stephen Charles, editors, *A History of the Ecumenical Movement, 1517-1948,* third edition, (Geneva, 1986).

Rouse, Ruth, "Other Aspects of the Ecumenical Movement, 1910-1948," in Ruth Rouse and Stephen Charles Neill, editors, *A History of the Ecumenical Movement, 1517-1948,* third edition, (Geneva, 1986).

Rouse, Ruth, "Voluntary Movements and the Changing Ecumenical Climate," in Ruth Rouse and Stephen Charles Neill, editors, *A History of the Ecumenical Movement, 1517-1948,* third edition, (Geneva, 1986).

Runblom, Harald, and Norman, Hans, editors, *From Sweden to America: A History of the Migration,* (Minneapolis, 1976).

Rupp, E. Gordon, and Watson, Philip S., translators and editors, *The Library of Christian Classics, Volume XVII, Luther and Erasmus: Free Will and Salvation,* (Philadelphia, 1969).

Ryden, E. E., "Augustana Quits Merger Negotiations," *Lutheran Companion,* v. 97, (Nov. 26, 1952).

Ryden, E. E., "Dissolution or Expansion," *Lutheran Companion,* v. 97, (Dec. 3, 1952).

Ryden, E. E., "Heroes of Faith: A Dramatic Pageant at Centennial Observance," *Lutheran Companion,* v. 56, (June 2, 1948).

Ryden, E. E., "A Hopeful Church Faces World Task: 3. Synod at Des Moines Asks for Total Lutheran Unity," *Lutheran Companion,* v. 97, (July 16, 1952).

Ryden, E. E., "Lund at Augustana: Noted Swedish Scholars Address Ministerium," *Lutheran Companion,* v. 56, (June 30, 1948).

Ryman, Björn, *Nordic Folk Churches,* (Grand Rapids, 2005).

Safstrom, Mark, "Defining Lutheranism from the Margins: Paul Peter Waldenström on Being a 'Good Lutheran' in America," *Swedish-American Historical Quarterly,* v. 63, (Apr.-July, 2012).

Safstrom, Mark Daniel, *The Religious Origins of Democratic Pluralism: Paul Peter Waldenström and the Politics of the Swedish Awakening 1868-1917,* Ph.D. dissertation, University of Washington, (2010).

Samling af Augustana-Synodens, dess konferensers och inrättningars oktrojer, stadgar och ordningsregler, (Rock Island, 1918).

Schjørring, Jens Holger et al., editors, *From Federation to Communion: The History of the Lutheran World Federation,* (Minneapolis, 1997).

Schlesinger, Arthur, Jr., "Forgetting Reinhold Niebuhr," *New York Times,* (Sept. 18, 2005).

Scott, Franklin D., *Sweden: The Nation's History,* (Minneapolis, 1977).

Schweitzer, W., Review of Conrad Bergendoff, *Christ as Authority,* in *Ecumenical Review,* v. 1, (Spring, 1949).

Sillen, Walter, "Nathan Söderblom," *Journal of Religion,* v. 28, (Jan., 1948).

Söderström, Hugo, *Confession and Cooperation: The Policy of the Augustana Synod in Confessional Matters and the Synod's Relations with Other Churches up to the Beginning of the Twentieth Century,* (Lund, 1973).

Södling, Maria, *Oreda i skapelsen,* (Uppsala, 2010).

Solberg, Richard W., *Lutheran Higher Education in North America,* (Minneapolis, 1985).

Stauderman, Albert P., *Our New Church,* (Philadelphia, 1962).

Stephenson, George M., *The Founding of the Augustana Synod, 1850-1860,* (Rock Island, 1927).

Stephenson, George M., *The Religious Aspects of Swedish Immigration,* (Minneapolis, 1932).

Stone, Glen C., "Conrad Bergendoff as Churchman," *Augustana Heritage Newsletter,* (Oct., 1996).

Stone, Glen C., Interviews with Conrad Bergendoff, June 22-23, 1977, Oct. 4, 1979, Archives of Cooperative Lutheranism.

Suelflow, August R., and Nelson, E. Clifford, "Following the Frontier, 1840-1875," in E. Clifford Nelson et al., editors, *The Lutherans in North America,* (Philadelphia, 1975).

Sundkler, Bengt, *Nathan Söderblom: His Life and Work,* (Lund, 1968).

Swanson, Byron, "Conrad Bergendoff as Ecumenist," in Hartland H. Gifford and Arland J. Hultgren, editors, *The Heritage of Augustana,* (Minneapolis, 2004).

Swanson, Byron R., *Conrad Bergendoff: The Making of an Ecumenist,* Th.D. dissertation, Princeton Theological Seminary, (1970).

Swanson, Byron R., Transcript of interviews with Conrad Bergendoff, June 23-24, Dec. 7, 1966.

Tappert, Theodore G., Review of Conrad Bergendoff, *The Church of the Lutheran Reformation,* in *Church History,* v. 37, (June, 1968).

Tatlow, Tissington, "The World Conference on Faith and Order," in Ruth Rouse and Stephen Charles Neill, editors, *A History of the Ecumenical Movement, 1517-1948,* third edition,

(Geneva, 1986).

Tergel, Alf, *Från konfrontation till institution: Ungkyrkorörelsen 1912-1917,* (Uppsala, 1974).

Tietjen, John H., *Which Way to Lutheran Unity?* (St. Louis, 1966).

Toynbee, Arnold, *A Study of History,* v. 4, (London, 1937).

Tredway, Thomas, and Blanck, Dag, "Interpreting One Hundred Years of Augustana History: Fritiof Ander, Conrad Bergendoff, and the 1960 Centennial," *Swedish-American Historical Quarterly,* v. 61, (Oct., 2010).

Tredway, Thomas, *Coming of Age: A History of Augustana College, 1935-1975,* (Rock Island, 2010).

Vecoli, Rudolph J., "'Over the years I have encountered the hazards and rewards that await the historian of immigration': George Malcom Stephenson and the Swedish-American Community," *Swedish-American Historical Quarterly,* v. 51, (Apr., 2000).

Walker, Williston, *A History of the Christian Church,* (New York, 1918).

Watson, Philip S., *Let God Be God! An Interpretation of the Theology of Martin Luther,* (Philadelphia, 1947).

Weigert, H. W., "Luther and the Germans," *Christian Century,* v. 59, (Jan. 21, 1942).

Welch, Claude, Review of Conrad Bergendoff, *Christ as Authority,* in *Christendom,* v. 13, (Summer, 1948).

Wentz, Abdel Ross, *A Basic History of Lutheranism in America,* revised edition, (Philadelphia, 1963).

Wentz, Abdel Ross, Review of Conrad Bergendoff, *Christ as Authority,* in *Lutheran Quarterly,* v. 1, (Feb., 1949).

Wentz, Frederick W., *Lutherans in Concert,* (Minneapolis, 1968).

Wesley, John, *Sermons on Several Occasions,* (New York, 1833).

Westin, Gunnar, *Mina unga år i skola, baptistsamfund och universitet,* (Stockholm, 1967).

Wilkinson, Rupert, "'The Lonely Crowd,' at 60, Is Still Timely," *Chronicle of Higher Education,* (Sept. 12, 2010).

Wittke, Carl, "Fissures in the Melting Pot," in J. Iverne Dowie and J. Thomas Tredway, editors, *The Immigration of Ideas: Studies in the North Atlantic Community: Essays Presented to O. Fritiof Ander,* (Rock Island, 1968).

Yoder, Don Herbert, "Christian Unity in Nineteenth-Century America," in Ruth Rouse and Stephen Charles Neill, editors, *A History of the Ecumenical Movement, 1517-1948,* third edition, (Geneva, 1986).

Zuckerman, Phil, *Society without God: What the Least Religious Nations Can Tell Us about Contentment,* (New York, 2008).

INDEX

A

Abelard, 109

Abrahamson, L. G., 42, 260, 264

Acheson, Dean, 25

Ahlstrom, Sydney, 280

Almen, Louis, 280

Almer, A. F., 73

American Council on Education, 285

American Lutheran Church, 35, 188, 196, 284, 288

American Lutheran Conference, 154, 180 188, 207, 221, 231

Amsterdam Assembly, 111, 210, 213

Anabaptists, 90, 112

Ander, Oscar Fritiof, 20, 72, 136, 142, 146, 247, 272, 294, 319, 323; Bergendoff, relation to, 136, 140-141, 152, 167, 255; Esbjörn, assessment of, 16, 144-145; Hasselquist, treatment of, 15-19, 136, 146; Pietism, 139; Sweden, judgment of, 256

Ander, Ruth, 255

Anderson, Carl A., 59

Anderson, E. T., 42

Anderson, O. V., 298

Anderson, Philip J., 150

Andreen, Gustav, 28-29, 35, 55, 63, 64, 164, 297

Andren, O. C. T., 19

Aquinas, 91, 108, 125, 159

Apostolic Succession, 222-224

Arden, G. Everett, 20, 41, 60, 72, 136, 152, 194, 275, 319; ecumenism in Augustana Synod, 183, 185, 235; Esbjörn, treatment of, 16, 140, 144-145; Pietism, 72, 148; seminary, history of, 35, 37; separation of college and seminary, 64, 160-164, 168

Augsburg Confession (Confessio Augustana), 61, 73, 74; ecumenical function, 179-180, 186, 188, 198-199, 205, 211, 214, 22-227,

246, 309-310, 317-318, 325; Pietists and, 139, 314; role in early Synod history, 18, 19, 36, 141, 174-177, 226; role in LWF, 198-199

Augustana: A Profession of Faith, 134, 168, 194, 200, 286, 306

Augustana Book Concern, 26, 74, 95, 100, 136

Augustana College: Board of Directors, 7, 31, 48, 56, 59, 63-64, 126, 157, 161-163, 170-171, 184, 213, 277-278, 293-300, 307; Chapel, 1-4, 30, 80, 83, 90, 118-119, 170, 257, 288-289, 295, 301, 320; curriculum, 30, 284-285, 289-290, 295, 321-322; dancing at, 98, 155-157, 293, 325; enrollment, 293; faculty, 3, 9, 25-29, 50, 83, 96, 128, 130, 146, 153, 167, 170, 240, 282, 287-295, 299, 303, 305, 308, 321-323; finances, 277, 296-199; Greek letter groups, 3, 30, 96, 98, 155, 293-294; panty raid 157, 171

Augustana Historical Society, 303

The Augustana Ministerium, 194, 306

Augustana Quarterly, 48, 57, 59, 73, 89, 104, 108, 109, 111, 118, 127, 140, 144, 178, 210, 211, 257, 299

Augustana Theological Seminary, 316: Board of Directors, 58, 159, 165, 167; curriculum, 62-63; faculty, 35-37, 56, 59-64, 159-161, 324; separation from college, 158-171, 144, 276, 280-281, 295-296, 308-309

Augustine, 73, 83, 86, 87, 91, 156, 284

Aulén, Gustav, 62, 99; ecumenical influence, 236; referred to by Bergendoff, 67, 72, 190, 221, 263; treatment by Hedenius, 262

B

Bacon, Francis, 118

Bagge, Gösta, 261

Bagger, Henry H. 31

Baptists, 30, 204, 214, 319

Barth, Karl, 62, 80, 82, 217, 229, 230

Bartholomew, E. F., 29, 44, 49

Barton, Bruce, 47